NO STRENGTH WITHOUT UNION

AN ILLUSTRATED HISTORY OF OHIO WORKERS 1803-1980

"There is no safety where there is no strength;
no strength without Union;
no Union without justice;
no justice where faith and truth are wanting.
The right to be free is a truth planted in the hearts of men."

William Lloyd Garrison

NO STRENGTH WITHOUT UNION

AN ILLUSTRATED HISTORY OF OHIO WORKERS 1803-1980

By
Raymond Boryczka
Lorin Lee Cary

Published by The Ohio Historical Society

Copyright 1982 Ohio Historical Society
ISBN 0-87758-015-4
Library of Congress Catalogue Card Number: 82-62218

Published by The Ohio Historical Society

DEDICATION

To Marg and Joc—
for never losing faith in the powers of a Polish Rabbit.

To June and Harry—
for never losing faith in the powers of an Anglo-Irish Rabbit.

CONTENTS

PREFACE

hrough nearly eighteen decades of statehood, Ohio has earned considerable prominence for its remarkable economic maturation, cultural diversity, technological achievements, and pivotal contributions to American development. As a primary component of the nation's industrial and agricultural heartland, as a traditionally crucial hub of political activity, and as a well-trodden crossroads for the continuous flow of peoples and ideas, the state has nurtured an imposing heritage. Yet, when the numerous volumes of Ohio history are examined, it soon becomes apparent that perhaps the most essential elements in that heritage have been consistently neglected—namely, the key roles and complex experiences of the vast working-class majority who customarily bore the brunt of the burden.

A major step toward rectifying this glaring deficiency finally was taken in 1975, when various concerned organizations and individuals established the Ohio Labor History Project under the primary auspices of the Ohio Historical Society. Over the past seven years, the Project has made impressive strides in preserving, illuminating, and commemorating the state's labor legacy. In addition to the erection of several historical site markers, the Project has gathered and inventoried nearly 325 collections of union records, personal papers, and photographs; conducted more than eighty oral history interviews; and microfilmed dozens of labor newspapers. The fertile information contained in these extensive materials provided the nucleus for this brief survey of Ohio's working classes.

As the book's format and style suggest, our efforts have been guided by several ambitious aims. Adapting recent trends in the field of labor history, this study has attempted to implement a "cultural approach" on a statewide basis. The complex quality of working-class life and the long-term interactions of laboring people with their diverse environments have been examined from such perspectives as economic standards of living, social and geographic mobility, leisure activities, family structures, housing, health, working conditions, spontaneous and organized militancy, political action, as well as the development of labor unions. At the same time, a sensitivity to the distinct experiences and contributions of women, racial minorities, and individual ethnic groups has been applied. In order to generate among a targeted non-academic audience an improved understanding of, and greater interest in, the history of working-class

Ohioans, we endeavored to avoid ponderously "analytic" frameworks. However, we have also been conscious of the necessity to demonstrate solid standards of scholarship, which are too frequently sacrificed in most cursory "narrative" accounts intended for popular consumption. Consequently, our intention in the text has been to steer an "interpretive" course between these two extremes. For casual readers and those who ardently insist that "a single picture is worth a thousand words," a more vivid sense of the multifaceted and extremely personal working-class experiences has been conveyed through a careful selection of graphics, pictorial essays, and sidebar quotations from plain-spoken but articulate toilers. For those who either are curious about available resources on specific topics or prompted to pursue further investigations, detailed bibliographies and statistical data have been provided.

The degree to which these objectives have been accomplished depended, in large measure, on a combination of factors both novel and endemic to a project of this nature and scale. Though aware from the outset of tremendous gaps in the literature, we have still been consistently amazed at the uneven and sparse research which has focused upon Ohio's labor history. Unlike the attention devoted to workers in such states as Massachusetts, New York, Pennsylvania, or Michigan, working people in Ohio have remained on the fringes of historiographic investigations — apparently presumed, but rarely proven, to be active participants in the broad trends supposedly typical of each era. While a smattering of valuable information could be gleaned from the published and unpublished studies cited in the bibliography, a thorough examination of available primary sources was exceptionally crucial in order to gain even a general overview of developments. The sheer volume of that raw material, however, posed additional practical problems of selective research and synthesis within the relatively limited time-frame alloted for the project. Ironically, the primary sources themselves also suffered significant shortcomings which affected the final product. For example, the concentration on industrial workers in most manuscript collections limited our ability to deal more fully with other segments of the state's extremely diverse labor force. Furthermore, we soon discovered that quality graphics depicting various aspects or time periods of Ohio labor history are sorely lacking. Although line art and photographs are abundant for strikes and for the 1870-1940 period, for instance, far fewer images are available — either due to technological considerations, fears of legal liability by potential donors, or a sad failure to preserve materials in a modern "throw-away" society — for leisure activities and the years prior to the Civil War and following World War II. Finally, these assorted difficulties have been compounded by the same dilemma which has repeatedly plagued the very workers we discuss — economic "hard times."

Of course, we recognize that various hurdles have not been completely overcome. Nonetheless, we trust that evident omissions and flounderings will not overshadow the uniqueness of the study. To our knowledge, this volume represents the first effort to measure decades of working-class life within the parameters of a single state, rather than within one community or the entire nation. The balanced format of graphics, text, sidebars, and statistical tables offers unusual opportunities to present labor's story from numerous perspectives. Hopefully, the challenges peculiar to this approach will stimulate increased efforts to expand and enhance our understanding.

A project of these dimensions invariably acquires a long list of debts, most of which can never be fully repaid. Without the love, understanding, and sacrifices of our dear ones, this book would have floundered long ago. For selflessly offering consul, support, and a soft shoulder; for enduring lonely evenings and working weekends; for being the best possible colleague and wife; as well as for repeatedly dispelling the clouds of cynicism with reason, a smile, or a tinkling laugh — Margaret Boryczka will always enjoy my gratitude and admiration. Equally special has been the continued encouragement, trust, and devotion of Jocelyn Boryczka whose intelligence, maturity, and sensitivity have made a fatigued father very, very proud. Francine, Elissa, and Michelle Cary, in ways that make each of them unique and special people, sustained, cajoled, and persevered, and were themselves. Close friends provided Joy, sprinting over time and distance at low moments during the arduous and lengthy process.

The Ohio General Assembly provided exclusive funding for this project. Sincere thanks are also owing to the individuals who provided crucial research assistance at various critical junctures: Vickie Congrove, David Holford, David Gray, Brian Klopfenstein, Raymond Stokes, Ann Kettles, Jose Asencio, Barbara Floyd, David Chelminski, Laurie Winters, and Tana Mosier. Dr. Dennis East supervised the project's tedious administrative aspects and bore the brunt of our grievances and inadequacies. The support of Warren Smith, John Thomas, and George DeNucci of the Ohio AFL-CIO enabled us to overcome a variety of stumbling blocks. Roger Meade, Director of the Ohio Labor History Project, lent valuable advice, expertise, and encouragement to our efforts. William and Marjorie Myers of the Ohio Historical Society's Manuscript Department repeatedly demonstrated that the all-too-common gulf between harried archivists and demanding historians can indeed be bridged, both professionally and personally. James Richards flourished his editor's pencil with great sensitivity, while the remarkable quality of many graphics resulted solely from Chris Duckworth's photographic wizardry. Though the entire staff of the Ohio Historical Society — past and present — contributed their efforts in countless ways, certain persons merit particular mention: William Keener, Carolyn Smith, Mark Mederski, Robert Jones, Sue Defenbaugh, Frank Levstik, Gary Arnold, Kit Leary, Arlene Peterson, Ed Lentz, Marilyn Bosen, Vernon Will, Robert Daugherty, Jane Touvell, and Sharon Edgar. Marianne Emsminger diligently transformed most of our scrawlings into a typed manuscript. Al Goldberg, Lois Kennedy, and Linda Cunningham helped to provide access to several corporate archives. With imagination, patience, and the highest professional standards, Gene Hite and Dean Kette of Design Communications, Inc. accomplished the feat of weaving text and graphics into a distinctive finished product. Finally, acknowledgement is also due the self-appointed critics, the crapehangers, the marplots, and the historiographic sciolists who unfortunately possess the collective ability to inhibit worthwhile endeavors. For, unintentionally to be sure, they have taught us the true value of cooperation, empathy, vision, and perseverance.

R.B.
L.L.C.

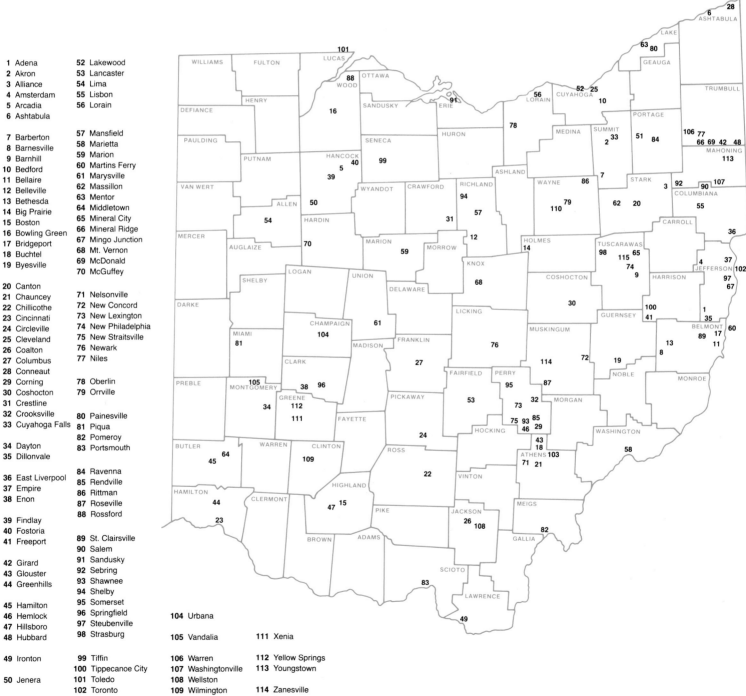

1 Adena
2 Akron
3 Alliance
4 Amsterdam
5 Arcadia
6 Ashtabula

7 Barberton
8 Barnesville
9 Barnhill
10 Bedford
11 Bellaire
12 Belleville
13 Bethesda
14 Big Prairie
15 Boston
16 Bowling Green
17 Bridgeport
18 Buchtel
19 Byesville

20 Canton
21 Chauncey
22 Chillicothe
23 Cincinnati
24 Circleville
25 Cleveland
26 Coalton
27 Columbus
28 Conneaut
29 Corning
30 Coshocton
31 Crestline
32 Crooksville
33 Cuyahoga Falls

34 Dayton
35 Dillonvale

36 East Liverpool
37 Empire
38 Enon

39 Findlay
40 Fostoria
41 Freeport

42 Girard
43 Glouster
44 Greenhills

45 Hamilton
46 Hemlock
47 Hillsboro
48 Hubbard

49 Ironton

50 Jenera

51 Kent

52 Lakewood
53 Lancaster
54 Lima
55 Lisbon
56 Lorain

57 Mansfield
58 Marietta
59 Marion
60 Martins Ferry
61 Marysville
62 Massillon
63 Mentor
64 Middletown
65 Mineral City
66 Mineral Ridge
67 Mingo Junction
68 Mt. Vernon
69 McDonald
70 McGuffey

71 Nelsonville
72 New Concord
73 New Lexington
74 New Philadelphia
75 New Straitsville
76 Newark
77 Niles

78 Oberlin
79 Orrville

80 Painesville
81 Piqua
82 Pomeroy
83 Portsmouth

84 Ravenna
85 Rendville
86 Rittman
87 Roseville
88 Rossford

89 St. Clairsville
90 Salem
91 Sandusky
92 Sebring
93 Shawnee
94 Shelby
95 Somerset
96 Springfield
97 Steubenville
98 Strasburg

99 Tiffin
100 Tippecanoe City
101 Toledo
102 Toronto
103 Trimble

104 Urbana

105 Vandalia

106 Warren
107 Washingtonville
108 Wellston
109 Wilmington
110 Wooster

111 Xenia

112 Yellow Springs
113 Youngstown

114 Zanesville
115 Zoar

NO STRENGTH WITHOUT UNION

AN ILLUSTRATED HISTORY OF OHIO WORKERS 1803-1980

PART 1 FOSTERING A NEW ORDER 1803-1843

O hio's first four decades of statehood marked a significant preliminary stage in the social and economic transformation of the populace, their environment, and their institutions. Beginning gradually, yet rapidly gaining momentum by the early 1840s, the interrelated influences of immigration, transportation, urbanization, and industrialization swept across the state. A relatively homogeneous population became more ethnically and racially diverse. Primitive modes of transportation gave way to better roads, canals, and steamboats. Bustling urban centers replaced isolated family farms and frontier settlements. A rudimentary factory system gradually supplanted domestic and craft-shop manufacturing. A society of pioneer egalitarianism faded into one with sharpened class distinctions. These trends did not develop evenly or completely in all areas of the state, of course, and at times changes were only vaguely discernable. However, for Ohio's working classes—the primary initiators, participants, victims, and beneficiaries of these currents—the ramifications became increasingly obvious. For they would bear the brunt of the burden.

Population growth was a vital, catalytic ingredient in Ohio's maturation from frontier to preindustrial society. Entering the Union in 1803 with approximately 50,000 inhabitants, the state experienced a meteoric increase over the next forty years. Ranked thirteenth among the states in 1810 with 230,760 residents, Ohio climbed to 581,434 in 1820, and 937,903 in 1830. By 1840, only New York and Pennsylvania exceeded the state's population of more than 1.5 million. Thus, while the total U.S. population rose about thirty-four percent per decade during this period, Ohio swelled at a remarkable rate of 152 percent between 1810 and 1820, and nearly doubled the national average during the 1820s and 1830s.

In an era when early marriage and large families were common, much of this expansion stemmed from natural causes—the surplus of births over deaths. Equally important, however, was the phenomenon which some easterners referred to as "Ohio Fever"—the mania to migrate westward. Of the estimated 1.8 million settlers who poured into the undeveloped Northwest between 1800 and 1840, nearly ¾ million (or forty-one percent) found roots in Ohio. This massive influx peaked between 1810 and 1820, with the arrival of more than ¼ million people who represented nearly seventy-two percent of the state's total population increase for the decade. The wave of newcomers continued thereafter, but at a relatively declining rate. Natural factors far

surpassed migration after 1820 as the primary explanation for population growth. In fact, by the 1840s a drastic alteration of the migration pattern itself occurred. Maturing rapidly, Ohio began to lose more residents to newer frontiers than it gained from new arrivals.

Despite the scarcity of records regarding these early settlers, some general characteristics—affecting generations of workers to come—may be sketched. Pennsylvania and the upper South apparently served as the main sources of migration to Ohio throughout this period, with Scotch-Irish constituting the largest ethnic group. Starting in the 1820s and steadily increasing for the next two decades, foreign-born Germans and Irish joined the influx of settlers. Blacks never comprised more than one percent of the state's total population between 1810 and 1840; but their absolute numbers rose from under 2,000 to over 17,000 in those years. Further, while average population density per square mile increased from six persons in 1810 to thirty-seven in 1840, the growth was not distributed evenly throughout the state. By 1830 most Ohioans had begun to settle within a broad geographic crescent stretching from the northeast to the southwest, containing dense pockets in the Steubenville, Zanesville, and Cincinnati areas. Sections such as the Black Swamp region of northwestern Ohio, by contrast, were only beginning to move past the frontier stage. Finally, while individual motives for locating in Ohio varied, one commonly shared stimulus seemed to take precedence among the working classes—an almost compulsive thirst for economic opportunity.

By the mid-1820s the mobility and ambitions of the predominantly agrarian inhabitants were being severely frustrated. In spite of extraordinary population growth and abundant fertile soil, Ohio remained a poor state, chiefly for want of profitable markets for its surplus products. Inadequate local markets consisted of scattered towns and small cities whose residents suffered from a shortage of hard currency. Venturing out upon the few available roads to trade locally, in any case, could be an arduous undertaking; most were little more than frequently-flooded bridle paths. Potentially rich markets lay to the east, but the prohibitive costs of transporting goods across the formidable Appalachians largely shut off that outlet. The only other alternative was to ship via water to New Orleans. But, that avenue was time-consuming, barely profitable, and available only to settlers near the Ohio River or its tributaries. For those producers pressing into the state's interior, the means of selling any surplus were practically non-existent. Thus, it became painfully obvious that development of an efficient transportation system was an absolute necessity if Ohio was to mature beyond the subsistence stage.

Ambitious efforts to remedy the situation launched Ohio's transportation revolution. After years of popular agitation for internal improvements, the state government in 1825 began construction of an extensive canal system. Intended to provide cheap access to the eastern

markets through New York's recently completed Erie Canal, two main canals linked the Ohio River and Lake Erie. The Ohio Canal, completed in 1832, wound its way from Cleveland to Portsmouth; the Miami and Erie Canal opened from Cincinnati to Dayton in 1829 and to Toledo in 1845. A combination of federal and state government funding and limited private initiative financed a series of branch canals which further penetrated the state's hinterlands. By 1845, when the state terminated its internal improvements program, Ohio could boast over 900 miles of canals, built at a total cost of $17,000,000. Matching this tremendous accomplishment was the construction of almost 900 miles of badly needed turnpikes and plank roads for areas not serviced by the canals. The National Road crowned the new transportation network. Financed by Congress to integrate the expanding west with the established east, the macadamized roadway finally extended from Wheeling, Virginia to Zanesville in 1825, to Springfield in 1838, and to the Indiana line a few years later. Numerous state-chartered turnpike companies, meanwhile, crisscrossed the state with additional thoroughfares. Nor were improvements on Ohio's great natural waterway ignored. The advent of the steamboat era on the Ohio River, about 1817, conquered river currents, thus enabling trade with the South to flow in both directions at last. Finally, although still in their infancy, railroads began to make their first appearances in Ohio in the 1830s. Only thirty-nine miles of track had been laid within the state by 1840, but Ohioans already recognized the train's importance for future development. This revolutionized transportation system—canals, roads, steamboats, and railroads—provided the greatest single impetus to the state's continued growth.

Efficient transportation played a particularly vital role in Ohio's urban awakening during the preindustrial era. As the volume and diversity of goods flowing through the land and water network increased, so too did the number, size, and significance of urban locales along its routes. Commerce provided the early life-blood for these frontier towns and cities. Functioning as trading and distribution centers for crops sold in the national markets and finished

Overleaf—page 3. Candle-making remained a key "household industry" prior to the 1840s.

In 1820, travel over Ohio's few rough roads could be a very jolting experience, even under ideal conditions.

The Dayton Aqueduct enabled animal-drawn boats on the Miami and Erie Canal to cross the Mad River. Canal boats were often given names like "Experiment," which were symbolic of the expansive, innovative age in which they flourished.

products imported from the East, towns also became important sources of credit for chronically cash-starved area farmers. These settlements further served as jumping-off points to the interior for the constant influx of immigrants. Many newcomers stayed, especially as the availability of cheap, fertile land diminished and job opportunities in the cities' incipient manufacturing enterprises grew.

While the rural-agrarian sector would retain numerical and economic predominance through most of the century, urban areas began to expand steadily by the 1830s. In 1820 Cincinnati and Steubenville qualified as the state's only legitimate "urban areas" (locales with a minimum of 2,500 residents). Akron and Toledo were yet unborn. In contrast, by 1830 Zanesville, Dayton, and Chillicothe joined the urban ranks, as city dwellers increased 270 percent over 1820 and accounted for nearly four percent of Ohio's total population. Cleveland, Columbus, Lancaster, and Newark gained city status as the urbanization trend continued upward in the 1830s. An additional 124 percent population increase pushed the cities' share of the state total to well over five percent by 1840.

From Alexis de Tocqueville to Frances Trollope, a number of contemporary travelers commented, with varying degrees of approval, on Ohio's impressive urban transformation. Unsurprisingly, most focused their attention on Cincinnati—the "Queen City of the West." Far surpassing all other interior U.S. cities in size and economic influence by 1840, Cincinnati had attained a commercial preeminence and cultural veneer which compared favorably with older eastern cities. Few observers captured the frontier flavor of Ohio's towns and cities as realistically as Cyrus P. Bradley. A young Easterner

leisurely traveling the state by steamboat, canalboat, and coach during 1835, Bradley confided his daily, and not unbiased, observations to his journal:

. . . Have just returned from a perambulation about the streets of Cincinnati . . . The population is of a heterogenous character, very few, comparatively speaking, of the inhabitants being natives of this region . . . There is a good deal, far too much, of mud and dirt and stagnant water about the streets; if the cholera approaches, it will set them a scrubbing. Swine are here in abundance— to be expected in this vast pork market. . . .
Arrived at Portsmouth . . . it is a vile place, or its looks belie it . . . the character of the population is that of a community of drunkards, at least that part of it which has fallen under my observation, and the whole town seems to be contaminated with it . . . the filth, the nastiness, is perfectly disgusting. The soil is hard clay, impervious to everything. Pools of stagnant water, and swine, their hides encrusted inch deep with putrefaction, infest the ways . . . No wonder the cholera makes dreadful havoc when it enters such a place. The wonder is, they escape so well . . . The population is of a mixed character, and a large portion of them do not separate Sabbath from the rest of the week . . . I have seen more drunken men to-day than for the last six years. . . .
We were in Chillicothe, the ancient seat of government of the Ohio, and the canal runs directly through it and is lined on either side with shops and stores . . . am much pleased with it, but there is displayed much of the same negligence in building and the outskirts are filthy. In fact, all the towns in this State are defiled by swine. The streets have the smell and appearance of a pig-yard. . . .
Bid adieu with some regret, to [Columbus] this pleasant little village, or city, as the inhabitants in anticipation, persist in terming it . . . This would

be a cleanly place, were it not for the pigs—as it is, it is an improvement on other places I visited. Its streets are broad and laid out in right angles. One, the main street, on which are the public buildings, forms a part of the National Road and will be macadamized this season. . . .

Sandusky is not so large a place as I had anticipated, judging from its early settlement and notoriety . . . Other settlements, such as Cleveland, etc., have been at first nearly as unhealthy, but have improved in process of time . . . But in this respect, Sandusky does not improve . . . I was struck with one singularity—the air was filled and every sunny wall or building was covered with myriads of a disgusting fly, about an inch long, with large wings and feelers . . . The inhabitants did not appear to notice them, and gentlemen and ladies as they passed the streets were covered with these reptiles. They find their way into the houses and infest everything; even the table where we dined swarmed with them . . . They are considered as certain forerunners of the cholera, and were never known here till just before the arrival of that disease. . . .

The urban environment hardly appeared idyllic, even at this early stage.

Of the various forces transforming Ohio through the early-1840s, none had greater ultimate impact upon the state's future—and that of its laborers—than embryonic industrialization. Changes in production methods did not occur suddenly. Nor did the evolution proceed evenly or universally in all geographic areas or manufacturing fields. Nevertheless, in this era the basic foundations were laid for the accelerated diversification and expansion of manufacturing commonly associated with the mid- and late-nineteenth century.

Prior to 1815, manufacturing was an overwhelmingly domestic endeavor. Relatively isolated from markets and skilled artisans, pioneer farm families relied on their own labors to provide such basic necessities as clothing, flour, salt, candles, lumber, and many farm implements. Families initially produced these "homespun" articles for their own use. But as population increased, villages and towns appeared, primitive transportation links emerged, and farmers developed some expertise and surplus, they began bartering and selling their products for other necessities in the local market. This "household industry" form of production remained important until the 1860s, especially in food processing and garment making, although new manufacturing methods increasingly supplanted it.

A sustained shift away from household manufacturing started after the War of 1812. Specialized establishments such as shops, mills, and furnaces had been few and far-between since the turn of the century, but by the 1820s their growth signified a modest industrial stirring which steadily gathered momentum through the 1830s and early 1840s. Several factors converged to trigger this process. First, geographic barriers separating Ohio from the East spurred the initial development of local manufacturing. The high cost of importing finished products across the mountains before the transportation revolution stimulated the formation of diversified local industries to satisfy the needs of the local market more cheaply, promote provincial self-sufficiency, and thus remedy the unfavorable commercial dependence upon the East. At the same time, distance and high shipping costs functioned as informal tariffs by protecting Ohio's infant enterprises from ruinous outside competition. Secondly, the population surge occurring during this period sparked industrial growth in various ways: local demand for manufactured products increased; new businesses attracted badly needed hard money; skilled craftsmen became more common; and cultivation of additional land made more agricultural products, by-products, and raw materials available for processing and fabrication. Finally, the improved accessibility of waterpower from newly constructed canals, together with the introduction of the steam engine, inspired further industrial development.

Countervailing influences, however, sufficiently blunted these expansionary stimuli to prevent a full-blown industrial acceleration until the mid-1840s. One primary cause was the labor shortage which plagued the entire nation, but which was accentuated in predominantly agrarian Ohio. Too few of the new settlers were skilled craftsmen, and the majority had farming rather than manufacturing occupations in mind. Insufficient capital also frustrated further development. Local businessmen and merchant-capitalists generally considered prospects for quick returns on their investments to be better in land or commerce than in industry. This reluctance, in turn, flowed in part from the managerial and technical inexperience of many individuals who ventured into manufacturing. With the exception of gristmills producing for the national market, Ohio's locally oriented industries also experienced damaging competition after 1830, as the transportation revolution lowered shipping costs on manufactured products from the East. To these handicaps must be added a distinct anti-industrial prejudice. Farmers and merchants, especially, feared that manufacturing would threaten their economic status in the community. When coupled with

In 1800, Cincinnati was still a village, huddled on the banks of the Ohio which linked it to the world beyond its boundaries.

Millstones were among the first of Cleveland's manufactures that required bulk carriers to reach distant markets. By the mid-'thirties, steam and sail were already competing on Lake Erie for Cleveland cargoes.

Dealer in Bolting Cloths and Mill Furnishing generally.

the widely-held distrust of industry as a corruptive and degenerative menace to society's moral and physical fiber, such bias exerted potent force.

These obstacles to industrialization also hampered the evolution of a factory system. Used quite loosely in the early nineteenth century, the term "factory" was often applied to enterprises better classified as craft-shops or mills. Certain characteristics distinguish true factory organization: concentration of a large number of workers in one or more buildings; the imposition of a definite work discipline regulating hours and tasks; a considerable investment of capital; mechanization and the use of non-manual power; and sizable output intended for a wide geographic market. Few manufacturers in Ohio fit these broad criteria, even by the minimal standards of the early 1800s. Steubenville boasted a three-story, steam-powered, woolen factory employing 115 workers and producing for eastern markets; a Zanesville iron works with 158 employees ranked as one of the nation's largest concerns; and the nine-story Cincinnati Steam Mill, built in 1814 for $120,000, used steam engines to process wheat, wool, cotton, and pork for markets as far away as the West Indies. But these and several other examples in textiles and meat-packing were exceptional for this time, for the vast majority of manufacturing establishments were small-scale enterprises. Typically, they used little power machinery, produced limited amounts for a local market, lacked adequate capital, and relied upon fewer than a dozen employees in an atmosphere devoid of strict work discipline.

Manufacturing firms fell into two broad categories: resource-processing industries and craft or shop industries. Because they directly relied on agricultural products and raw materials, processing industries appeared early, and dispersed widely throughout the state. A variety of types emerged: grist, lumber, and textile mills; iron furnaces; salt works; asheries; distilleries and breweries; brickyards; and, particularly in Cincinnati, packing houses. An impressive array of diversified shop industries also arose to serve the needs of maturing localities: machine shops, shipyards, potteries, carriage and wagon works, boot shops, tailor shops, woodworking shops, glass works, and more. Even before 1820, processing and shop industries had attained significant proportions, particularly in Cincinnati, Steubenville, and Zanesville. By 1840 an urban-based industrial pattern had been established, with basic manufacturing extended from the early industrial centers to Akron, Dayton, Columbus, East Liverpool, Newark, Canton, and Chillicothe. Industrialization was clearly on the ascent.

Ohio staggered and stumbled, rather than soared, through these dynamic decades. Mirroring national economic patterns, recurrent periods of depression and distress interrupted upward surges of growth and prosperity. These cyclical fluctuations of "boom and bust" bedeviled all segments of society, but especially exposed the rising insecurity and vulnerability of the working classes.

Two crises severely marred early industrial development — the depressions of 1819-25 and 1837-43. Several boom years preceded the Panic of 1819. Increased overseas demand for American agricultural products after the War of 1812 had fueled a sharp escalation in prices and land values. Prosperity was more apparent than real. Over-optimism led to the issuance of excessive credit and unsound money by weak local banks (the number of state-chartered banks in Ohio multiplied from eight to twenty-five in three years) and consequent over-speculation in land and commodities. Unbalanced trade with the East aggravated the precarious situation even further by draining local money supplies. When foreign demand fell by 1819 and the Second Bank of the United States initiated a contraction of credit, a deflationary spiral began. The money supply quickly dried up, leaving speculators overextended and local economies undermined. Ohioans did not feel the full force of the collapse until 1820, at which time land values plummeted, commerce stagnated, immigration declined, and manufacturing badly deteriorated. Although the depression hit all levels of society, workers in infant manufacturing centers such as Cincinnati experienced the worst effects. The fact that the unemployed and bankrupt could at least return to the land or barter for sustenance minimized acute physical suffering. Still, as Betsy Green Deshler, wife of a Columbus carpenter, explained in letters to her family, conditions were grim:

> David works every day, and for the last five months has not got one dollar in money. . . . All the work that is done in Columbus is for trade, trade, and no money. It makes it difficult to get along. . . . In the spring David had considerable business, but for some time past he can't get a dollar's worth of work to do, and not only he but all other mechanics in town are in the same condition. . . . Many families have gone to the Wabash [near the Indiana-Illinois border]. . . . Owing to the depreciation of paper money, and the scarcity of specie, merchants cannot collect their debts, and therefore replenish their stores. . . . Mr. Deshler has not in eighteen months received twenty dollars in cash for his work. We get produce of every kind for work, but more than what we can eat must be thrown away, for it cannot be sold, and produce will not buy store goods, except for a few articles such as whiskey, feathers, beeswax, and wool, and these the country people keep for themselves.

Recovery began in 1825, stimulated in large measure by the launching of the transportation revolution, which, most Ohioans believed, would at last generate profitable trade with the East. With minor fluctuations, the state's economy did prosper for the next dozen years. Yet, the underlying structure remained unstable with tremendous economic expansion, rising incomes, and full employment being paralleled by inflation, excessive land speculation, and chronic money shortages. The shaky financial edifice collapsed again in the Panic of 1837, followed until 1843 by one of the worst depressions of the century. The causes were similar to those of the earlier crisis, but the effects far harsher. Since the urban-industrial sector had expanded and agriculture had become more intregrated into the national economy, only remote areas of Ohio remained untouched by hard times. Personal deprivation and social tension were more widespread, particularly in the

cities where soup kitchens appeared and unemployment rates probably corresponded to the estimated national average of six to eight percent. Although relatively mild by today's standards, these cyclical depressions and consequent hardships contributed substantially to the distinctive instability of these turbulent transition years.

Generations of Ohio workers personally experienced the pervasive and enduring repercussions of these major trends. Successive waves of foreign-born and native workers with rural, non-industrial backgrounds encountered an increasingly urbanizing, industrializing, and economically unstable environment. They did not jettison former habits, values, skills, and relationships in the process, but instead gradually altered and adapted them to a setting which itself was continually being reshaped. A new working-class world was in the making, one from which labor would reap rewards as well as problems.

A distinct working class began taking shape early in the nineteenth century. During Ohio's earliest frontier years the forces of wilderness privation and a subsistence economy tended to mask class distinctions. By the 1820s and 1830s, however, such egalitarianism — a theoretically perfect equality of opportunity and material condition which lowered class barriers and produced a fluid society without rigid extremes of wealth and poverty — was more illusion than reality, especially in urban areas. Considerable social and economic mobility did blur class lines, but could not conceal the well-defined stratification then crystalizing in tandem with urban-industrial growth. Differences between the wealthy, who technically worked due to preference or taste, and the wage earners, who labored out of necessity, became conspicuous. Although workers demonstrated little class consciousness, in the sense of viewing themselves as members of a permanent, cohesive social group with definite economic interests, they could not avoid an awareness of emerging social distinctions.

Despite diverse backgrounds and occupations, wage earners shared several common characteristics — their relative scarcity being perhaps the most important. Even though Ohio's population increased rapidly, it did not keep pace with the demand for labor in all sectors of the growing economy. This scarcity, especially of skilled workers, in manufacturing, commerce, construction, and agriculture tended to generate high wages in comparison with the eastern states and Europe. Job opportunities and good pay, in turn, helped to stimulate geographic mobility, as workers not only moved to Ohio in search of better positions, but frequently relocated within the state as well. In addition, the composition of the labor force shifted, with workers increasingly attracted to non-agricultural occupations. Whereas over fifteen percent of all employed persons in Ohio engaged in non-agricultural pursuits in 1820, the proportion expanded to nearly twenty-four percent by 1840. Finally, Ohio's working class exhibited remarkable versatility. Many "jack-of-all-trades" semiskilled, and common laborers moved from canal construction, to crop harvesting, to mining, or to factory employment as the need or opportunity arose.

This heterogeneous and complex working class, which comprised the bulk of preindustrial Ohio society, was divided along various cultural, occupational, and social lines. However, three broad categories are most distinguishable: resident wage-earners, transient laborers, and black workers.

Resident white laborers were regarded as the "respectable backbone" of every community. Generally ranked below the merchant and professional classes, but above blacks, the assorted skilled craftsmen, apprentices, common laborers, clerks, and factory hands who lived in towns and cities shared similar economic conditions and social status. In an era of almost habitual geographic mobility and fairly common social fluidity, these laborers were not

Cincinnati's expanding metal industries played a leading role in the city's economic growth during the 1830s.

a static segment of society. It is not clear how many workers rose to higher jobs, but skilled individuals occasionally established prosperous shops and businesses of their own. Others failed and descended the ladder of success. Immigration and migration also swelled the number of resident urban workers, for urban areas acted as magnets. Some workers came to earn money to buy a farm. Others had failed at farming and sought alternative occupations. The relative steadiness of town jobs, compared with seasonal agricultural labor, seemed attractive to some workers, many of whom employers actively recruited. Still others had formerly lived in Eastern cities and hoped to practice their crafts in similar western environments. Whatever the motive for their arrival, these workers established roots, raised families, built schools and churches, and led active social lives. Dreams of greater success lured many workers to other locales, but many others tended to spend a lifetime in one town. In fact, by the early-1840s, as the factory system and economic uncertainty began tightening their grips on workers' lives, not all resident laborers who wanted to relocate could do so easily. Spinners at a Steubenville clothing factory, for instance, explained why they did not seek opportunities elsewhere, even during hard times:

> The land in Ohio is dear, generally, and we could not travel to the west without money, and we cannot save money; it is as much as we can do to provide our families with necessaries. We should want money to travel, then money would be wanted to buy seed, and then we should want more to support us till we could dispose of part of our crops, and we have no money at all. But, suppose we had all these means, we know nothing about the cultivation of land — we have all our lives worked in a factory, and know no other employment, and how is it likely that we should succeed? besides which, we have always been used to live in a town, where we can get what little things we want if we have money, and it is only those who have lived in the wilderness, who know what the horrors of a wilderness-life are.

The diversity evident among wage earners and their communities covered a broad spectrum. Nonetheless, the resident labor forces in "iron plantations" and in Cincinnati stand out as significant illustrations of existing conditions and as forerunners of long-term economic and social patterns.

Ohio's iron industry dated from the opening in 1804 of Hopewell Furnace, auspiciously located near the future steel complex at Youngstown. Within four decades, dozens of other furnaces appeared in a wide belt stretching from the northeast corner of the state, southwestward to Adams County. As a processing industry dependent upon accessible and abundant ore, limestone, lumber, and water, iron production concentrated within three rich resource areas: the Mahoning Valley, the Hanging Rock Region of southern Ohio, and along Lake Erie. Primitive operations, these charcoal-burning furnaces manufactured pig iron for the casting

EAGLE IRON WORKS,

M. GREENWOOD, PROPRIETOR,

Nos. 383, 384, 385, 386 & 396, Corner Walnut and Canal Streets,

CINCINNATI, OHIO.

The Eagle Iron Works was established in 1832, by the present proprietor, in connection with Mr. Joseph Webb, for the purpose of a general Foundry business, although in a limited way, as the means of the proprietors would not admit of an extended business; and the articles of manufacture relied upon principally, were Stoves, Hollow Ware, Sad Irons, Dog Irons, Wagon Boxes, Plow Moulds, and some other ordinary, articles in every day use; to which additions were made from time to time, of such things as were generally wanted, or made for special purposes.

The business was continued in this manner, and extended as the demands increased, for eight years, when Mr. Webb withdrew from the firm. The same year, 1840, it was determined to commence the manufacture of

BUTT HINGES.

This undertaking, for a time, met with but little favor from dealers, from whom it was but reasonable to expect a liberal patronage; but builders becoming aware of the superior quality of the Hinges made at this establishment, soon created a demand for them, which placed the manufacture and sales on a substantial basis, and has brought them into general use throughout the country.

and forging of necessities like kettles, tools, and machinery. Initially isolated in rural areas, they eventually became absorbed into growing industrial centers such as Portsmouth, Zanesville, Massillon, Warren, Canton, and Cleveland.

Early blast furnaces served as focal points within vast iron plantations. Because of the tremendous amounts of timber and minerals needed and the surface mining methods used, companies by the 1830s commonly owned tracts of ten to fifteen thousand acres. Clustered about each furnace were secluded communities of fifty or more families — 300 to 500 people entirely dependent on the furnace for their livelihoods. Housing for the wood cutters, charcoal burners, ore diggers, ox-drivers, furnace hands, blacksmiths, and carpenters consisted of company-owned, one-room log cabins with earthen floors. "Quality" residences reserved for company officials, a company store, church, and school completed the typical, largely self-contained town.

The ironmaster dominated this little empire like a feudal lord, residing in the "palatial mansion house" and ruling on all aspects of life within his domain. Meager wages ranged from fifty cents to one dollar per day. A newspaper advertisement placed by Brush Creek Furnace in 1826 read:

> Wanted: Fifty or Sixty wood choppers, to whom prompt pay and liberal wages will be given. Also— ox drivers and ore diggers. High wages will be given, and none but steady and industrious men wanted. Ox drivers will get twenty-eight dollars per month—five of it in cash. Men with families would be preferred, to whom houses will be furnished.

In fact, however, iron plantation workers rarely received cash wages. Ledgers kept by furnace owners indicate that they commonly paid employees partly in whiskey or even pig iron. The balance came in the form of scrip (promissory notes payable by the company in five or ten years) or credits redeemable at the company store, where employees generally had to shop as a condition of continued employment. Workers called these places "pluck-me" stores with good reason. Due to their monopoly in the community, arbitrary over-charging, and shady bookkeeping, they frequently enjoyed higher profits than the furnaces themselves. More often than not, workers discovered that they had exceeded their credit and were actually indebted to the company after a year's labor.

Iron plantations were Ohio's earliest precursors of the notorious company towns which sprang up later in the century. Highly dependent upon their employers; trapped by financial obligation; and living in socially stratified, tightly controlled, isolated, and self-contained communities — these laborers were among the state's most victimized residential wage earners.

A glimpse at preindustrial Cincinnati — the most populous, economically diverse, and industrialized urban area in Ohio—provides additional insights into early characteristics of resident working-class life usually attributed to later industrial society. Attracted to the Queen City in droves, laborers and artisans made up the majority of the city's booming population. Twenty-five hundred people lived there in 1810, nearly 25,000 in 1830, and over 46,000 by 1840. Cincinnati contained the state's largest and most heterogeneous concentration of urban workers. By 1841, less than ten percent of the adult male population had been born in Ohio. Almost half were foreign-born, about twenty-eight percent having immigrated from Germany and another sixteen percent from Great Britain. As the region's chief distributing center, the city remained dependent upon commerce throughout the period. Nevertheless, the manufacturing sector made great advances, producing goods for the growing local market and the entire West. Contemporary sources estimated that the value of manufactured products rose from $1.5 million in 1826 to over $17,000,000 in 1841. Increasing numbers of businesses accounted for only part of this growth. Equally significant was a widening assortment of specialized manufacturing enterprises. To the approximately seventy-five types — from potteries to tanneries to breweries—already operating in 1820, fifty more varieties of shops were added by 1841.

Economic growth and diversification offered expanded employment opportunities as well. Workers of all degrees and types of skill were in constant demand in commercial, construction, and service occupations, and apparently moved from job to job with ease. But Cincinnati's resident labor force was developing a predominantly industrial character; after the mid-1820s more and more wage earners concentrated in manufacturing. Numerous small craft shops — all averaging under a dozen workers toiling alongside their employers — provided jobs for the vast majority of residents, from iron workers and plumbers to shoemakers and machinists. Employment in large-scale establishments was still exceptional; the most sizeable in 1841 being five steamboat yards operating with 306 hands, thirteen foundries and engine shops with 563 workers, and two rolling mills with 148 employees. Despite the great influx of workers, labor remained in short supply. Prior to the 1830s, this situation forced employers to offer average daily wages of $1.00 for laborers and $2.00 for journeymen, minus room and board —rates almost double those paid in the East. Although skilled workers continued to command premium wages, after 1830 increased population density and the disappearance of cheap farmland brought the wages of common laborers into line with rates paid in eastern cities.

Manufacturers developed several responses to labor scarcity and high labor costs. Since the traditional apprentice training system could not fulfill the city's pressing need for skilled artisans, employers founded an Apprentices' Library in 1821 and the Ohio Mechanics' Institute in 1828. As part of a national movement for workers' education, these institutions aimed to

Producing soap from boiled animal fat became a large-scale offshoot of Cincinnati's meat-packing industry by the late 1830s.

supplement (or perhaps supplant) the traditional system by providing vocational training for the city's unskilled workforce. Although concerned craftsmen complained that these efforts merely produced "half-trained journeymen" at best, young workers could learn sufficient skills with which to advance within the infant factories then being established. Although the factory system was still in its rudimentary stages during this era, some Cincinnati manufacturers already recognized its advantages. Whereas in handcraft production the skilled artisan performed all operations in manufacturing a single item, in a factory system the various processes were broken down into mechanical operations, each performed by minimally skilled workers. With this new specialization and division of labor, machines owned by the capitalist-industrialist partially displaced skill. This reduced the manufacturer's dependence upon craftsmen, generated mass-production, and lowered labor costs. Several large pork-packing plants in Cincinnati were among the first to use primitive factory systems. They implemented a division of labor in their "disassembly lines" by having hogs move past stationary workers, each of whom were assigned a particular slaughtering task. By 1840, the system had become so efficient that a hog could be butchered, weighed, and trimmed in less than a minute — with a dozen fewer men than it had taken only three years before. In some industries, such as textiles, the factory system stimulated employment of poorly paid, unskilled women and children. During the 1830s, for example, twelve-hour shifts at the Colerain Cotton Mill earned men weekly wages of $4.00 to $10.00, while women and children received $1.00 to $1.75; and the Miami Cotton Mill employed four men

at $1.00 per day and sixteen women and children at 22¢ per day. Exploitation of female labor extended to the "ready-made" clothing shops. Between 1826 and 1841, the number of women engaged in the "putting-out-system" (piecework sewing done in the home) mushroomed from about four hundred to nearly 4,000. Most rarely earned as much as 40¢ per day.

As early as the 1830s, then, large segments of Cincinnati's resident labor force found that earning a living had indeed become an arduous and precarious endeavor. Despite expanding opportunities, many workers may have justly questioned the poetic license of a booster who rhapsodized in 1840:

The sound of her workmen in every street,
Is heard—and contentment we everywhere
    meet;
And each one is striving to get all he can;
For money, dear money's the making of man.

Tho some may be poor, and some rich
    there may be;
Yet all are contented, and happy and free.

May each trade and profession join heart
    and hand;
To cherish the arts and keep peace in the land.
Each apprentice and journeyman join in the
    song,
And let the brisk chorus go bounding along.

In fact, urban and economic growth intensified class distinctions in Cincinnati much earlier than in the other less-populous areas of the state. Occupational diversity, increasing concentration of wealth in the hands of a small elite, and a corresponding shift in the city's distribution of power in favor of the wealthy stimulated an increasing awareness of status among rich and poor alike. Residential patterns and living conditions laid bare the city's often vague social hierarchy. By the 1830s, class lines could be plotted on a city map, with wealthy residential districts carefully separated from the predominantly working-class wards and riverfront slums. Resident wage earners lived in congested, noisy, hazardous, and unsanitary areas due to a perpetual housing shortage and the inability of city officials to provide even basic police and fire protection. As early as 1815, dwellings housed an average of ten persons. Most "workies" paid high rents for run-down accommodations, and those eventually able to buy homes often found them so flimsily constructed that rapid dilapidation became a serious problem. Such living conditions, so different from those in comfortable upper-class neighborhoods, provided one source of working-class irritation. When combined with residents' rising concern over deteriorating employment conditions, working-class discontent would begin to flare.

Transient laborers comprised a second broad category within Ohio's working class. Spurned, snubbed, and often feared by respectable townfolk, who viewed them as "footloose and fancy-free," shiftless, brawling drifters, migratory wage-earners nevertheless played crucial roles in the state's development. Their primary characteristic was mobility, both geographic and occupational. Whether by choice or necessity, these young, typically single workers moved about regularly, living only briefly in any one place. Commonly capable of performing tasks from the most menial to the semi-skilled in their efforts to climb the ladder of success, they epitomized occupational versatility. Most itinerants eventually settled down to join the ranks of farmers or urban wage earners, but in the interim they depended on casual employment — frequently as agricultural workers, canal laborers, or teamsters.

Contrary to popular nostalgia, Ohio did not attain agricultural preeminence solely through the exertions of self-sufficient farm families. In an era when labor-saving machinery was still rare, hired hands supplied much of the manpower and skill crucial to the emergence of commercial farming. Agricultural workers were, by all accounts, a diverse lot — easterners, southerners, Europeans, and native-Ohioans; some were lazy, dishonest, and dangerous, but mainly they were hard-working transients temporarily selling their labor as a stepping-stone to farm ownership. Their ranks were sizeable, but, typical of the times, never sufficient to meet demand. Farmers relied on hired hands for help in accomplishing all of the unglamorous, tedious, yet necessary tasks common on farms in all areas — clearing land, chopping wood, plowing, cultivating, and, especially, harvesting. But, not all transient farm workers were mere common laborers. Some pursued specialized occupations such as carpentry, drainage ditching, well digging, cellar excavating, and horticulture, which required considerable skill. The scarcity of farm labor generated high wages, although the duration and type of task caused some variations. Prior to 1830, hands earned a monthly average of $9.00 plus board, rising steadily thereafter to $12-$15 in the early-1840s. Despite abundant opportunities and high wages, however, agricultural employment had an overriding drawback: the endemic seasonality of farming denied workers any long-term job security. Thus, necessity set in motion a seasonal migration of hired hands to the South or into towns and cities, where they sought to ride out the slack winter months. Such drifting depleted savings, forcing even the frugal to labor two to five years before earning enough to start their own farms. After 1830 the increasing costs of establishing a farm considerably prolonged the wage-earning period, therefore compelling more and more agricultural workers to settle for tenancy or alternative occupations in urban areas. By the 1840s, moving upward to farm ownership became an unfulfilled dream for all but a few of Ohio's hired hands.

Of all the filthy, hazardous, backbreaking ways to make a living in preindustrial Ohio, few could compare to canal building. Often wading ankle-deep in mosquito-infested muck from dawn to dusk, a small army of workers with ax, spade, pick, shovel, and plow hacked and

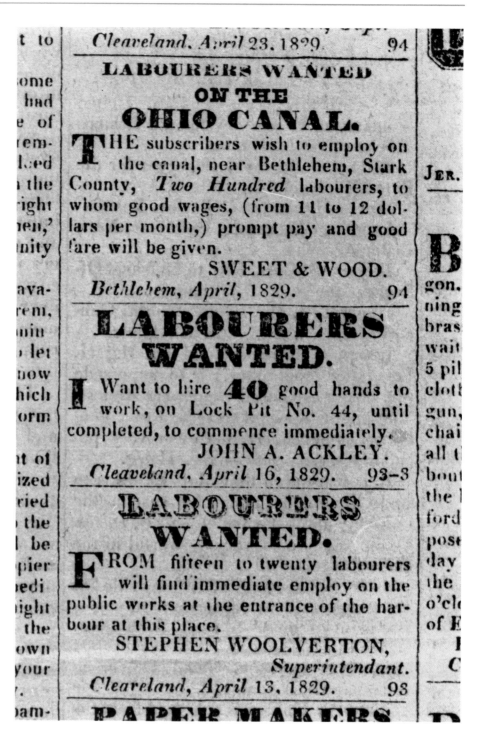

gouged over 900 miles of navigable ditches through the stubborn terrain. Thousands of farmers and hired hands along the canal routes risked the dismal working-conditions for a chance to earn scarce cash-wages, at least for a time. Local laborers frequently proved unreliable, however, for they tended to drift away during planting and harvesting seasons. In addition, many farmers apparently would only accept chopping or hauling jobs, due to a common native-American distaste for digging work which they considered degrading. Consequently, contractors bolstered their construction gangs with Irish and German itinerants drawn from overseas and the East to perform much of the actual excavating. Despite such recruiting efforts, workers remained in short supply, in part because of intense competition from canal projects in neighboring states and construction of the National Road through Ohio. Labor shortages and a high turnover rate caused an upward trend in pay scales as building of the canal system progressed. Typical daily rates for a common laborer were 30¢ in 1825, 50¢ in 1830, and 62¢ in 1840. But wages varied considerably between locales and remained low relative to comparable occupations. Moreover, "canalers" repeatedly discovered that contractors either failed to meet their payrolls, paid in depreciated currency, or even absconded with the funds. Although the State Canal Commission ironically advised disgruntled workers that the situation was "more frequently caused by the negligence of the laborers in not taking the proper measures to secure their pay, or by not laboring faithfully," spontaneous work stoppages and widespread desertions forced the Commission to guarantee payrolls in 1827. Numerous contractors nevertheless continued to cheat on wages and to charge canalers exorbitant prices for supplies. Sketchy evidence

NOTICE

TO LABOURERS ON THE CANAL.

Notwithstanding the exertions which have been made to insure punctuality in the payment of labourers employed on the Canal, complaints of a failure in this respect still continue. This difficulty originates in some instances from a disposition on the part of the original contractor either to defraud the laborer himself, or to connive at the fraud practised by the sub-contractor under him: but it is more frequently caused by the negligence of the laborers in not taking the proper measures to secure their pay, or by their not laboring faithfully so as to earn their wages.

To prevent a repetition of these evils in future, men who work on the canal are *advised* and *requested* to observe the following rules :

First, To enquire as to the character and responsibility of the person for whom they propose to work ; and not to work for any one who does not sustain a good character for honesty and responsibility :

Second, Not to work for a sub-contractor unless the original contractor will agree *in writing* to be accountable for the wages agreed on :

Third, Not to work for any person who suf his ha to be idle, inattentive to their work do the work unfaithfully, or who does not atte to his business himself ; for such a man will probably be unable to pay his laborers :

Fourth, To be in sober and careful to earn the wages that the contractor agrees to pay ; remembering that the surest way to get your pay is first to earn it :

Fifth, To settle with your employer as often as once a month and demand your pay ; and if not paid, to give immediate notice of such failure to the Acting Commissioner, or the Engineer who has charge of the work, who will inform the Commissioner :

Where no notice is given to the Commissioner of a want of punctuality on the part of the Contractor in paying his hands, the Commissioner takes it for granted that they are regularly paid and continues to pay the contractor, and when the money is once paid to the Contractor it cannot be paid again.— The laborer, thefore, looses his pay by neglecting to attend to it in season. He who will take *promises* instead of *payment*, should be contented with promises ; and not grumble if he gets nothing else.

The Acting Commissioner will not hold himself under any obligation to interfere in securing payments to any person for money lent, goods, provisions, or other articles sold or furnished to any contractor, sub-contractor or laborer on the Canal.— Persons who sell or furnish any property of any kind to a contractor, sub-contractor or laborer, must look out for themselves ; and if they give a credit, do it at their own risk.

No persons will be considered as laborers on the Canal except those who actually work thereon, or labor in procuring materials, or tools, necessary in its construction. Persons employed in making articles of clothing for those who work on the Canal, and those who sell tools, ready made, to contractors, are not considered laborers on the Canal. It is at their option to trust a contractor or not, as they please.

No original contractor will be held responsible for the payment of exorbitant or unusual wages, which a sub-contractor has agreed to pay, unless such original contractor has e ly agreed so to do.

The Commissioner will no fere in procuring payment to laborers who a le, unfaithful, insolent, or disobedient to their employer—such men do not deserve their wages.

If laborers will follow the advice which is given above, the Commissioner will use his best endeavors to secure to them their wages ; and few, if any, instances will occur in which they will fail to receive it : But if labourers will not attend to the advice of the Acting Commissioner it is unreasonable that he should be troubled with their complaints.

ALFRED KELLEY,
Acting Commissioner.

JUNE, 1827.

Known as "Gilmore's Row," this tenement house was erected in 1825, originally for workers recruited to dig a section of the Miami and Erie Canal through Dayton.

suggests that some Irish diggers may have formed secret societies, as they had in the old country, to combat exploitation with violence and intimidation. In general, however, factionalism and high turnover effectively undercut possibilities for ogranized collective action. As the experience of one Welsh immigrant illustrated, ethnic and religious antagonisms, for example, could be just as volatile in the ditches of Ohio as they had been in Europe:

> . . . I and an Englishman were working for three months in January 1830 on the Canal among three hundred papist Irishmen; they rubbed their knives in our waistcoats almost every night before going to bed, saying, "here is a knife that will rip the belly of an Englishman or a Welshman. George the Fourth is not in America; this is a free country.["] We were bound to stay there, having no money nor shoes. . . . I was very near death many a time among them, but thanks be to God, He in his great mercy has saved me. . . . from the hands of the bloodthirsty beast. . . .

Recurrent epidemics of typhoid, malaria, and cholera—popularly termed "canal fever"—not only compounded workers' woes but also depleted their numbers. So many were stricken or frightened off during an 1827 outbreak, for example, that the state legislature authorized the use of convict labor on the Columbus Feeder Canal; and in 1829 disease temporarily halted construction throughout the state. Unsanitary conditions in the jerry-built shanties commonly provided by employers aggravated the situation. Under such trying hardships, cheap whiskey often became the canal workers' prevalent remedy and consolation. Whiskey dens sprang up around construction sites and, at least in the early years, contractors customarily provided three daily "jiggerfulls" in order to mollify and retain their crews. Drunken brawls were the "unhappy consequences," frequently between rival Irish clans rekindling ancient hostilities

from the homeland. Little wonder that after stints as canal builders, many transient laborers sought out even the most arduous city jobs.

Before railroads spun their iron webs over Ohio's landscape in the 1850s, the vital flow of overland commerce hinged on the abilities and endurance of teamsters. Wagoners were always in great demand, especially from farmers, merchants, and manufacturers to whom water transportation was either inaccessible or infeasible. Two types of teamsters engaged in this form of itinerant employment—"regulars" and "sharpshooters." "Regulars" were the notorious wagoners of popular lore—stereotypically portrayed as "a unique breed" of short-tempered, hard-drinking, shockingly profane, burly, brawling, boisterous, brothel-patronizing drifters who appalled their more refined fellow-Ohioans. In reality the teamster was generally a diligent, semi-skilled toiler whose daily appearance and demeanor differed little from most other workers of his day:

> He was only a colorless drayman . . . a nobody. His face was streaked and his hands calloused. When he edged into a taproom, he smelled of sweat and horse and fish. He pulled off to the side of the road to rest his strong-shanked teams and to snatch a moment's sleep. He drove whenever he could prop his eyelids open. He was the man who kept commerce and profits moving. . . .

Regulars specialized in long-distance hauling over the state's turnpikes and the National Road. The majority owned their own horses, but hired out to established companies or freight lines to transport goods of every description in ponderous Conestoga wagons. "Sharpshooters," on the other hand, were part-time wagoners who handled short-hauls, mainly in rural areas. Hired hands and prospective farmers seeking to raise capital, these temporary teamsters used conveyances of every shape and size to pick up odd-jobs moving commodities and settlers or hauling on canal projects. Part-time wagoners were the highest-paid itinerants — commonly earning $1.50 to $2.00 per day in the 1830s — but jobs were sporadic and had to be supplemented with other forms of employment.

No matter how menial the job, how inferior the status, or how miserable the living conditions, the most unskilled white laborer could take comfort in the knowledge that white society reserved the degraded bottommost depths of the social order exclusively for blacks. To thousands of blacks condemned to permanent subservience in the slave South, antebellum Ohio appeared to be a haven of freedom. Slavery had been prohibited in Ohio since the Northwest Ordinance of 1787. Consequently, free blacks, in constant danger of reenslavement in the South, migrated northward in large numbers. Many escaped slaves also arrived through the state's extensive underground railroad network, operated by Quakers and numerous other abolitionists. In some instances, entire groups of manumitted slaves settled on land purchased for them by former masters. Largely as a result of this influx, Ohio's black population increased steadily from slightly under 2,000 in 1810, to nearly 5,000 in 1820, almost 10,000 in 1830, and over 17,000 by 1840. Most blacks settled in counties along the Ohio River, often establishing new settlements such as Guinea, Poke Patch, and Boston. Chiefly from rural Southern backgrounds, blacks once in Ohio, tended to cluster in the expanding urban areas which promised economic opportunity and safety. While Cleveland, Columbus, Oberlin, and Springfield all had early black communities, from the first Cincinnati drew the largest proportion. By 1840 the Queen City contained thirteen percent of the state's black residents.

Black immigrants soon discovered distinct limits to the freedom they had envisioned in Ohio. Blacks never accounted for more than one percent of the population, yet intolerant whites feared that the state would become a dumping ground for indigent members of the "naturally inferior race" and that they would corrupt the society, drain its resources, reduce job opportunities for whites, and strain relations with southern customers. To discourage free blacks from migrating to or residing in Ohio, the General Assembly enacted a series of Black Laws from 1804 to 1838 restricting their rights and activities. Patterned after southern slave codes, these statutes obliged blacks to furnish proof of freedom in order to live or be employed in the state; required free black immigrants to post $500 bonds signed by two whites willing to guarantee their good behavior and support within twenty days of arrival; established stiff fines for harboring fugitive slaves; barred blacks from the state school system, the militia, jury duty, and testifying against whites in court; and prohibited interracial marriage. Despite weak and inconsistent enforcement, the Black Laws posed a continuing threat to black security and served as constant reminders of their subordinate position. As free blacks became focal points of an intensifying debate among whites over the moral, economic, and political ramifications of slavery, their anxieties deepened. By the late 1820s, Ohio was a hotbed of abolitionist and pro-slavery agitation. Tensions mounted in various communities, particularly as the race issue became intertwined with recurrent economic and social problems. Violence against blacks frequently resulted, most graphically dramatized by the Cincinnati race riots of 1829, 1836, 1841, and 1843. Despite this, the flow of blacks out of the South continued—more an affirmation of slavery's repellence than Ohio's attractiveness.

Within this circumscribed, often hostile, environment, blacks occupied the lowest rungs of the social, economic, and occupational ladder. Some blacks had learned skilled trades in the South, but in Ohio white prejudice severely curtailed their employment opportunities. The overwhelming majority were relegated to the poorest-paid drudgery — some as day laborers in construction, manufacturing, or commerce; others in menial service-occupations such as household and steamboat servants, porters, shoe-blacks, and waiters. During economic depressions even these jobs became scarce, especially as competition from Irish and German immigrants mounted. The inability of black males to find any employment commonly compelled black women to support their families by working for paltry wages as domestics or laundresses. Blacks may have enjoyed relatively wider job opportunities in northern than in southern Ohio, primarily because their fewer numbers aroused white fears and prejudice to a lesser extent. Yet even in sparsely populated Cuyahoga County, after 1820, the proportion of blacks tended to decrease in the skilled trades and increase in menial service-related jobs. Wherever they lived, black workers were ill-housed and overcrowded. Although rigid residential segregation was not yet enforced, the origins of modern ghettoes clearly emerged in larger urban areas. Cincinnati's blacks, for example, concentrated in notorious neighborhoods known as "Little Africa" and "Bucktown." Available housing in these districts consisted of wooden shacks, shanties, and tenements owned by white landlords who resisted municipal attempts to improve the area. Erratic employment bred crime, vice, and violence, while growing congestion and continual neglect caused disease and fire. A small number of successful blacks moved to better districts; most remained trapped by their poverty. John Malvin, a free black who migrated to Ohio in the late-1820s, captured the pathos of the situation: "From the treatment I received by the people generally, I found it little better than in Virginia."

Workers had flocked optimistically to Ohio, dreams to be fulfilled, and opportunities to be tapped. Armed with a self-help gospel, they ardently believed that with hard work, self-discipline, and virtuous character, an ambitious individual would succeed. Personal success meant different things: shop, home, or farm ownership to some; financial security, independence, professional advancement, or some degree of social status to others. Many workers did act out their hopes and achieve their goals.

Yet for significant numbers of workers even modest dreams proved illusory. Ohio's dynamic transformation did not always benefit its laborers. The interplay of immigration, urbanization, transportation expansion, industrialization, and boom-bust economic cycles constantly disrupted workers' personal lives, their communities, and their role in the emerging economic order. Most workers adapted to the complex changes; others pursued their dreams elsewhere. But among the remainder coursed undercurrents of bewilderment, disillusionment, and resistance. As problems mounted, a faint suspicion brewed that effort would not necessarily be rewarded, that opportunities for success were narrowing, and that workers were losing control of their destinies to employers' whims and to impersonal economic forces. Particularly in urban areas such as Cincinnati, where social and economic disruptions were most pronounced, frustration and insecurity generated heightening tensions both among workers and between classes. Beneath the bustle and excitement of transforming a frontier, these were troubled times.

Although only vaguely understood at the time, profound alterations occurring in the economic system would have serious long-term consequences for the working class. Expansion of the transportation network opened up new markets, but also exposed producers to greater competition. As manufacturers gradually shifted from serving local needs to contending for larger statewide, national, and even international markets, increased production and decreased labor costs became crucial to their success. Thus, ambitious master craftsmen expanded their shops, hired more workers as cheaply as possible, and introduced rudimentary factory systems. This industrial transformation often required large sums of capital and credit which were not readily available to most small manufacturers. At this stage, merchant-capitalists entered the scene. They neither owned shops, employed laborers, nor involved themselves in actual manufacturing. Rather, they possessed the crucial capital and credit (gained from land speculation or overseas trading) with which to purchase raw materials, contract with craftsmen to produce finished articles, and conduct the final market transactions. Within this emerging economic order, the master craftsman bit by bit became dependent upon the merchant-capitalist. No longer was he an independent artisan, but instead a contractor for the capitalist, who incessantly demanded that prices for manufactured products be kept at a minimum. This pressure, and a desire to protect profits, prompted many masters to use sweatshop methods. They installed machinery to replace the hand-tools customarily owned by

Sheldon Kellogg (1809-1886) migrated with his family from New York to Cincinnati in 1818. His autobiographical account of the Queen City of his youth, the family's brief stay in the Owenite colony at New Harmony, Indiana, and his early work experiences provides rich insights into the lives of early Ohioans.

... our neighbors showed their kindness at once to us friendless newcomers. Several came to see us, offering to lend what we were in need of, and often sending us some savory morsel to eat....

...Social relations were of a delightful character in those primitive days in Cincinnati. There were no very rich nor very poor. I don't remember seeing a beggar there...except one old grey wooled negro, nearly bent double, with a long stick in his hand to support him, who visited the market places, asking of the public in general for "one cent fo poh ole nigga." He was quite a pet and had the run of the town, amusing the children much, and making a good living....

It must have been in the autumn of 1821 that I was bound apprentice to Sol Smith to learn the art and mystery of printing....He was then publishing...a weekly paper called the Independent Press. *...I became very useful as compositor, paper carrier, printer's devil, and so on. My mind was occupied in congenial pursuits—I could learn something—a very different employment from picking up apples or shelling corn....I was an apprentice about two years, and I look back upon the time so spent as about as valuable to me as of any two years of my life. My mind became set upon higher things than mere grubbing and hoeing. I began to appreciate the power that one has to elevate himself in society and in his own self-respect through a good knowledge of [the] mother tongue....*

I was again adrift after the breaking up of the newspaper concern. I cannot recall what I did for the next year or eighteen months—probably this was the time I spent in Samuel Stibb's chair painting factory—when I learned a good deal about paints and chair ornamenting....

In 1824 Robert Owen, the philanthropist, of New Lanark, Scotland, came to Cincinnati preaching his communistic doctrines. Father and fifteen to twenty families of our acquaintance became enamored of Mr. Owen, I now think, more than his communal notions....These families agreed to migrate to New Harmony, in Indiana, on the Wabash River, a nice rural town that Mr. Owen had purchased....So, in the spring of 1824 a lot of families started for our Heaven on Earth....

...at about the end of a year, we found it necessary to leave, and permit the jarring elements, now so prominent, to work out their own salvation, if possible. We had lost faith in any successful result....

...I wanted to do something for myself—all ideas of a general share and share alike division of the results of labor having by this time been quite knocked out of me. I soon concluded to go to Cincinnati, and, with my father's consent, I took a deck passage on a steam boat....This was about June 1825. I trudged the town for something to do, and found a situation in the pottery of Jas. K. Ogden....I went to work in earnest, proud of my independence. Grinding clay in a one horse mill: helping to fire the kilns: aiding in glazing the milk pans and dishes: and learning to turn pots and pans. I became very soon quite useful to my employer. But it was hard work for one so young. Working so much in the damp and cold clay, and, I suspect, being poorly fed by my employer, I broke down....

...I was taken home exceedingly ill, and for a month or so, the physicians despaired of my recovery....The good doctor Lorne said, that I must not go back to the Pottery—that the lead poison and work amongst the cold clay would kill me. His advice was, that a situation

artisans; further divided production into simpler tasks, which enabled them to hire unskilled women, children, and convicts for a fraction of a journeyman's wage; and instituted speed-ups, cut wages, and increased hours.

should be found for me when I could stand over kettles where lard and tallow were being tried out. He said my whole system had been poisoned, and that I absolutely needed this in order to strengthen my general health and strength....

...an old friend of my fathers, Mr. Simon F. Leonard, came to Cincinnati and went into the general grocery and dry goods business. He had become instated in a large soap making establishment ... about the time that I needed a situation in just such business....Dirty and unsavory as it all was to me, I did my best, and was rewarded for my honest and industrious efforts by daily increasing health and strength and the good will of my masters. I soon became able to do a man's work, whether in trying out beef fat, in making soap, or in turning out "dipped" candles....

In the course of 8 or 9 months ... my kind and just friend Mr. Leonard, said to me—"the object for which you came here has been attained. I dont want to see you end up in this calling. I think you can do better. I have a situation for you...." This was the first time in my life, that I became aware that anyone outside of my immediate family felt any interest whatever in my welfare.... Of course I took his advice, and he at once relieved me from any obligation I was under to remain any longer in his establishment....

The place obtained for me by Mr. Leonard was in the large provision and grocery establishment of C. Macalester Jr. and Co.,...the business being really carried on by Andrews and Shays....

I here had a stimulant to my ambition. I could see that here was room and scope enough to bring into active use all my energies of mind and body.... And this idea never faded in the heart, and my labors and careful attentions to the interests of my employers went on unflaggingly until the very last day in my twenty first year....

...My duties were very various, and quite exacting as to the hours of labor. The notion of the business was such that it required constant watching and attention both by night and by day, Sunday not excepted. Our business was divided into five departments. That which required...the most minute attention on each day and night throughout the entire year, was the supplying of Steam Boats with their stores of provisions....This created a vast quantity of night labor — and as I slept on a loft, over the store, in a small bunk, the greater portion of it fell upon my shoulders....It was a wearing and exhausting business—no vacation ever having been allowed during my whole service....

The other department of the business just alluded to, was the packing and conserving the meat of from sixteen to twenty thousand hogs and three to four hundred beef cattle in the course of each autumn and winter. When my time was not needed in the store department... it was fully consumed by exacting duties in the "pork house"....

Such is a general view of my course of life from 1826 to 1830. On the 18th of December of the latter year, I became "free"—that is, I attained my majority. I had been laboring during these four years, receiving as compensation, my clothing and boarding. It now became necessary to have an understanding with my masters, as to whether I should remain with them, and if so, what they would be willing to pay me as wages....So, I took occasion to call the attention of Mr. Shays to the fact that my "time was up" with his firm, and that having fulfilled faithfully all my obligations to it, that now I wanted an understanding as to the terms upon which I could serve him in the future....

...I did not like to leave the old house and would have remained if he would have given me what I asked $365.00 per year. But he would not do so. I went over to the Broadwells', and told them that I would accept their offer—and the matter was immediately settled....

By the 1830s these modifications in the economic system, still in their infancy and largely confined to Ohio's urban areas, deeply concerned skilled journeymen and created friction on the shop floor between them and the master craftsmen. The two groups had traditionally enjoyed a close rapport—living together, working side-by-side, sharing personal tribulations, and bound together by pride in their craft. To the journeyman mechanic, the master craftsman was often a respected mentor, a confidant, and man to be emulated. Journeymen viewed masters, although of higher rank, as fellow-members of the "productive class," distinct from "aristocrats" who lived off the labor of others. However, with the rise of the factory system and merchant capitalism, the bonds weakened. As some shops became larger and mechanized, relations became depersonalized. To the affected journeyman, the master was no longer a trusted friend, but a "boss"—a supervisor rather than a worker; constantly striving to cut labor costs and to increase production; uninterested in the worth of the individual; and worse, attempting to strip the journeyman of his tools, to demean the value of his skill, and to reduce him to a common wage earner. A rigid adversarial relationship between employers and employees did not immediately result. Small shops still prevailed, skilled labor remained in demand, and traditional ties did not easily wither. Nevertheless, as the shifts toward full industrialization accelerated, the chasm between masters and journeymen widened steadily. Agitated skilled workers soon banded together to protect their status and economic interests from what they regarded as the onslaughts of their employers.

While hours do not appear to have been a major concern, wages did present another source of unease for skilled and unskilled workers alike. The generally higher rates offered in Ohio, relative to those in the East, often proved deceptive. During periods of prosperity, inflation constantly pushed the cost of living upward at a faster pace than wage increases, thereby eroding real wages. The *Cincinnati Advertiser* noted in early 1837, for instance, that within the previous three years alone, "The common necessaries of life have been increased from two to four fold. . . . yet the means of securing these necessaries have not increased in the same proportion." During periods of economic depression, as struggling employers cut labor costs in order to survive, wages plunged faster than prices. The wages of Cincinnati's skilled mechanics fell thirty percent between 1839 and 1840, for example, and another forty-three percent in 1843. While workers' incomes were thus buffeted by a fluctuating economy, the scarcity of stable currency further aggravated their financial problems. Wage earners commonly discovered that the paper money with which they were paid at face value was either badly depreciated or totally worthless when they tried to spend it. Derisively referred to as "wildcat," "red dog," or "shinplasters," such currency chronically menaced economic security. In some cases, money in all forms was so scarce that employers eliminated cash wages altogether. Instead they utilized the "truck system," a version of barter which obliged laborers to accept wages in goods or credit slips.

Though generally associated with rural company towns, this arrangement spread by the 1830s to some urban areas as well. In 1843 Cleveland workers staged a public demonstration in opposition to the system. Elsewhere a Cincinnati nail works paid laborers in kegs of nails, and in Steubenville, clothing manufacturers used cloth for that purpose. If workers received credit slips, they could only "spend" them at stores wholly or partly owned by their employers, who ironically would often not accept their own notes for "cash only" necessities. Besides causing workers obvious inconvenience, the truck system enabled unscrupulous employers to defraud laborers of an estimated twenty-five percent of their wages.

Perceived challenges to their job-security further fueled working-class anxieties. Despite the labor shortage, wage earners became increasingly concerned over the ability of employers — as a result of immigration, industrialization, and better transportation — to tap cheaper sources of labor. From the workers' viewpoint, an influx of newcomers to local labor markets not only undermined existent pay-scales and jobs, but also endangered potential employment opportunities. Job competition, accordingly, appeared on various fronts. The use of cheap convict labor in private industry was one such source of concern. The Ohio State Penitentiary's implementation of the "contract labor system," by which manufacturers "hired" convicts to produce such articles as shoes, clothing, and harness in prison workshops, provoked considerable agitation by "free labor" in the vicinity. From the institution's opening in 1834, Columbus workers repeatedly staged large protest meetings, vainly petitioning the state government to end the system. As unemployment grew after the Panic of 1837, demonstrations against "unjust" job competition from convict labor spread to Cincinnati. There, aroused workers formed the "Hamilton County Association for the Reform of the Penitentiary System of Ohio" in 1841. State legislators repeatedly failed to confront the problem and prison labor thus remained a volatile issue for many decades. Skilled and unskilled males also encountered rivalry from unskilled women and children, whose increased employment at low wages corresponded to the spread of the factory system. Especially visible in the textile and garment industries, they gradually began to contend with men in other fields as well. Journeyman printers found, for example, that boys supposedly being trained as apprentices really learned only separate operations, thereby reducing demand for skilled craftsmen. Additional job competition directly resulted from the transportation revolution, which enabled employers to recruit in outside labor markets. Resident wage earners, particularly in Cincinnati, began to express apprehension and resentment over incursions by German mechanics, Irish laborers, transients, and, in rare instances, strikebreakers. Finally, tensions arose between blacks and whites. In their desperate search for even me-

ONE CENT REWARD.

RANAWAY from the subscriber on the 27th of last month, an indented apprentice to the Tanning business, by the name of

GEORGE WASHINGTON TIMMONS

between the age of 19 and 20 years, had on when he went away, a brown coat, yellow snuff vest, grey fulled linsey pantaloons, and a white fur hat; whoever will take up said boy and deliver him to the subscriber in Moorefield township, Clark county, near the Pretty Prarie, shall have the above reward, but no thanks or charges, it being the fifth time he has ran, four times away and once back.

JOSHUA CANTRALL.
Nov. 23.

A notice published in the *Springfield Western Pioneer* in November 1829, offering a paltry reward for the return of an habitual runaway-apprentice. The advertiser's wry tone suggests that occasionally masters, as well as apprentices, found the system troublesome.

Most artisans in nineteenth-century Ohio had acquired their skills and respect for master craftsmen through the time-honored apprenticeship system. By this method, parents or guardians contracted with masters to teach boys (but rarely girls) a useful trade. A typical contract — or "indenture" — from Portage County listed the mutual responsibilities of master and apprentice, in language inherited from the eighteenth century:

This indenture made on the fith day of Nov. 1831 witnesseth that Nelson, son of Benjamin Wait, aged eleven years, by and with the consent of the said Benjamin, Father, Hath, of his own free and voluntary will, placed and bound himself apprentice to Oliver O. Brown, Tanner, To learn the art, trade, mistery, or ocupation of Tanner which he the said Oliver O. now useth and with him as apprentice To dwell, continue, and serve from the day of the date unto the full end and term or age of twenty one years from thence ensuing and fully to be completed and ended. During which term years the said apprentice his master will and faithfully shall serve, His secrets keep, His lawful commands do and obey. hirt to his master he shall not do nor willfully sufer it to be done by others but of the same To the utmost of his power shall forthwith give notice to his master. the goods of his master he shall not embezle nor waste. At cards, dice, or any unlawful game he shall not play. taverns or ale houses he shall not frequent. Fornication he shall not commit. Matrimony he shall not contract. from the service of his master he shall not at any time absent himself without his master's leave but in all things as a good and faithful apprentice shall and will demean himself towards his master and all his during said term. And the said master, in consideration of the above, shall instruct his said apprentice in said trade, mistery, or ocupation whiche he useth with all things apertaining thereto, shall and will instruct or cause to be well instructed after the best maner he can and shall and will also find and allow his apprentice meat, drink, washing, Lodgeing, and physick and apparel, both Linen and woolen, and all other necessaries during said term of years and shall allso send the said apprentice to a good English school to be instructed in reading, writing, arithmetick, and bookkeeping; in short to give his a good common education. in witness wereof we have here unto set our hand and seal this 5th Nov. 1831.

It was not unusual, however, for masters such as Oliver Brown to subject young apprentices to physical abuse or exhorbitantly long hours of toil. Although such conditions made runaway apprentices commonplace, Nelson Wait was not forced to that extreme. Learning of his son's plight, Benjamin Wait obtained legal annulment of the indenture two years later. Nelson was then bound to a more kindly architect, under whom he served a full apprenticeship.

BILL OF PRICES,

AGREED ON BY THE

BRICK-LAYERS OF CINCINNATI,

MARCH 1, 1814.

	Dolls. Cts.
Brick laid (labor only) for brick & half walls, per thousand,	3 00
Do. for all exterior 9 inch walls, per thousand,	3 50
Do. for the 3d story of houses, per thousand, extra,	1 00
For finding lime, sand, loam and water, per thousand,	1 00
Outside arches, in front, common size, extra,	1 50
Back and side arches, outside, do. do.	1 00
For all inside arches, do.	50
Brick cornice, per foot, running, do.	25
Oiling and Penciling per yard, superficial,	12 1-2
For setting door sills,	1 00
For trimmers, common size,	1 00
For laying hearths, do.	1 00
Brick pav... yard, superficial,	18 3-4
For filling-in with brick, do.	18 3-4
Ovens, 3 feet by 2 feet 6 inches, or under, each,	5 00
Do. larger, per foot in depth,	2 00
Chimneys to frame houses, per thousand, counted solid,	4 00

Walls, laid Flemish bond, to be counted solid in all cases.
All other walls, doors and windows *only*, to be deducted.
The number of brick to be ascertained by counting them after they are laid.
Scaffold-boards and cords to be found by the employer.

We, the subscribers, have duly considered the above prices as low as can be worked for.

ISAAC STAGG,	SAMUEL BROADWELL,
LOFTUS KEATING,	NATHAN DICKS,
JABEZ C. TUNIS,	ELIAS FISHER,
JONATHAN PANCOAST,	JOSEPH PANCOAST.
HENRY CRAVEN,	

CINCINNATI—PRINTED BY LOOKER AND WALLACE.

During the early nineteenth century, journeymen stubbornly maintained their self-image as independent craftsmen, refusing to consider themselves lowly wage-earners. Consequently, they commonly preferred to call their labor rates "prices" rather than "wages," as illustrated by these minimum wage demands issued in 1814 by a society of journeymen bricklayers.

nial employment, blacks collided with white transients and immigrants seeking the same unskilled jobs. Each feared that the other would further depress wages and job opportunities. Animosity flourished most bitterly between blacks and Irish immigrants, even though both were victims of prejudice. Competing daily for the lowest drudgery, their intense frustrations often flared into violence.

As early as the 1830s, then, job competition contributed to the splintering of the working class into antagonistic groups. With increasing frequency, skilled were pitted against unskilled, black against white, native against immigrant, men against women and children, resident against transient, free against convict — with additional combinations for conflict on individual levels. Of course, this was not the only wedge driving workers apart, generating factionalism. But when combined with racism, nativism, sexism, the success gospel, and strains resulting from the cross-pressures of social and economic growth, job competition became a potent divisive influence — a readily understood issue within the impersonal maze of forces affecting workers' lives. The vast majority of workers viewed and reacted to these problems moderately, their basic optimism prevailing. Even the minority who actively attempted to correct inequities demonstrated little class consciousness or sense of overwhelming urgency to halt a permanent deterioration of

their conditions. Workers in these decades were at times bewildered and anxious, but rarely desperate or irate, and, above all, not radical. Various working-class efforts to deal with emerging difficulties clearly reflected these traits.

The formation of labor organizations was one such method. In conformity with national patterns of development, skilled craftsmen provided the initial impetus for Ohio's early labor movement. Prior to 1820, artisans began to establish small, local associations for their respective trades. Although masters organized first, journeymen in various crafts soon followed. Some associations embraced both groups, an indication of the minimal alienation of workers from employers. These labor bodies functioned primarily as fraternal and benevolent societies. Membership dues supported widows, furnished loans, provided relief to the ill or unemployed (though sometimes with the stipulation "that his disease or disability arise not from intemperance or other vicious or improper conduct"), and protected standards of craftsmanship. Occasionally societies supplemented mutual aid with efforts to protect members' economic interests. Masters' organizations adopted lists of uniform prices for their crafts in order to diminish the effects of unfair competition and rising costs of raw materials. Journeymen's societies, in turn, exhibited early characteristics of trade unions by issuing demands for minimum wages, piecework standards, and apprenticeship regulations.

With the exception of a Mechanics' Society founded in Dayton in 1813, and millwrights' associations at Zanesville in 1815 and Mt. Vernon in 1817, embryonic organizational activity centered in Cincinnati. Small masters' groups of one or two dozen members each appeared throughout the Queen City's infancy: millwrights in 1802, coopers in 1805, cordwainers in 1812, a Society of Master Taylors (sic) in 1818, and carpenters and joiners in 1819. Although the bricklayers and the Mechanics' Cotton Manufacturing Society evidently included both masters and journeymen, there is no record of separate journeymen's organizations until 1819, when the Mutual Relief Society of Journeymen Hatters, the Union Benevolent Society of Journeymen Taylors (sic), and the Journeymen Cabinet Makers' Society were formed. Approximately thirty-two craft associations of various types had been established in the city by 1819.

Despite these stirrings, however, labor activity remained relatively dormant in Ohio prior to 1820. Social and economic conditions were not yet sufficiently ripe, even in Cincinnati, to stimulate the level of militancy already displayed by eastern craftsmen. Shop-floor relations seemed harmonious; journeymen negotiated with masters personally; masters consented to demands readily because of economic prosperity and the labor shortage; and no recorded strikes occurred. None of the organizations enjoyed more than brief, fitful existences, and all were wiped out by the Panic of 1819.

A gradual revival of organizational activity

began as economic prosperity returned after 1824. Reinforcing pre-depression patterns, the reawakened labor movement continued to be an urban affair and was confined to the white, resident, skilled elite of Ohio's working class. However, notable changes also emerged. Some journeymen's societies shed benevolent aims, exluded employers, focused on economic concerns, and became more militant. At the same time, a spreading recognition of the need for broad labor unity led to early experiments with city-wide and national unions.

Local workers' organizations sprang up in many of the state's growing towns during the 1820s and 30s. Industrialization and its corresponding problems did not advance as rapidly in these places as in Cincinnati. Thus most artisans still felt secure and optimistic about their opportunities, and retained the benevolent features of their societies longer. In Columbus, two such bodies appeared: the Mechanics' Beneficial Society in 1830 and a Typographical Society in 1832. A unique development in the former was the members' decision in 1838 to enter the banking field, by founding the Mechanics' Savings Institute. In Cleveland, journeymen printers formed a short-lived Typographical Association in 1835, and in 1837 the Ohio General Assembly incorporated the Carpenters' and Joiners' Benevolent Society. In 1835, the state also granted a charter to the Mechanics' Union of Springfield, though strictly for "literary, scientific, and benevolent purposes." Organized militancy in these outlying urban areas was evidently rare before the 1840s. "Turn-outs" by Steubenville weavers for higher wages in 1835 and union recognition in 1836 were the only documented strikes.

In Cincinnati, Ohio's largest, most rapidly industrializing and problem-plagued urban center, workers forged the state's most aggressive and developed labor movement by the 1830s. Following the depression of the early 1820s, a mild organizational resurgence began among skilled craftsmen. The revitalized groups initially continued to function as mutual-aid societies of printers, bricklayers, hatters, wagonmakers, harnessmakers, tailors, cobblers, and other artisans. Although every important trade had established some form of labor organization by 1836, total membership represented only about four percent of the city's 16,000 artisans. A minority movement, organized labor also displayed the racist overtones so common at the time. Organized white craftsmen barred black artisans from membership and refused to work in integrated shops. In 1830, one society tried its president publicly "for the crime of assisting a colored young man to learn a trade."

Despite such limitations, several Cincinnati labor societies made important organizational advances during the 1830s. Gradually reacting to the pressures of merchant-capitalism, the impersonal factory system, and strained relations with masters, concerned journeymen began to transform their old mutual-aid associations into aggressive trade unions to collectively protect their wages, hours, and working conditions. In place of personal dickering between journeyman and master, united economic action appeared with increasing frequency. The Journeymen Tin-Plate Workers of Cincinnati, for example, may have won the first collective-bargaining agreement in Ohio, when, in 1830 they negotiated a signed contract for wage scales with a group of masters. In 1831 the Journeyman Carpenters and Joiners' Association warned masters not to undermine their wages by attempting to import "distant journeymen carpenters" and publicly declared that henceforth their members would only work a ten-hour day. By mid-decade, workers' anxieties peaked and journeyman-master relations deteriorated further. Fueled by the inflationary spiral which caused "turn-outs" across the nation during 1835 and 1836, Cincinnati unions staged several "defensive" strikes to protect wages. The Harnessmakers' Union struck in the summer of 1835, for example, and a reorganized union of journeymen tailors turned out that December. Apparently without success, the tailors demanded "more wages, fewer apprentices, no tailoresses, and [use of] the back shops on Sundays for beer and cards." And, in a display of unity remarkable for the period, nearly all building trades' journeymen struck successfully in 1836 — after Philadelphia workers refused to serve as strikebreakers.

Weavers in the Steubenville textile mills were among the most militant workers in early Ohio. During their 1836 "turn-out" for union recognition by R.H. Orth and Company, the strikers' Society issued a public appeal for support, in which they described their cause in song:

A STRIKE SONG
By the Society

Shall tyrants reign and rule us all?
Shall truth and reason cease to smile?
Ah, no! says Justice, they shall fail,
And Love and Union guard us all,
Truth and Justice hear our Call,
Defend our rights and guard us all!

Reward for toil by us is craved,
And Fortune has a scheme contrived:
Then why should Weavers be enslaved
And basely of their rights deprived?
Weavers, be firm, and never flee,
We have been bound but will be free!

By foreign yoke we're not oppress'd,
By evils laws we're not annoy'd,
Through war at home we're not distress'd,
Nor is our country's trade destroy'd,
Through drones and tyrants, we are poor,
We've suffer'd long, we'll bear no more.

Be firm and keep your point in view;
For one false step may lead astray
A noble club; but those are true
That's firm, but cowards soon give way.
Be firm, for Reason's on our side
And Justice will for us provide.

Cincinnati's journeymen printers were the most militant and progressive unionists in Ohio's infant labor movement. Although originally founded as a mutual-aid society between 1825 and 1827, the city's Franklin Typographical Society was the first trade union in Ohio. Drastic changes in the printing business, particularly the threat posed to small shops by larger enterprises owned by newspaper publishers who functioned as merchant-capitalists, caused deep concern among journeymen by the 1830s. As in other trades, some masters became mere bosses seeking to reduce costs, especially by replacing expensive journeymen with partially trained apprentices, called "two-thirders," or with transient "rats." Roused to resistance by these dangerous developments as well as wage reductions, journeymen struck in June 1835. Masters crushed the effort by importing strike-breakers, an ominous portent of things to come. In reaction to the bitter defeat, printers issued a national circular which stands as one of the era's most revealing statements regarding the moderation, problems, and potential of the labor movement:

> Our association, as societies, is not to oppress others, but for self-defence. To secure a living compensation for our labor, and to sustain the generous and liberal employer who is willing to allow such compensation. To defend ourselves from undermining and base-spirited journeymen; and thereby protect our friends among employers, from those of their number who would take advantage of their liberality—who would under-work master's prices, by dispensing a beggarly pittance to their journeymen. We have still another and a higher motive—it is benevolence. ... Against resident journeymen, we have had but few cases of complaint; but we have been seriously annoyed by unprincipled persons from a distance; and we fear that a considerable part of the floating mass of journeymen printers is composed of such characters. ... Let us seek for a constant and regular communication with our sister societies, that we may give and receive advice of unworthy persons of the craft, and pursue the same rigid rules of exclusion towards the enemies of other societies, that we do towards those who oppose us. And let the certificate of membership in a typographical society, be no longer looked upon as a mere evidence of regular standing; but let it call forth active friendship for the bearer — our zealous efforts to get him into employment, in preference to those who have no such claim upon us. ... We believe the signs of the times imperatively call upon us to arouse to action. ... And we would hail with pleasure, as the opening prospect of a bright day to our profession, the establishment of a chain of societies from one extreme of the Union to the other, governed by such regulations, and marked by such spirit and firmness in action, that the unprincipled may no where find a foothold, and the scurvy principle of ratting be for ever extinguished.

In November 1836, in part because of these proposals for unity, a printers' convention met in Washington, D. C., and founded the National Typographical Society. One of the first national labor unions, the organization lasted only two years. Despite its brief life span, however, Cincinnati's printers had established themselves as heralds of future "chains of societies" which would spread across the country.

The city's skilled workers recognized by 1836 that their small trade unions could not individually match the growing strength of employers. Therefore, like their counterparts in eastern cities, artisans united their various organizations into a city-wide central association—the General Trades' Union of Cincinnati. Reflecting the working class concern with social stratification and the increased concentration of wealth and power in the hands of an elite, the preamble to the union's constitution declared:

> ... Of what advantage is it for us to exult, that our admirable system of government knows no difference between individuals, if distinctions obtain in society, almost as broad as [those] between the Russian lord and his serf?. ... "Wealth is power"—and no where is the truth of this adage oftener exhibited, than between the rich employer and the poor working men — the freeman by our laws, becomes the bondsman by his necessities. But "in union there is strength". ... On the *individual* system, in ninety-nine cases out of a hundred, the employer will have the power of dictating, and the workingman be left the only alternative of submission or starvation, as has been fully exemplified by the oppression in some of the large manufactories of this country. ... That such evils may not be perpetuated, or come upon us, we unite. ...

The extent of the central union's local activity during its brief existence is obscure, lost in unrecorded pasts. However, the organization did play a role in national labor affairs through its membership in the National Trades Union. Established in New York City in 1834, the NTU was the labor movement's first attempt to form a national federation of unions. Above all, it voiced the artisan's anxiety over the menace of merchant-capitalism. At the 1836 convention, Cincinnati delegate David S. Snellbaker gained recognition for his ringing denunciation of the "great system of speculation, by which they who produce nothing receive nearly all the products of the labor of those that produce."

This "flush period of trade unionism" abruptly terminated with the Panic of 1837. Unemployment and economic hardship crushed local and national labor organizations, but neither the notion of unionization nor the deep-rooted causes which gave it sustenance disappeared. By 1839, agitation and organization began to reawaken in Cincinnati. In that year, local printers reactivated the Franklin Typographical Society; in addition, a loose, unnamed workers' body held regular meetings in which they discussed the depression's causes and effects. Journeymen tailors opened their own Union shop in 1840, asserting that they could not survive on the curtailed wages offered by employers; and in 1841 the butcher's and brick makers' societies reappeared. By 1843, with the worst of the crisis passed, Cincinnati's journeymen woodturners, shoemakers, and carpenters struck to recover the sizeable wage cuts which they had suffered during the depression. As the

People's Paper of Cincinnati noted in October, 1843:

> It gives us unspeakable pleasure to observe the progress the workies are steadily making. We have hitherto contended that it was impossible, in large cities, for mechanics to redress their grievances, unless they formed societies, resolved to firmly adhere to each other, and boldly demand their rights. Experience proves that we were correct in our opinions. . . .

Rumblings of organized labor unrest had thus revived.

Unlike their counterparts elsewhere, few Ohio workers turned to political activity as a means of remedying their difficulties. Vocal workingmen's parties arose throughout the East during the late-1820s and early-1830s, often playing vital roles in area politics. Not so in Ohio. The Workingmen's parties which appeared in Canton, Columbus, and Zanesville between 1827 and 1834 attracted few followers and made no discernable impact. Cincinnati's mechanics had shown early political promise by publicly endorsing a successful candidate for the General Assembly in 1822, but that promise remained unfulfilled. A Working Man's Party materialized, still-born, in 1828, and throughout the 1830s labor's political activity in Cincinnati was conspicuous only by its absence. While workers in other states began pressing after 1835 for legislation such as the ten-hour day, no such movement emerged in Ohio. The General Assembly did pass laws currently being demanded by labor across the nation — an act ending imprisonment for debt in 1838, and a Mechanic's Lien Law in 1843 — but not as a result of any evident political pressure by Ohio workers. A political spark ignited in the early-1840s, only to fizzle quickly. A Working Man's Association which briefly appeared in Cincinnati's third ward in 1841, for example, ironically opposed trade unionism. In 1842 another Working Man's Association sprang up in Dayton; composed of businessmen and mechanics, it collapsed in six months due to factionalism. The following year artisans formed the Toledo Mechanics Association and elected almost their entire slate to city offices, then immediately disbanded.

While political action slumbered in labor's arsenal of tactics, some workers regularly resorted to means other than unions to solve their grievances. Mob violence, unfortunately, was one such weapon. The causation, composition, and behavior of mobs are complex issues. A look at several Cincinnati riots shows that while racial hatred and anti-abolitionist sentiment generally triggered mob action, riots mirrored deeper social and economic tensions which flowed from the inability of contemporary authorities to respond adequately to the city's multifaceted growth. White rioters, moreover, had several specific characteristics. Most were mature men, not young delinquents. Although skilled and unskilled workers participated, chiefly because of what they saw as threats to their economic security, ranking members of the professional and commercial classes led and made up the bulk of mobs. Some mechanics may have been anxious over industrialization and sweatshop conditions; yet they did not view themselves as a "displaced social elite" hoping to regain lost status through violence. It is significant to note, finally, that white workers were not unanimously racist, as the membership of many artisans in the Cincinnati Anti-Slavery Society testifies.

Tensions reached the breaking-point on several occasions. In 1829 unskilled and transient whites acted on fears that the large numbers of blacks who had entered Cincinnati over the last three years would force down wages and take available jobs. Joined by non-workers, they demanded enforcement of the state's black laws, hopeful that this would drive blacks from the city. Before legal steps could be taken, however, impatient white mobs attacked black neighborhoods. Eventually nearly half the black population fled. When black migration accelerated again in the mid-1830s, white worries about job competition resurfaced. Warf laborers, foundry mechanics, and skilled machinists, whose jobs depended on southern trade, also feared that the city's growing black population and the presence of highly vocal anti-slavery agitators might cause offended southerners to do business elsewhere. Consequently, in 1836 workers joined in several mob attacks on blacks and the local abolitionist newspaper. As the depression gripped Cincinnati, racial tensions intensified, partly due to job competition between blacks and immigrants. By 1841 passions boiled over. Fueled by news of racial clashes in Dayton and repeated brawls between Cincinnati blacks and Irish, the city exploded into bloody warfare. City officials proved incapable of containing such repeated mob violence until 1843, when they prevented mob attacks on abolitionists from escalating into another full-blown riot.

Racial issues were not the only sources of mob violence. The Cincinnati Bank Riot of 1842 demonstrated that although the deepening economic depression affected all segments of the population, the working classes especially suffered. Already faced with financial uncertainty and rising unemployment, workers now had to bear the additional burden of wages paid in depreciated currency. This left employees, the editor of the *Cincinnati Republican* concluded, with few alternatives: ". . . for the last two or three years they have been glad to get hold of anything with which to buy bread for their families; they could not afford, they did not *dare,* to refuse it so long as it would pass." The brewing rage of workers who saw themselves as victims of ruthless bankers erupted on January 11. When one bank collapsed and merchants refused to accept the currency of others, panic swept the streets. Working-class mobs descended on the city's banks throughout the day. Demanding redemption of notes in hard money, they plundered banks which could or would not comply. Nativism briefly surfaced in the aftermath of the riot, when some residents publicly

blamed German mechanics for the violence. Suspicion and resentment of the clannish and growing German community, which by early 1843 comprised over one-quarter of the city's population, lay behind the charge. No serious violence followed, but the incident pointed ominously toward nativist riots which would flare in the following decade.

The strains and inequities arising from the new social and economic order also induced some disenchanted workers to explore alternatives to the prevailing system. By the late 1820s, a variety of communal and cooperative experiments had been launched in Ohio, all of which basically rejected the principles of individualistic, acquisitive capitalism. Participants attempted to eliminate or diminish the hazards of industrial society through collective ownership, production, and distribution of life's necessities. They hoped that in this way a more humane, just, prosperous, and satisfying way of life would emerge. Some ventures—such as the communitarian settlements established by the Shakers in 1805-06 and the village of Zoar founded by German Separatists in 1817— stemmed from sectarian efforts to withdraw from the corrupting influences of an imperfect world. Secular reformers seeking to regenerate society by establishing model cooperative socio-economic systems initiated other utopian experiments. Of the two movements, secular

A sample of Josiah Warren's ''labor-for-labor currency.''

reform had a more direct, if limited, appeal to urban workers concerned with the worldly hardships imposed by industrialization.

The associationist ideas of Robert Owen formed the base for one secular reform experiment which briefly sprouted in Ohio. A successful manufacturer, Owen had become deeply committed to correcting the shocking effects of industrialization on the working classes in his native Scotland. In 1825 he arrived in America with plans to build collectivist communities in the West to serve as utopian prototypes for a new social order. Two Owenite settlements were attempted in Ohio: the Yellow Springs Community in Green County from 1825 to 1827 and the Kendal Community in Stark County from 1826 to 1829. In these small communities of under one hundred families each, skilled artisans, common laborers, farmers, professionals, and merchants experimented with a communal system in which all were to share collectively in production, benefits, and responsibilities. As Owen had warned, however, the transition from an individualistic to a socialistic mode of living could be difficult. Soon after their founding, both communities fell prey to personal jealousies and factional squabbles. Skilled workers at Yellow Springs insisted that they should only have to work half as long as farmers because their efforts were twice as valuable. Such bickering, along with mounting debts,

You never will find any satisfactory solution of the great problem now up between LABOR and CAPITAL, or SLAVERY and LIBERTY, until you understand what Justice *is*, and what a circulating medium, or money, ought to be.

MAY 18, 1827.

CINCINNATI, OHIO.

The most disagreeable labor is entitled to the highest compensation.

LABOR for LABOR

Due to *Bearer,*

EIGHT HOURS LABOR
IN SHOE-MAKING, OR ONE HUNDRED POUNDS OF CORN.
Number —, F—street. *William Morton.*

Time is Wealth.

The above is one specimen of what money ought to be. It should be issued by those men, women, and children who perform some useful service, but by *nobody else*. It should command LABOR FOR LABOR in equal quantities, and the most disagreeable should be highest paid.

Perhaps no class or person is to blame, but the most fatal element of confusion, oppression, and violence ever introduced among mankind is the passing off of metals or any other natural product of the earth, or the earth itself as *pay for labor!* It defrauds, starves, and degrades, and then insults labor, and makes it a thing to be shunned and avoided, and forced upon whoever can be made to bear it. This is the origin of all forms of slavery, in all civilized countries, and of all poverty and crime, the *insecurity of condition*, the worship of money, the antagonisms of classes, and the crisis of these times. Whereas, if Labor were equitably rewarded (with an equal amount of labor), the hardest worker would be the richest man, and all would choose a portion of labor as a means of health and pleasure. For further explanations, see the works mentioned on the opposite page.

This is addressed in a friendly spirit to all parties and nations. *YOU HAVE NO TIME TO LOSE!*

forced both settlements to disband. Despite their failures, however, the notion of communal living survived to be rekindled in the 1840s.

Cincinnati musician and inventor Josiah Warren devised the most novel secular reform endeavor. Described as the "first American anarchist," Warren had been an early follower of Robert Owen. After participating in Owen's ill-fated colony at New Harmony, Indiana, he returned to Cincinnati convinced that a system based on total individual liberty, rather than Owenite principles of self-sacrifice and conformity, offered the only viable alternative to the developing system in which

> . . . we see the labouring and useful members of Society, who have produced every thing, starving in the streets for want; while some are rendered equally miserable from the anxieties of speculation and competition, and others for want of an object worthy of pursuit, are destroying their health, and shortening their lives by inactivity and apathy, or by luxuriously revelling upon the labour of the depressed. . . . Already have we in this country, made alarming progress in the road to national ruin. . . .

In Warren's view, collective equality could only be achieved when sovereign individuals were completely free to dispose of their labor and property as they saw fit. Advocating an early version of the labor theory of value, he stressed that workers should determine the worth of their own labor on the basis of the time spent, rather than accepting the arbitrary monetary values imposed by employers, bankers, or merchants. Only in this way could workers be assured of a more equitable share of the profits from the expanding capitalist order. As a means of demonstrating the applicability of his theories, Warren opened a "Time Store" in Cincinnati in 1827. In conducting this new enterprise, he used "labor-for-labor currency" and barter for the exchange of goods and services by local workers. As he described his experiment:

> . . . Time is the real and natural standard of value. . . . Here upon this single and simple principle, all exchanges of articles and personal services are made, so that he who employs five or ten hours of his time, in the service of another, receives five or ten hours of labour of the other in return. . . . He who deposits an article, which by our estimate costs ten hours labour, received any other articles, which, together with the labour of the [store] keeper in receiving and delivering them, costs ten hours, or, if the person making the deposit does not wish at that time, to draw out any article, he receives a Labour Note for the amount; with this note he will draw out articles, or obtain the labour of the keeper, whenever he may wish to do so. . . .

For his role as storekeeper, Warren received a fixed rate for the time and labor which he expended in each transaction. The store served not only as a marketplace for goods and an employment bureau for laborers, but also as a trade school for unapprenticed individuals willing to pay labor notes for training by skilled craftsmen. After a slow start, the Time Store eventually attracted a sizeable number of working class and professional customers. Satisfied that his experiment was a success, Warren closed the store in 1829, without having gained or lost any money, and moved east to spread his reform message.

While these cooperative ventures were short-lived and involved few laboring-class participants, they signaled a significant early link between workers and social reformers. Confronted with the increasingly serious challenges of industrial capitalism to their personal welfare, workers would intermittently flirt with various reform schemes throughout the remainder of the century. In the process, the basic moderation of Ohio's working classes would be sorely tested.

After four decades of multi-faceted transition, Ohio's diverse working class remained in a state of flux. Large segments of the toiling population began to encounter fundamental alterations in their personal relationships, living conditions, and means of earning a livelihood. Social and economic problems and tensions had emerged which, in various forms, would haunt workers for generations. Yet neither the composition, the cohesiveness, nor the responses of Ohio's working class had been determined. Although many workers had been sobered by the preindustrial trends, only a tiny percentage of the skilled elite had turned to unionization and even fewer had been radicalized by their experiences. Inclinations toward job-consciousness and militant action had been displayed, but the debilitating influences of factionalism and individualism inhibited the development of class consciousness. The working class had only begun to explore its potential options and capabilities. The avenues of response to Ohio's accelerating urban-industrial transformation remained open.

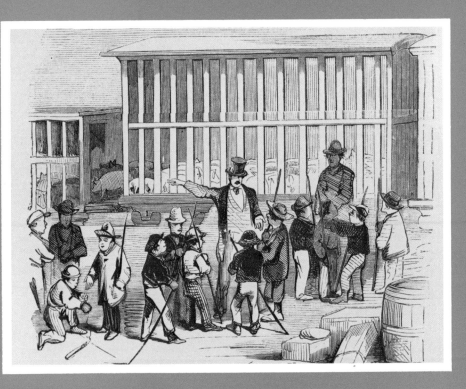

By 1841, the railroad brought tens of thousands of hogs to Cincinnati's stockyards, where young boys were hired to drive the animals to the slaughterhouses.

Boys herded the squealing hogs through the city's streets. Some invariably escaped from the doomed droves to roam freely in alleys and backyards and under houses.

Human Chopping Machines

A more gruesome occupation than hog-slaughtering would have been difficult to find in early Cincinnati. Blood soaked through shoes and clothing, coated the slippery floors, smeared tools, spurted into unguarded faces. Nauseating stenches filled the air. Since owners compensated for the lack of sufficient ice and mechanical refrigeration by operating only during the winter months, workers labored in biting cold. Oftentimes, only by plunging their arms into the warm entrails of a steaming carcass could they ward off frostbite. And always there was the danger that a razor-sharp blade would miss its mark, severing a finger or slashing an arm. Unnoticed nicks on numb hands could erupt into festering infections, blood poisoning, and agonizing death.

Charles Fenno Hoffman observed this grisly working environment in 1834. In *Winter In the West*, he subsequently described the grim efficiency with which laborers managed to perform their tasks:

The most remarkable, however, of all the establishments of Cincinnati are those immense slaughter-houses where the business of butchering and packing pork is carried on. The minute division of labor and the fearful clarity of execution in these swinish workshops would equally delight a pasha and a political economist; for it is the mode in which the business is conducted, rather than its extents, which gives dignity to hog killing in Cincinnati, and imparts a tragic interest to the last moments of the doomed porkers. . . .

Imagine, a long, narrow edifice, divided into various compartments, each communicating with the other, and each furnished with some peculiar and appropriate engine of destruction. In one you see a gory block and gleaming axe; a seething cauldron nearly fills another. The walls of a third bristle with hooks newly sharpened for impalement; while a fourth is shrouded in darkness. That leaves you to conjure up images still more dire. There are 40 ministers of fate distributed throughout these gloomy abodes, each with his

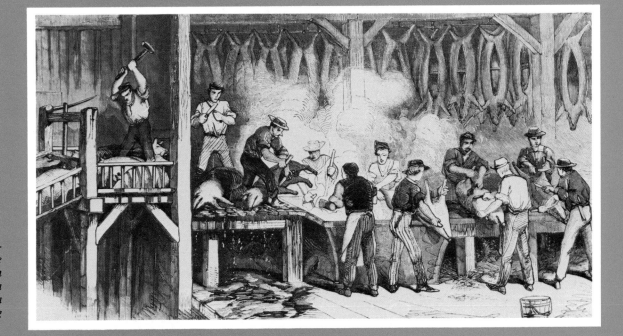

With machine-like precision, five hogs per minute were killed, moved through a scalding vat, and given a preliminary cleaning on a twenty-five foot scraping table.

In the second stage of the slaughtering process, the carcass was moved on a primitive overhead conveyor to the "gutting room" for final dressing.

particular office assigned him. And here, when the fearful carnival comes on, and the deep forests of Ohio have contributed their thousands of unoffending victims, the gauntlet of death is run by those selected for immolation.

The scene commences in the shadowy cell whose gloom we have not yet been allowed to penetrate. Fifty unhappy porkers are here incarcerated as one together, with bodies wedged so closely that they are incapacitated from all movements. And now the grim executioner ... leaps with his iron mace upon their backs and rains his ruthless blows around him. The unresisting victims fall on every side; but scarcely does one touch the ground before he is siezed by a greedy hook protruded through an orifice below. His throat is severed instantly in the adjacent cell, and the quivering body is hurried onward, as if the hands of the Furies tossed it through the frightful suite of chambers.

The mallet, the knife, the axe, the boiling cauldron, the remorseless scraping iron, have each done their work; and the fated porker, that was one minute before grunting in the full enjoyment of bristling hoghood, now cadaverous and "chopfallen," hangs a stark and naked effigy among his immolated brethren.

Indeed, as Hoffman's account vividly suggested, Cincinnati's butcher workmen were among the first "factory workers" in Ohio. As early as the 1830s, several factors combined to spur the introduction of mass-production methods in slaughtering and packing operations: the industry's brief seasonal character, which prompted proprietors to achieve large-scale output in the shortest possible time; the ready availability of transient laborers, who drifted into the city seeking temporary winter employment to tide them over until construction and farm jobs resumed in the spring; canal and railroad expansion, which provided rural hog-raisers with access to Cincinnati's slaughterhouses; and growing demand for pork from national and international markets. Intensive division and specialization of labor soon appeared in each of the three primary processing steps — slaughtering, cleaning, and cutting.

Each worker or crew performed a specific task as hogs passed through the various stations within the plant. While one man spent his day monotonously removing bristles, another cleaned ears, another hacked off rear legs, another gutted, another carved out shoulders, and so on. Although the operations remained basically manual, a "disassembly line" atmosphere developed through the implementation of large-scale, high-speed, and systematic teamwork. In fact, observers noted that workmen toiled with such precision, as to resemble "a sort of human chopping machine." By 1837, mass-production techniques were so refined that, without machinery, a team of twenty workers could kill and clean seventy-eight hogs per hour.

Further progress in the evolution of a modern factory system followed. During the 1840s, formerly separate slaughtering and packing operations became physically integrated into single, extensive enterprises employing dozens of workers. Hogs were driven up a ramp to the top floor of multi-story buildings for slaughtering, proceeded downward through the disassembly

The cleaned hogs hung in a "cooling room" for twenty-four hours prior to being cut and packed.

The final slaughtering stage — the "cutting room."

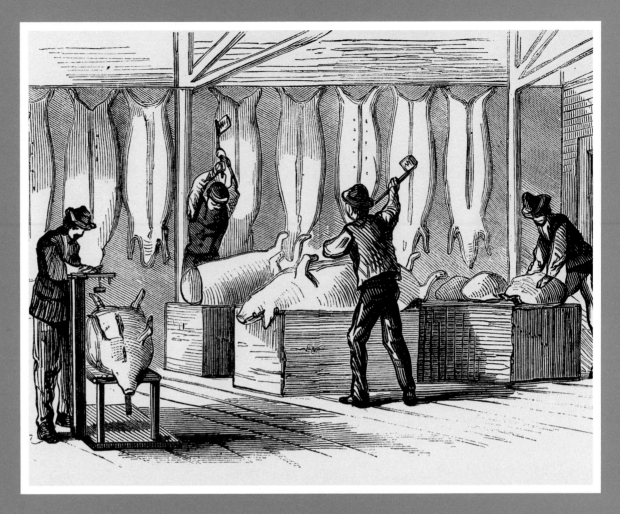

Within thirty-five seconds, a hog was chopped into hams, shoulders, and prime for the world's consumers.

Workers packed the pork in salt for preservation during shipping.

process on the lower floors, and emerged at ground-level as a variety of pork products. The complex, irregularly shaped carcasses continued to defy the use of machinery in the slaughtering and cutting stages. However, primitive mechanization did prove feasible in the gutting rooms, where the introduction of horizontal wheels in the 1850s, and overhead railway loops in the 1860s foreshadowed the massive conveyor lines, which later distinguished American industry. With these new devices, the killed, scalded, and scraped hogs were hoisted onto hooks attached to the rails or wheels, rapidly passed to workmen for washing and gutting, and then moved into the cooling room.

The immediate and long-term impacts of these technological and organizational innovations were tremendous. In the 1820s, Cincinnati had already earned the title, "Porkopolis," by annually processing 25,000 to 30,000 hogs for local and regional markets. However, by the 1850s, 350,000 to 450,000 hogs were efficiently slaughtered and packed every year for local, regional, national, and international markets. More importantly, by initiating the development of large-scale conveyor systems, pork producers also made Cincinnati the "birthplace of mass production." Decades later, Henry Ford and other manufacturers would successfully adapt the same techniques and principles to dozens of modern industries. And, as a result, generations of factory workers would wearily toil before ever-more-rapidly-moving assembly lines.

PART 2 ENTERING THE URBAN-INDUSTRIAL MAINSTREAM 1844-1885

During the mid- and late 1800s, massive industrialization, urbanization, and immigration catapulted Ohio into social and economic maturity and, in the process, indelibly dyed the fabric of working-class life. These were decades of phenomenally rapid and extensive expansion, beside which the developmental strides of the preindustrial period paled in comparison. However, economic growth and social transformation did not necessarily advance in tandem or in an orderly pattern. Although a formidable force, "progress" was not a juggernaut crushing all preindustrial methods, habits, and cultures in its path. Rather, kaleidoscopic change was the dominant motif—with transitions occurring at different times and paces, in different industries and communities, with varying degrees of impact. Ohio's laboring people, in turn, displayed multifaceted responses to the diverse alterations affecting their personal, social, and working lives. Some accepted the new urban-industrial order and its values, while some adapted without accepting. Still others rejected such change, seeking instead to retain preindustrial customs or to explore further the alternative avenues of response which had been charted earlier. But most of all, workers clearly demonstrated that, despite the insecurity, consternation, and dislocation which increasingly colored the era, many would refuse to be passive victims. In workplaces, streets, and homes throughout the state, they strove to assert or retain some control over the seemingly impersonal forces buffeting their working-class world.

George Garner arrived in East Liverpool, Ohio during the summer of 1844. A native of Burslem, England, he had joined an exodus of fellow-potters who were alarmed by unemployment and new labor-saving machinery in the famous Wedgewood Potteries. Writing to friends in the Burslem Emigration Society five months later, Garner related his initial experiences and impressions:

> ...In three days after we got in, Bradshaw, Cartwright, and myself began to work. Cartwright was turning after me; and Bradshaw began in the kiln, at John Goodwin's. John Goodwin wanted me to take a share with him, in the business, but I declined. I told him, I did not intend to go into business until spring. By that time, I shall know a little more of the country. It would be unwise of me to commence in business, as soon as I got in. There are those that have and have lost their money to teach them sense.... [I]n farming, the situation is a great deal better.... But I feel more favourable to the potting business.... East Liverpool is full of clay and coal, and contains about 700 inhabitants....[Recently] I have engaged with the

Bennetts that were potting here, to do their throwing until spring. Cartwright has engaged with them also, to turn for them. They, together with us, are leaving East Liverpool, and going to Birmingham [Pennsylvania]. The Bennetts have built a factory, to the amount of $4,000 dollars, which is now in operation at Birmingham. I shall have a good situation. I will not recommend any potters to come out, unless they have situations to come to; but as the trade spreads, potters will be wanted. But there are none wanted at present. If any potters come here, they will be in each other's way; and give the masters an opportunity of reducing wages.... To work here as you do would be considered by the Americans, as being worse than beasts....

There is none of that lordlyship as in England. Some of you are obliged to worship your masters, when meeting them on the road; I mean by almost ploughing the road up, with bowing and scraping to them; and perhaps just at the entrance of a place of worship. There is no such thing here. I have seen men worth double the amount of those you idolize, working side by side of their men, during the week and, on a Sunday, sitting by their side in a place of worship....

...Cartwright's lathe-turner is the son of a magistrate; his father is nothing but a tailor; but having character that bears the strictest investigation he is elected. Just so with other offices of the State. The people seem to be alive to their own interest....

As Garner's account vividly testifies, native and foreign-born workers alike were indeed "alive to their own interest" — whether individually defined in financial, occupational, social, or political terms. But equally significant, was the manner and extent to which so many pursued their personal "interest" through migration — a phenomenon which had a profound impact upon the diverse interactions of Ohio's laboring people with their swiftly maturing environment.

Changing migration and settlement patterns were among the first signs that Ohio was "coming of age" as a developed state. During its embryonic expansion, Ohio had been a primary frontier-destination for hundreds-of-thousands of migrants. But as the state became well-settled by mid-century—with growing families, rising agricultural production costs, and relatively little cheap land available—the trend began to shift. Increasing numbers of residents as well as potential newcomers, left or bypassed Ohio in pursuit of opportunities further west. Departing migrants outnumbered new arrivals by an estimated 76,000 during the 1840s, and by nearly 275,000 during the 1850s. Consequently, while natural population increases continued, such net migration losses caused Ohio's overall rate of population growth to slow dramatically —from thirty percent in the 1840s, to eighteen percent in the 1850s, fourteen percent in the 1860s, and twenty percent in the 1870s. These relatively modest increases fell well-below national growth rates, at the same time that younger states experienced population booms as the frontier pushed westward. Thus, even though its total population climbed to nearly 3.2 million by 1880, Ohio lost its rank as the na-

THE PIONEER POTTERY OF EAST LIVERPOOL, OHIO.

tion's third most populous state, slipping to fourth position behind Illinois.

Shifting migratory currents also had conspicuous effects upon the overall composition and nativity of Ohio's population (see Appendix — Tables 2A and 2B). Most noticeably, the populace became overwhelmingly indigenous to the state, as the proportion of Ohio-born residents rose sharply from sixty-two percent in 1850 to seventy-four percent by 1880. In contrast, during the same timespan, inhabitants born out-of-state steadily declined from twenty-seven to fourteen percent of the total population. Blacks, however, were exceptions to this trend. Largely due to migration from the South, especially during the Civil War decade, the black community expanded from one to three percent of all Ohioans between 1850 and 1880. Ohio attracted substantial numbers of European migrants as well, the vast majority of whom came from Germany, Ireland, England, and Wales. The influx peaked during the 1850s, when the addition of 110,000 immigrants accounted for over thirty percent of the state's total growth, and established the foreign-born as a sizeable minority of fourteen percent. Thereafter, the flow considerably slackened, resulting in the leveling-off of the foreign born populace at twelve percent by 1880. By and large, therefore, as Ohio reached maturity, the basic character of its population appeared remarkably uniform, with an increasing majority of its inhabitants being either Ohio-born or long-term residents.

Nevertheless, beneath these broad skeletal trends, the "maturation" of Ohio's populace was an uneven, dynamic process. High residential mobility among the working masses, expanding transportation systems, and a rapidly evolving urban-industrial structure combined to generate a constant ebb and flow of population redistribution within the state. The extent and complexity of this movement has been indicated in a recent study which geographically sampled heads of Ohio households in 1860 and found, not only that seventy percent were migrants; but also that thirty percent were Ohio-born who had migrated to another state, but then had returned to Ohio. With people con-

The Bennett Pottery in which George Garner toiled during the early 1840s.

Overleaf—page 29.
Section crews posed at the opening of the Lake Erie & Western Railroad crossing at Arcadia in 1881. These men labored for 11¢ per hour, ten hours per day.

tinually moving in, out, back into, and around the state, Ohio became a virtual patchwork of demographic diversity. For example, while such counties as Lucas and Cuyahoga enjoyed tremendous population expansion between 1840 and 1880, others such as Licking, Columbiana, and Muskingum counties endured extended periods of relative stagnation. Few areas experienced similar growth patterns, since expansion frequently came in intermittent spurts (see Table 2C). Generally speaking, however, aside from the northwestern counties, significant population increases occurred only in locales where manufacturing and mining developed. In addition, various patterns of racial and ethnic concentration emerged. Blacks continued to cluster primarily in traditional areas of black settlement within central and southern counties like Hamilton, Ross, Franklin, and Belmont. On the other hand, the foreign born tended to disperse more widely. Outside of Hamilton and Cuyahoga counties (which contained the state's largest foreign-born communities throughout the period), sizeable ethnic pockets appeared in a broad range of counties by 1880—English and Welsh in Trumbull, Mahoning, Columbiana, and Summit; Irish in Lucas, Franklin, and Montgomery; and Germans in Butler, Stark, and Washington counties (see Table 2D).

Amidst the swirl of continuous population movement during the mid- and late nineteenth century, one major factor provided an element of cohesion—the spectacular growth of Ohio's cities. As focal points of the state's commercial and industrial expansion, urban areas attracted unprecedented numbers of opportunity-seeking factory hands and farm youths, artisans and professionals, natives and immigrants. Throughout the state, villages swelled into towns and towns into cities. Although rural residents maintained numerical and proportional superiority, that dominance steadily dwindled. For, as indicated in Tables 2A and 2B, urban growth rates far-surpassed rural rates in every decade from 1840 to 1880, thereby enabling towns and cities to claim ever-larger portions of the total population. A significant turning-point was reached during the 1860s and 1870s, when surges of nearly 283,000 and 348,000 urbanites accounted respectively for eighty-seven and sixty-five percent of the state's total population increases for those decades. By 1880, one of every three Ohioans lived in an urban area, a figure well-above the national average of twenty-eight percent. The shift toward an urbanized Ohio was accelerating with incredible swiftness.

One of the nation's most extensive urban networks emerged during this era. Within little more than a generation, an impressive array of interrelated regional metropolises, large manufacturing-commercial centers, and smaller secondary cities of varying size and function had blossomed across Ohio. Cincinnati continued to reign as the state's premier metropolis, rising from 46,000 inhabitants in 1840 to over a quarter-million in 1880. However, its rapid economic and population growth had peaked by mid-century. Thereafter, the Queen City's dominance began to falter, its gradual maturation eclipsed by the larger expansionary spurts of younger, more vibrant urban areas. By 1880, Cincinnati's share of the state's urban populace slipped to twenty-five percent from a high of fifty-six percent in 1840. In fact, Ohio's entire urban hierarchy was in flux, as migration, new transportation links, and the industrial revolution selectively benefited some cities at the expense of others. Thus, while Cleveland,

By 1848, Cincinnati had grown from a sleepy village into a hurly-burly manufacturing and commercial center. Up-and-down-bound steamboats had replaced the flatboats of the city's infancy.

Columbus, and Dayton prospered, other older cities like Chillicothe, Lancaster, Newark, Steubenville, and Zanesville were outstripped by youthful rivals such as Sandusky, Akron, Canton, and Springfield. None could match the pace set by Toledo. From a struggling village of 1,200 in 1840, successive decennial population increases of 213, 260, 129, and fifty-nine percent transformed Toledo by 1880 into a bustling industrial-commercial center of 50,000 residents and the fourth largest city in Ohio. However, the era was marked not only by the rise of large urban areas, but by the proliferation of smaller cities as well. Between 1840 and 1880, while the number of Ohio cities containing more than 25,000 residents increased from one to five, the number of urban places with 2,500 to 10,000 inhabitants mushroomed from eight to seventy-five. One-third of all Ohio urbanites in 1880 lived and worked in such subordinate, but economically essential, cities as Nelsonville, Massillon, Lima, Findlay, East Liverpool, and Ashtabula.

Perhaps no city better epitomized Ohio's diverse urban transformation than Cleveland. Willard Glazier — army captain, author, and rather perceptive observer of nineteenth-century urbanization — marveled at the extent and the often contradictory manner in which Cleveland had developed from a lake-port of 6,000 in 1840, to the state's second-largest metropolis with 160,000 inhabitants forty years later. Writing in the mid-1880s, he could recall that:

> ...In 1845...Euclid Avenue and Prospect street extended for a few squares, and were then lost in the country. The flats through which the river wound its devious way were occupied as pastures for the cows of persons living in the heart of the city. The business portion of the town was contained, for the most part, in the two squares on Superior street....
>
> In the fall of 1852 the first whistle of the locomotive was heard down by the river side....It started the city into new life....
>
> ...Since 1860 the city has rapidly developed in the direction of manufacturing industries. The headquarters of the giant monopoly, known as the Standard Oil Company, Cleveland is the first city of the world in the production of refined pe-

troleum. The old pasture grounds of ...1850 are now completely occupied by oil refineries and manufacturing establishments; and the river, which but a generation ago flowed peaceful and placid through green fields, is now almost choked with barges, tugs and immense rafts. Looking down upon the Cuyahoga Flats, from the heights of what was once Ohio City, but is now known as the West Side of Cleveland itself, the view, though far from beautiful, is a very interesting one. There are copper smelting, iron rolling, and iron manufacturing works, lumber yards, paper mills, breweries, flour mills, nail works, pork-packing establishments, and the multitudinous industries of a great manufacturing city, which depends upon these industries largely for its prosperity....

Twenty or thirty years ago nothing more desolate or devoid of beauty can be imagined than was the lake and river approach to Cleveland. The cars ran along the foot of the cliff, while the space between the tracks and the table land upon which the city is built was given up to rubbish and neglect. Little huts, the size of organ boxes, were perched here and there, swarming with dirty, half-clad children and untidy women, and festooned with clotheslines, from which dangled a motley array of garments. Blackness, dirt and decay were visible everywhere; and the vestibule of the most beautiful city in America presented to the visitor the opposite extreme of repulsiveness....

The business portion of Euclid avenue extends from the Park to Erie street, beyond which it is lined with handsome residences, elegant cottages and superb villas, the grounds around each being

By the mid-1870s, Toledo was one of the state's leading industrial-commercial cities. Lake and rail carriers brought raw materials to the smoking workshops and carried away their products.

By 1878, Cleveland was a city of smoke, soot, and bustling businesses.

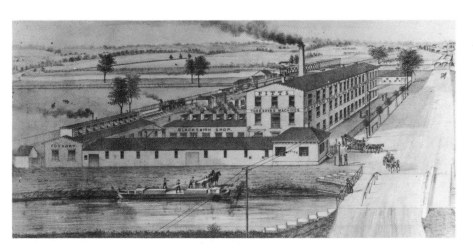

Nearby transportation arteries were crucial to the growth of Dayton's Woodsum, Tenney & Co. during the 1860s and 1870s.

Steamboats, such as these docked at Marietta, provided vital links in Ohio's transportation network.

The "Queen City" and the "Virginia" at Marietta wharf.

Rapidly being overshadowed by the railroads, canals and boats fell into disrepair. These boats were moored on the Ohio Canal at Lancaster in 1872.

more and more extensive as it approaches the country. It is one of the finest avenues in the world, and is not less than ten miles in length....

As Cleveland's climb to prominence vividly illustrated, the ongoing transportation revolution played a pivotal role in Ohio's economic and urban development. Canals, railroads, turnpikes, and natural waterways furnished towns and cities with access to the manpower, markets, capital, foodstuffs, and raw materials necessary for growth. Interlaced arteries linked urban and rural areas, bound sprawling cities and smaller urban satellites into a functional statewide network and made Ohio the crossroads of an increasingly integrated national economy. In keeping with the capricious tenor of the times, this transportation system also was undergoing dramatic alterations.

Although canals had provided yeoman service during Ohio's preindustrial evolution, their "glory years" were abruptly cut short in the early 1850s by overpowering adversaries, better suited to the needs of a new industrial age—the railroads. To farmers, merchants, and manufacturers who dealt in the increasingly competitive regional and national markets swift, inexpensive, and efficient transportation became a major concern. Canals, however, were unable either to meet the accelerating industrial and commercial demand, or to match the technological superiority of railroads. Steam locomotives could haul thousands of tons, at twelve to thirty miles-per-hour, and in almost any weather. Horse-drawn canal boats, on the other hand, had capacities of merely thirty to sixty tons; could travel at only two to eight miles-per-hour; and were commonly delayed for weeks by drought, floods, and ice. Numerous additional handicaps further plagued the canal lines: mismanagement by public and private officials: entanglements in party politics; "cut-throat" competition and rate discrimination by the railroads; and the canal operators' tendency to focus upon local trade, rather than the increasing through-traffic across the state. Canal business peaked in 1851. Thereafter began a prolonged period of progressive decay — traffic shifted to railroads; tonnage carried by canals steadily declined; annual expenditures exceeded income; as debts mounted, channels, locks, and reservoirs fell into disrepair. With increasing rapidity, section after neglected section was abandoned and faded back into the landscape. As early as the 1860s, cities like Toledo and Cincinnati were converting portions of the canals into sewers and streets. By the 1880s, despite some halfhearted proposals for rejuvenation, few segments remained in operation.

While outmoded canals deteriorated, new iron and steel rails enveloped the state. Only 455 miles of track were in use in 1850, but during the following decade "railroad mania" reached epidemic proportions, resulting in the completion of nearly 2,600 additional miles, and making Ohio the nation's leader in total railroad mileage in 1860. After a subsequent lull, another construction spurt during the 1870s extended the railway network to over 5,600 miles by 1880. Most railroad lines did a vigorous business — between 1860 and 1880 alone, passengers increased from an estimated 3.6 million to twenty million, freight tonnage rose from three million to forty-eight million, and reported net earnings swelled from $4.5 million to $15.7 million. With startling suddenness and completeness, the iron horse had doomed the once-teeming inland waterways to obsolescence and oblivion.

Relentless railway expansion proved to be a mixed blessing for Ohioans, ultimately generating as much anxiety as optimism in the public mind. Despite the undeniable benefits of rail-

roads, their growth patterns and business practices often adversely affected the economic, and even physical, well-being of individuals and entire communities. Failure to attract a rail line could mean economic stagnation, depopulation, and withered dreams for isolated interior towns; while municipalities which did succeed in luring a railroad with financial incentives frequently found themselves subject to its domination afterwards. Linkage with the nation's growing web of major trunk lines expanded potential markets, but also exposed the state's producers to a competitive crossfire from western as well as eastern rivals. Although greatly exaggerated then and since, some railroads blatantly utilized a wide variety of unscrupulous "business" methods: stock manipulations, excessive and discriminatory rate structures, political corruption, reckless speculation, monopolistic combinations, and outright fraud. But perhaps the most distressing aspect of the railroad boom was the dreadful toll in human lives and limbs. As the volume and speed of rail traffic increasingly overtaxed inadequately maintained equipment and right-of-ways, the corresponding rise in train collisions, derailments, locomotive explosions, grade-crossing accidents, and less spectacular (but equally

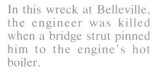

In this wreck at Belleville, the engineer was killed when a bridge strut pinned him to the engine's hot boiler.

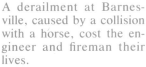

A derailment at Barnesville, caused by a collision with a horse, cost the engineer and fireman their lives.

tragic) daily mishaps became a public menace. From 1868 to 1885, 6,140 employees, 4,143 bystanders or trespassers, and 1,027 passengers were killed or injured by Ohio's railroads — figures made all the more appalling by the fact that these reported casualties represented only absolute minimums! State commissioners repeatedly complained that railroad officials refused or neglected to file accurate accident reports, as required by law. Inquests were seldom held; small payments to victims, friends, or relatives could settle an incident "quietly;" and employees hesitated to complain for fear of losing their jobs or the negligible compensation which employers might offer. Railroads cavalierly attributed four out of five reported deaths and injuries to the victims' "want of caution" (a condemnation seemingly applicable to almost everyone who purchased a ticket, crossed a track, stood on a station platform, or joined the payroll). Nevertheless, even the incomplete accident data reveals the gruesome side of the railroad age — particularly for trainmen. Railroading ranked as one of the state's most hazardous occupations. In 1872 at least one out of every sixty-eight employees was killed or injured on the job, a grisly rate which climbed to one in forty-seven by 1882. Accidents could have been diminished by safety devices, but few were as yet in use. Consequently, for decades, brakemen risked death by scurrying across the roofs of bucking, and often icy, boxcars to spin the primitive brake wheels of each car whenever deceleration was necessary. No less dangerous was the train-coupler's job, which called for a man to step between cars and manually engage or release heavy, swaying, unaligned link-and-pin devices. As the state railroad commissioner somberly observed in 1873,

... nearly one half [of] the accidents to [employees] comes from "coupling cars".... Injuries from this source, as a rule, are more than ordinarily severe, many of the victims being maimed for life—an arm, a hand, or the fingers taken off, or so crushed as to be a permanent disability....A large per cent are reported "for want of caution," which in the abstract may be true, but when any part of the employe's duty is attended with such fearful and certain danger to life and limb, ought not there to be at least an effort made to diminish the cause?....It is at least to be hoped that some invention ... will soon be substituted for this dangerous duty.

Unfortunately for couplers and brakemen, however, the commissioner's call would not be answered until the 1880s, when the introduction of automatic couplers and air brakes gradually eliminated these high-risk tasks. For train engineers, the strain of working long hours, under dangerous conditions, with often defective equipment also took a psychological toll which the casualty lists only indirectly reflected. As the superintendent of the Little Miami and Columbus and Xenia Railroads admitted in 1867,

There is no doubt but that the service required of locomotive engineers, wears out the health and shatters the constitution of a man very rapidly. I know of engineers who, after long and continual running of their engines, have become entirely disqualified for the business—it producing in them fear and apprehension to such an extent, that they were afraid to run an engine at any considerable speed . . . .

Small wonder that, as the litany of grievances grew longer through the century, an outraged and anxious public focused upon railroads in its demands for governmental regulation of business practices.

Extraordinary industrialization was yet another key facet of Ohio's turbulent maturation. Building upon foundations laid during the preindustrial era, the predominantly agricultural state of the 1840s was transformed into a primary component of the nation's "core industrial area" by the 1870s. The stunning economic shift did not occur as a result of any simple cause-and-effect relationship. Instead, change emerged from a complex, dynamic, and highly uneven process in which industrialization, population growth, the transportation revolution, and urbanization each nourished and fed upon the other in reciprocal relationships. While these interacting forces generally benefited agriculture and commerce, they provided an especially strong impetus to manufacturing, which became the most rapidly growing sector of the state economy. Between 1850 and 1880, the number of Ohio's manufacturing establish-

ments nearly doubled (from 10,622 to 20,699), and the amount of capital invested in industrial production more than quintupled (from $533,000,000 to $2.8 billion). Table 2E demonstrates that the value of products manufactured by these enterprises also made impressive gains, either matching or surpassing national growth rates. As a consequence of tremendous bursts of industrial development—a phenomenal rise during the 1850s, further acceleration during the Civil War decade, and continued expansion (despite a severe economic depression) in the 1870s — Ohio ranked among the nation's three or four leading manufacturing states throughout the period.

Increased diversification of the state's manufacturing sector was a primary characteristic of the modern industrial order. During the preindustrial era, the processing of farm and forest products had dominated manufacturing activities. Even as Ohio moved into the industrial age, production of processed resources — like flour, meat, beer, bricks, and lumber — continued to expand, stimulated by rising demand from an increasingly urban population, a construction boom, and improved access to regional and national markets. Nevertheless, the supremacy of these established industries steadily dwindled after 1850, in the wake of accelerated growth by new or previously underdeveloped branches of manufacturing. Factory production of finished consumer goods, assem-

A rear-end collision at New Concord.

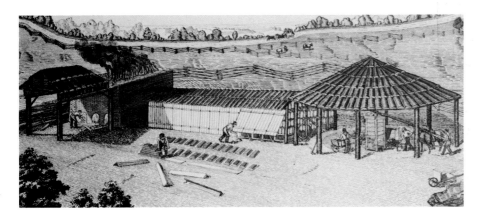

A construction boom in nearby Cleveland provided a thriving market for this primitive brick plant in rural Lake County.

Iron workers outside the cast house at Olive Furnace. In these early furnaces, man and animal power were supplemented only by primitive mechanical contrivances such as the slag wheel behind the ox-team.

Interior of Olive Furnace cast house, where molten iron was cast into pigs.

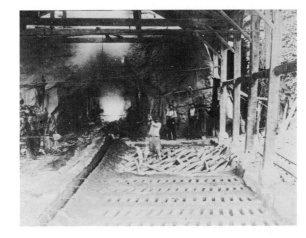

Olive Furnace, founded in 1847 in Lawrence County, was typical of the ''iron plantations'' located in Ohio's industrial hinterlands. Over fifty families depended on the furnace for their livelihood.

bly industries, light metals fabrication, large-scale woodworking, and ''heavy'' industries — generally classed as ''modern'' types of manufacturing—accounted for an ever-greater share of the state's industrial output (see Table 2E). An amazing variety and quantity of products began to flow out of Ohio's shops and factories: from clothing, shoes, soap, and furniture; billiard tables, corsets, window glass, and rubber hose; to agricultural implements, sewing machines, steam engines, bridges, carriages, and railroad cars.

The mainsprings of this diverse modernization movement were coal and iron—the crucial elements needed to stoke the furnaces, run the steam engines, forge the machinery, and, to a large extent, manufacture the finished products. Nature had endowed Ohio with vast coal resources. Bituminous deposits underlay more than 12,000 square miles in thirty eastern and southeastern counties, stretching in an immense arc from the Tuscarawas Valley and Mahoning Valley districts in the northeast through the Hocking Valley region in the south. Although discovered early in the century, the state's abundant coal seams had been barely tapped prior to the industrial age. In 1840, for example, Ohio's 434 miners extracted only an estimated 140,000 tons of coal, primarily for local consumption. Beginning in the 1850s, however, annual production spiraled upward, exceeding 1,000,000 tons in 1860, and reaching nearly 3,000,000 tons in 1870. By 1885, the labor force had swelled to approximately 18,000 miners, who picked, shoveled, blasted, and hauled to the surface almost 8,000,000 tons of coal. The relatively low costs of opening and working the rather shallow coal beds, critical transportation links provided by canals and railroads, and industry's seemingly insatiable need for fuel strongly contributed to coal mining's rapid growth. But by far the major single factor was rising demand from the simultaneously expanding iron industry.

Faced with depleted timber supplies, and gradually recognizing the practicality and superiority of mineral fuel, ironmasters during the 1850s began to adopt coal and coke for smelting and refining, in place of traditional charcoal. This shift fostered improved efficiency and greater manufacturing capacity, thus helping to transform Ohio's relatively backward iron industry into the nation's second largest producer by 1870. While the state's nineteen primitive furnaces had produced merely 26,000 tons of iron in 1840, by 1880 output from sixty-seven modern furnaces had soared to 930,000 tons of iron and steel (which was still in its infancy). Most progress occurred in the northeastern Cleveland-Mahoning Valley district, which, by the early 1870s, permanently surpassed the southern Hanging Rock district as the state's chief iron-producing region. The northeastern counties contained no significant iron ore deposits. However, they did enjoy a key locational advantage—accessibility to the rich ore fields of northern Michigan and Minnesota, provided by the opening in 1855 of the Sault Sainte Marie

Canal between Lake Huron and Lake Superior. A constantly increasing flow of ore poured into the lake-ports of Cleveland, Lorain, and Ashtabula, either for smelting in local furnaces or for further transport to inland centers like Youngstown, Canton, Niles, and Massillon. Emblematic of the state's industrial diversification, various specialized branches of iron and steel manufacturing evolved during the period. Eventually concentrated in the northeastern counties, blast-furnaces soon spawned nearby rolling mills, foundries, forges, and steel works, which turned pig or cast iron into rails, bar, sheet, and plate. A large proportion of this 'intermediate' iron and steel was then distributed to foundries, machine shops, and other establishments across the state for further refining into a wide assortment of finished metal products — of which pipes, stoves, plows, machine parts, and wheels were but a small sampling.

In contrast to developmental patterns in other core industrial states, no single manufacturing center or region could claim absolute dominance in Ohio. Once again diversity reigned, as tumultuous industrial growth occurred in numerous urban strongholds scattered throughout the state. Cincinnati had been the earliest Ohio city to exhibit industrial stirrings. Manufacturing had expanded so extensively that, by 1860, only New York and Philadelphia surpassed the Queen City in output. Although slipping to sixth position by 1880, Cincinnati continued to prevail as the state's foremost industrial producer. Nearly 3,300 establishments in over 125 types of industries—led by clothing, meatpacking and slaughtering, foundry and machine-shop products, whiskey, and carriages and wagons—operated in the metropolis, thereby qualifying Cincinnati as the most diverse manufacturing center in the West. Relentlessly challenging the Queen City for the state crown, Cleveland swiftly rose to manufacturing prominence after 1850. A bustling hub for iron and steel production, oil refining, and assorted dependent industries, Cleveland also became a key clothing, brewing, meatpacking, machine-tool, and shipbuilding center by the 1880s. However, Cincinnati and Cleveland were only the most conspicuous examples of the era's urban-industrial eruption. Individually dwarfed in scale, but cumulatively mammoth in the quantity and variety of their production, an impressive list of smaller cities also enlarged their manufacturing sectors. Dayton, Toledo, Columbus, Springfield, Akron, Canton, Youngstown, Sandusky, East Liverpool, Portsmouth, together with dozens of additional factory and mill towns along developing transportation routes busily (if not always confidently or enthusiastically) carved out their distinct niches in the modern industrial empire.

Yet, Ohio's march toward industrial eminence involved much more than an expanded variety of manufacturing cities, enterprises, and products. Closely interrelated, but highly erratic, developments in production methods, technology, business organization, and manpower also characterized industrial progress.

An iron miner and his young helper, perhaps his son, at the mouth of an ore drift at Olive Furance.

Furnace crew at the Bessie Furnace in Perry County, 1870s.

At the heart of these advances was the maturation of an early factory system. As described previously, factory production remained a rarity prior to the mid-1840s. However, with the rapid decline in household production (whose value plummeted sixty-five percent, to less than $600,000, during the 1850s alone), manufacturing in Ohio had irrevocably shifted to specialized craft-shops by the outbreak of the Civil War. It must be emphasized that the vast majority of these shops — and, in instances such as glass and construction, even entire industries — continued to operate on a small scale, and with little mechanization,

The Hecla Furnace complex in Lawrence County, ca. 1870. Hecla became one of the nation's most noted iron furnaces by casting the "Swamp Angel," a cannon which hurled 100-pound shells over five miles during the Civil War siege of Charleston Harbor.

Winding through the heart of Cleveland's manufacturing and commercial district, the Cuyahoga River in 1874 provided the city's diverse industries with easy access to Lake Erie and expanding national markets.

The Bessemer-Kelly furnace, first utilized in Ohio by the Cleveland Rolling Mill Company in 1868, helped to make steel production the cornerstone of the state's industrial economy.

The steam-powered rotary press revolutionized the printing industry. By 1880, it was capable of automatically feeding, printing, separating, and folding 5,000 sheets per man-hour, compared with 50 sheets using more primitive methods.

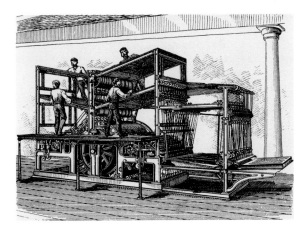

pendence on manual exertion, shops and factories were steadily transformed by more minute divisions of labor, greater mechanization of production, and technological progress. Decade after decade, revolutionary innovations emerged on countless interacting fronts — the conversion from water power to steam engines; the invention of the Bessemer-Kelly converter and the open-hearth furnace, which propelled the steel industry to prominence; the incipient but vital development of a specialized machine-tool industry, which both served and symbolized the manufacturing sector's growing demand for more advanced machinery of every type; the introduction of sewing machines in the shoe and garment industries; continual technological improvements in paper-making, printing, food processing, and even umbrella production. Just as the extent and the pace of technological change varied widely between individual localities, industries, and establishments, so too did the motivations of manufacturers who adopted modern production methods. For some industrialists, increased output was the primary stimulus, due to the fact that machinery could accurately produce 200 to 300 times faster than manual methods. Others were driven to change by fierce competition in expanding markets. And for still other employers, mechanization offered opportunities to cut labor costs, since the use of readily available, cheap, and unskilled "greenhands" to perform simple machine operations could reduce reliance upon higher-paid, and sometimes scarce, skilled workers.

Whatever the particular impetus, massive industrial plants abounded in Ohio by the 1870s — enterprises such as the Barney & Smith Company's eighteen-acre railroad car factory in Dayton; the Champion Machine Company of Springfield, whose 2,000 workers turned out one reaper every four minutes in the world's largest agricultural-machinery factory; Cincin-

throughout the century. Nevertheless, beginning in the 1850s and quickly gaining momentum after 1865, initially modest establishments in almost every line of manufacturing blossomed into large-scale factory operations, each employing hundreds of workers. While some manufacturers began to pioneer the mass-production-line techniques which would dominate twentieth-century industry, most plants in this early factory era utilized a system of fixed stations. Workers, machines, and tools were grouped in separate areas of the factory floor, to which components and materials were intermittently brought, in order to perform each fabrication or assembly step. Though this increasingly regimented system *still* necessitated a heavy denati's Proctor & Gamble Company, which produced more soap and allied products in its sixteen buildings than any firm in the nation; and the Melburn Wagon Works in Toledo, which manufactured sixty-five types of vehicles in a sprawling multi-story plant, so fully mechanized by 1876 that, according to one observer, "the forming of every part of the wagons is done entirely by machinery . . . [t]he men only control the machine and guide the material." Industrial expansion on such a grand scale required huge amounts of investment and operating capital — sums frequently beyond the means of even the most successful entrepreneur. In order to raise these substantial funds through stock sales, as well as to limit their legal liabilities, a rising number of manufacturers converted their individually-owned firms or partnerships into corporate organizations. Approximately 4,000 corporations were set up in Ohio from 1851 to 1874, thereafter multiplying at a rate of 400 to 900 per year into the early 1880s. Foreshadowing a trend which would accelerate toward the end of the century, corporate enterprises after 1870 continually grew larger, more complex, and — in the view of alarmed critics — too politically and financially powerful, too monopolistic, too impersonal, and too concerned with profit at the expense of the public welfare. For good or ill, many industries in Ohio, as throughout the nation, rapidly became dominated by "big business."

Industrial expansion, new technologies, and spreading factory production generated a tremendous need for labor of all types and levels of skill. Native farmers and foreign immigrants alike flocked to these fresh job opportunities, and, in the process, nourished radical changes in the state's employment patterns. As the figures in Table 2F indicate, between 1840 and 1880 Ohio's swelling labor force shifted from farming to nonagricultural occupations. Especially during the 1840s and 1850s, this transformation in the way Ohioans earned a living was startling. In 1840 only twenty-four percent of the workforce was engaged in nonagricultural pursuits — well-below the national average of thirty-one percent, and indicative of the state's industrial infancy. Over the next two decades, however, the number of workers drawn to these occupations quadrupled, thus making nonagricultural wage-earners the majority of Ohio's labor force by the Civil War. Not until 1880 would fifty-one percent of the national workforce be employed outside farming — by which time the proportion in Ohio had jumped to sixty percent! Since new wage-earning opportunities generally materialized in urban-industrial arenas, changing employment patterns were most dramatically displayed in the state's principal cities (see Table 2G). While a significant share entered domestic service or commerce, the bulk of the urban labor pool (which included rising numbers of female, adolescent, and native-born workers) was absorbed by rapidly expanding industries. This striking redistribution of manpower into facto-

Steam engines, such as this model manufactured in Salem, Ohio in the 1850s, provided the crucial energy for Ohio's increasingly mechanized industries.

ries, mills, mines, and shops had profound consequences, not only for the nature of work itself, but also for the status and the welfare of industrial toilers.

All these interwoven changes — population growth, native migration, foreign immigration, urbanization, the transportation revolution, and industrialization — inaugurated significant modifications in the social and economic fabric. Layer upon grimy, sooty layer, the texture of working-class life in the 1880s had become more complex and a bit more bewildering than it had been only forty years earlier. It was a time of chaos and upheaval in many Ohio communities, as modernization encountered, and all too frequently clashed with, tradition. Warnings of tradition's imminent demise proved premature. But, whether reluctantly or eagerly, Ohioans experienced alterations in cherished values, habits, behavior, and relationships. In a very real way, the emerging urban-industrial environment was an alien world — not just to the immigrant German brewer, English iron-puddler, or Irish factory hand, but also to the native migrant and long-term resident who were equally unaccustomed to the new odors, sounds, sights, congestion, regimentation, and isolation which daily assaulted their senses. For workers from Cincinnati to Painesville, and Cleveland to Buchtel, exposure to the whimper or the roar of progress would leave an indelible mark.

What specific impacts did these transitions have on the character and quality of working-class existence? Within the continual flux of an evolving urban-industrial society, how were concerns of daily life such as housing, health, cultural traits, leisure activities, and the "standard of living" affected? How extensively and rapidly did adjustments occur in the workplace, the workforce, the nature of work, and the status of working people? Were these men, women, and children able to maintain some semblance of security in the face of altered living and working conditions? How did the strains, demands, and

A portion of the workforce at the world's largest agricultural-machinery factory in Springfield, ca. 1880.

rewards of a changing environment ultimately influence working-class consciousness and cohesiveness?

Precise responses to such crucial questions are difficult to make, given the magnitude and diversity of the changes, the settings, and the participants, as well as the complexity of working-class expectations. Nevertheless, as elusive as many details remain, any attempt to gain at least limited insights into the shadowy world of the laboring classes must begin with an awareness of a basic, yet frequently overlooked, fact — working people were much more than producers and employees. Of course, earning a livelihood was a dominant aspect of everyday life. But outside the workplace, these toilers were also homeowners, renters, commuters, consumers, patients, teammates, fans, neighbors, family members, church-goers, saloon regulars, members of fraternal organizations, and civic volunteers. Ohio's developing communities contained robust working-class subcultures, which both affected and reflected social and economic progress. Glimpses of living conditions and life styles within the urban and small-town environments to which workers thronged, thus provide a fuller understanding of the flavor and character of their world.

Since most Ohioans continued to dwell on farms and in small towns from the 1840s through the 1880s, Cincinnati and Cleveland were not typical communities for the era. Rather, these urban giants were early locales for environmental situations which would later be duplicated in other cities throughout the state. At mid-century, both had been relatively compact "walking cities," in which residents generally lived only short distances from their work. In succeeding decades, however, economic growth, population increases, and the introduction of horse-drawn streetcars sparked tremendous physical expansion. Boundaries were constantly pushed outward, as urban residents and businesses occupied formerly rural areas on the fringes of the original cities. The wealthy, who had the time and means to travel the greatest distance, fled the increasingly congested downtown centers to take up residence in the farthest suburbs. Less successful urban dwellers—including many white-collar, skilled, and semi-skilled workers — also fled, but to more modest neighborhoods situated between the affluent outskirts and the downtown areas. Growing numbers of industrial and commercial enterprises likewise began to locate in these outlying middle-class districts. The poor, the unskilled, the recent immigrants, and the criminal elements soon drifted into the once prosperous inner-city neighborhoods, where they clustered in badly deteriorated buildings which had been vacated by the middle and upper classes.

By the 1870s, Cleveland and Cincinnati had thus been transformed into modern, sprawling, diverse metropolises. Immigrants continued to comprise major segments of the expanding populations, but the rising proportion of Ohio-born inhabitants (partially due to the great influx of rural migrants) was even more conspicuous (see Table 2H). Although ceaseless residential turnover among the highly mobile metropolis-dwellers impeded the growth and persistence of homogeneous communities, neighborhoods did become more clearly fragmented along income, occupational, ethnic, and racial lines. In the midst of these increasingly complex, drastically altered surroundings — where home and job became geographically separated; where fellow workers were not necessarily neighbors, friends, or fellow countrymen any longer; where streets were crowded with unfamiliar faces; and where (outside the family or immediate neighborhood) daily human relations became more impersonal — the individual worker was cloaked in a certain anonymity and isolation. Furthermore, the environment in which laboring people spent their non-working hours was too often beset with aggravation, tribulation, and downright danger.

Housing was a major problem in both metropolises. Since new construction simply could not keep up with the needs of the continuously expanding populace, overcrowded, expensive, and run-down quarters became a basic fact of working-class life. Although toilers and their families yearned for cheap, cozy accommodations (preferably within walking-distance of work), they had little choice but to settle for any available shelter — which unfortunately ranged, as a rule, from uncomfortably cramped at best, to abysmally congested at worst.

For the "working poor" — unskilled, underemployed, and low-income laborers — conditions were especially deplorable, even by the accepted standards of the time. In Cincinnati (by 1869, the nation's most densely populated city, with over 37,000 persons per square mile) lower-class lodging primarily consisted of multi-family tenements — old downtown warehouses, mills, and mansions hastily converted into tiny, one and two-room apartments. As early as 1868, the Cincinnati Board of Health counted more than 1,400 slum-tenements, housing nearly 40,000 persons:

> These buildings are almost always in a bad sanitary condition, due to . . . faults in the original construction . . . and . . . due to over-crowding and neglect. There are many large tenement-houses in this city without one square yard of air space, excepting that used as an entrance. A single privy is provided, in most instances, for the occupants of the building, and it is commonly placed at one end of the entrance way, so that it is almost impossible to prevent the gasseous exhaltations arising from it from being disseminated through the entire building, poisoning the atmosphere, and causing discomfort, disease, and death.

The Ohio Commissioner of Labor Statistics found that, during the following decade, even more squalid, flimsy tenements had been built by unscrupulous landlords. In 1878 he concluded that,

> An average of over 70 per cent of the deaths in the city occur in tenement houses. . . . Two rooms, front or back, in the second, third, fourth, and even fifth story of a barracks, hemmed in on all sides but one, is the average home of the working-man in the Queen City of the West, and for these two rooms he pays an average rent in excess of the rent of four-roomed tenements in most of the towns and smaller cities of the State.

Nor had conditions improved by 1881, when a shocked reporter for the *Cincinnati Enquirer*

described his tour of such infamous tenements as Diamond Alley, Gilligan's Barracks, and the Broadway Hotel:

> . . . tenement houses . . . [are] managed by unscrupulous and exacting agents, who know that the greater the rents the larger their commissions, the better satisfaction they give their employers. Some are huge tumble-down structures, with narrow, dark and dingy entrances. The rooms are small, illy ventilated, badly lighted, and yet in them are found families of five, six and seven people, sometimes four beds in a room, containing people living together in promiscuous confusion, regardless of sex or age. . . .

In Cleveland, tenements were not common until the late 1870s. Instead, the working poor in this metropolis squeezed into more traditional, but equally ghastly, slums which consisted of shanties, shacks, and dilapidated houses. An investigator in 1873 provided an appallingly graphic description of such housing in the city's "Flats" district:

> . . . [In] the next shanty . . . a man and woman, three children and a boy were all in a room about eight by nine feet in size. In a small room to the rear were three or four others. All the windows were closed, and the same damp, sickly smell prevailed. The "Hole in the Wall" was next visited. It is a boarding house under the basement of the New England Block on Broadway . . . and has a commanding view of a couple of soap factories and the Cuyahoga river. . . . The room which is spoken of opens from a low, damp and dark hall or cellar, which is lighted only by the few straggling rays of sun or moonlight which are able to penetrate the gloom. . . . The scene which was presented on entering beggars description. The room was small and low, a swarm of flies hung on the dirty, filthy ceiling, small amount of light was admitted through the window, while all of heaven's air was completely barred out. Rags, filth, squalor and wretchedness were everywhere. . . . To think that human beings could

A section of the Cleveland "Flats" known as "Irish Bend," 1885.

By 1880, Cleveland's primitive water and sewer systems had become serious hazards to public health. In his annual message to the city council, Mayor Herrick vividly explained the urgent need for repairs and expansion:

... Under the present system of sewering the city we have what is equivalent to two large open sewers, one, the Cuyahoga river, traversing the city from north to south its entire length; the other, Wolworth run, from east to west through the westerly half of the city. Into these pours all the house and surface drainage of a large portion of the city—the filth from the slaughtering-houses, oil-refineries, and manufactories which line their banks. Their waters become impregnated with the foul mixtures, and when exposed to the summer's sun can not but exhale a noisome and unhealthful odor. Some of the filthy substances which find their way into the river settle to the bottom, and there remain until brought to the surface by the action of the wheels of some passing steamer, when they give forth a disease-breeding stench and sink back to await the next opportunity to rise.

Another ill-effect of the deposit of so much nastiness in the river was seen in the condition of our drinking-water from the lake at the time of the ice gorge at the mouth of the river this winter. The ice in the lake prevented the egress of that in the river, so that when the latter broke away it was forced by the current under the lake-ice until it reached such a depth as to plow up the concentrated filth at the bottom of the river and in the lake just at its mouth. This was carried out toward the water-works crib, and a considerable quantity found its way into the water-pipes and was distributed throughout the city .... Much, too, of the offal that is thrown into the river and Wolworth run is carried by the current into the lake, and is then washed landward and deposited along the shore and there left to putrefy and decay, emitting in the mean time noxious odors and rendering the neighborhood disagreeable both to sight and smell.

exist thus for any length of time seems almost impossible. . . .

. . . On Spring street below Water are from forty to fifty shanties perched up on the hill-side and filled to their utmost capacity with men, women and children whose existence in such quarters seems almost an impossibility. The houses are small, dirty and wretched. Most of them are mere sheds boarded up and provided with a floor. The woodwork is rotten, the real estate lies thick on the floor and the windows are stuffed with rags. The houses are ranged so that the floor of one on the hill-side is on a level with the roof of another and so the refuse water and filth from those above finds its way upon the tables and into the beds of those beneath. . . . In these old shanties there ranges from one to three families each, and to each one is accorded space sufficient only for a bed. . . .

Fortunately, not all workers dwelled in such festering "squalor and wretchedness." Those able to secure steady employment at decent wages, obtained moderate-quality housing in the many working-class residential neighborhoods which dotted metropolitan Cleveland and Cincinnati. Here were located the "citadels of the working people"—row after closely packed row of neat, modest, rectangular, frame houses, most rarely having enjoyed the luxury of paint, but some with a treasured patch of untrimmed yard out-back. Although comparatively comfortable and clean, these single or multi-family accommodations were hardly considered spacious. Each five-room residence commonly housed an average family of five, plus assorted relatives, plus (in order to pay the high rents) an inevitable boarder or two. As William Foster, a Cincinnati printer, commented in 1883, "their comforts are not what they ought to be. A man ought to have a room where he could go and sit down and read without his children climbing all over him and making a nuisance of the house." Somewhat roomier, less expensive "cottages" on larger lots were available in the suburbs. However, for workers employed in downtown areas, suburban living necessitated the added daily expense of five-cent trolley-fares, or dawn and dusk hikes to and from work — prohibitive drawbacks for many workers existing on limited incomes and toiling long hours. Moreover, regardless of the location, the overwhelming majority of working-class families rented their cramped quarters. The financial drain of these steep rents, combined with low wages and relatively high purchase costs, made it extremely difficult for workers even to attempt to purchase a house. Available evidence indicates that, by the 1880s, even with the 'cooperative' aid of numerous ethnically, religiously, and racially organized Building and Loan Associations, no more than one in five wage-earning families owned or paid mortgages on their dwellings. Owning one's own home — the common-man's traditional symbol of middle-class success, independence, and stability — remained only a frustrating dream for the mass of metropolitan working people.

Not only were living conditions overcrowded, they were also filthy, stinking, unhealthy, and hazardous. Chaotic physical expansion, tumultuous industrialization, and mushrooming populations — together with widespread apathy and ignorance — bred monumental sanitary, environmental, and social problems in both metropolises. Overwhelmed by the magnitude of the difficulties, inadequately financed and often corrupt local governments simply could not provide basic public services and protection. Consequently, conditions rapidly worsened, especially after mid-century.

Cincinnati and Cleveland became blanketed in smoke and soot — dingy consequences of burning increased amounts of bituminous coal in factories, homes, and locomotives. Air pollution in the Queen City was so severe by the mid-1880s, for example, that one visitor disgustedly observed:

Cleanliness in either person or in dress is almost an impossibility. Hands and faces become grimy, and clean collars and light-hued garments are perceptibly coated with a thin layer of soot. Clothes hung out in the weekly wash acquire a permanent yellow hue which no bleaching can remove. The smoke of hundreds of factories, locomotives and steamboats arises and unites to form this dismal pall, which obscures the sunlight, and gives a sickly cast to the moonbeams. . . .

To Cleveland's foul air was added the unique stench emanating from the city's oil refineries. Rotting garbage, raw sewage, and industrial

waste were everywhere — oozing from un-
sealed and overflowing outhouses (publicly
referred to as "the privy nuisance"), clogging
alleys and gutters, contaminating water-
supplies, piling up in yards and vacant lots, and
accumulating on slimy streets and sidewalks.
Until the 1860s, Cincinnati residents depended
on packs of scavenging hogs and heavy rains to
dispose of garbage and waste. When local officials subsequently assumed responsibility
sanitation deteriorated further, since the mis-
managed and corrupt street-cleaning department neglected the busiest avenues for weeks at
a time and ignored many residential areas
altogether. Sewer systems were woefully in-
efficient and inadequate — most property owners would not or could not install expensive
connections with the main lines; sewer pipes
emptied into open streams and ditches; and
large portions of densely populated working-
class neighborhoods remained entirely un-
drained. Because the stock-yard and slaughter-
house districts along Cincinnati's Mill Creek
and Cleveland's Wolworth Run lacked sewers,
for instance, vast amounts of waste were often
washed directly into the streams, which then
flowed blood-red through residential areas.
Streets were sanitary calamities. By 1880, barely half of Cincinnati's 402 miles of streets, and
only sixteen percent of Cleveland's 370 miles,
had been paved in any way. Busy thoroughfares
thus became fly and mosquito-infested quag-
mires of filthy muck; potholes were usually
filled with a mixture of coal ashes and garbage;
and during dry-spells, the entire mess turned to
a sickening dust which blew into nostrils, eyes,
and lungs. Animals compounded the problem.
Tens-of-thousands of horses each deposited
fifteen to twenty pounds of manure a day along

metropolitan streets. In 1879 alone, nearly
12,000 dead hogs, cows, sheep, goats, and
horses were removed from Cincinnati's avenues. The incredible filth and contaminated water contributed to the many dreaded diseases
which flourished among the masses. Tuberculosis, diphtheria, croup, dysentary, measles,
whooping cough, consumption, and meningitis
took fearful tolls every year. Cholera, typhoid,
scarlet fever, and smallpox epidemics regularly
terrorized residents. No group of citizens was
immune from disease, but, as the Cincinnati
Board of Health concluded in 1878, the
"greatest mortality, in proportion to population
. . . [was] found among the working classes."
Improved sanitary habits by the inhabitants
themselves surely could have diminished the
disease-breeding filth. Unfortunately, however,
public indifference and ignorance prevailed.
Perhaps unwittingly, a Cincinnati resident ex-

Though not all as elaborate
as Wielert's, Cincinnati's
saloons provided welcome
relief from the dreariness
of nineteenth-century
urban life.

Neighborhood saloons played integral roles in working-class life. To the laborer, the bar was an oasis of brief relief from the strains, harshness, and insecurity of crowded homes and demanding jobs. Here could be found fellowship, understanding, and cheer among those who shared his dreams and disappointments—not to mention rare credit, when times were tough. Despite the dire warnings of temperance advocates, the beer continued to flow. William C. Smith nostalgically remembered the Cincinnati saloons of his boyhood as a "home away from home" during the 1880s:

The saloons in the West End were not as gaudy as the gilded palaces of sin located farther down town ... a bar with a brass rail usually took up half of the room; a shelf backed by a mirror held a display of whiskey of various brands, gin, wine, etc. ...

In most neighborhoods, the bucket trade was a considerable factor in the day's business; a nickel's worth of beer provided two good-sized glasses .... Bakers, thirsty souls, would several times a day develop a yen for the amber fluid. It was the chore of any lucky boy who happened to be on hand at such times to be sent to Longinotti's in quest of refreshment. Frequently, through foresight, I was the lucky boy .... A broomstick was utilized with nails driven part way into the wood at six inch intervals. Strung along this contraption were five or six home-made buckets .... For this chore, or rather public service, the usual compensation was a doughnut, a cake, or a slab of zwieback, warm, with a hole punched in the center in which was placed a lump of sugar ....

All saloons provided something in the way of free lunch. In most places a simple spread of cheese, sausage, pretzels, pickles, etc., was tendered. Others, operating on a more elaborate scale, served soup and hot meat in addition to the customary layout. A hot dog—which was a good-sized bologna sausage—with two slices of rye bread and plenty of mustard, sold for five cents, with a scuttle of suds at the same price. Ham and cheese sandwiches were five cents each, and the ham was not carved with a safety razor .... Pig's knuckles and kraut were offered in some saloons—fifteen cents for a man's size serving and with a reasonable amount of foaming balloon juice to wash it down. This was a treat for the gods ....

Saturday nights, with the sidewalks crowded, the saloons on Central Avenue did a land-office business. The night trade was good on other evenings, and in most cases accounted for the bulk of the daily receipts, but Saturday night was the gala night of the week. Saturday was pay day, and after five days of economy the inhabitants had a feeling of opulence that sometimes lasted through Monday but not often .... Nearly all the saloons on Central Avenue could be classed as neighborhood enterprises .... An expenditure of fifteen or twenty cents was sufficient to provide an evening's entertainment .... Such places as had a side entrance maintained what was called a sitting room. It was sometimes in the rear end of the saloon but more often a separate room that insured some degree of privacy. Such places were patronized by the women in the neighborhood, singly and in groups, oftener with a male escort. Sitting rooms were operated in an orderly manner; you could take your wife or best girl for a libation without fear of molestation by any of the less couth habitués ....

Nearly all the saloons at that time had their floors covered with sawdust and as tobacco chewing was an almost universal habit, gaboons were placed at strategic intervals for the chewers' use. But most masticators of the weed were either nearsighted, blind, or just didn't give a damn ....

A credit system was in operation in most saloons in a limited way: any of the regular patrons known to be reliable could, at the tail-end of the week when funds were low, get their regular libations and have it "put on the slate" until Saturday ....

pressed the apparently dominant attitude, when, with 'tongue in cheek,' he later recalled:

Sanitary safeguards were few and primitive but as germs had not yet been invented and all diseases were considered acts of God, there was probably little need for them.

The "darker side of urban life" also included the constant menace of fire. Metropolitan fire departments were badly undermanned, poorly equipped, overrun with inexperienced political appointees, and unable to enforce primitive fire codes. Closely packed, refuse-filled, highly flammable, and lacking sufficient exits, nineteenth-century factories and residences were potential firetraps for their inhabitants. Cincinnati probably had the best fire protection in Ohio. Nevertheless, citizens repeatedly endured disastrous blazes, causing approximately $1.5 million in damage between 1853 and 1881. In 1877, for example, six workers burned to death in a factory fire which lasted only twenty-five minutes; and, in 1881, flames raged through thirty factories before being brought under control. Fanned by winds off Lake Erie, fires in Cleveland were even more dangerous. One of the city's most spectacular blazes broke out in 1884 in the "Flats" — a congested area of slums, factories, refineries, packing houses, docks, and working-class neighborhoods along the Cuyahoga River. Before it could be contained (only with the aid of equipment sent by rail from a score of other cities), dozens of people were injured, nearly $900,000 in property had been destroyed, and thousands of workers had abruptly become homeless and unemployed. More than 3,300 serious fires erupted in Cleveland between 1865 and 1880, resulting in nearly $4.4 million in property losses and immeasurable hardship for their victims.

But though problems were plentiful, working-class life in Cincinnati and Cleveland was not all dreariness and distress. The metropolitan environment also radiated a unique excitement and allure — streets teeming with a constant frenzy of human activity; new technological wonders such as telephones and electric lights; every imaginable necessity and tantalizing luxury beckoning from hundreds of display-windows; prayers, curses, and conversations uttered in strange foreign tongues or curious native accents; the raw power of machinery throbbing within hundreds of mills and factories. Especially attractive were the seemingly limitless leisure activities, which provided welcome outlets for the tensions and insecurities of daily existence. As had been the habit of many previous generations, laboring people spent their idle hours patronizing favorite saloons (which, by the 1870s, outnumbered grocery stores in some neighborhoods), enjoying a game of poker or pinochle, placing a bet at the rat-pits or cock fights, attending church functions, or just relaxing at home. Reflecting the public's mounting interest in leisure, however, additional activities began to spring up in unprecedented numbers during the mid- and late nineteenth century. Hundreds of new voluntary associations appeared, offering various types of mutual protection, self-improvement, and recreation. These benevolent societies, religious organizations, social clubs, educational groups, cultural societies, and ethnic associations — from the Catholic Aid Society, the Ancient Order of Hibernians, and the Turnerverein to volunteer fire departments and the Cincinnati Labor Lyceum — became important facets of working-class lifestyles. For more lighthearted amusement, nothing quite sparked the interest of the masses like the circus — the grandest of which only played to the huge audiences available in cities such as Cleveland and Cincinnati. For the sports enthusiast, there were roller and ice skating rinks, pool halls, and race tracks. With the founding in 1869 of the nation's first professional team, the Cincinnati Red Stockings, baseball became a popular mania. And, finally — for those simply craving a bit of tranquility, fresh air, and pleasant scenery — the post-Civil War development of parks on the urban fringes offered peaceful strolls, boating, concerts, and, of course, the customary picnic.

While the best and the worst aspects of nineteenth-century urbanization emerged in Cincinnati and Cleveland, smaller Ohio cities began to feel growing pains of their own. Urban-industrial expansion in places like Dayton, Canton, and Steubenville obviously was not as diverse, vigorous, or extensive as metropolitan development. Yet, in many respects, living conditions in these primary and secondary cities increasingly resembled metropolitan environments, with differences being largely of degree. Disease-breeding filth, foul air, and polluted water were prevalent. Pedestrians became skilled at dodging scavenging animals and decaying carcasses. Municipal services were primitive and totally insufficient for the needs of swelling populations. By 1880, for example, seven of Ohio's ten largest secondary cities lacked sewer systems; while only nine percent of Columbus' streets, and less than four percent in Dayton, Toledo, Akron, Steubenville, and Zanesville, had been paved. Inhabitants of virtually all other Ohio cities invariably slogged through mud and dust. Street-cleaning was usually a semi-annual event, and sanitation remained a matter of individual or corporate discretion. Public water systems were deplorable — in one illuminating instance, enraged Ironton residents in 1867 smashed the city's thirteen street-corner pumps, in order to force local officials to construct an effective waterworks. Fire also posed a continual threat, as typified by Akron, which suffered at least one catastrophic blaze in seven of the ten years between 1848 and 1857.

Although larger cities like Columbus and Toledo experienced sprawling physical growth, especially after the Civil War, most urban areas maintained their compactness. Distances between home and job tended to be shorter in these "walking cities" than in metropolises, and neighborhoods were less rigidly fragmented. Every urban community contained slums, but, at least through the mid-1870s, adequate housing was not a severe problem. Laboring families most often found simple, moderate-quality, single-family dwellings to be

Zanesville was still a "walking city" in 1870, with working-class residential areas located within the gloomy shadows of the city's iron furnaces.

Smaller cities like Canton also experienced vigorous growth by the 1870s.

Massillon, in 1855, still had much the appearance of a farming village.

Compared to Cleveland or Cincinnati, a much slower pace of life prevailed in small industrial towns like Marietta in 1860.

readily available. Compared to Cleveland or Cincinnati, typical working-class accommodations in industrial centers such as Warren or Hamilton may have been just as drab; but they were also generally cheaper, less crowded, and, apparently, more frequently owned. By the early 1880s, however, these advantages began to diminish, as continued growth spawned deterioration, housing shortages, higher rents, and dreaded tenements. A glassblower in Bellaire voiced complaints being echoed by urban workers throughout Ohio:

> The health of this neighborhood would greatly improve if dwellings for the working classes were more liberally provided with ventilation, higher ceilings, more light and better drainage.
> There is also a scarcity of small houses here, in consequence of which the families of working classes are compelled to crowd into tenement houses, much against their will, so as to live within reasonable distance of the work-shop.

Daily life in primary and secondary cities lacked much of the social diversity and rich cosmopolitan flavor which enlivened metropolitan environments. Leisure activities, for example, were neither very commercialized, cultured,

nor plentiful. Laboring people usually centered their pastimes around traditional family and church functions, saloons, amateur baseball, occasional appearances by small tent shows, and a few social and fraternal organizations. Since diversions were often sparse, the preoccupations and routines of the work-world tended to dominate everyday existence and personal relationships. In part, this rather humdrum atmosphere resulted from the relatively homogeneous composition of the populations. With notable exceptions — such as significant immigrant communities in Toledo, Youngstown, and Sandusky, as well as black concentrations in Columbus, Portsmouth, Springfield, and Chillicothe — the overwhelming majority of residents were distinctively native-born and white (see Tables 2H and 2I). Thus, at the same time that complex economic expansion and mounting public problems transformed the urban landscape, a certain tenacious, small-town "sameness" continued to characterize most inhabitants and their lifestyles. Despite stunning economic inroads, "modernization" hardly appeared triumphant in the social realm.

For the multitude of workers who dwelled in small industrial towns and mining villages, an overriding simplicity marked many aspects of day-to-day life. Here in Ohio's "industrial hinterlands," change ordinarily proceeded in modest fashion — a few dozen additional inhabitants per year; a handful of new houses on the edge of town; the long-awaited completion of a railway spur or canal branch; the opening of a mine, another carriage works, or perhaps a brick yard. Unlike urban areas, small towns like Wellston, New Straitsville, and Canal Dover did not have complex economies. Although some boasted several manufacturing enterprises, most towns depended solely upon one business for their economic existence. After the Civil War, numerous boom-towns sprang up with furious spurts of initial growth, particularly in the southeastern coal fields. Yet, overall progress seemed to occur bit-by-bit, frequently generating adjustments in prevailing living patterns, but generally without undermining existent social and cultural foundations. Except for scattered pockets of immigrants and blacks, townfolk remained predominantly native-white, most having come from the surrounding countryside and nearby counties in search of jobs. There were no "faceless crowds" in these closely knit environments, as were found in large cities. Residents knew each other, maintained strong personal relationships, shared common backgrounds and values. The simple pleasures of small-town environments — a beer at the local saloon, old-fashioned ice cream socials, spelling bees, square dances, holiday celebrations, participant sports, and lodge meetings — may not have offered the dazzling variety of urban leisure activities, but they did promote a personal sense of homespun solidarity with one's neighbors. Laboring people usually comprised large, highly visible, and homogeneous segments of the populations; living and working close together, as well as

actively participating in public affairs. Available evidence also suggests that home ownership among small-town workers may have been more extensive than in the cities, thereby reinforcing a certain working-class independence and respectability which often characterized these grass-roots communities.

Despite its outward simplicity, however, working-class life in non-urban environments was hardly romantic. Living conditions in cities could be harsh, but in remote towns and hamlets they were frequently far worse. Public sanitation, health, and safety efforts were not just primitive or inadequate — they were practically nonexistent. The cozy vine-covered cottage surrounded by rose bushes and a white picket fence was little more than a nostalgic ideal on a picture postcard. The typical reality (even when owned) was a dank log cabin or rickety frame dwelling with no insulation, no paint, no conveniences, and probably a hog wallow instead of a rose garden. Cramped quarters in rundown, wooden barracks — the small-town equivalent to urban tenements — commonly housed workers in many communities. Especially bleak were the company towns which arose around secluded coal mines and iron furnaces. Coal dust and cinders filled the air, coated inhabitants, and infiltrated homes. Much like the iron plantations of the preindus-

trial era, employers retained predominant ownership and control of these self-contained communities, thereby also functioning as landlords, merchants, and bankers. The workers consequently paid high rents for deteriorated "company housing," were obliged to purchase exhorbitantly priced necessities in the "company store," often received "company scrip" for wages, and remained trapped in a cycle of poverty resulting from their inevitable indebtedness to "the company." Finally, for all the seemingly uncomplicated appeal of small towns, daily existence could also be oppressive, monotonous, and frustrating. Limited job opportunities, relatively few social diversions, and the constant grinding toil caused numerous workers to seek a wider range of perceived alternatives in the cities. Laboring people in the isolated industrial hinterlands, therefore, may not have reaped many of the benefits of progress, nor escaped exposure to much of the hardship which it generated.

Whether workers made their homes in urban settings or small towns, the quality of their lives was further shaped by chronic economic instability and uncertainty. Repeated, spurting cycles of 'boom and bust', as well as long-term inflationary and deflationary spirals persistently afflicted America's maturing industrial-capitalist system. As the state's economy be-

Periodic street-grading to facilitate water drainage and lessen the accumulation of manure was one of the few sanitation efforts in East Liverpool during the 1870s. Horse- and manpower still did most of the work with the aid of simple tools, sometimes, like the plow in the foreground, adapted from other purposes.

came increasingly integrated and ever more closely linked to the national economic structure, few communities, industries, or occupations in Ohio escaped the impacts of these erratic national trends. Though bewildered by the ambiguous causes of these complex, and seemingly impersonal, economic forces, workers did understand the consequences. For they touched the hard realities and concerns of everyday existence — their employment, their pocketbooks, the food on their tables, the clothes on their backs, the houses in which they lived, and the security of their families.

The broad cycles of fluctuating economic activity were clear. After seven harsh years of depression, the economy gradually began to revive in 1844. Gathering momentum by the late 1840s and early 1850s, a dramatic upswing brought business expansion, increased prices, and rising money wages. The surge of prosperity staggered briefly during the recession of 1854-55, and finally ground to a halt in 1857-58. Caused by overspeculation in real estate and railroad stocks, the shortlived, but nasty, depression resulted in widespread business fail-

ures, production cutbacks, and a national unemployment rate of approximately six to eight percent. Recovery remained sluggish through the outbreak of the Civil War, but heavy government spending on military supplies of every description soon triggered a wartime boom. From 1861 to 1865, business thrived, prices climbed above antebellum levels, and labor shortages rapidly pushed money wages upward. The end of hostilities and reconversion to civilian production brought another recessionary slump in 1866-67, and ushered in a drastic deflationary slide in consumer prices which continued through the rest of the century. From 1867 to 1873, renewed prosperity swept the nation — industry resumed vigorous expansion, jobs were abundant, and money wages rose or held stable. Unfortunately, in 1873, excessive stock speculation and a collapse of the weak banking structure suddenly plunged the soaring economy into severe depression once again. Hard times gripped the country until 1878 — prices tumbled, profits plummeted, factories and mines shut down or drastically reduced production, business competition sharpened,

Olive Furnace was typical of the company towns found in Ohio's industrial hinterlands. The workers' company housing (right) stood in stark contrast to the manager's "palatial" residence (far right). The company store (below) dominated the workers' lives.

employers slashed wages, and an estimated twelve to fourteen percent of the nation's workers were unemployed. The economy recuperated by 1879 and flourished through 1882. In all too familiar fashion, however, from 1883 to 1885 the nation slipped into yet another mild depression, with unemployment rates reaching six to eight percent.

Although the broad economic cycles were evident, their specific impacts on working-class standards of living in nineteenth-century Ohio remain rather blurry. The general scarcity of reliable wage and price data — compounded by significant cost-of-living variances between communities; complex wage differences between regions, industries, companies, occupations, and skill levels; as well as the irregular effects of cyclical, seasonal, or technological unemployment — make precise measurements of changing standards of living very difficult. The first crude attempts to gather detailed information on the economic conditions of Ohio's working classes began in 1877, with the creation of the Ohio Bureau of Labor Statistics. For earlier periods, frequently only national estimates or isolated local figures are available. Nevertheless, with these qualifications in mind, some tentative observations can be ventured, in order to understand more fully the economic dimensions of workers' lives.

During the 1840s and 1850s, most American workers experienced generally rising wages. Average annual money earnings increased approximately 11.7 percent nationally, from about $226 in 1840 to $297 in 1860. Available evidence indicates that wages especially climbed in the late 1840s and early 1850s. For example, after dipping from an estimated 95¢ in 1840 to 85¢ in 1845, national daily rates for the unskilled masses climbed to 91¢ in 1850, $1.00 in 1855,

and $1.03 by 1860. Even the average wages of low-paid domestics improved between 1850 and 1860, rising from $1.08 to $1.34 per week. In Ohio, rough estimates suggest that advancing money wages continued to lag behind national rates in many categories. From 1850 to 1860, daily earnings for Ohio's unskilled laborers grew from 78¢ to 98¢, and weekly wages for domestics jumped from 96¢ to $1.22 — both still below national averages. So too in the cotton textile industry, where, between 1849 and 1859, annual wages rose from $141 to $180 in Ohio, while increasing from $176 to $201 nation-wide. In iron and steel manufacturing, the state's annual rate of $312 in 1849 exceeded the industry's national average of $292, but ranked slightly lower by 1859 with $344. Nevertheless, during the 1850s, greater wage increases in Ohio did significantly reduce or eliminate most differences with eastern industrial states such as New York and Massachusetts. Skilled workers appear to have enjoyed the largest income-gains. Whereas Ohio journeymen made no more than $5.00 to $8.00 per week in 1845, by 1860 they appear to have averaged slightly under $12. Finally, overall wages continued to be higher in cities than in small towns and villages. Cincinnati and Cleveland, for instance, set the pace for the state in 1860, and apparently surpassed national rates as well, with daily earnings of about $2.00 to $2.50 for skilled and $1.10 to $1.30 for unskilled labor.

However, rising money wages alone did not signify improved working-class standards of living, since consumer price increases could rapidly erode the "real" purchasing power of any wage-hikes. In fact, between 1840 and 1860, prices escalated nationally by an estimated fourteen to nineteen percent, with the greatest increases occurring from 1845 to 1855 — ironi-

Construction crew at an East Liverpool pottery. Few of the bottle kilns, which once dotted the landscape, remain.

Samples of ''company scrip'' used to pay the wages of nineteenth-century iron workers.

Samples of ''company scrip'' used to pay the wages of nineteenth-century iron workers.

cally, the very period in which workers experienced their greatest boosts in wages. Inflation climbed even more rapidly in the nation's cities, to which growing numbers of native and foreign workers were being lured by relatively generous money wages. In Ohio, the cost of living shot up at least as high as the national average, and possibly higher. Housing and clothing expenses apparently remained fairly stable, but food prices soared. Since food probably accounted for fifty to sixty percent of a working-class family's average expenditures, and since the proportion of earnings spent on food tended to increase as income decreased, rising grocery costs particularly affected laboring people. A sampling of prices for eight basic items in six Ohio cities illustrates the inflationary pattern (see Table 2J). The average total cost of these staple foods in Cincinnati, Cleveland, and Columbus rose 126 percent betweeen 1845 and 1855, declined thirty-nine percent over the remainder of the decade, but were still thirty-eight percent higher in 1860 than in 1845. While prices in these large cities were among the highest in the state, increases in smaller localities like Springfield, Zanesville, and Canton from 1855 to 1860 indicate that mounting living expenses afflicted workers throughout Ohio.

From the mid-1840s to 1860, therefore, most workers appear to have suffered from the rising cost of living. According to one estimate, ''real hourly wages'' — the actual purchasing power of money earnings — grew at an average annual rate of less than .5 percent. For many groups, especially among low-paid, unskilled laborers in big cities, real wages probably declined. Economic downturns in 1837-43, 1854-55, and again in 1857-58 further diluted any improvement in standards of living by draining precious savings, generating increased personal debt, and thereby delaying working-class recovery when inflated prosperity returned. These were indeed years of economic vulnerability and frustration for Ohio's laboring classes.

During the Civil War, the gap between wages and prices widened dramatically. With labor in short supply due to the military draft and curtailed immigration, annual money earnings for nonfarm employees increased about forty-one percent. By 1864, daily wages of $1.75 for un-

skilled labor and $3.00 for craftsmen were common in Ohio cities. More importantly, however, between 1860 and 1865, a seventy-six percent leap in consumer prices far outstripped the rise in money wages. The consequences for nonfarm labor were disastrous — real annual earnings (measured in 1914 dollars) plunged approximately twenty-eight percent, from $457 in 1860 to $328 in 1865. In the wake of such an enormous economic setback, which was further aggravated by a brief postwar recession, many years would pass before most workers could fully regain their prewar standards of living.

Labor began to recover some lost ground during the welcome burst of national prosperity in the late-1860s and early 1870s. The primary cause was a drastic reversal in cost-of-living trends. From 1865 to 1872, overall consumer prices declined nearly forty percent, led by sharp drops in food and clothing expenses. At the same time, money wages for the nation's nonfarm workers generally hovered at about $1.50 per day and $490 per year. By 1872, the combination of stable to slightly rising money wages and deflated prices pushed up real annual earnings twenty-seven percent to $416 — an impressive gain, but still below 1860 levels. Ohio's economy also experienced price slumps comparable to the national norm, though with considerable variation between communities (see Table 2J). Limited evidence suggests that average daily wages for unskilled, urban-industrial laborers held firm at about $1.60 throughout the period, while many skilled workers apparently enjoyed an increase in weekly wages from approximately $16 at the end of the war to $19 in 1872. Although these money earnings roughly equalled national rates, as well as pay-scales in the East, incomes were much lower for Ohio workers in industries such as steel and textiles. Therefore, with significant exceptions, steadily employed Ohio workers — especially among the skilled elite — appear to have shared in the extensive upgrading of real wages and standards of living which marked the era.

In the autumn of 1873, gloom and distress replaced optimism and prosperity, as the roller-coaster economy suddenly plunged into severe depression. Over the next six years, nationwide unemployment and wage-cuts caused annual money earnings to slip twenty-three percent. Another twenty-one percent decline in prices eased working-class losses, but not enough to prevent a general reduction in real annual earnings of six percent. The long depression hit laboring people in Ohio very hard, essentially because average wages fell much more steeply than prices. Whereas the statewide cost of groceries dropped about twelve percent, clothing thirty percent, and rents ten percent, average money wages plummeted thirty-three percent. Unskilled workers, who ordinarily had earned $1.60 per day or $450 per year in 1872, received only $1.00 per day or $300 per year by 1878. When employed, skilled artisans averaged $2.00 per day, compared to earnings of more than $3.00 during earlier "good times." Even by conservative estimates, Ohio workers probably suffered an average drop in real annual wages of fifteen to twenty percent. However, decreases did not strike all wage-earners equally. Between 1872 and 1879, the sharpest slashes in money wages occurred among the state's common laborers (forty percent) and skilled factory employees, such as cigarmakers (forty-one percent), shoe workers (thirty-two percent), and furniture workers (thirty percent). Pay-cuts were somewhat milder in less industrialized occupations like iron molding (twenty-five percent) and the building trades (twenty-eight percent). Nor were working-class standards of living affected uniformly. As illustrated in Table 2K, by the tail-end of the depression, the most steadily employed artisans still managed to save a bit of money. On the other hand, most unskilled laborers faced a hard choice: either go into debt — at least $60 per year simply in order to maintain pre-1873 standards of living — or reduce their living expenses substantially. The urban unemployed received little public assistance, since middle and upper-class residents, who held political power, firmly believed that depressions were normal and necessary adjustments in a competitive economy. Public unemployment relief was viewed as a dangerous socialist concept, "alien" to the capitalist system. Instead, workers were expected to endure any hardship with patience, with staunch "individualism," and — if absolutely necessary — with private charity. Consequently, numerous working-class families were compelled to exist as best they could, generally at bare subsistence levels. In 1878, the Ohio Commissioner of Labor Statistics summarized the stark reality of their lives:

One dollar per day to the laborer is absolute poverty even if work is to be had every secular day in the year; it may purchase bread, and water is cheap, but man as well as society can not live on bread alone. . . . One dollar per day means children forced from school and into a workshop; it means the wife and mother leaving her children all day while she toils over the wash tub of a more favored neighbor. . . .

Two dollars per day to the mechanic, counting the days he must lose for lack of employment, keeps the masses of them in poverty; it may not be so absolute or so glaring as that of the common laborer, yet it exists, and is made painfully appar-

Having just weathered a grueling depression, an anonymous Akron carpenter in 1879 eloquently expressed the dismay and frustration felt by thousands of workers who had flocked to Ohio's cities in search of opportunity:

I think that one reason of so much idle time in factories is owning to an unreasonable crowding and gathering to the cities and staying there half starving, when the country offers so many inducements to the industrious poor. It seems strange to me that our young men do not strike out for the West and secure homes for themselves. I would gladly do so if I could. I am 45 years of age and have a family of four children to keep and no means. But I see homes in abundance for the young and strong and persevering. I was raised on the blooming prairies of Wisconsin, and God knows that I do love the wild, free country. But at present I am like a bird whose wings are clipt—I can sigh for the freedom that I can not enjoy.

ent in the houses of thousands, who, when work was steady, were able to keep the wolf from the door, and live in apparent comfort. . . .

When the crisis finally passed in 1879, working people began their accustomed task of repairing battered living standards. National statistics seem to indicate that they generally succeeded. During the business upswing of 1879-1882, prices crept up about four percent, but average annual money wages increased fifteen percent, thus producing an overall ten percent rise in real earnings. In 1883, when real annual wages reached $459, the nation's nonfarm workers had at last restored their pre-Civil War income levels. Despite a mild depression from 1883 to 1885, real wages improved another seven percent, due to resumed declines in consumer prices and slight increases in average money wages. In the case of Ohio's working classes, however, national averages were somewhat deceiving. Daily wages for the state's unskilled labor grew to approximately $1.30 by 1880 and $1.50 by 1883, while annual money earnings for craftsmen evidently rose over thirty-five percent between 1878 and 1882. Although these increases were roughly equal to nationwide rates, consumer prices in Ohio jumped approximately fifteen percent over the same timespan. At the very least, therefore, inflated prices curtailed real wage gains and clearly hampered workers' efforts to recover from the depression. Furthermore, as Table 2K demonstrates, the supposedly "mild" national economic downturn of 1883-1885 was actually a calamity for many working-class families in Ohio. Even renewed deflation could not offset declining annual earnings, which by 1885, for example, had fallen to $265 for common laborers and $523 for skilled machinists. Thus, from 1879 through 1885, the mass of Ohio workers found decent standards of living difficult to achieve, and even harder to retain.

Three primary conclusions can be drawn from this brief survey. First, in purely economic terms, working-class standards of living did advance during Ohio's urban-industrial maturation. From the mid-1840s through the mid-1880s, the overall progress of real wages — perhaps averaging .4 percent per year — could most accurately be described as "moderate." Second, while workers made moderate economic headway over the long term, over shorter intervals improvements in wages were highly erratic. As the business cycles gyrated wildly, gains achieved during prosperous years could suddenly be rolled back in an unexpected crisis. At times the setbacks outpaced advances, as occurred from 1860 to 1883 — a full generation without a net improvement in real annual wages. Finally, economic progress was not only staggered over time, it also was not shared equally by all groups of workers. Considerable variation in personal incomes appeared both between and within communities, industries, occupations, and skill-levels. Many Ohio workers did achieve relative prosperity, but for some the next rung on the ladder of success seemed to remain just out of reach. Poverty in the midst of plenty — that unique reality of life in the emerging industrial-capitalist order — became as characteristic of the era as smoke-belching factories, corner-saloons, and the iron horse.

Yet, it is essential to recognize that the quality of a worker's existence cannot be evaluated solely in economic terms. Past experience and future expectations were also key factors in shaping a worker's estimation of his living standards, as well as his responses to those conditions. Even depressed wages could satisfy a new factory hand, if, as often happened, he had recently earned only half as much on a farm, or

Public breadlines for the needy and unemployed were rare during the nineteenth century.

perhaps less in a foreign homeland. In contrast, a similar situation could provoke great alarm in a veteran industrial worker, who had not seen improvement in his fortunes for many years. The significance of such factors was unmistakable, for example, in the revealing responses of two anonymous craftsmen to an 1878 questionnaire from the Ohio Bureau of Labor Statistics.

A skilled wheel-maker — whom we shall call "Jeremiah" — resided with his wife and four children in Tippecanoe City, a small town in rural Harrison county. In 1872, Jeremiah had started out as an unskilled hand in the local carriage and wagon wheel factory, making daily wages of $1.25. Despite the depression, he apparently worked his way up to journeyman status by 1877, when (although laid off for five weeks) he earned $500, or about $1.75 per day. During the following year, his pay for a ten-hour day rose to $2.00 — the very level, remember, which the Commissioner of Labor Statistics described as keeping most skilled workers in "poverty." Jeremiah, however, was obviously pleased with his own personal progress, and with his employers:

. . . When I went to work at this factory I had no credit, and not a dollar in the world. To-day I own my own property, worth, say ten to twelve hundred dollars; owe about $400 on that, which is all I do owe in town, and have a good chance to pay it; have as good credit as laboring men generally have, and earned every dollar [that] I am worth in this factory.

. . . They have employed about the same amount of men ever since they . . . started in business about ten years ago. They pay from $1.25 per day to $3.00, which is good in country towns. There has never been a strike in this firm. Every man in the factory seems perfectly satisfied with their present employment and wages, and are only afraid that it is too good to last. . . .

The superintendent and treasurer are both live young men of good business capacity, and desire to live and let live. They pay good wages promptly, and desire good work . . . do not make allowance for any one, but require a steady day's work. And I believe if all manufactories were run as this one is, there never would be any strikes in this country.

On the other hand, consider the rather grim account of "Ezra," a machinist who made his home in the rapidly industrializing city of Springfield. Married and without children, Ezra appears to have been somewhat older than Jeremiah. In 1872, he already earned journeyman's wages of nearly $3.00 per day. The subsequent depression, however, took a heavy toll. By 1877, when he was out of work for more than four months, his daily wages had plunged sixty-six percent, to slightly over $1.00. An increase to about $1.85 per day in 1878 could not make up for five years of periodic unemployment, which, as Ezra pointed out, "has run me in debt $680." Due to these experiences — and, one suspects, various additional hardships — Ezra's perspective on a worker's "lot-in-life" was much different than Jeremiah's:

There are thousands of young men running idle . . . they can not even support themselves, much less . . . think of enjoying the blessings (if there are any) of married life, for the simple reason of being unable to earn money to either get what is necessary to commence house-keeping or to support a wife after that. I have seen families that did not have a solid chair in the house, the husband and father being unable to provide anything during the time of employment but the commonest kind of food, let alone getting decent clothing or furniture. *What good does it do the working man to know that things are cheap, if he has not the money to buy them?* Employers here seem to make it a point to get their work done as cheap as it is possible to have it done, regardless of consequences to employes — that is, they want much done in a short time, for the lowest wages. One of the rules in my shop gives notice that my employers will not be responsible for accidents that may happen to employees. (emphasis added)

These plainspoken statements also call attention to the diversity of working-class experiences in the daily world of work. As described earlier, technological advances, mechanization, and the factory system gradually transformed production processes, though at varying paces and to different degrees in individual industries. The specific effects of these complex alterations — on working environments, on shop-floor routines, and on the shifting roles and status of laboring people — merit closer examination.

A conspicuous feature of Ohio's industrial development during this transition era was the relatively modest size of the typical workplace. As late as 1870, for example, Ohio boasted over 9,000 more manufacturing establishments than Massachusetts, but operated them with only half as many hands. To be sure, the average working arena grew larger after 1840, as craft shops gradually and unevenly evolved into moderate-sized plants and sprawling, multi-storied factories. Not until the century's last decades, however, would enormous factory complexes, each employing thousands of laborers, begin to emerge as the prevalent production setting in Ohio. Prior to the 1880s, the vast majority of small-town and urban industrial workers earned their livelihoods in cramped, one or two-story establishments, which usually employed from a dozen to a hundred hands. The changing scale of production in Cincinnati, Ohio's most diversified industrial center, illustrated the statewide pattern. From 1850 to 1880, large factories employing more than 100 wage earners multiplied from twenty-two to 109. Nevertheless, over the same timespan, the average number of workers per shop for the

Many manufacturing firms were small family-run operations. B. Mehlberth, a German immigrant, opened Dayton's first brush factory in 1855. Production took place on the first floor and the family occupied quarters upstairs.

Working in traditionally formal attire, a skilled cigarmaker could hand-wrap about 250 cigars per day. Mechanization expanded daily production to approximately 3,700 cigars per employee by 1880.

entire city rose from roughly ten to seventeen hands. By 1880, none of the Queen City's major industries averaged more than forty-five workers per establishment. Obviously, mammoth factories had not instantaneously banished smaller shops from the industrial scene.

Of the various shop-floor problems which accompanied industrial expansion, perhaps the most troublesome stemmed from employers' efforts to impose greater work-discipline on their wage earners. Drawn from agricultural and preindustrial backgrounds, the growing army of blue-collar laborers had been accustomed to spasmodic work habits. Grueling workdays had often extended from sunrise to sunset, but, more importantly, the tempo of production had been set by laboring people themselves. In practice, this usually meant spurts of strenuous activity, interrupted by periodic breaks which might last from a few minutes to several days. Especially in skilled occupations, irregular styles of work often became time-honored and fiercely guarded rituals. Coopers and glassblowers, for instance, had enjoyed three-day weekends, beginning on Saturday morning (payday) with beer, cards, and conversation on the shop floor; and ending on "Blue Monday," when the craftsmen did little more than casually prepare their tools for the week's work. Potters had commonly left their jobs for unannounced "holidays," whenever exhaustion or a whim struck them. Cigarmakers continually drifted in and out of the shop during the day; and, while at work, listened to a fellow artisan reading aloud from a newspaper or book. Even outdoor laborers like construction workers and longshoremen expected frequent breaks, complete with beer or sweets. Despite their stubborn persistence in many shops throughout the century, such loose work habits were increasingly viewed by profit-minded manufacturers as abominations of confusion and inefficiency which had to be controlled. In order to succeed in highly competitive markets and cover the cost of expensive new machinery, employers felt it crucial to keep production operating continuously and to tighten work discipline. Relatively rigorous time-schedules became their principal weapons. Wage earners were required to labor at the specific times and paces dictated by a new taskmaster, one almost totally alien to successive waves of factory newcomers — "the clock." In contrast to traditional practices, breaks became fewer and shorter. The clock would no longer tolerate tardiness, recreation, or relaxation during working hours. The dreaded "speed-up" — more output within the same amount of time — began to appear more frequently. The working world was now to run on a unique and demanding "industrial sense of time." In this setting, the steady reductions which occurred in the length of the average workday — from almost twelve hours in 1850 to just over ten in 1880 — could be very deceptive, since breathing spells were more infrequent and toil more intense.

Long hours and intensive labor practices combined to produce extremely hazardous working conditions. Packed into buildings with few fire escapes, meager ventilation, and inadequate sanitary facilities — and operating poorly maintained, improperly safeguarded, and often overworked machinery — fatigued industrial workers continually jeopardized their health and lives. The "human" cost of industrial progress tragically mounted, as, year after year, thousands of wage earners were killed or maimed by machines, slain in steam-boiler explosions, or trapped in factory blazes. For example, in 1881 alone, an insurance company counted 159 boiler explosions in Ohio workplaces, resulting in 251 deaths and 313 injuries. Many accidents were regrettably unforeseen, but, given the predominance of unsafe shop conditions, a large proportion were surely preventable. Henry Dorn, Chief State Inspector of Workshops and Factories, reported that, during 1885, investigations of 1,469 establishments (employing over 85,000 workers) had revealed that nearly half were in violation of even the weak safety and fire statutes then in force. Of those firms ordered to make improvements, only half subsequently complied. Yet, as Dorn further discovered, workers themselves contributed to high accident rates by often spurning safety devices on their machines:

> . . . strange as it may seem, there are persons operating stationary engines who object to these simple means of protecting themselves. In one instance I found a so-called engineer who was bitterly opposed to fencing in the fly-wheel of his engine. In answer to the question why he opposed it, he said it was unnecessary; though, on being further questioned, he acknowldged that he had himself been caught by the wheel three different times, the last time having his clothing torn off. . . .

Though not as dramatic as instantaneous amputations or violent deaths, a variety of job-related diseases also caused immeasurable suffering and countless fatalities. Noting in 1878 that workmen over the age of fifty were rarely found in the city's factories, the Cincinnati Department of Health concisely described occupational illnesses which afflicted laboring people in every corner of Ohio:

> Workers in iron, exposed to clouds of fine dust and minute particles of metal, suffer from phthisis [tuberculosis] to a marked degree. Molders especially, and all other classes working in metals, are subjected at times to high temperature, and are liable to contract rheumatism and subsequent heart disease, bronchitis and pneumonia from sudden exposure to cold draughts of air while overheated. Workers in copper and other metals, requiring use of acids, suffer from chronic asthma, chronic bronchitis and subsequent cardiac disturbances, from exposure to poisonous vapors and fumes. . . . Tailors, shoemakers, blacksmiths, printers, counting house clerks, seamstresses die early from consumption engendered by the physical position they assume while occupied at labor.

While industrial environments were never particularly safe or pleasant, during this era they were utterly treacherous.

Nothing in the course of my inspection has more strongly impressed me than the necessity of requiring all shops and factories, of a greater elevation than two stories, to be provided with a safe and efficient system of fire-escapes. The duty of supplying safeguards against the terrible casualties always likely to occur in the event of conflagrations in crowded shops and factories is so obvious and imperative, that there can be no difference of opinion respecting it . . . . Nevertheless it is a fact, amply demonstrated, in the observation I have had, that very many owners and proprietors of shops and factories are wholly indifferent to this important duty, and I have found some so utterly destitute of all concern for the safety of employes, as to refuse to provide proper escapes when their attention was called to the necessity for such provision . . . . The frequent occurrence of fires which have their most serious result in the loss of human lives, furnishes fearful warnings that should not be heedlessly dismissed from attention . . . .

In Cincinnati many of the buildings used for shops and factories are from five to nine stories high, and generally the first three or four floors of the building are used as store-rooms, the employes occupying the upper floors, escape from which would in most cases be extremely difficult in the event of a rapidly spreading fire, and loss of life or serious bodily injury almost inevitable. Most of the buildings are improperly constructed with reference to means of egress, the ingenuity of the architects having apparently been exerted to secure the greatest possible economy of space in the matter of stairways. Some of these buildings are provided with but a single stairway, and where there are two or more they are generally located so near together that a fire which would render any of them useless as an avenue of escape would be very likely to do so with all. In many cases, also, these stairways are located near elevators, which are most potent aids to the rapid progress of fire . . . . I found Cincinnati to be a great field of labor, and during the necessarily short time that I was there, I ordered the erection of about fifty fire-escapes on shops and factories . . . .

First Annual Report of the State Inspector of Shops and Factories, 1884.

Technological advancements generated new jobs, as well as eliminating outmoded occupations. Here, a diver outfitted in a new pressure-suit prepares to descend into the Ohio River at Cincinnati in 1872.

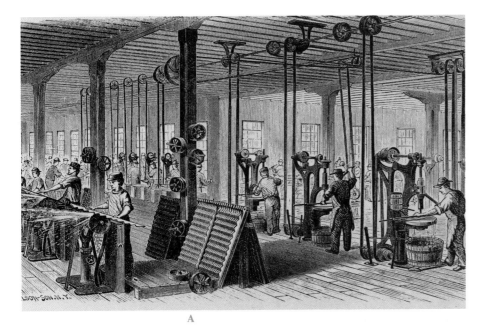

A

B

C

D

E

By 1876, the Champion Machine Company of Springfield was probably Ohio's largest and most advanced manufacturing enterprise. The firm's numerous buildings contained approximately fourteen acres of floor space and employed well over one-thousand workers. Row upon row of machinery — joined to central steam-powered drive shafts by a maze of belts and gears — produced as many as twelve-thousand farm implements annually. From the Polishing and Drilling Department (A) to the Grinding Room (B), the work force consisted primarily of semiskilled and unskilled machine-hands. In operations such as sawing slots in guards (C), once-skilled metal workers now idly observed machines perform their tasks, while young boys sharpened tools nearby. Yet, despite extensive mechanization, an integrated factory system had not fully matured. For example, the fabrication of "finger bars" (D) remained a bench-work operation, the sledge hammer was as necessary as a drill-press in the machine shop (E), and the movement of material between departments still depended on manual labor. Thus, even the era's most advanced factory production was a curious blend of modernity and tradition, machine and muscle, efficiency and cumbersomeness.

Just as industrialization bred diverse alterations in work environments and routines, so too did it gradually generate complex shifts in the roles and make-up of blue-collar workers. Mechanization and new managerial techniques tended to dilute the overall skill-levels required of the individual worker. Tasks formerly performed only by a skilled artisan were frequently divided up among teams of semi- and unskilled laborers, who performed simplified operations with the increasing assistance of machines. Implemented in various ways and at different stages in the evolution of each industry, changing production methods set in motion an ongoing restructuring of the industrial work force. Many independent artisans were relegated in status to factory wage earners; manual laborers advanced to semiskilled machine operators; and an influx of cheaper women and children filled tedious unskilled jobs. Keeping in mind that these occupational transitions were hardly simple or clear-cut, the emergence of four broad categories of industrial workers may be distinguished: independent craftsmen, factory artisans, factory laborers, and "sweated pieceworkers."

Especially in Ohio's numerous secondary cities and towns, independent skilled workers continued to practice their trades in traditional craftshops. Here, preindustrial work habits reigned supreme. Shops were small, each employing under a dozen journeymen and apprentices. Rigid schedules, shop-floor regimentation, division of labor, centralized supervision, and mechanization seldom appeared. Instead, craftsmen enjoyed great autonomy over the method, pace, and quality of their own production, generally recognizing custom as their only limitation. Because of their vital skills and knowledge, these proud artisans also commanded considerable status and high wages. Furthermore, by owning many of their own hand tools, they retained substantial control over the means of production. Though their numbers slowly declined after the Civil War, independent craftsmen steadfastly refused to be swept aside by industrial progress.

Another breed of skilled worker appeared with the rise of factory production. Like the transitional environments in which they toiled, factory artisans were curious blends of the old and new. The typical factory of this period, it will be recalled, more closely resembled a collection of craftshops than a highly integrated plant. The artisan continued to perform crucial tasks, but instead of turning out a complete finished item, exercised fewer skills while performing only certain steps in the manufacturing process. Still not totally subservient to machines, factory artisans even used their own hand-tools on occasion. Many retained considerable shop-floor power, continually waging — and often winning — skirmishes with employers who attempted to alter customary work habits. Nevertheless, in piecemeal fashion, mechanization and standardized production eventually diminished the factory mechanics' independence, status, and traditions. Control of

Apprenticeship agreements stipulated various obligations to be fulfilled by master and apprentice. In this case, the master harness-maker was to provide William Harry with a "freedom suit" upon completion of his apprenticeship.

the means, quality, quantity, and tempo of production gradually slipped from their hands, and into management's grasp. With their skills subdivided and their autonomy reduced, factory artisans increasingly became mere wage earners selling their time, rather than the crafted fruits of their labors. Despite these serious drawbacks, factory employment also held out attractive benefits to skilled wage earners. Mechanized factories tended to offer higher wages and better job security than small shops. Moreover, large plants employed numerous laborers to perform the more tiresome chores, thereby permitting artisans to focus on the most gratifying aspects of their trades. Therefore, the transition from traditional to modern workworlds posed perplexing choices for many skilled craftsmen.

The experiences of two groups of skilled workers illustrate how the transition from independent craftsman to factory artisan could vary widely between industries and plants. The Barney and Smith Company was founded in Dayton in 1849 to produce freight and passenger cars for the vigorously expanding railroads. However, the totally inexperienced owners quickly discovered that skilled workers who possessed the necessary knowledge of car building were not to be found in the vicinity. Consequently, in 1850 they recruited four master craftsmen from the East — a wood worker, a blacksmith, a machinist, and a painter. For at least the next decade, while the owners occupied themselves with obtaining raw materials and arranging sales, these artisans enjoyed almost complete shop-floor control of production. Using the traditional "cut and try" method of car designing and construction, they made all technical decisions; set the pace of production; and also hired, trained, and directed their own workers. By the end of the Civil War, the management of the rapidly growing company began to implement conspicuous

By virtue of their unique knowledge and skill, ship builders at the Knox Boat Yard in Marietta maintained their status as independent craftsmen.

Charles Cist was an early Cincinnati booster and avid proponent of industrialization, who also tended to overlook the inequities in the emerging factory system. Using the furniture industry as an illustration, he argued in 1851 that mechanization was an absolute blessing for workers and consumers alike. The factory hands who toiled under these conditions may not have been quite so enthusiastic.

Two or three popular errors exist, respecting the making of furniture by machinery, which it may be well here to refer to. One of these is, that the ware is not as exact in fit, or reliable for durability, as that made by hand; the reverse of this, is however, the fact. The least exercise of the reflecting powers, must suggest that work performed by machinery must be the more accurate. Another erroneous prejudice is, that the employment of machinery lessens not only the number of persons employed, but reduces their wages and profits. The fact, in reality, is, that the machinery, as a general result, takes the coarsest, hardest, and most unprofitable work out of the journeyman's hands—such as rough planing and ripping—and enables him to make his customary wages, at more pleasant employment. It is true, at the same time, that a great reduction in the price of these articles, is effected by the use of machinery, but this is done by the increase of product, which is both the cause and effect of low prices. But a comparison between past and present wages, will show clearly that the journeyman has been no loser, but in fact, gainer, by the introduction of machinery in the fabrication of furniture. . . .

One of the most remarkable of our manufacturing establishments, is the bedstead factory of Clawson and Mudge. . . . The building, which is of brick, is five stories in height, and one hundred and ninety by seventy feet, on the ground. The machinery consists of seven planing and two tapering machines, sixteen turning-lathes, six boring, and two tenoning machines, four splitting, and four buff saws, all which are driven by steam. One hundred and thirty hands are employed in this establishment. A very vivid impression of the power of machinery is given in this case, by the fact, that one hundred and thirty bedsteads are made and finished, as an average, every day, or one bedstead to each workman; while under the hand system of manufacture, a first rate bedstead is more than a week's work for one journeyman . . . .

In other articles, reference has been made to the benefit of machinery to the interests of the working-man, in taking the roughest and hardest of the ripping and planing out of his hands, and leaving to him only those delicate operations, which give play to the exercise of skill and judgment. It may be added, on the same subject, that the low prices at which machinery permits articles to be sold, so increases the quantity made, that more hands are now needed in these factories, than found employment under the old order of things, and at an average of better wages than heretofore . . . .

changes. Basic car designs were standardized, supervisors assumed control over the speed and method of production, more machinery was introduced, the factory mushroomed into a complex of forty buildings, and the number of employees swelled to nearly 2,000. By the mid-1880s, the skills of the four original craftsmen — who had since become foremen and stock holders — had been subdivided among more than fifty categories of factory artisans and semi-skilled wage earners. Developments were quite different for skilled rollers in the smaller Columbus Iron Works. In the mid-1870s, the iron mill owners still limited their activities to purchasing equipment and raw materials and obtaining orders for their finished rails. Actual production decisions were largely left to the firm's three rolling gangs, whose members had formed a small local union to negotiate the amount which management would pay for each order. The work-gangs then decided collectively how the rates should be divided per worker, the allocation of production among the three crews, the amount of rail to be rolled each day, and even hiring and promotions within the gangs. While little else is known about the company's history, it is clear that the firm's skilled iron rollers did retain the traditional autonomy which the skilled car builders had steadily lost.

Factory laborers comprised the largest and most vulnerable portion of the new industrial work force. These were the masses of men, women, and children who flooded into the countless varieties of tedious jobs spawned by the division of labor. Initially attracted by opportunities to earn higher wages than they had previously known, they performed the manual tasks and simple machine operations which gradually predominated in moderate-sized plants and large factories. Though their experiences varied widely, most were raw greenhands who required minimal training to execute their daily drudgery. Consequently lacking essential skills, factory laborers were the most susceptible to lay-offs, wage cuts, and the various restraints of factory discipline.

Finally, tens-of-thousands of laboring people fell into the rather disparate category of "sweated pieceworkers." Particularly common to the clothing, cigar, and shoe industries, this form of labor was an expanded version of the preindustrial putting-out system. Manufacturers frequently subcontracted production to small entrepreneurs. The subcontractors, in turn, would hire the workers, provide them with necessary materials, sell them machines on credit, and pay them a few cents for each completed piece. The skill-levels of the male and female pieceworkers ranged from the experienced artisan to the untutored child, depending on the task. Subcontractors sometimes provided workplaces in cramped "sweat-shops," generally located in highly flammable and poorly ventilated tenements. More often, pieceworkers carried their work home, where several family members toiled long hours, in order to produce enough pieces within the allotted time, to pay for the bare necessities of life.

As a reporter for the *Cleveland Herald* sadly concluded in 1879, after a lengthy investigation into the conditions under which female pieceworkers labored: "Those who thus become successful at it would be another striking illustration of 'survival of the fittest,' did they not in turn break down at last, utterly worn out, and burdened with chronic ills conduced by the endless tread of a sewing machine."

These broad alterations in work forces and workplaces did not affect all laboring people in the same manner, to the same degree, or at the same time. Working-class encounters with industrial progress varied significantly, as illustrated by the experiences of brewers, window-glass workers, and coal miners.

Ohio's brewing industry exemplified the unique blending of tradition and modernity which distinguished this period. Prior to the

1850s, brewing typically had been a rather primitive affair — a few crude kettles and vats in a small log-building, where an English or Scotch brewmaster personally directed several journeymen and apprentices in the ancestral art of concocting ale and porter beer. With the vast influx of German immigrants to the state during the 1850s, however, the character of the industry began to change dramatically. The newcomers introduced, as part of their cultural baggage, a German brew which promptly gained widespread popularity in America — lager beer. In contrast to the manufacture of ale or porter, lager brewing was an expensive process requiring slower fermentation and lower temperatures for production and storage. Furthermore, because it soon grew stale, a tapped keg had to be consumed quickly. These factors combined to make lager brewing a distinctively urban phe-

Following the Civil War, technological advancements and standardized production steadily transformed the brewers' working environment. The Hauck Brewery in Cincinnati, for example, grew into a massive operation, including boiler room (A), granary (B), cooper shop (C), and shipping department (D).

A

B

C

D

Predominantly comprised of German immigrants, the labor force at the Hauck Brewery typically put in fourteen to eighteen-hour workdays in 1870.

nomenon, since only in the growing cities could brewery owners be assured of local markets large enough to generate sufficient profits. While Cincinnati and Cleveland thus became leading brewing centers, by the 1880s hardly any large Ohio city lacked a brewery of its own. From sixty-four establishments employing an average of four hands each in 1850, the industry expanded by 1880 to 163 firms and approximately eleven workers per brewery. After the Civil War, standardized production methods and a variety of technological improvements appeared, from ice machines and steam boilers to mechanized keg-washers, elevators, and pumps. Traditional craft structures and proce-

dures gradually broke down as well. By the 1880s, managers of modern breweries had divided the skills of independent craftsmen among as many as a dozen classifications of factory artisans and laborers. Small local breweries continued to turn out limited batches for a handful of nearby saloons. But, particularly in larger cities, the neighborhood brewery was increasingly dwarfed by the massive factory complex employing dozens of hands and containing miles of pipe, giant kettles, carpenter shops, ice houses, and even stables for the teams which hauled the brew throughout the city.

Yet despite technological advances and the rising scale of production, working conditions within Ohio's breweries remained deeply rooted in an almost feudal traditionalism. The ethnic homogeneity of the labor force was a significant cause. Of all the occupations in American manufacturing, brewing had the highest proportion of foreign-born workers — the overwhelming majority of whom were German. In fact, after introducing lager beer in the 1850s, Germans became so entrenched in the business that, by 1880, two out of every three brewery hands in Ohio — and three out of four in Cincinnati — were German-born. Not only in brewing techniques, but in labor practices as well, the familiar old-world standards were consequently applied in even the largest Ohio plants. For instance, in keeping with the craft's "masculine" traditions, women and children were very rarely employed. Wages were higher in Ohio than in the fatherland, but, in order to earn them, brewery hands still had to work the extremely long hours which custom dictated. Thus, while the average hours of labor steadily declined in most other industries between 1840 and 1880, brewers continued to put in preindustrial workweeks. An arduous schedule of fourteen to eighteen hours from Monday through Saturday, plus another six to eight hours on Sunday, was only the average. For, as the Ohio Commissioner of Labor Statistics pointed out in 1878, "laborers in a brewery work whenever necessary, day or night, or both, if called on. Sometimes required to be on duty twenty-four or more hours at a time." Employers also utilized traditional — and certainly distinctive — methods of enforcing shop-floor discipline. Although it has not been proven conclusively that brewmasters and foremen continued the notorious custom of beating unproductive or dissatisfied workers, another long-standing practice did thrive — keeping wage earners docile by encouraging excessive drinking on the job. So pervasive was this practice, that drunkenness became as much of an occupational hazard for brewers as tuberculosis and rheumatism. The autocratic control to which workers had traditionally been subjected did not diminish when successful brewmasters were transformed from craftsmen to capitalists. Rather, their powers were simply passed on to foremen, whose authority extended even to the brewery hands' living conditions. In a unique version of company housing, all workers were obliged to reside either on the brewery premises, in specially selected tenements nearby, or in the foreman's house. This arrangement enabled management to enforce discipline both on and off the job, to keep their hands on 24-hour call,

Like their fellow-immigrants who toiled in Ohio breweries, German-born butchers encountered a working world in which modern production methods were combined with almost feudal labor practices. In an 1880 statement to the Ohio Commissioner of Labor Statistics, John Ehmann, a Cincinnati sausage-butcher, provided a fascinating description of conditions in the plants and the workers' reactions:

There are ten sausage factories in the city, employing from 2 to 20 persons each, a total of 110 men. The employers are all Germans, and the employes are nearly all Germans, only five or six, who were born in this country, of German parentage being employed.

Up to October, 1879, the average working hours per day were 18, beginning at 3 o'clock in the morning and ending at 9 o'clock in the evening. Wages were, for foremen, $12.00 per week, and for others from $6.00 to $9.00 per week, including board. Some few received less than the above wages.

Whenever the employer is prepared to board the employe, he must accept, whether married or single, so that the married man has little chance to join his family, except after 4 o'clock on Sundays. On Sundays they worked from 5 o'clock in the morning until 4 o'clock in the afternoon, or eleven hours. No extra pay was allowed for Sunday work, and if the men worked less than 18 hours per day, or did not work on Sunday, the lost time was deducted from their weekly wages. Occasionally they were obliged to work 22 hours without intermission and without extra pay, except a glass of beer or cider.

In October, 1879, the Butchers' Benevolent Association organized a protective union. At their first meeting nearly every butcher in the city was present, the meeting being held on Sunday evening, and many of those present were in their working clothes, having come from their work to the meeting. The speakers present urged an immediate attempt to regulate the hours of labor and to abolish Sunday work, the result being the adoption of resolutions demanding that 12 hours per day constitute a day's work, and that 15 minutes be allowed for breakfast, 15 for dinner, and 15 for supper. All time worked over 12 hours to be paid extra, and Sunday labor to be abolished; but if necessity compelled work to be done on Sunday, it was to be paid extra.

Employees at Cincinnati's Jackson Brewery, ca. 1870.

The resolutions were presented to the employers next day, the men refusing to work for any employer who refused to sign an agreement to abide by the resolutions. In three days all had signed, with one exception, whose men had not joined the union, but the moral effect was such that for a time his men were given the benefit of the change. The effect of the change was immediate; wages increasing because of the extra time worked over 12 hours, the men not realizing the danger of working over time, although pointed out to them at every meeting. The men did not object to overtime, because of the extra pay; and, in time, the custom of working over 12 hours had grown so that pay for overtime was refused. A few promptly struck work, others remained at work, and extra pay for overtime disappeared. The men neglected the union after a few months, the membership falling from 90 to 30. Although many of the employers have repudiated the agreement they signed, yet the condition of affairs is not as bad as it was before the men organized. Four factories are still working under the resolutions.

The machinery in this trade has made the work easier for the workmen. Although it had not previously lessened their hours of labor, there had not been any less employed because of the machinery, but the work was easier.

The only dangerous machine is the 'chopper;' the least slip on the part of the 'feeder' would make mince-meat of his hand or fingers.

Besides the dangers of chopped fingers, rheumatism seizes every butcher; their limbs become stiff at thirty-five, and they are unfit for the trade; but one man is known to have worked at the trade 25 years, and he is yet working at it.

Few of them have any opportunity to learn English, so narrow is the circle of their daily experience; and some, who have been in this country for 15 years, cannot talk in English, and have some difficulty to understand it.

These men say that the custom, or conditions under which they are employed, are not those of Germany, but purely of American growth, and that it is worse in St. Louis than in Cincinnati. They claim it is impossible to earn or save a competence at the trade; that those of the present employers, who were workmen, became employers when there was but little competition and when prices were high; others were assisted by relatives.

An oval tank furnace used in the delicate glass-making process in 1880.

and to minimize exposure to more modern ideas of workers' rights. Stringently controlled, exploited, and isolated from the larger society, most brewery workers therefore endured as vassals within a modernizing industry.

While selective change occurred in even tradition-bound breweries, window-glass manufacturing was virtually unaffected by the industrial revolution. Throughout the nineteenth century, glassmaking remained a handicraft industry, stubbornly immune to new technology, mechanization, and the factory system. Production methods and work settings were essentially identical to those utilized two centuries earlier. The lack of innovation stemmed, in large part, from the peculiar physical properities of glass and the complexities of the glass-forming process. As a very fragile substance, glass was quite difficult and expensive to manipulate mechanically. In addition, since the physical qualities of each batch varied considerably, glassmaking required flexible production techniques which could adjust swiftly to changing situations and defects. Until twentieth-century technology sufficiently resolved these complex problems, manufacturers found it cheaper and more efficient to rely on skilled workers who used crude, but highly adaptable, manual methods. Four types of craftsmen thus comprised the backbone of the window-glass industry: "gatherers" who removed the molten glass from the pot, "blowers" who then shaped the glass into long cylinders, "flatteners" who smoothed the cylinders into sheets, and "cutters" who slit the sheets into desired sizes. Because of the industry's handicraft character, the typical glass works remained small, averaging from thirty to sixty skilled and unskilled workers per plant. Though a variety of glass products were manufactured in half-a-dozen Ohio shops by the 1850s, a specialized window-glass industry did not expand appreciably in the state until the 1870s, primarily due to rising demand by the construction industry. Most new glass works located in secondary cities in eastern Ohio — such as Ravenna, Kent, Bellaire, and Zanesville — in order to be near the abundant deposits of sand, lime, and coal which were essential for production. By 1879, five small window-glass firms operated in the state, employing a total of no more than 250 hands.

Window-glass artisans were among the most tightly knit, highly skilled, well-paid, and independent craftsmen of the nineteenth century. Numbering fewer than 2,000 men throughout the nation by the 1880s, members of this exclusive craft possessed an exceptionally strong sense of group solidarity and tradition. The trade actually resembled an extended family, since not only did sons of artisans customarily enter one of the industry's four crafts, they also commonly married the daughters and sisters of fellow glass workers. Habitual migrations from shop to shop further reinforced their sense of camaraderie, by placing them in regular contact with most of the trade's other "cinderheads." Long years of training and the fact that relatively few men successfully mastered the glassmaking art bred intense pride in their workmanship. As one historian has described these elite artisans, "their work was highly skilled, requiring some knowledge of the chemistry of glass, the lung capacity of a prima donna, and the heat-resisting qualities of a stoker." Vigorous competition between glasshouse owners for the

Second National Convention of Window Glass Workers' Assembly, No. 300, K. of L., held at Pittsburgh, July 10th to 13th, 1883.

services of these scarce workmen generated considerable geographic mobility, insured substantial job-security, and kept wage levels high. Skilled window-glass workers generally earned two to three times more than unskilled laborers, and from one-third to two-thirds more than craftsmen in most other industries. Wage rates were particularly high in Ohio, where gatherers, blowers, flatteners, and cutters consistently received twenty-five to thirty percent more than their counterparts in the East. From approximately $400 in 1850, the average annual incomes of Ohio's skilled glass workers rose to about $1,500 in 1867, and remained relatively high at nearly $1,200 during the depression-year of 1877. Hardly surprising in light of such comfortable earnings, the majority of these shop-floor aristocrats easily weathered economic downturns and even achieved the working-class dream of home ownership. However, as one might also suspect, monetary rewards were not gained without a price. Arduous labor in frequently excruciating heat, the constant menace of fire, and — to quote a state investigator's 1877 report — "consumption, lung disease, and a general breaking down of the system, [were] the penalties for the wages received."

As a reflection of their indispensable skills, their scarcity, and their conspicuous job-consciousness, window-glass workers retained control over production to a degree unmatched by most other tradesmen. Though in no immediate peril of being displaced by machines, skilled cinderheads did perceive two potential threats to their influence and security — overproduction and a surplus of labor. In order to prevent employers from using these means as

disciplinary weapons, craftsmen strictly enforced their own formal and informal codes of shop-floor behavior. Window-glass artisans, for example, independently determined the quality and quantity of daily production. By staunchly preserving the industry's traditional "summer stop" — a novel practice in which all glasshouses shut down during July and August — they not only further restricted output and avoided unexpected layoffs, but also enjoyed a leisurely vacation from the oppressive summer heat in unventilated shops. Furthermore, local trade societies of gatherers, blowers, flatteners, and cutters effectively regulated employment through restrictive apprenticeship systems which customarily admitted only members' relatives. Since craftsmen also zealously protected their long-standing right to hire, supervise, and pay their own unskilled helpers, they had a virtual monopoly on the industry's labor supply. In the late 1870s, employers in Kent, Zanesville, and other glass centers attempted to break the artisans' grip by accelerating their recruitment of cheaper crews of European glassmakers. The cinderheads responded in 1880 by uniting their scattered trade societies into probably the era's strongest labor organization — the Window Glass Workers' Union, Assembly 300 of the Knights of Labor. After organizing most of their Belgian, British, and French competitors as rapidly as they arrived, and after finally defeating the employers in an 1883-84 strike, the union could justifiably boast: "We absolutely control the production of window glass in this country."

The working world of the Ohio coal miner defied clear-cut comparison or simple classifica-

An 1877 account by a Mahoning Valley miner revealed that company housing in Ohio's coal camps could be as stark and squalid as any urban slum:

There are two kinds or classes of dwellings in Church Hill. The first are built of frame, have four rooms—two on first floor, and two on second floor. On the first floor the rooms are lined with pine lumber; on the second floor there is no finish of any kind, the bare weatherboarding keeping out the heats of summer and the frosts of winter. These rooms are fit for two purposes only—breeding vermin in summer, and as a skating rink in winter. They are painted on the outside. Each of these houses contains two families.

The second class of houses are harder to describe, being what are known as shanties, with no plaster or paint inside or outside. They contain two rooms, one up and one down stairs. To each house there is about one-fourth of an acre, but no fences, consequently useless for garden purpose. The houses have no cellars, and any repairing must be done by the tenants. One well of water supplies the occupants of sixty houses.

tion increased, so too did the number and size of bituminous mines. In 1850, the state's 124 small-scale enterprises produced primarily for local consumers with an average of under ten miners per pit. By 1879, the industry had grown to over 600 mines, now selling in state and national markets, and employing underground work forces which had more than doubled to an average of twenty-three diggers per mine. Many of the largest coal companies to emerge were controlled by absentee owners who, beyond their annual profits, had little concern or contact with daily mining operations. Others were "captive mines," run by iron firms essentially to provide fuel for their blast furnaces. Since the bituminous deposits were located in areas remote from established communities, coal operators provided basic housing and stores within walking distance of the mines. However, because these dwellings were initially intended to serve only as temporary shelters and because profit, rather than the employees' comfort, was the primary concern, company-owned housing generally consisted of stark, jerrybuilt, multi-family structures which rapidly deteriorated into permanently squalid shacks. Like the early iron masters, many mine owners quickly learned that excessive rents, the use of scrip, and monopolistic price-gouging in the company store furnished generous profits, as well as powerful economic weapons with which to assert control over their workers. Despite such drawbacks, thousands of native and foreign-born laborers swarmed into Ohio's coal camps after 1850. During the 1870s and '80s, a large proportion of the newcomers consisted of Swedes, Germans, Italians, and blacks, whom employers recruited through Cleveland's notorious contract-labor exchanges to serve as strikebreakers. But even more significant to the industry's evolution were the experienced British-born colliers, who not only comprised

tion. Like brewery hands, for instance, miners endured an almost feudal relationship with their employers; but, in contrast, remained relatively untouched by technological advances. Like window-glass artisans, they also cultivated an intense camaraderie and a stringent "code of honor;" but, lacking the cinderheads' degree of skill and sense of craft consciousness, miners never achieved the same autonomy or control over production. Secluded in the remote coal fields of Ohio's industrial hinterlands, faced with subsistence standards of living, and haunted by ever-present danger, members of this underground fraternity justly deserved their distinction as "a people apart unto themselves."

Ohio's coal industry underwent extensive transformations during the mid- and late 1800s. As the fuel needs of the urban-industrial revolu-

Even when newly constructed, multi-family company housing in this Hocking Valley coal town was stark and primitive.

one-third of all Ohio miners by 1870, but who also brought strong traditions of militant unionism.

Economic insecurity became a pervasive feature of this turbulent industry. Cutthroat competition and chronic overproduction, together with the industry's seasonal nature and exceptional susceptibility to fluctuations in the national economy, resulted in irregular profits for mine owners, and recurrent unemployment and low wages for employees. Miners could never count on steady work, losing fifteen to twenty weeks every spring and summer during prosperous years, and even more during strikes or depressions. Erratic employment patterns were further aggravated by a constant surplus of workers—a condition largely caused by the conscious efforts of employers to generate job-competition and dissension among the miners, as well as to provide more customers and profits for their company stores. Annual incomes of coal miners consequently remained among the lowest in the state, ranging from an average of $270 in 1850 to $325 in 1880—a rise which barely kept pace with the cost of living. Besides being meager, wages paid per ton were also very unpredictable, depending on such widely varying factors as the quality and size of a coal seam, current market prices, and an employer's wage policies. Owners commonly paid employees in company scrip, from four to six weeks after the coal was mined. While awaiting their wages, workers had little choice but to purchase high-priced necessities on credit at the company store. When payday finally did arrive, dismayed miners often learned that their earnings had been insufficient to cover their accumulated bills. After several such experiences, many miners found themselves trapped in a cycle of economic bondage to the company — perpetually indebted to employers for their food, homes, and supplies, as well as their jobs. Thus, three out of four Ohio miners who were

The depression of the 1870s struck coal miners and their families with a particular vengeance. In 1877, an anonymous miner described the deprivation and suffering endured in Hubbard:

My two little girls have been going to school all summer, but God knows they cannot go this winter, for want of shoes and clothing. The plastering is coming down in my kitchen, and I can not repair it for want of money to buy shingles for the roof. There is a glass out of the window in my front room, and a piece of paper fills the vacancy. We used about two-thirds of corn meal for our bread last winter. I never used such in my life before. The food of miners consists mainly of corn meal bread, mush, with skim milk or molasses, potatoes, pork, cabbage, with occasionally some wheat bread, tea or coffee, sugar, whatever the store pleases to let them have.

I have neighbors to-day who are industrious, sober, and honest men, whose children are going from door to door begging, because the stores are closed against them.

Three weeks ago I helped to carry home a man who was badly injured in the back by a fall of coal in the mine, who last winter, with a wife and six children, lived in a house without a stove and without a bedstead.

surveyed in 1879 reported that their family expenses had exceeded their incomes in each of the previous five years. Even for those fortunate enough to avoid debt, standards of living were low, as illustrated by the experience of a Trumbull County miner with a wife and seven children. Assisted by two teenage sons, he managed to earn $538 during 1878. From this sum, however, the company deducted $36 for rent, $25 for coal, $16 for lamp-oil, $74 for blasting powder, and $5.00 for tool-sharpening. The balance of $427 left him with less than $1.00 per week to feed and clothe each family member at the company store.

As bleak and insecure as their lives above ground remained, the dismal conditions which coal miners confronted in their subterranean working world were without parallel. Miners toiled in the gloomiest and loneliest of environ-

The company store in Coalton, ca. 1880, was operated by John Patterson, the future founder of the National Cash Register Company.

The gloomy working world of the Ohio coal miner.

Miner using an early drilling machine at the coal face.

ments, at the most grueling and most hazardous of all occupations. During the winter months of peak employment, when they descended into the pits before dawn and surfaced after dusk, miners seldom saw the sun. Miles underground, only the faint rays of a flickering lamp disturbed the awesome, enveloping blackness. Since few coal-cutting machines appeared before the 1880s, these gloomy chambers remained the domain of the "practical pick miner," who used methods and tools which had persisted for four hundred years. Each miner was assigned an individual "workroom," never more than five feet high, but always ankle-deep with water. Lying on his side in black slime, with a shoulder resting on his thigh, he began by undercutting the coal face with short, powerful strokes of the pick — a contortionistic feat described by one authority as "the most exhausting work to which the human frame can be put." Holes were then drilled into the face, black powder inserted, and the coal blasted down onto the floor. With an assistant, the miner hand-loaded the heavy chunks into cars, which mules or husky youths hauled to the surface for weighing and sorting. In addition to digging coal, miners performed arduous "dead work" for which they usually received no pay — bailing water, shoring up the roof with timbers, shoveling debris, and repairing rails. Despite primitive

safety precautions, underground workers were ceaselessly hounded by the grim certainty that death or crippling injury could strike at any moment. Though obviously commonplace, accidents were not well tabulated during this era. The State Inspector of Mines counted 285 reported fatalities and 362 serious injuries between 1874 and 1885, but admitted that these were only very minimal estimates. With the exception of an 1872 mine fire in Portage County which claimed ten lives, the coal industry remarkably escaped spectacular disasters. Rather, Ohio miners typically met their fates alone and unnoticed by the outside world. Casualties occurred in a variety of grisly ways. Most were crushed or suffocated when cave-ins converted workrooms into tombs. Others perished due to "fire damp"—pockets of invisible, odorless, tasteless, toxic, and highly flammable methane gas released by cutting into the coal vein, and resulting in unexpected asphyxiation or, if ignited, immediate cremation. Still other miners died "by inches" over many years — maimed by crippling accidents; wracked by painful rheumatic diseases; gradually poisoned by noxious gases in poorly ventilated mines; or slowly strangled by the solidification of inhaled coal particles, known as "black lung."

A miner's occupational status in this treacherous industry was a complex issue and a source of considerable controversy. In a sense, for example, pick miners possessed many of the characteristics of 'independent craftsmen.' Although subject to the dictates of employers on the surface, miners enjoyed substantial autonomy when below ground. Without any direct supervision, they controlled the method and pace of their own production, determined their own working hours, and hired their own helpers. They were rarely threatened by machines, owned their own hand-tools, and even developed notions of proprietorship over "their" assigned workrooms. Besides brute strength, coal mining required a certain degree of delicacy and experience in the various intri-

As this "blackleg" learned during an 1874 coal strike at Washingtonville, violations of the miners' sacred code of honor brought bitter condemnation from neighbors and fellow-workers.

cacies of properly sighting, undercutting, drilling, and blasting, so as to produce a high percentage of valuable lump coal instead of worthless pea-coal and slate. But, in another sense, miners also resembled semiskilled 'factory laborers.' Their jobs were basically tedious and routine. Unlike highly skilled crafts such as glassblowing, digging coal required little creativity and minimal training — as partly reflected in the abundance of miners, the relative ease with which they could be replaced, and their low wages. Despite their understandable feelings of proprietorship, the fact remained that — like factory laborers — their workplaces were assigned by a boss, who thereby exerted significant power over individual productivity and earnings. And yet, in still another sense, miners were also similar to "sweated pieceworkers," since they labored for a certain price per ton of coal produced. These three occupational distinctions were quite important, because, in large measure, they accounted for the industry's ongoing hostility between miners and employers. Miners tended to view themselves as independent craftsmen, and therefore felt entitled to the respect and economic benefits which accompanied that status. On the other hand, most coal operators considered miners to be mere factory laborers or sweated pieceworkers, and thus qualified only for subordinate status and exploitation. These contradictory perceptions were rarely resolved. Consequently, grievances accumulated, animosities grew, and labor-management relations deteriorated so completely that, in 1877, the Commissioner of Labor Statistics concluded: "There appears to be no understanding among the operators and miners upon any question. There is a mutual distrust — a mutual belief that justice can only be had by taking every advantage when opportunity offers." As we shall see, this bitter adversarial relationship flared into violent confrontation with tragic frequency.

Amidst the danger, hardship, strife, and isolation which uniquely marked their lives, miners forged a strict code of conduct for their mutual security. Though total compliance was never achieved, several unwritten rules of honor were universally understood. No man had the right to work for less than the prevailing rate received by fellow-miners. No man ever had the right to become a "blackleg," or strikebreaker. No man could shirk his duty to assist fellow-miners during an accident, a depression, or a strike. Violations of this simple miners' code brought disgrace, ostracism, threats, and physical attack — prices few inhabitants of closely-knit coal towns were eager to pay. The extraordinary working-class solidarity which emerged became the miners' most formidable defense against unending challenges to their personal welfare.

For the mass of Ohio workers, however, solidarity proved elusive. As with American labor generally, widespread cohesion among the state's diverse working classes was effectively inhibited by a complex web of interrelated obstacles.

One of the most pervasive and durable barriers to working-class unity was the American "gospel of success." Passed on from generation to generation since colonial days; ingrained in every schoolchild through the McGuffy

Readers; praised in popular novels and self-help manuals; absorbed by immigrants as a supplement to their own European versions; and continually reinforced by church sermons, newspaper editorials, and political speeches, the gospel permeated the American mentality. More than a set of lofty ideals, this influential creed was considered a practical formula for achieving upward social and economic mobility — namely, that with hard work, talent, and a virtuous character, every deserving American had an equal opportunity to become a "self-made man." The key was "individual" effort, for material advancement or failure would be determined by one's own actions. According to the success ethic, therefore, class lines were not rigid and every worker was a potential entrepreneur, capable of escaping his wage-earning status through individualistic endeavors. To join in collective action with fellow-workers was a radical contradiction to the gospel, as well as a tacit admission that workers would probably remain workers — unappealing heresies which ambitious laboring people were extremely reluctant to accept. Even when distinct flaws in the success formula appeared during the last half of the century, most workers did not discard the gospel's basic principles, but instead adjusted their goals to changing conditions. Rather than advancement to entrepreneurial status, success became increasingly defined in terms of home ownership, promotion to a supervisory position, or simply a secure job at adequate wages. Consequently, the majority continued to be "alive to their own interest" — pursuing success individually, competing rather than cooperating, depending on their own abilities, but continually fearing that another worker's advancement might threaten their own opportunities.

The highly erratic nature of Ohio's economic and industrial transformation further weakened solidarity among workers. As we have seen, uneven change produced a wide variety of working-class experiences. The strains, demands, and rewards of a changing environment were not felt equally. Thus, while the factory

Though still a tiny segment of the state's work force, public employees such as Lima's first mail carriers in 1884 began to increase with urban development.

A Cincinnati delivery man in the early 1880s.

system might threaten skilled tailors and iron puddlers, it also provided job-opportunities for unskilled seamstresses and heavy laborers. A depression might bring destitution to Hocking Valley miners, while Kent glassblowers lived in relative comfort. Nor did workers within a single plant necessarily share similar plights, since they were divided by skill, wage, and age levels, as well as being split into separate departments with different conditions. Furthermore, when the swelling number of workers in transportation and service occupations are also considered, contradictory experiences with progress became endless. The diverse impacts and perceptions of seemingly widespread problems therefore tended to undermine any strong sense of mutual concern among laboring people who, at the same time, were being fragmented by the gospel of success.

Intertwined with these ideological and economic influences were complex social and demographic forces which deepened the cleavages between workers. For instance, overlapping ethnic, religious, racial, and sexual differences often blended with job-competition to stimulate bitter tensions among workers, both within their communities and their workplaces. Mutual suspicion and hostility could take many forms. Native-born white males often refused to work with immigrants, blacks, or women. Squabbles arose between ethnic groups, such as the continual conflicts in the Cleveland diocese between German, French, and Irish Catholics who insisted on governing their own parishes. Frictions within ethnic groups were also commonplace, as exemplified by the violent religious disputes during the 1880s among Polish-Catholic workers in Toledo. The nativistic anxieties of Anglo-Saxon Protestants

As expressed by an anonymous skilled machinist in 1884, many artisans bitterly resented their declining status in the modern industrial world:

Socially, in this town, a mechanic earning fifteen dollars a week is looked down on by many of what we call society people, while a counter-hopper, earning one-half as much, is regarded as a very much better man, not because he knows any more, but because the former is a "greasy mechanic." I admit that many mechanics waste their time and money foolishly, especially on theaters and drink, but many are sober, economical men, kind husbands, and tender fathers. Almost all have a common school education, and many improve their time in reading, drafting, etc.

spurred various types of discrimination against "radical" foreigners and Catholics, especially during the Know-Nothing movement of the 1850s. Numerous race riots broke out, such as the clashes in 1862 between Irish and black dockworkers in Cincinnati and Toledo. And, of course, there were the repeated incidents of strife between skilled natives and unskilled immigrants, particularly during strikes. Moreover, high rates of geographic mobility hindered efforts to overcome this rampant factionalism, since it was obviously difficult to develop strong bonds among neighbors or fellow-workers who were habitually "moving-on" — across town, across the state, or across the country. Within the sprawling industrial cities to which more and more workers migrated, the insecurities of natives and immigrants led to the creation of isolated ethnic communities. While these enclaves may have relieved the personal anonymity of urban life, they also physically reinforced a sense of separateness among workers. Even leisure activities tended to hamper

Operating telephone exchanges was stereotyped as "women's work" as early as 1879.

working-class consciousness, not only because they diverted attention from common problems, but also because they were usually organized along ethnic, religious, and racial lines.

Perhaps it should not have been surprising that, amidst the constant disruptions of an evolving urban-industrial society, Ohio's diverse workers were pitted against one another so frequently and in so many ways. Perhaps the greater wonder was the degree of solidarity which they did achieve, despite the stresses and obstacles. For, expanding upon the perceptions of preindustrial toilers, an awareness gradually spread among many laboring people that they indeed faced common adversaries and similar problems which required cooperative action. Though hardly outweighing factional impulses, these relatively feeble notions of solidarity would have significant consequences for the quality of working-class life.

Anti-union propaganda during the nineteenth century warned workers that union membership not only contradicted the gospel of success, but also undermined their families' security.

Concerted working-class efforts to deal with advancing social and economic problems followed four main paths: trade unionism, political activism, reformism, and mob violence. Though tentatively explored by a handful of aroused workers prior to the 1840s, these avenues were more fully expanded and tested by scores of laboring people over the next four decades. The efforts developed simultaneously and intersected repeatedly. Unions commonly participated in reform movements, labor organizations delved into politics, and strikes or political concerns could flare into mob insurrections with disturbing regularity. From their somewhat meandering search for effective courses of action, however, Ohio workers gradually learned valuable, if often unpleasant, lessons in the use of collective power.

For most nineteenth-century workers, participation in labor unions was a drastic step, born out of desperation, and loaded with potentially adverse consequences. In a society which viewed unions and collective economic action as "conspiracies" against the capitalist system and the individualistic gospel of success, membership exposed workers to scathing denunciation from pulpits, press, and a generally unsympathetic public. More importantly, union activism could pose grave risks to their very livelihoods. Managers seldom approved of organization among their employees and openly used firings, blacklists, spies, and yellow-dog contracts (agreements not to join a union as a condition of employment) in order to purge "agitators" and suppress collective action. If these methods failed to prevent a strike, management had even more weapons at its disposal: employers' associations to provide financial aid and strikebreakers; "lockouts," whereby owners closed the plant or mine until hunger and debt forced disgruntled workers either to drift away or to submit to the employer's conditions; the power of state and local governments which supplied troops, police, and court injunctions to quell labor disturbances. Finally, unionists discovered that their chances for success were further diminished by factionalism among fellow-workers, who were as likely to break ranks and take their jobs, as to stand shoulder-to-shoulder during a dispute. Despite this incredibly hostile environment and against formidable odds, a growing number of workers were still disturbed enough to launch Ohio's modern labor movement.

The movement began feebly during the 1840s. In Ohio, as elsewhere in the nation, labor organizations had been badly disrupted by the depression of 1837-43; and, for many years thereafter, workers tended to focus their energies on various idealistic crusades for social and political reform. Nonetheless, sporadic rumblings of trade unionism also revived, though concentrated almost entirely in Cincinnati—the state's oldest, largest, and most problem-plagued industrial center, as well as foremost hotbed of early labor activism. With the return of economic prosperity from 1843 to 1849, local organizations were spasmodically reactivated

or established by a wide range of Queen City craftsmen — from woodturners, carpenters, stone masons, bricklayers, plasterers, and coopers, to cordwainers, bakers, tailors, cigarmakers, printers, and ironmolders. While these tiny trade societies generally maintained traditional goals of fraternalism, benevolence, and a "community of interest" with employers; many demonstrated a growing concern with the economic problems of journeymen, together with a willingness to strike for better wages and working conditions. In most cases, unions sprang up suddenly, staging defensive strikes for immediate economic demands. After the usual defeat or rare victory, they quickly disappeared or reverted to purely benevolent functions. Occasionally, even unskilled laborers displayed an interest in unity, as exemplified by the spontaneous walkout of female employees at the Cotton Factory in 1849 to protest a wage-cut. It should be pointed out, however, that the cultivation of working-class solidarity was not the principal intent of every labor group. For instance, in 1847 the Order of United American Mechanics of the State of Ohio, Washington Council, No. 1 was founded in Cincinnati. Comprised of "mechanics and workingmen," the Council ostensibly was formed for fraternal and benevolent purposes and "to assist each other in obtaining employment." In actuality, the Order was a secret nativistic association

which appeared in numerous states prior to the Civil War as part of the Know-Nothing movement. Stating in their constitution that they "felt the peculiar disadvantages under which we labor from foreign competition and foreign combinations," Council members surreptitiously spread hatred and fear of immigrants and Catholics. They underscored their prejudice by stipulating that "no person shall be admitted to membership unless born in the United States of America." Fortunately, this shadowy organization typified an offshoot of the labor movement which, as a rule, the mass of workers declined to follow.

The evolution of trade unions reached a critical turning point in the 1850s. After a half-century of preparation, the labor movement at last embarked on a course of organizational activity whose scale, aggressiveness, and orientation would ultimately have decisive impacts on Ohio's new industrial order. It was, of course, no mere coincidence that that new order burst forth during this same tumultuous decade. Urban, industrial, and transportation expansion was occurring at a phenomenal pace. Technological advances appeared, manufacturing diversified and modernized, the factory system spread, and the radical shift of workers into industrial occupations accelerated. Money wages rose, but so too did the cost-of-living: thereby causing workers' real wages to stagnate

Protected by armed guards, scabs ran a gauntlet of angry strikers' wives during the Hocking Valley coal dispute of 1884-85.

or decline, especially in the state's larger cities. Bewildered, frustrated, and alarmed by the threats which these changes posed to their economic security, laboring people attempted to cope by increasingly resorting to trade unionism. Though still basically composed of skilled craftsmen from the same trade, still representing only a very small proportion of the state's work force, and still short-lived, the unions of the 1850s differed in several fundamental respects from their predecessors. First, members abandoned the idea that workers had a "community of interest" with employers. Not only did journeymen often exclude masters from membership, they also began to accept their inevitable wage-earning status within the emerging factory system. Second, because they recognized the permanence of capitalism and the irreversibility of the industrial revolution swirling about them, trade unionists became less and less interested in sweeping reforms which sought to restore preindustrial conditions. Third, unions consequently began to minimize their fraternal and benevolent functions, and instead stressed the achievement of immediate economic objectives through collective bargaining and organized strikes — characteristics which would eventually be termed "business unionism." As these new conceptions of labor's role gradually took hold and combined with militant impulses, trade unionism became a force to be reckoned with in Ohio's rapidly maturing, urban-industrial society.

Maintaining a pattern which had prevailed in the state for over two generations, Cincinnati was again the hub of aroused labor activism. From 1850 through 1854, an upsurge of organization and militancy swept the city. Practically every skilled trade formed at least a temporary local union, which demanded wage increases, shorter hours, and occasionally a "closed shop" (an agreement that only union members would be employed). In some instances, collective action in the form of clamorous mass meetings or street parades were sufficient to persuade employers to concede. More frequently, however, bosses remained obstinate and walkouts resulted. Sketchy records indicate that these strikes — by hodcarriers, barbers, chairmakers, porkpackers, stonemasons, omnibus drivers, and many others — occurred almost weekly, and were remarkably successful. Strike-fever also spread to female, adolescent, and unskilled laborers. For example, in 1850, female trimmers in the city's hat factories walked out for higher wages; and, in 1853, brief strikes were staged by a group of day laborers, waiters at the Broadway Hotel, and even the boys employed in a bagging factory. Violence was not widespread, but — as demonstrated by striking railroad workers who assaulted a particularly belligerent boss, and by strikers at a bedstead firm who stoned the factory and attacked scabs—neither did Cincinnati workers avoid the use of force, if desperate enough. By 1855 and 1856, labor militancy began to fade away. Apparently satisfied with the gains which they had achieved, Cincinnati workers neglected their unions, allowed many to dissolve, and undertook few strikes. For all intents and purposes, the city's staggering trade-union movement then collapsed during the depression of 1857-58, and remained relatively dormant until the economy spurted again after the outbreak of the Civil War.

Despite their overall impermanence during the decade, Cincinnati's unions did make notable strides in the development of labor solidarity. Perhaps recalling the lessons learned by their predecessors in the mid-1830s, some unionists recognized that isolated and weak local unions could not effectively confront the growing power of employers. Consolidation and coordination between locals were obvious remedies. Toward that end, delegates from numerous unions throughout the city met in 1853 to establish the General Trades' Union. While militantly declaring "that if one stone in the arch of labor be destroyed, the whole must fall," the organization actually generated little city-wide labor cooperation, and vanished in 1855. Renamed the "Trades Assembly", this city-central was resurrected in order to conduct an 1859 political campaign, after which it again dissolved. Of greater long-range significance, was the participation of several local trade unions in the national labor movement. Cincinnati's printers had a long, but fitful, tradition of organization which stretched back to the mid-1820s, and included taking part in the trade's first national society during the 1830s. In 1850, the local printers' society began to urge the formation of another national union, an idea which reached fruition when they hosted the founding convention of the National Typographical Union in 1852. Since that date, Cincinnati Typographical Union, No. 3 has been one of the organization's most prominent locals.

Iron miners at Ohio Furnace, Scioto County, pause at the scale where the day's production of ore was measured, ca. 1882.

A second group of local craftsmen affiliated with the National Hat Finishers Association in 1854, although far less is known about their activities. Finally, Cincinnati's role in the national trade-union movement was especially enhanced by the efforts of the iron molders. After many years of sporadic experimentation on the local level, in 1859 a number of molders joined with counterparts from across the country to establish the National Union of Iron Molders. Cincinnati Local No. 4 subsequently enjoyed considerable success. Furthermore, from its permanent headquarters in the Queen City, the NUIM grew into probably the single most influential union in Ohio during the turbulent years ahead.

Outside Cincinnati, the labor movement continued to slumber. In Cleveland, organization and militancy appeared less frequently and achieved fewer successes. A revealing indication of trade-union weakness was the formation of a City Industrial Congress during the early 1850s. Though technically a city-wide federation, the Congress was actually an attempt to compensate for the lack of effective trade unions by uniting individual workers for political action. The most significant development on the city's labor scene occurred in 1850, when seamstresses decided to join a walkout by the Journeymen Tailors' Union of Cleveland. This was a very rare step. Nineteenth-century workingwomen were virtually barred from the skilled trades as well as the male-dominated unions. Therefore, they usually had few qualms about crossing a picketline in the hope of attaining permanent employment — even though the job generally paid only $1.50 for a 96-hour workweek. It is not known whether their refusal to serve as strikebreakers in this case resulted in victory, but thereafter women were granted union membership. In Columbus, trade unionism languished. The only notable activity apparently occurred among the printers, who were chartered as National Typographical Union, Local No. 5 in 1852. Weak membership caused the local to disband almost immediately, not to be revived until 1859. The following year, it conducted a vigorous, but futile, strike against the city's newspapers, demanding a wage hike and the closed shop. In Dayton, the formation of a secret molders' union in 1857 represented the sole manifestation of labor activism. Signs of unrest among the coal miners of the Hocking and Mahoning Valleys were far more auspicious. In 1859, for example, 150 miners at Nelsonville struck against a reduction in wages—the first of countless upheavals to erupt in the coal fields over the next century.

It was strangely ironic that Ohio's labor movement should finally gain permanence while the stability of the entire country tottered on bloody Civil War battlefields. In only a few short years, from 1862 to 1865, fledgling unions made their power felt in communities across the state, and forged stronger links with the growing national unions. Organized labor won a solid foothold in Ohio's rising industrial order, which it would never again relinquish.

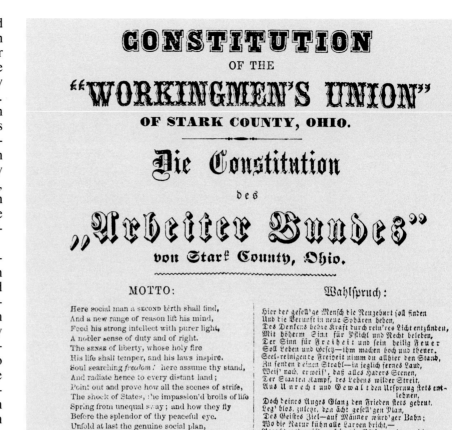

After weathering yet another recession in 1861 and early 1862 (which left about 30,000 people unemployed in Cincinnati alone), workers began to stir. For the next several years—despite such serious impediments as the formation of local, regional, and even national employers' associations—conditions were ripe for unionization. The economy boomed, the military draft caused labor shortages, and prices shot up seventy-six percent. Outraged at the rapid decline in their real earnings, and recognizing that profit-minded employers could ill-afford interruptions in production, workers united primarily to obtain wage increases. Many unions were purely local, but examples also abounded of successful organization and collective action by groups affiliated with national unions. In 1863, coal miners in the Tuscarawas, Mahoning, and Hocking Valleys formed district branches of the American Miners' Association, the first national miners' union. Notorious as ''terrible fighters,'' these Ohio miners evidently never needed to strike in order to reach agreement with their employers. A national union of iron puddlers, the United Sons of Vulcan, had established several locals in Ohio by 1862. Shortly after its founding in

Prior to the Civil War, labor organizations outside Cincinnati were rare and primarily oriented toward fraternalism rather than trade unionism. The Workingmen's Union of Stark County was one such example, founded in 1861 by Canton's German workers for purely educational and beneficial purposes.

1864, the Cigar-Makers' International Union organized locals in Cleveland and Cincinnati. In 1863, the newly formed Brotherhood of Locomotive Engineers set up headquarters in Cleveland. Locals sprang up all along Ohio's rail lines, despite the union's unfortunate constitutional restriction, that "no person shall become a member of the Brotherhood, except he is a white man." The first union in Toledo, National Typographical Union, Local No. 63, was chartered in 1863. But the state's most flourishing and militant union was the Iron Molders. By 1865, in the course of a nation-wide organizing drive, molders had formed locals in ten Ohio iron centers — Columbus, Dayton, Springfield, Akron, Painesville, California, Ironton, Hamilton, Cleveland, and three in Cincinnati. Of the numerous strikes conducted by these locals, the most notable was a lengthy city-wide walkout of Cincinnati molders in 1864, which only partially succeeded due to factionalism among the rank and file, and the intransigence of an employers' association. As in most major cities at the time, Cincinnati's central trade-union body also reappeared in 1864. This revived General Trades Assembly further demonstrated the rising sense of solidarity among at least some unionists, by sponsoring a boycott in support of the city's striking shoemakers, by parenting an influential labor newspaper (the *Workingman's Advocate*), and by sending delegates to the only meeting of the International Industrial Assembly of North America — an abortive attempt to unite unions throughout the country into a national federation. By the end of the war, therefore, Ohio unionists were firmly anchored within the mainstream of the national trade-union movement.

Rank-and-file apathy ranked as one of the most serious difficulties plaguing Ohio's early union movement. As a Cincinnati molder complained in a letter to the *Iron Molders International Journal* in October, 1873, active participation in local union affairs was not a favorite working-class pastime:

What can be done to induce members to attend the meetings of the Union? ... They can find time to go to the theatre, concert-saloons, or worse, bar-rooms, and there spend half the night in listening to silly plays that do not benefit them a cent's worth, or play cards and drink until intoxicated and spend the earnings of the week .... [They are] that kind of Union men that proclaim their unionism on street corners and in rum-shops, but never show any of it by putting their shoulder to the wheel and helping along the Union car .... When they do come [to the meetings], they often are in no fit condition to do business, as they have seen the 'brown jug' too often .... But should there be a strike, they are the first and loudest in the cry for money, and never pay dues until the secretary notifies them to pay or be suspended .... When will the men wake up to their interests and take pattern after the employers unions. How united they are ... what active interest they take in the business of their association. That is the reason they are so successful in all their efforts to reduce wages. Men, wake up; attend your Unions regular, take an active interest in its affairs ... treat every member as a brother ... then, indeed, we will have a union in which there is strength, and we will be able to fight our battles with success, and reap the reward that is due us.

Yet, organized labor did not have long to relish its wartime accomplishments. Almost as soon as peace was restored, unions faced a new round of challenges to their existence and legitimacy. The postwar recession of 1866-67 caused widespread unemployment and, consequently, a drop in union membership. Determined to reassert their power, employers launched a concerted anti-union offensive which crushed local after local. In addition, the traditional demons of the labor movement—internal factionalism and rank-and-file apathy—hobbled union efforts. Workers did continue to organize and strike against management's assaults, but, in the ebb and flow of extended battle, the unions' casualty rates were high.

Developments in the Ohio coal fields illustrated labor's plight during the postwar period. In 1865, miners at Mineral Ridge struck to protest a substantial wage reduction. The stubborn mine owner reacted by locking out the strikers until they finally agreed to abandon their union, a local lodge of the American Miners' Association. Because of many similar defeats at the hands of determined employers, the depressed state of the coal industry, and factional strife among its members, the AMA disintegrated by 1868. Far from abandoning unionism, however, militant miners simply changed tactics. In order to protect themselves from discrimination by owners, miners set up new locals masked as "Benevolent Associations" — a maneuver introduced by experienced British-born miners. By 1869, numerous lodges in the Tuscarawas and Hocking Valleys joined with groups in the Pennsylvania fields to form the loosely structured Miners' and Laborers' Benevolent Association. Although the locals' long and bitter strikes during 1869 and 1870 met with varying success, the union made a more lasting contribution to coal unionism. In contrast to the elitist "trade unions" which each accepted only skilled workers within a particular craft, MLBA lodges organized all toilers in and around the mines, regardless of their skill or trade. By thus instituting the tradition of "industrial unionism," the MLBA not only invigorated the miners' spirit of solidarity, it also provided a valuable source of strength in future conflicts.

Workers in the maturing industrial centers experienced a similar pattern of sporadic triumphs mixed with recurrent setbacks. The state's most prominent union, the Iron Molders, was a revealing case in point. During the "Great Lockout" of 1866, molders' locals in Cincinnati and Cleveland played crucial roles in defeating an attempt by the National Stove Manufacturers' and Iron Founders' Association to break their national union. The following year, however, these same locals seriously weakened the entire national union by staging a disastrous wildcat strike. After nine futile months, the walkout collapsed, primarily due to scabbing molders, leaving the union nearly bankrupt. Disillusioned with subsequent efforts by union leaders to restrict strikes and to shift the organization's orientation from business unionism to social and economic reform, "wage conscious" members dropped out in droves. Not until the union resumed its aggressiveness in a series of successful local strikes for better wages in 1871-72, did the Iron Molders begin to recover their membership and prestige. Cincinnati cigarmakers faced a somewhat different fate. In 1869-70, two local unions won a strike against the city's Cigar Manufacturers' Association, which had attempted to impose a cut in wages. The victory proved hollow, however, since the larger owners immediately responded by introducing cigar-moulds into their factories. Men who refused to use this new labor-saving device were dismissed and replaced by cheaper female and child labor. The cigarmakers never fully recovered from this technological assault, and remained on the defensive throughout the century. On the other hand, a string of losses to organized employers caused some unionists to seek broader solidarity of their own, through the creation of city-wide Trades Assemblies in Columbus (1866), Dayton (1867), and Cleveland (1868). When frenzied prosperity returned in the early 1870s, labor unrest escalated again in a strike wave which included coal miners at Nelsonville and New Straitsville; Springfield iron molders: stone cutters in Columbus and Dayton; Cincinnati telegraphers, shoemakers, ship carpenters, harness makers, and coopers; and printers in Dayton and Cleveland.

Beleaguered by unemployment and management's anti-labor campaign, many Ohio unionists turned for assistance to the nation's first "permanent" labor federation, the National Labor Union. The NLU was created in 1866, primarily to press for the eight-hour workday, an end to the contract labor system of importing cheap alien workmen, the formation of consumers' and producers' cooperatives, and the orga-

nization of all working people into defensive trade unions. Initially composed of seventy local, city, and national trade unions and a few reform groups, the federation subsequently underwent a vast expansion, in which dozens of trades were organized into loosely knit local and national bodies. A wide variety of Ohio labor groups actively participated, ranging from the coal miners of the Tuscarawas Valley and the Machinists' and Blacksmiths' Union of Mt. Vernon, to the Iron Molders and the Colored Teachers' Co-operative Association of Cincinnati. Reflecting Ohio's new-found status as a center of the labor-reform movement, NLU national conventions were held at Cincinnati in 1870 and Cleveland in 1873.

Within five years of its founding, however, the NLU began to disintegrate. A major cause was the federation's weak organizational structure. Since constituent unions jealously guarded their individual autonomy, they refused to grant the NLU strike support, arbitration functions, boycott powers, or adequate funding. Consequently, the uncoordinated federation failed to accomplish many concrete objectives, member unions had little reason to maintain active participation, and apathy quickly set in. Furthermore, differences arose among participants over such issues as the admission of female and black members — a practice which most unions would not permit even in their own separate organizations. But the most serious controversy emerged over political tactics to be used in pursuing their reform goals. Although the federation had been established expressly to serve as labor's national political arm, unionists had a strong ambivalence about mixing strictly trade-union activities with potentially debilitating political action. A solu-

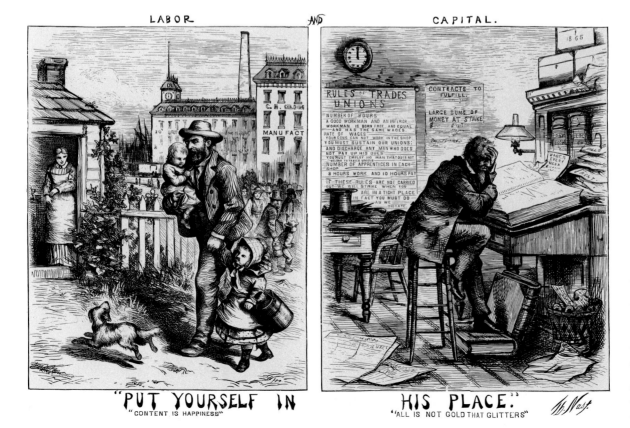

LABOR AND CAPITAL.

"PUT YOURSELF IN HIS PLACE."
"CONTENT IS HAPPINESS"   "ALL IS NOT GOLD THAT GLITTERS"

Despite the movement's overall weakness, trade unionism was continually under attack by most of the nation's press. This popular cartoon in the March 4, 1871 issue of *Harper's Weekly* propagandized that unions forced exploited employers to 'burn the midnight oil' so that contented workers could enjoy the comforts of vine-covered cottages.

Bread or Blood !!!!

Thunder! Lightning! Earthquakes!

War, Panic and Revolution!

Now Starving in a Land of Plenty; 12 000 000 Workingmen and Women. The Day of Deliverance is Near at Hand!

Workingmen, Pay No Taxes!
Stand the Battle, Grind your Axes!
The only thing to save the nation,
Is immediate Repudiation.
Down with Monopolies! Down with Kings!
Down with Party! Smash up Rings!
Rise Workingmen and Battle for your lives,
Your Children are Starving, So are your Wives!

LOOK OUT FOR THE FAMOUS

TRAIN LIGUE,

To be published simultaneously on the First of January, 1874 in Cincinnati, O., and Covington and Newport, Ky.

The revolution is near at hand! 12 000 000 Starving, Hungry, Blood thirsty, Down-trodden and Oppressed—Slaves—Workingmen and women are now on the point of rushing through the land demanding *BREAD or BLOOD!*

The TRAIN LIGUE demands immediate

REFORMATION or REVOLUTION!
REFORM or REBELLION!
BREAD or BLOOD!

And is ready to join the honest sons and daughters of toil in waging war, war, war, upon the heartless wretches that have monopolized the cream of their labor.

Look out for the 100,000 copies of the TRAIN LIGUE; Chief of the Workingmen and Champion of the Down-trodden Poor and Oppressed of every Land and Nation. Ready for sale by noon, December 31st 1873.

Price, Ten Cents per copy or One Dollar per dozen.

Sample copies to any part of the United States, post-paid for Ten Cents.

Train Boys, News Boys, Dealers and Agents supplied with this Startling Paper at $7 per hundred copies, returnable if not sold.

Send all money and orders to

SYLVESTER FRANKLIN WILSON,
Editor and Manager of the

TRAIN LIGUE,
CINCINNATI, O.

As the century's worst economic depression caused increased hardship, calls for radical working-class action began to appear in Cincinnati.

tion was finally found in 1870, when NLU leaders created a separate National Labor Reform Party. Unfortunately, by the time a national convention met in Columbus in 1872 to nominate a presidential candidate, ambitious politicians had gained control of the infant party. As a result of their manipulations, the campaign was a total calamity. The party collapsed, followed shortly thereafter by the neglected NLU.

By the early 1870s, organized labor had been severely weakened. Strikes had been lost; rank and filers ignored impotent union leaders who tried to curtail their militancy; an admirable effort to establish a national labor federation had misfired; and union membership remained small in proportion to the state's growing industrial work force. But, far more importantly, the labor movement had survived the postwar turmoil. Rather than being left isolated and virtually unprotected, Ohio's workers remained among the most well-organized in the nation.

The most critical test of the labor movement's sturdiness was yet to come — the depression of 1873-78. Workers had known hard times before, but never of this magnitude. As we have seen, businesses closed or curtailed production, multitudes were totally or partially unemployed, and incomes dropped. Organized labor activities were consequently impaired. Thousands of members began "tramping" in search of jobs, while many who remained justifiably felt that food and shelter took precedence over union dues. Although some unions survived through mergers—such as the 1876 consolidation of three small trade societies into the Amalgamated Association of Iron, Steel, and Tin Workers — far more perished. National unions dwindled from thirty to eight, and membership plunged nationally from 300,000 to approximately 50,000. Cincinnati, a union stronghold during prosperous years, had only about 1,000 members by 1878, and Cleveland virtually became a non-union city.

Distress and unemployment, however, did not extinguish either organized or spontaneous militancy. During late 1873 and 1874, for example, a succession of brief, but often violent, upheavals swept the state, as workers sought relief from their mounting economic hardships. When unions were nonexistent or unresponsive, toilers took matters into their own hands. Cleveland utterly churned with labor unrest. A strike by 200 unorganized sailors demanding a wage increase was broken in a bloody riot with police. Two weeks later, a walkout by 800 coal heavers and dock workers did succeed in preventing a wage reduction, despite another tense confrontation with police. Even the city's sewer diggers paraded through the streets, assaulting any fellow-workers who refused to join their spontaneous walkout. In Newark, unorganized mechanics struck a B & O Railroad repair shop. At Ironton, Portsmouth, Pomeroy, and other iron centers in the Ohio Valley, members of a tiny national union of skilled heaters and rollers walked out over a wage-cut imposed by the regional employers' association. The strike was especially noteworthy because of the support provided by unskilled hands and sympathetic townspeople, which enabled the unionists to win a compromise. Aside from fruitless wildcats by railroad engineers and furniture workers, Cincinnati's local unions generally remained silent. Nevertheless, thousands of the city's unemployed staged a mass demonstration demanding public relief. The Common Council responded with soup kitchens and a small number of public-works jobs at $1.25 per day. In the acutely depressed coal fields, misery and exploitation sparked renewed outbursts by the inveterately militant miners. Many formed locals of the Miners' National Association, which had

Delegates donned their 'Sunday best' for the founding convention of the Miners' National Association, held at Youngstown in October, 1873.

been established in 1873 as a successor to the MLBA, and which boasted nearly 5,000 Ohio members at its peak. MNA locals called two major, ill-fated strikes during the year: a walk-out in the Tuscarawas Valley, after an attempt to arbitrate a wage dispute failed; and a violent, three-month shutdown of Hocking Valley mines. The latter was particularly significant for the strike-support displayed by middle-class residents, and for the first large-scale use of black strikebreakers in Ohio. After a string of such defeats—marked by deepening splits between cautious union leaders and aggressive rank and filers—the MNA collapsed in 1876.

Agitation in 1873-74 foreshadowed an uprising of greater dimensions in 1877, the lowest point of the depression and one of the most turbulent years in American labor history. Accumulated frustration and suffering had intensified working-class discontent in countless communities. Within this highly-charged atmosphere, a seemingly minor railroad strike at Martinsburg, West Virginia, on July 17 unexpectedly ignited spontaneous walkouts all along the nation's extensive railway network. The fact that no labor organization called or coordinated the strikes indicated not only the weakness of the unions, but also the pervasiveness of dissatisfaction among the workers. Like so many other disputes, the railroaders' specific grievances were primarily economic: an announcement by most railroads that wages would be cut again by 10-12 percent; paydays delayed as long as four months; and the requirement that employees pay their own fares and stay in company-owned hotels when working along the rail lines. A striker in Newark, Ohio, explained: "We were driven to this. It's only $1.58 a day for the best man, and none of us get over three day's work in a week. The longer we work the deeper we are in debt, and it is awful on them with families." But, as the Ohio Commissioner of Labor Statistics perceptively pointed out, the causes went much deeper:

> . . . these men devoting their lives to the several companies, justly considered that they were entitled to some consideration, some recognition more than would be given to a piece of machinery

or a dumb animal. The tendency of railroad managers to entirely ignore these men as men, to issue orders cutting off their supplies of bread and meat, just as they would the supply of coal for an engine, could not . . . be received without at least a mental protest.

This quest for personal dignity in an increasingly impersonal industrial world—as much as the extensive economic distress and the fact that the railroads were already targets of public resentment for their abusive and monopolistic business practices—aroused the sympathies of masses of workingmen and many middle-class Americans. Consequently, the railroad strike quickly escalated into more than a mere labor-management dispute. It became a "social rebellion." Tens-of-thousands took to the nation's streets to protest their worsening conditions. In Baltimore, Pittsburgh, Chicago, St. Louis, and dozens of towns between, demonstrators engaged in pitched battles with police and troops. For a few tense weeks, many citizens wondered whether a second civil war had not, indeed, begun.

The "Great Labor Uprising" rapidly spread through Ohio. At Zanesville, Crestline, Alliance, Steubenville, and Lancaster the tracks were blocked and disturbances broke out. The general excitement prompted a walkout by Coshocton miners. Approximately 4,000 Dayton workers staged a mass meeting to complain of low wages. In Columbus, rampaging mobs caused millions of dollars in property damage to businesses and factories—for which the striking railroaders offered to help pay, if they won. When Governor Young ordered the militia to regain control of the crucial rail yard at Newark, the sympathetic soldiers refused to confront the strikers. Instead, they became the guests of workers and businessmen who paid the troops' lodging in a local hotel. Bloodshed seemed imminent when hundreds of miners from Shawnee and New Straitsville began to march on Newark, upon learning that the frustrated governor had dispatched additional militia companies from Dayton and Cincinnati. The crisis passed, however, when appreciative railroaders intercepted the miners and explained that assistance was unnecessary. In Cleveland, tensions had been simmering since the beginning of the year. Violent strikes had broken out earlier on the waterfront, at several iron mills, and at the Standard Oil Refinery — the latter also having stimulated a partially successful call by immigrant coopers for a general strike. Special police details had been permanently assigned to guard various shops and factories against labor strife. However, the alarms proved unwarranted. During the futile, two-week walkout by the city's railroaders, neither a general strike nor widespread violence materialized. On the other hand, a brief general strike did occur in Toledo, where firms were peacefully shut down by an *ad hoc* labor group demanding a minimum wage of $1.50 per day for all classes of workers. Though both the mayor and the commander of the local militia initially encouraged the strikers, pressure from the business interests evidently caused city officials to have a change of heart. Leaders were arrested and the strike ended. In Cincinnati, the strike hardly caused a ripple. Local railroaders did walk out and a mass meeting offered verbal support, but very little collective action emerged and the disturbance died within two days.

The unrest of 1877 had a broader significance that went beyond the strikers' overall failure to achieve their immediate demands. Perhaps their greatest accomplishment was to demonstrate forcibly that serious problems emerging in the new urban-industrial order could no longer be ignored. But the outburst also had a profound negative effect, as illustrated by a representative headline in the *Cincinnati Enquirer* during the strike — "The Red Flag, It Casts Its Ugly Shadow Over Our Queenly City." Although violence had been minimal in Ohio (especially in comparison to other states), the huge number of participants and the depth of their discontent were unprecedented occurrences, which generated widespread hysteria among the middle and upper classes. An enduring fear developed that the strikes signaled the

first incursion of a "Communist menace" from Europe. This association, in the public mind, of labor militancy with a foreign revolutionary movement created an atmosphere of hostility toward unionism, which would prevail for many years. Ironically, rather than any "revolutionary" potential, this "social rebellion" had actually displayed the basic conservatism of Ohio's working classes. Strikers had repeatedly stressed their respect for law and order as well as property rights, and had rejected suggestions that the conflict be expanded. The "great uprising" had clearly demonstrated that working-class solidarity in the nineteenth century was, at best, only a tenuous phenomenon.

The transitory nature of working-class unity was also manifested in the political realm. As problems associated with the new urban-industrial order steadily mounted after mid-century, workers had gradually begun to press for governmental policies which would protect labor's interests and ameliorate working and living conditions. Their consequent attempts to exercise political power at the state and local levels took several directions. The vast majority chose to participate in mainstream party politics, developing strong allegiances to the dominant Democratic and Republican parties. Within this traditional American channel for political action, workingmen tended to behave as "citizens" taking part in the democratic process with all other members of the community; rather than as "workers" consciously pursuing distinctive economic concerns. However, an increasing number of laboring people became disenchanted with the traditional two-party system, and formed independent third parties to promote specific working-class interests. Appearing sporadically during the era in various Ohio communities, workingmen's parties ran candidates in local elections, advocated measures such as a state eight-hour workday law, and attempted to cultivate political cohesion among working-class voters. Despite waging heated campaigns, these independent parties met with little success, due to cooptation by the major parties and an inability to break down the workers' Democratic and Republican loyalties. On occasion, aroused workers also resorted to interest-group politics by conducting nonpartisan lobbying efforts at the state level. One of the earliest and most effective examples occurred in 1860. After a series of strikes by Mahoning Valley coal miners, David Tod — a prominent Democratic politician and mine owner — proposed legislation in the Ohio General Assembly backed by Youngstown businessmen, making it a felony for any worker to conspire to prevent a business from operating. Since the bill seriously threatened to cripple labor's strike weapon, an extraordinary outburst of working-class protest swept the state. Led by unionists from Cincinnati and the coal fields, workers launched intensive lobbying campaigns, which killed not only the Tod bill, but also a similar version introduced in 1865. Coal miners proved especially adept at implementing pressure tactics, by securing pas-

Reflecting the nation's anti-communist hysteria of the late 1870s, the labor agitator was stereotyped as a shiftless, immoral loafer content to live off the toil of others.

sage in the early 1870s of legislation to regulate and enforce state health and safety standards in the mining industry. Nevertheless, these concerted efforts were exceptional. Prior to the late 1870s, Ohio workers had habitually failed to use their potential power as the majority of the electorate, either to alter the political system or to secure consistent governmental assistance.

The upsurge of the greenback movement during the late-1870s, however, caused anxious leaders of the major parties to wonder whether workers would finally flex their collective political muscle. Popularly called the "Ohio Idea," greenbackism initially had been proposed in 1868 by state Democrats seeking a politically advantageous cure for the postwar recession. Though eventually assuming numerous ramifications as it gained support across the country, the greenback program essentially demanded inflationary monetary reform through increased circulation of paper currency, or "greenbacks." Advocates believed that a greater supply of 'cheap money' would allow the government to retire the federal debt, enable individuals to pay off creditors, as well as stimulate business expansion and jobs. After waning in the early 1870s, the movement revived after 1873 when economic depression and discontent gripped the nation. The Ohio Idea soon acquired moral and class overtones, as greenbackers argued that their program would curtail the greed of "big business" and "the money powers," and thus save the common man from the massive influence of the "non-producing classes" which were blamed for the economic crisis.

Disgruntled with Republican opposition and Democratic vacillation toward their demands, greenbackers convened in Indianapolis in 1876 to form the National Greenback Party, which nominated Peter Cooper of New York for president and Samuel F. Carey of Ohio for vice-president. Comprised almost exclusively of angry farmers, the Greenback Party discovered during the subsequent election that considerable sentiment for cheap money had also spread to hard-hit manufacturing and mining areas. In fact, in Ohio the new party tallied its greatest strength among industrial workers and coal miners in the northwestern and northeastern counties. The time seemed ripe for the state's agrarian greenbackers, urban workers, and miners to join forces in the political arena.

The railroad strikes of 1877 triggered that alliance. Many workers had been outraged by the government's use of military force during the dispute, and subsequently set up workingmen's parties throughout the nation to increase their political influence. The movement toward independent political action especially gained momentum in the industrial centers of Ohio, where a strong state organization also appeared. At a September convention held in Columbus, labor formed a state Workingmen's Party. Building upon the cooperation between workers and farmers which had emerged during the strike, a common hatred of the railroads, and the appeal of greenbackism to financially

HARPER'S WEEKLY.
JOURNAL OF CIVILIZATION

VOL. XXII.—No. 1113.] NEW YORK, SATURDAY, APRIL 27, 1878. [WITH A SUPPLEMENT. PRICE TEN CENTS.

Entered according to Act of Congress, in the Year 1878, by Harper & Brothers, in the Office of the Librarian of Congress, at Washington.

CONFUSEDISM.

HONEST LABOR. "You must not do any work; they say it will depreciate mine."
CONVICT LABOR. "All right. If you, your wife, and children will work for me, and be taxed by high rent, dear food, etc., to keep me in board and lodging, I don't object."

pinched urban laborers, the Workingmen's Party immediately fused with the Greenback Party. The new organization nominated the greenback candidate for governor, but the rest of the state ticket was filled by workingmen. Delegates agreed to an almost wholly greenback platform, which included demands for a graduated income tax, governmental control over corporations, and legislation prohibiting the payment of wages in company scrip. Although the Democrats captured the gubernatorial election, the Greenback-Labor candidate polled nearly 17,000 votes — over five times the greenback tally in 1876. The majority of the new party's support was concentrated in the railway and manufacturing centers of Lucas, Franklin, and the northeastern counties. The Greenback-Labor coalition scored its greatest victory in Toledo, where the entire city ticket, several county officials, and two state legislators were

The convict labor issue generated considerable debate throughout the century. A sketch which appeared in *Harper's Weekly* on April 27, 1878 ridiculed organized labor's position as "confusidism." The caption read:
Honest Labor. "You must not do any work; they say it will depreciate mine."
Convict Labor. "All right. If you, your wife, and children will work for me, and be taxed by high rent, dear food, etc., to keep me in board and lodging, I don't object."

By 1884, labor was a recognized force in the American political mainstream. During the scurrilous presidential campaign, workers were urged to reject the vague promises of Republican candidate James G. Blaine that he would protect their interests.

Labor uprisings during the 1870s sparked hysterical reactions in the nation's press. Blatantly ethnocentric propaganda, such as this personification of working-class militancy on the cover of *Harper's Weekly* — complete with caption in Irish brogue which read, "Is Sercierty To Be Reorganized? Is The Wurkin'-Man To Hev His Rights? That's Wot I Wants To Know!"—fueled public fears that immigrant workers would use brute force to achieve their supposedly revolutionary aims.

swept into office. Encouraged by these gains, 800 delegates from twenty-eight states gathered in Toledo in 1878 to organize the national Greenback-Labor Party. While farmers, radical businessmen, and lawyers dominated the convention, the party's working-class element was strong enough to insist on several platform planks of distinct concern to labor—demands for the eight-hour day, abolition of the contract system of prison labor, and the establishment of national and state bureaus of labor. In the congressional elections of 1878, the Greenback-

Labor Party reached peak strength, winning more than 1,000,000 votes nationwide and over 38,000 in Ohio.

By 1879, however, the promising, yet fragile, alliance rapidly began to crumble. Labor became disillusioned when state greenback leaders proposed a merger with the Democratic Party, which had once again officially embraced the Ohio Idea. But, more importantly, renewed prosperity in the fall of 1879 diffused much of the economic discontent upon which the political coalition had been based. Though the Greenback Party survived for another five years, it was only a negligible force in state politics. Having exhausted their brief flirtation with large-scale, third-party politics, Ohio workingmen returned to the Democratic and Republican folds.

As the long and bitter depression finally drew to a close in 1879, workers again turned toward collective economic action to improve their conditions. Hundreds of thousands flocked into various types of labor organizations, generating an unprecedented resurgence of unionism. Moreover, workers demonstrated a militancy rarely seen before, staging hundreds of strikes which often assumed large proportions and sometimes resulted in violence and bloodshed. Their efforts would not be easy. The atmosphere of hostility toward organized labor became even more strident in the 1880s. Employers aggressively exhibited a staunch resistance, which was made more formidable by increasing cooperation in the anti-union fight. But most importantly, the working classes would have to combat their own factionalism—perhaps the most serious obstacle of all.

The primary beneficiary of this post-depression organizational spurt was the Knights of Labor, by far the largest and most extensive labor alliance of the nineteenth century. Founded in 1869 as a secret society of Philadelphia workers, the Knights expanded after 1874 into every state and into every type of community — from mining camps and county seats to small industrial towns and sprawling metropolises. Especially after secrecy was abandoned in 1879, membership climbed nationwide, reaching a peak of close to one million in 1886. Like its predecessor, the National Labor Union, the organization was a curious amalgam of skilled trade unionists, unskilled women and blacks, reformers, and small shopkeepers. Though resembling an industrial union in structure, it certainly was not a trade union in function. For, rather than trying to protect the economic positions of pure and simple trade unions, the Knights attempted to unite all workers into one organization in order to lead them, somehow, into a reformed society based on preindustrial economics. Their program centered upon winning the eight-hour day, establishing various consumers' and producers' cooperatives, and pressing for such political reforms as the graduated income tax. While never totally successful, they also tried to persuade workers to abandon the strike weapon, and replace it with arbitration and boycotts.

The Knights first spread to Ohio in 1875. By 1880, Ohio's membership ranked fifth in the nation with heavy concentrations in Cleveland and Cincinnati. Despite being condemned by the Catholic bishops of Cincinnati, Cleveland, and Columbus, 182 local assemblies functioned across the state by 1885. The Knights were especially active in the coal fields after the demise of the Miners' National Association in 1876. Over the following decade, 83 miners' local assemblies were formed. However, total membership evidently never exceeded 1,300, or fourteen percent of the state's employed miners. Initially attracted to the Knights because of its aura of secrecy, most miners rapidly became disenchanted with the organization's no-strike policy and its inability to improve their wages or working conditions. Consequently, local assemblies seemed to fall apart as rapidly as they were established. The militant miners preferred to take matters into their own hands, and staged numerous strikes during the period, most of which ended in defeat. Recognizing that their isolated, local efforts were no match for the powerful mine operators, the state's miners formed the Ohio Miners' Amalgamated Association in 1882. The following year, however, the operators in the Hocking Valley also united into the Columbus and Hocking Coal and Iron Company, popularly known among the miners as "the Syndicate." In 1884, the Syndicate severely slashed wages in a deliberate attempt to

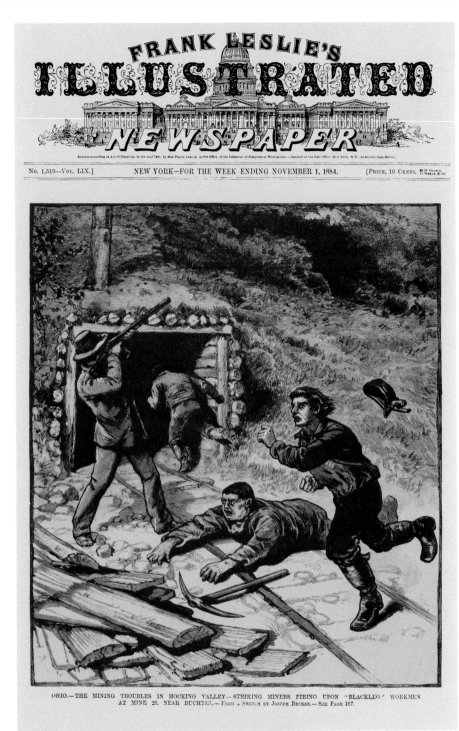

OHIO.—THE MINING TROUBLES IN HOCKING VALLEY—STRIKING MINERS FIRING UPON "BLACKLEG" WORKMEN AT MINE 25, NEAR BUCHTEL.—From a Sketch by Joseph Becker.—See Page 167.

B

A

C

The Hocking Valley coal strike of 1884-85 attracted national attention for its bitter violence. As depicted in magazine sketches, tensions especially mounted at Buchtel, where the strikers' sniper attacks on "blackleg" workers (A) repeatedly roused hired Pinkerton guards (B) to protect the strikebreakers (C).

IRON-CLAD CONTRACT

FOR THE LOCK-OUT POTTERS OF EAST LIVERPOOL.

I, A. B., hereby agree to work for C. D. at my trade at the regular established prices, doing my work in a good, workman-like manner, withdrawing from the Knights of Labor, and ignoring all outside parties, committees, and trade or labor associations, and also agree not to connect myself with the Knights of Labor, or any similar organizations, or to join in any meeting or procession of such organizations while in the employ of the said C. D.

In consideration of which the said C. D. agrees to pay the said A. B. for his services every two weeks, as is customary, the necessary stoppages excepted.

The above agreement can only be terminated by either party giving the other two weeks' notice, unless for bad workmanship, violation of this contract or the rules of the factory, or interference with other workmen.

Signed and sealed this —— day of ——————, 1882.

WEST, HARDWICKE & CO.,
WM. BRUNT, JR. & CO.,
HOMER LAUGHLIN,
KNOWLES, TAYLOR & KNOWLES,
WILLIAM FLENTKE,
GOODWIN BROS.,
WALLACE & CHETWYND,
GEO. S. HARKER & CO.

EAST LIVERPOOL, O., June 2, 1882.

provoke a strike, break the Amalgamated, and introduce new coal cutting machinery. The miners obliged, staging a violent nine-month walkout, which the Syndicate defeated with the assistance of foreign-born strikebreakers, Pinkertons, and the state militia. The Amalgamated survived, however, and went on in 1885 to be one of the primary forces behind the formation of the National Federation of Miners and Mine Laborers.

During the 1880s, the Knights of Labor was equally unable to contain the militancy of other workers. Several examples are illustrative. Prior to the Panic of 1873, Cleveland axemakers had been content with their lot, earning $1.00 per hour for a five-hour day. As one observer noted, "they used to be at liberty in the afternoons, and people wondered if they worked at all." Obviously, they felt no need for a union — until employers doubled production and cut their pay during the depression. About 1877, the Knights secretly organized an Axemakers' Assembly and obtained a ten percent wage increase without a strike. However, when the workers demanded a twenty percent increase in 1880, the owners responded with a forty percent cut. Against the advice of their conservative leader, the axe-makers struck for nine months, denouncing the Knights' leadership as scabs. The companies failed to weather the strike by hiring unskilled workers, the strikers scattered, and the union collapsed. A more complete employer-victory was won in 1882-83 in East Liverpool. In order to crush the local potters' assembly, the employers demanded that all workers sign an "iron-clad," or "yellow-dog," contract which made union activity sufficient cause for dismissal. When the potters struck in protest, the employers locked them out. With only meager financial assistance from the Knights, the workers surrendered, thus eradicating unionism in the potteries for

nearly nine years. One bright spot in a string of such defeats was the national telegraphers' strike in 1883, which involved employees throughout Ohio.

Generally more successful than the Knights' reluctant involvement in strikes were their peaceful endeavors. For instance, when the Dueber Watch Case Company of Cincinnati fired all employees who were union members, the Knights imposed a boycott on the firm which forced the owner to relent. Several cooperative banks in Ohio, primarily intended to help members purchase homes, were successful. Cooperative foundries, however, apparently had only mixed success.

The growth of the Knights was complemented by an organizational spurt by the trade unions as well. One of the most militant, though nominally a member of the Knights, was the Amalgamated Association of Iron and Steel Workers. The union staged numerous strikes after 1878, some against wage cuts, but many others against the "contract system" — a nefarious policy by which workers were obliged to permit the company to retain their wages for the first month of employment, plus twenty-five percent of all wages earned thereafter, to be paid at the end of the year only if the owner felt that his profits had been sufficient. The union staged nationwide strikes in 1880 and 1882, affecting mills in Cleveland, Cincinnati, Janesville, and Portsmouth. Both these and various local strikes, however, were usually defeated. The basic weakness of the union was rampant factionalism, ranging from animosities between different trades, to splits between native and foreign-born workers. The latter was glaringly evident, for example, in strikes at the Cleveland Rolling Mill Company in 1882 and 1885.

A rather unique reversal of the usual pattern of trade union development was provided by laborers in Ohio's Great Lakes ports. Unlike most industries, where the skilled organized first, in the maritime industry the unskilled and semiskilled workers (sailors and longshoremen) led the way. The Lake Seamen's Benevolent Association had established locals in several Ohio ports by 1879, to fight low wages, long hours, poor food, unsanitary living quarters, and abusive treatment from officers. Members of the aggressive union attempted to enforce a closed shop by refusing to sail with non-members. Rather than negotiating with shipowners for wages, they used a more primitive approach — simply posting the terms under which they were willing to work. Surprisingly, they were successful at first. By 1880, however, the shipowners had had enough. Forming the Cleveland Vessel Owners' Association, they established their own hiring halls in Cleveland and nearby ports to ban union members. Compounding the unionists' problems were technological change and factionalism. Steam vessels were rapidly replacing wooden sailing ships, but the stubborn sailors refused to accept men who contaminated their craft by serving on iron steam ships. Such divisiveness facilitated the employers' efforts to break the union,

which collapsed within the year. At the same time, longshoremen organized locals in Cleveland, Toledo, and Sandusky, but generally maintained a low profile. In contrast, the aristocrats of the industry—the marine engineers—were content with a purely fraternal and benevolent organization formed in Cleveland in 1875. Not until the 1890s, would they attempt to influence wages, hours, or working conditions through collective bargaining or strikes.

Finally, in addition to the various city-central labor bodies which again sprang up across the state, unionists took the significant step in 1883 of forming an Ohio State Trades and Labor Assembly. This development stemmed from several factors: the influence of the politically oriented Knights of Labor; the frequent failure of collective bargaining and strikes; and the growing recognition among unionists that an effective labor lobby was necessary in order to protect the workers' interests and combat business' political clout. Thus, the State Assembly became the lobbying arm of the state's labor movement, pressing such issues as an eight-hour day law, abolition of convict labor, "equal-pay-for-equal-work" for women, restrictions on child labor, and mine safety laws.

While detailed information on the growth of labor unions during these years remains sparse, an admittedly incomplete federal survey in 1880 provided some sense of the movement's scope in Ohio. Of an estimated 2,440 labor organizations in the United States, 252 were located in Ohio, ranking it second only to Pennsylvania. As a reflection of the shifting composition of the work force, the emergence of the industrial order, and the consequent areas of greatest working-class difficulty, seventy-nine percent of these organizations were in manufacturing and mechanical industries and thirteen percent in coal mining. Professional and personal services had less than one percent of the state's total, while eight percent were found in trade and transportation. Moreover, breaking down these categories more specifically suggests that organization was most prevalent among the

state's most militant workers. Approximately forty-five percent of all trade societies in Ohio were formed among iron and steel workers (twenty-two percent), coal miners (thirteen percent), and building tradesmen (ten percent). During the same year, out of an estimated ninety-three strikes and lockouts in Ohio, forty-two percent occurred in coal mining and twenty-seven percent in the iron and steel industry.

As indicated in Table 2L, the level of working-class militancy in Ohio generally escalated during the early 1880s, and was increasingly organized rather than spontaneous. After declining slightly from 1881 to 1882, the number of disputes rose again with the outbreak of another depression in 1883. The pattern for 1884 is particularly interesting: while the total number of disputes dropped, their average duration soared (137 days compared to eighteen days in 1881), and their success rate plummeted. Fortunately for the labor movement, however, that unusual trough did not continue in 1885, when the number of walkouts and participants reached epidemic proportions, and victories multiplied.

Ohio's labor unions had become firmly entrenched by the mid-1880s as an important vehicle for voicing and protecting working-class

Founders of the National Marine Engineers Beneficial Association at their first convention, held in Cleveland in 1875.

interests. Indirectly, they had assisted many non-members as well. Nevertheless, certain overwhelming weaknesses remained. They still represented only a small minority of the industrial work force, probably no more than the national average in 1880 of four percent. Union membership was still concentrated among the white, male, skilled elite. Although women had been admitted to the National Labor Union, the Knights of Labor, and a few trade unions, the vast majority continued to be shunned. Unionization among black workers was even more dismal. Consigned primarily to unskilled labor and service occupations, largely shut out of factory employment, and suffering racial dis-

Hod-carrying on construction projects was one of the few occupations in which large numbers of black common laborers regularly obtained employment during the nineteenth century. This black hod-carrier shouldered bricks and mortar in Oberlin in the 1870s.

crimination in hiring, black workers were apparently limited to token union membership in a few isolated locals. Even in those rare instances when job advancement was offered by liberal white employers, resistance from white workers was usually strong. Such was the case in Springfield, for example, where the efforts of a prominent manufacturer in the 1880s to provide job opportunities for blacks in his foundry caused a furor among the all-white iron molders union. Additional cleavages along ethnic, religious, and skill-level lines, further debilitated the movement. Finally, the crucial ideological conflict within the unions—whether to concentrate on social reform or "pure and simple" economic activities — remained unresolved. These multifaceted flaws in working-class solidarity—as much as business and governmental opposition — effectively inhibited the full realization of labor's potential to influence the direction and structure of their new industrial world.

Thus, by the 1880s, long-term transitions were reaching their climax. With the completion of a far-flung transportation network, Ohio's economy transcended local or regional lines. In order to take advantage of this national market, employers invested increasing amounts of capital in machinery and expanded the size of their enterprises. The factory system relentlessly advanced, cutting off the mass of workers from their employers. Skill became less and less important, as reliance on unskilled and semi-skilled labor accelerated. Immigration and the movement from farm to city further weakened the working classes, stimulating job-competition and overcrowding within grimy industrial centers. Basically, therefore, the social and economic condition of Ohio's working classes had not improved appreciably by the 1880s, and in many ways had deteriorated. A new working-class experience had emerged in Ohio, but the degree of acceptance and the avenues of response by laboring people remained in considerable doubt.

Militia guarding one of many barricades erected in a seven-block circle around the Cincinnati jail and courthouse.

The Great Cincinnati Riot of 1884

Among the numerous distinctions which working people helped Cincinnati to earn during the nineteenth century, none were as lamentable as the title, "Queen City of Mobs." As Ohio's oldest, largest, most congested, and most industrially developed metropolis, Cincinnati was a focal point where the strains of the emerging urban-industrial order were concentrated and magnified. Economic insecurity, squalid living conditions, immigration, disease, and a host of additional problems generated tremendous tension among the city's working classes. Their attempts to resolve difficulties were generally peaceful and orderly. But, when unresolved grievances accumulated—as they did with disturbing regularity — simmering discontent frequently exploded into mob violence. Even in an era when riots were common to the nation's cities, Cincinnati seemed particularly volatile—an anti-abolitionist riot in 1843, an attack on the city jail by a lynch mob in 1848, a series of riots between rival volunteer fire departments in the early 1850s, religious and nativist violence in 1853 and 1855, a race riot in 1862, and repeated election brawls during the post-Civil War period seemed characteristic of the city. While all elements of the city's residents participated, workers comprised the majority of insurgents in almost every incident.

By early 1884, public passions had once again been aroused to a feverish pitch. Already suffering from yet another economic depression, residents experienced additional adversity when a catastrophic flood devastated homes and businesses in February. Moreover, hardpressed citizens were increasingly outraged at the political bosses who had controlled local government for over a decade. Under their reign, Cincinnati had become a "wide open" city with rampant corruption, rigged elections, juries packed with political cronies, and disgraceful miscarriages of justice. Over the previous year, conditions appeared to worsen as a

Main Street barricade.

In blind passion, the mob burned and gutted the courthouse.

Soldiers guarding the Main Street viaduct.

Military firing on the mob from the stairs in the center of the jail.

Soldiers outside the burned-out courthouse.

crime wave swept the city. Nearly 57,000 arrests had been made — 284 for shooting with intent to kill, and ninety-two for murder or manslaughter — but relatively few convictions resulted. As one contemporary noted, "public exasperation, especially among the workingmen, has been extreme. The cry has been that a man with money could commit murder and get away, and there was too much truth in it."

In this setting, one more instance of perceived injustice spontaneously triggered the most massive and most violent civil disturbance in Cincinnati's history. On March 28, approximately 20,000 rioters stormed the city jail, intending to lynch a confessed murderer who had received a light sentence as a result of a political deal. Unable to find the prisoner (who had been secretly moved to the state penitentiary in Columbus), the furious mob turned its wrath on the public buildings which symbolized their indignation and on the militiamen who attempted to quell the violence. Two nights of street warfare followed, as thousands of rampaging residents battled with more than 7,000 troops. Before the riot finally subsided on March 31, fifty-four men had been killed, hundreds were wounded, and the courthouse laid in smoldering ruins.

Of course, all segments of Cincinnati society had participated to some degree. However, there was no mistaking the specific overtones of working-class anger which marked this frenzied protest against government corruption and the use of military force. A recent study has revealed, for example, that, out of 135 casualties and arrests for which records have survived, over ninety-five percent were comprised of skilled artisans, factory workers, and common laborers. Furthermore, the majority of troops in local regiments refused to obey orders to defend the courthouse, declaring that they would not march against fellow workers. Combined with several earlier instances across the state in which the military was used to suppress strikes, this incident confirmed the suspicions of many workers that government was indeed as much an adversary as employers. Thus, Cincinnati's laboring people had demonstrated with glaring clarity that their discontent and fervor for reform extended beyond shop floors, into the larger social and political arenas as well.

Ohio Potters—From Independent Craftsmen to Factory Artisans

Ohio's pottery industry exemplified the complex and uneven transformations which occurred in nineteenth-century workplaces. Prior to the Civil War, pottery-making was conducted in small craft-shops, each employing an average of five workers who produced plain dishes and basic household items for local and regional markets. In order to be near clay deposits and other necessary raw materials, most early potteries located in Cincinnati, Akron, Zanesville, and East Liverpool. The English immigrants who dominated the trade were ambitious and highly independent craftsmen, characteristically intent on earning a stake in an established pottery with which to start their own competing businesses. Consequently, while there were only 556 potters in the state by 1850, they were spread out in 120 separate shops, none of which achieved more than minor success. Beginning in the 1860s, however, the industry enjoyed rapid expansion and prosperity due to two factors—the federal government's imposition and perpetuation of high protective tariffs on foreign pottery, and increased public demand for china and various ornamental objects. Though pottery remained a secondary Ohio industry compared to clothing or iron manufacturing, its relative growth was impressive. Between 1860 and 1880, production rose dramatically, as the number of potteries increased from 130 to 179, the work force more than quadrupled from 654 to 2659, and average workers per plant tripled from 5 to 15. Production for national and international markets especially boomed in East Liverpool — an isolated, one-industry city which soon became America's leading pottery

Machine shop at Knowles, Taylor & Knowles Potteries, one of East Liverpool's largest firms.

An operative dish-maker and his helpers.

Women and girls applying decals in the decorating department.

Despite increased mechanization, some traditional skills survived, such as hand-painting delicate artware.

By the 1870s, mechanization had transformed operative potters into factory artisans and had increased the employment of cheaper, unskilled youths.

Packing the pottery for shipment.

center. By 1877, East Liverpool's twenty-four potteries were among the largest in the state, employing an average of thirty-two workers in imposing, multi-story, brick buildings. Despite nagging problems with cut-throat competition, the industry was so strong by the 1870s, that— unique among Ohio manufacturers — pottery firms weathered the decade's severe depression without any plant closings, significant production decreases, lay-offs, or large wage-cuts.

The evolution of pottery-making from craft-shop stage to mass-production industry obviously had tremendous impacts on the work force. Traditionally, the "practical" potter had been skilled in every step of his trade — from digging and preparing the clay mixtures by hand, to "throwing" pieces on his wheel or "pressing" them in molds, "turning" the rough objects into standard form, applying decorations, glazing, and finally firing the pottery in a kiln. For simple but tedious tasks, practical potters utilized the "helper system" which had been introduced to Ohio potteries by English immigrants. In this arrangement, the skilled craftsman served as manager as well as worker, hiring his own assistants or "helpers," and paying them from the fixed price which he received from the owner for each acceptable piece. By the late-1840s, however, traditional craft structures and manufacturing practices began to change. As public demand for a greater variety and volume of ceramic products increased, a more efficient division of labor also emerged. Practical potters gradually moved into the formal ranks of management, while their customary responsibilities were divided among "operative" potters—skilled specialists trained in only one aspect of the trade such as

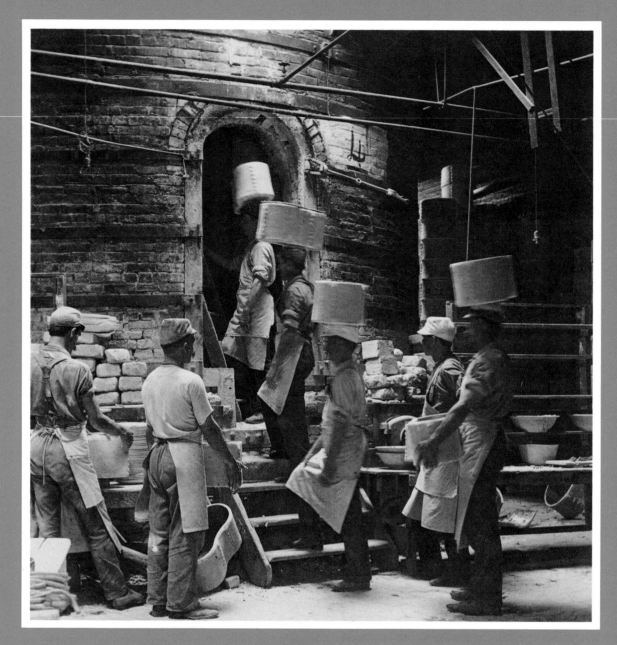

The ancient craft of "throwing" pottery on a wheel driven by footpower.

mold-maker, presser, thrower, or kilnman. Though operative potters continued to function as independent craftsmen and maintained the helper system, they did not possess the status or complete skills of the old practical potters.

Advances in technology, mechanization, and the factory system, which accompanied the industry's accelerated expansion after 1860, not only transformed production processes and working environments, but also generated further job-specialization and skill-dilution. Like most nineteenth-century factories, modern potteries were not highly integrated operations. Instead, they consisted of a collection of craftshops or "departments," each performing a particular phase of pottery-making. Production still depended heavily on manual labor. For example, in a single workday, youths employed as "runners" typically covered over fifteen miles while carrying an average of 35,000 pounds of molds and materials between departments. Nevertheless, new labor-saving machinery steadily appeared, such as plungers, hydrostatic presses, and pug mills for clay preparation, and jiggers, lathes, and jollies for

Women and children performed the menial tasks of brushing and smoothing the finished ware.

fashioning uniform pottery ware. By the 1870s, many potteries had installed steam-driven machinery to replace operations customarily run by hand and foot-power, and began to utilize natural gas in place of wood and coal to fire their kilns. While these changes increased, standardized, and simplified production, they also transformed operative potters from independent craftsmen to factory artisans. By the late 1870s, the potter's skills had been subdivided into as many as a dozen distinct job categories, many of which were filled by semi- and unskilled workers. As one operative described the trade's declining skill-levels: "They can take a green boy fourteen years old, and in a week's time, with the use of their machinery, he can turn out fifteen teacups a minute, more perfect in form and uniform in size than could be made by hand."

Industrialization also caused adjustments in the composition of the labor force. Although practical potters had occasionally employed wives and children as helpers or apprentices, the craft had remained an adult male occupation. By 1880, however, nearly one out of every four pottery workers in Ohio was a woman or child. From 1850 to 1880, female pottery hands increased from sixteen to 226, a rise from three to nine percent of the total work force. Many were wives and daughters of operative potters, who used them as helpers in order to supplement family incomes. But, more commonly, they were hired by plant owners themselves, generally to handle menial and routine tasks like brushing, smoothing, and finishing pieces. While women often outnumbered men and developed considerable skill in decorating departments, they were seldom permitted to operate jiggers, lathes, or presses. Sexual discrimination also extended to female wages, which were rarely comparable to rates received by males performing the same skilled or unskilled jobs. Employers began to exploit child labor as well,

Though women occasionally worked as skilled jiggermen, they earned only half the wages of their male counterparts.

Women invariably outnumbered men in decorating departments, but, just as surely, men operated the machines.

especially during the 1870s, when the number of pottery workers below fifteen years of age doubled from 193 to 391 and comprised about fifteen percent of the labor force. Frequently ignoring traditional apprenticeship and helper systems, pottery owners employed children as machine-hands to replace higher-paid skilled artisans. Thus, entire families often toiled side-by-side within the same pottery — a somewhat unusual occurrence in Ohio's increasingly depersonalized factories.

Pottery work presented serious health hazards. Poor lighting and ventilation, exposure to temperature extremes, overcrowded conditions, and constant fatigue were common problems which state inspectors blamed for the high rate of "industrial alcoholism" among pottery workers. In addition to lead-poisoning and colic, employees suffered from two chronic diseases peculiar to the industry — "potters'

Job-specialization began at an early age in East Liverpool potteries. Here, teenage toilers depended solely upon sunlight for illumination as they carefully decorated ware at the Knowles, Taylor & Knowles Potteries.

Preparing one of the countless molds utilized in the mass-production of pottery.

While a helper prepared the clay, an operative potter used a jigger machine and molds to shape pitchers.

asthma'' caused by continual inhalation of the fine clay dust which filled the air; and "potters' paralysis,'' a temporary but recurrent ailment of the arms which afflicted dippers who manually immersed ware in huge tanks of chemical solutions during the glazing process.

Yet, traditional craft attitudes and work-habits proved stubbornly resistant to change. Even as mass-production techniques threatened their trade, operative potters continued to perceive themselves as skilled craftsmen, and consequently used various means to protect their accustomed influence, status, and independence. They were especially successful in counteracting management's efforts to impose regimentation and work-discipline. Operative potters had traditionally controlled their own working hours, generally choosing to alternate long periods of intense labor with several days of complete idleness. Since they were paid on a piece-rate basis, the potters had just worked as long as it took to earn a desired amount of money or until they felt in need of a rest. However, such sporadic work-habits disrupted the efficiency of pottery factories, and in the 1870s employers repeatedly attempted to impose standard ten-hour days on their workers. The potters simply ignored management's demands, and not until companies adopted hourly wages in the early twentieth century were these old habits broken. Intentional absenteeism was also an effective weapon against the "stretch-out,'' whereby employers sought to increase production quotas under the piece-rate system, in order to force employees to make more for the same wage. On the other hand, preservation of the time-honored helper system benefited the potters and the owners. Operative potters preferred the system because it enabled them to maintain their semi-managerial status, to protect craft traditions, and to influence the entrance of newcomers to the trade. Companies favored the arrangement, since it undermined solidarity between operatives and helpers, while stimulating productivity. In other instances, such as mechanization, skilled potters had little choice but to compromise. They strongly resented the introduction of the "wooden men'' and tried to block their use, but ultimately could only request the right to work at these very machines which diminished their skills. Therefore, throughout the century, the pottery industry remained a curious mixture of the old and the new.

A skilled jiggerman at work.

Dippers commonly suffered temporary paralysis of the arms from chemicals used in the glazing process.

PART 3 RESPONDING TO THE URBAN-INDUSTRIAL ORDER 1886-1918

Ohio stood center stage in 1886, heralding the genesis of a new force in the history of American labor. On the evening of December 10, a small band of dissident trade unionists gathered in Druids' Hall in Columbus. Convinced that they understood the direction in which workers had to head in order to find collective solutions for common problems, the assembled delegates created the American Federation of Labor. For the next five decades, the AFL maintained a tenuous reign over the nation's labor movement. Moreover, like the state which gave it birth, the federation would embody the best and the worst of working-class responses to an urban-industrial world.

That this highly significant event occurred in Ohio was hardly a simple coincidence. For, in many ways, developments in the Buckeye State both reflected and shaped the dominant trends transforming the entire nation. Ohio cities were among the most strongly unionized in the country. Strikes regularly swept the state's manufacturing and mining centers, but always stopped short of the revolution which the propertied so deeply dreaded. A politically pivotal state, by the late 1880s Ohio had also established one of the nation's foremost "smokestack" economies based on heavy industry. Though the transition to an industrial economy was substantially complete by the 1890s, the forces of change did not diminish. The ongoing industrial revolution, technological advances, and new forms of job organization relentlessly reshaped factory, mine, and office work. Industrial cities grew ever larger, drawing more and more job-seekers from rural areas and abroad. The influx of immigrants, increasingly from southern and eastern Europe now, profoundly altered the composition of the work force, injected new traditions into working-class culture, and further complicated efforts to unite. Finally, all of the processes which had already converted an agrarian and rural society into an urban and industrial order were accelerated by the First World War. Ever so briefly, it also appeared as if the war might be an irreversible turning point in the history of Ohio's working classes.

Ohio remained a leading agricultural state between 1880 and 1920, but population movement, expansion of industrial cities, and growth of mining areas all testified to the further development and maturation of the industrial sector of the economy. Still the fourth most populous state in the nation, Ohio boasted a population of 5.7 million people in 1920. Compared to the post-Civil War years, the overall growth rate slowed appreciably and exceeded the national average only during

the last decade of the era; then population rose by twenty-one percent. Large increases in the numbers of immigrants and persons born outside Ohio fed growth, but until 1900 the tendency for the proportion of persons born in Ohio to increase persisted. With some minor fluctuations, too, the other major components of the population remained essentially in balance until the World War I era. The combination of massive immigration and, once World War I began, the influx of native-born migrants from elsewhere in the U.S. altered that mix (see Appendix—Tables 3A and 3B). The uneven pattern of county growth attested to the magnetic pull of the state's industrial and mining centers, for it was agricultural areas which consistently had the smallest increases in population (see Tables 3C and 3D). Although long underway, this tendency was especially marked now. Rural Ohioans outnumbered other Buckeyes for the last time in 1900; indeed, the rural population barely grew at all between 1880 and 1890 and thereafter declined steadily. Thus, in every decade except the 1880s urban dwellers accounted for practically all population growth. In all, the urban population more than doubled and rose from thirty-two to sixty-four percent of the state's total population in these critical years (see Tables 3E and 3F).

The urban network well underway after the Civil War developed further between 1880 and 1920, although until the 1890s, only Cincinnati and Cleveland had populations over 100,000. The Queen City's decline persisted; it grew by an average of only twelve percent a decade. By contrast, Cleveland expanded dramatically and by 1920 accounted for twenty-two percent of the state's urban population. Together the two cities were home to forty percent of Ohio's urban population in 1880 and thirty-seven percent in 1890. Thereafter—Columbus and Toledo by 1900, Dayton by 1920, Akron and Youngstown by 1920 — more and more cities joined the ranks of those with 100,000 population (see Table 3G).

Other secondary cities also expanded throughout these years, although at uneven rates. Youngstown and Lorain boomed in the eighties, with the latter continuing at an even faster pace in the nineties. Akron was more typical—until 1910. A good-sized small city of 16,512 in 1880, it expanded steadily for thirty years. By then the growing appetite of the auto industry utterly transformed the diverse manufacturing community; rubber, a relatively minor industry until the turn of the century, now dominated Akron. From 1910 to 1920 the city's population rose from 69,067 to 208,435, a 202 percent increase, the largest of any Ohio city in the early twentieth century (see Table 3H).

The development of particular industries, or clusters of related industries, generally explained growth patterns: rubber in Akron, glass, autos and auto parts in Toledo, steel and related products in Cleveland and Youngstown. Sometimes the arrival of a single company could make a dramatic difference. Canton, for instance, had only 12,258 inhabitants in 1880.

Whether in secondary cities such as Lima in 1891 (top), small mining communities such as Rendville in 1906 (middle), or major cities such as Cleveland in 1917 (bottom), organized labor's presence was a visible factor in community life, especially on Labor Day.

Overleaf—page 95.
In the NCR machinery department, ca. 1910, where components for different products were actually made.

The 1888 arrival in Canton of Dueber-Hampden Watchworks employees.

Repairing a Cleveland streetcar line, 1907.

and blacks alike, moreover, clustered increasingly in Ohio's cities, those dynamic urban frontiers of opportunity. Thus, most cities had higher proportions of blacks, recent immigrants, and their children than statewide figures relating to these groups suggest. In Cleveland in 1920, for instance, the ethnic community of first and second generation immigrants totalled seventy-five percent of the city's population, although the state average was only thirty-four percent. Blacks made up under two percent of Cleveland's population in 1920, below the state average, but in more southerly cities the figure was considerably higher: five percent in Cincinnati and Zanesville, seven percent in Columbus, and eleven percent in Springfield.

Knitting together this urban fabric was a highly integrated transportation system which had long made Ohio a crossroads in the national economy. Canals and riverways still figured in the shipment of goods and raw materials, but other forms of transportation eclipsed them long before 1920. The railroad dominated the scene throughout the period. Between 1880 and 1912, Ohio's system enlarged by sixty-three percent to 9,233 miles of track, most of the additional lines related to the vast expansion of Ohio's coal production. Within most cities, meanwhile, new technologies rapidly displaced the commonplace horsedrawn street cars.

Cincinnati added a cable system similar to San Francisco's in the 1880s. More common was the spread of electric streetcars. They made it easier for workers to reach their jobs and this in turn encouraged the spread, already underway, of suburbs. By 1912, Ohio cities had 781 miles of street and suburban lines.

Electric interurban lines, carrying both passengers and freight, were a logical extension of these streetcar systems and they further linked

Seven years later the population stood at about 13,000. At that point the Dueber-Hampden Watchworks, attracted by free land and a $100,000 gift, began constructing its new plant. In short order it brought in its 2,000 workers. With their families, the total influx amounted to 7-10,000 people. By 1890 Canton's population exceeded 26,000. The general pattern was obvious. By 1920 fully sixty-four percent of all Ohioans lived in cities, and increasingly in cities which exceeded 100,000 in population. In 1900 forty-eight percent of all urbanites lived in such cities, and in 1920 fifty-nine percent.

Racial and ethnic groups, meanwhile, continued to spread across the state in varying patterns. The English, Welsh, German and Irish, who predominated among the foreign born in former times, were gradually supplanted by southern and eastern Europeans. Immigrants

Ohio's cities. The first of these interurbans, the ABC Line (Akron, Bedford, and Cleveland), began its 27-mile run in 1895. By 1912, Ohio boasted 2,118 miles of interurban track.

Even as the interurbans spread to meet the demands of Ohio's burgeoning population, a new form of transportation emerged: the automobile. Although the number of registered motor vehicles in Ohio increased from 10,649 in 1908 to 643,897 in 1920, the auto did not assume a dominant role in transportation until after World War I. Nor did the rapidly spreading trucking industry entirely supplant the horse and wagon for local cartage. In 1915, for instance, Cleveland cartage occupied 10,000 men, 20,000 horses, and 5,000 motor vehicles. Still, the new machine had an impact. A good roads movement developed during the 1890s, and as motorized vehicles spread in popularity the demand for better roads intensified. In 1920 the state highway department reported maintenance and repair work on nearly 2,800 miles of roadways at a cost of almost $2,000,000.

Few other states mirrored American industrial development as fully as Ohio. Between 1880 and 1890, the number of manufacturing establishments jumped from 20,699 to 28,673, but by 1920 declined to 16,125, one result of the remarkable series of combinations and consolidations which marked the emergence of the modern corporation. Even as this far-reaching concentration occurred, the value of manufactured products and the number of workers ballooned. While this growth (see Table 3I) was uneven, there was never any question as to the direction. Agriculture provided a living for forty percent of all Ohioans who worked in 1880, only sixteen percent forty years later. Ohioans concentrated more and more in manufacturing, mechanical, and construction jobs, the latter fed by city building. The Ohio workers involved

A grocery delivery boy and his wagon, Massillon, ca. 1890s.

The first delivery truck in Lima, 1908.

A streetcar maintenance crew in Springfield, 1913.

Sensitive to the ways in which mechanization and the sub-division of work were repeatedly remolding the nature of factory, mine, and craft work, the Ohio Commissioner of Labor in 1894 pointed out that something of the same sort had happened to Great Lakes sailors.

Beeson's Inland Marine Guide for 1894, credits to Ohio 475 vessels. This . . . would place the number of employees on shipboard at about 6,300. Unusual interest centers about this body of wage earners, because of the nature of their calling, concerning which the mass of people, who do not come in contact with it, are apt to have impracticable ideas. A few months' association with the lake sailor man has the effect of dispelling certain illusions. Not that he is altogether lacking in adventurous and heroic attributes, or that at one time they may not have been his characteristics, but candor compels the statement that the Lake Erie sailor of to-day is much like men of other occupations, barrring the fact that certain requirements of his business place a check upon his full social and political development. He is neither picturesque nor untrammeled, neither conspicuous by his habits nor his lack of interest in matters which absorb the attention of citizens generally. In fact, whatever may have formerly been the distinguishing peculiarities of his life, they have become subdued through the changed condition of his surroundings. During the wonderful development of navigation his calling has been virtually snatched from his hands, and his very name, in its true sense, threatens to become a tradition.

Sacks of flour come off a conveyor belt at the Cleveland Milling Company, 1911.

A worker shovels sand to form a mold at the Buckeye Steel Castings foundry, 1916.

in this process rose from twenty-four to a staggering forty-eight percent of the non-agricultural labor force between 1880 and 1920. Extracting coal, oil and gas from the earth boomed as well, but since the total workforce enlarged so much, this segment of the non-agricultural sector never exceeded four percent of the workforce (see Tables 3J and 3K).

Coal was central to the revolution in the manufacturing world, for it powered much of the machinery involved and, with coke, was crucial for the production of iron and steel. Output skyrocketed, reaching 20.5 million tons in 1902 and 35,000,000 tons in 1919. Even as this occurred, new power sources assumed important roles. Oil and gas discoveries in Northwest Ohio made Toledo, as well as Cleveland, a refinery center during the 1890s. But the most dramatic new power source was electricity. It had begun to change the face of cities by 1900 — electric wires multiplied in startling confusion — and even earlier had begun to displace oil and gas lighting in factories. Gradually it altered industrial machinery as well, enormously speeding the internal transformation of the factory. Electric motors accounted for under two percent of the power used to drive industrial machinery nation-wide in 1899, thirty-two percent by 1919 — and by then industry used more electricity than any other sector of the economy.

Other changes in the occupational structure slowly became apparent, especially the gradual expansion of the non-manual portion of the wage-earning classes and a proportionate decline of workers in domestic service. Shifting census classifications, themselves signs of the rapidity of change in this era, make it difficult to be precise regarding the exact dimensions of this change. What contemporaries noticed most, in any case, was the obvious — the large increases in manufacturing and related industries.

Ohio remained an important producer of goods such as flour, meat, lumber and beer through World War I, and still ranked first in the production of pottery, but other kinds of manufacturing assumed larger and larger roles. Iron and steel, miscellaneous iron and steel products, and foundry and machine shop products had figured prominently in the 1880s; forty years later Ohio still ranked number one or two in the nation in the production of these goods and they now represented an even greater proportion of the state's output — sixteen percent in 1880, twenty-three percent in 1920. And, by 1920, a series of new mass-production industries had arisen. In 1890, Ohio had been the country's leading producer of carriages and wagons, a fact which helps explain its later prominence in the auto industry. By 1920, the state ranked first nationally in the production of rubber tires, second in automobiles, auto bodies and auto parts, and third in glass. In addition, Ohio placed second in the manufacture of electrical machinery, apparatus and supplies.

Between 1886 and 1920, Ohioans experienced the turmoil that invariably accompanies rapid

By the 1890s, oil production had become one of Ohio's most highly complex and integrated industries. If initial exploration was successful (upper left), the oil then had to be transported from oil fields (above), through miles of pipe line (left), to massive refineries in urban areas (below).

change. Only rarely were old ways and values completely rejected or effaced. More often the new was grafted upon the old with a resultant hybrid vigor. Still, many of the uncertainties of former times remained. Ohio workers still grappled with the problems of material well-being, psychic security and human dignity. One of the most pressing needs confronting workers in the new industrial era was for living space. In the rapidly growing cities this posed a perpetual problem. Prejudice and restricted budgets kept the poor in the worst sections of most cities, often in low lying areas near the central business district. City services were often poor here —streets unpaved, sewers non-existent, drainage poor, open privies common. Congestion was often intense, especially in the older and larger cities. By 1912, indeed, forty-five percent of all Cincinnatians lived in apartments and divided houses, chiefly in the packed downtown wards. Proportionately, these wards had more people living in tenements than any other city in the U.S. Although reformers on occasion experimented with model housing, these ventures had a limited impact on most workers.

Investigators for Cleveland's Hiram House graphically described numerous places they visited in the early twentieth century. In one instance, in 1907, they found:

. . . a little shack overhanging the Nickel Plate railroad on Broadway. The house is built into the side of the embankment and shelters within its miserable walls four families, the landlord receiving eighteen dollars per month rent. In three small rooms live a Polish family, consisting of the father, mother, and eight children, the oldest of whom is thirteen years of age. When the home was first visited the baby was ill of pneumonia. He was being nourished on condensed milk, coffee being substituted if the supply of milk ran short. We learned that the father worked for the American Shipbuilding Company for two dollars and five cents per day, that sum feeding and clothing a

Working-class children pose and play in the Orange Avenue slum area near the Hiram House settlement in Cleveland.

Washington Terrace, a model home development for blacks in Cincinnati, ca. 1910.

family of ten, paying rent and buying fuel. The home was reasonably neat and clean, the mother had evidently done her best, but work and worry had driven her almost to desperation.

Proud people, these Poles refused private charity aid, except for milk. "Both father and mother," the investigator concluded, "realize that the house where they live, with its miserable environment, is not fit to be inhabited by human beings, yet they say they know of no place they could get where the rent would be within their means."

In a few instances, urban enclaves of a different sort developed. The Kossuth Colony in Dayton, for instance, housed Hungarians who worked at the Barney and Smith Car Works. Run by a Hungarian-born labor contractor between 1906 and 1915, the colony had forty homes and an imposing two-story clubhouse where workers and their wives found stores, offices, a bank and postal station, as well as a dance hall and beerhall. While such amenities were far superior to those available to slum dwellers, Kossuth residents experienced many restrictions. Guards allowed visitors through the single gate in the twelve-foot high fence which surrounded the community only on Sundays and holidays. Housing hinged on employment, and payment of the $10 for fifty-five hours of work came in the form of brass scrip usable only in the colony's store.

The typical working-class neighborhood was not static. Large numbers of people moved frequently. Since housing was expensive and in short supply, workers with seasonal jobs or irregular employment patterns commonly moved from apartment to apartment. Among blacks in Toledo forty-six percent changed residence between 1891 and 1892, about thirty percent in 1899-1900, forty-two percent in 1903, and twenty-four percent in 1906.

This constant sense of motion made institutions such as neighborhood churches, social clubs, bars, and stores which catered to particular groups all the more important in shaping a sense of community life. "Buckeye Road," a Cleveland Hungarian remembered, "was a wonderful territory, just like . . . [your] town. People would all know each other and all like each other." Even so, over time some of the enclaves shifted entirely. In Cincinnati the German and Irish neighborhoods moved outward from the center of the city as newcomers, blacks and eastern and southern Europeans, flowed into the Queen City between 1893 and 1920.

In city after city similar scenes unfolded. An everchanging mosaic of ethnic and racial enclaves characterized Ohio's expanding cities. Cleveland, the nation's tenth largest city in 1890, became a metropolis split along ethnic lines. Poor Irish settled in the Whiskey Island section, Hungarians in Buckeye, Jews around Orange Avenue and East 22nd street. Cincinnati had its Over the Rhine district, a German residential area; Irish settled in The Bottoms, and gradually moved westward as blacks moved in; by 1910, Russian-born Jews clustered in the West End. In Toledo, Hungarians settled around Irontown on the East Side and Polish workers in two distinct areas to the North and Southwest; the Irish around Irish Hill near downtown; and the Germans in nearby Lenk's Park. In Akron the foreign-born made up smaller proportions of residents in each ward, but as elsewhere concentrated near their work or trolley lines. Most wage earners would not buy cars until the 1920s. When a Toledo developer advertised Homeville before World War I, he stressed that it was "less than ten minutes' walk" from the giant Overland plant. And when the Cincinnati Consumers' League opened a Room Registry Bureau in 1916 it learned that most applicants wanted to live within walking distance of the business section to save both time and car fare, "an item to be considered when the income is none too large."

As late as 1920, where workers lived depended very much on where they worked. Streetcar suburbs developed at an early date in most Ohio cities, but the working-class character of in-city residential districts remained a notable feature of city life through World War I. A study conducted in Columbus indicated as much:

Although the west side neighborhood is primarily a workingman's district, still it by no means represents a uniform standard of living. Many of the heads of households, such as skilled laborers, railroad conductors, etc., belong to the higher income groups and could easily afford to live in one of the superior economic areas of the city. Proximity to work doubtless accounts for their residence here.

Fully fifty-one percent of the adult male workers in a sampled group walked to and from work.

Despite the various problems confronting workers, goodly numbers were able to purchase their own homes. Throughout the U.S. in 1900,

The poorest workers in Cleveland lived in lakefront shanties such as this one "on the dump," ca. 1905.

thirty-six percent of non-farm families owned their homes; within Ohio forty-four percent did so. Home ownership patterns varied considerably, in both major and secondary communities. In 1900 about fourteen percent of the blacks living in Toledo owned their own homes, a lower proportion than did so in Columbus and Rendville but more than did so in Cleveland. There only ten percent of the blacks owned. Among foreign-born whites home ownership was much more extensive. In 1900 fully fifty-seven percent of Toledo's foreign-born owned their homes, a figure even higher than that of native-born whites. Germans, Irish, and immigrants from Great Britain had the highest proportions of homes, for they had been in the city the longest. Newcomers tended to rent. Among

Street market places such as this one in Cleveland ca. 1900 were hubs of daily working-class life, providing the necessities of life as well as diverse social contacts.

National Cash Register sales agents perfect their skills.

Poles in 1900, for example, only seventeen percent owned their own homes. Among Italians ninety percent rented. By 1920 nearly fifty percent of all Toledoans owned their homes. In Hocking Valley coal towns, the proportion of miners who owned their homes in 1900 averaged forty-two percent and in some towns it was considerably higher — New Straitsville, sixty percent, Trimble, sixty-four percent, Corning, fifty-six percent, Hemlock, fifty-five percent.

The ownership of single family homes hinged in part on location, as well as earnings. In Akron eighty-four percent of inhabited homes were single-family structures and the city, in 1913, had one of the highest rates of home ownership in the country. This reflected, in part, the aspirations of city workers and in part the concern of manufacturers such as Firestone and Goodyear to encourage stability in their labor forces by facilitating home ownership. Goodyear launched a housing project in east Akron in 1912, and similar plans existed elsewhere as well. In the coal fields of southeastern Ohio company towns such as Congo still existed. Earlier, Bauscher's Bicycle Factory in Toledo had developed Bicycleville, In 1915, Youngstown Sheet and Tube began a two-year project to build nearly 500 homes which would be sold to workers, part of a plan to cement the loyalty of workers to the firm. Revealingly, the plans called for five distinct groups of houses: for American workers, foreign-born workers, "colored" workers at the main plant, miners at Nemacolin, and foreign-born workers at Highview.

Even where workers owned their own homes they often had to use them as sources of income — by renting out rooms. Since many new arrivals and low income workers could not afford to buy a house or rent an apartment, boarding with a family was a convenient alternative. Incoming immigrants, on the other hand, often placed an enormously high priority on owning property and achieved this, despite low salaries, by renting out every available inch of space. The practice was widespread, but varied from group to group, reflecting not only differing wage levels but also attitudes toward familial privacy or communal living. Fully fifty-one percent of Cleveland Hungarian households surveyed in 1909 had boarders or lodgers, for example. A similar pattern existed in Akron and houses at the Kossuth Colony in Dayton came equipped with dormitory attics for single male boarders.

At bottom, where people lived hinged heavily on how much they made — and wages varied by

The first filling station in Findlay, 1913.

A canal boat family near Massillon, probably during the 1890s.

industry, age, sex, skill, race and nationality. Men commonly received twice as much as women and children, blacks and recent immigrants less than native-born whites, and skilled workers more than the non-skilled.

The range of hourly wages can be seen by briefly looking at the Cleveland auto industry in 1915. Twenty-three percent of the workers made less than 25¢ an hour — ranging from 18.3¢ for women sewers and pasters to male heat treaters who earned 24.9¢ an hour. Fully fifty-nine percent — all in machine occupations, and all of them male — earned between 25 and 30¢ an hour — with chassis assemblers, fender fitters, and flask makers at the bottom and sheet metal machine operators at the top of the scale. The remaining workers, "the aristocracy of the labor force," consisted of two groups. Ten percent earned 30-35¢ an hour: floor molders, gear shaper operators, and carpenters earned the 30¢ figure; top makers made 34.8¢ hourly. Only eight percent of Cleveland's auto workers earned over 35¢ hourly — back hangers, bench molders and machine molders, tool makers, cutters, finish varnishers, and stripers.

Overall, real wages (the amount of goods which could be actually bought per dollar) rose substantially in the late nineteenth century — by ten to twenty percent in the 1870s, and twenty-five percent in the 1880s. By 1890, real wages in manufacturing were about fifty percent higher than they had been just before the Civil War. Thereafter, until 1914 at least, real wages increased more slowly than did labor productivity and the cost of living. One reason for this was that employers, increasingly concentrated, had more power in the marketplace; another is that because wages were still higher than in Europe, they attracted immigrants. The millions who poured into the country found opportunity they sought, but also created a labor surplus which allowed employers to keep wages down.

The overall increase in real wages did not mean that all workers benefited equally. What counted, ultimately, was how much a worker, or a working class family, made annually. Much employment was irregular, either because it was of a seasonal nature, such as construction, or because manufacturers cut production periodically. During times of depression, too, the number of days in the year that a worker actually toiled fell precipitously, and thus annual earnings plummeted — even as real wages rose. These factors lay largely beyond the control of individual workers.

The cost of living rose between 185 and 200 percent between 1890 and 1920. Nationwide figures on average annual earnings, which conceal regional and yearly variations, suggest that many workers fared fairly well; their average annual earnings increased more than the cost of living. Among wage earners in manufacturing annual earnings climbed from $439 to $1,407, for example, an increase of 221 percent, while railroad workers saw their average annual earnings rise from $560 to $1,817, a 225 percent increase, and bituminous coal miners' earnings leapt from $406 annually to $1,386, up 241 percent. Not all workers did so well. Street railway employees averaged $560 in 1890 and $1,608 in 1920, a 187 percent increase. Clerical workers' earnings rose from an average of $848 in 1890 to $2,160 in 1920, an increase of only 155 percent, and gas and electricity workers fared even more poorly — their average annual earnings rising from $687 to $1,432, an increase of but 108 percent.

These figures, of course, are averages and thus reflect general trends rather than what happened within Ohio. What is clear, however, is that high hourly rates were no guarantee of high annual earnings. In Cleveland in 1915, for instance, such building trades workers as structural iron workers and stone masons and bricklayers netted 70¢ an hour. Tool and die makers made 40¢, by comparison, and general machinists between 35 and 31¢ an hour. Even unskilled workers in the building trades made more than machine operator "specialists," and general machinists less than hod carriers and longshoremen. Yet the machinists were not as badly off as this comparison of hourly rates suggests. Normally they worked year round and for 9-10 hours daily, one or two more than in the highly seasonal building trades.

Bituminous coal miners also worked extremely irregular schedules. Ohio miners averaged 208 working days in 1901 and thus trappers made $189 and machine cutters $655 that year. Yet even this considerable range of annual earnings does not reveal the disparities among miners, for what miners made varied from county to county. The nineteen machine cutters who worked in Athens county in 1901 averaged $4.30 a day (243 days) and $1,044.90 a year, while in Belmont daily earnings for ten machine cutters averaged $3.50 daily (220 days) and $770

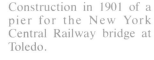

annually. Nine years later, in 1910, Athens county had 431 machine cutters and their circumstances had changed considerably. No longer the highest paid inside workers, they averaged only $2.39 daily (196 days) and $468 annually. The county's loaders, by contrast, earned an average of $593 annually. In Belmont county the number of machine cutters had also risen, to 733, but here they remained, at an average of $3.70 a day, the highest paid inside workers. Working 235 days they earned $870. Belmont's 5,890 loaders, meanwhile, worked 248 days, averaged $2.84 daily, and thus earned an average of $704 in 1910.

Since annual earnings varied so widely, so did the standard of living. Evidence is fragmentary, but comparing two sets of budgets allows us to look within the world of late nineteenth-century workers. Interviews with a number of working women in Cincinnati in 1888 revealed that their average annual earnings amounted to only $257. Out of that sum they spent $152, fifty-nine percent of their income, on room and meals. Another $60, twenty-three percent, went for clothing, while $31 went to other expenses (twelve percent). What is remarkable is that average expenses totalled $245, meaning many of these women saved something out of their paltry incomes.

The situation was slightly different among working women polled in Cleveland at the same time. Their annual incomes averaged $280. Room and meal costs ate up $148, fifty-three percent of what they earned, clothing $81, or twenty-nine percent, and other costs $41, or fifteen percent of their annual earnings. On the average, expenditures totalled $275, meaning an even smaller margin for extras than in Cincinnati.

By comparison with these women, Ohio glass workers enjoyed relatively high wages. Interviews with over two hundred glass workers in 1891 showed that only seven percent earned under $300 annually. Fully fifty-three percent made between $300 and $699 a year, twenty-five percent between $700 and $999, and sixteen percent over $1,000. Wives and children contributed to these rather substantial incomes in only a tiny proportion of cases. Virtually none of the wives in the 232 families worked, and in only twenty-five cases did children, forty-three in all, toil — and their annual earnings ranged from $16 to $1,406.

The variations among Ohio working-class families which derived their income from the glass industry were notable and suggestive of the range within the working class as a whole. Take the case of an American-born glass blower, aged fifty-seven, who lived in a six-room "Good rented house" with his wife, aged forty-nine, and their six children. The father earned $976, while four children, ages twenty-five, twenty-two, nineteen, and seventeen, earned an additional $1,406, meaning a total family income for the year of $2,382. The family spent $526 on food, twenty-two percent of the family income, $204 on rent, nine percent, $41 on fuel, two percent, $345 on clothing, fifteen percent, and $610 on all other expenditures, twenty-six percent — including $24 on labor organizations and $73 on books and newspapers. Attesting to the family's cultural interests and material well-being was the brief comment of the investigator: "have a piano, organ, and sewing machine."

Clearly, this family had a life style which set it apart from the working women of Cincinnati and Cleveland. Yet not all glass workers were so fortunate. One American-born laborer earned considerably less than the man described above. Aged 54, he earned $398 and had an additional $25 in income from other sources. He and his 64-year-old wife lived in four rented rooms, described as "poor, no comforts." For these sparse rooms, he and his wife spent $96, twenty-three percent of their annual earnings. Food cost $260, a whopping sixty-one percent of their earnings, while they allotted only $25 for clothing, six percent, $16.40 for fuel, four percent, and $33.45 for all other expenditures, eight percent. The extras included $18.20 for life insurance, $5.80 for taxes, $1.25 for organizations, $1.75 for books and newspapers, and $1.95 for tobacco. For this glass worker and his wife, life was a precarious struggle.

Such workers confronted harsh circumstances due to their low wages and long hours. A federal government survey of working women in 1888 unwittingly pointed to the conditions common among the ill-paid and overworked members of the laboring class:

> The percentage of working girls living at home is higher in Cincinnati than in any other city visited . . . , but the homes are unusually uninviting, even in the newer quarters. The streets are dirty and closely built up with ill-constructed houses, holding from two to six families. Many poorer parts of Cincinnati are as wretched as the worst European cities, and the population looks as degraded.

Although the urban environment altered dramatically over the next several decades, poverty and disease persisted as common features in the lives of many working-class families. Depressions and recessions regularly added thousands of unemployed workers to the ranks of those whose work was seasonal or irregular and whose annual earnings thus were insufficient to provide a decent standard of living. Unsanitary living and hazardous working conditions remained the plight of such workers, moreover, for while medical knowledge advanced rapidly during this era, implementing reforms proceeded slowly and unevenly. Despite an increase in social services, the powerless often benefited least from the changes which were made.

As was generally true throughout the United States, in Ohio the death rate fell dramatically and life expectancy increased substantially in the early twentieth century. Between 1909 and 1911 the mortality rate was 12.13 per thousand population, below the national average of 14.7 in 1910. But urban areas consistently showed higher death rates. Portsmouth, for instance, had an average annual death rate from all causes of 14.65. And nineteen of Ohio's eighty other cities had even higher rates. Contagious and infectious diseases remained the most prevalent causes of death. Measles, diptheria and whooping cough afflicted many and while these years did not see the epidemics of scarlet fever and cholera and occasionally typhus, which characterized the nineteenth century, croup and pneumonia were commonplace. At the turn of the century, indeed, nearly one in every four deaths was caused by tuberculosis, influenza, and pneumonia. Diseases such as influenza singled out no particular class, as a disastrous epidemic in 1918-19 demonstrated, yet other contagious diseases affected the working class disproportionately because of the links between environment and health.

The cost of correcting environmental health hazards was high, and construction of modern sewerage and water filtration systems lagged, with poorer districts generally the last to receive adequate service. By World War I progress had been made, but it was distributed unevenly. As a result, even as the gross figures for contagious diseases declined, they disproportionately infected workers and their children. A 1916 study of Portsmouth confirmed that:

> poverty and tuberculosis are found together. Not all persons who have tuberculosis are poor. Nevertheless tuberculosis is known as a poverty

Down and out in the Over-the-Rhine section of Cincinnati, about 1900.

Before World War I ice was still the main source of refrigeration. Here Portsmouth ice cutters pose with their tools, ca. 1900-1910.

Poor distribution and storage systems and the fickleness of nature frequently resulted in ice famines in major cities, as it did in Cleveland in 1912.

disease, for it follows undernourishment and overwork or work under unhealthful conditions, it is associated with bad housing conditions, and it thrives among the ignorant.

What was true in Portsmouth was true in Cleveland as well. There, in 1912, 3,247 cases of tuberculosis were reported, seventy percent of them estimated to be "charity cases." That same year residents of the 19th and 20th wards, a heavily working-class district inadequately serviced by sewage service, contained fully seven percent of all Cincinnati typhoid cases.

Poorer districts in urban areas also suffered in other ways which affected health. When Cincinnati's Mayor Henry Hunt toured the crowded, tenement-filled 18th ward in 1912, he was appalled by the "simply horrible" amount of garbage lying about. Reflecting a widespread attitude, he blamed ward residents "for the atrocious state of affairs," calling them "filthy in their personal habits and manner of living." Neither the attitude nor the situation was unique to major cities. As the social survey team which visited Portsmouth in 1916 learned:

The frequency of removal varies with the neighborhood. A housewife was heard to congratulate herself that her garbage was removed regularly and often because she lived in the same block as a city official. Only four or five blocks away people who did not feed their garbage to their own or their neighbor's hogs were in a number of cases carrying it to the dump.

And the Portsmouth dump itself proved a source of disease. Unlike Zanesville, which burned its refuse, Portsmouth just dumped it. "It forms a breeding place for flies, and mosquitoes," the survey team reported. "In damp weather the odors are overpowering."

An increased awareness of occupational diseases paralleled the growing understanding of public health. Many workers toiled in unhealthy and accident-conducive conditions. The extent of dust, dirt, dampness, poor air, extremes of temperature, fatigue, inactivity, danger of infection, and exposure to poisons differed from place to place, even within a given industry. Whatever the attitude of particular employers, common practices in some industries often contributed to poor health. Workers in industries where work processes made for dusty or polluted air — machinists, glass, pottery — had substantially higher rates of tuberculosis and bronchial infections than those in industries that did not. (By 1915, the National Brotherhood of Operative Potters had established a Tuberculosis Fund and begun to keep careful records on the disease among its members.) Where work processes exposed workers to sharp changes in temperature — as in foundry work, some glass, and rubber work — then pneumonia ranked high.

The situation was especially bad in the rubber industry. Harvey Firestone openly admitted that the curing pits were especially poor places to work. Only "big, husky men could stay" in them, he said, "and they could not stay for long." Looking back on this era later, two Akron authors described the situation prior to 1920:

It was still the era of dust and flying soapstone loading the lungs; of workers nodding drunkenly in the benzene vapors above cement tanks; of unventilated calendar rooms below the street level where men withered in the heat and the skin peeled from their bodies; of hell-hot pits where the toilers yet slopped about in the wet underfoot. Mills had no hoods to carry poisonous fumes away, and the result was lassitude and loss of appetite on the job, a splitting headache to carry home every day. 'Blue men' baffled physicians who had yet [sic] compounded the jealously guarded compounding secrets of the gum mills to discover that aniline was in use. Lead poisoning doubled up compounding and mill room workers with agonizing colic and fuddled them mentally.

Safety hazards were another feature of the workplace. Significant improvements in machine design during the 1880s were not paralleled by changing attitudes among employers about industrial accidents. Although some

Safety hazards affected all workers. This 14-year-old boy had his right arm cut off by a veneering saw in a Cincinnati box factory in late 1907. Luther Watson's mother then sent him to school "So's he won't have to work."

A Portsmouth blacksmith shop in the 1890s.

Saloons were centers of working-class life in Cleveland in 1910.

progressive employers mounted intensive safety campaigns, especially after 1910, more commonly they blamed employees for on-the-job accidents. In some instances such assumptions may have been justified. In 1917, a 66-year-old grandmother was killed and her 15-year-old daughter severely injured while eating lunch on the tracks in the middle of the busy Lorain B&O yard where they worked as section hands.

But accidents due to such negligence were not as common as some suggested. The fact that hazards varied among industries and within industry by job points to peculiarities of each workplace. Night workers in all jobs were injured more often than those who worked during the day. Iron and steel making were especially hazardous among the manufacturing industries — in 1909-10 one in every four full-time workers were injured. Railroading remained a dangerous occupation, too, but it was coal mining which had the highest accident rates and the longest periods of subsequent disability.

Whatever their causes, both temporary and permanent disabilities prevented working and thus inflicted enormous hardships on many working-class families. In this sense the twin issues of occupational safety and environmental health hazards overlapped. It was only in the years just before World War I that recognition of this link and of the need to deal with the related social problems developed. Prior to passage of the Ohio workman's compensation laws of 1911 and 1912 employers had no legal liability for their employees and workers could have no realistic expectation of success if they sought redress in the courts. Most firms handled accidents on an individual bases, although companies such as Goodyear and Firestone with welfare schemes encouraged the formation of relief associations. Trade unions and various voluntary organizations also developed benefit and insurance programs, including sick and death benefits, but these two approaches only partially met the situation. For, despite some interest in safety programs, not until passage of the workman's compensation act did all employers have to consider the monetary benefits of preventing accidents.

Middle-class fears, that the mounting human cost of progress might cause underprivileged and desperate workers to turn to radical alternatives, provided a primary impulse for the Progressive reform movement which swept the nation during the century's early decades. The Progressives were a diverse coalition of elitist reformers, chiefly comprised of young, college-educated, financially-secure, native-born Protestants engaged in professional occupations. Though some were motivated by a thirst for social justice or greater efficiency in public affairs, the main concern of most Progressives was to somehow preserve the traditional social, economic, and political order without sacrificing the benefits of progress. Faced with serious challenges to those ideals by urbanization, immigration, corporate growth, labor unions, socialists, and corrupt politicians, Progressives launched social and political action campaigns to relieve misery and modify inequitable conditions. Their reform efforts at municipal, state, and federal levels covered a broad spectrum, ranging from banking and industrial regulation, anti-trust action, environmental conservation, and factory safety laws to establishing settlement houses, the legal prohibition of alcohol, housing reform, and electing reformers to public office — such as the famous administrations of Mayors Tom Johnson and Newton D. Baker in Cleveland, and of Sam "Golden Rule" Jones and Brand Whitlock in Toledo. Despite the Progressives' extensive activities and considerable energy, however, their reforms proved inadequate, either to contain discontent, or to establish a national consensus on values and behavior for a complex urban-industrial society.

The workers' world was not all grimness, poverty, industrial accidents, and poor health, to be sure. Few workers took vacations — only six percent did so in 1901 — but the length of the average work week fell steadily, and the varieties of leisure-time activity became more diverse. Saloons, the "poorman's club," and their adjacent pool halls maintained their popularity. Baseball and boxing reigned sovereign as spectator sports despite a growing enthusiasm

Cincinnati newsboys and supply men waiting for the 5 p.m. "baseball" edition.

for football, basketball, and auto racing. Dance halls and theatres catered to working-class audiences. An old Akron "canaler" recalled in the 1930s: "For us canal men . . . our great ambition was to reach Cleveland. It was there we had our fun taking in the shows. . . ."

Outdoor activities also boomed. The city park movement, which began in the state well before 1880, spread in this era. Among the notable additions were Toledo's Ottawa Park Golf Course in 1900, the second municipal golf course in the nation. Older forms of recreation which retained their popularity included boating, ice skating, and sledding. These were now joined by bicycling — a craze directly responsible for a good roads movement in the 1890s. Starting in that decade, too, private entrepreneurs began to develop amusement parks, casinos, and commercial beaches. By the early twentieth century they were commonplace on the outskirts of most cities.

Increasingly, group activities became a feature of urban working-class life. Ethnic communities hosted numerous voluntary associations modeled on those of the old country and patriotic, social and fraternal organizations blossomed. Individual firms and unions organized sports teams, musical groups, reading clubs and so on. And an increasingly common form of entertainment was the day-long company-sponsored excursion into the country or to a nearby park, a jaunt often taken by street car or interurban. Settlement houses, which became common in most Ohio cities before 1920, also served as centers for leisure activities. Dora Silverman, who emigrated to Cleveland from Russia shortly after 1900, for instance, told a social worker that she not only learned English at Hiram House but that "she also went to parties and dances! 'All the pleasure I had was at the Hiram House!' "

Without question the most important and all-pervasive form of entertainment to sweep Ohio and the nation in these years was the movies. In 1890, Thomas A. Edison mistakenly thought that moving pictures would be used primarily

Elaborate showboats such as the "Cotton Blossom" brought entertainment to residents of towns along the Ohio River.

The "Virginia," a popular excursion boat on the Ohio River.

Two Youngstown steel workers enjoy stereoscopic slides during a break.

by the wealthy, yet they developed into a uniquely working-class form of entertainment. A 1910 handbook for prospective nickelodeon operators explained: "The ideal location is a densely populated working-men's residence section, with a frontage on a much-traveled business street." Shows conveniently fit work schedules; they lasted only 15-20 minutes in the early days and in time were shown continuously starting in the afternoon. Much to the displeasure of middle-class critics, as one historian has noted, they allowed working-class audiences to master by their imagination the time and motion they could not control in their daily lives. Interestingly, when the Ohio General Assembly created an Industrial Commission in 1913 one function assigned it was to censor movies.

In 1910 there were 10,000 theaters nationwide and each week they played to an incredible ten million people, more than packed into all other kinds of theaters, circuses, museums, carnivals, variety and lecture halls put together. Portsmouth, a small city of about 28,000 in 1916, may have been fairly typical for the period. It boasted seven movie theaters which collectively seated 2,000 people. Films ran from 6:30 to 10:30 or 11:00 every evening and on some afternoons as well. In 1916 an estimated 4,000 people saw these shows daily, a remarkable one-seventh of the city's population.

The Hippodrome in Marietta, a popular entertainment center.

While the hours Ohio workers spent on the job declined somewhat between 1880 and 1920, the world of work still occupied major portions of each week. Precisely how workers spent that time varied considerably. If not all workers had the same experiences, certain groupings within the work force can be identified — women and children, blacks, new immigrants — as having been exposed to somewhat similar conditions. Workers in particular industries, moreover, shared certain common features in their work lives.

Clustered chiefly in the state's cities, Ohio blacks in 1890 constituted over five percent of the population in only three places — Columbus, Springfield, and Zanesville. Thirty years later the proportions of blacks in those locations had grown somewhat and both Cincinnati and Dayton now had sizeable black communities. In virtually all Ohio towns and cities the numbers of blacks increased most dramatically between 1910 and 1920 as the severe labor shortage of the war era opened new opportunities.

The precise pattern of economic opportunity for blacks varied from city to city, and changed over time, but tended to be broader in communities such as Springfield, Xenia, and Columbus where immigrants made up smaller proportions of the work force than in Cincinnati and Cleveland. Generally, too, blacks were excluded from manufacturing jobs until the World War I era. In Springfield and Columbus blacks secured a foothold by 1890 in the expanding metal industries, which used large numbers of unskilled and semi-skilled workers, and by 1900 some opportunities had opened in Steubenville and Youngstown steel mills and Salem, Canton, and Lisbon iron and tin works. As early as 1910, twenty-seven percent of Columbus' black workers had jobs in manufacturing and mechanical industries. Where cheap immigrant labor was available blacks had less luck. Cleveland's booming metal industries employed only three blacks in 1890, for example. Two decades later several hundred blacks worked in mills and foundries and smaller numbers had jobs in cigar, tobacco, and furniture factories, but the overwhelming majority of Cleveland's black males toiled in unskilled positions outside of factories.

In 1890, three of every four black males in Ohio worked as laborers or service workers. Most toiled in non-skilled, and often outdoor, jobs as hod carriers or general laborers in the building and construction trades, as teamsters and draymen, as stokers of furnaces, or as general labor in warehouses and at loading platforms, and as stevedores for canal, river and, to a lesser extent, lake boats. Nearly two percent labored as miners and mine laborers in the coal fields. Although more densely concentrated in areas such as Sunday Creek in Perry County, overall blacks made up only 2.5 percent of all Ohio coal miners.

Domestic and personal service provided the key areas of employment for blacks, especially females. In 1890 blacks made up only three percent of the total work force, but twelve percent of the workers in the service sector. Nine percent of white workers toiled in domestic and personal service jobs; forty percent of blacks did — twenty-eight percent of the men and eighty-nine percent of the women. Competing against first and second generation immigrants, blacks were represented disproportionately in a range of service jobs: twenty-four percent of all Ohio barbers in 1890 were black, as were ten percent of the domestics, servants, waitresses and waiters, and thirty-two percent of the laundresses.

In many Ohio cities black males had formed an important, if small, component of the skilled work force in the hand trades during the nineteenth century. Thirty-two percent of Cleveland's black males worked in the skilled trades in 1870, but this proportion dropped to eleven percent by 1910. Nineteenth-century traditions, formed when blacks were not numerous, made room for blacks and whites to work together in such jobs as carpentry and masonry. Here the numbers of blacks employed

Newsboys outside the Cincinnati Daily Times Star.

Workers in front of a Xenia
factory.

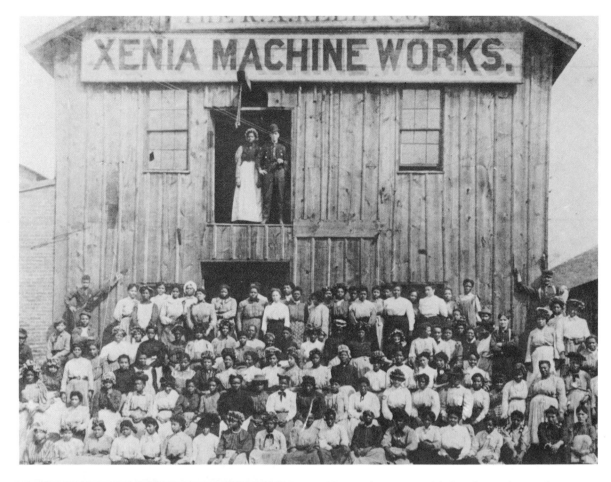

Cleveland barbers proudly
display their political loyalty to the Republican party,
1896.

1886, only twenty-eight throughout the state three years later, and of 1,700 men in Cleveland apprenticeship programs in 1910, only seven were Negroes.

A similar pattern of gradual exclusion occurred in several other occupations that had been important within the black community in the nineteenth century. Being a waiter, especially a headwaiter at an exclusive restaurant, was an opening that closed steadily. The number of black servants and waiters grew slightly in Cleveland and Columbus between 1890 and 1910, while declining a bit in Cincinnati, and in all three cities the percentage of blacks in the total job category fell. By 1918, only two of Cleveland's posh restaurants still hired black waiters. In barbering much the same thing happened. In 1870, forty-three percent of the barbers in Cleveland were black and they served a predominantly white clientele. By 1890 that proportion had dropped to eighteen percent and by 1910 to ten percent, the tendency now being for black barbers to operate solely within the black community. In cities with less substantial influxes of immigrants, blacks retained their position in barbering and catering for longer periods of time. In Columbus, for example, over thirty percent of the barbers in 1890 were black. But here, too, racism intensified, especially as more and more southern blacks moved into the capitol city. By the second decade of the twentieth century, when one observer noted that "the feeling against Negroes is bitter in the extreme," the percentage of blacks among local barbers had fallen by fifteen percent.

Still, blacks made some progress. In Cleveland, the proportion of black males who held

actually increased over time and when those two trades unionized at the end of the century they did at first exclude blacks. In other trades the drop off in black employment was sharp because older trades such as blacksmithing declined, because young blacks shifted to areas with less direct competition from hostile whites, and because many unions that developed in new or specialized skilled trades such as cabinetmaking, typesetting, baking, electrical work, and paperhanging had exclusionary policies from the outset. There were only three black apprentices in Cleveland in clerical positions, one of the growth areas of the economy, rose from two to four percent between 1870 and 1910. And among females the proportion rose from zero to 1.4 percent. Yet these increases scarcely paralleled those made by whites and were offset, as well, by declining opportunities for black women in areas such as department stores and communications. By and large black women remained relegated to low-status, personal-service jobs. Throughout Ohio, indeed, black women increasingly came to dominate female service work. They represented forty-six percent of women service workers in 1890 and sixty-two percent in 1910, even as the total number of such positions declined.

During the decade of World War I, the number of black Ohioans rose by seventy percent. Cleveland's black population quadrupled, that of Toledo and Youngstown tripled, Columbus' and Dayton's doubled, and Akron's rose by more than ten times. The war did nothing to alter the prejudice against blacks in Ohio cities, but the labor scarcity of the era did dramatically, if temporarily in some cases, change the occupational structure of the black community. By 1920, in Cleveland, for example, nearly two of every three black males now worked in an industrial job; only twelve percent remained in domestic or personal service jobs, compared with thirty percent in 1910. The bulk of the positions opened to black males involved unskilled work, but there were also substantial increases in the numbers of semi-skilled and skilled factory jobs. Black women benefited from the wartime opportunities, too, but in their case the move into semi-skilled manufacturing jobs was shortlived. As veterans returned, they rapidly displaced black women.

Women and children, whatever their race, shared with blacks a lowly position in the work force. Their wages were low, hours of work long, the jobs to which they could aspire were limited. The proportions of children under sixteen in the labor force declined over the years, in part because of state protective legislation — in 1890 (barring children under sixteen from hazardous jobs), 1891 (preventing the employment of those under fourteen in manufacturing), and laws in 1910 and 1913 stipulating the minimum ages at which children could leave school (fifteen for boys, sixteen for girls).

In the late nineteenth century child labor was commonplace, although sometimes even con-

Photographed by Lewis Hine, 13-year-old Joe, an Italian boy, works at his parents' Cincinnati fruit stand on a Saturday night.

Employees of a Clay Shop in East Liverpool, ca. 1890.

A laundress in the posh Walnut Hill area of Cincinnati, 1904.

temporaries were shocked by the abuses involved. In the late 1880s, for example, orphan children of twelve were discovered being imported from Brooklyn to work in Fostoria and Findlay glass factories. Children had long worked as helpers in the industry, but these youngsters would have no future in glass. The inspector of workshops and factories explained why:

> The glass workers' organization controls the internal government of these workshops, and by its rules prohibit any but the sons of glass blowers from learning the trade, and even limits the number of apprentices then. These orphan boys are not considered apprentices. They 'knock off' the rough edges of bottles while heated and carry them to the trimming tables. It is hot and tedious work. These boys, as fast as they grow up, will be turned loose without the first rudiments of a trade, and younger ones put in their place.

Protective legislation evolved slowly during this age of reform and did not preclude abuses. Not until 1900 did state law prohibit boys under fifteen from working as trapper and breaker boys in coal mines. The 1890 law covered manufacturing, but not other fields. The inspector of workshops and factories lamented this loophole in his 1895 report, pointing to a tobacco warehouse which employed children as young as eight. A decade later John Spargo, in an influential exposé of child labor, remarked

that although Ohio prohibited night work for those under sixteen "the law is not very effectively enforced . . . in the glass factories."

Reformers also fretted about the effects of street selling on the large numbers of very young children involved in these trades. A Cleveland study of 1908-1909 pointed to examples of under-nourishment and school absenteeism among the 1,210 boys under twelve and another 1,231 between twelve and fourteen, mostly children of the foreign-born. By World War I Cincinnati and Cleveland had passed regulations restricting such employment. The Cincinnati ordinance of 1911 prohibited boys under ten and girls under sixteen from selling newspapers and merchandise or working as bootblacks. Cleveland's 1912 law was similar, but unenforced.

Meanwhile the proportion of females in the Ohio work force rose steadily. Women made up fifteen percent of the work force in 1890 and eighteen percent in 1920. Typically women workers were young and single, contributed to their families' earnings, left the work force upon marriage, and returned to it only if their husband's earnings were insufficient or if they were deserted or widowed. While these broad characteristics remained essentially stable down to 1920, they mask crucial differences among women workers.

Black and immigrant women were disproportionately represented in the lower levels of the female labor force. Immigrant women competed with black women for domestic and personal service jobs, the two groups comprising most of the women in those fields. As already noted, over time, black women came to dominate the domestic field, although where the immigrant population was especially high that was not the case. As late as 1915, sixty-nine percent of the laundresses and fifty-five percent of the servants in Cleveland were immigrant women. Immigrant women, however, also worked in a range of manufacturing occupations which, until World War I at least, largely excluded blacks.

The expanding needle trades, where sweating tactics were often used, are a key example of the conditions women often faced in manufacturing. Under this system employers contracted with individuals who worked at home or with sub-contractors who in turn hired women at minimal wages. In 1892, Cleveland alone had some 6,000 people, most of them women, working under such conditions. Although a state law sought to regulate sweat shops, a 1918 investigation of home work in the Cincinnati clothing industry revealed that in some ways little had changed:

> Light is good in the rural shops, but is only fair in most of the shops in private dwellings and tenements. Ventilation is poor in nearly all the shops inspected, especially in the larger shops, where gas irons are used for pressing. Many of the workrooms connected with living rooms are used both for cooking and sleeping purposes. Frequently the family washing is hung in the workroom. Children, too young to go to school, are usually kept

Rose Dickhoner, a Cincinnati shirtmaker and the only female delegate to the 1905 Ohio State Federation of Labor convention, spoke for many women when she explained her attitude about trade unions.

"There is just as much to be gained by the women as for the men in this idea of labor organization. We labor just as hard, we have the same conditions to contend with, identical desires and similar ambitions in our work, and the only way to obtain them, we believe, is in organization. After our Union is formed and affiliated properly we feel it is our duty to have a part in that which is planned for the good of labor generally, regardless of sex. That is why I am in this convention."

Decals are applied to pottery at the Harker & Knowles, Taylor & Knowles Potteries in East Liverpool, ca. 1901.

Packaging and labelling in the food processing industry were commonly handled by women, but the conditions under which they worked varied considerably over time and from plant to plant, even in the same city. At Kahn Meat Company in 1896 the job was done by hand. By 1910 Streitmann Baking Company (bottom), also in Cincinnati, had mechanized the task with technologically advanced equipment.

there that the mother, who assists with the sewing, may take care of them. It is only in the *custom* tailor shops that workrooms are connected with living rooms. The operators in this branch of the trade are now principally Italians who live in rather congested quarters in old tenements. Their helpers, outside the family, are usually young immigrant girls and boys who do not speak English.

Wages were also low for the women who found work in garment and millinery factories. The situation varied a good bit, in some cases pieceworkers averaging more per week than those who toiled at set rates. In either case, wages of $1-3.00 a week were not uncommon in the early 1890s although many women made $3-5.00 weekly. By 1914 more than two-thirds of Cincinnati women in the industry made between $5.00 and $10.00 per week, while the majority of girls under eighteen made $3-8.00 weekly.

As a rule factory work paid more and provided better working conditions than the sweating system. Outside of the garment industry, women formed an important part of the labor force in a range of manufacturing fields. Cleveland chewing gum factories used women as wrappers, kneaders, rollers and cutters by the early 1890s, for example, and by then women had already also made deep inroads into the previously all-male domain of cigar making. Women also played an important role in the pottery industry, working as ware selectors, wrappers, Bisque brushers, stampers, dippers' assistants and drawers. A contract negotiated by the ware-room girls' independent union of East Liverpool in 1913 shows wage rates ranging from $1.15 to $1.30 for a nine-hour day.

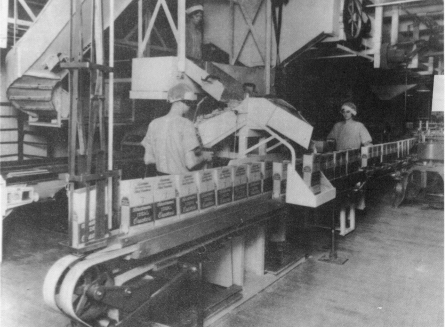

Over time the shape of the female occupational structure gradually changed. The most rapidly growing area for female employment, particularly for native-born whites, was in the service sector of the economy — in banking, insurance, advertising, mail order houses and department stores, for example, as well as com-

Machine operators follow a pattern to engrave NCR cash register parts in 1910.

Building beads for pneumatic tires at Firestone in Akron, about 1913.

The NCR indicator department, about 1900. The presses in the foreground stamped numbers.

munications. Closely linked were clerical positions in these and other businesses and industries. Between 1870 and 1910 the feminization of this occupation took place. Ohio, with thirty-seven percent of its clerical work force female in 1910, closely approximated national trends. In sales occupations, as department stores spread, a similar increase occurred. Women represented four percent of sales workers in 1870, eight percent in 1880 and twenty-five percent in 1910. Precise comparative figures are hard to come by for Ohio due to changing census classifications, but in general paralleled the tendencies nationwide.

World War I stepped up each of these trends. The decline of domestic and personal service continued, service positions such as sales expanded, the proportion of women in clerical jobs nearly doubled, and while more women found jobs in manufacturing the proportion of women in manufacturing jobs continued to decline. The war did offer a chance for some women in low-paying areas to shift to higher-paying manufacturing jobs. Although many who did so were replaced by returning veterans, the shape of the female occupational structure by 1920 bore few surprises. Women now comprised forty-six percent of the clerical and sixty-two percent of the domestic and personal service work forces. In transportation women now formed twelve percent of the workers, up from five percent in 1910.

Ethnicity provided another distinguishing characteristic among state workers. The waves of immigrants who reached the United States between 1880 and 1920, 24,000,000 in all, sought work above all else and thus selected regions where economic growth maximized their opportunities. A fair number of immigrants therefore chose Ohio.

The bulk of new immigrants who entered the labor force did so at the lowest levels, often competing with blacks for positions as day laborers. In 1894 fifty-three percent of the

By 1900, when these pictures were taken at NCR in Dayton, the clerical work force had become predominantly female.

sailors on the Great lakes, and nearly all of the dockmen at Ohio ports, had been born abroad. Workers who toiled to pave streets, build street car and interurban lines, and to haul goods within bustling communities tended to be predominantly foreign-born. Yet unlike most blacks, the foreign-born were not excluded from factory jobs. Indeed throughout the United States, unskilled and non-skilled positions in nearly all industries took on an increasingly foreign complexion. Indeed, the foreign-born came to comprise the overwhelming majority of workers in industries such as textiles and clothing, iron and steel, and coal mining in 1890. By 1910 the proportions were even higher in some industries. Seventy-one percent of the workers at Youngstown Sheet and Tube in 1915 were foreign-born, for example, and in Cleveland, in 1910, ninety-one percent of the common labor in blast furnaces and rolling mills and seventy-one percent of all semi-skilled labor was foreign-born.

Roughly one-third of all immigrants who came to the United States during this period returned to their home countries rather than settling here. For the most part this had been their intention from the outset. From depressed sections of southern, central and eastern Europe, these workers regarded their time in the U.S. as a period for intense labor during which it would be possible to earn enough money to allow them to return home and live in comfort. That expectation was not always fulfilled, but it affected the experience of many immigrants because it shaped attitudes about work, working conditions, and labor organizations, often dulling sensitivity to immediate circumstances in the anticipation of long-range satisfaction.

A willingness to work hard, of course, was not the only reason so many immigrants secured low-paying general labor and low-skill factory or sweat shop jobs often characterized by irregularity. A large portion of the new immigrants came from backgrounds which prepared them poorly for clerical and sales jobs which required fluent English, advanced educa-

An early phone exchange in Mentor, perhaps 1900.

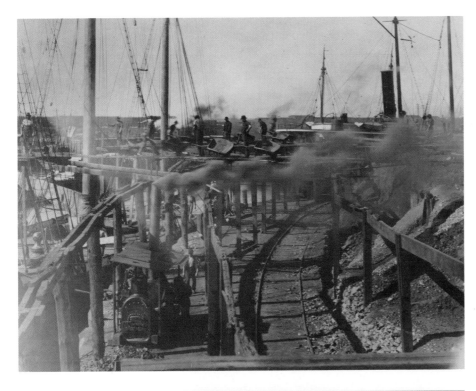

Hand unloading iron ore, probably at Conneaut in the late 1880s.

Using a cement gun, a worker at Buckeye Steel Castings in 1917 lines a ladle to prepare it to receive molten steel.

Sheet steel being cut by a clipper shear machine at Youngstown Sheet and Tube.

tion, or knowledge of American business methods. Service positions in and even outside of ethnic communities provided opportunities, as the large numbers of foreign-born peddlars and domestics suggest, but in an age of burgeoning Anglo-Saxon consciousness new immigrants often found themselves cruelly stereotyped and discriminated against on the job, restricted to certain kinds of work and barred from others.

During times of economic downturn, especially the 1890s, unspoken fears and real competition for jobs wound tight the springs of opposition to immigration and immigrants. Literally thousands of Ohioans joined the anti-Catholic American Protective Association, discriminated against Catholic workers, and sometimes panicked. In Toledo, in 1893, rumors of a Catholic invasion prompted the mayor and

In 1916, the Industrial Commission of Ohio studied the problem of job selling in industrial establishments and found it to be relatively widespread. As this segment of the Commission's report suggests, immigrants were most affected by the practice.

In plants where the custom of paying foremen for jobs has been in existence for a number of years there has been a gradual but very decided advance in the amount paid the foreman with the general increase in the price of other necessaries of life. With some foremen a box of cigars or a bottle of whiskey was a sufficient 'present' to secure a job ten years ago; then the applicant learned that money was more acceptable and $5 was the usual fee for the unskilled laborer; the applicant next learned that $2 or $3 extra . . . would help him to get a job without waiting, or in other words, it would place him on the preferred list; then the price rose to even money, $10, and from that to $15; and at the times these investigations were begun the fee 'expected' was generally $15, $20, or $25 for a job paying approximately 25 cents per hour.

According to the information obtained, the payment of fees to foremen for furnishing jobs is a well established custom in a number of plants....The employes paying these fees are almost altogether non-English speaking foreigners, and those who profit from the fees are usually English speaking, or able to speak English, and quite generally of a different race from those who are exploited....The immigrant gains his first and his lasting impressions of America during the first few months of his residence . . . and these impressions are usually gained from the industrial establishment in which he secures work, and if there he finds graft and is exploited by his foreman, his lasting impression of America is that it is a land where the strong live by exploiting the weak.

several other city officials to buy rifles. Slavs, Italians, and Jews, all prominent among the new immigrants to Ohio by the 1890s, especially felt the bite of nativist sentiments.

Rampant nativism, especially of the anti-Catholic sort, faded with the return of prosperity by 1897-98, but recurrent cyclical downturns and the massive number of immigrants entering the country in the first decade of the twentieth century kept anti-immigrant sentiment alive. The composition of the immigrant population was now decisively tilted toward southern and eastern Europe. This fact, and the resurgence of both militancy and radicalism in parts of the working class, reinforced a brand of Americanism which encompassed several strains of nativist thought — anti-radicalism, anti-Catholicism, Anglo-Saxon supremacy — and affected the lives of immigrant workers in diverse ways.

Blacks, women, and immigrants shared specific kinds of experiences which bound them as groups within the working class despite the differences which separated them. Other workers were linked by work experiences. A "sense of kind" among coal miners — whatever their origin—flowed from exposure to hazardous underground conditions, for example, while in handicraft trades such as carpentry workers commonly manifested a pride of craft which rested on a sense of independence, highly-developed work skill, self-direction on the job, and a mutualistic ethical code. In the nineteenth

century workers in numerous jobs displayed such characteristics. Mechanization partially undercut this cluster of values and when employers tried to control their work skill knowledge such workers were further threatened. The struggle over skills control, indeed, would contour much of the history of trade unionism down to World War I.

A garment "homeworker" sews in his kitchen.

A scissors grinder in the exclusive Walnut Hill area of Cincinnati, ca. 1904.

Mary Gilson, who worked at the Clothcraft Shops in Cleveland for over a decade after 1913, offers some insight into patterns of immigration and the difficulties which sometimes arose because of the ethnic mix of the work force.

Applicants often applied because their friends and fellow countrymen worked in our plant. Jimmy Nolan was the first native of County Mayo we employed and in the course of a few years County Mayo had contributed over a hundred workers to us. I began to think that all the inhabitants of Bohemia had been tailors, for there was an endless stream of cousins and uncles and aunts of our Bohemian workers who said they had worked as tailors in the old country.

You had to exercise some discretion in the initial placing of the members of certain nationalities. An Irish girl who had been in the United States one month complained bitterly to me about being assigned to a work table with 'thim furriners.' The 'furriners' happened to be pleasant English-speaking Hungarian girls. The old feud between Czechs and Germans occasionally flared up, and woe be unto you if you placed a Sicilian girl under a Neapolitan foreman. But the factory demonstrated its functions as a melting pot when time was given for the melting. Evidently melting was welcomed in some quarters. 'My mother was a Pole and she married a Pole,' said a girl to me one day. 'Now she says we got enough Poles in the family and I should marry Antonio Augustino if I want to.'

The company store in Modoc, around 1912.

Harvey Firestone considered his twelve employees "a big family" in 1902. Eleven years later the "family" numbered 1,800 and Firestone admitted that he no longer even knew the names of his foremen.

Although the pattern of industrialization remained varied, by World War I the shape of Ohio's industrial world was quite different than it had been four decades earlier. Not only had the key cities changed, the work force grown in size and become more ethnically and racially diverse, but the factory itself had altered in important ways. Larger factories and work forces had been a commonplace development throughout industrial America after the Civil War. What occurred after 1880 built on these developments.

The growing concentration of manufacturing workers in capital-intensive industries was but one ingredient in the constantly-changing world of Ohio workers. In nearly every line of work, three related developments, each in process for some time, shaped workers' lives. The place of work itself altered, became larger. The application of machinery and new technologies to the productive process intensified, further subdividing skills. And, in industry after industry, managers wrestled with complex problems involved in handling enlarged work forces; their solutions restructured existing forms of supervison, the flow of work, and the autonomy of workers.

The increasing size of manufacturing establishments had long been underway. During the thirty years before 1920, modern mass-production techniques came to the fore. The average work force in iron and steel works and rolling mills leaped from two or three to 849 between 1890 and 1919, in rubber from ninety-four to 663, in glass from 109 to 249, in the boot and shoe industry from ninety-one to 235, in electrical machinery, apparatus and supplies from thirty-two to 141. These averages mask the enormous size of some individual plants. The work force at the Barney Car Works in Dayton increased from 900 to 2,004 between 1880 and 1887, for instance.

Within these large plants the application of new technologies proceeded rapidly. What happened in the glass, steel, and auto industries is illustrative. Glass production processes remained basically unchanged until the mid-1890s, when Michael J. Owens, the inventive genius of Toledo's Libbey Glass Company, developed a semi-automatic machine that could turn out glass chimneys and tumblers with an astonishing rapidity, certainty, and uniformity. By 1905, Owens had perfected the machine, which had already displaced various workers, making it automatic and thus eliminating the need for gatherers and pressers. Skilled glass blowers found work for a time in the electric light bulb industry, but there, too, technology undercut their acquired skills. Semi-automatic and then automatic machines appeared well before World War I, again developed by Owens and his associates. Not surprisingly, the proportion of Ohio workers who toiled in the glass industry declined over the years, the absolute numbers rising only from 6,435 in 1890 to nearly 11,000 in 1919.

The methods of smelting, refining, and rolling steel — which had largely supplanted wrought

A

B

C

D

In 1910 auto assembly at the Willys-Overland plant in Toledo took place in individual stalls. By 1913 the firm had a moving assembly line. Auto bodies were lowered from one floor to another by crane (A) for workers to guide onto a frame (B). Despite such automated techniques, manual methods reminiscent of carriage production had not yet been totally eliminated (C & D).

iron during the 1890s — had been developed earlier in Europe. American engineers, goaded by the economizing pressures of competition, tackled the problem of mechanizing every step from material handling, to the linking of iron smelting, Bessemer converters, and rolling mills, to continuous steel rolling. The quest to cut per-unit labor costs succeeded, both in boosting productivity by eliminating the need for large numbers of hand workers at each stage and, as in glass, in reducing dependency on highly-skilled workers. Machine tenders and semi-skilled operatives replaced iron puddlers and hand rollers in rolling mills, and while skilled blowers and melters in blast furnaces and converters did not fall to technological advances, there too the ranks of the semi-skilled expanded.

In the auto industry, the tendencies toward largeness, mechanized procedures, and reliance on semi-skilled machine operatives converged in a fashion which suggested the direction of the economy for the rest of the century. For, of all the industries which rose from the sprawl of a burgeoning population and expanding metropolitan areas, none better symbolized the new era of mass-production. Although Detroit ultimately became the leading auto center, in these years Ohio was an important producer of autos, auto bodies, and auto parts. By 1909, there were seventy-five establishments in the industry, a decade later 281. In that same period, the

number of auto workers in Ohio rose from 12,130 (sixteen percent of all U.S. workers in the industry) to 45,882 (thirteen percent). Cleveland alone accounted for thirty-two establishments and 6,408 workers in 1909, and eighty-five plants and 18,873 workers ten years later.

If the proportion of auto workers in Ohio fell somewhat by 1920, the industry in Ohio none the less epitomized the extent to which mechanization and sub-division of labor proceeded. No one understood this at the time better than R.R. Lutz, who studied the Cleveland industry in 1915. Automatic and semi-automatic machines, he noted, were used more extensively here than in other industries and in no other had "the subdivision of labor and simplification of machine processes" gone further:

The technical knowledge and skill formerly demanded of the workers have been transferred to the engineering and designing departments, where practically all the thinking, planning, and experimenting are done, and as a result the head work in the shop is limited to that involved in carrying out simple instructions. The fact that production is on a large scale, requiring thousands of pieces of the same shape and size, still further simplifies the operator's task. This system has enabled the manufacturers to produce one of the most intricate machines known to modern manufacturing with a working force composed in the main of semi-skilled labor.

Some assembling occupations required considerable skill, he added, but most did not. Some could be learned in a day or two, including the job "described by an assembler . . . who, when asked what kind of work he did, replied that he 'assembled nut No. 5.' "

The subdivision and systematization of labor were ongoing processes across the nineteenth century and not unique to the 1880-1920 era. The direction of management control, however, did alter. Initially managers gathered workers under a single roof and set the hours of labor. Gradually attention turned to supervision to ensure diligent, intense, uninterrupted work; rules prevented talking, smoking, drinking, and leaving the work-place. Setting production minimums was another form of control managers sought. The pattern varied and depended on how much discretion management had, given the technology involved, with production methods and handling workers.

In both situations, however, delegation of authority represented the normal form of management. Foremen managed production, watched quality control, kept track of costs, and handled all personnel relations except contract negotiations. They usually also had responsibility for what employees actually did, and thus controlled the crucial hiring, training, supervising and disciplining functions. In factories with hourly or daily rates, too, they could vary rates, and where piecework prevailed they set the rates. Abuses — such as the widespread practice of job selling — were commonplace and persisted into the twentieth century.

Poor working conditions, tight discipline, and the abuses and insecurity which spun out of the powerful foreman system generated considerable antagonism between workers and managers. Strikes and sporadic violence reflected this tension, but it surfaced as well in efforts by workers to assert control on the job by various means, restriction of output the most common. Concern with both kinds of conflict, with technological and economic change, and with the increasing "foreignness" of the work force, led during the 1880s and thereafter to a two-pronged movement which reshaped the world of factory workers.

Professional mechanical engineers and labor reformers together produced the managerial revolution, although they approached factory reform from different angles. Engineers focused on production problems. They regarded inefficiency and restricted output as results of unsystematic management and overreliance on foremen. Devising various systematic plans in areas such as accounting, production scheduling, and incentive wage rates, engineers gradually cut away the foreman's managerial and personnel functions. Some plants — such as the Barney Car Works in Dayton — began doing this in the 1880s. The most widely-known of the planners was Federick W. Taylor. Meshing numerous schemes for handling issues ranging from tool design and work flow to productivity and worker satisfaction, he presented his ideas as a system and did more to make "scientific" management a catchword of his era than any other single individual.

Although Cincinnati slaughterhouses had long been noted for their highly subdivided disassembly lines, by 1896 foremen also carried stop watches.

A Cleveland garment worker being timed by an efficiency expert.

Few companies initiated plans which incorporated all elements of scientific or systematic management plans. In any case, the most revolutionary aspect of these schemes — the absolute necessity for management to dictate to workers the precise manner in which work would be done — contained a fatal flaw. Engineers assumed that workers would respond to economic stimuli alone and willingly give up traditional production practices which had, even in large factories with powerful foremen, left considerable control over the work process to workers. Instead, workers often rejected incentive and premium pay plans because they violated existing shop practices and seemed merely clever variations of piece rate systems, which workers saw as devices to sweat them. When the Bickford Tool and Drill Company of Cincinnati tried to introduce such a system in 1899, for example, union machinists struck and their international union upheld rejection of the plan. During the next two decades thousands of other workers would engage in such "control" strikes which had at their heart resistance to management efforts to assume total control over precisely how employees performed each task.

Labor reformers had narrower concerns than engineers. They wanted to eliminate the roots of labor discontent, and often to uplift workers morally, and thus focused on programs to minimize the gap between employers and employees, improve morale, and in the process to increase productivity. Systematic 'welfare work,' as it came to be called, encompassed a variety of programs: clean rest rooms and bath facilities, dining rooms, libraries, athletics, safety programs, neighborhood clubs, even kindergardens.

Although scientific management schemes became increasingly common, most workers in

Samuel M. "Golden Rule" Jones, an enlightened employer and reform mayor of Toledo between 1897 and 1904, wrote a number of songs which reflected the kinds of views common among many labor reformers. This one is entitled "Industrial Freedom."

Sing aloud the tidings that the race will yet be free,
Man to man the wide world o'er will surely brothers be;
Right to work, the right to live, let every one agree,
God freely gives to the people.

Hurrah, hurrah, the truth shall make us free!
Hurrah, hurrah, for dear humanity!
Right to work let all proclaim till men united be,
In God's free gift to the people.

Tell the story over to the young and to the old,
Liberty for every man is better far than gold;
In the sweat of labor eat thy daily bread, we're told,
As God's free gift to the people.

Chorus:

Shorter days for those who toil will make more work for all,
For a shorter workday then we'll sound a trumpet call,
And thus the fruit of labor on all alike will fall,
As God's free gift to the people.

Chorus:

Let us grant to every man the right to have a share
In the things that God has made as free as sun and air;
Let us have free land for all, then free work everywhere
God's gift will be to the people.

Chorus:

With justice done to every one then happy shall we be;
Poverty will disappear, the prisoners will be free;
The right to work, the right to live, the love of liberty—
All God's best gifts to the people.

In March, 1882, workers on both sides of the Ohio River in the industrial belt around Wheeling, West Virginia formed the Ohio Valley Trades and Labor Assembly. Although the Ohio locals withdrew and organized a separate central labor union in 1897, the preamble to the Assembly's revised constitution of 1894 mirrors attitudes widespread among organized workers at the time.

Aggregated capital has combined to govern the industrial interests of the country, to the detriment of the producing classes, and through machinery, concentration of capital, the power of corporations and corruption of our legislatures are forging a chain, link by link, which . . . will bind and intensify the oppression we suffer to-day.

The history of wage workers . . . is but the history of constant struggles and misery, engendered by ignorance, greed and indifference. The past history of trade unions proves that small organizations . . . have accomplished great good; but the results of their efforts have not been of that lasting character which a thorough unification of all the different branches of . . . workers is bound to secure . . . . We deem it to be our right and imperative duty to follow the examples set and practiced by capitalists to organize and unite in one common interest all labor organizations, without regard to nationality, sex, color or creed, for mutual protection against the unjust demands of capital, and by concerted action to so shape the industrial interests of the country that the laboring classes . . . shall receive their just reward and proper and manly treatment from their employers; to adopt such measures and disseminate such principles among the wage earners that a wrong to one . . . shall be the concern and interest of all . . . and by organization, agitation and education, to advance the social, moral and financial status of the toiler.

the evolving mass-production sector of the economy were not affected by them. The bulk of such workers were semi-skilled machine runners who had no artisanal skills to lose. Corporate welfare plans did bear a special relevance to the large numbers of immigrants in these positions, for they included language classes and other efforts aimed at breaking down the array of customs and values which management regarded as standing in the way of carrying out simple industrial tasks.

The common feature of the mass-production work experience, whatever the workers' background, was performing specific tasks, ones increasingly defined by job control engineers and supervised by watchful inspectors. At the Goodyear Rubber plant in Akron, where only one in three of the 20,000 employees were foreign-born, there was one inspector for every ten workers. Where production work was done on a piece rate basis, the result was a furious pace. Even where factory workers were paid a flat rate pegged to what common labor received in the area, the pace could be intense, for the power of foremen in many plants remained supreme.

Regardless of the industry in which they toiled, then, Ohio workers in manufacturing came to share certain similarities in their jobs. Not until the 1930s would that commonality form a sufficiently strong base for trade unionism in the mass-production industries. Prior to that time, however, these shared experiences helped to define one of the numerous lines which criss-crossed and shaped the working class.

Precisely how workers responded to the conditions they confronted in this era of rapid change and increasing complexity hinged on many things. Economic cycles — especially downturns — and the presence or absence of labor shortages provided basic parameters molding workers' behavior, but within these limits a host of other considerations figured: the background and expectations of the workers, the precise situations to be dealt with, the kind of grievance involved, the extent of employer power, and such things as "traditions" among particular groups of workers or in specific localities. In a general sense, the ways in which workers approached solutions to the problems in their lives after 1886 displayed direct links to the patterns evident earlier. Individuals acquiesced, rebelled, or coped as best they could, groups spontaneously expressed their unrest in various ways, and workers also continued both to refine the economic institutions they had been creating and to explore the political avenues open to them. Yet as always is the case, as conditions alter so do responses.

The conditions workers confronted generated a host of grievances. Irregular employment, poor wages, heavy, hot, or hazardous work, long hours, and repressive foremen were only the most prominent of the complaints workers had. And while they often grumbled, most workers either accepted their lot or expressed their discontent in essentially individualistic ways which did not overtly threaten their employers. The kinds of expectations they had accounted for much of this, as did the decidedly hostile environment shaped by employers, government, and the press in those places where a majority of industrial workers toiled— the major cities. In the early part of the period industrial workers were in a minority, and in a nation where individualistic and rural values still held sway. Workers hopeful of moving upward, whether out of the working class altogether or to a higher level within it, may have felt inhibited from expressing their discontent, viewed it as a temporary matter, or explicitly identified with the values of their employers. Immigrants who anticipated returning to their homelands after several years of intense labor, on the other hand, ruled out noticeable or persistent protest because it seemed to them to be an obstacle to their goal.

Fear also held protest in check, and with good reason. The ups and downs of the economy and the irregularities of the work year made insecurity a common feature in the lives of most workers. From the 1880s on, economic power became more concentrated, moreover, and thus the ability of employers to resist unionization intensified. Coal miners in company towns had long been subject to pressures such as discharge from their company-owned homes if they proved uncooperative. As corporations assumed more prominent roles and employed greater proportions of the industrial work force, more and more workers came face to face with similar sorts of pressures, all of which aimed to undercut the willingness to organize by playing on fears of being fired. In the late nineteenth century these pressures were chiefly forceful and openly coercive — yellow dog contracts which made jobs contingent upon promises not to join a union; the use of blacklists to keep track of agitators and disgruntled workers; the presence of paid spies within the work force; the brutality of foremen; the willingness to lock-out employees who expressed discontent; the use of hired thugs, state militia, and federal troops in strike situations.

Coercive tactics did not disappear in the twentieth century. If anything, they became more sophisticated. Specialty firms such as Corporations Auxiliary of Cleveland were hired to place informants in the work force, and by 1908 the federal government had entered the field of domestic surveillance with the creation of the Bureau of Investigation, precursor of the FBI. In addition, a number of firms used welfare work to bind workers to them more closely and so undercut the willingness to strike. These programs did not explicitly foster fear, but they did seek to mold values antithetical to unionization and radicalism.

By 1920 industrial workers were no longer a minority in the work force, organized protest was far more widespread, and many immigrants had given up the dream of returning home because of the war. Despite this change in circumstances, most workers remained outside unions and either apolitical or tied to the major parties. They expressed their discontent in other ways, however.

Absenteeism was one form individual workers used to show their discontent, assert their autonomy, or act out cultural traditions brought with them from another country. As factory production assumed a larger and larger share of all manufacturing jobs, absenteeism persisted as a problem, from the perspective of management, in some cases because immigrant workers retained traditional holidays and other "premodern" ways, in others because economic conditions instilled irregular work habits even as employers tried to create time-conscious workers. Manufacturers had long imposed fines on factory workers who voluntarily absented themselves from the job, or who arrived late, and such fines remained a persistent feature of industrial life throughout the era before firms devised modern personnel relations departments in the World War I era. Absentee rates varied widely, but by 1920, factory experts were happy if only six percent of all workers were absent on a given day.

An even more common way in which workers expressed discontent, one not really recognized as such by most employers until the World War I era, was simply to quit their jobs. Skilled workers in the nineteenth century were a highly transient lot, carpenters being only one group noted for "tramping" from job to job. The seasonal rhythms of factory production only partially explained why factory workers also moved about at an astonishing rate. Typically one-third of all factory workers in the early twentieth century stayed on a single job less

THE FEDERATED TRADES.

OPENING OF THE SIXTH CONGRESS.

The Relations of the Unions with the Knights of Labor — Preparing to Amalgamate with the Labor Union Conference.

The sixth annual Congress of the Federation of Organized Trades and Labor Unions of the United States and Canada was called to order by President Gompers in Druid's hall, South Fourth street, at noon yesterday. D. P. Boyer, chief organizer of the International Typographical union, introduced Grafton Pearce of this city who, as the representative of the Columbus Trades assembly, delivered an excellent address of welcome, in which he ably discussed the objects to be attained, urged harmony, deliberation, freedom from politics and the wisest course of procedure.

President Gompers returned the thanks of the congress for the cordial welcome, referred to the mistakes of organized labor in the past, the good it had done and the purposes for the future. He discussed the eight-hour law, the struggles of the past year, and urged harmony in all meetings and co operations.

than one year, and the majority did so for under three years, a fact which may have muted unrest in some instances by siphoning off people who otherwise might have formed a core of union activists. Not all of those who left quit, of course, yet the majority did so, with dissatisfaction with wages and having gotten a better job being the reasons most often cited. Generally it was the youngest, least skilled, and most recently hired who chose this route. Where work was especially dirty, heavy, hot, or low paid, turnover rates were highest. One Cleveland foundry in the World War I era, for instance, found that of 2,273 men who left, two in every three had been there less than thirty days and that fully ninety percent had worked there less than four months.

The *Ohio State Journal* of December 8, 1886 notes the opening of the convention which led to the formation of the A.F.L.

At times perceived injustices produced collective action rather than individual responses. Depressions and downturns in the economy closed tighter the safety valve of transiency and hard times, repeated wage cuts, and various indignities could ignite workers, provoking sometimes violent outbursts of spontaneous activity which alarmed even the most sympathetic middle-class supporters of labor. These spontaneous expressions of outrage were sometimes linked to union drives for recognition, shorter hours, or improved wages, but that was not always the case. In a number of situations workers joined together, without the aid of union organizers or even of a local union, to forge their own transient links of solidarity.

Collective but unorganized activity cannot be easily documented for there are few direct references to it by workers and press reports seldom provide an accurate guide to what happened. A sense of the dimensions of rank and file self-activation may be suggested by the statistics on the proportion of strikes not ordered by labor organizations. In Ohio between 1881 and 1905, thirty-eight percent of all strikes were of this sort, but over time that proportion fell steadily—one index of the growing importance of labor organizations. Whatever the dimensions of rank and file self-activation, its most important expressions came in the conscious efforts to build unions. These both shaped public perceptions of "the labor question" and had the most lasting impact (see Table 3L).

In retrospect, 1886 marked a turning point in the history of the labor movement, though not in the sense that many of those at the time regarded it. The magnitude of labor activity was not in doubt, for there were more strikes that year than ever before in American history—1,572 involving 610,000 workers. In Ohio strikes numbered eighty-three (only thirty-five of them ordered by unions) and they involved 16,276 workers. Foremost among those who struck were factory artisans, the specialized workers created by the intensified mechanization and further subdivision of labor which characterized the age. For leadership they turned to the Knights of Labor.

The focal point of organizing in 1886 was a May 1 strike for a universal eight-hour working day, an issue which reflected the overlapping of economic and political routes workers used to achieve their goals. Although the weak Federation of Organized Trades and Labor Unions had originally shaped the campaign, Knights of Labor chieftain Terence Powderly had reluctantly agreed with the tactic. At the last moment, however, he secretly ordered Knights not to participate. Nonetheless, 340,000 workers turned out nationwide. In Cincinnati alone nearly 18,000 men and women, almost twenty percent of the city's working population, struck.

The strike did not achieve its desired goals, despite such massive support, but it did dramatize the changing structure of America's work force, intensify the tension between traditional craft unions and the rapidly expanding Knights, and expose some of the weaknesses of that organization. Unorganized workers, enthralled by various Knights of Labor victories during the past two years, viewed the strike as a way that they, too, could taste the fruits of victory. As journalist Oscar Ameringer, a Cincinnati participant in the strike, recalled later: "the cause of less work and more pay" had captured the imagination of his fellow workers at the time.

Powderly's last-minute opposition to the strike was just the sort of behavior which alienated the independent national unions, leaders of the Federation of Organized Trades and Labor Unions, and the trades element within the Knights. Tension had been mounting before the May 1 strike, but it was during May that the groundwork was laid for the emergence later that year of an organizational challenge to the Knights. When the General Assembly of the Knights met in Cleveland on May 25, a trade union group presented a "treaty" designed to force the organization to stop competing with the craft unions. No solutions appeared when the Knights met that fall, so the disgruntled trades element within the Knights called for a December 8 meeting in Columbus to create "an American Federation of Labor or Alliance of all National and International Trade Unions." At this point Samuel Gompers of the independent Federation of Organized Trades and Labor Unions, many of whose affiliates had never been in the Knights or else had withdrawn from it, moved that organization's meeting from St. Louis to the Ohio capitol city. When further efforts to reconcile differences with the Knights failed, the two trades groups merged on

Poster announces a Springfield trade union meeting, 1893.

LABOR!

Trades Assembly and Carpenters' Union

Have United in Securing

R. C.

LONGSDON

Of St. Louis, who will discuss

The Merits and Value of Trade Unions

—AT THE—

CITY HALL,

THURSDAY EV'G, AUG. 10

All Labor Organizations are requested to meet at Trades Assembly Hall at 7 o'clock for the purpose of being escorted to the City Hall by

BIG SIX BAND.

☞ Everybody Invited. Admission Free.

Barrett Publishing Co.

December 10, 1886, to create the American Federation of Labor.

The new organization, with cigar maker Gompers at its head, had a different conception of organization than did the Knights. The Knights had an inclusive philosophy grounded in a belief in the common interests of all producers—"an injury to one is an injury to all" was their slogan. They thus accepted into their ranks all who did "productive" work, excluding only lawyers, stockbrokers, saloon keepers, and gamblers. The basic organizational unit was the mixed local assembly: all workers in a given locale were members. There were also local assemblies which organized only one craft, the most prominent ones in Ohio being among glass blowers, coal miners, and shoe workers.

The AFL asserted the notion of exclusive jurisdiction—one trade union per craft—rather than the industrial model proposed by the Knights. The philosophical base for this and other components of what came to be called "business" or "pure and simple" unionism was an amalgam of Marxist ideology and commitment, British and German trade union pragmatism, with injections of Knights of Labor fervor. The leadership of the AFL had few illusions about the direction of the economy. They neither expected a return to a working-world of small shops nor assumed that most workers would rise out of the working class to become farmers or entrepreneurs. They stressed the here and now.

Commitment to limited goals such as improved wages and working conditions did not mean that AFL unions triumphed immediately or that the new labor center rapidly displaced the KOL. Not all trades left the Knights. The four window glass trades—gatherers, blowers, flatteners, and cutters — had combined into Local Assembly 300 of the Knights between the mid-1870s and early 1880s, for instance, and there they remained, despite periodic rivalries and tensions, until the early twentieth century. During the 1890s the flatteners and cutters did form trade unions and attempt to organize others of those crafts into their unions, but for the moment they retained their affiliation with the Knights. So did a number of other unions, the mine workers and the brewery workers among them.

It made sense to do that, for it had been the Knights which had grown so dramatically between 1884 and 1886. And that growth did not stop everywhere even after a bomb thrown by an unknown person at a labor rally in Chicago's Haymarket Square killed several police and generated massive public opposition. Gradually, however, Powderly's aversion to strikes and his unwillingness to support those on the picket line, led to an erosion in the strength of the Knights. Among the crucial incidents which soured trade unionists was one involving iron workers at Mingo Junction, Ohio. Although loyal to the Order, when the District Assembly, in early 1887, refused to sanction a strike, or even understand the need for it, the men turned to the Amalgamated Association of Iron, Steel and Tin Workers. Such conflicts chipped away at the KOL's strength. The organization persisted through the depression of 1893-97, but increasingly as a political ally of the Populist and other third parties. By then the majority of unionized workers had given up on the Knights as a labor organization, if not on all of its visions of a future commonwealth.

It was the depression of 1893-97, one of the most severe in the nation's history, which confirmed the direction of the labor movement. The KOL shied away from economic confrontations. Few trade unions made collective bargaining gains until the economy recovered, but at least the national unions survived—a feat not often accomplished in previous depressions— and in a number of locales so did the locals (see Table 3M).

FIRST NATIONAL CONVENTION UNITED MINE WORKERS OF AMERICA
JANUARY 22, 1890, COLUMBUS, OHIO

The UMW's 1898 strike included a quest for the eight-hour day. That issue had long served as a focal point for union organizing. This song, set to the tune of "The Lea Rig," appeared in the *United Mine Workers' Journal* and was written by a miner named Scott from Wellston, Ohio.

HAIL TO THE EIGHT-HOUR DAY

Ye miner lads, come gather round,
And listen to my roundelay;
Ye lads who labor underground,
Where never shines the light of day,
We fought and won a gallant fight,
Threw our enslaving chains away;
United labor's peerless might,
Brought shorter hours and longer day.

Then make the welkin loud resound,
Triumphant came we from the fray;
Unfurl our flag, let mirth abound,
And joyfully hail the eight-hour day.

From Eastern hill to Western plain,
United labor's signal ran,
From sunny South to northern Maine,
Came forth the brotherhood of man.
Mark well the patriotic tide.
Can nobler, braver hearts be found
Than those who crushed the tyrant's pride—
The lads who labor underground

Chorus:

Ye labor friends from every craft,
Who helped the miners' cause along,
With grateful hearts we fondly waft
Returning thanks in simple song.
Oh, soon may reason's sway enfold
The homes of labor far and near;
For right we fought and will uphold
Our rights with every coming year.

Chorus:

No Eolian harp on Grecian isle,
Awoke of old such grand refrain;
In bygone age no minstrel wile
Attuned the lyre to sweeter strain.
From mountain peak to sheltered vale,
Let maid and miner lad be gay,
Proclaim with joy o'er hill and dale,
United labor gained the day.

One of the most important unions in Ohio throughout this period was the United Mine Workers of America. Founded in Columbus in 1890, it merged the National Progressive Union and National Trades Assembly Number 135 of the Knights of Labor. The two had bargained jointly in the Central Competitive Field between 1887 and 1889 and shared an emphasis on strong district and state organizations, a preference— despite an increasing willingness to strike—for arbitration and conciliation, and a commitment to political and legislative action to secure gains for mine workers. These commonalities led directly to the merger of 1890.

Fragile at the outset—it had but 17,000 dues-paying members among the nearly 200,000 bi-tuminous coal miners — the UMW eventually proved to be an organization with which to be reckoned. Unlike most other AFL unions, the UMW from the first adopted an inclusive or industrial structure; it represented all men in and around the mines. The conditions and grievances unique to coal mining made it essential for coal miners to do this to maximize their bargaining power. Equally important, the union's influence extended beyond its membership. When the president, John McBride of Massillon, called a national strike for April 21, 1894, the UMW had only 13,000 members. And yet fully 160,000 miners struck. In Ohio eighty-three percent of 21,731 miners at 178 mines joined in the call for a new scale; in the Hocking Valley nearly all 12,000 miners turned out.

Wage cuts as high as thirty percent sparked sporadic violence, most of it related to attempts to block the shipment of non-union West Virginia coal through the mining districts. Glouster miners achieved that aim, but, because of failures elsewhere, by mid-June national leaders ordered the strike ended and negotiated a compromise settlement. The adopted scale was lower than hoped for and that led some Ohio miners to hold out longer. Massillon area miners, who had begun their strike in February, held out until early October, 225 days in all.

But ultimately it was to no avail. In the midst of the depression few employers could honor even the compromise contract and the young union, financially drained from its long struggle, found itself unable to police the agreements. To compound this problem the mechanization begun in the 1880s intensified, creating a further surplus of labor at a time of unprecedented unemployment. By 1898 Ohio had 579 undercutting machines, 451 of them in the crucial Hocking Valley. Six years earlier there had been only 129 machines in use in Ohio. Because of their heavy capital investment in machinery, Hocking Valley operators increased their production despite the depression, cutting sharply into the traditional work styles of coal miners. As late as 1889, eighty-five percent of Ohio's coal miners worked in the traditional fashion with a pick at the coal face. Generally they labored with a paid assistant in a separate "room." By the mid-1890s this mode of production was on the way out. By 1896 machine runners made up thirty-eight percent of the labor force in Ohio's coal fields but produced fully fifty-three percent of its coal.

The transformation of the work force was but one part of the story of coal mining in Ohio during the nineties. Perhaps no other single group of workers were so adversely affected by the depression. Average annual earnings plummeted as the number of days fell and employers instituted cuts which ultimately dropped tonnage rates from 79 to 45 cents. By 1895, poverty and suffering were widespread in the Hocking Valley and adjoining coal districts.

A strike in 1897 marked a turning point for the union. Nationwide, membership had fallen to barely 10,000 and the decline was severe in Ohio, where Irish-born Michael Ratchford presided. Yet loyalty to unionism persisted and when the strike began on July 4 the turnout, again, was high. A long battle, the strike involved considerable suffering among Ohio miners. Fortunately, the state government provided relief to the striking miners, as did numerous communities.

Contract negotiations covering Pennsylvania, Indiana, and Illinois, as well as Ohio, began in August, but it was not until January of 1898 that an interstate agreement went into effect. Besides the eight-hour day, it provided wage scales which reflected the different mining conditions in each state. A sign of things to come, union membership, which had sagged sharply after 1894, surged upward. In Ohio the number of union miners doubled between 1898 and 1900.

The introduction of mechanization and electricity transformed the nature of mining in Ohio by the late 1890s. Whether in hauling coal from the face or raising cars to the tipple, Ohio's most productive mines replaced the mules of former years with electric power.

The individualism so characteristic among Ohio potters is evident in this 1894 poem of the National Brotherhood of Operative Potters. Evident too is the influence of British trade unionists' interest in arbitration and the powerful pride of craft which distinguished workers in the skilled trades.

TO ONE AND ALL

There is trouble in the atmosphere
the strike is in full play.
Rumors are rife upon the streets,
Rumors by night and day.

Don't put your trust in them, my lads,
But use your mother wit;
Conform at all times to the law,
Be with your brethren knit.

In unity is strength, my lads
Union of hearts and hand.
Be sure you're right, then go ahead,
From home and native land.

Yes, join the Potter's Brotherhood,
And battle for the right.
True men will back you up, my lads
And in you take delight.

Don't dare to be oppressors men;
Deal ever in fair play.
The employer has his rights, my lads
You will not say me 'nay.'

And if we want on middle ground,
And each his side will state,
Then act the part of honest men,
And aim to arbitrate.

Let each one make concessions — don't
Seek for petty flaws,
But aim to set the wheels awhirl,
The wheels of labor's cause.

And thus bring peace and plenty,
No longer need to roam,
But, thank our God, bring happiness
To every hearth and home.

The UMW story was not unique. In trade after trade, the nineties witnessed a high level of strike activity and of union building. The number of strikes peaked in 1894 and declined after that until prosperity returned in 1897 and 1898. As in coal, trade union membership rose substantially. In 1898 it stood at 37,941. Two years later 79,884 Ohio workers were union members, an increase of fifty-four percent. The pace of unionization picked up as well. Of the 956 locals in existence in Ohio in 1900, only forty had been organized before 1880 and 126 during the eighties. Fully 710 had been organized in the nineties, 300 of them in 1900 alone.

The expansion of trade unions came between 1897 and 1904. A combination of factors—adverse Supreme Court rulings, concerted and collective employer opposition to unions, increased immigration, and intensified mechanization — stalled the drive to unionize. Ironically, this coincided with the outburst of reform known as Progressivism. Between 1904 and World War I most unions expanded little, made few gains, lapsed into what secure niches of the economy they could find. As the mass-production sector of the economy expanded, the proportion of trade unionists in manufacturing declined.

Another gauge of union strength was the renewal of central labor unions. During the late 1880s centrals were organized in Cincinnati and Toledo, but the depression short-circuited this process elsewhere until the late nineties. Youngstown unions organized a city central in 1899, for example, and it was not until 1902 that unions in Cleveland did so.

Union-building required tenacity. In the documents which follow some of the problems common in early twentieth-century organizing are apparent. Selected from the reports of Thomas Rumsey, the business agent of the Toledo Central Labor Union, they reflect an attempt in 1907 to unionize semi-skilled workers at the Pope Motor Company. Under AFL policy such workers were to be organized first into a federal local, one directly affiliated with AFL headquarters rather than a particular craft union.

April 4, 1907. "With B.A. David of the machinists held two meetings with the men at the Pope plant who were not eligible to any organization. Vice President Keegan addressed them and advised them to get together and form an organization. After considerable discussion it was advised that they apply for a Charter from the A.F. of L. to be known as the Federal Labor Union. This was unanimously accepted by the men and enough names and money for charter was received and the application sent to the A.F. of L. and expect to form a permanent organization next week.

May 2, 1907. "Attended two meetings of the Federal Labor Union, and with the assistance of B.A. David have succeeded in getting them going in good shape, have elected a good staff of officers and delegates to CLU."

June 13, 1907. Having attended a meeting of the Federal Labor Union, Rumsey noted that there was a good crowd and that the members were "very enthusiastic. New members are being initiated every meeting."

October 17, 1907. "Attended meeting of the Federal Labor Union and was surprised to be informed that unless they received the help promised them at the time of organizing they would have to disband, the officers claimed this on account of the dullness in trade and another union in the Machinists taking in members that rightfully belonged to them, that they did not see how they could make any headway. I finally got them to at least hold together till their next meeting and in the meantime to get busy themselves, that they could not expect others to do the work that belonged to them."

In union after union, the years after 1886 also witnessed substantial regularization of trade union practices. Ohio workers, like those elsewhere, had long been reluctant to turn over much authority to elected or appointed officials. It was only during the 'eighties and 'nineties that paid officials became a common feature in unions. By the turn of the century, as union collective bargaining agreements mushroomed in number, trade union bureaucracies became ever larger. Unions would not for years duplicate the extensive professionalization and clericalization of staff which occurred in manufacturing. But, by 1900, election or appointment to union office — whether at the local, state or national level — began to become a recognized path of upward mobility within the working class.

Union-building involved creation of formal structures, work rules, and the gradual emergence of an increasingly professionalized group of labor leaders. Yet trade unions remained more than a business—at a time when the term "business unionism" first came into being. While top leaders often emulated Gompers in his quest for respectability in the eyes of the public and business world, others, generally at lower and often unpaid levels, regarded trade unionism as a cause, a mission. It was this evangelical spirit which had infused so many rank and filers in the KOL and which carried on into the next generation of workers.

A union newspaper which described Richard L. Davis—a Negro mine organizer and member of the Ohio and national UMW executive boards from Rendville—as a man with a special gift for preaching "the gospel of trade unions" touched on this strain so crucial in the union movement, one which paralleled the development of a professional cadre of trade union officials. For Davis and many others, unions served as a kind of "secular church," an institution which promised ultimate redemption. Like missionaries, such men and women dedicated their lives to the union cause and their vision of truly democratic unions. Individuals such as Davis formed the backbone of local organization; they were the keys to animating workers in a given locale.

While professional organizers might provide guidance, inspiration, spark enthusiasm, local activists bore the brunt of the day-to-day work it took to build unions. Two strikes, different in nature, illustrate something of this process and reveal as well the kinds of obstacles which confronted those who tried to erect trade unions.

The first strike took place in 1901 at Dayton's National Cash Register Company. The focal point of the controversy was brass foundry foreman James McTaggart. An overbearing, abusive man known as a "driver," he so alienated the proud molders that they unionized in 1897. McTaggart fired the union leaders, forced others to quit, and by intimidating the rest caused the small union to fold. Two years later the increased work pace and reduced piece rates led twenty-one of the thirty-three brass foundry molders (most of them "new" men) to

unite once more, inspired in part by other organizing in city plants. McTaggart fired several men but failed to crush the union spirit. The molders joined the Metal Polishers and, after a brief strike in early 1900, won a union shop and reinstatement of the discharged men. Patterson, hopeful that unions would eliminate similar grievances and production delays among other workers, then recognized over twenty other unions. Dayton's anti-union business community was shocked, for NCR suddenly had become the most important organized company in Ohio.

Patterson's desires for labor peace dimmed as newly-organized workers probed the limits of their power, but it was McTaggart who again provoked the controversy which profoundly reshaped labor-management relations at NCR. The man refused to accept the 1900 contract, badgered the molders, slashed piece rates, added extra hours in the summer, and in early 1901 discharged four union men. When Patterson upheld this action, the molders struck and, in sympathy, so did the metal polishers. Faced by disruptions in key departments and thoroughly exasperated with unions, Patterson closed the plant, locking out 2,300 production workers.

Patterson used several tactics to cut the strength of the strikers. He played on fears about jobs and on divisions among the various unions. Rumors spread that the plant might move and these, as well as threats of an open shop, immobilized the Metal Mechanics, the largest non-striking union. AFL president Gompers sought a compromise, but Patterson, now a member of the rabidly open shop National Metal Trades Association, refused to rehire the discharged molders and the molders

NCR machinists making patterns for various parts, ca. 1900.

NCR's final assembly room, 1900. Note the highly individualized styles of the various cash registers.

Between February 28 and March 1, 1913, a committee of Ohio senators, headed by William Green, took over 3,500 pages of testimony from dozens of rubber company workers and their employers. The following excerpts illuminate some of the conflicting points of view evident throughout the strike.

Harvey Firestone, like other employers, insisted that he was open to hearing complaints:

We want them to come [in with grievances]. . . . Up until last October I was acting superintendent. I was through the factory almost every day; and any complaints could be brought to me. I think your record rather speaks more than you can tell about yourself. That it is perfectly free for any man to come to me, don't make any difference what position he occupies; and we always . . . were looking to the human side, and trying to make our men feel a part of that organization. We are handling expensive material, and we want them interested; and we used every effort; and I believe that we have as loyal and as fair a body of men as you can find in any factory. . . .

H.F. Pollock, a Firestone rubber worker, disagreed and pointed to a variety of problems, among them the speed-up, the operation of the piece-rate system, and the difficulty with expressing grievances. The speed-up started, he explained, when the company sent in "some fellow with a stop watch."

He will go into the foreman and ask for the best man in the room, the fastest man in the room. . . . Maybe there is not another man . . . that can work like him, one of these greedy fellows working as fast as he can work; stand there with a stop watch and get the time it takes him to make that article . . . and they set the price of all the rest of the room according to him. There is how they speed you up. . . . It is like this, that speed up system, they get such a bonus on, premium as they call it, get a person going, get all the men going at a good fair rate, get a fair stock of goods ahead, and then they are ready for a slash. They don't care who quits or not. They advertise all over the world for help. They don't need it. Help comes here to town, standing around possibly from fifty to a hundred at these employment offices. If you don't do just what they want you to do, or the way they want it done, they go to the employment offices, and hire a couple of other men.

The senate committee did not lambast the employers in Akron, but among the principal findings was an observation which said much about the different perceptions of the period:

The most striking feature . . . was that the employes refrained because of fear of discharge to submit grievances for adjustment to the foreman or superintendent. The employers testified that they never knew of the existence of complaints such as shown in the evidence, and supposed that they had a contented body of workers in their employ.

refused any settlement which did not include that.

By mid-June most NCR employees lost patience with the molders and on June 19 the Metal Mechanics and non-union workers returned to work. Only 300 molders, polishers, machinists and carpenters remained on strike. NCR conceded Machinists the nine-hour day, refused any concessions to the molders and then affirmed that henceforth NCR would be an open shop plant. On July 2, half of the striking molders resumed work, as non-union men. New employees filled the remaining positions.

The strike broken, Patterson refined his management system. He sent McTaggart on "vacation," revised his welfare program, and established a Labor Department, the first modern personnel department in American industry. Patterson intended the new unit to win worker participation without the trouble of unions. By reducing the power of foremen, keeping a careful record of workers' sympathies, and weeding out potential activists NCR in time remolded the loyalties of its employees. It was a lesson other employers did not miss; by World War I the personnel management movement was spreading rapidly.

The 1901 NCR strike was not unique. Shop-floor conflicts were commonplace and often key factors in precipitating larger confrontations. In no place was this more evident than Akron, the booming center of the U.S. rubber industry, where in 1913 fully 22,500 men and women toiled in rubber factories. Despite the good intentions of most employers, the presence of all-powerful foremen in most plants meant regular shop-floor conflicts. Yet neither these clashes nor other grievances automatically provided fertile ground for collective action. Unions had made little progress, for neither native-born workers, predominantly from West Virginia, Kentucky, and Tennessee, nor foreign-born English, Serbian, Italian, or Hungarian workers would risk membership. Given the transiency of the labor force and the policies of the rubber companies, that is not surprising.

Akron's rubber barons had no intention of letting unions get a foothold in their industry. When women in the Goodrich speciality department and bicycle tire makers at the India Rubber company walked out in 1899, they were replaced immediately. Isolated walkouts at Goodyear in 1900 were also unsuccessful. And two years later Goodyear and Diamond fired all who dared join the International Association of Metal and Rubber Workers. That union could not win reinstatement, nor could its successor, the short-lived Amalgamated Rubber Workers' Union of North America. Akron manufacturers countered union sentiment by raising wages, installing welfare plans, and creating an anti-union open-shop organization, the Akron Employers' Association. The AEA coordinated anti-union activity and hired spies from Corporations Auxiliary of Cleveland. These moves did not halt all worker resistance, but when tire builders in 1908 and 1911 walked out over wage issues the companies involved just hired new men.

Grievances did not disappear. Foremen remained arbitrary, working conditions poor, annual earnings lower than those of comparable workers elsewhere, benzine fumes ever present, and fines for "spoiled rubber" a persistent problem. By 1913 a new grievance emerged—mechanization and the speed-up. The key development was the introduction at Firestone of a tire-building machine which permitted the displacement of the highly-skilled hand tire builders by numerous machine runners who constructed tire carcasses which other workers cured and finished.

This situation triggered the great Akron rubber strike of 1913. With efficiency experts now in place and piece rates reduced, tire builders—no matter how fast they worked—found they could not earn what had been customary. When Firestone announced a thirty-five percent cut in the rate for tire finishers in early February, a shop delegation won a compromise agreement which most tire finishers refused. About twenty-five finishers stayed out in protest on the 14th, but most continued working. When Firestone fired those who had stayed out, this triggered a walkout of some 300 more workers. Gradually the strike spread outward from the tire department, ultimately engulfing all rubber plants in the city. At its peak, strikers numbered some 15,000 in Akron and close to a thousand in Cleveland. "The men in town was all ready to come out," one striker explained to an Ohio Senate investigating committee. "All that was necessary was a starter."

The spontaneously-kindled walkout quickly gathered strength with the assistance of the era's most militant, innovative, and colorful labor organization—the Industrial Workers of the World. Founded in 1905 by an assortment of socialists, anarchists, revolutionaries, and disgruntled trade unionists, the IWW represented the radical strand of the American labor movement. Though the "Wobblies," as members proudly dubbed themselves, never formulated a monolithic philosophy, they were guided by a set of specific animosities and revolutionary visions which could be loosely categorized under the heading of "syndicalism." Outraged by the existing distribution of wealth and power in American society, Wobblies advocated the abolition of the capitalist system. Militarism was denounced as a brutal capitalist ploy to increase profits at the expense of workers' lives. They vehemently opposed the conservative "business unionism" of the AFL, and believed that, since mechanization and technological advancements were rapidly diluting the craftsmen's skills, workers should be organized into integrated industrial unions rather than by individual trade. Membership was open to any wage-earner, regardless of occupation, skill-level, race, nationality, or sex. Their ultimate goal was to replace capitalist society with a new utopian order (the Cooperative Commonwealth) consisting of "One Big Industrial Union" controlled by labor. In order to achieve that class-conscious revolutionary aim, as well as to struggle for the workers' immediate needs, Wobblies espoused direct action at the point of production and the general strike as their principal weapons. They rejected contracts with employers, viewing them as impediments to labor's right to strike whenever necessary. Furthermore, the IWW set extremely low initiation fees and dues, and refused to create a well-defined organizational structure for fear of spawning a rigid union bureaucracy which would become isolated from the workers. At its peak in 1912, total paid-up membership probably did not exceed eighteen thousand. Despite repeated accusations by businessmen, politicians, and AFL leaders that the IWW encouraged violence and industrial sabotage, members were never convicted of any overt personal assault or destruction of property. Wobblies were extremely fond of threatening imminent revolution and making blistering condemnations of any and all opponents in voluminous speeches, songs, and poems. But, beneath the rhetoric and propaganda, their use of "sabotage" consisted exclusively of work slowdowns and the novel "sitdown strike"—the first in American history having been staged by the IWW at the General Electric Company plant in Schenectady, New York in 1906. Striking fear in the nation's establishment with their defiance, militancy, and revolutionary zeal, the Wobblies were as much a social movement as a labor union, spreading among migratory workers, tradesmen, and factory hands, both across the U.S. and abroad.

Wobblies had established Rubber Workers' Industrial Union 470 in Akron in 1912, but had been able to recruit only 150 members prior to the 1913 strike. One week later, the IWW local claimed to have signed up more than half of the city's twenty thousand rubber workers. The organization willingly worked with recent im-

The transformation of tire building from manual methods (left) to semi-automatic machine processes (below) sparked discontent among Akron rubber workers.

Vulcanizing tires in Akron, 1907.

Such workers were both susceptible to pressures on them and impatient for quick results. As pressures mounted and financial resources dried up, the ranks of the strikers thinned. By mid-March some 4,500-5,000 workers had left Akron. Too few had the stamina of an old tire finisher, one of the first to join the strike:

> I made up my mind that the factory officials were going to keep on cutting down the earnings so long as I and others would stand it, and that the only chance to keep even what we have was to strike. I don't think much of the philosophy of the I.W.W. but they came to help us when we were without leadership of any kind, and I am going to stick to the finish.

The motives of the employers were never in doubt. Rubber company officials regarded the strike as an outside attempt to seize power. Taking the threat seriously, they erected board and wire stockades, organized fire companies, advertised widely for strikebreakers, and made plans to house them inside the plants. The companies also refused to meet with either the State Board of Arbitration or union representatives. Nervous local authorities failed to get Democratic governor James Cox to send in the National Guard, so it was left to them to deal with the strike in general and the IWW specifically. As the strike persisted police harassed pickets, broke up picket lines, gave strike breakers safe passage, and arrested IWW leaders. Meanwhile Akron businessmen formed a Citizen Welfare League to step up publicity designed to win over the public and "reliable" workers and to drive out "the small but active group of agitators."

To compound problems for the strikers, divisions began to appear within the ranks of organized labor as well. The Akron Central Labor Union had promised financial and moral support and opposition to any rival union, but when an AFL organizer arrived he reversed direction, tried to block contributions to the strike committee because of its IWW ties, and attacked a proposal for a general strike. In late February, too, the AFL chartered Rubber Workers Union No. 14407, but not even the

Female strikers in 1913 reply to plant manager Shaw's threat to move the B. F. Goodrich Co. from Akron.

migrants and other workers often shunned by AFL craft unions. However, as the number of strikers in Akron leaped from 3500 to 16,000, the local found its financial and organizational resources severely strained. With the help of the local Socialist party, the Wobblies struggled along until the national IWW began to send in skilled organizers. Yet, there were limits to what could be done. for a smaller but better publicized strike in Paterson, New Jersey drew off both donations and organizers. Ten days after the strike began, grievances had still not been formulated.

The evidence is somewhat contradictory as to what membership in the IWW meant to strikers. Most workers who joined did so for practical rather than ideological reasons. As the Ohio Senate Committee which investigated the situation reported: "very few [workers] knew the principles, doctrines and methods of the Industrial Workers of the World, and scarcely any had read their constitution or declaration of principles." They lined up with the IWW, many told the committee, "because they hoped through collective action to increase their wages and improve their conditions of employment."

talented young John L. Lewis, sent in to handle this federal local, could get it off the ground. Despite such directions the Bricklayers Union did donate $700 to the IWW strike fund.

By February 21 the strikers had formulated their demand. Key proposals included reinstatement of strikers, an eight-hour day, double time for overtime, and a minimum wage of 22.5¢ an hour. The companies still flatly refused to bargain with the workers. The insistent and incessant pressure of the companies and the Welfare League, moreover, gradually lodged seeds of doubt in some strikers' minds about the wisdom of associating with the IWW. Splits developed among those who wanted to compromise and more militant workers. One outcome of this conflict was that by early March IWW speakers were barred from the platform at strike meetings on the grounds that several of them had used inflamatory language. Shortly thereafter the chairman of the strike committee resigned, saying he knew the strike would collapse and that he did not want to be associated with it. Some activists claimed he had been booted out because he was a paid informant for the rubber companies, a charge later proven correct, but which made little difference. By now the strike was fading.

Even so, for the first time the confrontation now led to violence. Prior to March 7 there had been no serious trouble. But when 500 marchers picketed in front of Goodrich on the 7th and police ordered them off and then charged, that set off two days of repeated clashes between strikers and police and strikers and nonstrikers. Police then arrested some key leaders and by March 12 virtual martial law existed. One thousand members of the Citizens League were deputized and patrolled streets, driving out of town forty or fifty people linked to the IWW. Now it was the strikers who urged Governor Cox to send in the National Guard. He refused. The strike persisted only as long as Senator William Green and his investigating committee stayed in town. Six days after they left on March 24 the strike ended.

Reports filed by operatives for one Akron rubber company suggest the ways in which employer tactics and union weakness ensured the failure of the strike. In a typical entry, operative No. 148 reported that "several men from Paterson, N.J., were around the waiting room, seeking employment. No. 148 told the employment agent that there was a strike in Paterson and the men did not receive employment." In another instance No. 148 heard from another employee that "there is a man working in the machine shop now...who has been there for some time, who is a strong Socialist and I.W.W. man...." Both of these reports were dated May, 1913. Less than two months after the strike the companies had things firmly in hand. In September operative 141 attended a Rubber Worker's union meeting which confirmed the degree of control, for he reported that he had been "appointed Recording Secretary." In going over the books he "found that there is only about thirty members in good standing." By

late 1913, one man later admitted, all of the officers of the Akron IWW were paid informers.

Other strikes of the era were equally inconclusive for the workers, even when no spies were employed and local circumstances seemed more favorable for the workers involved. When U.S. Steel announced in July, 1909, that it would operate only under open shop conditions, this provoked a lengthy strike in a subsidiary, the Aetna Standard mill of the American Sheet and Tinplate company. The plant straddled the boundary between Bridgeport and Martins Ferry, two strong union towns. The mayor of Martins Ferry, indeed, was a former employee of Aetna, a steelworker, and the brother of strike leader Llewlyn Lewis, vice president of the Amalgamated Iron Steel and Tin Plate Workers. That union had operated for years under union scales at all American Sheet and Tinplate plants, and reacted vehemently to the U.S. Steel proposal.

By early winter tension in the two towns was high. Mayor Lewis, who amazingly lost his bid for reelection during the strike, had been accused by the county sheriff of being blatantly pro-labor, but he himself found it impossible to recruit volunteers into a peace-keeping force from in-town or from the surrounding area. When violence erupted after the company imported armed guards in preparation for resuming operations with strike breakers, the sheriff called for, and the governor dispatched, some 1,500 troops to the scene. The strikers, however, remained determined and an impasse seemed probable. "The conditions existing in Bridgeport are unusual," the *Ohio State Journal* explained:

National Guard troops positioned on a bridge during the American Tin Plate strike at Bridgeport, 1909.

Instead of the customary assortment of ignorant foreigners, the officials are dealing with Americans, the majority of whom are of Welsh, Irish and Scotch stocks. They have the ability not only to plan well but to carry out their plans in an intelligent manner.

The strikers petitioned for arbitration and eventually the company agreed to pull its guards out and not to try to run the plants with strikebreakers. Under this situation the governor withdrew the troops, which even the strikers agreed had played an important role in restoring peace. But nothing came of the effort to block the open shop; U.S. Steel won that bid.

Another area of conflict involved street car strikes. Although the Street and Electric Railway Workers shaped a constitution which stressed "conciliation and arbitration in the settlement of all differences between labor and capital," language quite different from that evident in most union documents of the era, street car strikes often involved violence because lines frequently crossed working-class neighborhoods where support for the strikers was strong. Company intransigence, of course, figured as well.

Refusal to recognize the Amalgamated Association of Street Railway Employees, for instance, generated the 1910 Columbus strike of streetcar employees. Temporarily halted by intervention of the state Board of Arbitration, it flared anew when the company deliberately fired a number of union men. Some police initially refused to protect strikebreakers and strikers seized the opportunity to harass operators, harangue scabs and, in some instances, to cut wires. The arrival of 450 guards and strikebreakers from Cleveland only worsened the situation. Cars were stoned and blown up and on one occasion strikers stormed the barracks where strike breakers were housed. In July local authorities called in the National Guard and the presence of the troops both restored peace and caused the strike to subside.

The tenacity of strikers was evident in the 1911 strike of 6,000 garment cutters in Cleveland. Pauline M. Newman, a national organizer for the International Ladies Garment Workers, summed up the situation as she saw it:

> Despite the fact that the strikers have about seven nationalities amidst their ranks and the deaf and dumb to take care of, the police department against them, guards to annoy them, thugs to assault them, judges to fine them—the strikers are bound to win; are bound to come out the victors! For the strikers possess one power—that of making cloaks! Guards can annoy the pickets, but they cannot make cloaks; the police can arrest the girls, but they cannot finish skirts; a judge can render a decision in favor of the manufacturers

Colt gun mounted on an automobile which was used by troops during the 1910 streetcar strike in Columbus.

Obstruction on track during Cleveland streetcar strike, 1908.

that cuts the law into pieces, but he, too, cannot cut garments, and garment cutters are what the employers need.

After manufacturers rejected a bid by the state Board of Arbitration to mediate the dispute, the strike continued. Arrests — some 737 of them during the strike — served only to fire up the sense of solidarity. One jailed group of women sang repeatedly:

All we ask is bail,
All that we get is jail,
All that we want is to fight
Until we get what is right.

That took six months.

Throughout these years the tempo of strikes increased, and in Ohio it was no different. In 1913 strikes occurred in nearly every occupation. In Cincinnati alone streetcar men, icemen, teamsters, cigar makers, stationary engineers, tailors, and laundry workers all struck. The highly-organized cigar workers, teamsters, and stationary engineers had more success than those workers who sought recognition as well as redress of grievances. The tailors' strike, for instance, involved 500 unorganized custom tailors who had struck first with members of the United Garment Workers for a 48-hour week but then had been excluded from the compromise settlement of fifty hours. The Journeymen's Tailors union sent in several organizers — Arthur Caroti to work with the Italian men, Emma Steghagen of the National Women's Trade Union League "to 'handle the girls,'" and a third for general work with the Jewish and German workers. The strike lasted thirteen weeks and ended in defeat.

Between 1914 and 1916 union activity picked up dramatically, reflecting the improved economic conditions which came with the onset of World War I. Among those striking in 1914 were

Portsmouth and Cincinnati shoe workers, Canton phone operators, retail clerks in Zanesville, buffers and polishers in Wooster, clay workers in Empire and Toronto, miners in Dillonvale. In 1915, the list of 115 strikes included paper makers in Middleton, molders in Hamilton, machinists in Cincinnati and Columbus, and munitions workers in Youngstown. The following year 276 strikes swept the state. Clay workers in Toronto and Empire struck again, as did molders in Springfield and Tiffin, machinists in Columbus, Cincinnati and Hamilton, Queen City brewery workers and shoe workers, electrical workers in Cleveland, Alliance cash register makers, machinists, electricians and rubber workers in Youngstown, coal miners in the Hocking Valley, and streetcar men in Toledo, Cleveland, Cincinnati, East Liverpool, and Alliance. Women had participated in Ohio

The bullpen at the Cuyahoga County Jail, ca. 1910.

strikes before, but, in 1916, strikes involving women seemed to be everywhere: garment workers in Cleveland and Cincinnati, pottery workers in Sebring and Alliance, office workers in Cincinnati, cigar makers in Cleveland and Cincinnati, nurses in Massillon (in a short-lived but possibly momentous first), soap wrappers in Cincinnati, telephone operators in Toledo.

Perhaps the most significant developments of 1916, however, were the strikes which occurred in January at Youngstown Sheet and Tube and at Republic Iron and Steel. Together they idled over 16,000 workers, the bulk of them unorganized and foreign-born. Economic conditions lay at the heart of these strikes. The predominantly foreign-born machine runners earned wages too low to support their families, a surplus of labor had generated fear, and over the years the companies had resisted any efforts to air grievances, had, one labor leader said, engaged in "industrial depotism" and treated their employees no better than "cattle." "They leave home...expecting to return within a few years with a fortune," observed a sympathetic Cincinnati labor newspaper; "they reach the promised land and become slaves." Social and political exploitation was also involved. According to one paper East Youngstown had a population of 10,000 but only 400 voters.

Gradually grievances piled up. When war orders and expanded production created labor shortages and a faster work pace in the city, frustrated workers mobilized spontaneously. AFL organizers provided some guidance once the strike started—despite problems finding interpreters — but could do nothing to hold the workers in check when company guards panicked and fired into a crowd, killing one man and wounding twenty-five others. This provoked widespread rioting which led to over a million dollars in property damage. The state rushed in 2,000 National guardsmen, the Industrial Commission issued a report sympathetic to the workers, and the companies made some concessions. Meanwhile some 1,500 Republic employees had joined craft unions and a federal local set up for unskilled workers. The winds of change were blowing.

This upsurge in strike activity reflected the impact of World War I. As the European war progressed, the economy, which had sagged in a series of sharp recessions prior to 1915, entered a period of dynamic expansion. Labor surpluses, which had retarded collective action and encouraged individualistic forms of protest, melted as immigration to the U.S. dropped precipitously. This enhanced the bargaining power of even nonskilled workers. With war orders piling up, employers granted concessions previously resisted.

Police on guard during the 1913 Cincinnati streetcar strike.

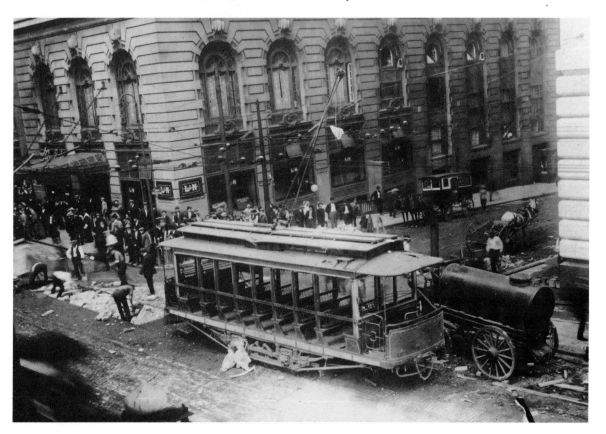

Cincinnati streetcar strike, 1913.

Striking coal miners and their families, Dillonvale, 1914.

Coal miners in Dillonvale protest the 1914 arrest of organizer Joseph Ettor of the IWW, then trying to organize in the area.

Steelworkers leaving Youngstown Sheet and Tube at the end of a shift during World War I.

The war — which the United States did not enter until April 1917 — thus had a profound, if short-lived, impact on labor-management relations. The federal government, intent on avoiding production delays which might hinder the war effort, gradually constructed a framework of agencies and policies which enormously enhanced the opportunities for organized labor and set precedents for the New Deal era. Creation of the Federal Mediation and Conciliation Service in 1914 provided an early indication of the direction the Democratic administration of Woodrow Wilson would take. In late 1916, labor representatives joined the Council of National Defense and, in 1917, the War Industries Board. In Ohio, AFL officials—Thomas J. Donnelly, secretary of the Ohio Federation of Labor, and John P. Frey, editor of the Iron Molders *Journal,* among them—served on the state CND, a form of recognition long sought by organized labor. Such representation did not alleviate pent up grievances. Workers, in 1917, staged more strikes than ever before in the nation's history, and increasingly they won closed

Delivery trucks, old and new, during World War I.

shop agreements and representation even in industries earlier impervious to union drives.

By late 1917, the Council of National Defense moved to deal directly with the labor turmoil. It created a War Labor Conference Board, and out of its efforts came the War Labor Policies Board, established in May, 1918. Another offshoot of the CND's advisory committee was the National War Labor Board. Relying on conciliation and mediation techniques, it sought to resolve industrial disputes peacefully, arguing throughout that both strikes and lockouts should be barred. In return, workers were to be allowed to organize without interference from their employers, a right trade unionists had battled for years to achieve.

Such policies, the changed legal context for organizing, the enthusiasm of unorganized workers to organize in a time of staggering inflation and labor shortages, and the willingness of established unions to organize, dramatically increased trade union membership. Nationwide, trade unions claimed 2.8 million members in 1916, 3.5 in 1918, and 5,000,000 in 1920 — an increase of eighty-two percent in four years.

Not all segments of the work force unionized at an equal pace and employer resistance certainly did not evaporate. Still, the striking fact about World War I is the breadth of the union experience. While craft unions remained strong and expanded in size, the most significant development of these years was the penetration of unions into the mass-production industries and the growing numbers of blacks, women, and immigrants who were exposed to unionsim.

The severe labor shortage in the North created new opportunities for southern blacks. As a Cleveland manufacturer explained: ''Colored

AGREEMENT

Agreement, made and entered into between...

....known as the Employer, party of the First Part, and Local No. 407, I. B. of T. C. S. and H. of A., party of the Second Part.

ARTICLE I

Party of the First Part agrees to employ members of the I. B. of T. C. S. and H. of A., Local 407, carrying the regular working card, when in their power to do so, and in case the Party of the First Part hires a teamster or helper who does not belong to Local 407, said teamster or helper must become a member in two weeks' time.

ARTICLE II

The wage scale for Teamsters shall be as follows: $11.50 for light singles for the first year of this agreement; second year, $12.00; third year, $12.50. $12.50 per week for heavy singles for the first year of this agreement. Second year, $13.00; third year, $13.50. $13.50 per week for light doubles, for the first year of this agreement; second year, $14.00; third year, $14.50. $15.50 per week for two horse trucks for the first year of this agreement; second year, $16.00; third year, $16.50. $17.50 per week for three horse trucks for the first year of this agreement; $18.00 for second year; $18.50 for third year. The above to be considered a weekly wage, day work to be figured accordingly. Six days to constitute a week's work. Working hours for Teamsters shall be 11 hours per day, allowing one hour for dinner during the day, thirty minutes allowed contractor on day's work. Overtime for teamsters and helpers shall be at the rate of time and a half after 10½ hours to 8 o'clock, double time after 8 o'clock. Extra helpers shall receive 30c per hour, a lee way to be given grocery houses of one hour.

ARTICLE III

Wage Scale for Chauffeurs shall be as follows: $19.50 for the first year of this agreement; $20.00 for the second year; $20.50 for the third year. Helpers shall receive $14.50 for the first year; $15.00 for the second year; $15.50 for the third year. Working hours for Chauffeurs shall be 11 hours per day, allowing one hour for dinner during day. Overtime for chauffeurs and helpers shall be time and a half until 8 o'clock, double time after 8 p. m.

ARTICLE IV

Should any member receive any more than this scale of wages, he shall not suffer reduction during the life of this agreement.

ARTICLE V

Should any difference arise between the Employers and Local Union 407, it shall be referred to the Grievance Committee of Cartage Club and Local Union No. 407 in joint session; and the decision of these Committees shall be final and binding to both parties.

ARTICLE VI

Sunday and Holiday Work

Drivers shall clean horses only on Sundays and Holidays. Drivers shall not clean harness, wash or grease wagons on Sundays or Holidays. Drivers shall receive double time on Sundays and Holidays.

ARTICLE VII

Members of Local Union 407 not notified by employers night before of a lay-off, shall receive two hours' pay for care of horses. Members of Local Union 407 who do not notify Employer the night before of a lay-off, shall be subject to the deduction of two hours' pay. After first year of this agreement, members of Local Union 407, shall not go to the barns on Holidays.

ARTICLE VIII

There shall be no dissension between van and truck drivers as to working conditions.

ARTICLE IX

Members of Local Union 407 shall receive pay for the following holidays: New Year, Decoration Day, 4th of July, Labor Day, Thanksgiving and Christmas.

ARTICLE X

Members or Employers agree that all men employed by them shall be paid upon or before the 10th of each month after report of steward.

ARTICLE XI

Riggers shall receive 50c per hour. Foremen shall receive 55c per hour, 5c an hour increase for each year.

ARTICLE XII

Local Union 407 agrees not to tolerate members of Local 407 stopping and congregating over 10 minutes in saloons or elsewhere.

ARTICLE XIII

This agreement goes into effect February the 1st, 1915, and terminates February the 1st, 1918.

ARTICLE XIV

Thirty days' notice to be given by either party prior to the expiration of this agreement in case of any changes in new agreement. Otherwise this agreement shall remain in full force and effect.

....

....

A 1915 Teamsters contract reflects the changing conditions in that trade.

As a result of wartime shortages of labor and housing, the Youngstown Sheet and Tube Company built a "labor camp" to attract and retain newly recruited workers. Complete with a central kitchen (upper left), the camp consisted of crude barracks (upper right) and segregated accommodations for black families (left). Company police maintained constant vigilance.

labor is the only available class of labor at this time, and the manufacturers have made up their minds to employ it permanently." In 1916 and 1917, the U.S. Department of Labor estimated, at least 37,500 blacks entered Ohio seeking work.

Organized labor did not relish this influx. The Ohio and Cleveland AFL units jointly sponsored a resolution at the Federation's 1916 convention which pointed with alarm to the possibility that union wage levels would be undercut. Although the resolution, which called for the organization of blacks, passed, the Federation did little to organize blacks in either the North or the South.

Meanwhile, racial tension mounted in a number of northern cities as poor blacks and unskilled whites competed for jobs and housing. By 1918, acute housing shortages had developed in Cleveland, Akron, Dayton, Lima, Portsmouth, Toledo and Youngstown. As early as June 1917 the Ohio Council on National Defense fretted about "the negro problem." At its June meeting the Committee on Labor and In-

dustrial Relations discussed "handling the problem" but could reach no agreement on any specific plan. The Committee did authorize establishing a subdivision in the Cleveland Free Labor Exchange, one of the state employment offices, "for the placement of negro women."

Ohio experienced no riots, but racial animosities persisted, and unionized blacks remained few in number, concentrated in the barber's, musician's, hod carrier's, building laborer's, teamster's, chauffeur's, printer's, and miner's unions. Most black migrants found work as common laborers in construction and on the railroads as freight handlers.

The severe labor shortage of the war years also had a dual effect on women workers. It permitted many women to move into jobs from which they had previously been barred, and at which they could work at much higher rates, and it also exposed them to the direct discrimination of male workers and employers. Walter Leiserson, then a professor at the University of Toledo, worked during the war as an investigator for the Ohio CND. His report on

Assemblers at Sunlight Electrical, a division of General Motors, in Dayton, ca. 1918.

Relations between unions and black workers were not always harmonious. The fact that blacks had been involved in strike-breaking left an imprint as did the fact that many whites were openly hostile. During World War I some attempts were made to unionize black workers. As the following excerpt from a report by a business agent for the Toledo Cental Labor Union indicates, considerable ambivalence continued to mark relations.

September 20, 1917. "In conjunction with the organizing committee circulars were distributed calling for a meeting of the Colored workers for the purposes of organization . . . for Saturday evening Sept 8, 1917. About Thirty . . . colored people were present. Bro Ames, Grames, Powers and your Business Agent explained the purposes of the meeting. There were representatives of the colored people present including two Lawyers, two ministers and several others prominent in uplift work amongst the colored people. They expressed themselves as being rather pleased at my Frank method of explaining our method of organization and why it was necessary and our motives in devoting our time to this organization work. They all more or less wanted to know if by organization new avenues of employment would be opened to the colored people and mentioned several industries that these people could not gain employment at. In answer to these queries . . . we made it plain that it would depend almost entirely upon the activity of the colored people as Trade Unionists as to the scope of their employment that that trade Union movement recognized no race, creed or color lines and that any prejudices that might exist in so far as Colored labor was concerned would be handled better through an intelligent, efficient Labor Union than by some so-called uplift representative who sometimes may be more interested in his own particular welfare than that of those whom he was chosen to represent. Arrangements were made at this meeting to call another meeting . . . but through lack of co-operation in the past of those present and the fact that some employers had cautioned their colored workers to Stay away the meeting was not successful. The organizing committee and your Business Agent intends to keep in touch with this situation and we might say are gathering a good deal of valuable information as to who and how the colored workers are being exploited in Toledo that will be of immense value to the Central Labor Union."

conditions at the B&O railroad yard at Lorain in mid-1917 suggests something of the dilemma for women workers:

The B. & O. claims that there is a shortage of labor and that women must help. But no attempt had been made to pay the prevailing rates of wages for men for this work, although cost of living and wages have risen even where the wages here have not gone above 20¢ an hour. This was the rate for common labor four and five years ago. Not being able to get capable workers at this rate the company had recourse to poorer and poorer grades of labor until they got to the lowest class of floating hobo and negro labor. Whether they would be better or even cheaper than good laborers who might be secured at 30¢ an hour is a question that ought to be investigated. . . . If women are to enter industrial occupations hitherto closed to them, the process should be watched . . . and they should not be permitted to enter industry merely as a cheaper grade of labor than the worst paid 'hob' and negro labor. That would be merely encouraging exploitation.

Women experienced resistance similar to that which confronted blacks as they moved from low paying jobs into ones traditionally dominated by males. The conflict was especially marked where their introduction meant skill dilution, a subdivision of production processes, and thus directly challenged established shop craft traditions of control. Although the International Association of Machinists decided to organize women workers (by mid-1918, women made up over six percent of the union's 229,500 membership), opposition to that policy developed in some railroad machine shops. For its part, the Ohio Molder's and Foundry Worker's Union aggressively urged further protective legislation in order to limit opportunities for women workers in foundries.

Even where skill dilution was not involved

male workers often felt threatened, as the case of the women employed by the Cleveland Railroad Company illustrates. The powerful Amalgamated Association of Street and Electric Railway Employees of America had blocked company attempts to hire white women and black men, but in the summer of 1918 the company nonetheless hired 150 women conductors. The union protested and the Department of Labor ruled, without consulting the women, that the women should be discharged as the company had created an artificial labor shortage. This prompted Laura Prince, a former secretary of the Cleveland Waitresses' Union, and others to found the Association of Women Street Railway Employees. The women hired Ohio suffragist Florence Allen as their attorney and mobilized support among feminist organizations.

This did not protect their jobs. Although Secretary of Labor William B. Wilson deferred the women's dismissal and the National War Labor Board agreed to hear the case, the male union decided to enforce its own will by striking on December 2, 1918. Intense pressure forced a number of the women to resign and eventually the union got its way. The remaining women appealed in the spring of 1919 and the NWLB upheld their contention that their contractual rights had been violated and their social rights to seek employment where they desired unfairly circumscribed. The company simply ignored a NWLB reinstatement order, however, when the union indicated it remained opposed to the women conductors.

Occupations already feminized were also affected by the war. The demand for telephone operators soared, for example. Since wages did not keep pace with pay scales in other industries, labor turnover increased as women sought better paying work elsewhere. Militancy among operators also rose. In August, 1918, the telephone system, like the railways, came under federal control. Postmaster General

Albert S. Burleson took charge of the wires and unlike William McAdoo, who controlled the railways, Burleson reinforced existing anti-union policies and ruled with an autocratic hand. The International Brotherhood of Electrical Workers thus had considerable success organizing phone workers in a number of cities, including Cleveland and Youngstown. Yet until June 1919, when threatened by a system-wide general strike, Burleson did not extend to phone workers rights conceded earlier to other workers.

The labor shortage of the war era also affected attitudes toward immigrant workers. In industries heavily dependent upon immigrants, executives moved to reduce labor turnover which they had previously ignored. Unilateral and regular pay increases, sometimes opposed by the War Labor Policies Board, were one approach used in the steel industry. Steel companies also targeted immigrant workers for the same policies originally designed to bind skilled workers to their firms. Youngstown Sheet and Tube launched a housing program for its immi-

Immigrant workers in Youngstown received free English lessons and other study classes in this community hall.

In Cleveland, Hiram House provided Americanization classes.

grant workers and so did the American Rolling Mill Company in Middletown.

Americanization programs, which spread in 1916, also aimed at retaining the immigrant worker. In Cleveland the Mayor's Advisory Committee established an Americanization Information Bureau which typified the direction of such efforts. The program aimed, a flyer explained, "to enroll as many as possible of the 80,000 non-English speaking peoples of Cleveland in Americanization classes in order that they may learn the English language and prepare for American citizenship." Another flyer was more explicit:

The first step to Americanization is learning the common language of our country....The 'One language City' and the 'One language factory' means fewer misunderstandings, fewer accidents, no interpreters and increased efficiency. Learning the American language will assist our foreign born population to help themselves and will materially aid in stabilizing and increasing the efficiency of our industries in this war for 'world democracy.'

Not all immigrants benefitted from the war, of course. An investigator of privately-run labor camps for transient workers learned, for instance, that in some cases practices common in the post-Civil War era among contract workers still existed:

Most foreigners make gang movements from job to job and the business incident to such transfer is transacted by one of their leading English-speaking members, who acts as a straw-boss but who is in very truth a help hunter in disguise and the collusion, if any, that exists between him and the real work-boss in their negotiations about taking on or letting off men is easier in suspicion than in proof....Enough has been learned...to justify the conclusion that hundreds of men in our large and freely circulating camp element live and work under sub-standard conditions equally deplorable whether considered from the standpoint of their own welfare or their employers' profits.

Labor shortages and the heightened demand for American industrial goods left organized labor in the strongest position it had been in for years. The UMW signed up 50,000 coal miners in the summer of 1918 alone, the Machinists grew threefold, and the Amalgamated Association of Iron, Steel and Tin Workers, long dormant, made an important come back. In Girard, Ohio, over 300 workers at the A. M. Byers Company, the largest puddling mill in the U.S., formed an Amalgamated Lodge in June, 1917. Much of the organization had been underway before the federal government started to erect its essentially pro-labor agencies, but the war had a decisive impact, one wholly apart from the changed organizing climate and unintended by government planners. Wartime propaganda — especially the notion that this was a war to make the world safe for democracy — led more than one worker to conclude that there should be economic as well as political democracy within the U.S. By the fall of 1918 the quest for industrial democracy was well underway.

Even as trade unionists unfurled their banners and launched a series of organizing drives, there were signs of an impending counterattack. Company-initiated employee representation plans in the steel industry served as an opening beach head, an effort to siphon off the dangerous grievances which might foster independent trade unionism. For the trade unions it was a sign of things to come. The Armistice in November 1918, ironically, also undercut the meaning of industrial democracy as trade unionists understood it. The pressing need which had led the federal government to intervene in labor-management relations now gone, the government disbanded the War Industries Board and the War Labor Policies Board. The National War Labor Board remained in operation to deal with cases still before it, but its powers were seriously diminished — as the Cleveland women conductors learned. In this context employers prepared to regain the prerogatives which, they believed, they had lost to organized labor during the war.

World War I represented the peak of organized labor's economic influence and the high point of its membership between 1886 and 1920. During this period a number of unions had made important gains at the collective bargaining table, but for most of the era had not been able to dent the bastions of the mass-production industries. For much of the time, however, workers sought relief by taking another route, a political one. Working class political action and the practical work done by trade unions were always interwoven.

The late nineteenth century was an intensely political age, with high levels of voter participation. Workers neither shied away from expressing their opinions at the polls nor from seeking laws which would right the evils of the workplace. Persistent agitation at the local and state level for safety, child labor, and sanitary housing laws characterized the entire period. Equally sought-after were bars to convict labor, the abolition of anti-tramp laws, and legislation which would restrict the issuance of injunctions. Passage of an eight-hour law in April, 1886, reflected the potential power of Ohio organized labor in the political arena, but also the reality of pro-business Republican control— the bill proved too loosely drawn to be effective. For the next three decades, debate would continue over this and other pieces of legislation labor sought.

Much of the initiative for action in 1886 stemmed from the ranks of factory artisans in trades which had undergone rapid change over the past decade. The eight-hour campaign had specific short-range hour and wage goals, but also served as a vehicle by which workers hoped to redirect the course of industrialization. The bonds of unity which resulted transcended the lines of ethnicity, race, religion, sex and craft which fragmented the working class and provided the basis for a major movement to shape a working-class political party.

The United Labor Party originated in New York in mid-1886. Reformer Henry George ran for mayor of New York City as its candidate. Although he lost that race, his call for land and tax reform, homes for workers, the end of oppressive monopolies, and endorsement of Irish home rule galvanized a broad base of support and prompted workers elsewhere to set aside their loyalties to the Democratic and Republican parties and form local ULP organizations.

The impetus for organizing a Cincinnati ULP, in late 1886, came from the largely German-controlled Central Labor Union. Local leaders of the Knights of Labor soon joined the coalition, as did the Amalgamated Council of Building Trades, with 17,000 members in sixteen construction unions. With between thirty-two and fifty percent of all manufacturing workers

in the city in unions, making it one of the most powerful labor centers in the U.S., Cincinnati workers seemed on the verge of an important breakthrough.

They shaped a program which reflected the influence of George and their own disenchantment with contemporary America. And when the national ULP convention met in the Queen City in February, 1887, delegates adopted a similar platform. It urged the creation of a cooperative industrial commonwealth in which government would prevent the abuses of power so evident at the time. The ULP also called for strong child-labor laws, abolition of convict labor, compulsory arbitration of labor disputes, a graduated income tax, direct election of U.S. senators, a bar against corporate use of private armies, and establishment of agricultural and industrial coops.

Despite its strengths, the Cincinnati ULP could not overcome an alliance of major manufacturers with the Democratic and Republican parties. The ULP won nine seats on city council and seven on the board of education, but in subsequent elections the vote for major ULP candidates declined sharply, and by early 1889

A ULP broadside typified the sort of labor political activity which swept the country in 1886 and 1887.

Coxey's army is escorted, quickly, through a town enroute to Washington, D.C.

Like so many other events in American labor history, Coxey's "army" found a place in contemporary songs. The following one, "Marching With Coxey" (sung to the tune of "Marching Through Georgia"), appeared in 1894.

We are marching to the Capital, three hundred thousand strong,
With live petitions in our boots to urge our cause along,
And when we kick our congressmen, they'll feel there's
*   something wrong.*
As we go marching with Coxey.

Hurrah! hurrah! for the unemployed's appeal!
Hurrah! hurrah! for the marching commonweal!
Drive the lobbies from the senate,
Stop the trust and combine steal
For we are marching with Coxey.

We are not tramps nor vagabonds that's shirking honest toil,
But miners, clerks, skilled artizans, and tillers of the soil
Now forced to beg our brother worms to give us leave to toil,
While we are marching with Coxey.

the organization was defunct, torn apart by political divisions.

During the 1890s, trade unionism was the chief focus of working-class activity. Yet adherents of direct political action never passed from the scene. In 1889 they backed the nationalist party and subsequently the People's party, both of which called for the nationalization of certain key industries.

The depression of the 'nineties prompted a quest for solutions, one which attracted considerable attention being proposed by Jacob Coxey, a wealthy Massillon quarry operator long interested in reforms. Among other things, he considered public works a solution to the problem of unemployment. To bring this idea to the attention of Congress, Coxey formed the

"Commonweal of Christ" and in 1894 marched on Washington — a "living petition," one of several such industrial armies that year. Carefully observed by Secret Service agents — Attorney General Richard Olney feared industrial revolution — the "army" made its way to Washington, D.C., arriving there on May 1 with some 500 members. Its leaders ingloriously arrested for carrying banners on capitol grounds, the movement collapsed quickly.

The discontent did not go away so easily. The People's party, formed in 1891 by farmers in the South and West, demonstrated this when it sought in 1894 to forge an alliance with workers in the mines and the mills. While this quest proved less successful in Ohio than Illinois, a coalition did emerge with influence as far south as Cincinnati. Coxey, whose anti-monopolist attitudes meshed well with those of many workers, ran for Congress on the Populist ticket and got twenty-four percent of the vote. Fellow Massillon resident John McBride, president of the United Mine Workers, urged his supporters to vote the Populist ticket. In all, Ohio Populist candidates for all offices polled a disappointing 49,496 votes despite a coalition of various labor and reform groups.

The persistence of the depression and the presence of large numbers of British and German workers in key industries helps to explain the continued interest in third party movements despite limited successes at the polls. German and British workers — prominent among brewery workers, miners and machinists — were inclined to independent politics, willing to operate outside the confines of the two-party system, and bolstered in this inclination by the emergence of labor parties in both England and Germany. These served as evidence that trade unionists could operate successfully in political as well as economic spheres. In late 1893, the program of the British Independent Labour Party won applause at the AFL's convention, despite Gompers' opposition, and affiliates were urged to study its program and consider the issue of independent political action. This accounted in part for the election of John McBride as AFL president in 1894, the only time Gompers lost that post between 1886 and his death in 1924. Endorsement of independent political action by the AFL itself, however, lost at the convention, as did a plank calling for "the collective ownership by the people of all means of production and distribution."

Although city centrals, local trade unions and state organizations tended to pull back from direct party politics for a time after the ULP experience, they scarcely removed themselves from the political process. The AFL officially endorsed a non-partisan "reward your friends and punish your enemies" stance toward political action in 1906. Many affiliated unions, city centrals, and individual workers assumed more partisan stances. And while Gompers advocated "voluntarism" — the idea that labor's interests were served best by self-organization and collective bargaining rather than government action — at the state and local levels organized labor proved adept in its quest for protective legislation throughout the Progressive Era. Over the years organized labor in Ohio would emerge as a powerful interest group in state politics, successfully lobbying on a range of issues to benefit workers, often with great success. Legislation was one path to industrial justice.

The Knights of Labor in 1883, and other labor groups thereafter, tried repeatedly to control the job market by restricting the output of contract and piecework by Ohio convicts, for example. Laws did pass in 1892 and 1893 which

limited such work, but they do not appear to have been enforced. Efforts to deal with the issue renewed in 1900 but the campaign was not entirely successful given current theories of work reform and the fact that it was regarded as profitable. "Idleness is a vice everywhere," one defender of the system explained, "but to the prisoner it is more than ordinarily harmful." By then, in any case, the system was well-established and the Ohio penitentiary turned out bolts, nuts, cigars, brooms, hollow ware, stoves, hoes and rakes, stamped metal products, and soap. In 1907, a bill more tightly controlling contract prison labor did pass. Periodically thereafter unions visited prisons to ensure

Writing in 1894 about a Cincinnati tenement ward largely populated by Germans, an investigator for the Ohio Bureau of Labor Statistics reported some of the social effects of the depression:

The late business depression fell with great severity upon these people. When the factories closed down and the shops shut their doors, the population of the third ward was idle. Numerous examples can be found where men were out of work for many months, and there is scarcely a man who was not out of work for a longer or shorter period ranging from a few days to a few weeks. Most of them had accumulated a little saving which tided them over the crisis and kept them from appealing to charity for help. When the investigation was begun, almost every man, it seemed, was out of work, but by the time the investigation closed in October, a very marked difference was observed. Many men were yet unemployed, but the number was small as compared with the earlier reports. The slight improvement in business had resulted in work for the majority although many were working considerably less than full time. During the summer, families were found where strong, able-bodied men remained in enforced idleness while the wives and children supported them by washing and scrubbing. They could find work of that kind to do while the men could find nothing.

Coxey's army at Canton, March 1894.

Ohio was a crucial battleground in efforts to win the vote for American women. Warren, Ohio briefly served as National American Women Suffrage Association Headquarters, as treasurer Harriet Taylor lived there. These broadsides, issued during a losing 1912 referendum bid to amend the state constitution, reflect the common linking of suffrage with broader social reform issues.

It is Bad for Working Men

to have women forced to take low wages.

IT LOWERS ALL WAGES

Give Ohio Working Women

the right to Vote for

A MINIMUM WAGE!

Give Ohio Working Women the power to HELP THE WORKING MEN. No class has more to gain and less to lose by giving *Votes to Women* than the workers.

THEIR CAUSE IS THE SAME

"WE BELIEVE IN VOTES FOR WOMEN"

HARRY THOMAS,
Sec'y Ohio State Federation of Labor.

MAX HAYES,
Editor Citizen, Cleveland

JAMES ROBINSON,
Canton, Ohio.

WM. P. HALLENKAMP,
Con. Con. Labor Delegate.

PERCY TETLOW,
Con. Con. Labor Delegate.

WM. DAVIO,
Con. Con. Labor Delegate.

FRANK P. LAMBERT,
Con. Con. Labor Delegate.

Workers, Vote for the Equal Suffrage Amendment Number 23 on September 3.

Ohio Woman Suffrage Association, Warren, O. [OVER]

Workers and Women

Women Are Wage Earners

There are 8,000,000 working women in the United States.

They Must Help Support the Family

Often they work at home *with the children* as SWEATED LABOR, mother and children *together making as a day's wage*

49 cts. for finishing pants at 7 cts. a pair;
60 cts. for making violets, 144 for 3 cts.;
45 cts. for tying feathers, 237 knots for 5 cts.

In Shops and Factories

they work long hours, *often without pay for over-time*, earning as low as $4 and $5 a week, often amid unsanitary and unhealthful conditions.

WOMEN MUST TAKE THESE WAGES OR STARVE!

What Can Help These Conditions?

GIVING WOMEN THE VOTE

to protect themselves by electing the men who make the laws.

OHIO WOMAN SUFFRAGE ASSOCIATION
MASONIC BLDG.,　　[Over]　　　　WARREN, OHIO

One of the principal shapers of Ohio's workmen's compensation laws was William Green, senator from Cochocton and future president of the AFL. A former miner, he knew the hazards of that occupation first hand. In this 1916 interview with *The* (Cincinnati) *Labor Advocate,* Green discusses some of the background and passage of the legislation.

I have worked in the mines of Ohio and know what labor conditions were a few years ago. . . . It isn't necessary to remind you of the fate of the injured workman in Ohio for fifty years prior to 1914. We have all seen them carried out of mills, mines, and factories, many crippled for life. Many of our friends and comrades lost their lives. The wounded men were plunged into a law suit, and if they got anything at all, it was after a fight that lasted for years in the courts. In most cases they got nothing. In some instances where men lost their lives, the widows and orphans inherited law suits, and if they got anything at all—in most instances they did not—it was after the fight had gone on in the courts for years, and they were worn out and compelled to compromise. . . . Labor saw the injustice of this, and we tried to correct it by legislation, but the courts held that under the constitution it could not be done. Finally we determined to change the constitution and make the accomplishment of our hopes possible. In 1912 the amendment to the constitution of Ohio, making the passage of the Workmen's Compensation Law a duty of the legislature, was submitted to the vote of the people (and passed). . . . The law was passed. After it had been in operation one year employers who had opposed it were loud in its praise and labor lived in a day they thought would never dawn.

that operations there would not compete in unauthorized ways with outside union labor.

The legislative program of the Ohio Federation in 1915 typified the other kinds of bills organized labor sought: regulation and limitation of the use of injunctions; prohibition of the importation of strikebreakers; a ban on the exercise of police authority by anyone except those

in control of the state; a workmen's compensation bill amendation; an eight-hour day for women workers; the Australian ballot system in primary elections.

Another pressing problem involved compensation for job-related accidents. Civil actions generally were the sole recourse for injured workers in the nineteenth century, and court interpretations of common law seldom favored workers in such cases. In 1904 and 1910 the Ohio General Assembly narrowed the defenses available to employers. A 1911 bill introduced in the Senate by William Green, former president of the Ohio UMW, represented a compromise between the Ohio State Federation of Labor and the Ohio Manufacturing Association, headed by S.P. Bush, the progressive head of Buckeye Steel Castings. Aiming for the social harmony so cherished by both middle-class reformers and non-socialist trade unionists in an era wracked by social conflict, the act incorporated the labor position that employers bear the bulk of the cost of industrial accidents, as well as the employer desire to make the cost of accidents predictable. But the program remained elective. In 1912, the Ohio Federation pushed for a compulsory bill shaped the following year by Green. The new measure created an Industrial Commission which — in addition to handling the compensation system — served as a centralized body to establish safety rules, provide arbitration and conciliation services, set up state employment agencies and license private agencies, investigate issues relating to unemployment, and censor movies.

Throughout these years, interest in third-party politics percolated, principal attention focusing on the Socialist Party of America. Founded in 1901 and committed to gradual

Painting the foundry roof at Buckeye Steel Castings. Note the safety railing.

Liberty Hall, on the corner of Orange and East 22nd Street in Cleveland, 1907. "Here," an anti-Socialist said, "the local anarchists met."

triumph via the ballot box, it attracted many Ohio workers because it advocated curbs on monopolies, accident and old age insurance, unemployment programs, and a 48-hour work week. The charisma of Eugene Debs, who had been jailed during the American Railway Union's 1894 strike against the Chicago-based Pullman Company, also swayed voters. His tireless campaigning for the presidency drew growing numbers of voters. In 1904, Ohio ranked fourth among the states in the total number of Socialist votes; by 1910, Ohioans cast more votes for the Socialist party than any other state.

Socialism made its greatest gains at the local level prior to World War I. Party candidates for governor and secretary of state were never elected. Until 1911, only two communities had Socialist administration and there were only nine Socialist officials throughout Ohio. But in the fall elections fifty-four small urban and industrial centers elected one or more Socialist officials—among them Amsterdam, Barberton, Barnhill, Canton, Conneaut, Cuyahoga Falls, Fostoria, Lima, Linden Heights, Lorain, Martins Ferry, and Mineral City. While most of these administrations fell two years later, new ones were elected in Martins Ferry, Canal Dover, Coshocton, Conneaut, Hamilton, Shelby and Talen. This represented the peak of Socialist electoral success in the Buckeye State. Thereafter, although the total number of Socialist votes would rise, fewer candidates would be elected. The fusion of Democrats and Republi-

cans behind one candidate explained that in some places, while in others adoption of the commission or manager form of government had the same effect.

Party strength varied around the state, industrial centers being the key areas of activity. In northwest Ohio, Toledo's party enjoyed modest success—bolstered in part by members of Russian and Polish background — although

During the war, labor activists were carefully watched by federal authorities, it being suspected that they were linked to the Bolsheviks who had gained power in Russia. Toledo was one Ohio city targeted for such an investigation. Socialists had garnered thirty-five percent of the vote in 1917 municipal elections and the city had a large eastern European population as well. In this report of April 11, 1918, a Bureau of Investigation agent indicates the extent to which surveillance extended.

Agent had important conference with the highest official of the IWW organization in Toledo, at which were present Mr. L.C. Van Vleck of the American Protective League, Mr. W.H. Birchall, Superintendent and general manager of the Willys-Overland Automobile plant and Mr. Charles Krausberger who is in direct charge of the particular lines of investigation for that plant. . . . At this conference it was learned . . . that Charles Stevenson . . . secretary of the Rationalists' Society of Toledo . . . is one of the most active IWW workers. . . . Also that there is being organized . . . what is to be known as 'The Hoboes' . . . composed of the members of the IWW, the radical Socialists, Rationalists and anarchists and other bad classes and organizations. That the purpose of this organization is to get back into the ranks old members of the I.W.W. who have been afraid to attend the IWW halls on account of governmental activities. . . . This agent is glad to report that his informant will be initiated (into 'The Hoboes') next Sunday . . . after which this office will be in a position to get all information direct from the secretary of the new organization. . . .

the popularity of reform mayors Golden Rule Jones and Brand Whitlock limited it somewhat. Cleveland Socialists dominated the state organization and Cleveland's United Trades and Labor Council, but the popularity of reform mayor Tom L. Johnson from 1901 to 1909 limited electoral gains here as well. Bohemians, Poles, Slavs and Germans provided the ethnic dimension in Cleveland and the party operated a sophisticated ward level organization. Max Hayes of the Typographical Workers was the most prominent Socialist in the state and he regularly clashed with Gompers at AFL annual conventions. Dayton, Cincinnati, Portsmouth and Columbus in the southwestern part of the state each had strong organizations with close links to the labor movement. In Martins Ferry, long linked in activism with Socialists in Wheeling, West Virginia, the tie with labor was equally strong.

The Ohio Socialist party's downfall came with World War I. Most Ohio Socialists favored neutrality and supported a strong anti-war platform, but among those who quit over the issue prior to the declaration of war in April 1917 were Max Hayes and a number of other prominent members. During this period the composition of the party altered, partly as a result of the Russian Revolution, and membership in the special foreign language federations mush-

Preparing to erect more buildings at the expanding NCR complex, 1900.

roomed. This put the party on a collision course with the federal government. In July 1917 leaders began to be arrested for giving anti-war speeches or, it was alleged, for urging resistance to the draft.

The pressures of patriotism put a severe strain on the relationship of various unions to the Socialist party. The Brewery Workers by this time were not as militantly socialist as they had been in the late nineteenth century and younger workers lacked a strong socialist tradition. National ties with Germany became an embarrassment during the war and although the union endorsed the Socialist party's anti-war platform in 1917 it also praised the AFL's backing of Wilson. Gradually the union moved to a pro-war stance and drifted from its socialist moorings.

Something of the same thing happened within several other unions. The International Association of Machinists regularly supported Socialist candidates before 1912, but Woodrow Wilson's reform program eroded this support even before the war began. Predominantly Anglo-Saxon, the membership supported the war. The mine workers' evidence of radicalism and dissent persisted, but by 1916 the more conservative forces which would ultimately elevate John L. Lewis to the presidency were on the ascendancy. The union also benefitted from government reforms, and that too had an impact.

Paradoxically, even as membership slipped and its strength faded among unions, the Socialist party gained at the ballot box. In Cleveland Charles E. Ruthenberg ran for mayor in 1917 and won over nineteen percent of the vote—up from six percent in 1915. Two other Socialists won election to city council and one to the school board. In Toledo four Socialists gained council seats. Dayton Socialists polled better than forty-four percent of the total vote cast for city commissioners. In each instance working-class wards made the heaviest contributions to the Socialist vote. Cincinnati Socialists also increased their vote substantially. Massillon elected a Socialist mayor and one councilman, Piqua a mayor and two councilmen, Jenera (a heavily German community) and Byesville nearly the whole Socialist slates. In Hamilton two Socialists won council seats and only fusion of Democrats and Republicans blocked the Socialist candidate's bid for the mayorship.

By 1918 and 1919 it was a different story. Several Socialists had been ousted for anti-war stances in Cleveland, Toledo, and Piqua. Elsewhere efforts were diverted into campaigns to raise money for the legal defense of imprisoned members and that made it difficult to focus on elections. Federal suppression also played a role. The Post Office barred Socialist papers from the mails, the Bureau of Investigation repeatedly raided offices and disrupted meetings. Ultimately a slate for state offices could not get enough signatures to win a place on the 1918 ballot. By that time, what had once seemed a viable political option for many now seemed a closed door.

These had been dynamic, decisive, and yet immensely perplexing decades for Ohio's working classes. With dazzling bursts of activity, transformations which had been in the making throughout the nineteenth century at last reached fruition during the dawn of the twentieth. Henceforth, the state would be predominantly urban, and manufacturing would be the primary fulcrum upon which the economic welfare of its residents rose and fell. Though workers did not share equally in the resultant benefits, many did realize discernable improvements in their lives — increased incomes, fewer working hours, a greater diversity of leisure activities, expanding opportunities for jobs, education, and home ownership. If not total acceptance or formidable power, trade unionism had at least achieved a distinct stability and direction. However, modernization had only reached a critical turning point, rather than its fullest limits. This social, economic, and technological revolution was ongoing, feeding upon itself to generate ever more growth, increased complexity, and new problems to compound existing difficulties. Nowhere was the human price of progress more clearly demonstrated than in continually expanding workplaces. In an amplification of long-brewing trends, the traditional craftsman's autonomy, skill, initiative, and control had been thoroughly undermined in increasingly intricate ways. Mechanization, subdivision of labor, scientific management techniques, and integrated mass-production methods — together embodying the relentless quest for speed, efficiency, and automation — threatened to convert industrial workers into depersonalized servants to the rhythms of machines.

Perhaps because expectations and experiences varied so widely, the responses of laboring people were as complicated as progress itself. Undeniably, there had been an abundance of working-class casualties. Nevertheless, relatively few had been radicalized by their experiences, as both the Wobblies and Socialists could attest. Whether tacitly or overtly, whether lulled or compelled, the mass of workers had accommodated themselves to their changing world. Clinging to personal versions of the success ethic, they steadily became habituated to new environments, modes of production, status, and paces of life. Of course, efforts were made to ameliorate the harshest conditions, but they were invariably channeled into moderate, "progressive" courses. As most reform efforts attained only imperfect success, workers began to develop a sense of narrowing alternatives, of powerlessness, of manipulation by anonymous and uncontrollable forces which menaced personal dignity and individual recognition. Resultant tensions generally remained submerged. But when accumulated grievances became intolerable, workers were fully capable of resorting to desperate measures. Such circumstances had arisen on a massive scale by 1919. The outcome would be explosive.

NCR provided employees with this fully-equipped library, ca. 1906.

"Welfare Capitalism In Ohio Industry"

The tensions generated by the rapidity of industrialization in the late nineteenth century raised unsettling questions, stirred fears and qualms, and ultimately created what has come to be called welfare capitalism. As workers mobilized to act collectively on a broad variety of grievances, strikes mounted steadily. By the mid-1880s, it seemed, an epidemic had hit the country. At the same time thousands of newcomers poured into American work places. Frequently of different origins than those already there, the immigrants attracted an increasing amount of attention. Their willingness to work long hours for low pay, some feared, would undercut American standards; others fretted that the presence of so many aliens in industrial America posed a distinct threat to American values. Economic instability compounded the tensions which flowed from this mix and focused attention on different ways to solve "the labor question." Rooted in a fear that intensifying social divisions and labor discontent would lead unique America toward a polarized European form of society in which class strife was endemic, there emerged in the 1880s a movement to reform the harshest aspects of industrial life.

Ohio manufacturers were early leaders in the movement. Procter and Gamble near Cincinnati, makers of Ivory Soap, was one of the first. It introduced a profit-sharing plan in 1887 after fourteen strikes and constant pressure by unions to organize the workforce. Designed, the company said, "to create an economically secure, steady, loyal and prospering working force," the plan was but one part of an ambitious welfare scheme. Included were such things as stock purchase and pension benefits, a savings and loan association, a cooperative store, and a lunch room. Although the company dropped profit sharing in 1903, by then welfare

NCR employees checking out books from the circulating library truck, 1907.

The women's dining room at NCR, 1902.

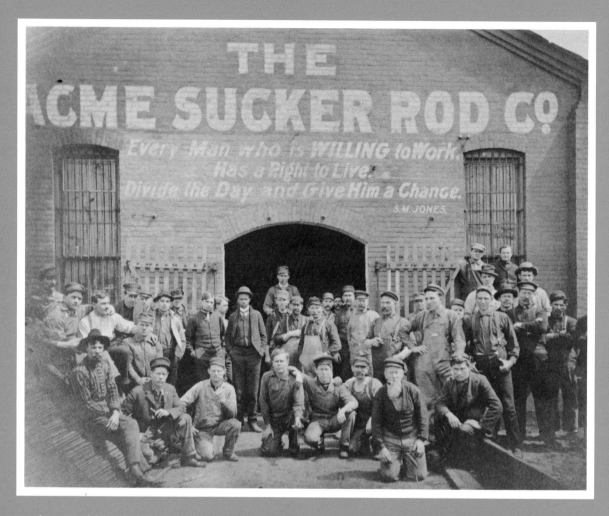

Employees at "Golden Rule" Jone's Toledo factory, ca. 1898.

work was widespread and had in fact become a profession.

The depression of the 1890s hastened that development by deepening the sense of social chaos. Profoundly affected by labor turmoil and the effects of the 1893-97 depression, Samuel M. "Golden Rule" Jones made his Acme Sucker Rod Company unique in the city of Toledo. His company motto indicated as much: "The business of this shop is to make men; the making of money is an incidental detail." Jones insisted that only one rule governed his factory, the Golden Rule. Workers kept track of their own time, enjoyed annual picnics, a company band, and access to an in-plant library and lunch room.

Jones's attitude about money, if not the contents of his program, was unique. In most instances practioners of welfare capitalism had more pragmatic aims. John H. Patterson launched his elaborate program at National Cash Register in Dayton, for example, as part of a general revamping of plant layout and production methods — but also after several strikes and lockouts, and three mysterious fires, suggested the need to pay more attention to the labor force. Patterson was not the first to hire a "welfare secretary," Filene's department store in Boston was, but the NCR program had a broad impact. Between 1897 and 1901 Patterson employed Lena Harvey to carry out his belief that labor and capital could work "together for the benefit of both." To secure harmony, the NCR scheme included suggestion boxes, a heavy stress on safety, baths for employees, physical culture classes, a highly developed

A black porter holds towels for NCR employees in the men's bath room, 1900.

NCR provided fully-equipped bathing rooms for its male workers.

155

(Left) The NCR kindergarten, in the House of Usefulness, ca. 1900. Patterson bought the building when he learned that a saloon was going to be opened in it.

(Right) An NCR employee using an Autographic Register to make a suggestion, about 1904.

NCR employees, in the indicator department here, did calesthenics daily.

The Buckeye Steel Castings foundry baseball team, 1915.

club system, numerous athletic outlets, and grounds landscaped by John Olmstead. Patterson had a ready answer for critics who considered this program too costly: "There is no charity in anything we do. Isn't it just good business to lose three cents on a girl's lunch and get back five cents worth of work." "Why does the National Cash Register Company spend thousands of dollars annually for the comfort, education and health of its employees?," he said on another occasion. "Because it pays. That is the practical reason."

Cleveland, the state's most important industrial city, also witnessed a number of welfare programs. Starting in 1898 the Cleveland Chamber of Commerce, eager to harmonize labor and management relations, spearheaded an effort to spread welfare work. Sherwin-Williams, Cleveland Hardware, and Cleveland Trust had highly developed programs and by 1901 another seventy-five companies added them as well. Welfare work spread still further before World

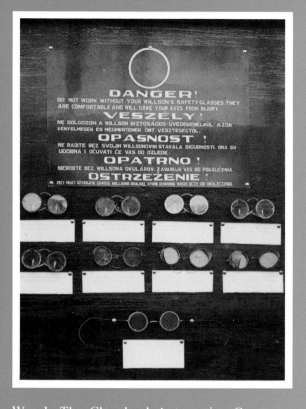

(Left) Safety signs at Buckeye Steel Castings in Columbus testify to the makeup of the workforce.

(Right) Steve Majesky of Buckeye Steel Castings in Columbus displays the steel fragment that shattered his safety goggles, 1915.

War I. The Cleveland Automotive Company had one of the largest programs. An admirer of company president Arthur L. Garford hoped other manufacturers would copy his attitude about capital and labor because "the example of pioneers like yourself is so shining, and spells so much for better conditions in industry—the substitution of understanding for suspicion, of love for hate—that it cannot long be ignored, especially, also, since ultimately it pays better."

The mixture of pragmatism and idealism reflected welfare work at the Buckeye Steel Castings Company in Columbus and the Youngstown Sheet and Tube Company as well. A 1915 pamphlet issued by the Youngstown firm pointed with pride to the extensive safety and welfare work it did. The company had two "emergency hospitals" on the premises and another under construction. In addition, the company tried to educate foreign-born workers in English. Since seventy-one percent of the 19,000 workers in the company's three plants were foreign born—twenty-three nationalities, forty-two distinct dialects—this was a matter of practical importance. Buckeye had similar concerns and company president Samuel N. Bush early introduced medical facilities, safety programs, and washrooms, as well as leisure activities. During World War I the firm added life insurance benefits and started, as did Youngstown Sheet and Tube, to provide housing.

In some firms welfare capitalism merged with the other management approaches of the day—scientific management and personnel relations. John Patterson pioneered in the latter, creating in 1901 a labor department which assumed a number of hiring and firing functions previously handled by foremen. Although the personnel management movement did not spread significantly until World War I, as early as 1913 the Clothcraft Shops of the Joseph and Feiss Co. in

The track team of Buckeye Steel Castings, 1919.

The Firestone basketball team of 1911-12.

Construction in 1917 of company-sponsored housing for Youngstown Sheet & Tube Workers.

Leaving downtown Dayton on an interurban for the annual Delco picnic.

An outing of garment workers at the Joseph Feiss Co., Cleveland, 1914.

Cleveland put into operation a rather unique program. Richard Feiss, a devotee of Frederick W. Taylor, approached professional personnel manager Mary Barnett Gilson that year and she found Feiss ''sincerely and genuinely interested in integrating personnel work with factory management'' and thus accepted his offer of a job. Welfare work, personnel relations, and scientific management went hand in hand and Gilson, who stayed with the firm until the mid-1920s, found it a happy place to put into operation her ideas. Workers generally seemed pleased too. Through World War I the shop remained basically contented, workers even somewhat puzzled when the advanced management created a company union in 1917. The inherent limits of that institution, however, were already apparent. As Gilson explained it, one of the unions' chief functions appeared to be handling grievances among the various ethnic groups about the food to be served in the cafeteria.

World War I accelerated the felt need to develop welfare programs. The events of the era reinforced ideas current decades earlier. Fear of labor turmoil, for example, stemmed not only from the disruption of defense production but from the example of the Russian revolution of 1917. That event—as well as the quest for labor stability and the desire to avoid surrendering management prerogatives to unions, which grew so much during the war — spurred the spread of welfare capitalism during the twenties. Refinements in particular programs appeared, of course, but the outlines remained largely those shaped by Ohioans and other pioneers in welfare work.

An Americanization class in the Community Hall, a Youngstown Sheet & Tube project.

PART 4
CONFRONTING PROSPERITY, DEPRESSION, AND WAR
1919-1945

Ohio's working classes played key roles in the social and economic tug-of-war which marked the nation's fitful evolution between 1919 and 1945. Both as active participants and hapless victims, workers encountered repeated challenges—concerted employer belligerence and economic hardship in the immediate aftermath of World War I; the supposed "normalcy" of uneven prosperity and the reign of the open shop in the 1920s; extended deprivation and revived labor militancy during the Depression years; economic recovery and curtailed unrest induced by another war crisis. Moreover, upon these broad, skeletal trends were layered the intense personal struggles of laboring people to make the necessary adjustments, to understand the perplexing problems, and, above all, to retain some mastery over their lives. Like so many previous generations, their resiliency would be continually tested.

Much of the tenor and many of the undertones of this complex quarter-century surfaced at the very outset. Fueled by widespread disillusionment—in this instance, that the war-effort had failed to fulfill the various Wilsonian promises to improve conditions at home and abroad—one of the most massive displays of American working-class insurgency erupted in 1919. With the termination of governmental controls and the elimination of wartime's patriotic constraints, labor and management resumed their long-standing struggle. Militant rank and filers were staunchly determined not only to consolidate the gains that had been won during the war, but to achieve even greater recognition of their rights. However, as in the early years of the century, the spread of unionism and labor's assertiveness again stimulated aggressive opposition by organized employers who eagerly awaited the opportunity to reaffirm their power. With emotions and resolve running high on both sides, the strife which broke out in 1919 attained unprecedented dimensions. More than 4,000,000 laborers—comprising an amazing one-out-of-five American workers and ranging from Broadway actors to Cincinnati clothing workers—staged over 3,600 work stoppages. Equally remarkable, diverse strikers often managed to unite across slowly fading boundaries of skill, sex, race, and ethnicity in their confrontations with corporate and government adversaries.

Among the various causes of these disputes, wages and union security were the most common. The high wages which Ohio workers had enjoyed during the war years continued into 1919. Between 1914 and 1919, for example, the average money earnings of the state's factory workers rose 143 percent. Furthermore, despite a national inflation rate of seventy-three percent over the same timespan, Ohio factory employees still realized a thirty-six percent increase in their annual real earnings—twice the national average. However, laboring people recognized that their bounty had been temporary, resulting largely from the artificial demands of war-production. With reconversion to a peacetime economy, hours were slashed, wages cut, and layoffs ordered, thereby heightening fears that continued inflation would rapidly chip away at their gains. (In fact, from 1919 to 1921, those same Ohio factory workers — particularly in major cities like Cleveland — saw the earlier increases in their purchasing power totally wiped out as the inflationary spiral and a thirty-two percent drop in manufacturing employment caused a twenty-seven percent slump in their real earnings.) Far more difficult to settle than wage adjustments, however, was the key question of union security. Though some employers were at least disposed to compromise on wage demands, most bitterly opposed any expansion of collective bargaining as a challenge to their right to manage their own enterprises. As organizers from Toledo to Cleveland soon learned, employers adamantly refused to recognize unionists, and revoked many of the concessions granted under the pressure of war.

Employers were aided by a postwar surge of anti-radical hysteria which swept the nation. Fears of foreign revolutionaries generally, and of the 'communist menace' in particular, had festered in the American mind since the late nineteenth century. But, bolstered by residual war passions and fanned by the boasts of Bolsheviks that their successful Russian Revolution of 1917 would spark the worldwide overthrow of capitalism, these deep-rooted anxieties flared anew in 1919-20. The public became more and more alarmed that mushrooming labor disputes not only endangered economic reconversion, but also threatened the very stability of American institutions. As the nation's coal miners and steel workers walked out, as a general strike broke out in Seattle, as Boston police refused to work unless their demands were met, and as the level of violence increased, fears were aroused that labor strife had indeed been instigated and orchestrated by Moscow in order to achieve the downfall of the capitalist system. Workers' civil liberties and legitimate grievances were quickly ignored in a frightening zeal to link communist subversion to every labor dispute. Management took full advantage of this "red scare," ceaselessly seeking to brand all strikers as communists. Despite high wartime expectations, laboring people now found themselves continually on the defensive, faced with the unappealing predica-

ment of attempting to justify their concerns within an extremely hostile atmosphere. The sympathetic public attitudes of the Progressive Period hardened during the immediate postwar years into popular demands for federal, state, and local suppression of the striking working classes. In the process, the American businessman returned to his pedestal to be respected and emulated by every "true American."

Overleaf—page 159.
Bonded together by unique occupational hazards, a construction gang casually posed atop the girders of Toledo's Anthony Wayne Bridge, c. 1930.

In 1919 and 1920, Toledo became a hotbed of political and social strife. Battle lines had emerged even before a strike wave, the government's anti-radical Palmer Raids, and management's open-shop drive rocked the city. Surveying the scene in January, 1919, John Quinlivan — business agent of the Toledo Central Labor Union — provided this perceptive analysis:

. . . Computing our membership on the government basis of 4 to a family and the workers will average at least five to a family, we represent almost directly fifty percent of the total population of Toledo. However it will not be amiss at this time to call your attention to the fact that organized labor will have the severest test of their existence in the next six months. There are thousands of men out of employment in Toledo and more are being added each day. Employers of labor are busy lining up their forces and labor will have to battle to maintain its standard of wages and working conditions. The Merchants and Manufacturers have opened an employment office on Huron St. and will seek to control employment in their various factories through this institution as well as establish complete methods of tabulation of workers resulting eventually in the Blacklist systems and other evils well known to the workers. At least three new strike breaking detective agencies have established themselves in Toledo and anyone who knows the history of these strike breaking agencies know that they . . . operate only where there promises to be a big field for their activities. Already some of the employers of labor in Toledo who laid off men during the holidays and after cancellation of government contracts are attempting and in many instances succeeding in rehiring their labor at from ten to twenty cents an hour less than before the layoff. In many cases active members of labor unions are not employed and their places filled by new faces or men. These are some of the conditions that confront labor in 1919 and if persisted in will result in an industrial war in Toledo that will make all other disputes seem like a mole hill in comparison with a large mountain . . .

By April, on the eve of extended hostilities which would severely weaken labor in the city, Quinlivan revealed that simmering tensions had reached boiling-point:

. . . Merchants and Manufacturers employment office are running true to form. Despite the fact that there are still thousands of men unable to secure steady employment, the M & M office is advertising in other cities for help . . . We have repeatedly stated that this office was installed to blacklist labor, to reduce wages by flooding the town with labor from other cities and is a positive disgrace to the community. This institution and its supporters are a bigger menace to the welfare of Toledo and its future than all the I.W.W. and Anarchists that they spend pages in newspapers raving about and I think it is about time that local unions got busy and increased their donations to the M & M picket fund so that we can enlarge the scope of this work. Counter advertisements . . . should be published in all outside newspapers, labor papers advising labor to stay away from Toledo because of the already overcrowded labor market and the exploitation of the Manufacturers and Merchants organization . . . I believe that if this is done you will hear some loud squacking and apologizing from this gang of exploiters.

Ohio was a major arena for labor-management confrontations and anti-radical hysteria. During 1919, the state was rocked by 237 strikes — an annual total which remained unsurpassed until the momentous battles of 1937 (see Table 4-A). The majority of walkouts — whether by Toledo machinists or Columbus carpenters for higher wages, or by male street-car conductors in Cleveland to force female co-workers out of jobs acquired during the war — were purely local in scale and lacked any radical aims. Nevertheless, frantic middle and upper-class Ohioans pointed to supposedly ominous signs that a left-wing conspiracy with foreign overtones was being launched among the working classes—IWW agitation in Toledo, Rossford, Akron, and Cleveland; several new-ly-elected Socialists on the Toledo City Council and a Socialist mayor in Massillon; the increased combativeness of tiny radical groups such as the Soldiers, Sailors, and Workers Council (an organization of unemployed veterans). Especially disturbing was a bloody May Day riot in Cleveland, when 5,000 marchers carrying red banners and placards which read "Workers of the World, Unite!" battled in the streets with 700 policemen and countless thousands of hostile spectators. To many, a total collaspe of the "American way of life" seemed imminent.

A furious outcry arose from various sectors for loyal citizens and governmental officials to take drastic action to protect the state from revolutionaries, Bolsheviks, radical aliens, and militant unionists. In Cleveland and Cincinnati, chapters of the Loyal American League — successor to the wartime American Protective League, a volunteer vigilante group of private citizens who spied upon suspected enemy aliens and provided information to government authorities — were formed to fight the Red menace and to guard the nation against "treason, lawlessness and disorder." Members disrupted radical meetings and submitted sur-

veillance reports to city, state, and federal officials about suspicious "un-Americans" in their communities. Anxiously lining up with the forces of patriotic conservatism, the Ohio State Federation of Labor also loudly proclaimed its condemnation of both the IWW and Bolshevism. In March, 1919, local AFL leaders even established a weekly *Columbus Labor News,* "for the purpose of combatting the Bolsheviki menace in the United States of America, [and] to combat the IWW element in all, or any organized, or unorganized groups of wage-earners." As the anti-radical movement gathered momentum, the Ohio General Assembly responded in May by unanimously passing the Criminal Syndicalism Act, which penalized the advocacy of "malicious injury or destruction of the property of another; violence; or unlawful methods of terrorism as a means of accomplishing industrial or political reform." Surprisingly, while hundreds were tried under similar laws in other states over the next decade, no individuals were prosecuted in Ohio. However, the federal government did continue the offensive in late-1919 and early-1920 by conducting the notorious Palmer Raids. Coordinated by the U.S. Department of Justice and carried out with the assistance of local authorities and the Loyal American League, the coast-to-coast raids of private homes and union halls in thirty-three cities — including Cleveland, Youngstown, and Toledo — led to the arrest of more than 7,000 alleged communists, the overwhelming majority of whom were ultimately found innocent of any radical involvement. Much to the embarrassment of conservative alarmists, the feared "reign of terror" failed to materialize.

Often rabid public hostility and the cautious responses of union leaders did not diminish rank-and-file discontent, however, nor did they dissuade workers from forcefully asserting their right to protect their interests. Two particularly notable strikes — the Willys-Overland dispute and the Great Steel Strike—illustrated the unrest which wrenched the state.

Toledo was a hotbed of labor ferment in 1919. The city's jobless ranks had swelled to approximately 17,000 — roughly fifteen percent of the labor force — as thousands of recently discharged soldiers joined laid-off workers in a vain search for employment in local industries striving to reconvert to peacetime production. For those fortunate enough to find work, the escalating cost of living rapidly ate away at wages. Furthermore, many workers grew disenchanted with conservative AFL spokesmen who urged prudence and cooperation with increasingly antagonistic employers. Consequently, significant numbers of laboring people turned to the IWW, the Socialists, and various tiny communist groups for leadership, with Eastern European immigrants apparently among the principal recruits. So dangerous did this combination of radical politics, labor militancy, and alien activism appear to federal authorities that the Bureau of Investigation dispatched agents to Toledo to investigate and infiltrate local left-wing organizations. Much

Although generally satisfied with working conditions, by 1919 many Willys-Overland employees strongly resented management's efforts to hold down wages, increase hours, and discourage unionization.

The Willys-Overland plant's Enamel Department.

of the information which they uncovered, ironically was provided by private undercover operatives employed by the Willys-Overland Company.

Willys-Overland had gained a popular image as one of the most progressive employers in the city, by implementing the precepts of welfare capitalism on a broad scale and with much fanfare. In 1918, the company had opened the Overland Hotel to provide comfortable room and board for 350 male employees at the reasonable rate of $8.00 per week. In 1919, a program was announced to place workers on jobs which best suited their individual abilities, and to inaugurate a profit-sharing plan based on seniority and individual output. In order to facilitate upward job-mobility and efficiency, the company also established its own school to train employees in the skilled trades. However, these attractive benefits were not granted without a price. Due to anticipated post-war competition in the auto industry, management further proposed an increase in the workweek from forty-five to forty-eight hours, with only small wage-gains which supposedly would result from a new piecework system.

Employees were hardly enthused by the company's policies. The profit-sharing plan, the increased hours, and the piecework system were viewed as mere camouflage to hold wages down, and many resented the job-placement plan by which they could be moved to lower-paying positions in unfamiliar departments. While conservative leaders of the Automobile Workers Council — an umbrella group comprised of eight trade unions in the plant — insisted that collective bargaining was the proper course of action, a small radical faction instead demanded an immediate strike to force the company to accept a forty-four hour week and to concede larger wage increases. The proponents of prudence prevailed initially, but during fruitless negotiations from February through

In *An Autobiographical Novel*, Kenneth Rexroth recalled that the Toledo of his youth was a gritty, rough-and-tumble, wide-open, blue-collar town which teemed with street-gangs, gambling dens, burlesque houses, brothels — and passionate working-class activism. As a teenager during the World War I era, Rexroth abandoned his upper-class background to support himself as a 'street-wise' hustler and gang leader. His immersion in the workers' daily world led to participation in the Willys-Overland dispute of 1919. Deeply radicalized by his strike-experience, Rexroth subsequently joined the revolutionary Industrial Workers of the World.

One of the finest adventures that my association with this gang involved me in was the Willys-Overland strike . . . one of the most bitterly fought strikes of the time. Who led it, I don't know. Possibly the IWW. It had all the characteristics of a strike under revolutionary leadership — a big rank-and-file strike committee, soup kitchens, a mass picket line, dozens of soapboxers. The kids of the strikers got jobs as runners. This was a necessity because the plant covered a good many acres and the mass picket lines were concentrated at several gates, considerable distances apart. We went on our bicycles carrying messages from one picket captain to another, general orders from the strike committee, bundles of bulletins, and big sacks of sandwiches. . . .
. . . the strike came to its climax in the most spectacular battle I was ever to see in my years in the labor movement. Tear gas had just come in and I believe the Army loaned a supply of canisters to the city police. The mayor ordered the mass picketing stopped, and the strikers, of course, ignored the order.
The next day the street in front of the main gate was a solid mass of cops, stretched for more than a block past the next factory, the De-Vilbis Atomizer plant. First were a couple of platoons of mounted police, armed with long sticks. . . . Behind them were foot police and amongst them a detail of tear gas hurlers. The mounted police rode very slowly toward the gate, pushing the strikers back a foot at a time with the breasts of their horses, but not using their sticks. The strike committee was prepared for them. They had gone up to the carbarns across the street and taken the junked poles — whole pine trees rotted out at the base and presumably stacked up with the rest of the junk to be sold as firewood. Each pole was manned by about eight heavyweight Slav and Hungarian strikers, and they were planted behind the picket line, just in front of the bridge across Ten-Mile

April, company spokesmen refused to compromise. Moreover, management authorized the election of a shop committee by employees to discuss working conditions, safety, health, discipline, or any other grievances. Outraged at the creation of this company union and especially frustrated by management's continued insistence on longer hours, 7,500 union members —nearly two-thirds of the workforce—walked out on May 5.

Violence erupted a few days later, when workers who had remained on the job ended their shift. The typical exchanges of angry insults between pickets and strikebreakers this time ignited a riot which the small police squad assigned to protect the strikebreakers was powerless to stop. Before the workers' passions had been exhausted, dozens laid injured, the plant was bombarded with rocks, and streetcars had been overturned. Realizing that available police power was insufficient to protect their property or employees, company officials shut down the factory. Reinforcements immediately appeared, however, as Toledo's business and commercial interests rallied to Willys-Overland's support. Numerous newspaper advertisements appeared in which the city's banks and the Merchants and Manufacturers Association proclaimed their firm endorsement of the company's fight for the open shop, and branded as "un-American" anyone who would force workmen to join a union. The Kiwanis and Rotary Clubs also published statements which blasted "outside agitators, who having no interest in the welfare of our city or of our citizens, are seeking to stir up trouble in the ranks of labor, harass and interfere with the production of our factories and by their revolutionary doctrine, ferment in the minds of many misguided foreigners a class hatred and a disregard for all law and authority."

In fact, the city's sizable Slavic population became trapped in a nativistic crossfire, as charges of foreign influence in the strike flew from all sides. Frustrated strikers tended to perceive all scabs as aliens. At the same time, the company repeatedly blamed the dispute on foreign instigators who were bent on destroying the "American way of life." Prevalent xenophobia and anti-radical hysteria even emanated from Toledo's pulpits, with ministers warning their working-class congregations to ignore the raving aliens. While subsequent research has demonstrated that very few members of the Slavic community actually served as strikebreakers — though at least half remained passive observers — and that Poles were especially active strike-supporters, such exaggerated accusations did weaken working-class solidarity and fortify management's efforts.

Meanwhile, the company had reopened its doors with the aid of 500 former soldiers deputized by the mayor. The move backfired, however, when strikers engaged the strikebreakers and the untrained deputies in repeated battles over the next several days, ultimately forcing the company to shut down again. Governor James M. Cox refused the mayor's request to mobilize the national guard. Finally, federal officials stepped into the breach to halt both the bloodshed and the strike. On June 5, the United States District Court issued a temporary restraining order which severely limited the number of pickets and stated that they all had to be American citizens. Subsequently, the court also ordered members of the radical Soldiers and Sailors Council to leave town and confiscated the strikers' newspaper. Willys-Overland quickly resumed production, and strapped workers — unable to withstand the combined power of employers, the federal court, and public opinion—were forced either to concede defeat or to seek employment elsewhere. Though picketing would continue into February, 1920, the strike effectively collapsed. The workers' hopes for recognition of their right to bargaining equality would have to await another day, when hysteria had abated and the use of government power had shifted.

Perhaps the most significant strike of 1919, both in scope and ultimate impact, raged in the nation's steel industry. Union activism in the

Creek, invisible to the cops, who were a couple of blocks higher up the street.

Now, as the street . . . went down the hills to the bridge it passed between cut banks about thirty feet high, so there was a narrow canyon rising straight out of the sidewalks. When the strikers had been pushed away from the main gates, a mounted police officer fired a shot in the air and shouted a proclamation ordering them to disperse. Instead, the picket line surged back against the horses and the mounted police charged. . . . The picket line ran back toward the bridge and the cops were drawn down into the canyon, between the masses of strikers on the sidewalks. The picket line opened up and the boys with the poles came through. When this happened the tear-gas detail hurled the canisters over the heads of the mounted police into the front ranks of the strikers. Unfortunately, scientific warfare had not reached the point it was to achieve in World War II. There was a gas detail, but there were no meteorologists in the police force, and a couple of hundred cops had not noticed that the wind was blowing in their faces.

The pandemonium was indescribable. The horses were enveloped in clouds of tear gas, which made them scream with the bloodcurdling scream of horses in a fire and they took off up the steep banks, spilling their riders, as the boys with the poles, with wet handkerchiefs wrapped round their faces, charged.

Considerable time passed before order was restored. The cops were shooting in all directions but lucky for us they didn't shoot one another or anybody else. I think a few strikers got flesh wounds, but they were hauled away to safety and the only serious damage was done to the horses, some of whom broke their legs on the cut bank and had to be shot. When the battle was at its height, out the gate came [company guards] . . . on the run with fixed bayonets and the strikers vanished like snowflakes. . . . A few strikers who had been thrown into the muck of the creek were fished out and locked up. The press exploded and demanded that everybody in the union be tried for attempted murder, but a few days later the strike was settled.

This was my first strike and, except for the poor horses, that I can still hear screaming, certainly my most enjoyable. When I look back on it one of the most significant things, it seems to me, is that at the age of twelve or thirteen, like all of Engels' "Members of the upper class who cut themselves loose from their own class and go over to the workers," I got on the payroll. I started off in the labor movement as a pie-card artist.

mills had been dormant for nearly a decade, ever since walkouts by the Amalgamated Association of Iron, Steel, and Tin Workers were crushed in 1901 and again in 1910. Though the Amalgamated managed to maintain a small membership among skilled workers, the growing mass of unskilled laborers had been totally neglected. Wages and working conditions ranged from poor to abysmal. The average work week lasted sixty-nine hours, with most of the labor force putting in twelve-hour shifts, and one-third working seven-day weeks. When changing from the day to the night shift — a mandatory monthly or weekly procedure — thousands of laborers worked a twenty-four hour day. Wage rates had advanced by an estimated eighty-one percent during the war, reaching an hourly average of 30 to 42¢ for common labor in 1918. But such increases barely kept pace with, and frequently fell behind, the steadily mounting cost of living. In 1919, an investigator for the Interchurch World Movement's Commission of Inquiry reported on typical conditions in Youngstown:

> Timekeeper in the sheet mill department of a large 'independent' stated: that among the men whose time he kept there were about 45 rollers who worked eight hours, 110 laborers who worked ten hours and 190 who were on the twelve-hour basis, seven days a week. They changed every week from day to night turn, making a 24-hour shift... In the sheet galvanizing department the men worked a twelve-hour day with no rest spells and no lunch hour. Their rates were 42, 42½, and 44 cents. So many men gave out under the strain and had to be fired for not being able to do the work that checks for these men gave out in the time department, and the timekeeper begged the foreman not to discharge so many. There were about 100 men in the department, and from 35 to 50 were hired and fired each month.

As this statement suggested, in addition to the excessive hours and arduous conditions, steelworkers toiled under a system of absolute and arbitrary management control in which they had no "say" — a system which became an especially important source of shop-floor unrest.

In mid-1918, the AFL at last resolved to improve conditions and to rectify its lack of influence by launching a National Committee for the Organizing of the Iron and Steel Industry. Comprised of representatives from twenty-four unions claiming jurisdiction in the plants, the National Committee was headed by William Z. Foster—a talented organizer, a former member of the IWW, an exponent of direct economic action, a subsequent leader of the communist movement, and a spokesman whose obvious left-wing leanings would provide ammunition for management's charges of radical subversion in the strike. Despite efforts of employers to discourage membership by firing and blacklisting unionists, the organizing drive achieved remarkable success. Within a year union leaders claimed over 150,000 members nationwide, approximately thirty percent of whom worked in Ohio mills. The Cleveland and Youngstown districts proved especially fertile recruitment

areas. Flushed with success and faced with growing rank-and-file pressure for action, in July, 1919 the National Committee asked for a meeting with Elbert H. Gary—chairman of the board of the massive United States Steel Corporation and head of the industry's employer-association—to discuss its demands for abolition of the twenty-four-hour shift, a reduced eight-hour day and forty-eight-hour week, as well as wage increases. Since the granting of a conference would have implied recognition of the union, Gary ignored the request. By September, grassroots militancy had reached boiling point in steel centers across the country. From Youngstown, for example, dismayed organizers notified Foster, "we cannot be expected to meet the enraged workers, who will consider us traitors if the strike is postponed." On September 22, the momentous struggle began.

Within a week, approximately half of the industry's labor force—more than a quarter of a million steelworkers—had walked off their jobs in nine states, including an estimated 100,000 in Steubenville, Cleveland, Youngstown, Niles, Canton, Alliance, Massillon, and Warren. Though not a total shutdown, the strike surpassed in scale and intensity any similar out-

As the Willys-Overland strike began to falter in the face of concerted employer-opposition and federal court injunctions, the Toledo Central Labor Union warned of dire consequences for the city's entire labor movement, if workers did not provide immediate support.

Toledo, Ohio,   June 18th, 1919.

Help Financially and Morally!

Pay and Forward Your Assessment Promptly! Seven Weeks Assessment Now Due! Are You Doing Your Bit?

TO ALL LOCAL UNIONS:

GREETING:—

Every business interest in Toledo that is opposed to progress is fighting the Locked-Out Overland Workers and Organized Labor in Toledo. This fight means much to every man and woman in Toledo who works for a living. Federal court has restricted our picketing and has THREATENED to STOP picketing entirely. ONE HUNDRED AND FIFTY MEMBERS of the COMMERCE CLUB HAVE BEEN SWORN IN AS U. S. DEPUTY MARSHALS in the last few days. THERE IS no DISORDER IN TOLEDO. WE WORKERS are LAW ABIDING. "THEN WHY THE INCREASED DEPUTIES ALL BUSINESS MEN" and most of them KNOWN enemies of LABOR. WATCH the NEWS-BEE and BLADE for some more PEACE editorials all in the interest of the OVERLAND COMPANY. THEY may tell you the Overland Company can't work forty-four hours per week because of competition, that the OVERLAND COMPANY is going to move out of Toledo and a hundred and one other reasons. WATCH COCHRAN of the NEWS-BEE and his EDITORIALS and then watch the BLADE and TIMES follow suit. You notice how they now elaborate on any statement the FEDERAL judge makes that is detrimental to aLbor and their CAMPAIGN of SILENCE as to LABOR'S side. READ THE UNION LEADER for the FACTS, SUBSCRIBE FOR IT.

IF PICKETING IS PROHIBITED BY FEDERAL COURT, DO YOU FAVOR A GENERAL STRIKE OF ORGANIZED LABOR IN TOLEDO. IS YOUR LOCAL IN POSITION TO DECLARE A GENERAL STRIKE. WE MUST BE PREPARED FOR THE WORST AND WE WANT LABOR TO BE PREPARED.

This is your fight. If the OVERLAND LOCKED-OUT WORKERS are forced back to work because of lack of funds Labor in Toledo will suffer. PAY AND FORWARD YOUR ASSESSMENT PROMPTLY. FIND OUT IF YOUR LOCAL IS DOING ITS BIT.

WE NEED FUNDS BADLY FOR RELIEF AND WE NEED IT NOW. TWO WEEKS FROM NOW IT MAY BE TOO LATE.

ACT ON THIS APPEAL AT ONCE, DON'T DELAY. THE LOCKED-OUT WORKERS CAN'T FIGHT WITHOUT FOOD. NOW IS THE TIME TO HELP, TOMORROW IS TOO LATE.

TOLEDO CENTRAL LABOR UNION COMMITTEE.

JOHN J. QUINLIVAN, Secretary.

Rank-and-file factionalism remained one of the most serious problems plaguing the labor movement after World War I. In the Great Steel Strike of 1919, for example, intimidation and coercion contributed to the workers' defeat. But so too did sharp divisions along lines of ethnicity and skill that split the workforce. Skilled Anglo-Saxon steelworkers with secure status were particularly antagonistic toward strikers who were unskilled and recent immigrants from Eastern Europe. John Martin, a skilled heater at the McDonald Works in Youngstown who had refused to join the strike, expressed such animosities in testimony before a U.S. Senate Investigating Committee in 1919:

The Chairman. And how many of those men are out on strike?
Mr. Martin. Well, I think that that question ought to be qualified, Senator. That is a hard question to answer because we do not understand the foreigners.
The Chairman. You do not understand the foreigners?
Mr. Martin. We do not understand them.
The Chairman. And about how many of them are foreigners?
Mr. Martin. About 70 per cent, I should judge.
The Chairman. Well, when they are working in the mills don't you understand them, then?
Mr. Martin. Yes, sir.
The Chairman. And if you understand them, then, why is it you do not understand them when they are out?
Mr. Martin. Well, it is so hard to get their sentiments and their intentions in regard to the strike . . . There is one point that I would like to emphasize in my testimony, and it is that question of intimidation, because it has to do with our Americanism. I believe that we ought to be entitled to all the lawful rights that are coming to us, and these men have carried on a system of intimidation that has been thoroughly un-American by the massing of thousands of men at the gate and by the threatening of the burning down of homes and killing of families. . . .
The Chairman. Do most of these people you speak of as foreigners own their own homes?
Mr. Martin. A great many of them, and right there, in our town, Youngstown, the Steel Corporation has built them homes, a cement house, that they are selling for $5,000, to these foreigners, well worth the money, based on present values of real estate in Youngstown. They have instituted this home-building plan, and many Americans complain that they always give it to the foreigner first. . . .
The Chairman. If conditions were so favorable there, how do you account for 85 per cent of the men going out?
Mr. Martin. I account for it by the un-American methods used by the organizers. . . .
Senator McKellar. How are living conditions there? Are they good or bad?
Mr. Martin. The sentiment of the Americans — and I believe we are backed up by the foreign element there — is that we do not want more wages . . . you will find as fine homes in Youngstown as anywhere owned by workingmen. You would be surprised to see them . . . in fact, a good many of them approach what you might designate as a mansion. . . .
The Chairman. Do you really mean that the American Federation of Labor is not asking the Americans to join, and is asking the foreign workers to join?
Mr. Martin. Yes, sir.
The Chairman. You were a member of the Federation of Labor once, were you not?
Mr. Martin. Yes, sir.
The Chairman. Was that true at that time?
Mr. Martin. No, sir.
The Chairman. Do you think then that the American Federation of Labor has changed and has become foreignized as to some of these industries?
Mr. Martin. My personal opinion is this: Somebody got in and scuttled the American Federation of Labor. . . .

burst in the country's long labor history. Moreover, this was a distinctly grassroots effort, instigated on the industry's shop-floors, and involving at least twice as many non-unionists as signed-up members. To these disgruntled steelworkers, issues of wages, hours, and conditions actually seemed symbolic. Foremost in their minds, was an apparently deep-rooted desire for "industrial democracy" — namely, for recognition by employers of their right, not only to organize unions, but also to maintain some personal dignity and control in their working lives. A veteran of the Youngstown mills summed up the feelings of many fellow-strikers, when he stated:

I had relatives in the Revolutionary War, I fought for freedom in the Philippines myself, and I had three boys in the army fighting for democracy in France. One of them is lying in the Argonne Forest now. If my boy could give his life fighting for free democracy in Europe, I guess I can stand it to fight this battle through to the end. I'm going to help my fellow workmen show Judge Gary that he can't act as if he was a king or kaiser and tell them how long they have got to work.

As the mightiest capitalistic power on earth, the American steel industry was fully capable of resisting this upsurge. While local officials in a few communities such as Cleveland attempted to assist the strikers, in the majority of cases government authorities at all levels were firmly allied with management in its efforts to suppress the walkout. Deputized private guards, together with local and state police, attacked pickets and broke up strike meetings. An army of strikebreakers was hired, largely consisting of blacks so as to aggravate racial tensions. Labor spies infiltrated the union ranks, forewarning employers of strike-strategy, fomenting factionalism, and disrupting the conduct of the walkout. In most steel centers, the companies could count on the support of friendly newspapers whose reporting often became blatantly slanted against labor. As only one example, assailants in strike clashes were invariably identified as "foreign" or "union members," and all victims were described as "American." Management also used the press to launch a tremendous propaganda campaign to win public support. Daily advertisements appeared, claiming that the strike was a communist plot contrived in Russia to generate revolution throughout the U.S., rather than a mere labor-management dispute. Union spokesmen in Ohio feebly tried to counteract these distortions by asserting that, in fact, "failure of the A.F. of L. to win the nation wide steel strike would mean a rapid growth of Bolshevism, IWW disorder and civil war." But the employers' ceaseless stress upon the strike's supposedly radical and subversive aims, together with Foster's left-wing views, effectively reduced public sympathy for the workers. Reports that "reds" arrested during the concurrent Palmer raids had urged the use of sabotage in Ohio steel mills, overshadowed uncontradicted accounts of brutal working conditions in the same plants. For many Ohioans, the sole fact that seventy-one percent

During the Great Steel Strike of 1919, the Youngstown Sheet and Tube Company converted boxcars into sleeping quarters—appropriately dubbed "Hotel DeCop"—for its army of local police and deputized guards.

of all steelworkers were immigrants or of foreign parentage was sufficient proof that they also had to be un-American and revolutionaries.

The atmosphere grew especially volatile in the Youngstown district. In contrast to most other mill towns, the local clergy actively supported the strike. However, city officials openly sided with the employers, prohibiting any strike meetings, arresting organizers, and charging them with criminal syndicalism. On one occasion, police arrested an entire local union of the Amalgamated Association merely for holding a standard business meeting. Citizens' vigilante committees were formed, which threatened to tar and feather all union leaders and run them out of town. Violence accelerated when thousands of scabs were brought in, especially blacks recruited from the South. Despite the opposition's strength, strikers stubbornly persevered. Local newspaper accounts described with grudging admiration how the strikers—the majority of whom were foreign-born—had built up their personal savings and food supplies in order to weather a long walkout, and selflessly assisted fellow-workers in need. A reporter for the *Youngstown Vindicator* sarcastically noted that American women could take a lesson from the thrifty wives of immigrant steelworkers:

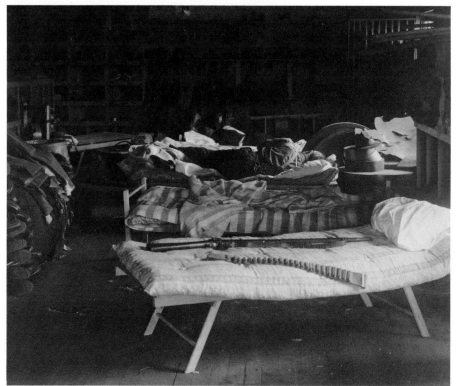

The difference between the foreign-born and American worker is in the women. The modern American wife, especially if she is young, spends four and five times as much for clothing as the foreign-born wife. To keep up with Dame Fashion is the ambition of many a woman and nobody denies that it costs a pretty penny. Friend wife likes to drive an automobile and indeed there are many who are driving their husbands to work every day and calling for them in the evening. Expensive automobiles and pretty dresses on the one side and nice fat savings bank accounts on the other, that is the real reason why the picket lines around the plant gates are composed of foreign-born.

Nor did strikers' wives restrict their support to the domestic front. When rising numbers of imported workers seriously threatened to defeat the walkout at Youngstown Sheet and Tube in early November, crowds of women attacked police and strikebreakers, hurling pepper and mustard into their faces, while yelling "Me men no work. You scabbage!" One of the arrested females—collectively portrayed in the press as "Amazons from the Slavish community"—firmly stated her resolve: "I like angel and devil, angel pull devil, devil pull angel, you pull me, I pull you. Me Mrs. Union. Me not Mrs. Scab."

As cautious union leaders had feared from the outset, such instances of local cohesiveness

In mute testimony to the volatile atmosphere in the 1919 steel strike, company guards at Youngstown Sheet and Tube even napped with guns and ammunition at-the-ready.

and insurgency could not effectively combat the power of the steel corporations. Unions represented on the National Committee began to withdraw, the AFL renounced Foster's leadership, hopes that the coal strike in late-1919 would curtail steel production soon faded, and factionalism spread through the ranks. In desperation, the National Committee agreed in late-November to binding mediation by the Interchurch Commission, but management refused to participate. Discouraged strikers drifted back to work, and the walkout was officially called off in January, 1920, without having gained a single concession from the steel magnates. Not only did their defeat mean a return to long hours and arbitrary paternalism, it also crushed unionization in the nation's most important industry for seventeen years, thereby crippling the entire labor movement.

The setbacks of 1919, plus an ensuing string of labor defeats from 1920 to 1922, commenced another unique phase in the evolution of working-class life. According to previous patterns, the prosperous years between 1922 and 1929 should have been marked by widespread labor unrest and union expansion. Instead, working people generally seemed mired in apathy and disillusionment, while an inert labor movement flirted with collapse. No single factor adequately explained this turn of events. The initial strike failures and

employer obstinance, for example, surely contributed to deflated militancy—but workers had experienced serious reversals before and soon regrouped to continue the struggle. Nor could conservative, weak, and unimaginative union leaders solely bear the blame, though they obviously exerted an inhibiting influence. Rather, this state of affairs must be viewed within the era's larger context, in which a complex array of social, economic, and political forces interacted to reshape the perceptions, the status, and the environments of laboring people.

Of primary importance, were the various impacts of shifting migration patterns on the composition, nativity, and residency of the state's population. As Tables 4-B and 4-C indicate, whether new developments or part of long-term trends, the resultant adjustments were substantial. One highly significant change, for example, was the decline in Ohio's foreign-born inhabitants. Spurred by wartime xenophobia and nationalism which carried over into the postwar wave of anti-radical hysteria, the federal government enacted immigration restriction laws in 1921 and 1924. Especially intended to curb the flow of aliens from southern and eastern Europe, the legislation caused immigration into the U.S. to drop by a startling sixty-five percent from 1921 to 1929, and slowed the overall growth of the nation's foreign-born to a mere two percent during the entire decade. Acute reverberations appeared in Ohio — a traditional destination for job-hungry immigrants — where the foreign-born population actually declined by four percent. Consequently, between 1920 and 1930, the proportion of foreign-born Ohioans slumped from twelve to ten percent — the lowest ratio of immigrant residents in the state's 127-year history. Meanwhile, the native-born population rose sixteen percent, partially due to natural increases, but also because of geographic mobility. Continuing an already familiar course, the number of residents who had relocated from other states jumped thirty-eight percent during the 1920s, ultimately accounting for more than one-out-of-five Ohioans by decade's end. Blacks comprised a major contingent of this movement, as their swelling exodus from the South stimulated a sixty-six percent increase in the state's black inhabitants. Therefore, with the sole exception of race, a certain uniformity increasingly characterized the overall composition of Ohio's populace. Though hardly a complete transformation, much of the cultural and ethnic diversity which had enriched the texture of working-class life for decades perceptibly diminished in the "Roaring '20s," as earlier immigrants and their children became assimilated—ever so gradually—into the "American way of life."

Bustling cities remained the pivotal hubs for ongoing migratory activity, particularly attracting masses of native-born newcomers from within and without the state. While failing to match the growth rates of prior decades, Ohio's urban population advanced twenty-three percent during the 1920s, largely as a result of the

While profits and production soared during the 1920s, health and safety hazards continued to plague the workforce. Addressing the 1927 All Ohio Safety Congress, P. F. Casey, Chairman of the Industrial Commission of Ohio, voiced the concerns of many that the human price of economic prosperity was excessive:

. . . In the year 1926, 1,124 industrial workers were killed in Ohio. 219,661 injuries were reported to the Industrial Commission . . . sixteen of these men were permanently totally disabled, by which we mean totally incapacitated for work forever. There were also 1,843 of these injured persons who were permanently partially disabled, meaning that they have lost a leg or an eye or an arm or a hand or some other member of the body.
I sometimes think that the reason we are not as much concerned about these accidents as we should be is because we do not visualize the real seriousness of the situation. We hear of an accident here and there or we see one occasionally, but we do not get a picture of what the real situation is. Suppose we were to see all of the people who are killed and injured in the industries of Ohio together in a parade or procession of some kind. What a sight it would be!
Such a parade would be led by the 1,124 coffins. These would be followed by a number of stretchers or wheel chairs to take care of the totally disabled. Then the blind would come along, being led. Then would follow hundreds of men on crutches and with canes. Then would follow along the men with the empty coat sleeves and the empty trouser legs, and hundreds and hundreds of them without fingers and hands, or with artificial fingers and hands. what gruesome sight that would be! And, by the way, what an indictment against industry and what a reflection on our boasted civilization!

constant influx of former rural inhabitants. In an abrupt turnabout after thirty years of decline, the state's rural population finally achieved a modest three-percent increase during the decade. But, with agriculture suffering from persistent depression and with mechanization steadily reducing the number of required farm-hands, many agrarian and small-town residents "picked up stakes" and flocked to the job-opportunities, dazzle, and apparent luxury of industrial-commercial cities. The ranks of urban-dwellers swelled in primary centers from Dayton to Youngstown, as well as in secondary cities like Hamilton, Lakewood, and Portsmouth (see Table 4-D). Of course, the consequent make-up of the populations also underwent dramatic change. Paralleling statewide demographic trends, foreign-born inhabitants decreased in the vast majority of cities; native-born whites enlarged their numerical superiority; and black residents multiplied, more than doubling their number in Cleveland, Toledo, Akron, Youngstown, Canton, Warren, and Steubenville (see Tables 4-E and 4-F). The pressures of population growth stretched the very physical dimensions of urban centers, as residents spilled out into adjoining areas. Facilitated by the public's new-found "love-affair with the automobile" — which enabled more middle and working-class urbanites to escape the geographic limitations habitually imposed by trolley lines or the need to live within walking distance of their jobs — urban sprawl and suburban expansion accelerated. However, growth also generated problems. Mounting demand for more of everything — police and fire protection, water and sewer lines, paved streets, sanitation, housing, education, parks, and hospitals — placed tremendous financial strains on taxpayers and municipal govern-

By 1920, mechanization had facilitated the arduous task of paving Massillon's streets.

As they had for over eight decades, pottery kilns continued to dominate East Liverpool's landscape and economy in 1925.

Called "the prototypical industrial city," Youngstown drew its lifeblood from steel production. As demonstrated by this view of a portion of the vast Youngstown Sheet and Tube Company complex, the mills devoured massive quantities of raw materials, shrouded the city in smoke and soot, and dwarfed nearby working-class neighborhoods.

Teamsters posed with their rig in Canton, 1929.

During the 1920s, postal workers in Dayton manually sorted the swelling volume of mail piece-by-piece.

ments. Frustrated city officials often had little recourse but to follow the example of Cleveland's mayor, who suspended garbage collection in 1922 and 1923 for lack of sufficient funds. Creeping blight in the inner cities and "white flight" to the suburbs thus became familiar characteristics of maturing urban environments.

Furthermore, the composition of the labor force as well as occupational structures experienced extremely significant alterations. Though workforces expanded in each sector of the economy except for the severely slumping coal industry, a profound occupational redistribution was underway. Primarily because of tremendous technological advances, the proportion of Ohio's total labor force employed in manufacturing slipped by four percent from 1920 to 1930. At the same time, the service in-

dustries, trade, and transportation absorbed larger shares of the state's workers, often transforming displaced factory hands into "white collar" employees (see Table 4-G). These profound transitions had readily apparent impacts in Ohio's major urban-industrial centers. While a plurality of the increasingly native-born workers continued to earn their livelihoods in industrial occupations during the decade, rising proportions of local labor forces from Cleveland to Youngstown found jobs in the non-manufacturing sectors (see Table 4-H). Moreover, employers now drew from an immense pool of native workers arriving from depressed rural areas to replace depleted foreign sources. Habituated to low farm incomes and irregular employment, these new recruits thus relieved pressures on employers to maintain or increase wages and to provide steady jobs. Since most were also semi- and unskilled, the replacement of skilled labor with machines tended by these new urban workers was expedited. Perhaps most importantly, migrants from farms and small towns possessed personal traits which were quite attractive to management: customs of geographic rather than occupational mobility, fundamentally conservative outlooks based on old rural values, firm beliefs in the individualistic gospel of success, and (once again with the exception of former coal miners) a critical lack of union traditions.

The overriding factor shaping and conditioning most aspects of working-class life, however, was the era's distinctive economic upswing. After a sharp dip in 1920-21, the economy staged a quick recovery which launched an extended period of prosperity from 1922 to 1929. Although prosperous years are usually characterized by some inflation, during this era prices remained remarkably stable, rising only a bit more than one percent. Consequently, real annual earnings rose from an average of $672 in 1920 to $834 in 1929. The output of Ohio industries surpassed even the national growth rate, with an eighteen percent increase during the 1920s (see Table 4-I). Furthermore, a transition in the nature of manufacturing occurred, which generally benefited working-class consumers. Since the mid-1800s, industrialists had focused upon the production of "capital goods" such as steel and machinery, which were intended to generate further wealth. But, by the 1920s, the economy had matured sufficiently so that a much greater proportion of industrial activity could be devoted to the production of "consumer goods." Therefore, even though capital production continued to rise — as evidenced by the thirty-one percent growth in the output of Ohio's mighty steel mills — greater proportions of manufacturing concentrated on durable goods for mass consumption. New mass-production industries like automobile, chemical, and electrical appliance manufacturing experienced spectacular expansion. From washing machines, refrigerators, and vacuum cleaners to radios and automobiles, more and more consumer items appeared on the market. With production booming, prices remaining relatively stable, real wages generally rising, and modern conveniences becoming increasingly available, more Ohioans than ever before apparently improved their material well-being.

Ohio wage earners were swept along in the decade's powerful tide of conspicuous consumption. For working-class families without sufficient cash, credit was easily obtainable. In fact, a new mass-advertising industry emerged urging ordinary people to cast aside traditional aversions to debt and instead buy "on the installment plan." With not only the trappings of affluence now within their grasp, but with shorter working hours also providing greater leisure time and opportunities for community involvement, growing numbers of Ohio laboring people appeared—at least superficially—in the process of being absorbed into the middle class. Their social activities, political leanings, and standards of behavior increasingly seemed to conform to nationwide patterns. Workers piled into family cars to join the weekend crowds flocking to beaches and parks, avidly attended local movie theaters, and gathered around their new radios every evening. Their sons and daughters enrolled at Ohio State University with those of the upper classes. Though cheaper, their clothes were identical in style to fashions worn in higher income brackets. Shrinking immigrant communities proudly retained their cultural distinctions longer, but even for the foreign-born, pressures to assimilate were not always subtle or easily resisted. An Akron observer noted, for instance, that "some Russians even shaved their beards and used English names in order to get jobs as Americans." The illusion, if not always the substance, of upward social mobility and a more homogeneous society seemed to be manifested on every front.

Responding to the tremendous demand for consumer goods during the 1920s, refrigerator manufacturing became one of Ohio's fastest growing industries. At Dayton's Frigidaire plant in 1926, assembly-line methods stimulated increased production.

Though laboring people did not share equally in the material prosperity of the 1920s, many did enjoy more leisure time with which to savor life's simple pleasures — as illustrated by an Ohio River boatcrew relaxing with ice cream (below) and a Chillicothe paper worker proudly displaying the rewards of a day spent with his son (left).

Blacks did not fully experience the prosperity or opportunity of the 1920s. James Culver recollects:

. . . I came to Ohio when I was seventeen years old . . . I came looking for two things: number one, better wages, higher wages and number two, a chance to escape racial discrimination; I'd heard that there was less of it in the North . . . I started in Massillon working for the Fidelity Tire and Rubber Company . . . and when the factory at Massillon was shut down and moved to Warren, I came to Warren with the company . . . in 1926 . . . Blacks were restricted in the rubber industry at that time, the same as they were in others, so far as job opportunities were concerned, but I did fairly good considering the restrictions that they had in some of the other factories. I was a machine operator most of the time; semi-skilled work . . . Job and wage restriction, but in the plant in which I worked, it was a small plant, it was mostly job restrictions . . . blacks were not allowed to build tires . . . we worked in the tire-making process, but we were not allowed to build tires . . . It was a higher-skilled occupation, and it was also considered to be a white job . . . They would tell you specifically that this is a white man's job . . . they made no bones about it . . . I was familiar with that sort of thing in the South, so it was no surprise to me. Actually, I was more interested in the wages, the higher wages that I got, than anything else . . . In fact, at Goodyear Tire and Rubber Company, in the 1920s, blacks were restricted to janitorial work, and at Firestone they were mostly restricted to work in the mill, and at Goodrich they were mostly restricted to janitorial work. . . .

Lest the picture appear too rosy, however, it is important to recognize that serious flaws existed. Economic growth during the 1920s did not proceed without hitches, even in prosperous years. In mid-1920, a relatively brief, but extremely steep, depression caused unemployment to more than double by 1921 to 4.9 million workers—nearly twelve percent of the national labor force. Minor business slumps occurred as well in 1924 and 1927. In addition to cyclical fluctuations, other defects marred the image of general prosperity. Low farm prices, for example, kept agriculture depressed, and entire industries staggered through the period. Coal, a prime Ohio industry, was particularly crippled by the shift toward gas and oil for home heating and the gradual displacement of coal-burning trains by automobiles and trucks. Thus, while the state's output of refined petroleum increased fifty-eight percent during the decade, coal production shrank by approximately ten percent. Since advances in mining technology enabled owners to operate with fewer employees, nearly one-out-of-four coal miners were discharged between 1923 and 1929. With few sources of alternate employment available, workers in isolated coal towns faced grim prospects. Even for the state's bituminous miners fortunate enough to be steadily employed, average annual earnings dropped twenty-one percent between 1920 and 1929. In the textile industry, markets declined due to changing styles, and production costs in the garment industry rose due to the introduction of synthetic materials. Consequently, employers in both industries cut labor costs, imposing a financial crunch on employees in Cleveland and Cincinnati shops. In the men's clothing industry alone, annual wages in Ohio diminished from an average of $1249 in 1921 to $995 in 1929.

Material prosperity and social mobility did set the decade apart, but their distribution among the various segments of the workforce was very uneven. Glaring inequalities and insecurities remained. As perhaps the most obvious example, general economic expansion did not appreciably improve conditions for black Ohioans, who remained locked in menial jobs and inner-city ghettoes. But even among native whites, unemployment had not been eliminated, and actually rose in some industries and areas of the state. Technological progress and mechanization enabled manufacturers to pro-

The depressed state of the coal industry during the 1920s compelled many Ohio miners to eke out a living in marginal operations which could ill-afford expensive machinery. As conditions in this small mine near Roseville exemplified, a revival of more arduous, less efficient, but cheaper pick-mining methods (right) and animal-power (above) became increasingly widespread.

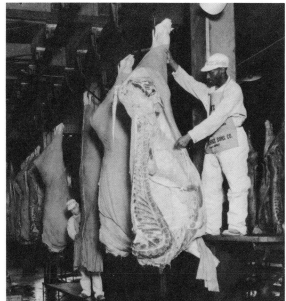

By the early 1920s, unskilled rural blacks from the South had gained tenuous footholds in Ohio's urban industries, such as metal working in Columbus (upper left), and meatpacking in Cincinnati (upper right). However, blacks were invariably the 'last-hired and first-fired,' were restricted from skilled or supervisory jobs, and received less pay. A disproportionate percentage occupied the lowest rungs of the occupational ladder, like these custodians in a Chillicothe paper mill (lower right). In Columbus, Tom Lawrence posed with the "tools" of his trade (lower left).

duce more with less labor, thereby resulting in diminished payrolls in many basic industries. Table 4-J illustrates that, while employment grew in many key industries—especially among salaried personnel—job opportunities for wage earners dwindled in such manufacturing areas as tires, machine tools, foundry products, tobacco, and railroad cars. Shifts into new jobs in the trade or service sectors helped to ease the situation. Nevertheless, a surplus of labor invariably remained, causing persistent unemployment and hardship within many working-class communities and families. A 1926 description of reported economic conditions by the Ohio Council on Women in Industry pointed out the irony and poignancy of enduring deprivation in the midst of plenty:

> ...Ohio conditions very good. All plants running on practically full time schedules and only a slight labor surplus. Cincinnati has a large surplus of unskilled labor and surplus of carpenters though all plants running full time with some overtime. Dayton surplus of sheet metal workers, welders, and cabinet makers with almost all plants running full time. Toledo plants likewise with surplus of unskilled labor and clerical help. And so it goes in the larger cities and in the smaller towns, the same

story of prosperity and a state busy making goods for the consumption of themselves and others. It is a splendid picture for everyone: except those surplus workers. I wonder who they are, how they live and what they would think of this report should they happen to see it?

In April, 1927, members of United Brotherhood of Carpenters and Joiners Local 200 received a note from the local recording secretary in East Liverpool which stated: "I have your circular telling all carpenters to stay away from Columbus as work is scarce there. I have been instructed to answer it and tell you the same thing of East Liverpool . . . we have plenty of men here to take care of all the carpenter work and would appreciate it very much if out-side men stay away." Thus, even high wages while employed could not eliminate the pervasive insecurity of the industrial worker. Just keeping the job seemed to carry greater importance than the wages or the hours—or union membership.

Perhaps no issue during this decade of prosperity aroused as much public debate in Ohio as the employment of female workers. Much of the controversy stemmed from popular misconceptions of the involvement of women in

After the labor unrest and economic depression of the postwar period, overall prosperity and labor-management peace became the dominant themes of the 1920s. However, there were serious flaws in the popularly-held image. Not all workers shared in economic security and harmony did not always characterize relations between workers, their employers, and their unions. Unemployment carried an especially strong social stigma in an era when jobs seemed plentiful, wages high, and success guaranteed for diligent workers. But when Toledo police acted on that narrow view in April, 1924, and arrested unemployed workers, the Central Labor Union took strong exception:

The attention of the Central Labor Union has been called to the recent arrests of unemployed by the Police Department. It is barely possible that some of these individuals could be classed as so-called suspicious persons but you will invariably find that the great majority are simply workers out of a job . . . I just concluded an investigation and find that . . . some of our largest concerns have recently laid off part of their help. Such wholesale arrests of unemployed even under periods of industrial prosperity are not in keeping with our conception of liberty as American citizens and invariably result in discrimination to the worker. Assuming even that some of these individuals do not or will not work they are no different than those who are blessed with plenty of the world's goods and live from the labor created by others, without work. It is possible that newspapers may have exaggerated those wholesale arrests but we feel that it is not amiss to protest against any tendency in this direction. . . .

To which the City Director of Public Safety replied:

. . . these arrests were made upon complaint of citizens in the vicinity . . . The men arrested were mostly white men who associate with negros in that vicinity and have no visible means of support. It is not the policy of this department to arrest unemployed men who honestly endeavor to secure employment, but we do believe, there [are] enough honest men in Toledo, who are out of employment at this time that should be taken care of and we do not intend to allow other Cities to make Toledo the dumping grounds for their undesirables. . . .

Until modern machinery transformed the handling of crude rubber, workers in many Ohio plants manually shoveled the material into processors.

the labor force. Many believed that women were flooding into shops, offices, and factories as a result of the suffrage and a supposed new degree of freedom from the restrictions which had formerly bound them to males and the home. The fear was rampant that in their strivings for economic equality, women were undermining the very institutions upon which society was built — the home and the family. In fact, however, the 1920s did not comprise a watershed in the history of women at work. No revolution in women's economic role occurred. Despite the fears of commentators, preachers, and unionists alike, females achieved very little progress toward the twin goals of economic equality and diminished sexual divisions of labor.

A few pertinent facts regarding the status of Ohio's female workers illustrate the hard reality that they generally continued to be restricted to traditionally inferior roles as second-class citizens attempting—without much success—to improve their positions. In 1920, women comprised eighteen percent of the state's total workforce. Of these 410,000 females, nearly twenty-five percent were employed in manufacturing, approximately twenty-three percent in domestic and personal service, and twenty-one percent in clerical positions. Only thirteen percent had broken into professional service fields such as teaching, medicine, and law, and but seven percent were engaged in trade and transportation. Primarily as a result of overall growth in population and the economy, rather than any radical change in their economic activity, the number of working women rose to nearly 540,000 by 1930 — a mere three percent increase in their total proportion of the labor force. Moreover, the percentage of women in manufacturing had slipped to nineteen percent, while increasing in menial service or clerical occupations. Within the new urban workforces, similar trends emerged (see Table 4-H). Midway through the decade, a study of working women in forty-four Ohio cities by the U.S. Department of Labor revealed details of the developing pattern: most were white, native-born, and had sixth to eighth-grade educations; nearly half were married or divorced; single women most often worked in electrical products plants, the garment industry, 5&10-cent stores, and candy factories where their manual dexterity or skills traditionally learned in the home were thought to be applicable; a woman's peak earning years were between the ages of twenty-five and thirty, when a gradual decline in wages then occurred, until by age sixty a woman earned less than a twenty-year-old girl; and finally, females were able to increase their earnings through education only to sixth-grade levels, after which no correlation could be found. Women's wages throughout the decade averaged only about half of that paid to men. In 1922 and 1925 the median weekly income for all Ohio women workers remained at $13.80. By 1927, over forty-three percent of all female wage earners were paid under $15 per week. Although most women expressed desires to find full-time employment, they found it very difficult. A 1922 study found, for example, that only about half of those females employed in bakeries, men's clothing mills, electrical products, shoes, and cigarmaking, worked full-time. The poorest record was among rubber and metal workers — heavy industries traditionally restricted to men. Typical of the modern working-woman's lot, the Ohio Consumers League reported in 1925 that self-supporting females in Cleveland averaged monthly earnings $10 below the amount needed to remain above poverty levels.

Women also received scant assistance from the men who dominated organized labor. Only a scattering of female workers were admitted to trade unions — garment workers, musicians, pottery workers, railway clerks, cigarmakers, cooks and waitresses, printers. Occasionally, a woman was permitted to act as secretary to a city central union, but, by and large, except in the garment trades, their organized strength and union participation remained negligible. Ohio unionists were also deeply ambivalent about women entering the workforce. On the one hand, these males resented the job competition posed by these largely unskilled and unorganized females who threatened their wage levels, and who were only expected to remain in the labor force for a short time before marriage. But, on the other hand, they felt an obligation as protective males to shield the women from any health, safety, or moral threats in the workplace which would endanger their abilities to bear and nurture future generations. This con-

tradition was especially illustrated by the positions taken by the Ohio State Federation of Labor on various pieces of legislation dealing with women workers. For example, in 1919 the State Federation sponsored — at the behest of the rabidly anti-female Iron Molders Union — the passage of a state law which barred women from supposedly corrupting or dangerous jobs in over sixteen different areas, including not only iron foundries, but also: taxi cabs, blast furnaces, shoe-shine parlors, bowling alleys, pool rooms, saloons which catered exclusively to males, delivery services, and baggage handling. These restrictions far exceeded the total to be found in any other state in the nation. However, when women's groups repeatedly attempted to secure passage of a female minimum wage law, they faced staunch opposition by State Federation leaders, who argued that such action by the government would undermine the organization's traditional insistence that only unions could protect a worker's economic interests. The dream of working women for equal-pay-for-equal-work remained unfulfilled. The image of the newly emancipated woman of the 1920s — at least on the state's shop floors—was an illusion.

Reinforcing and even encouraging the cumulative influences of widespread material prosperity, the geographic mobility and shifting composition of the new urban labor force, frequent job insecurity, and subtle changes in workers' habits and perspectives, employers launched an extensive campaign to assert their

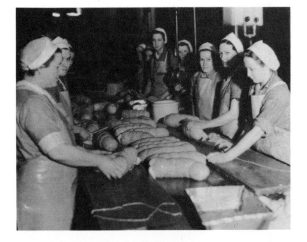

Whether processing meat in Cincinnati (upper left), making paper in Chillicothe (upper right), assembling refrigerator controls in Dayton (lower left), or building vacuum cleaners in Canton (lower right), few female industrial workers during the 1920s experienced job-security, opportunities for advancement, or "equal-pay-for-equal-work" with male counterparts.

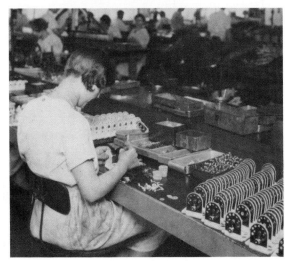

During the early 1920s, in order to maintain continuous production in Youngstown's cavernous steel mills, employees commonly put in twelve-hour shifts and seven-day workweeks.

Simply having a job in the 1920s did not necessarily guarantee security. Charles Beckman describes conditions in a Cleveland automobile plant:

. . . I looked for work for quite some time and came over and got a job at the Fisher Body when they were building it (the present Fisher Body here on Coit Road) . . . That must have been about 1919. I worked there for about one year until they came to the completion of the job . . . Then I was out of work for quite some time. On January 22, 1922 I hired out at the job that I have retired from—a trimmer at the Coit Road plant. At that time I hired out at 35¢ an hour. That was a common wage at that time. However, on piecework you made more. I think piecework was 85¢ . . . But you worked for it. I worked there and always had in mind the hopes for the place to be organized. However, there wasn't any attempt by the legitimate unions to organize the place . . . Conditions were ridiculous. We did not have any security. If I recall correctly if you were to work seven days a week, you worked seven days a week whether it was a holiday or non-holiday . . . We worked for straight time . . . Originally nine hours was our standard day's work but we worked much overtime and including Satudays and Sundays. If you did not come in, you might as well go out and look for another job. You had no security. You were at the will of the supervisor. In layoffs you had no seniority as to coming back or any security from the time you hired out. On many occasions you would come in and they would run out of stock as soon as you got into the plant and the foreman would tell you to go home . . . Then the layoffs would come. We had seasonal layoffs lasting from three to five or six months at that time. If you could not get a job you would come around to find out how your working status was coming along. There would be hundreds of people standing out in the winter. Some foreman would come out to the employment office and say, ''Hey you, come on in,'' disregarding seniority or your honest ability to work . . . Likely it would be that the guys that was called in would go out and do some work on the supervisor's house or something of that nature. They were what we called the ''Red Apple Boys.'' Conditions were intolerable. Many of the foremen borrowed money from the workers and if the workers resented giving it to them, they would look for a new job. Those were the conditions in the early 1920s up to the time that they knew that the movement was on for organization. . . .

control within and beyond factory gates. While the degree of success enjoyed by individual employers is still open to debate, their collective efforts undoubtedly swayed the nature of labor-management relations, organized and spontaneous protest, as well as the working environment itself.

Management termed the cornerstone of their drive ''the American Plan'' in an obvious effort to link the primary targets of their wrath—labor unions—with un-Americanism. Begun in 1919, the plan aimed to promulgate the ''open shop'' doctrine that an employer had the right to hire anyone he chose, whether or not the person was a union member. In essence, it urged that the traditional tenets of the individualistic gospel of success be applied with a vengeance in order to defeat ''foreign'' concepts of collective action. However, in practice the doctrine meant blatant discrimination against all union members, and refusals to grant union recognition even if a majority of employees had joined. In the eyes of fiercely anti-union employers, therefore, the open shop argument became a legitimate strategy to deny the entire collective-bargaining process which organized labor had struggled for since the nineteenth century. Open-shop associations sprang up across the nation, with seventeen formed in Ohio alone to promote the campaign against unions. Citizens' alliances like Cincinnati's No-Strike Association and local chambers of commerce vocally endorsed the effort, and behind them stood powerful and wealthy employers' groups such as the National Association of Manufacturers, the National Metal Trades Association, and the League for Industrial Rights. In 1926, Ohio was surpassed only by New York and Pennsylvania in NAM membership. Nor was propaganda the employers' only weapon. The old yellow-dog contracts were revived, hired spies were planted on shop floors and within working-class

A

B

C

D

E

G

F

H

Welfare capitalism achieved peak popularity among Ohio employers during the 1920s. Ostensibly intended to boost labor-management cooperation, the "new gospel" was embraced for various reasons: a sense of paternalism; improved efficiency; sensitivity to public opinion; the promotion of company loyalty and contentment among workers —thereby diffusing class-consciousness, union organizing, and labor disputes; and, most importantly, management's desire to maintain power over the workforce. Welfare programs took numerous forms. In Columbus, Buckeye Steel Castings Company provided wokers with time off to celebrate Flag Day (A) and to conduct Bible classes on the shop floor (B). Firestone Tire and Rubber Company's plan included assisting their employees' acquisition of property in Akron's Firestone Park (C), and operating a library for their children at the Firestone Clubhouse (D). National Cash Register in Dayton supplied a dining room for female employees (E), while the Youngstown Sheet and Tube Company promoted plant safety (F). In order to make the workplace more tolerable, the Mead Corporation provided a cafeteria and lunchwagon in its Chillicothe paper mill (G) and The General Tire Corporation sponsored a baseball team (H).

The expanding automobile industry of the 1920s also generated jobs in Akron's rubber plants. But as with their fellow workers in auto, rubber workers like Harley Anthony experienced little prosperity or security on the shop floor:

I started to work at the B.F. Goodrich plant in Akron in 1922. My job was supplying the tire builders with treads, beads, liners, etc. Three weeks after I started to work there was a lay-off . . . and even though I was the youngest employee in point of service in the group, I kept on working for three months longer . . . I remember quite vividly the case of the fellow with whom I worked, who had been at Goodrich for several months before I was hired. He received a telegram from his folk in Tennessee that his father was quite ill and he asked the foreman's permission to go home for a few days to see his father — permission was granted. His father passed away and he returned to Akron to his job, only to be informed when he reported to work that he had been laid-off. Such instances was quite common at Goodrich and other rubber plants in Akron before we organized a Union. There was no such thing as **seniority** *in any of the plants. When a seasonal lay-off would occur (and they occurred quite frequently) the oldest employee in point of service in the department would be "shaking in his boots" the same as the youngest . . . It was a common occurrance those days for employees to slip the foreman a sizeable piece of "dough" to keep from being laid-off or to get a better job. Then there was the Klu Klux Klan with thousands of members in the rubber shops in Akron, including foremen and other officials who would give their fellow-Kluxers the breaks on lay-offs and preferential jobs . . . One could be fired on the slightest provocation and without recourse . . . "Blackballing" was commonplace in those days. If you were fired at one shop in Akron, the only possibility of finding employment elsewhere was to tell the other employer that you had never worked in any other shop and that you had just arrived in Akron from the South and of course, give an assumed name. Life under Hitler's iron rule was undoubtedly intolerable, however, I seriously doubt whether it was much worse than slaving under the conditions prevalent in the rubber shops in Akron. . . .*

neighborhoods to identify malcontents, blacklists of unionists circulated freely between companies, and openly discriminatory hiring practices weeded out unionists. If unrest among job-conscious workers still managed to erupt despite all their precautions, employers often resorted to intimidation and coercion. Professional strikebreaking agencies thrived during the era, providing hired thugs in the guise of company police to beat up troublemakers and

imported scabs to maintain production. Through their political influence, management easily obtained injunctions and local police assistance to squelch any die-hard militants.

Management also utilized the slightly more subtle techniques of welfare capitalism and company unionism. As described at length in earlier pages, welfare capitalism schemes had been pioneered by Ohio firms at the turn of the century. During the '20s, their programs were accelerated and refined by a new generation of professional "industrial relations experts" in order to instill company loyalty among the workers, to promote efficiency, and to remove annoyances which could potentially escalate into conflict. To complement these efforts, as well as to increase production and efficiency through improved labor-management cooperation, many employers also set up "employee representation plans" — better known as company unions. The activities of these bodies were generally restricted to conducting athletic and social programs or requesting better toilets or locker rooms, representatives were often selected by managers themselves, and employers retained veto-power over any decisions. By 1926, the number of these employer-controlled unions had expanded to over 400, with a national membership of roughly 1.4 million. In Ohio, some of the largest corporations utilized this technique, including the Procter and Gamble Company, Youngstown Sheet and Tube, Willys-Overland, Goodyear Tire and Rubber, National Cash Register, and the Printz-Biederman Company.

Yet another development which had strong bearings on working-class life during this decade was the resurgence of the Ku Klux Klan as a social and political power. By endorsing the American Plan, exploiting racial fears, branding all aliens and Catholics as subversive "un-Americans," and by cloaking their cause in a unique weave of patriotism and Protestant moral reform, KKK leaders won recruits in every Ohio county. Initially a middle-class movement, the Klan also gained strong support from less successful white and blue-collar workers — especially among small-town Ohioans and those who had flocked from rural areas to urban-industrial centers. Statewide membership grew to nearly 400,000 — the largest KKK branch in the nation. While never influential in Cleveland, Toledo, or Steubenville, local Klaverns in industrial cities like Akron, Youngstown, Columbus, Marion, and Newark attracted wide followings and exerted considerable political clout. Rural Knox, Licking, and Muskingum counties became hotbeds of agitation. Although the organization's impact crept into various aspects of working-class life, its most unfortunate effect was to trigger a renewed surge of grassroots factionalism. Differences of race, religion, nativity, and ideology which had weakened working-class solidarity for generations surfaced once again. Not even labor unions were immune from the Klan's divisive influence. Within Ohio locals of the United Mine Workers District 6, for instance, serious

Due to constantly wet working conditions, many Chillicothe paper workers had the unusual habit of toiling barefoot.

With the nation's largest membership by 1923, the Ohio Ku Klux Klan publicly demonstrated its strength in Springfield.

controversy arose when Klan recruits openly defied the union's ban on membership in the organization by refusing to work with non-members and by appearing at the funerals of fellow-miners in hoods and full regalia. Hoping to avoid confrontations which would further debilitate the union, UMW leaders refused to impose penalties on Klan members and finally reached a truce with Ohio KKK officials at a Columbus conference in 1923.

Despite all of these hurdles to labor activism and organization, more assertive and progressive leadership at national, state, and local levels may have at least enabled unions to hold their ground. Instead, union heads remained paralyzed and the movement began to retreat. National membership plummeted twenty-eight percent from over 5,000,000 in 1920 to slightly more than 3.6 million by 1929. While some union gains were achieved—as when Cincinnati's "Golden Rule" Nash abandoned the open shop in 1925 and startled the business community by urging his employees to join the Amalgamated Clothing Workers of America — they were few and far between. Pervasive job insecurity, fear of reprisals by belligerent employers, community pressure, and a misguided sense of patriotism deterred many workers from joining or retaining membership in unions. But many others simply believed that membership was unnecessary, concluding that there was no point in paying union dues or agitating when paychecks grew larger and affluence seemed assured.

Labor leaders did little to change the opinions of these apathetic, and even hostile, workers. In fact, the distinct conservatism and timidity of the AFL — the largest labor organization in Ohio and the nation — weakened the entire movement. Far from seeking to revive labor militancy, the AFL made every effort to encourage labor-management cooperation. Especially after the defeats of 1919 to 1922, the organization stressed its customary commitment to craft unionism—a structurally obsolete method of organizing the huge new industries such as automobiles, rubber, utilities, chemicals, and

Labor unions of the 1920s offered little assistance to most black workers. As Daniel Blakely explains, they could be their worst adversaries:

. . . I went back to school and eventually I got around to graduation in 1928, at which time one of the local concerns [in Warren] . . . had asked Mr. Davis, who was then principal of the high school, to send down two of his most apt students. He'd give them a job in the sheet metal works. So I and Howard Wolfs were selected and we went down, and . . . he gave us the jobs. I was sent out with the roofing and spouting group, and Howard Wolf went downstairs where the sheet metal workers were working. So this goes on for about two or three weeks . . . So one day, for some reason or the other, me and my partner came back to the shop to get some material. We were setting up a furnace, and there was something we needed. We came back to get it and everybody was at work, and I didn't know it but I evidently wasn't allowed to go downstairs where this craft union was working. So I went down, and all of a sudden I find everybody's stopped working, standing. Very shortly thereafter, the owner of the place, Mr. Woodward, came dashing down the stairway and says, "Come on Blakely, let's get out of here . . . And he got me upstairs, and then he gave me a few startling facts . . . "You know I'm having a lot of trouble keeping you here. Those fellows down there are liable not to work at all, they're liable to shut my place down if you go down there." So, he says, "On Friday, I'll have to let you go." . . . I says, "Why? Why is it that way?" He says, "Well, that's the union; that's the way they work, and I don't question. I just find it convenient to get along with them, and they do good work for me, and I like them all, they're good workers, but I want to keep my promise to Mr. Davis . . . I can put you to work for the rest of the week. I'm going to do as much as I can to see that you get your just desserts because I asked for you, I didn't ask for any color, or anything like that, I just said two apt people, and you're one of them. Your work is all right, no complaint about that. It's only the situation existing here in the plant." So this went on for two or three weeks, and there was only one guy that would work with me . . . and we were always out on some farm. So, eventually, one day the boss came to me and he says, "If I keep you, they're gonna shut down, so I think I'll have to let you go." I said, "Well, I understand it now." . . . But I left that plant with my first impression of a labor union, and it was a sour taste in my mouth; I had no use for 'em . . . I kind of nursed on that idea, thinking about it as I looked for work . . . as far as I feel today, Mr. Woodward was right. He meant to keep me there, but the force of the union forced me out of that job. . . .

A

Having pioneered in mass-production techniques during the mid-nineteenth century, Cincinnati's meat-packing houses had further refined their "disassembly-line" methods by the 1920s (A & C). Nonetheless, certain grizzly tasks such as gutting carcasses were still performed by hand (B).

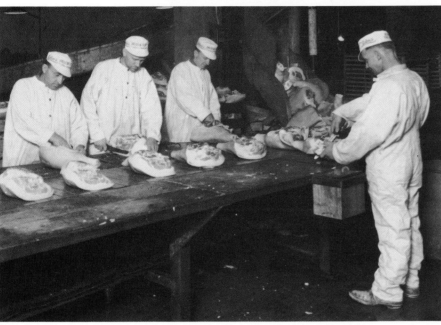

C

B

electronics, which employed either broad varieties of tradesmen or unskilled and semi-skilled labor. Large segments of the new urban workforce thus could not be accommodated within the existent craft system. Furthermore, although mechanization and repeated divisions of labor had been diluting and transforming traditional skills for decades, AFL unions generally proved unable or unwilling to adapt to these changes. Rather than launching a major drive to sign up these potential recruits, conservative AFL leaders concluded that they were unorganizable. With disastrous short-sightedness, they merely attempted to hold on to their technologically threatened skilled members. Such caution and a growing financial inability to service their members apparently even soured many trade unionists. By 1929, for example, half of the city's local unions had disaffiliated from the Columbus Federation of Labor, "complaining that the Federation is doing nothing to better their conditions."

In large measure, this stagnation was due to the pervasiveness of the ideas of the long-time president of the AFL, Sam Gompers. In brief, Gompers pragmatically accepted capitalism, within which he perceived labor's role in terms of simply trying to secure a maximum wage. He believed that highly paid skilled workers had the shared-interests and financial ability to build strong unions in their individual trades, and that once established, the sovereignty and jurisdiction of that international union were inviolate. Consequently, he felt that industrial unions — comprised of all workers in an industry—would always be the weak link in organized labor, and therefore should not be stressed, at the expense of violating the jurisdictions of the craft unions involved. When Gompers died in 1924, his presidency and his philosophy were passed on to William Green. Green had begun his union career in Coshocton, Ohio, where he entered the coal mines and became a local union officer. Eventually he rose to the presidency of the Ohio district of the United Mine Workers. Also elected to the Ohio Senate, he successfully sponsored several labor laws, including the state's basic workmen's compensation statute. After rising within the UMW hierarchy and becoming an AFL vice-president, he was chosen to succeed Gompers as a compromise candidate. Under Green's gentle leadership, the AFL shifted even further from a position of militancy to a quest for respectability. He repeatedly stressed throughout the decade that, with business supreme, labor should avoid adversarial relationships and resign itself to being a cooperative partner at best. Such policies as these would hardly stimulate the slumbering labor movement.

In light of these varied, complex, and overwhelming obstacles, it was little wonder that the strike as an instrument of collective bargaining, to say nothing of social protest, fell into almost total disuse. This does not mean that no strikes occurred—as exemplified by the violent and catastrophic nationwide coal strike of 1927-28, which resulted in tremendous hardship in already depressed coal towns, a victory for the open-shop campaign, average wage reductions of one-third for Ohio miners, and a startling drop in UMW membership. Nonetheless, the calm which descended over Ohio's workplaces was seldom, if ever, matched in the state's history. As indicated in Table 4-A, the number of disputes in Ohio fell from 237 in 1919 to only twenty-one by 1927. In 1929, a mere 6000 Ohio workers walked off their jobs. Capitalism had finally found the proper mix of ingredients with which to diffuse labor militancy—union debility, welfare capitalism, repression, an adverse social climate, a stable cost of living, modest increases in real wages for those employed, resurgent factionalism, and a large part of working-class apathy. It would take a major jolt to reawaken labor insurgency.

After seven delirious years of accelerated expansion, the era of affluence expired in 1929. Under the assault of the century's most calamitous economic depression, the seemingly impregnable edifice of prosperity and complacency cracked, crumbled, and—by 1933—laid in shambles. Anxiety and hardship supplanted confidence and comfort, as the worldwide Great Depression raged with initially devastating fury, abated slightly at mid-decade, then resumed its spasmodic rampage until the outbreak of World War II. Individual experiences and responses varied, but, as a whole, working people eventually overcame their numbness to launch an offensive as unanticipated and consequential as the economic con-

No one needed to tell Mrs. Stella Wagner of Buchtel, Ohio that the coal industry was depressed or that the United Mine Workers of America faced organizational collapse during the 1920s. In early 1925, she wrote directly to President John L. Lewis seeking help:

*I wrote to you a short time ago in regards to conditions here among the miners, and it still exists. Mr. Lewis do you think a family of fourteen can live on four and eight dollars a week, that is clothing, food and send six children to school and in fact everything come out of this little pitiful sum. If there wasn't so many scab places around here, a union man, may stand some show of getting a job. And instead of sending Organizers out in West Virginia, send them around here in the Hocking Valley, for there is a mine, right in front of my door, just as bad, if not worse than any scab place in West Virginia, and the officials know it too. The case I wrote to you about has never been taken up. The officials were notified of this trouble to. They are paid to do this and are paid well I think. Mr. Lewis something will have to be done. I think the fellow that is the biggest crook, he is counted the union man. No a real, honest to goodness union man isn't called a union man. Aren't these officials supposed to settle grievances. Well they don't do it. It seems like they are great friends to some of the mine bosses or something and they won't bother with some mens complaints. **There must be something done.** There has to be. I know feeling is running high. Conditions are makeing some very good men, very bad ones. I know what I am talking about. The delegate that went from here to the convention about two years ago, and told them there that thirty five per cent of the miners were scabbing around here in the Hocking Valley did not tell the truth. If he had said all were scabbing, but thirty five per cent, he would have told the truth. I have been in West Va; I have seen some people come from W. Va that is called scabs. They had their big fine automobiles. Their families all were well dressed, and by their appearance, well kept. This is something, we haven't got. Just sitting around here year, after year, half fed, half clothed waiting on the big fellow to do, who knows no hardships of this kind; I say Mr. Lewis if it is going to be union, make it all union, and if it is non union, don't have it mixed. Just imagine a miner haveing a grieveance notifying the officials and they don't even show their faces, after the poor half starved miner is being checked off every two weeks, to pay them a large salary . . . The Organizer he will go into West Va. in a non-union field, and say, "Yes you stand by the union, and organized miners, and the miners will*

Led by President William Green (third from left), a delegation of AFL leaders met with President Coolidge, in a vain attempt to win governmental assistance in resolving the 1927 coal dispute.

take care of you." But I have never heard the same said to some that has always been a union miner. No he can "root hog or die." . . . Now I have always heard some people say, "John L. Lewis will settle it." So please settle this one grievance or see that it is settled. . . .

Lewis passed on her letter to the UMW District 6 president. In the best bureaucratic tradition, he chastised her for bypassing the chain of command, denied her accusations, and concluded his letter by stating, "I never have and I do not expect to begin now, to recognize grievances registered by the women folks. . . ." Mrs. Wagner, in the best tradition of rank-and-file independence, had different ideas:

*I received your frame up today. And I just want to inform you that I did not write or make any complaint to you whatever. I am down here in the Hocking Valley, right among the miners, and I am not deaf nor dumb. I can understand the American Language, and when I hear people talking I know what they are talking about. And that I can see, and am almost old enough to know right from wrong, That I wrote about a complaint to other officials and **not to you**. And these officials were gentleman enough to answer me very nicely. And I want you to plainly understand that I am just as truthful as **you**, or anyone else. And I wrote the complaint for Mr Wagner as I do almost all the writeing for him, and right now he says he don't know anything about his grieveance being settled, also to tell you **that it is not a personal affair** . . . And you or/no one else can say that I do not tell the truth that I and Mr. Wagner keep our children all to gether, and take care of them and no one can say a word against my reputation. That I know our liveing is hard earned. And if you would just take a trip down in the Hocking Valley you could see for yourself if you wanted to . . . I think I know a lettle of what is going on in America. And as far as the Organization is concerned, I am not even studying about it. I have greater things to study about that concern me a lot more. I was just telling John L Lewis what was up town. And as far as conditions being investigated that is news to me, but they wasn't investigated in the right manner. And I want to tell you that I don't consider it any of yours or any one's business who I write to, that this is a free country, but I think I'll enjoy my self showing your letter to the miners and other people around here . . .*
P.S.: About the women folks. I'll say if some of them couldn't do as well as some of the men as Officials, I'd get off the earth. So don't speak after this till you are spoken to.

vulsions which swirled about them. Though capricious, massive working-class militancy had finally been rekindled.

There never has been unanimity among experts regarding the complex causes of the Great Depression of 1929-1941. However, most do agree that one very basic weakness in the apparent prosperity of the 1920s directly affected workers and had long-range economic impacts — an unequal distribution of the national income. The intertwined ramifications of that influential factor merit brief description. An enormous capital expansion occurred during most of the decade, primarily in the form of relatively new mass-production industries such as electrical appliances and automobiles which depended heavily upon consumer demand. But, by the late 1920s, markets for these goods had become nearly saturated—not because demand had been satisfied, but because the purchasing power of consumers had diminished. Customers would have liked to purchase more, but lacked sufficient funds. The basic reason for

this dilemma was a distribution of national income which was totally inadequate to support a mass-consumption economy indefinitely. Annual per capita disposable income increased about nine percent between 1920 and 1929. However, while the share of that national income received by the nation's wealthy rose significantly, the proportions received by the middle and lower classes declined. The richest one percent of the nation's population increased their share of disposable income from roughly twelve percent in 1920 to nineteen percent in 1929; the top ten percent in 1929 controlled forty percent of the nation's disposable income. Obviously, therefore, purchasing power tended to concentrate in the hands of the wealthy few, who tended to place large portions of their money into stock speculation and the purchase of luxury items, thereby inhibiting the rapid flow of money back into the "real economy." More proportionally balanced incomes for middle and working-class customers would have stimulated greater consumer purchasing, since these individuals would spend almost all income out of necessity. At the same time, labor productivity increased forty-three percent, mostly due to improved machinery and industrial organization. Though the volume of available goods rose, prices did not decline, nor did wages increase in proportion to productivity. In Ohio, for example, industrial output jumped fourteen percent from 1920 to 1930, but the workforce increased only three percent, largely because of considerable job-displacement by machines. Many of these victims of technological unemployment took jobs in the lower-paying service and retail trade sectors, further reducing purchasing power. The net result was an alarming growth in inventories, which businessmen attempted to cut by frantically urging customers to use credit—only a temporary and economically dangerous solution. When combined with weak banking structures, monopolistic business practices, as well as overspeculation in stock and real estate markets, this core imbalance in income distribution caused serious flaws in the apparently prosperous economy, and probably made an ultimate collapse inevitable. Furthermore, since many middle and working-class consumers had participated in the bounty by using credit, they would be especially vulnerable to the economic disaster which followed.

As a critical segment of the nation's industrial heartland, Ohio reeled under the impact of the financial crash of October, 1929 and the economy's subsequent collapse. From 1930 to 1940, the state's industrial output slipped twenty-four percent, surpassing the sharp national drop of nineteen percent. While a few leading industries like chemicals and petroleum refining did manage to increase production, most suffered drastic reductions (see Table 4-I). Resultant discharges provoked a twenty-percent contraction in the state's industrial labor force during the decade. With the unusual exception of refrigerator manufacturing—where the number of wage earners more than doubled—employees

were slashed in industry after industry (see Table 4-J). Ohio's jobless ranks rose to an estimated total of 307,000 in 1930 (13.3 percent of all workers), to 576,000 in 1931, and 869,000 (an astounding 37.3 percent) by 1932 — and these figures did not include uncounted thousands who found only part-time employment or who worked for vastly reduced wages! In the state's major cities, unemployment reached astronomical heights — fifty percent in Cleveland, sixty percent in Akron, eighty percent in Toledo. The effects specifically felt among wage earners were even more stupefying. For instance, average annual wage and salary payments for all Ohioans dropped twenty-nine percent from 1929 through 1932. But, among wage earners, incomes plunged thirty-three percent overall — ranging from a seventeen-percent dip in wholesale and retail trade, to twenty percent in service occupations, thirty-six percent in manufacturing, and forty-one percent in construction. Average annual employment exclusively for wage-earning Ohioans sank forty percent overall between 1929 and 1932; while unemployment climbed to sixty-seven percent among construction workers, forty-four percent in manufacturing, fourteen percent in trade, and "only" nine percent in the service sector.

The depression also profoundly affected demographic patterns. With far fewer jobs to attract newcomers, Ohio's foreign-born residents dropped precipitously and natives from other states declined slightly during the 1930s. The black population expanded, but at a much smaller rate than in the previous decade. The most notable shifts were in the hard-hit cities. From 1930 to 1940, urban areas experienced the smallest population increase in the state's history — a mere two percent. Possibly because many unemployed urbanites returned to family

As the depression tightened its grip on Ohio's economy in 1930, employees from Youngstown Sheet and Tube Company's Campbell Works (above) to International Harvester's Springfield Truck Works (left) wondered how long the imminent layoffs would last.

farms where they might at least have food and shelter, and because rural residents now perceived little benefit in seeking relief from depressed agricultural conditions by joining the suffering masses in the cities, Ohio's rural population growth actually exceeded urban growth by five percent — an equally startling phenomenon, unheard of since the early frontier years. In contrast to the universal expansion of the booming '20s, primary and secondary cities across the state witnessed either population slumps or only minimal gains during the depressed '30s (see Tables 4-B through 4-F).

Yet, no matter how detailed, statistics alone cannot convey an adequate sense of the deeply personal nature of the ''depression experience.'' Concealed within the almost incomprehensibly massive percentages and figures, were human beings — people who often suffered exceptional deprivation, endured private trauma, and who bore their peculiar scars for a lifetime. With empathy and imagination, perhaps at least a broad understanding can be gained of this calamity's intensely human dimensions.

For the most serious casualties of the depression, the very basics of life became scarce commodities. After losing their jobs, vainly searching for other work, and exhausting savings and credit, the unemployed and their families had to resort to relatively desperate means of survival. For example, a 1931 study by Hiram House social workers revealed some typical coping methods in one working-class Cleveland neighborhood. Out of 234 families, forty four had no visible means of support, twenty-two literally lived on garbage, eleven were supported through illegal activities (bootlegging, numbers racket, gambling, theft, prostitution), nine entirely depended upon relatives, twenty-six were sustained solely by female breadwinners, and thirty-seven relied on the earnings of delivery boys. In one typical instance, investigators found that:

> The A. family have all been out of work for two years. Mr. A has not worked steadily for five years. He finally decided to make himself a little cart and collect paper, which he re-sells. On his paper rounds he picks up wood for fuel. Mrs. A. goes on the market and picks up food for the family. The second son lost his job when the depression came. He picked up junk and sold it, turning over the money to his mother. One day last November, he was caught taking plumbing from a vacant house and was arrested and sent to Mansfield. Another boy went into a vacant house to look for old bottles, was arrested and spent some time in the detention home. With so large a family, the various members have turned to anything that might bring in money.

Though many more-fortunate Ohioans were dubious, people commonly died of starvation in this supposed land of plenty. Particularly in major cities such as Toledo and Akron, doctors reported alarming increases in malnutrition-related diseases manifested in gastrointestinal afflictions, skin eruptions, and nervous disorders. A visiting nurse in Cleveland reported her observations of once-comfortable working-class families:

> In one case . . . the children were pale. They all showed the inevitable result of not having an adequate diet over a period of time sufficient to build them up physically. The mother plans well and can do a lot with a little food. When she was confined recently, the family lived for three days on potatoes, bread and cocoa. A few weeks before they had a three day stretch of cornmeal mush without milk or sugar. The new born baby has gained one pound in a month. The mother has plenty of milk but it is doubtful how nutritious it can be on such a limited diet. . . . [In another case] all they had in the house was some cooked oatmeal and lard, so the mother fried the oatmeal, gave it to her children and called it lunch. She sent her daughter, seven years old, to a neighborhood grocery store hoping she might get one quart of milk in advance on her next relief order, but the little girl came back and shook her head to her mother — no milk. In another home there was nothing to eat but plain corn meal.

By 1939, the Cleveland City Physician confirmed that such debilitating conditions were hardly unusual, and hinted darkly that deprivation left potentially dangerous psychological scars:

> . . . Lately I have been called in quite frequently to see people who are not really ill but whose complaint is referrable to a lack of food. I can recall quite vividly a number of such cases. Just the other day I went in to see a young woman of twenty-two who complained of general weakness.

Dorothy Burch poignantly described the Depression experience of her black working-class family:

. . . I was married in '29, and that's when the Depression hit, and my husband lost his job. He was working here in Fostoria, but he lost his job and it was necessary for us to go home and live on the farm with my mother, and we lived there then for five years before things picked up and we moved back to Fostoria. Then he got his job back here in the foundry, so then we moved to Fostoria . . . We never had the money to buy a farm, so we just stuck with working in factories . . . he worked in the foundry for forty years . . . In 1935, when we first came back here, if he would go to work and there wasn't any work, he'd just get sent home, and sometimes we would have $12.00 a week, sometimes $20.00 a week. It just depended upon whether there was anything out there for him to do, and if there were people out there that they liked better than him, they got the work and he still got sent home. I remember one time my husband went to work; he had to walk to work, we didn't have a car, and he walked to work from out on the south end of town out to the factory where he worked, and it was so cold that he froze his ears, and he had to come back home, he had to walk back home through that cold because there wasn't anything for him to do that day. When he got home his ears were just sticking straight out from his head, I think you could have broken them off, his ears were frozen solid. And this was some of the things — that's just one of the little hardships that people had to go through before there was organization in the plants, that they would have a system to go by. Then it was, oh, a few years after that they started organizing a labor union at the foundry, and at this particular foundry where the working conditions and all were just deplorable, after the union was organized there, not only did the people get treated better, but the working conditions were improved. So that was my first experience with labor unions . . . he was in there helping organize the union. . . .

Upon examination, I was unable to find any organic basis for complaints and in questioning her I obtained the information that for the past six days she had been living almost entirely upon potatoes and potato peelings. This is not an isolated case. I could multiply this one case many times over. . . . For example, today I visited a family of seven adults who receive seventy-five cents per day to feed all these individuals. Even under the most expert management, a housewife cannot possibly feed herself and her children on such an allowance. The *children*, especially, *become weak and emaciated and underweight, and as a result, frequently contract colds and other diseases* which they would not become subject to had they been eating an adequate diet. . . . The people are in a very bad frame of mind. They cannot understand that the city is unable to supply them with the barest necessities of livelihood. They see their children go about hungry and very poorly clothed, losing weight and frequently succumbing to colds and more serious complications. Hunger is not productive to logical thinking and people who are hungry cannot reason out this thing in a logical manner. . . . When people are hungry they want food, and they want it now! When they do not receive food right away, these people must resort to begging from their neighbors. This has a devastating effect upon the mind. It robs them of self-respect.

Of course, nagging hunger did not stalk everyone. Food prices had plummeted to very low levels, especially by today's standards. In many cities during the '30s, bread sold for as little as 7¢ per loaf, bacon for 20¢ per pound, eggs for 29¢ per dozen, and butter for 13¢ per pound. However, in order to take advantage of the situation, families had to maintain stable incomes. With more than one-out-of-three wage earners jobless and countless more working part-time or experiencing wage-cuts, that was not easily accomplished. While frequently making the difference between life and death, low prices surely offered little luxury to the majority of Ohio's working people.

Second only to food, decent housing was an extremely pressing problem for poverty-stricken families. As reflected in the fact that nearly seven-out-of-ten construction workers in Ohio had lost their jobs by 1932, the erection of new dwellings nearly came to a standstill. Ironically, however, there was no lack of available housing. Rather, numerous residences of every type sat empty, because people plainly could not afford to purchase or rent necessary accommodations. Families with jobless breadwinners often doubled up with friends or relatives in order to save precious dollars. Surprisingly, fewer evictions and foreclosures occurred than might have been expected. For many working-class people, "keeping a roof over their heads" was even more important than food, and they made extraordinary sacrifices to meet their payments. Oftentimes, when families still fell behind in their obligations, landlords concluded that to allow debtors to remain until times improved made better business sense, than to evict them forcibly and have the property remain vacant like so many others. Nonetheless, countless families were compelled to accept

Claiming to have only one resident out of 200 on relief and only two families without automobiles in October, 1935, the town of Big Prairie was a rare oasis in severely depressed Ohio.

For Italians on Cleveland's East Side, religious celebrations offered comfort and hope during the 'hard times.'

With millions of jobless transients "tramping" across the country in search of work, the 1936 Hobo Convention promised to be a well-attended affair.

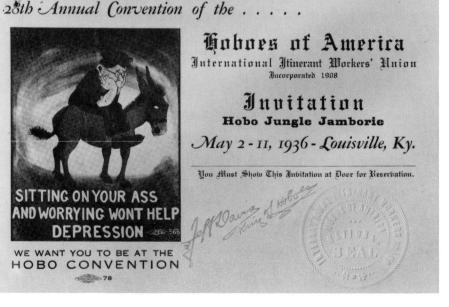

Whether found in Cincinnati (A), in the shadows of steelmills at Youngstown (B), in Toledo (C), or Cleveland (D), stark blue-collar neighborhoods testified to the traumatic depression-experiences of their occupants.

substandard housing, and distressed home-owners sadly watched their houses — which represented so many years of toil—deteriorate simply because they could not afford repairs.

No one knows, with any degree of accuracy, how many individuals became totally homeless, but scattered reports indicate that many were concentrated in jerribuilt "Hoovervilles" outside the state's major cities. In one of the few attempts to grasp the extent of the problem, the State Transient Committee requested various relief agencies in July, 1938 to conduct a one-day survey of homeless individuals in their respective cities. Cooperating agencies in Akron, Cleveland, Columbus, Dayton, Portsmouth, and Toledo were able to identify 3,617 such individuals. A similar effort the following year uncovered 6,520 homeless persons. But, far more significant were the tragic experiences represented by those numbers. One particularly poignant account from Cincinnati seemed emblematic:

> Both Mr. and Mrs. C. are persons of limited mentality who have been wandering from place to place in an effort to find some relative whom they thought would take them in. A police official in a small Kentucky town is said to have given them train fare to Cincinnati to live with an uncle

(whom Mrs. C. hadn't seen in fifteen years). Upon arrival here relatives refused to see the family. Two weeks prior to coming to Cincinnati, they had been in Indiana with a cousin. The cousin couldn't keep them so they started wandering again. No sooner then they had left the cousin's home, they stopped for the night on the front porch of a canning factory where the woman gave birth to a child. The township officials of that community sent the family by truck to another relative, approximately a hundred miles away in Kentucky.

Their first baby is dead. Burial was made by the mother and father "under a rock somewhere." They couldn't remember the name of the place.

The [new] baby was taken ill but the mother refused to allow her to be hospitalized. When last seen they had their knapsacks and were trudging down the road presumably to try to find another relative in Indiana to whom they had referred on several occasions.

Considerable public concern arose during the 1930s regarding the severe strains which prolonged deprivation placed upon family units. The emotional stress caused by repeatedly "hitting the road" in search of jobs, sending the kids off to live with more fortunate relatives, insufficient food, living in overcrowded conditions, and the consequent loss of personal dignity did create friction and threaten the cohesiveness of many families. Most managed to endure despite terrible odds, as illustrated by a case in Cleveland:

Mr. J. has for a number of years kept his family in terror, especially when he was drinking. Last winter Mrs. J. died, leaving the eight almost grown children with the cruel father. For a time after his wife's death, Mr. J. was kept in the workhouse but he is again at home with the children, adding to their burden of self support. The two oldest boys are unable to find work, the oldest probably gambles. The oldest girl, 22, works in a department store and is chief bread-winner. A 16 year old girl with the help of a 13 year old sister, takes the responsibility of the home, while two high school boys deliver the Shopping News. In this way the family has held together and is living in a very respectable fashion.

Others, however, failed to survive. Children drifted away and "the poorman's divorce" (desertion) became increasingly common. Many weddings and children were undoubtedly postponed due to unemployment and a lack of sufficient funds.

Marginal members of society were not the only people who suffered during this depression. While the unskilled lower classes bore the brunt of the disaster, the professional and upper classes were also affected — though to lesser extents. Many businessmen went bankrupt and even highly-trained experts were laid off, forcing them to descend the ladder of success and into relief lines. Ohio State University reported in 1933, for instance, that over 2,000 alumni had lost their jobs. College graduates painfully learned that they were not exempt from salary cuts. Teachers especially incurred financial losses, since depleted tax bases forced many school districts to shorten school terms, eliminate staff and programs, and pay remaining faculty members in scrip.

In its initial stages, the Great Depression did not stimulate mass anxiety. Business and government leaders assured the nation that the slump was only a normal cyclical fluctuation which would soon pass. Some spokesmen argued that the economic downturn was necessary and even beneficial, purging the capitalist system of its weaker components, and guaranteeing that prosperity's imminent return would be stronger than ever. As the weeks turned into months, as more and more businesses and jobs vanished, as savings dissolved, as befuddled public officials tried to ignore the growing problems, and as the burdens of unemployment became unbearable, those blustering promises began to fall on deaf ears. There seemed to be no end in sight to this unprecedented economic trough. Public confidence rapidly eroded, replaced by disbelief, bewilderment, and paralyzing fear.

By early 1931, working people gradually broke out of their stupor. Obsessed with survival and increasingly suspicious that government and business leaders were at best incapable, and at worst indifferent to their plights, thou-

sands of distraught Ohioans stirred into action. Rather than harboring any long-range, revolutionary goals, the vast majority of discontented workers were clearly motivated by immediate needs — jobs and public relief. Nonetheless, Communists and Socialists oftentimes provided inexperienced workers with the organizational expertise and leadership with which to press their demands, and repeatedly exhibited a willingness to endure danger and personal hardship. While relatively few became members and most rejected radical ideologies, some workers pragmatically welcomed the assistance of zealous left-wing agitators. To the desperate unemployed, an individual's politics seemed far less important in a crisis, than the person's eagerness and ability to help. Consequently, communists had achieved considerable success in their statewide efforts to organize local Unemployed Councils — affiliates of the Trade Union Unity League, a national communist organization headed by William Z. Foster. In the spring of 1931, the State Committee of Unemployed Councils announced plans for a "hunger march" on Columbus beginning on May 1. Under the watchful eyes of local law enforcement agencies, company spies, and Ohio National Guard intelligence officers, bands of demonstrators started from Toledo, Cleveland, Youngstown, and Cincinnati hoping to swell their ranks with sympathizers as they passed through communities along their routes.

Steelworkers and their families enjoyed a fleeting respite from their troubles at a Youngstown amusement park on Labor Day, 1939.

Fortunate to have found employment in 1935, black foundry workers in Cleveland performed manual tasks on a mold conveyor line.

In an interview published in Studs Terkel's *Hard Times,* "Dynamite" Garland vividly remembered her deprived childhood during the Depression, her father's struggles to provide for his family, and—at long last—the return of prosperity:

I remember all of a sudden we had to move. My father lost his job and we moved into a double-garage. The landlord didn't charge us rent for seven years. We had a coal stove and we had to each take turns, the three of us kids, to warm our legs. It was awfully cold when you opened those garage doors . . . my father was pretty sharp in a way. He always could get something to feed us kids. We lived about three months on candy cods, they're little chocolate square things. We had these melted in milk. And he had a part-time job in a Chinese restaurant. We lived on those fried noodles. I can't stand 'em today. He went to delivering Corn Flake samples. We lived on Corn Flake balls, Rice Krispies, they used to come out of our ears. Can't eat 'em today either . . . My father did the best he could. He used to stuff in the mailboxes those little sheets, "Pink Sheets for Pale Purses." I think it was for a left-wingish organization. My father disagreed with whatever philosophy was on there. He got $3 a week for this. 'Cause he got a job in Akron, delivering carry-out food, we moved there [from Cleveland]. That was a dandy place: dirt, smoke, my mother scrubbing all the time. We lived right on the railroad tracks. They used to throw us watermelons and things like that. When the trains slowed down, he used to jump on and have us kids pick up the coal . . . I finished high school and got sort of engaged. I thought maybe if I got married I could eat hamburgers and hot dogs all night, have a ball, play the guitar and sing . . . Eleven months later, I had a baby. I was pregnant with another when the war was declared . . . From $14 a week, we jumped to $65 a week, working in a defense plant. It sort of went to my head. Wow. Boy, we were rich. . . .

When the four columns converged at Columbus on May 10, however, only 182 marchers were left to present demands for unemployment insurance and old age pensions to the unswayed legislature. The unemployed council movement had more success at local levels, with such tactics as resisting evictions and staging demonstrations at relief offices and in city council chambers. More important than the fact that protests led by the state's various "radical" groups usually failed, was the publicity and public awareness which resulted. Furthermore, spontaneous mass action also began to erupt in major cities, small towns, and rural areas which clearly could not be dismissed as leftist agitation. For instance, community leaders in Akron were stunned in 1932, when unemployed members of the American Legion and the Veterans of Foreign Wars mobilized for relief. The rising number of reported incidents in rural areas was epitomized in 1933, when

. . . a group of miners, men who had been miners in the marginal mines of Athens County, marched into Glouster, Ohio which was the trade center of the surrounding area. Each man was armed with a gunny sack; each man was uttering demands for food—food for his family, food for himself. . . . This march was a spontaneous local move. There were no outside agitators. The group was composed of Americans of English and Welsh descent, grandsons and great grandsons of the miners who came at the opening of the Hocking Valley field in the [eighteen] fifties and sixties.

Alarmed officials began to recognize that the grievances of the jobless were real and widespread and could no longer be ignored.

Governmental action was plainly needed to deal with a tragedy of this magnitude. By early 1933, more than seventy percent of the populations in numerous counties depended upon some form of assistance. Residents of heavily industrialized counties like Cuyahoga, Lucas, Mahoning, Hamilton, Stark, and Summit were especially hard hit. Toledo alone had 30,000 families who had applied for relief, but sympathetic officials could only afford to allocate six cents a day to each adult. In the agricultural and industrial hinterlands, where relief organizations often had never existed or had quickly collapsed under the extraordinary demands for aid, the crisis was even more acute. Private charitable organizations had accelerated their efforts to assist the jobless, and in many communities *ad hoc* citizens' groups appeared to undertake a variety of ''self-help'' projects. In Trumbull County, for example, more than a dozen local committees — adopting the motto ''You Help Me and I'll Help You'' and hoping to counteract the influence of radicals among the unemployed — established programs to deliver free milk and bread to needy families, provide coal and firewood, and set up soup lines and garden projects. Despite such efforts, private groups could assist only a small portion of impoverished residents. The ever-swelling remainder had to turn to local governments. However, Ohio's anachronistic structure for public relief, dating back to the 1800s, did not encourage that alternative. The state's decentralized system legally allowed township trustees to provide residents with outdoor relief, while county officials were authorized to assist the disabled and transients. In the early years of the depression, policies emanating from Columbus manifested a glaring lack of consistency, innovation, or a willingness to commit the necessary funds. As a result, city, township,

and county officials were forced to wrestle with massive relief problems totally beyond their financial capacity. Not until the election year of 1932 — when political necessity and the rising volume of grassroots complaints made the issue unavoidable — did traditional resistance to public relief finally waver. Tacitly admitting that overwhelming relief problems could not be resolved by local government units alone, the General Assembly created a State Relief Commission. The SRC was given the responsibility of facilitating greater cooperation between national, state, and local relief agencies; assisting in the distribution of Red Cross goods; and funneling nearly $19,000,000 from the federal Reconstruction Finance Corporation into local communities. In practice, however, conservative state leaders continued to expect local authorities to administer relief programs.

Unemployed army veterans in Cleveland sign up for the Bonus March on Washington, D.C., June, 1932.

Yet another New Deal program, the Civilian Conservation Corps, provided training and wages for needy youths. In a Ross County CCC camp, boys chiseled stone for barbecue pits in a newly constructed recreation area.

Women manufactured overalls in Hillsboro at Ohio Relief Production Unit No. 8 in December, 1934.

The Public Works Administration was a key element in President Roosevelt's recovery program from 1933 to 1937. In order to stimulate employment and business activity, the PWA "pumped" federal funds into local economies through large-scale construction projects. In Cleveland, for example, PWA workers built Lincoln Park in 1936.

With the election of Franklin D. Roosevelt to the presidency in 1932 and the subsequent implementation of his administration's New Deal reforms, the relief situation altered dramatically. Millions of dollars in federal aid poured into Ohio — nearly $28,000,000 in 1933 alone — through a wide variety of programs intended to assist the state and local governments in coping with the depression's impacts. From 1933 to 1935, the primary wellspring for relief aid was the Federal Emergency Relief Administration, which channeled funds through the SRC. Approximately 1,000,000 Ohioans per month received direct relief during those years, generally in the form of allotments for necessities like food, clothing, and rent which were near or below subsistence levels. The FERA also established programs in Ohio to assist college students and rehabilitate rural residents. Work relief — in which recipients performed labor for their money — was implemented through the

creation of the Civilian Conservation Corps and especially the Civil Works Administration. In late-1933 and early-1934, the CWA spent nearly $58,000,000 and employed a weekly average of 205,000 unemployed Ohioans. The CWA sponsored about 6,000 "make-work" projects across the state, from constructing a new library in Yellow Springs, a city hall in Marysville, and community swimming pools at Orrville and Alliance to improving thousands of miles of roads, and building hundreds of public parks. Though conservative sceptics worried that these massive federal efforts would rob workers of their initiative and opportunities to become "self-made men," to the unemployed these programs meant hope and survival for their families.

Under FERA auspices, in 1934 the SRC launched a unique experiment in "state capitalism" by organizing the Ohio Relief Production Units, Inc. The ORPU was commissioned to lease idle factories and employ local relief recipients to produce necessities for fellow-Ohioans who were "on the dole." Workers received a combination of cash and credits which could be exchanged for items manufactured in other ORPU plants. Although the ORPU employed approximately 1,000 jobless workers per month in twelve plants, the experiment was dismantled in mid-1935, due to various problems. The credit wage-system proved burdensome to workers who, after quickly acquiring ORPU-produced clothing, blankets, furniture, china, and stoves, then accumulated unneeded labor credits. Instead, they preferred increased cash wages in order to pay off debts, obtain medical care, and purchase food and fuel. While this difficulty was corrected with higher wages and shortened hours, additional obstacles and objections emerged. Labor leaders feared that

A

C

B

D

E

The New Deal's diverse WPA projects furnished work-relief and services for hard-pressed Ohioans in every corner of the state. Cleveland women earned money piecing quilts in the Public Auditorium (A), while Columbus workers "on the WPA" repaired the city's streets (B). In Steubenville, a teacher employed by the WPA conducted literacy and citizenship classes for East European immigrants (C). Federal assistance even reached into isolated rural areas such as Laurel Cliff — a small coal community tucked away in a hollow in Meigs County — with a small lending library housed in a converted chicken coop (D & E).

the ORPU threatened jobs of unionists in private industry and might inhibit organizational efforts. In addition, since the ORPU did not produce for the mass-consumption market, its distribution system remained primitive. Furthermore, businessmen generally objected to the principle of governmentally sponsored competition with private industry, despite the ORPU's obviously limited purpose and scope.

Formation of the Ohio Transient Division in 1933 represented yet another aspect of the broad FERA campaign. Transients had customarily been viewed as social outcasts and shiftless derelicts, who preferred hand-outs to honest labor, and who deserved no sympathy and little assistance from respectable citizens. Consequently, these individuals were either jailed, run out of town, or, at best, provided with sparse shelter by private charitable groups. By the fourth year of depression, however, public recognition began to spread that, in fact, many of these homeless wanderers were plain work-

ing people temporarily "down on their luck." Studies discovered that the majority were native-born Ohioans who had been compelled to hit the road in search of jobs. With federal funding, the Transient Division established and supplied shelters in Cleveland, Cincinnati, Toledo, Columbus, Akron, Dayton, Canton, and Portsmouth. In addition, ten rural camps were constructed to provide work relief, medical attention, and educational facilities. Special efforts were made to keep families together and the children in school. By 1936, tens-of-thousands of desperate migrants had benefited from the program.

Unfortunately, numerous problems marred the effectiveness of federal relief projects in Ohio. Officials in rural areas, for instance, frequently lacked sufficient experience or training to deal efficiently with massive case-loads and the sudden influx of funds. In urban areas, such as Toledo, political corruption and patronage complicated relief efforts. Across the state, many community leaders seemed to favor cheaper over humane assistance for the needy — as reflected in the statewide average of five dollars per month in individual relief payments. Despite repeated prodding, federal officials generally failed to improve inadequate implementations of their programs, since the expenditure of funds necessarily relied on local participation and discretion. Finally, most politicians at the state level maintained cautious positions, often refusing to continue or expand proven programs, and apparently preferring to allow the initiative for public welfare policies to shift to Washington, D.C.

As substantial and wide-ranging as initial New Deal activities had been, they were but a prelude to the massive second wave of social reform inaugurated by the Roosevelt administration in 1935. Of the numerous government programs, two were particularly significant to the poverty-stricken and jobless. The historic Social Security Act established the nation's first comprehensive system for unemployment compensation, old-age retirement benefits, as well as aid to dependent children and the handicapped. But in immediate terms, creation of the Works Progress Administration had even greater impact. The WPA initiated federal work relief projects for a broad spectrum of unemployed job seekers. Ohio's skilled and unskilled laborers were put to work constructing streets, schools, sewer systems, parks, and public buildings. The WPA-sponsored National Youth Administration provided jobs for high school and college students in order to keep them in school and off the glutted labor market. Various additional programs enabled white-collar workers and professionals to utilize their training and skills in federally funded endeavors — writers, actors, artists, musicians, teachers, social workers, statisticians, and many more. At its peak in 1938, the WPA paid average monthly wages of $58.04 to more than 281,000 Ohioans— more than any state except Pennsylvania. By 1940, an estimated thirty-six percent of the state's unemployed depended upon the WPA for their survival.

Through dozens of measures such as these, the New Deal achieved a fundamental redirection in the course of the nation's development. Despite numerous shortcomings in implementation, New Deal policies firmly established the long-resisted principle of governmental responsibility for the welfare of needy citizens in an urban-industrial society. From 1933 through 1937, the federal government expended an estimated $787,000,000 in Ohio for recovery and relief, and another $793,000,000 in federal loans. By 1938, more than one-third of Ohio's

Miners on a WPA project in New Straitsville attempted to extinguish an underground fire which had burned since the late nineteenth century.

counties had *at least* one-out-of-four families on some form of public relief. While Roosevelt and most New Dealers asserted that such was hardly their intention, this large-scale and diverse involvement in the activities of so many individuals — from local administrators and businessmen to actual or potential relief recipients —began to generate a distinct willingness in the public mind to depend on federal assistance, not only during times of crisis, but in the normal course of their daily lives as well. Together with the consequent accumulation of political and economic power in Washington, this growing reliance on the federal government would affect working-class affairs for generations to come.

One of the most eventful and controversial aspects of New Deal activism was the transformation generated in labor-management relations. Prodded by a mixture of grassroots militancy, fears that the workers' revolutionary potential might be unleashed, and basic sympathies with labor's plight, New Deal politicians put the government's official stamp of approval on the principle of collective bargaining. In sharp contrast to previous administrations, freedom to unionize and resolve grievances on equal terms with employers were no longer viewed as working-class privileges to be occasionally tolerated, but rather as innate rights to be nourished and legally guaranteed. With this benevolent protection, an emboldened labor movement flourished as never before. After over a decade of dormancy, organized labor more than doubled its membership within the first five years of the New Deal, and finally gained firm footholds in steel, rubber, automobile, and other mass-production industries. By no means was this momentous watershed in working-class history achieved without bitter employer-opposition, considerable strife, or government efforts to curtail labor's more "radical" demands. Nevertheless, by the outbreak of World War II, it became apparent that the invigorated labor movement had finally won sufficient status and power to deal with organized capital on more equitable terms.

The resurgence of unionism was sparked, in large part, by the passage in 1933 of the Roosevelt administration's most important, initial measure to combat the depression — the National Industrial Recovery Act. Included within this complex legislation were provisions exempting from anti-trust laws any businesses which agreed to substitute self-regulation and industry-wide cooperation for cut-throat competition. To accomplish this goal, each industry was encouraged to draw up and abide by a "code of fair competition" which fixed prices, contained child-labor prohibitions, established minimum wages, and increased employment by limiting working hours. Furthermore, the law's famous Section 7-a stipulated that each code had to guarantee the right of employees to "organize unions of their own choosing" and to bargain collectively with their employers. A National Recovery Administration was set up to generate support, supervise formulation of the codes, and monitor compliance.

The totally unanticipated response of working people to the NIRA literally flabbergasted business, government, and union leaders alike. Now possessing the blessing of the federal

The famous "Blue Eagle" emblem displayed by companies which complied with the National Recovery Administration's codes of fair competition.

Hoping to rekindle public confidence in the American economy, the NRA launched its recovery campaign with massive publicity and morale-building efforts, such as this 1933 parade in Cleveland.

the coal fields telling the miners that they now had the right to organize; that it was guaranteed to them by their government; that operators who tried to stop them would be subject to the full wrath of the National Industrial Recovery law. Dazedly the miners listened. A brave few went to meetings. They had heard organizers before, but this was a new message. The Government of the United States guaranteed the right for them to have a union! They began to believe; then they did believe; then they started to move. Thousands upon thousands signed enrollment cards designating the United Mine Workers of America as their collective bargaining representative. . . . Local unions reappeared as if by magic, at mines where almost everyone thought they had been destroyed.

Wildcat strikes erupted throughout the state, as exuberant workers sought concessions from surprised employers. In Cleveland, the ranks of the Amalgamated Clothing Workers of America, the Teamsters, and various craft unions swelled, strikes multiplied, and dozens of firms agreed to contracts. Only the year before, the *Cleveland Plain Dealer* had asserted approvingly that "Today labor stands patient and hopeful. . . . Never has there been a period of depression so free from labor strife. Unemployment has harassed it. Closed factories have taken away its livelihood. But, in the face of enormous hardship, labor has showed its good citizenship and sturdy American stamina." Obviously, the patience, hope, and stamina of many rank and filers had been exhausted, as an estimated 25,000 Ohioans conducted ninety-six walkouts in 1933 — more than double the previous year's total.

However, it quickly became evident that the workers' drive for unionization and resolution of their grievances would not necessarily be easy or fruitful. Several factors tempered the initial enthusiasm of many newborn activists. In some industries such as rubber, the NIRA actually inhibited unionization, since employers pointed out that the vague mandate of Section 7-a did not expressly prohibit the formation of company unions. In other instances, employers utilized the fear of unemployment to deflate militancy. Though described by a social worker in humorous tones, an incident at Cleveland's Hiram House illustrated the serious extent to which the technique had even permeated into supposedly benevolent relief endeavors:

Everything progressed quite smoothly [on a brief make-work project], until an interesting problem presented itself. James, a young man of very low mentality — much older than the other boys — had absorbed some of the theories of the pool room and essayed to pass them on to the other boys. He urged them to strike for more money, suggested that there was graft along the line and to stand up for their rights. Most of the boys range in age from fifteen to seventeen years and are quite impressionable. Naturally this upset things. . . . As a result they declared a strike and walked off the job.

The leader called a meeting of the insurgents and for two hours gave them a serious talk on practical economics. It was pointed out how fortunate they were even to have work. . . . One boy

government, long-suffering workers suddenly clamored by the thousands for union membership. Not just toilers with union traditions like miners and clothing workers; not only the unorganized masses in the electrical, automobile, steel, and rubber industries; but even farm workers, motion picture actors, newspapermen, bartenders, and laundresses spontaneously flocked to the union cause. AFL local offices were flooded with recruits. In numerous instances, inexperienced workers organized themselves and sought AFL affiliation afterwards. Coal miners in the Ohio fields joined their brethren across the nation in reviving the gospel of industrial unionism and resurrecting the United Mine Workers from the brink of extinction to the pinnacle of the labor movement. As one participant recalled:

Every organizer in the union, and hundreds of volunteers from the mines began to sift through

In the highly-charged atmosphere of the 1930s, almost every labor-management confrontation in Cleveland threatened to explode into street-warfare.

was asked how much he had earned before he began the job in question. He replied, "Nothing." He was then asked how much he had earned since he began working. He said, "Fourteen dollars." . . . When told their places could be filled at a moments notice by boys who were clamoring for an opportunity to work, their enthusiasm cooled somewhat. A very chastened group of boys returned to their duties the next morning.

Furthermore, while the NIRA endorsed the principle of unionization, it failed either to provide any tangible means of enforcement or to prevent violent anti-union tactics. Many employers consequently ignored or violated the law with impunity. In fact, subsequent investigations by the U.S. Senate's LaFollette Civil Liberties Committee graphically revealed that the nation's leading firms were preparing for industrial warfare. As just one of many examples in Ohio, the Youngstown Sheet & Tube Company paid over $1300 for tear gas in 1933. In 1934, the company increased its arsenal with another $8,505 in tear gas and over $10,000 worth of munitions, including 424 police clubs, six 12-gauge repeating shotguns, 11,500 rounds of .38 caliber pistol ammunition, and 300 shotgun shells. In addition, the Committee documented the employers' extensive use of labor espionage networks (the general manager of the Associated Industries of Cleveland insisted that "spying always will be an essential part of warfare"), professional strikebreakers, private police forces, wire-tapping, and interception of personal mail in order to disrupt, intimidate, and defeat their employees. Witnesses described a typical perversion of police power in private hands, when, during a bloody 1935 strike, Republic Steel's private guards

. . . sallied forth into the city of Canton attacking with ferocity employees, nonemployees, strikers, pickets, bystanders, women, and children, with the same impartiality and lack of discrimination as the attacks on defenseless civilians in contempo-

George Roberts found that union organizing could be extremely dangerous, as he reported to AFL President William Green in late-1935:

. . . the Diamond Alkali Company and the F.P. and E. Railroad Officials have hired in the neighborhood of sixty guards. These guards being deputized by the Sheriff of Lake County and are to serve the Companies in anyway they see fit to use them. Some of these guards are assigned to guard the Railroad property and regular watchmen of the Diamond Alkali Company are used to intimidate the employees and myself. Knowing that my main purpose in being there is to organize their employees, they have had me watched day and night. Company guards have watched the Union Hall every meeting. Seeing that all this action on their part has not scared me out of town, the guards set about to try other methods to intimidate and embarass me, so they checked my license plates in the Akron courthouse and found that the automobile dealer with whom I made a trade had failed to have my license transferred . . . While I was being held pending the arrival of Attorney . . . the Sheriff himself, decided to search my car. He did so and found a gun in the pocket for which I had been authorized to keep in my car for protection by Officers of the Law in Summit County . . . I had been attacked by three unknown gunmen and left unconscious in the street and when I told the Police that I was going to carry a gun in my car to protect myself, they said I was absolutely right in doing so . . . Now the Sheriff and Prosecuting Attorney of Lake County, who are tools of the Ohio Rubber Company and the Diamond Alkali Company, are going to try to cause me trouble . . . I had been scheduled to address an Official Meeting of the Ministerial Association of Lake County and after this trouble occurred, the Prosecuting Attorney and the Officials of the Diamond Alkali Company started a movement through some of their Minister friends to prevent me from addressing the Ministers Meeting and almost succeeded . . . While the Ministers were debating the question, the Prosecuting Attorney of Lake County and an Official of the Diamond Alkali Company, the General Manager of the Ohio Rubber Company with the Vice President of the same Company and the President of the Chamber of Commerce of Cleveland Ohio pushed themselves into the meeting and took notes on what I had to say. I only tell you the latter incident to show you the coercion and intimidation that the workers of Lake County are faced with. . . .

A Cincinnati brewer drew a mug to celebrate the repeal of prohibition in 1933.

Cleveland police assisted strikebreakers through the picket line at the Fisher Body plant in April, 1934.

Iron, Steel, and Tin Workers — with little aid from the union's organizers. Clarence Irwin, a local insurgent and skilled roller at Youngstown Sheet and Tube asserted:

> There was a wave of organizing going on all around us in the Mahoning Valley. But the old-line lodges were refusing to take in the unskilled and semiskilled workers. . . . the mass of steel-workers wanted industrial unionism, and so did we. But it wasn't clear to us until we set out to get it that we would have to fight not only the companies but our own international officers and even the Government. The process of learning was slow and painful, and a lot of us dropped by the way.

In 1933, 1934, and 1935 the rank and file attempted to gain union recognition, but steel masters refused to negotiate and applied their customary union-busting tactics, while timid Amalgamated leaders refused to support the workers' fruitless efforts.

Despite the odds, a violent outburst of working-class militancy in 1934 signaled the beginning of a new era, as more strikes broke out in Ohio than in any year since 1920. The Toledo Auto-Lite walkout and the onion workers' dispute in Hardin County were two of the most dramatic.

Shop-floor unrest had been brewing at the Electric Auto-Lite plant for several months. Reflecting the surge of unionism which swept Toledo following passage of the NIRA, workers had formed United Automobile Workers Federal Labor Union No. 18384 and affiliated with the AFL. In February, the union had tested its strength, when 3,500 workers struck Auto-Lite and three other automobile-parts companies for union recognition and wage increases. The brief dispute ended with an agreement that outstanding grievances would be resolved through negotiations. However, subsequent discussions on wages and recognition stalled, causing frustrated employees to call another walkout in April against Auto-Lite and two local firms owned by the company. Auto-Lite management immediately responded by replacing the strikers with new workers, building up its arsenal with $11,000 worth of tear gas, hiring 150 specially deputized guards, and by launching a propaganda barrage which stressed that the existence of a company union proved the firm's compliance with the NIRA code. Since the AFL provided little assistance, strikers welcomed the support of left-wing groups like the Lucas County Unemployed League — a local branch of the National Unemployed League, led by the noted socialist A.J. Muste, and claiming 100,000 Ohio members. The strike appeared lost after the first month, but the issuance on May 14 of a court injunction prohibiting mass picketing quickly escalated hostilities. Thousands of unionists, radicals, and sympathetic workers from throughout the city defied the court order, marching in a massive picket line which imprisoned 1,800 strikebreakers inside the factory. Clashes between the pickets and the police, company guards, and strikebreakers expanded into ugly rioting

rary warfare. . . . [Guards] were rushing around the people, and beating the people to the brick pavement, and then beating them after they were down. . . . It did not occur to me that in a community that was supposed to be civilized such things could occur.

Finally, the inability of AFL leaders to respond vigorously to the upsurge of grassroots activism frequently stifled unionization. For example, thousands of rank-and-file steelworkers in Youngstown, Canton, Cleveland, Warren, and other centers organized their own lodges of the AFL's feeble Amalgamated Association of

which spilled into the surrounding neighborhoods. Hundreds of state police moved in, a state of emergency was declared, and Governor White sent in 1,350 National Guardsmen—"the largest military display in peace time in the history of Ohio." Though the plant finally shut down, mob action continued on an almost daily basis, the Guard fired on a crowd of demonstrators killing two and wounding dozens more, and a city in financial collapse deteriorated to the brink of anarchy. Tensions flared higher as outraged radicals and union leaders threatened to call a general strike. Through the peacemaking efforts of federal officials, a six-month truce was at last achieved in early June. In signed contracts with the three firms, the union did not win exclusive bargaining rights, but did gain wage increases, seniority rules in layoffs, and the removal of strikebreakers from the payroll. Six weeks after this partial union victory, Charles P. Taft — one of the special mediators assigned by Secretary of Labor Perkins to resolve the dispute — wrote to an associate: "It just happened that I was in Toledo last night . . . and I understand that trouble is still simmering at the Auto-Lite Plant. It is not surprising that there would continue to be some friction, but . . . I am a little afraid there may be another outbreak." His fears proved justified, though unduly circumscribed. Unabated discontent subsequently spread to auto factories throughout Toledo, and, in the process, the local union expanded into one of the most powerful in the emergent UAW.

McGuffey, Ohio seemed, to outsiders, an unlikely site for bitter labor-management conflict. Tucked within the rich marsh lands of rural Hardin County, the quiet farming community of 700 appeared to be isolated from the turmoil

---

The Communist Party of Toledo calls a

MASS MEETING

Roi Davis Auditorium (cor. Jefferson and Michigan)

Thursday, May 31st, — 7:30 P. M.

TO DISCUSS THE

Auto-Lite Strike

THE NEED FOR A

GENERAL STRIKE

AND THE

Danger Of a Sell-Out

The finest courage ever shown by men and women has already brought victory within the reach of the Auto-Lite workers. In the fumes of tear gas and the new deadly KOCS and DM gas, over the bodies of their murdered brothers, the Mass Picket Line has held firm and has ABSOLUTELY CLOSED DOWN THE PLANT.

Up to the beginning of this week the Auto-Lite strike has been the most outstanding triumph of strike action in closing down a scab plant in 15 years of American Labor history.

The Auto-Lite workers have not been without support. The many thousands of Unemployed in Toledo have NOT scabbed, but have been mobilized by the Unemployed Council to help on the picket line. This is an example for the whole country.

The TRADE UNIONS have voted by overwhelming majority to support the struggle with a GENERAL STRIKE. This splendid resolution, if carried out, would mean an unparalleled triumph for Toledo Labor.

Sixty-Eight Trade Unions out of 103 affiliated to the C. L. U. HAVE VOTED FOR THE GENERAL STRIKE.

But no General Strike.

Why?

Just at the time when an immediate General Strike could bring an overwhelming victory, we have "postponement" of the General Strike and, instead of the expressed desire of the trade unionists being carried out, we have a whole series of maneuvers and offers of "ARBITRATION" which can only mean surrender of the victory already within our grasp. The "offers" of the millionaire capitalist Chas. P. Taft are only offers to break the strike and to turn over all questions of Wages, Conditions, etc., to an "Arbitration" board—which means to Miniger and his friends.

"Arbitration" and "Postponement", of the General Strike are swindles intended only to snatch a victory—already won up to this time—out of the hands of the workers.

What are the Labor Officials doing behind the doors of the Commodore Perry Hotel? The Bosses KNOW EVERYTHING THAT IS BEING SAID AND DONE BEHIND THOSE DOORS! WHY CAN'T THE WORKERS KNOW?

The workers in every Shop and Local Union must take action themselves. Call the General Strike NOW. Elect rank and file committees in every Local Union and Shop. A General Strike Committee should be elected from the shops, with a decisive majority of workers on it that will energetically carry out the wishes of the workers. The local strike committee should immediately formulate DEMANDS FOR EACH SHOP AND TRADE in addition to supporting the demands of the Auto-Lite workers and for withdrawal of the National Guard. The General Strike must involve all workers and their organizations. Only the unity of employed and unemployed—of white and Negro workers—will carry thru this great battle to victory.

The Main Speech will be made by a member of the Central Committee of the Communist Party.

ROBERT MINOR

Other speakers will include:

John Williamson—State Organizer of the Communist Party.

I. O. Ford—Communist Candidate for Governor of Ohio.

Jim Wilson—Toledo Negro Leader.

K. Eggart—Local Communist Organizer.

Dorothy Cheyfitz—Young Communist League.

Re-establish the Mass Picket Line Thursday Morning!

Immediate General Strike Must Be Called.

National Guard Must Be Withdrawn!

Direct Negotiations—with the Open Knowledge of the Workers.

No Arbitration!

Settlement Only After National Guard Is Withdrawn!

Sheriff Krieger Must Be Removed!

Win the Wage Increase!

COMMUNIST PARTY OF TOLEDO   137½ North Erie Street

A communist handbill called for a general strike in Toledo to support the 1934 Auto-Lite strike.

National Guardsmen attempted to control the masses of Auto-Lite strikers and sympathizers who spilled into nearby neighborhoods.

which disrupted urban centers. Since the late-nineteenth century, local natives had depended for their livelihoods on the cultivation of onions —their primary cash-crop and, beneath the surface, an indirect source of strife. Onion growing required intensive seasonal labor, which had been supplied for decades by migrant workers from the hills of Kentucky and Tennessee. Although employed only part of the year, over half of the area's farmworkers and their families had chosen to settle down as permanent residents, despite deplorable conditions. Six to eight families crowded into each tar-paper hovel provided by the landowners, and most relied on public relief during the winter months. Sixty percent of the 1000 farmworkers who were employed during the growing season earned a total of less than $250. Moreover, their poverty and clannishness aggravated the prejudices and resentments of native residents, resulting in such rigid discrimination that one observer compared the community's social relations to a caste system. In June, 1934, these underlying tensions exploded, when repeated wage cuts, deteriorating working conditions, and the infectious militancy emanating from Toledo and Columbus sparked a strike in the onion fields surrounding McGuffey. Described as "one of the longest, most violent, and most highly publicized farm-labor outbreaks of the early thirties," the walkout had been called by the local Agriculture Workers' Union—the first such group in the nation to receive a charter from the AFL. Growers adamantly refused to discuss the union's demand for a 13¢ hourly wage-increase over the prevailing 12¢ rate. The importation of strikebreakers and evictions of the strikers' families widened cleavages within the community, and brought national attention. Reporters from around the country descended on the town, members of the Lucas County Unemployed League appeared with offers of assistance, the Ohio AFL vainly requested an investigation by the governor, and a federal conciliator arrived to attempt a settlement. State health officials became aroused when typhoid fever broke out among the evicted families, who had been forced to live in the streets of McGuffey. Although the county sheriff reportedly sympathized with the workers, most local residents and officials supported the powerful growers. In late August, for example, a mob of 200 vigilantes kidnapped union president Okey Odell from the sheriff's office, where he was being questioned about an earlier bombing of the mayor's house. Odell was driven into the countryside, severely beaten, and told to leave the county. However, he returned to McGuffey, only to find that local authorities refused to prosecute his attackers. Instead, after another angry mob of several hundred residents subsequently gathered outside his home, Odell was indicted by a local grand jury for threatening them with a gun. None of Odell's assailants were ever arrested, despite a $1000 reward offered by the American Civil Liberties Union. Additional violence and a sweeping court injunction prohibiting all gatherings by strikers severely crippled the walkout. By the end of September, Ohio's first farmworkers' strike collapsed, when vigilantes loaded insurgents into trucks and dumped them across the state line.

The hopeful jubilation with which workers greeted the NIRA turned to rampant disillusionment by early 1935. In confrontations at Auto-Lite, McGuffey, and countless other workplaces, labor experienced firsthand the inadequacies of the law — which the U.S. Supreme Court declared unconstitutional in May in the noted *Schecter* decision. If government was to maintain its commitment to protect workers' rights, as well as diffuse their militancy, stronger legislation was plainly needed. Congress responded in June with the Wagner Act — the most significant labor legislation ever enacted. After more than a century of working-class struggle, the measure finally legitimized the basic rights of working people to advocate unionism, to elect representative unions of their own choosing, to engage in collective bargaining in order to resolve grievances, and to express dissatisfaction with unfair practices by employers. More importantly, the bill also created the National Labor Relations Board to

During one of the many bloody Auto-Lite riots, Toledo police carried away an injured auto worker.

Disgruntled with the failures of the First New Deal, the Ohio Unemployed League delivered a "rattlesnake" warning to the White House in April, 1935.

conduct union elections, settle disputes, and enforce the act's provisions through the judicial process. Although the New Deal had corrected the shortcomings of the NIRA and had strengthened its pledge to protect workers, the Wagner Act did not immediately have a tangible effect. Many unionists remained leery that, like the NIRA, the bill would not be upheld by the Supreme Court, and employers hampered enforcement with court challenges. The law's effectivenes was not assured until May, 1937, when the Court declared the act constitutional in the *Jones and Laughlin* decision.

Meanwhile, Ohioans could not afford to wait for resolution of the legal questions, and continued to take matters into their own hands to improve their depressed conditions. Many of these efforts reached beyond the organized labor movement. For example, concerned residents in Toledo — where labor disputes had risen alarmingly, from merely eighteen involving 648 workers during 1928-33, to thirty-two involving over 13,000 people in 1934-35 — established an Industrial Peace Board in July, 1935, which gained nationwide attention. Comprised of moderate labor, business, and community leaders, the unique municipal mediation agency successfully averted and resolved many local disputes before its demise in 1943. During the summer of 1935, Cleveland was the scene of especially notable direct action efforts by black residents. Racial prejudice had not only barred blacks from many factories and labor unions, but also from jobs in the very white-owned stores which depended on their patronage. With unemployment causing tremendous suffering, local blacks formed the Future Outlook League for the express purpose of gaining jobs in these businesses. A community survey by the League discovered that, out of 3,000 firms operating in the Central Area, less than 100 employed blacks, usually in menial positions. Effectively marshalling their financial clout as the primary customers for these businesses, the FOL staged a picket and boycott campaign which won nearly 300 jobs for blacks during the year. This grassroots, non-violent, job-action movement subsequently served as a model for blacks across the country.

The organized labor movement had reached a critical crossroads by 1935. Conservative AFL leaders had failed to sustain the momentum of rank-and-file interest in union membership after 1933. With customary shortsightedness, they continued to maintain their outmoded insistence on the sanctity of craft unionism, as well as their preference for respectability over combativeness. In an attempt to ally unskilled industrial workers and beleaguered skilled tradesmen, some craft unions had been amalgamated or transformed into semi-industrial unions. But pure industrial unionism was still viewed as untenable, and as a threat to the jurisdictional sovereignty which each craft union so jealously guarded. As a result, dismayed mass-production workers who craved organization soon learned to expect little assistance from the AFL. Akron's rubber workers encountered

Inspired by President Roosevelt's New Deal policies, aided by revived union organizing drives, but primarily dependent upon their own initiative, rank and filers aggressively demanded that their conditions be improved. Automobile workers were among the earliest to display their militancy, as James Roland explains:

. . . I came to Toledo in 1929 and worked at the Auto-Lite for approximately seven or eight months, then I shipped out on the lakes . . . I worked for Chevrolet from November, 1931 to about 1942 . . . in 1931 [conditions] were pretty bad at the Chevrolet, very bad in fact . . . mostly it was the driving by the foremen always wanting more. The men were working to capacity. I know I was. It was more the working conditions, than the driving, than it was the wages although the wages were very small. I worked one time there for forty and forty-five cents an hour. At that time, of course, food was quite cheap at the time, but if you were laid off a week you still had to go on relief. You could not save enough to get by even a week's layoff . . . I think the confidence the working man had in Roosevelt and in the NRA led to the organization of the mass production industries, not only in Chevrolet but others and in Auto-Lite . . . I felt that there was a need for organized action and I felt that individuals could not deal with corporations or with foremen that represented the corporations. It needed the united action of a group. What one person could not accomplish, a group could . . . I joined . . . on September 15, 1933 . . . members were flocking to the organization to gain things that they could not gain bargaining individually . . . Then that led to . . . the big Auto-Lite strike in 1934 . . . A strike was called because the company would not even recognize them . . . Tom Ramsey being business agent was supposed to be directing the strike . . . the company went into court and got an injunction . . . limiting the pickets to twenty-five at each gate. In the meantime the interest in the strike was falling off. The employment office was wide open, the company was hiring, and I think it was estimated about 1,800 workers were in the plant working at the time, when there was a small group of five people who were dissatisfied with Ramsey's conduct of the strike and more or less took leadership of the strike. They violated the injunction and then came the mass arrest, court hearings, contempt of court charges and so forth. I happened to be one of the five that took over the leadership of the strike at that time . . . The strike was a lost strike at that time. There was nothing further to lose . . . To revive it and put some life into it, we took the strike over . . . There was rioting at the Auto-Lite plant which, of course, the leaders had nothing to do with it. This happened as I see it as a spontaneous gesture on the part of the public. I mean, they became so antagonized that nothing was done to settle it and what started the rioting, I actually do not know . . . a small group of us felt that unless the Auto-Lite strike was a winning strike, the labor movement would be set back for quite a few years in Toledo . . . By the way, at the time I was in the Auto-Lite strike, I was fired from Chevrolet for organizational work . . . shortly after the Auto-Lite strike was settled, I announced that I would conduct a one-man picket line at the Chevrolet. I being the only man on strike. Although we had a few members in there, they were advised not to put themselves on the spot by staying out . . . I carried a sign on a picket line alone and all I was demanding was a hearing before the National Labor Relations Board . . . I think I picketed one day or two days and . . . we had the hearing . . . The results of the hearing was that I was to be put back to work at the Chevrolet plant but not necessarily in the same job that I was fired from. So the company put me back to work after I complained a little bit of their being slow. . . .

While strikers marched in front of the Toledo Chevrolet plant in 1935 (above), a "silent picket" guarded railroad tracks in the rear (right). The novel device was intended to derail trains which attempted to enter or leave the factory.

frustrations and voiced sentiments which became typical in many shops and factories. Outraged by their employers' continual production speed-ups and cuts in piecework wage rates, the rank-and-file had flooded into AFL federal unions in 1933 and 1934. However, their demands for militant action to resolve their grievances met with criticism and obstructionism from AFL leaders, especially from Coleman Claherty, chief organizer and personal emissary of President Green. By late 1934, few gains had been made, morale sagged, and local membership dropped — from 6700 to 2000 at Firestone, from 8000 to 4000 at Goodrich, and from about 5000 to 2000 at Goodyear. Local activist

Wilmer Tate warned Claherty that the workers were "sore as hell:"

The men think we're bastards too. I tell you, I ain't going to sit through another meeting like the one last Sunday at Goodyear, with guys yelling for a strike all over the place and booing the very name of the A.F. of L. We got to do something. Conditions are terrible in the factories.

In the spring of 1935, desperate rubber workers had again voted to strike, but instead Green and Claherty negotiated an agreement in Washington which indefinitely postponed a walkout, without winning any concessions from management. Ruth McKenney, an Akron newspaper reporter, vividly described rank-and-file reactions:

. . . The fight seeped out of these men. Defeat lay heavy and sore on their minds. Already their shoulders slumped. What was the use now? The agreement was signed. If they voted to strike now, every man's hand was against them. . . .

Men cried on the streets of Akron. Gangling tirebuilders, men with blue eyes and big ears, shuffled along the dirty smoky streets and gouged tears out of their eyes with the backs of their big hands.

Men cried. But more stood on street corners and tore up their union cards, sending the pieces fluttering in the raw wind, fluttering into the gutters.

"Why didn't you vote no?" women asked their husbands.

"What good would that have done?" they answered heavily. "You can't do nothin' about that. They run the union, and they run it for the bosses, not for us. I'm through. I'd see myself in hell before I ever belonged to another stinking union."

A growing recognition that such experiences were rapidly sapping the labor movement's vitality and potential spurred a relatively progressive minority of AFL officials to urge an immediate shift toward industrial unionism. Led by UMW President John L. Lewis, the concerned union leaders carried their campaign to the 1935 AFL convention. It was a lively meeting, with furious and bitter debate punctuated by Lewis' eloquent pleas for a drive to organize the unorganized before the opportunity evaporated. Though the delegates rejected his proposed industrial-union strategy, Lewis remained undeterred. With his usual flair for theatrics, Lewis abruptly ended a fiery argument with William Hutcheson — president of the Carpenters union and vociferous exponent of craft unionism — by decking the burly labor leader with a single punch. Lewis had struck a symbolic blow for factory workers throughout the nation, signaling a break with traditional trade unionism and an organizing onslaught which would change the complexion of the entire labor movement. A few weeks after the convention adjourned, leaders of eight AFL unions — the United Mine Workers; Amalgamated Clothing Workers; International Ladies' Garment Workers' Union; United Textile Workers; International Union of Mine, Mill, and Smelter Workers; International Association

Reflecting his tremendous popularity among industrial unionists, a banner honoring CIO Chairman John L. Lewis led the 1938 Toledo Labor Day parade.

of Oil Field, Gas Well and Refinery Workers; International Typographical Union; and the United Hatters, Cap and Millinery Workers — organized the Committee for Industrial Organization, in order to "encourage and promote organization of workers in the mass production industries." Shortly thereafter, the committee was joined by four additional unions — the United Automobile Workers; United Rubber Workers; Amalgamated Association of Iron, Steel, and Tin Workers; and the Federation of Flat Glass Workers. The rebel faction had hoped initially to prod the more conservative AFL leaders into accepting industrial unionism, without splitting the Federation. Instead, the die-hard craft unionists branded the committee as a dual organization and ordered the insurgents to disband or be expelled. For the nation's reinvigorated industrial workers, such bluster fell on deaf ears. They now had an idol, a vitriolic spokesman, a man who exuded and instilled confidence. With charismatic daring, John L. Lewis would dominate and personify the CIO for five tumultuous years. Ultimately ejected from the AFL in May, 1938, the CIO — claiming over 4,000,000 members — reconstituted itself as the Congress of Industrial Organizations. A seventeen-year schism in labor solidarity had been formally declared.

As a key mass-production industrial state and pivotal area for potential union expansion, Ohio became a crucial battleground for internecine struggles between AFL and CIO unions. Led by representatives from United Mine Workers, District 6, a dissident faction within the Ohio State Federation of Labor had already begun to urge adoption of a militant industrial-union program in 1934. Although the conservative majority temporarily squelched the proposal,

From her perspective as a secretary for the AFL, and later the United Rubber Workers, Florence Lynch was keenly aware of the efforts and shortcomings of Akron's female workers:

. . . I would have to take affidavits from the people that would be fired, how it came about that they were fired. That was almost full time work. There were many people that got fired when they first signed up for a labor union. Whether it be Goodyear, Goodrich, or Firestone, any one of them . . . I don't think there was any such thing as women helping the Rubber Workers get organized. I really don't . . . They weren't aggressive and they didn't push in and they would always come to the men for help. Rather than represent themselves, push forward, they would always come to the men and ask them. They leaned on the men. I could count the committeemen on one hand that were women . . . there were quite a few women workers at Firestone in the Steel Products Building where they made milk cans and beer barrels and rims for tires. Oh, those women worked so fast, all on piecework and they would get their hands and fingers cut off. They really worked hard, oh mercy, they worked hard. And then, of course women in the tire room were service girls to the tire builders. They would see the stock was there ready for the tire builder so he would not lose any time getting stock to build his tires and so forth. That was one thing; tire builders always respected the girls that were their service girls. Because it helped them to earn more money, that was why . . . There used to be a lot more women working in rubber factories. Now, there is none to speak of . . . You never saw a woman tire builder, never . . . Women never had a place in the Rubber Workers. Outside of the bead girls and the service girls their jobs were very menial, other than those two classifications. Again, I say, the women didn't help themselves any . . . the majority of them were married. The American Federation of Labor frowned on married women [working] . . . They thought all jobs should be for men, not married women. They kept pushing that all the time. Married women took jobs away from men. That wasn't true. Because their jobs weren't men's jobs at that time. But they didn't have any married women. We've come a long way. . . .

Some unionists enjoyed relatively amicable relations with their employers during the 1930s. For Dick Coleman and thousands of other Ohio workers, the charisma of John L. Lewis provided the highlight of their unionizing experience:

. . . I . . . finally went to work for the Twin Coach Bus Company in Kent, Ohio . . . I spent many years at the bus factory and at the factory became acquainted with a George B. Roberts, a general organizer for the American Federation of Labor. This was back in 1933 after the NIRA when we all became anxious to organize a union. Mr. Roberts . . . was active in organizing our plant which became [UAW] Local 40, originally an American Federation of Labor Federal Local 18544 . . . One meeting organized the plant . . . 99% of the people in the meeting room signed cards . . . Recognition and some bargaining rights were hard to get in many cases. In our particular union, very easy. We had a very, very fine management. As a matter of fact, operated without a signed labor contract for several years. Management recognized the union. A contract was drawn up but not signed as the top management of the company said he trusted the employees and we in turn had a lot of faith in him. He said that he would operate under what he had agreed upon and each year it would be reviewed . . . 95% of the employees [were members]. The other five percent went slow in becoming union members but eventually they were sold on it . . . The membership remained quite stable all during that period and increased as time went on . . . Being a youngster and attending the meeting in Cleveland [in January, 1936] with the older members . . . from our local union, I met John Lewis for the first time. I had the opportunity to meet with him, talk with him and shake his hand. And as far as I was concerned he was as the boys would say today, "The greatest man that walked." . . . we came away with the feeling that we had found a leader that could lead the American working people into forming and organizing unions . . . he was the greatest labor leader and greatest speaker. And I think the feeling throughout the entire auditorium was the same. . . .

Strikers ringed Barberton's Ohio Insulator Company during a walkout by the National Brotherhood of Operative Potters for formal union recognition. With the remarkable financial and political support of local residents who were outraged by excessive police violence, the union successfully settled the eight-month strike in April, 1936.

the OSFL found itself increasingly embroiled in the escalating nationwide controversy. Following the 1935 convention, State Federation leaders officially supported the position of the parent AFL, but dreaded the diminished power and membership which would result from the loss of CIO unions. Hoping that unity would be restored, the OSFL tried to "ride the fence" between the warring groups in 1936, even seating delegates from the rebel United Mine Workers and the United Rubber Workers at its annual convention. Nonetheless, the CIO continued to build its base in Ohio with organizing

drives and mass meetings, such as an August gathering of 800 Columbus workers at which various CIO spokesmen preached the gospel of industrial unionism. Unable to ignore such defiance, the AFL ordered that the charters of organizations sympathetic to the CIO be revoked. The ax fell first on the Columbus Federation of Labor. The city federation had been torn for months by factional strife between the local Building Trades Council and a CIO group headed by George DeNucci, president of the CFL. Despite officially representing only about 900 auto and garment workers, the CIO faction gained sufficient support from other likeminded unions to pass a CFL resolution endorsing the CIO's historic strike, then underway, against General Motors Corporation. Enraged craft-union leaders complained to AFL President Green, who revoked the CFL's charter in February, 1937. Expulsions of more local bodies and unions from the AFL followed, but failed to check the CIO's organizing momentum. In February, 1938, representatives from forty-eight unions, as well as fifteen city and county bodies, established the Ohio CIO Council as a counterpoise to the OSFL, and elected UMW, District 6 President John Owens as their first president. By October, the Ohio CIO claimed approximately 500 constituent locals, with over sixty percent concentrated among auto, mine, rubber, and steel workers in Cuyahoga, Hamilton, Summit, Lucas, Trumbull, and Scioto Counties. Full-scale competition between AFL and CIO unions for members and contracts became nearly as commonplace as strikes during succeeding years. In 1940, Ohio CIO Secretary-Treasurer Ted Silvey reported that out of forty-three disputes settled by NLRB elections since 1935, the AFL won twenty-three (with thirty-four percent of all votes cast), while the CIO won nineteen contests (with fifty-six percent of the total votes). Though AFL and CIO members did frequently cooperate at grassroots levels, the energy and finances expended by the bureaucrats and officers of the rival unions certainly lessened organized labor's overall effectiveness and growth.

Ohio's pragmatic workers, however, were less interested in inter-union squabbles than they were in immediate resolution of shop-floor grievances. Venting pent-up frustrations on a scale and with an intensity unmatched since the uprisings of 1919-21, they enthusiastically joined in a nationwide rank-and-file rebellion in 1936-37. In two turbulent years, more than a quarter-of-a-million laboring people — the vast majority in mass-production industries and under the CIO banner — struck against employers across the state. Besides thrusting the new CIO into the forefront of the labor movement, this tremendous surge of militant industrial unionism also unleashed a provocative weapon which had been shelved since the heyday of the IWW — the sit-down strike. By "sitting down," workers discovered that they achieved much more than the physical occupation of a workplace. For, with this dramatic tactic, they could effectively exert control, regain a sense of personal dignity, minimize violent retaliations by police and guards, compel property-conscious employers to negotiate, as well as enhance the responsiveness of union officials to the membership's demands. An anonymous sit-downer perhaps described the primary significance of the technique when he admitted:

> We were nervous. We didn't know we could do it. Those machines had kept going as long as we could remember. When we finally pulled the switch and there was some quiet, I finally remembered something . . . that I was a human being, that I could stop those machines, that I was better than those machines anytime. . . .

The sit-down era began in Akron in June, 1934, when 1,100 General Tire employees staged a brief sit-down, planned by local union leaders to launch a month-long strike. Having demonstrated the effectiveness of the tactic by gaining better working conditions, increased wages, and abolition of the company union, the General Tire sit-down became a model for disgruntled workers during the upheavals of 1936-37. On January 19, 1936, John L. Lewis concluded a bombastic speech to thousands of angry Akron workers with the exhortation, "I hope you will do something for yourselves." Much to the consternation of union leaders and employers alike, rank-and-file rubber workers unexpectedly took him at his word. Nine days later, tire builders at Firestone spontaneously sat down at their machines to protest the suspension of a fellow URW member. According to one dramatized version of the incident.

> . . . in perfect synchronization, with the rhythm they had learned in a great mass production industry, the tirebuilders stepped back from their machines.
> Instantly, the noise stopped. The whole room lay in perfect silence. The tirebuilders stood in

Coal cutters operating at St. Clairsville in 1937 (left) and at Adena in 1941 (below). Faced with keen competition for dwindling markets, coal companies increasingly sought to cut labor costs through mechanization.

Among the most militant and pro-CIO groups at Toledo's Willys-Overland plant, auto workers in the Rear Axle Department spontaneously staged numerous sit-down strikes during 1937 to demand resolution of their grievances.

Renowned in American labor history as the first walkout assisted by the newly-formed CIO, the 1936 Goodyear strike in Akron helped to trigger a nationwide surge of labor militancy. Workers drew their famous battle line in February (right) and warned police and strike-breakers not to cross. The line held. In numerous shanties along the eleven-mile-long picket line, some strikers endured the sub-zero temperatures with music (lower right). After five tense weeks, pickets celebrated news of partial victory on March 21 (lower left).

long lines, touching each other, perfectly motionless, deafened by the silence. A moment ago there had been the weaving hands, the revolving wheels, the clanking belt, the moving hooks, the flashing tire tools. Now there was absolute stillness, no motion, no sound.

Out of the terrifying quiet came the wondering voice of a big tirebuilder near the windows: "Jesus Christ, it's like the end of the world."

He broke the spell, the magic moment of stillness. For now his awed words said the same thing to every man, "We done it! We stopped the belt! By God, we done it!" And men began to cheer hysterically, to shout and howl in fresh silence. Men wrapped long sinewy arms around their neighbors' shoulders, screaming, "We done it! We done it!"

The protest spread throughout the plant, with workers refusing to resume work until the suspended tirebuilder was reinstated four days later. Within three weeks of this successful exhibition of rank-and-file initiative, five more sit-downs erupted at Firestone, Goodrich, and Goodyear factories. The most significant outbreak occurred at Goodyear on February 17,

beginning as a sit-down but evolving into a conventional strike of 14,000 employees. While the final settlement was only a partial union victory, the walkout had triggered a tremendous jump in membership, and brought the United Rubber Workers into the CIO fold. Moreoever, the rubber workers had achieved a symbolic triumph for unionism in the mass-production industries throughout Ohio and the nation.

Sit-down fever swept Ohio. The most historic incident broke out in Cleveland in December, 1936, when employees at General Motors' Fisher Body plant surprised their new United Auto Workers officers by suddenly occupying the factory. Their action triggered the most important single confrontation of the century — the great sit-down strike at General Motors' key complex in Flint, Michigan, which in turn led to the unionization of the crucial automobile industry. Rank-and-file insurgency assumed the character of mass social protest, as sit-downs raged among factory workers, maids, stenographers, Great Lakes seamen, sales clerks, taxi drivers, printers, and WPA workers. Some

stoppages were coordinated by union leaders and lasted for weeks, but most were undisciplined "quicky wildcats" lasting only a few minutes or hours; most were called to resolve serious problems, but many were relatively frivolous outbursts sparked by personality conflicts with the boss or a simple craving for excitement. Whatever the duration or motivation, however, the net result was a new sense of strength among the working classes. For a time, society seemed in utter chaos, as workers collectively flexed their long-constricted muscles. Though unable to harness this raw power completely, labor unions did reap benefits in status and membership. By the end of 1937, the rash of militancy had caused CIO membership to rise startlingly to about 4,000,000, and even the AFL had added 886,000 new recruits nationwide.

However, the CIO's rise to power did not proceed without notable defeats, especially in the Little Steel Strike of 1937. An important segment of the CIO's overall strategy for industrial unionism involved a major campaign in the essentially unorganized iron and steel industry. The only industry-wide union was the nearly defunct Amalgamated Association of Iron, Steel, and Tin Workers, which represented less than one percent of the nation's 500,000 steelworkers, and whose stodgy leaders had hardly attempted to expand during the New Deal's early years. As part of Lewis' plans for conquering the industry, the CIO took over the Amalgamated and set up the Steel Workers Organizing Committee in June, 1936 to assume most of the old union's functions. Determined to control the shop-floor militancy which, from their horrified perspective, had gotten out of hand in auto and rubber, SWOC leaders imposed tight discipline on their recruits. Despite the lack of union democracy, by the end of 1936, a massive organizing drive had increased membership to over 100,000. SWOC's first victory could not have been more dramatic. In March, 1937, following secret negotiations between Lewis and Chairman of the Board, Myron Taylor, the

United States Steel Corporation—the nation's largest producer and formerly labor's most intransigent opponent—peacefully agreed to recognize SWOC as sole bargaining agent for its employees and granted the union's wage and hour demands. With the surrender of U.S. Steel, more than 100 other companies came to terms, and union ranks swelled to over 300,000 by May.

SWOC then focused its attention on the powerful companies collectively known as "Little Steel" — Republic, Youngstown Sheet & Tube, Inland, and Bethlehem. Since these firms operated mills in Canton, Warren, Youngstown, Cleveland, Massillon, and Niles, Ohio was a critical battlefield in the massive confrontation which ensued. Despite the example set by U.S. Steel, the Little Steel companies were convinced that the cost of defeating a strike was outweighed by the future gains that would result from the absence of unions in the mills. Consequently, company officials refused to negotiate at any level, and SWOC called a nationwide walkout of 75,000 steelworkers in May. The conflict developed into one of the bitterest disputes in labor history. The grisly details which shrouded this month-long upheaval — the riots, the vigilantee committees, the employers' utilization of the "Mohawk Valley formula" of propagandizing, the unbelievable armaments which the companies had prepared, the bombings, and the deaths of six Ohio strikers—are too numerous to describe briefly. Torn by factionalism among its leaders and splits among the rank and file, SWOC demonstrated that the CIO was not unbeatable. When Governor Davey sent in the National Guard to re-

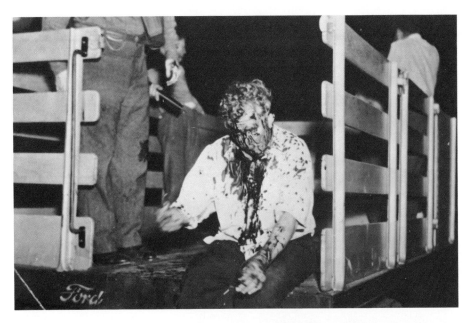

An injured striker (above) and a burned-out police car (right) demonstrated the ferocity of the June 20, 1937 riot in the "war zone" outside Republic Steel's Warren mill. The bloody clash between 1,000 strikers and 250 policemen left one striker dead and fourteen injured. By June 24, the National Guard grimly protected the company's property from further violence (below).

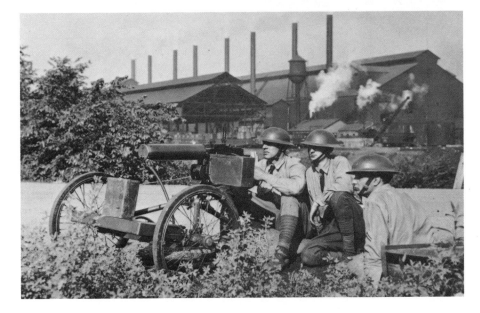

store order and protect company property, the strike was broken in Ohio and dejected workers straggled back into the mills. The impressive advance of the CIO had been halted, and at least one critic gloated that "CIO" now stood for "Collapsed In Ohio." However, SWOC proved tenacious. Diligently employing more conventional techniques, the union gradually rebuilt its support among the steelworkers. In 1941, their efforts finally paid off in a series of NLRB-election victories in Little Steel plants. Thus entitled by law to serve as the exclusive representative for all employees, SWOC at last negotiated contracts with the same companies which had imposed such a seemingly crushing defeat four years earlier.

In Cleveland, during the same summer of 1937, the CIO's International Garment Workers Union discovered that the AFL—now revitalized by the most severe threat in its history— also possessed considerable power with which to counterattack. Bitter inter-union warfare broke out in the city's garment district, as the AFL attempted to defeat ILGWU strikes at four knit-wear factories, claiming that its federal locals were the legitimate representatives of the workers. In an increasingly common tactic, employers exerted pressure on their employees to join the "respectable and responsible" AFL, rather than the more militant CIO. While the NLRB spent three months deciding whether to call elections to decide the issue, numerous picket-line riots erupted when mounted police attempted to sweep aside the female strikers for the AFL strikebreakers. Injuries numbered in the hundreds. The employers' effort to mount a back-to-work movement was countered by the flooding of CIO auto and steel workers into the city to help their union sisters. The union combatants reached a temporary truce, but hostilities continued as company thugs waged guerilla warfare on the women, attacking their strike kitchen and assaulting them in their neighborhoods. When the NLRB finally held elections in August, the ILGWU won certification in two of the four plants, but the human cost had been high.

By 1938, labor militancy and organizing began to taper off, as unionists concentrated on consolidating and formalizing their newly-won gains. Despite the dire warnings of imminent revolution by worried business and government leaders, the radicalism of most workers had again turned out to be largely rhetorical, ephemeral, and limited to immediate shop-floor concerns. Communists had played major roles in the militant upsurge, especially within several CIO unions, but converted few rank and filers into card-carrying idealogues. Nor had a lasting, radical political movement emerged. During the mid-'30s, "progressive" unionists had attempted to expand grassroots unrest into the political realm, but local efforts at third-party politics in Toledo and Columbus, as well as the formation of a statewide independent labor party — the Ohio Farmer-Labor Progressive Federation — gained only negligible support. The CIO achieved greater success through its Ohio Labor's Non-Partisan League, which confined labor's political activities to conventional channels by rallying members to the emerging Democratic coalition. However, to the dismay of all political organizers, workers habitually failed to extend their solidarity from factory gates to voting booths.

Disappointments and unfulfilled promises notwithstanding, workers did make enormous gains during the decade. Wage rates in unionized industries rose much more rapidly than in unorganized sectors of the economy, and union members received protection against arbitrary rulings by foremen and supervisors through institutionalized grievance procedures. At least a measure of industrial democracy had been achieved. As expressed by a Cleveland worker, the renewed sense of personal dignity was an especially important attainment—"We are now treated as human beings and not as part of the machinery." In terms of organizational growth alone, the CIO's maturation and the AFL's revitalization had been remarkable. The ranks of the nation's unionized employees more than tripled from 2.9 million in 1933 to 10.5 million in 1941—representing a startling jump from 11.5 to 28.2 percent of all nonagricultural workers. In testimony to the breadth of the organizational impulse, the proportion of unionized employees rose during the decade from twenty-one to seventy-two percent in mining, from fifty-four to sixty-five percent in construction, from twenty-three to forty-eight percent in transportation, and from nine to thirty-four percent in manufacturing. Furthermore, with the added protection of New Deal legislation, many of the rights and benefits won by organized workers extended to their non-unionized counterparts as well. More convincingly than ever before, working people had demonstrated that they were a powerful force to be reckoned with in shop-floor, community, and national affairs.

As impressive as these gains had been, however, their permanence was hardly guaranteed. Past generations of Ohio's working people could testify to the tenuousness of the toiler's lot. Footholds could disappear and hard-fought conquests evaporate, even before the victory-celebrations had ended. Within the constant flux of working-class experience, new challenges were sure to appear.

Women played important roles in union organizing throughout Ohio. Few, however, were black or as fiery as Pauline Taylor:

. . . Well, union was just a bad name in Youngstown . . . So people were afraid . . . some people came out and talked with my husband [who] didn't know anything about a union . . . I said, "You should not get the benefits of what somebody else struggled for unless you help. So if you don't help, you let me help." So that was the interest that I had. But most of the people that talked with me were white foreign people, you know. They were the people who had a better understanding of organized efforts than our people did. Our people was just scared to death of it. So I worked with them . . . And it was quite a struggle . . . when the committee was trying to get together or organize, this was a white committee. All except just . . . one colored fellow. There wasn't too many colored in it . . . Anybody who did anything different than what the company wanted was called Communist or Communist sympathizers. Yes. So we were called everything but what we were (laughter) . . . Some people were frightened off, some were paid off. And the ministers were all called into a conference by the mill heads to tell them that this organizing was going a little too fast . . . And if this city was organized, Communism would take over. And of course, the ministers just buckled under this threat, all but one white minister who defied them. And of course, he was fired from his church . . . So we went through 1937 through the strike . . . I was just a housewife. No, I just worked at home, but I would go out on the picket line and work, you know, where they served food and coffee. Wherever they would ask me to go and assist, I would do it. . . . The contact was made through people that I would know and then I would ask them if they would talk to somebody that they would know . . . And of course, the people who was in the company plant union, they were quite bitter against the union. They tried to get my husband to either put me out or stop me from being so flamboyant in this Communistic organization because that's all it was. He just kept silent. He didn't take any part with it, but he didn't fight against it, he let me just go ahead . . . My work with the foreign born was more than it was even with the black workers until they got used to what I was doing. Because they thought that I was either brain-washed or I was being led by people who had come from other countries that they didn't think it was very wise . . . they accused me of being a Communist. No, they never did seem to think that I was an "Uncle Tom." (laughter) No, no, no, I wasn't put in that category at all. But they felt like I had some Red ties because they felt like all foreigners are Red, you know, one way or the other . . . my husband let me work alone. And they couldn't make quite as rough for him as they could have if he had been active. They made it pretty hard for my son who was a millman. But they couldn't get me like they wanted to because I was not employed. And I could go on any picket line I wanted to go on.

T he turmoil of the 1930s had caused extraordinary disruptions in the long-standing relationships between labor, management, and government. The organization of traditionally open-shop industries had met strong resistance, and many union conquests were consequently precarious. Unionization did not automatically insure peace and cooperation, since numerous employers viewed initial contracts as only temporary setbacks in an ongoing battle, while many embittered unionists were unable to shake off their engrained

A young boy received curbside lessons in labor relations, while his disgruntled elders picketed Toledo's Cannan Cleaners.

In 1939, General Motors Corporation sought to take advantage of the factional strife wracking the United Automobile Workers Union, by refusing to bargain with any union representatives. The majority UAW-CIO faction responded with one of the shrewdest strike tactics of the Depression era. Rather than having all members strike, union leaders only called out the crucial skilled workers in strategic plants. In this way, critical retooling for the company's new models was stopped; while production employees continued to work, draw their pay, and financially support the skilled strikers. At GM's Cleveland Fisher Body plant, strikers also used the novel technique of bringing the picket line to a scab's doorstep (A). Violence flared in the dispute's final days, when strikers battled with police headed by the city's new safety director and former U.S. Treasury agent, Eliot Ness. However, despite tense confrontations (B), fights with tear gas and bricks (C), and numerous arrests (D), the UAW forced GM to submit to its demands on August 5.

A

B

D

C

suspicions and antagonisms. Furthermore, the inexperience of most unionists and managers in the art of collective bargaining generated understandable, but irritating, stumbling blocks in the resolution of even minor differences. The absolute authority formerly enjoyed by company officials now had to be shared with employees and union outsiders. A new working world had been created, in effect, but the spheres of influence between management and unions had not been clearly delineated. Continuing factionalism between the AFL and CIO added to the unsettled state of affairs. Yet another complication in the perplexing picture stemmed from new governmental involvement in labor relations. Management accused the NLRB of pro-labor bias, resisted its decisions, and vigorously attempted to obtain the repeal or revision of the Wagner Act. Nor was the NLRB immune from labor attack, as the AFL repeatedly claimed that board members favored the CIO in the administration of the law, while the CIO charged the reverse. Finally, the board itself became immersed in political controversy, as the resolution of complex labor-relations issues inevitably had broad social and economic repercussions. An adjustment period was urgently needed in order to enable all parties to assimilate and implement the new parameters of their respective powers and responsibilities. However, with the nation poised on the brink of the most cataclysmic war in its history, time for calm reorientations quickly ran out. Compounded by wartime pressures, controversy and confusion continued to dominate the labor scene.

Long-awaited prosperity burst forth in the wake of massive economic conversions to war production. In 1940, approximately 8.1 million Americans were out of work; by 1942, the jobless ranks had dropped to 2.7 million; and by 1944, unemployment had virtually disappeared. As an indication of Ohio's economic upswing, the average weekly number of workers receiving unemployment benefits plummeted from 50,043 in 1940, to 23,820 in 1942, and only 1,521 in 1944. Between 1940 and 1944, average employment jumped 209 percent in Ohio's converted auto plants, fifty-three percent in rubber, and fifty-seven percent in all manufacturing industries. Business profits soared, especially due to "cost-plus" clauses in military contracts, by which the government agreed to pay all production costs above original estimates. Workers' incomes rose to pre-depression levels. Average weekly wages of production workers in Ohio manufacturing, for example, increased from $29.55 in 1940 to $52.52 by 1944. Freed from the bonds of joblessness and poverty, elated defense workers with bulging wallets rushed to ministers, judges, and justices of the peace to be wed. During 1941, for example, marriages involving defense workers swelled by a reported fifty-one percent in Cincinnati, and seventeen percent in Youngstown and Akron. Yet, the anxieties and deprivations that had tormented unemployed working people during the Great Depression were soon exchanged for new difficulties and convulsions resulting from the social and economic frenzy of total warfare. In response to accelerating job-opportunities, an immense migration occurred from Ohio's rural areas and the South to mushrooming war-production centers like Youngstown, Akron, Cleveland, and Toledo. However, so great and sudden was the influx, that few cities could adequately house the newcomers, thus compelling thousands to live in flimsy huts, overcrowded rooming houses, slums, or automobiles. Rationing, curtailed production of consumer items, and rampant inflation caused considerable inconvenience and occasional hardship. When the federal government's Office of Price Administration announced imminent meat rationing in March, 1943, angry crowds in Columbus mobbed butcher shops and fought police, while 50,000 panicky Cleveland residents gathered outside three markets demanding scarce meat. As manpower shortages developed, the average work week in the state's war plants climbed from thirty-eight hours in 1940 to forty-seven by 1944, and seven-day work weeks became common. Employees relished the higher earnings which resulted, but hardly welcomed the associated fatigue, frazzled nerves, and disruption of family lives.

Such pressures frequently strained labor's keen sense of patriotic duty to the war effort, and contributed to numerous outbursts of militancy. In 1940, strikes in Ohio were generally brief and involved a sharply diminished number of workers compared with earlier years (see Table 4-A). But, as the nation geared up defense production in 1941, labor resumed its aggressive stance. Ohio experienced 341 work stoppages during the year involving 164,000 rank and filers — new records which even surpassed the levels achieved at the height of the 1936-37 sit-down movement. Several walkouts were lengthy, bitter confrontations with powerful and recalcitrant employers, particularly in the automobile and steel industries. In many other instances, striking unionists found themselves at odds with decreasingly sympathetic New Dealers, whose primary concern had shifted to national defense and the uninterrupted production of war material. Most prom-

When the nation conducted its first peacetime draft in 1940, eligible males —many of whom were jobless transients—lined up to register in Cleveland.

The economic stimulus of World War II finally ended the Depression. Yet, as Charles Beckman reveals in recalling what happened at a plant in Cleveland, the influx of new war-workers generated shop-floor problems which would have lasting effects.

. . . Our membership went way up [during the war]. That is when we started getting the colored people in . . . [Prior to the war] they had one man in there. He was a shoe shine boy in the front office. You would very seldom see them around the plant . . . When the colored fellows started coming in there they did a good job and they showed leadership. We got them in and started them on negotiation committees and tried to develop them as fast as we could because we had quite a number of them . . . In the later part of 1941 they laid off everybody. It came to a standstill. We knew they were going into war material and they had to reconvert the plant. They did it very expediently . . . War-time production . . . did not change the shop problems too much but it became more of a burden on the committeemen and union because we were getting in people who had worked in drug stores and soda fountains and all kinds of diversified work that had never had any training or discipline under the union. It made it pretty grim because we employed almost 11,000 people. We would have meetings and we could not house them. So we had to have three shifts of meetings. That is where it became a little bit cumbersome for the leadership . . . They had me crazy here for quite a while. Many of them took up grievances that were not normal shop grievances such as in peacetime because they were inexperienced and lacking in discipline and so on. We had a good union though . . . We had a certain force in here that would have liked to have had stoppages and we knew who they were and kind of controlled them . . . Naturally, all the Cleveland locals were for the no-strike pledge . . . In general, I think the boys thought from a patriotic point of view, "Well, we will withhold our resentment as long as we can and after the war is over then we will get it back on these boys. . . ."

inent were the successful walkouts staged by the United Mine Workers against "captive mines" owned by steel firms, in defiance of the government's war-mobilization program.

In a burst of patriotic fervor shortly after America's formal declaration of war on December 8, a conference of business and labor leaders voluntarily pledged to cease their own hostilities and avoid strikes for the duration. In January, 1942, President Roosevelt created the War Labor Board to facilitate that promise. The twelve-member WLB—equally divided among public, management, and labor representatives—was empowered to settle all labor disputes by compulsory mediation and arbitration. In an attempt to stabilize wages and remove a major source of labor-management friction, in mid-1942 the WLB devised the "Little Steel formula"—a policy which arbitrarily limited wage increases for all workers to supposedly predominant levels existent in January, 1941, plus adjustments for subsequent cost-of-living increases. Labor strenuously objected, arguing that the restrictive guidelines were inequitable, given the complex disparities in wage rates between industries, companies, and occupations, as well as varying cost-of-living impacts between geographic areas and income brackets. The WLB sought to placate union leaders by granting "maintenance-of-membership" clauses in contracts, by which a worker who did not resign from a union within a fifteen-day escape period had to pay dues for the life of the contract. In effect, therefore, unions received protection from any substantial loss of membership and an assured flow of new recruits (a camouflaged closed shop), in exchange for a virtual wage-freeze, compulsory WLB arbitration, and a no-strike pledge.

Pleas by government and union leaders for "equality of sacrifice" during the war-emergency met with increasing scepticism and rebuffs from discontented rank and filers. In 1942, Ohio workers curtailed their militancy and concentrated on "doing their bit on the home front for the boys overseas." However, with business profits reaching all-time heights, with consumer goods becoming scarcer and continuously more expensive, with wage rates frozen by the Little Steel formula, and with mandatory overtime taking an emotional and physical toll, many war workers began to perceive that they were actually shouldering a very unequal share of the sacrifices. Shop-floor rumblings steadily mounted about hazardous working conditions in hastily converted war plants, excessive hours, and low wage rates. Workers expressed their dissatisfaction in various ways. Taking advantage of critical labor shortages in most industries, workers often quit to take jobs in factories which offered better wages and conditions. Absenteeism became a

A Civilian Defense Parade in Warren, May, 1943.

popular form of personal protest, as laborers simply stayed home for a day or two, when they could no longer tolerate the strains of the workplace. Rank and filers also sought to gain relief through formal grievance procedures, which were soon bogged down with thousands of complaints. In other instances, rebellious employees staged slowdowns or blatantly disregarded their supervisors' directives. Work discipline and production schedules consequently broke down in many shops.

Union leaders had supposedly relinquished labor's right to strike in order to bolster production and retain government support, as well as to preserve and expand their organizations. By 1943, however, it was glaringly obvious that thousands of resentful Ohio workers no longer felt bound to honor the surrender of their most potent weapon. Taking matters into their own hands, nearly 300,000 rank and filers conducted an unprecedented 467 work stoppages, which cost the war effort more than 1,000,000 man-days of production. Efforts by union officials to impose discipline on the defiant wildcatters proved ineffective, as another 549 strikes involving 216,000 workers broke out in 1944. Toledo, Cleveland, and Cincinnati were storm centers of discontent. Working conditions triggered the overwhelming majority of wildcat strikes, especially in automobile plants which had been converted to produce aircraft, tanks, and other military equipment. Though some rebels were seasoned veterans, most were recent recruits from rural areas — individuals unfamiliar with the unique rigors of factory discipline, without personal loyalties to union leaders, and strongly resistant to attempted controls by unions which they had been compelled to join. To such workers, a spontaneous walkout, which often achieved results within a

A Navy inspector discusses the grievances of sit-down strikers at Goodyear's Akron plant in June, 1942.

few hours or days, made far more sense than tedious grievance and arbitration procedures, which were time-consuming and infrequently effective.

Accelerated rank-and-file militancy in 1943-44 threatened to shatter organized labor's facade of solidarity and patriotic cooperation. Factionalism within and between every sector of the union movement once again posed problems of crisis proportions. From the perspective of international union leaders, wildcat strikes were intolerable, since the WLB held them responsible for enforcement of the no-strike pledge and threatened to penalize continued violations by revoking maintenance-of-membership agreements. International officials consequently exerted strong disciplinary pressures, in some instances expelling rank-and-file wildcatters and removing local officers who

By 1944, strains resulting from years of sacrifice, frustrating governmental bureaucracy, and perceived obstructionism by management created widespread restiveness among war-workers. As a plant committeeman who daily bore the brunt of his fellow workers' hostility, Edward Gerchak apprised CIO President Phillip Murray that:

. . . we at Local 1298, Cuyahoga Works, American Steel & Wire Company, Cleveland, Ohio, are rapidly approaching a state of unrest that may well develop into something serious. Collective bargaining is rapidly becoming a memory. In the eight years I have been a grievance committeeman I thought I had seen all phases of management's adherence to the contract, but the present indifference in the matter of settling just grievances leads me to believe I have seen nothing . . . For two years now we have been contending with the so-called I.Q. Test. This method of grading mechanical men has been a source of dispute entirely too long. Hundreds of men have been denied wage increases because of it and a speedy settlement of it should be brought about. The workweek has kept us in hot water for a long time. If you recall—it is just a year ago that the American Steel & Wire Locals did stage a protest that threatened to throw the whole district into a walkout . . . The Company's latest maneuver over the holiday just passed may bring about another episode comparable with that a year ago. Management's brazen disregard of War Labor Board directives is another source of annoyance. That they were caught red-handed in a violation just recently had done nothing to prevent additional violations. This may be due to the fact that the penalty was no more than a slap on the wrist. The War Labor Board itself is not entirely blameless by allowing the Company to extend piece work rates without their (the W.L.B.'s) scrutiny. This blanket concession, you can rest assured, was exploited to the fullest extent. Supplementary agreements entered into by plant management and the committee are being ignored. The loss in earnings is not adding satisfaction to the picture. In some cases a loss of twenty-five cents an hour is not unusual. All this despite a wage freeze that is supposed to be in effect two years now. Just how long the officers of this Local will be able to avert serious trouble I cannot say, but it is going to take a lot more than promises and an appeal to process grievances according to the contract. We have been doing that religiously . . . A condition of this kind, I think you will agree, is not helpful. . . .

As the poster at Firestone's Akron plant suggested, absenteeism from the long hours and grueling pace of the helmet-liner line became a growing problem by 1944.

were unable or unwilling to control their members. Such practices alienated and embittered members, who grumbled that distant union bureaucrats were more interested in preserving their own power and pleasing government and business leaders, than in responding to the concerns of the workers. Local union officers were frequently caught in the crossfire—if they sided with militant rank and filers, they faced the wrath of their superiors; but, if they strictly enforced official union policy, they had to deal with angry members, many of whom were friends and co-workers, and upon whom they depended for their elected positions. Developments centering upon United Rubber Workers, Local 9 in Akron typified the factionalism which wracked many unions. Between August, 1943 and January, 1944, rank-and-file members at General Tire and Rubber Company had staged twenty-four wildcats, apparently with the acquiescence, or even encouragement of the local union president. However, when workers in the band building department pulled further stoppages over working conditions on January 5 and 6, International Union President Sherman Dalrymple abruptly expelled seventy-two participants. Strident protests by members and officers prompted the International, on January 16, to place the local in receivership and remove the elected officers. Irate members of Dalrymple's home-Local 5 in Akron responded by voting to revoke his membership for violating the rights of fellow-unionists. The Akron Industrial Union Council subsequently conducted an investigation into the incident at General Tire, and concluded that the actions of the International had been "hasty, ill-advised, illegal, and unconstitutional as most of their information came from the management;" and that the top union officers had consistently failed to assist the local in solving problems at the plant. Dalrymple then complained of this censure to CIO President Philip Murray, who sternly warned the Akron Council that their behavior could "lead to suspension or expulsion" from the CIO. Numerous factional squabbles such as this sparked strong grassroots opposition to the URW president which eventually compelled him to resign from office in September, 1945. The majority of leaders, however, survived internal splits and rank-and-file rebelliousness within their unions. With the weight of governmental authority behind them, international officers and their appointees effectively imposed discipline, thus restricting local autonomy, tightening their own control, and hastening the bureaucratization of the organized labor movement.

During these war years, factional cleavages also intensified along several additional lines. Though labor organizations purportedly had laid aside their rivalries for the duration, inter-union jurisdictional battles continually erupted, as unions competed to win maintenance-of-membership rights to prospective dues-paying workers. One of the most complicated examples developed at Toledo's Willys-Overland plant, where four separate groups—the CIO's United Automobile Workers, Local 12; the AFL's International Association of Machinists, Lodge 105; the International Die Sinkers' Conference, Lodge 160 (an independent union which had seceded from the IAM in 1941); and another independent union, the Mechanics Educational Society of America — waged repeated organizational skirmishes, staged wildcats against each other, and filed numerous election appeals with the NLRB. The Communist issue, which would cause havoc in several

CIO unions during the postwar period, also began to generate serious divisions, particularly within United Electrical, Radio and Machine Workers, Locals 801 and 755 in Dayton. Finally, further splits in Ohio's labor movement resulted from personality and policy clashes between John L. Lewis and his successor to the CIO presidency, Philip Murray. In 1942, their differences culminated in Murray's expulsion from the United Mine Workers and the UMW's withdrawal from the CIO. While most state CIO leaders remained loyal to Murray and the CIO, John Owens—a Lewis supporter and president of UMW District 6—immediately resigned as president of the Ohio State CIO Council, taking nearly 18,000 rank-and-file miners out with him. Thereafter, Lewis' UMW District 50 (a national catchall organization for all non-miners) actively competed with CIO and AFL unions for the state's membership. By mid-1945, conflicts between the UMW and CIO had become so heated in Ohio, that the Montgomery County Industrial Union Council proposed to CIO Director John Brophy:

> . . . we think it is time that the CIO through one of its Internationals carried the fight back to the Mine fields. We are positive that the best defense is a good offense. Let's tie up some of their organizers in their own territory, and go right into the Mine Fields, and organize them into the CIO. This will at least free us from their disruption in some areas.

Many of the problems confronting organized labor, as well as the changing attitudes and behavior of a new breed of war-workers, were exhibited in the glass factories at Toledo and Rossford, Ohio. After a lengthy sit-down strike in 1937, Local 9 of the Federation of Glass, Ceramic, and Silica Sand Workers, CIO, had achieved collective bargaining rights at four Libby-Owens-Ford plants in the adjacent cities. In 1941 contract negotiations, the union bargainers won an unusual "cooperation clause," whereby the company agreed to assist the local in the creation of a union shop. In return, local leaders consented to abandon their antagonism toward management and to accept without question the company's production decisions. Since the union, therefore, could no longer permit militant behavior or informal work patterns

Dirigible construction at General Tire in Akron.

Cleveland workers displayed their support for the war-effort in the 1942 Labor Day parade.

Employees of the Marion Steam Shovel Company received management's praise for their efforts in exceeding production quotas for the navy.

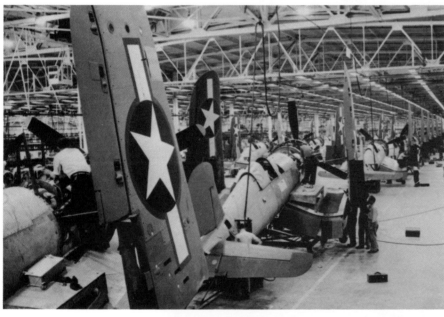

At the Goodyear Aerospace plant in Akron, assembly line methods were applied to production of the Corsair fighter plane by 1943.

Formerly discarded after passing their prime, older experienced workers were eagerly sought during the war in Dayton's scarce labor market.

which threatened the company's authority, the rank and file inevitably became disenchanted with their leaders' drift away from adversarial relationships with management. As working conditions deteriorated with the company's hasty conversion to war-production, shop-floor discontent accelerated into a crisis, which glaringly revealed the union's tenuous position as "arbitrator" between workers and management.

Following six years of depressed business conditions, production at LOF increased sharply in 1943, primarily due to military orders for aircraft glass. Employment immediately jumped fifty percent to 3,000 employees; average hourly wages were increased 11¢; and average take-home pay rose nearly forty percent by the end of the year, from $1,990 to $2,780. Growing incomes and the disappearance of unemployment seemed to spur rank-and-file aggressiveness. While only two walkouts occurred in 1941-42, LOF plants experienced ten work stoppages in 1943 and five more in 1944. Old unsettled grievances caused some wildcats, but the majority evidently arose from the large influx of female workers who demanded equal-pay-for-equal-work with men. The issue came to a head in early-1943, when management created separate seniority lists for male and female employees, which granted males preference in promotions and lay-offs. Despite complaints by the women, however, LOF refused to discuss its decision and submitted all wage questions to the WLB for resolution. In May, disgruntled female workers took matters into their own hands and staged a one-day wildcat to protest unequal wages. Subsequent efforts by local union officials to pacify the women failed, and they walked out again for three days. By August, female rank and filers had not received any assistance from either the WLB or the union, causing them to strike yet again for two weeks. When LOF management and the glassworkers' international president issued a joint threat to fire and expel any mem-

bers who did not call off the strike in twenty-four hours, only half of the women returned. Much to the frustration of the defiant females, however, repeated wildcats through 1945 never did solve their wage concerns.

Meanwhile, LOF management strove to expand its authority over shop-floor activities. In large measure, their offensive represented an attempt to circumvent existing grievance machinery and to regain concessions made to the union in the late-1930s, by exploiting labor's no-strike pledge. Having also relinquished any real control over working conditions by their cooperative policies, local union leaders were helpless to assist disgusted rank and filers. When management insisted on exercising its right to demand extended working hours, therefore, employees simply stayed home as a personal form of protest. During 1944, absenteeism rates reached eight percent of the workforce on weekdays and thirty percent on weekends. The company ignored the union's suggestion to reduce hours and filed a futile complaint with the WLB, but failed to curb the militancy of their fatigued workers.

Convulsions generated by the war-emergency hastened the most dramatic alteration in modern working-class life—the influx of women into the labor force. A War Manpower Commission survey of Ohio's war plants revealed that, between May, 1942 and November, 1943, female employment rose from 142,470 to 422,830—a remarkable increase from sixteen to

Of the numerous problems confronted by women war-workers, sexual stereotyping was one of the most difficult to overcome. For example, Whiting Williams — an "employee relations consultant" in Cleveland — gave the following confidential tips to male foremen in 1943, on how to deal with their female workers:

1. *Her **height** averages about five inches less than men's. (Many tools and benches are too high.) Besides having no Adam's apple, her joints at knee, elbow and finger differ from ours.*

2. *Especially the type now being hired has **less muscle, more fat,** than men. Also **thinner blood** — fewer red corpuscles for carrying oxygen. Hence more susceptible to bad ventilation, smells, noises; needs more frequent (not longer) rest periods than men.*

3. *She's not less intelligent but **weaker on arithmetic** — more likely to figure that two-fourths make one-eighth! (Well to post needed computations on desk or machine.) Also slower in making decisions. (Inspectors often helped by specific charts or photos showing Good —Bad.)*

4. ***More easily discouraged.** (Simplify your job-instruction. Explain one step at a time. Use the do's; avoid the don'ts.)*

5. *Needs much more **Praise**. More anxious to be noticed — and respected—as a distinct individual, **different** from others. "Hell hath no fury like a woman **ignored!**" Delights to be told "You do that better than a man!" (Make fullest use of her name, but shun partiality. Don't use nick-name or pet-name for one and formal name for another. Kidding is risky business; avoid it unless sure O.K.)*

6. *Greater **loyalty**—to family, country, company, department, chosen leaders.*

Women performed numerous jobs at General Tire's warplants, such as making military pontoons.

By January, 1944, women comprised 40 percent of the labor force in Dayton-area war plants — the highest proportion employed in any of Ohio's industrial centers.

Continual admonitions to maintain war-production even extended to factory bathrooms.

Uncle Sam Never Won A War By Loafing !

Use This Room For The Purpose It Was Intended

RETURN TO YOUR WORKPLACE AND BACK UP OUR FIGHTING BOYS

thirty-two percent of all workers. By January, 1944, women comprised thirty-six percent of all war-workers in Akron, thirty-four percent in Cincinnati, thirty-three percent in Toledo and Columbus, and thirty-two percent in Cleveland. Under pressure from businessmen faced with severe manpower shortages, the Ohio legislature, in 1943, relaxed minimum-age and maximum-hour standards for females, and repealed the 1919 law which had barred women from many occupations. As the military draft absorbed growing numbers of male workers, the government launched a massive propaganda campaign, urging women to show their patriotism by filling essential slots in war plants. Public opinion vacillated considerably on the issue of women abandoning traditional domestic roles to perform "men's work," but generally the change was accepted as another necessary sacrifice associated with war. Attracted by wages which averaged forty percent more than rates in customary female jobs, and freed of long-standing social and legal constraints, women flocked into war industries and occupations formerly dominated by men. Abandoning their household chores and leaving such menial jobs as waitresses, domestics, and laundresses, women became machine operators, factory laborers, auto mechanics, taxi and truck drivers, plant guards, welders, and heavy equipment assemblers. The available pool of single females was soon depleted, and large numbers of wives and mothers entered or returned to the paid labor force. By 1944, not only were about seventy-five percent of the nation's new women war-workers married, most also had children; thus raising the critical problem of child-care for working mothers. Although various communities worried about rising delinquency rates among unsupervised youths, Congress refused to provide adequate funding for child-care facilities. Left to their own devices by male government leaders who expected women to return home when peace was restored, most working mothers were forced to make informal child-care arrangements with friends and relatives.

Despite the alluring assurances of desperate employers and government spokesmen, women did not achieve full equality in status or opportunity in Ohio's war plants. Instead, prevalent sexual discrimination restricted female employees at every turn. Beginning wages for Ohio women averaged five cents below male rates, and they invariably earned about one-third less in total income than men who performed the same jobs. Male workers demonstrated considerable hostility to women employed in their departments, particularly when they competed for upgrading and promotions. Although UAW locals in Toledo and UE locals in Dayton actively attempted to support female rank and filers, their rather progressive efforts remained exceptional. By and large, male-dominated unions tended to view women members as only temporary constituents, and thus were unresponsive to female grievances regarding separate seniority lists; discriminatory wage, job-classification, and training policies;

sexist behavior among supervisors; and physical segregation within plants. Since the WLB also failed to enforce its generally egalitarian guidelines, women were frequently forced to assert their rights through spontaneous direct action.

As the end of the war and demobilization drew near in 1945, a study by the U.S. Department of Labor indicated that three-out-of-four female industrial workers, and more than half of the married women, intended to work during the postwar period. Moreover, contrary to the popular notion that women had only accepted war-work out of patriotism, eighty-six percent expressed strong desires to remain in newly acquired occupations. The fulfillment of their expectations, however, proved illusory. With reconversion to a peacetime economy and the discharge of men from the armed forces, women were quickly laid off from their remunerative positions. Disappointed with their subsequent relegation to lower-paying "female" jobs in service and clerical areas, tens-of-thousands of former war-workers nevertheless remained in Ohio's labor force, and continued the accelerating struggle for sexual equality in the workplace.

Labor shortages during World War II also expanded employment opportunities for black Ohioans; but, as in the case of women, resultant changes were tumultuous and often impermanent. In response to strong pressure from the civil-rights movement, President Roosevelt issued an executive order in 1941 prohibiting racial discrimination in war industries, and created a Fair Employment Practices Committee to investigate charges of bias. With at least formal governmental assistance, therefore, blacks managed to increase their share of total employment in Ohio's war plants from 3.5 percent in 1940 to 8.2 percent in 1945; while the proportion of skilled jobs filled by blacks rose from two to eight percent over the same timespan. However, advances were neither easy nor equitable. For instance, an inquiry by the War Manpower Commission revealed that, although about half of Ohio's employers in war industries favored the hiring of blacks, thirty-five percent expressed indifference, and thirteen percent were openly opposed. These attitudes were often manifested in discriminatory hiring, wage, and promotion policies, as well as in racially segregated working conditions. Many employers argued that they were reluctant to hire or promote blacks because white employees would object and cause disruption. Unfortunately, management's excuse was too often valid, as white laborers commonly refused to work with blacks, and even staged wildcats to protest the placement or advancement of blacks in their departments. These shop-floor hostilities actually reflected broader racial tensions which mounted in war-production communities during the period. In August, 1943, for example, the local Council of Social Agencies reported that Cincinnati was experiencing the same difficulties which had already sparked bloody race riots in Detroit, Los Angeles, and New York City—assaults on blacks by white gangs, interracial friction over the use of public facilities; wild rumors regarding impending violence, competition for housing and jobs, the racial bias of white workers from the South, and "a praiseworthy determination by the majority of Negroes to defend their new-found status."

Some CIO unions, like the United Automobile Workers, made notable progress in the improvement of race relations within their organizations. Nonetheless, especially at local levels, racial prejudice continue to plague black rank and filers. White members repeatedly frus-

The conversion of Dayton's industries to war-production and continual labor shortages opened new job-opportunities for blacks.

A rare sight prior to World War II, black and white women work side-by-side producing parts for military aircraft in Vandalia.

Reflecting the rising tide of labor discontent by July, 1945, local members of the National Maritime Union picketed the Cleveland offices of the War Shipping Administration protesting proposed wage-cuts.

With the end of the war little more than a month away, pickets cheered when Navy officers — acting under President Truman's executive order— took over the Akron Goodyear plant on July 5, 1945. The nineteen-day strike, which idled nearly 17,000 workers, was but a prelude to a massive surge of labor-militancy the following year.

James Culver personally discovered that, relative to conditions during the 1920s, black workers achieved some gains during the War:

. . . I was elected president in 1943, after I served five years as recording secretary. The man who had previously been president was elected financial secretary at the same election. He decided that he would make a racial fight out of it, so the following week he went throughout the plant and asked the other officers of the local, who had been elected when I was elected president, and he was elected financial secretary, to resign — "We don't want a nigger for president." Some of them did succumb to that, but interestingly enough, the man who was elected vice-president was a white southerner . . . This fella said to me, in this southern accent, "So far as I'm concerned," he said, "they can go to hell; you were elected by the membership, and you're the president, and that's the way it's going to be." Some of the members came to me and asked me to resign, and I refused. When we had our next meeting . . . I immediately reported to the membership that some of the officers had resigned, and I said, "We have two offices open here, two of the officers have resigned, and one of the orders of business that we have to take care of today is to elect some persons to replace them." We proceeded to do that; we elected two people to replace the two officers who resigned, and from that time on, for a period of many, many years, we never had another racial question . . . I was president for twenty-five years. . . .

trated efforts by union officials to overcome racial barriers, as the president of Columbus Local 5 related to International Typographical Union headquarters in May, 1945. At a meeting held to discuss applications for union membership by five black printers,

. . . A couple members of No. 5 spoke against the recommendation, bringing out the argument that once these colored printers were members of the Union they would be free to seek employment in any Union office. These members, of course, stressed that they did not wish to have to work beside a Negro. I, and others, defended the recommendation. After considerable argument, the recommendation was tabled. . . .

Perhaps I am not any more anxious to organize Negro printers than anyone else. But I do know that there are already some Negro members in the I.T.U. I also feel that the C.I.O. would not refuse to organize these workers—and I, for one, do not wish to sit back and permit the C.I.O. to make additional inroads into our jurisdiction. [The ITU had returned to the AFL in 1944.]

Both Secretary Brown and I are mindful of various Fair Employment Practices Laws (one is pending before the Ohio Senate at the present time). We realize that these laws make it impossible for any labor organization to refuse membership to any man or woman simply because of race, creed or color. Furthermore, we are anxious to prevent the Typographical Union from receiving a black eye on this score. . . . However, we are at a loss to know just which course should be pursued.

Of course, many other local union officers made little effort to represent black members. For instance, after investigating conditions at a Cincinnati firm which primarily employed black women to manufacture overalls for the military, a special committee of the War Manpower Commission concluded in February, 1944 that:

Employees received nothing from the Union. Meetings lasted about 10 minutes; long enough for dues to be collected. When employees insisted that their complaints be heard, the collecting officers listened and promised to report later from the white Union "upstairs". Two white women from the Union attended meetings. The function of one was to collect dues. The other said that she was President. Both refused to discuss grievances, saying that they could do nothing unless they took it to Washington and the Government. Meetings were conducted carelessly and with very little order. Girls were not acquainted with any of the officers of the Union. Meetings were held once per month as outlined above. Members are told that they are in good standing when dues are paid but know nothing about officers, bargaining committees and the usual functions of a Union.

As these cases illustrated, substantive gains by black war-workers usually occurred as a result of manpower shortages or government pressure, rather than union action. Few objections were heard from union leaders, when

Problems which would plague Ohio's labor movement after the war began to surface even before VJ-Day. In addition to rank-and-file discontent, inter-union factionalism accelerated. In August, 1945, an alarmed Edwin Brendel of the Butler County Industrial Union Council wrote to CIO Director John Brophy:

. . . I hear so much lately of prestige in our movement. Each affiliated group sparring and fainting for the most advantageous position over the other. While this political conniving goes on in our movement the workers in the shops, mines, and offices are paying the Bill. Industrial Unionism has been my philosophy ever since the World War No. 1. Since the inception of C.I.O. movement, some of our affiliates such as U.E. — Steel and Auto have made unthought of progress in numerical and financial strength. Now each group act as though they are unaffiliated with each other. They seem to have gone power crazy. Our C.I.O. program is being slowly but surely following the tactics of A.F. of L. in which one group is pitted against the other. Our present leadership should take stock of themselves and imagine they are back in the sweat shops of our country. See the workers as they exist today. Forget their egotism and false pride. All work as one C.I.O. group. It is a bad omen that we don't use one application card for all workers and eliminate segregation as it is now being done in our movement. Unemployment due to cut-backs and reconversion will have a tremendous effect on the morale of those members affected. By reason of these lay-offs we stand to loose some active members. Our finances will also be greatly curtailed. If we of the C.I.O. expect to survive our post-war period . . . Let us not wait until a "Pearl Harbor" hits our labor movement. . . .

black members began to face discriminatory layoffs in 1945, in order to make room for returning white servicemen.

Thus, in 1945 Ohio workers awaited the imminent resumption of peace with a mixture of eagerness and anxiety. Successive encounters with prosperity, depression, and war had vastly altered the patterns of everyday lives. The diminished flow of foreign-born workers, the gradual assimilation of second generation immigrants, as well as the accelerated infusion of blacks and women had transformed the character and composition of the labor force. Despite massive fluctuations in the economic climate over more than a quarter-century, technological innovations, depersonalizing divisions of labor, mechanization, and mass-production methods had continued to modify working environments and the very nature of toil. At the same time, laboring people had been jolted by extremes of prosperity and adversity; and both had left their imprints on working-class mentalities. For many individuals, personal expectations and ambitions henceforth would be guided by caution and an unquenchable thirst for security. Furthermore, labor had established a new interrelationship with government. New Deal policies provided the working masses with numerous safeguards against physical deprivation, authoritarian employers, and economic insecurity. Such unprecedented reforms kindled a legacy of governmental protection, which working people would sporadically attempt to maintain for decades, by exerting their political influence on behalf of the Democratic Party. But perhaps the most momentous change of all was the emergence of organized labor as a legitimate power. National union membership had soared from 8.3 million in 1938 to 14.8 million in 1945, significant contractual gains had been made in formerly open-shop industries, internal union structures had been consolidated, and labor leaders had achieved a degree of respectability and prominence in political and governmental circles. Observers began to note that the "iron law of oligarchy" seemed to be taking hold in many organizations, especially as conservative officials drifted toward business unionism and accommodations with employers. Yet, within the movement itself, debilitating factionalism endured. The lingering separation of the AFL and CIO was less important than multidimensional tensions between union bureaucrats and militant rank and filers, male and female members, blacks and whites, as well as Communists and anti-Communists. Particularly at the shop-floor level, solidarity could spontaneously evaporate, if union power was not used effectively to protect the interests of members. Although rank-and-file apathy remained a problem, it was hardly pervasive. Members clearly perceived that reconversion to a peacetime economy would trigger new problems, and they demanded that their unions respond on their behalf. Indeed, a surge of walkouts in 1945—by an unparalleled 418,000 Ohio workers—signaled the advent of renewed restiveness and turmoil in the postwar years to come.

Even workers fortunate enough to retain their jobs — such as these rugged employees of Youngstown Sheet and Tube Company (above) and Toledo's Willys-Overland Company (right) — did not escape nagging anxieties. Additional layoffs, wage-cuts, and grueling speedups were daily occurrences.

Unemployed blacks resignedly await the opening of a Cincinnati soup-kitchen in 1931.

"Human Contours of the Great Depression"

None of the nation's economic catastrophes prior to 1929 could have adequately prepared Ohio workers for the Great Depression. For never had "hard times" struck such multitudes, caused such severe distress, or persisted for so many years. Of course, some managed to evade calamity entirely, while others actually prospered. But even these fortunate survivors were affected — either by the pervasive anguish of neighbors, friends, co-workers, and relatives; or by justifiable fears that their turn might in-

As this rural black family could testify, poverty and squalor were not restricted to Ohio's depressed cities.

deed be next. Whether directly or indirectly, the tragic consequences of this disaster touched nearly every household.

The depression's countless casualties resulted not only from physical hardship, but from devastating psychological blows as well. For generations, workers had embraced the individualistic gospel of success. They had fervently believed that economic and social advancement depended upon an individual's hard work, sound character, and proper behavior. By the same token, failure was also perceived in intensely personal terms. Consequently, though many others suffered similar fates, each dispirited individual tended to blame himself for his own defeats. Somehow, he must have done something wrong to deserve the pink slips, eviction notices, overdue bills, exhausted savings, hungry children, and lack of job-prospects. More often than not, however, the grievous mistake or personal inadequacy could not be identified—thereby adding bewilderment and frustration to a consuming sense of guilt. As the depression stubbornly ground on year after year, 'just getting by' became a daily struggle. Fears mounted that losses of property, self-respect, and personal dignity might become permanent. Many former breadwinners finally had to face the ultimate humiliation — requesting public or private relief. With hat in hand, tormented workers had to swallow their remaining pride and admit that they were defeated, that they could no longer provide for themselves and their families. With that poignant step, throngs of desperate relief recipients staggered across the threshold of despair. An overwhelming numbness seemed to descend over the working-classes. As the popular and

Cincinnati street-children enjoying a rare curbside feast of watermelon.

Though disaster continually hovered about them, working-class parents in Columbus' Franklinton neighborhood managed a meager existence for their children.

During the summer of 1938, noted photographer Ben Shahn brilliantly captured the human contours of the Great Depression in Ohio. Standing in line outside an Urbana relief station, two desperate generations pondered their condition (A). At Circleville, Shahn encountered a despondent resident who asserted: ''No man in the United States has had the trouble I had since 1931. No man. Don't talk to me. I'm deaf. I lost my farm in 1931. I went into town to work with a painter. I fell off a scaffold and broke my leg. I went to work in an acid factory. I got acid spilt on me; burnt my nose and made me blind. Then I get these awful headaches. I've been to lots of doctors, but that doesn't help me '' (B). The depression respected no age barriers, as reflected in the melancholy gazes of children of an ex-farmer in central Ohio who was forced to join the WPA (C), and an adolescent inhabitant of a ''Hooverville'' outside Circleville (D).

A

B

D

C

Trudging home to the Cleveland "Flats" after a day's toil in the mills, some steelworkers masked their insecurities by wearing their "Sunday best."

For this anonymous veteran, the "hard times" of the 1930s posed yet further challenges in a life-long struggle to survive.

The unemployed in Toledo had nothing much to do but agonizingly bide their time.

Angry, embarrassed, and dejected Clevelanders wait for surplus commodity relief in 1938.

perceptive commentator, Will Rogers, noted: "Depression used to be a state of mind. Now it's a state of coma, now it's permanent. Last year we said, 'Things can't go on like this,' and they didn't, they got worse."

Long periods of enforced idleness compounded the dilemmas of the unemployed and dispossessed. Often for the first time in their hard-working lives, throngs of Ohioans had nothing to do, nowhere to go, nothing to spend. Waiting in gallingly lengthy lines for relief or a rumored job became a prevalent pastime. Tens-of-thousands spent their days 'squatting' in makeshift communities of tar-paper shacks, packing crates, and scrap-metal — universally called "Hoovervilles" by their embittered inhabitants—which sprang up on the outskirts of nearly every town and city. The 'free-time' which had once been a cherished luxury was now an oppressive enemy. For with little else to fill the hours, "the forgotten man at the bottom of the economic pyramid" (as Franklin Delano Roosevelt termed him) continually mulled over his condition, pondered his self-worth, deepened his pain. Sporadically, that pain burst into angry defiance. Growing numbers of working people overcame their lethargy and sense of anonymity to stage marches, strikes, and assorted protests. Yet—much to the dismay of ideological radicals, union activists, and political demagogues, and much to the relief of the propertied classes — high levels of working-class solidarity and militancy were rarely sustained. Any revolutionary potential eventually subsided.

Thus, the adults and children who suffered through the Great Depression were indelibly marked by their experiences. Neither statistics nor words alone can adequately convey the deep psychological and spiritual scars which would permanently affect their attitudes and behavior. In order to understand, one must search the faces, examine the haunted features, and—above all—imagine the inner feelings which the eyes reflect.

PART 5 SEARCHING FOR SOLUTIONS 1946-1980

The thirty-five year span following World War II comprised an era of unique paradox in the lives of Ohio workers. Conditioned by depression experiences, laboring people feared that they might again be engulfed by "hard times." As citizens of the world's foremost military and economic power, they initially felt more confident about the nation's supremacy in international markets and politics. Yet, evolving realities did not match their expectations. Ironically, American strength would prove to be severely limited in the international arena, displaying its greatest vitality on the domestic front. Much to their dismay, workers soon began to experience the shop-floor effects of foreign challenges to American pre-eminence—either in the form of industrial competition, the control of energy resources, or domestic hysteria resulting from Communism's global expansion. Meanwhile, an unfolding age of affluence assuaged earlier anxieties. Fed by an explosion in consumer purchasing, unprecedented economic growth combined with militant collective bargaining efforts to produce long-sought financial and job-security. Never before had the nation's laborers enjoyed the luxury of more than three decades without a major depression. Yet, neither prosperity nor opportunity were spread evenly among Ohio workers, and new challenges to seniority-conscious, white males emerged in workplaces throughout the state. Tensions would develop over the position of blacks, women, Hispanics, and other minorities in the workforce; automation would spawn fears of displacement; and levels of unemployment would rise gradually. As the structure of the labor force changed, moreover, the numbers of people in low-paying service positions mounted and the portion of the workforce that was unionized slowly contracted. Postwar assumptions about the power of organized labor were, from the perspective of 1980, naively optimistic.

In the momentous decades after World War II the structure and composition of the Ohio workforce changed, reflecting developments throughout the United States. The increasingly important role of jobs in the secondary labor market—poorly paid, less skilled, less secure, less unionized—highlighted the changing composition of the labor force. Women increased as a

TEACHERS ON STRIKE

CINCINNATI FEDERATION OF TEACHERS LOCAL 1520

proportion of the total workforce, for instance, and by 1980 more than half of all adult women were either working or looking for work. By that time, too, women represented nearly forty percent of all workers nationwide. The proportion of women who worked had climbed gradually throughout the twentieth century and peaked during World War II when labor shortages even opened well-paying factory jobs to black women. As soldiers returned and families formed at the most rapid rate in the nation's history, many women left the labor force under duress. But the long range tendency for more and more females to work rebounded and by the early 1950s, prodded by the labor demands of the Korean War era and the economic pressures of inflation, women again flocked to work. Women remained relegated to jobs in the secondary labor market, especially in the booming areas of clerical and service work. In the decade after the emergence of a strong feminist movement in the late 1960s women enlarged their proportion of professional and managerial positions, though chiefly in nursing and teaching. Perhaps more significantly, the pattern of female labor became more continuous rather than being broken by extended periods of child rearing. Still, in 1980 most working women toiled in sex-segregated lower level positions, on average earning barely fifty-nine cents for each $1.00 paid to a male; only twelve percent were union members, compared to thirty-three percent of all working men. Discriminatory patterns figured here, but so did a contracting job market in the 1970s. Affirmative action alone could not clear the hurdle. Ultimately, recognition of the existence of segregated job structures would give rise to demands for comparable-worth pay. As an AFL-CIO resolution passed in 1979 explained, "over 80 percent of women workers are segregated into 'female' occupations that are different in content from 'men's' jobs, but in many cases not different in skill, effort and responsibility required."

For non-whites the story was much the same. World War II opened a host of economic opportunities and stimulated further massive migrations from the South, a current which continued throughout the era and was soon reflected in the changing population of the state's industrial centers (see Appendix — Tables 5A and 5B). Unlike the situation after World War I, black factory workers tended to retain their positions. However, black males generally remained in the dirtiest, lowest paid, and least skilled jobs well into the 1960s. Civil rights challenges to restrictive apprenticeship programs started in the 1950s to loosen the hold on scarce skilled jobs somewhat and, as barriers to advanced education eroded, blacks moved into various white collar positions as well. Black women, however, continued to experience the dual discrimination of gender and color.

Though Hispanic workers had never comprised a major segment of Ohio's workforce, pocket communities had grown since the 1920s in cities such as Toledo along the routes migratory farmworkers traveled from Texas. While the spread of labor-saving farm machinery reduced the numbers of migrants each year, the activist currents which animated women and blacks in the 1960s also led farm workers in Northwest Ohio to forge a Farm Labor Organizing Committee and mount a campaign for economic justice. Chicanos who settled down were, like blacks, gradually able to improve their economic positions. Still, nearly four decades after Pearl Harbor, they were disproportionately represented in the secondary labor force and continued to experience the degradations which had characterized their lives for generations. By the late 1970s, the effects of this concentration in unskilled occupations and of the tightening job market were apparent. Although the percentage of the U.S. population

Overleaf—page 225. As the 1977 walkout by Cincinnati teachers illustrated, a new sense of militancy among public employees became a distinctive feature of the tumultuous 'seventies.

Like thousands of other Ohio firms by September, 1945, Delco Products had begun the task of reconverting its Dayton plant to peacetime production.

The tendency for women to work had increased steadily since the late nineteenth century. Nonetheless, for many women, the first experience could be difficult. Dorothy Burch, who subsequently became a union official, discussed her work at the Tiffin General Electric Plant starting in 1950:

When I first walked in that plant I had never had a job outside my home, and I thought it was the biggest thing I ever saw. It was very menacing to me, and the plant doesn't have windows, and having a background from the farm, it seemed like I couldn't breathe, I felt stifled, and it took me a long time to get used to that . . . . The work— the first job I had was tying wires in place, and we had quotas to meet, and it was pretty hard to get used to it in that when you start working . . . your hands get so sore . . . from pulling the string tight, and putting the wires in place right. At first, I wondered how in the world the women could stand it and work under all that pain all the time because I thought all their hands were hurting just like mine were, and it took me awhile to realize that you got used to it . . . . I got so that I could go right along with the rest. It was very interesting work, and the first paycheck that I drew I was so proud of it. I don't think it was more than around $50.00, but I just thought that was really something, that I had my own paycheck. I was, at that time, thirty-seven years old . . . . Some people to this day still look down on folks that work in factories . . . . I used to feel bad about it. I suppose that was my farm training, I don't know, but anyway, now, I, somehow, can't feel bad about somebody working, making refrigerator motors, because when you think about it, refrigeration is necessary for everybody's home, hospitals, and there's many, many places where if we didn't have refrigeration people wouldn't be living as nice as they are.

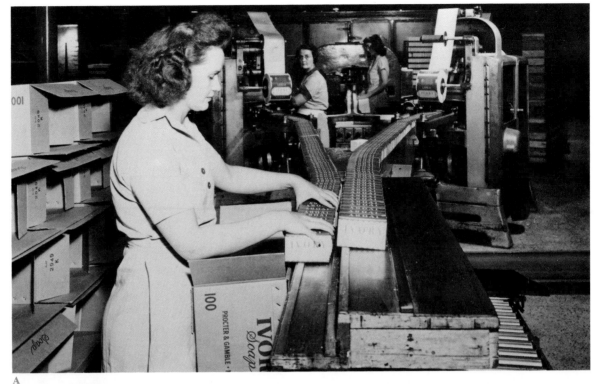

Female employment expanded steadily during the postwar years. Women continued to work in a variety of jobs they had long dominated — as Cincinnati soap packers and as Dayton Delco assemblers in the 'fifties (A&B), and as Cleveland garment workers and Columbus TV tube inspectors in the 'seventies (C&D).

A

B

D

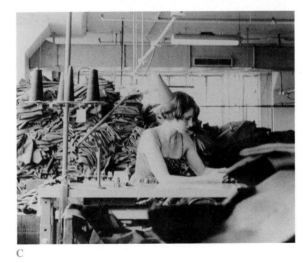

C

below the poverty-line had dropped to 11.4 percent by 1978, among black and Hispanic families the rates were 27.5 and 20.5 percent. For white families the rate was 6.9 percent.

The post-war era also witnessed a dramatic change in the structure of Ohio's workforce. Despite the richness of state agriculture, the proportion of workers in that field continued to slip downward, a tendency paralleled by the de-

cline in the ranks of the unskilled. By 1980 barely three percent of employed workers toiled on farms. Among non-agricultural workers fully half were employed in manufacturing in 1945— most in the production of durable goods in the so-called heavy industries. In the years thereafter manufacturing jobs remained an important but dwindling component of the workforce. The percentage of non-agricultural employees on manufacturing payrolls nationwide fell to forty percent in 1960 and to thirty-four percent in 1975. Trends in Ohio were comparable. At the end of World War II just over half of all employed nonagricultural workers in Ohio held jobs in manufacturing. Thereafter the proportion declined steadily—to 36.6 percent in 1950, thirty-seven percent in 1960, 33.8 percent in 1970, and twenty-nine percent in 1980. Continuing a trend underway since at least the 1920s, fewer and fewer manufacturing employees were actually involved in production. The situation varied from industry to industry, but in 1947 production workers represented almost eighty-four percent of all manufacturing employees, whereas by 1977 that proportion had dropped to just over sixty-nine percent. Gradually, the economy shifted from the production of goods to the production of services. In Ohio the goods-producing industries—manufacturing, mining and quarrying, construction—accounted for the bulk of the non-agricultural employed workforce until the early 'sixties. In 1963, for the first time, the number of workers in transportation and public utilities, wholesale and retail trade, finance, insurance, and real estate, in miscellaneous professional and service occupations, and on government payrolls surpassed the number of workers producing goods. The shift toward what one observer called a "post-industrial society" accelerated significantly in the 'sixties and 'seventies. By 1970 fifty-four percent of the employed workforce generated services and by 1980 nearly sixty-seven percent did. Developments within each of the state's major metropolitan areas reflected these broader tendencies (see Tables 5F and 5G).

The changing composition and structure of Ohio's workforce were but part of a persistent pattern of change evident from the earliest days of statehood. Through the years bracketed by the end of World War II and the election of Ronald Reagan another aspect of continuity with the past was also apparent—the enormous variety among working people in terms of hours, wages, and working conditions. The work week tended to stabilize at forty hours throughout this era, although the powerful building trades and some white-collar workers secured a thirty-five hour week. During periods of rapid economic expansion such as the mid-to late 1960s, labor scarcities in traditional blue collar jobs boosted overtime hours and increased the working week to an average of nearly forty-three hours. For a time, indeed, mandatory overtime became a principal grievance for many workers. Meanwhile, the upward trend of wages persisted. The average manufacturing worker in the United States earned $1.08 an hour in 1946, $2.26 in 1960, $3.36 in 1970 and $5.34 in 1980. Yet not all workers benefited from such increases. Although racial distinctions for the same work tended to disappear over time, the sex differential proved more resistant. For example, nearly a third of women laundry workers, but only five percent of the males, earned between $1 and $1.19 hourly in 1960. By 1970 male accounting clerks in Cincinnati earned between $113.50 and $142.50 a week while women doing the same tasks averaged from $92 to $122. In virtually every office occupation similar distinctions existed. Although by the early 1980s there were some indications that conditions were changing, the fact remained that women were clustered in lower paying jobs.

Increases in wages and salaries did not keep up with the cost of living. As the years passed,

Founded in 1956, the Governor's Committee on Migrant Labor sought to coordinate assistance to the roughly 18,000 migrant farm laborers who annually harvested crops in Ohio. The Committee's original statement of purpose succinctly summed up some of the problems confronting migrants.

Ohio is a highly industrialized State, and there are not sufficient qualified local agricultural workers to meet the demands of the agricultural economy at various seasons of the year. Therefore, agricultural employers depend heavily upon the services of a large mobile force of migratory agricultural workers to help plant and harvest certain crops.

The presence of thousands of migratory workers in Ohio propounds certain problems, not only to the migrant and his employer but also to the community in which migrants are temporarily domiciled and, in a broader sense, to all of the citizens of this State.

Due to the nature of their nomadic existence, migratory agricultural workers have been unable to secure for themselves and their families the decent living standards, adequate educational opportunities, and other social benefits which permanent residents of the community take for granted.

In 1978, while migrants from Florida worked in a Hocking County orchard (left), representatives of the Farm Labor Organizing Committee rallied on the steps of the statehouse in Columbus to seek legislative redress of their grievances (below).

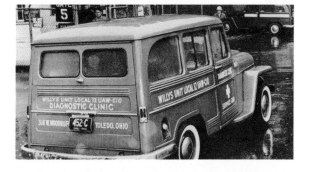

Postwar inflation ravaged consumers' pocketbooks. Some unions grappled with the problem directly. UAW Local 12 in Toledo, for instance, established a coop grocery store and a mobile health clinic.

In 1946 an unprecedented strike wave, greater even than that of 1919, swept Ohio and the nation as workers in industries such as auto, coal, electrical, railroad, and steel determined to recoup losses inflicted by inflation and wartime wage controls. Adamant about limiting wage increases, President Truman used powers granted during the war to seize several industries and thus bolster the resolution of strikes by appointed fact-finding committees. Military intelligence reports from the Ohio coal fields mirrored the complex issues at stake. Having visited Chauncey, Nelsonville, Glouster, Corning, and Crooksville, Lieutenant Alvan Talmadge filed this report six days after the government took over Ohio mines:

Public cautious, seemingly indifferent. Not sympathetic to miners & their demands, but remain intimidated & fearful. No public support likely to operation of mines by force until present wage negotiations should be broken off and until money becomes scarce. Miners are expecting work contract to be signed momentarily . . . . If force used to compel mining it must be overwhelming and determined. Perhaps regiment in Nelsonville vicinity—Perhaps must remain until all return to work, present funds being exhausted. Barracks at mines necessary, as workers could not be protected going to and from their homes, up to 12 miles distant from mine. In past, there have been shootings & bombings directed against the workers, their homes and other property. Guard units would be out a long time at much expense. Mine owners found it very costly to break previous strikes . . . . Defense of each mine is a separate problem. Prevent riotous assemblies. Road blocks were necessary. Guard all access roads & railroads to mines, also mine trackage—air reconnaisance. Arrest of agitators. Forest cover is protection to snipers. Extensive area must be securely held to protect each mine & access thereto . . . . No bread was seen for sale in any stores. No flour—one miner at Chauncey complained of no bread available for lunches. If we expect them to mine coal, they must have bread . . . . Miners said to be talking some against Lewis' demands as welfare funds already provided in Ohio through industrial Commission, but collectively the miners support Lewis and are proud of his success in dealing with Govt.

this central paradox of the age of affluence became more evident. Sustaining a moderate standard of living in an inflationary era when expectations were constantly being raised by an all-pervasive electronic media came to require overtime, moonlighting, and the income of other family members. By the 1970s, for the first time, the typical American family consisted of a husband and wife who both worked. The difficulty in Ohio was that opportunities in high-paying manufacturing jobs declined after 1970. Other sectors of the economy did expand, but jobs in government and service areas tended to pay less well. Thus purchasing power gradually eroded or levelled off. By 1979, the average Ohio factory production worker grossed better than $300 per week, while in non-manufacturing the gross was about $200 weekly. To compound problems, recurrent recessions struck with a vengeance. Unemployment notched upward and more and more often, when recessions hit, the rate of unemployment in Ohio exceeded the national average. The combination of declining purchasing power and rising unemployment had a deadly effect within the state—eating away at the tax base and accumulated manufacturing skills, while accelerating the decline of major urban centers. For the increasing numbers of workers on government payrolls, too, the gap between earnings and the cost of living made the notion of public service a cruel dilemma. Nor did financial pressures generated by the inflationary spiral cease once a worker settled into retirement. As a former employee of the Columbus Coated Fabrics Corporation complained to the president of the Textile Workers Union of America in October, 1974:

…I was president of the Local 487 when the pension system was put…in force. In 1958 I bought a farm in southern Ohio (Hocking County). Work on it weekend, holiday, vacation. So on Feb. 25, 1972 I retired [and] moved to farm. Things went along fine for 1 year. Then bottom went out with the Congress-Nixon-Ford inflation. Nixon was traveling around the world. Congress was playing around with Watergate. They are throwing the taxpayer money away. As I get around and exchange labor paper I have never seen one thing about the labor helping the retired man [and] woman. So I think T.W.U.A. should get started to think about the retired people as I paid dues in Local 487 [for] 25 yrs. You try to live on a fix income. I know you would holler like hell because I know. I have sold the farm. Going to move to a small town 30 miles south of Columbus and *try* to get work. Lets get labor on the ball to roll Congress around to help the retired as well as the one who works.…

The decline in the proportion of workers in manufacturing, so central to the Ohio economic crisis by 1980, occurred gradually. The number of manufacturing jobs actually increased annually until 1969, although at a rate below that of the national average. Even during the generally prosperous 'fifties, when tailfins sprouted and limousines lengthened, there were signs of the coming crisis. In that decade Ohio slipped to fifth place among industrial states as

measured by value-added by manufacture, although it ranked fourth in the nation in number of manufacturing employees and first in the East North Central Region into the 'sixties. Civic leaders in some cities, Toledo and Youngstown among them, nervously pointed to the loss of manufacturing jobs in such diverse fields as apparel, plastics, and fabricated metals and some observers urged the development of research facilities in order to attract specialized high-technology firms to the state. What was already apparent was that even in industries such as food and kindred products, where the number of jobs increased substantially during the 'fifties, most of the increase was not in actual production work. Indeed, production workers fell from seventy-two to fifty-nine percent of the employed workforce in that particular industry. The same thing happened in paper and allied products and chemical and allied products.

During the 'sixties, the state benefited by the general expansion of the economy and for a time held its leadership position. But the gradual trend for production workers to decline continued, and trouble spots evident earlier — textiles, tobacco products, and apparel, for instance — remained. There were exceptions, of course, given the expansive nature of the economy — employment in primary metals, transportation equipment, fabricated metal products, machinery, and electrical products all rose. Such gains permitted Ohio to retain its position of leadership in the industrial world, but the dependency on durable-goods production such as motor vehicles and equipment would, in the 'seventies, prove to be a disaster for the state's economy (see Tables 5H and 5I).

Between 1969 and 1977 alone Ohio's eight largest and most industrialized counties lost an average of 15.6 percent of their manufacturing jobs. The decline was sharpest in Montgomery County (Dayton), where such jobs fell by twenty-five percent. Mahoning County (Youngstown) manufacturing jobs dropped by twenty

percent, those in Cuyahoga (Cleveland) by eighteen percent. Of the some 140,000 manufacturing jobs lost, nearly 36,000 were in the area of electric and electronic equipment production, 27,000 in primary metals, 16,000 each in non-electric machinery and transportation equipment, and 5,000 or more in a host of industries ranging from the production of food and kindred products to stone, glass, clay, paper, and textile products. By the late 1970s the tempo of job losses accelerated, marked by the announcement in the fall of 1977 that Youngstown Sheet and Tube's Campbell Works, now owned by the Lykes Corporation, would close. In 1980 U.S. Steel closed two of its massive but aged mills in Youngstown — the Ohio Works and the McDonald Works. Unemployment in the Youngstown-Warren area mounted and by the end of the year stood at nearly fifteen percent, the highest level since the Great Depres-

A

Manufacturing remained one of the principal employers of Ohio labor after 1945. Assembling goods into finished products still relied on a diversity of techniques. Despite greater mechanization and automation, the moving assembly line was not all-pervasive. It was used to produce shock absorbers in Delco's Dayton plant in the 'fifties (A). Yet, in a number of other industries —at NCR for cash register assembly (B), and for the production of tires at Firestone in the 1950s (C) — assembly relied upon a series of linked but discrete steps, generally carried out at individual work stations. In some instances, as in the case of the Deisel-Weimmer-Gilbert Cigar Company in Lima (D), where cigar molding was still done by hand in 1963, the link to previous modes of manufacturing was readily apparent.

B

C

D

sion. A similar pattern developed in Akron, where over 8,000 jobs disappeared as one rubber giant after another shut down. Although other cities also lost numerous manufacturing jobs, by 1980 Youngstown stood as a symbol of weaknesses in the American economy and as a painful reminder of the price paid by Ohio workers. In less than five years over 10,000 Youngstown steel workers had lost their jobs.

The falling numbers of manufacturing workers stemmed from many causes. Mechanization and automation of the labor process in basic industries were partly involved. For over a quarter of a century after World War II, Ohio ranked first or second in the nation in terms of investment by manufacturers in new plants and equipment. The level of investment began to slip steadily after 1970, and by 1976 Ohio ranked sixth among the states. By then, plant closings and the flight of companies to the "Sunbelt States" and overseas in pursuit of lower labor costs accounted for a portion of the decline. Authorities disagree on all the causes, but several additional factors are pointed to most frequently. As federal defense needs shifted from ground-warfare equipment to sophisticated air, space, and underwater technologies, spending shifted to states with developed capacities in those areas. While providing a badly needed boost to the local economy, the recent channeling of federal funds into Columbus for production of the B-1 bomber project is an exception to long-term patterns. By the 1950s, competition from overseas began to have an impact as well, since substantially lower labor costs enabled foreign firms to manufacture and sell their products more cheaply than American producers. The merger movement of the 1960s also had debilitating effects, for conglomerate multi-nationals increasingly tended to plow profits into further diversification rather than plant modernization. Finally, persistent inflation and high interest rates since the early 1970s made doing business more costly and thus intensified the disinclination to modernize.

The energy crisis which flowed from the 1973 decision by OPEC to raise oil prices worsened the situation, driving fuel costs up, plunging the auto industry into the worst sales period since the depression of the 1930s, and severely affecting related industries such as auto parts, rubber, and glass, all of which figured importantly in Ohio's economy. In 1974 those out of work represented 5.6 percent of the nation's civilian workforce. The following year, the unemployment rate reached a staggering 8.9 percent, and averaged 8.5 percent, the highest level in any of the years after the Second World War. Most severely affected were two major goods-producing industries, manufacturing and construction. In the construction trades more than one in every five workers was unemployed, while in manufacturing the national average topped twelve percent.

Long-term trends in most Ohio cities intensified problems, for as whites and many businesses fled to suburban areas, the proportion of low-income blacks in the cities rose and tax bases, consequently, eroded (see Tables 5C, 5D, 5E, and 5G). As unemployment surged upward in the mid-seventies, Ohio cities verged on collapse and school systems across the state plunged into chaos. The gradual return to a more stable economy did not alleviate the situation. In 1978 Cleveland defaulted on its loans, the first major city to do so since the thirties. By 1980 a major recession was underway, further deepening the urban crisis. Inflation reached an annual rate of 12.4 percent that year, the prime lending rate soared to a record high twenty percent, and unemployment climbed to 8.4 percent, compared to 7.5 percent nationwide. In some areas of the Buckeye State the rate was even higher, with no indication of relief in sight. An employee laid off after seventeen years when Clark Equipment closed its Lima plant expressed the anguish of many Ohio workers: "It's kind of like when you get sick. There's nothing you did to cause it, but you wonder if

you should have done something different. You're not in control of your own destiny."

Difficult though plant closings and high unemployment were, not all workers felt out of control. Indeed, many working-class neighborhoods displayed an intensely cooperative approach to dealing with these problems. Youngstown, for example, had been populated in its halcyon days by eastern European immigrants and the patterns of ethnic settlement evident by World War I persisted well into the early 1980s. Generations of the same family had worked together in the steel mills and in troubled times such families and their neighbors helped one another. Communal efforts to save the uniquely working-class community also lay

Soaring gas and oil costs fueled inflation after 1973, squeezing workers' pocketbooks, and prompting demonstrations such as this at Sohio's corporate offices in Cleveland in October, 1979.

By the early 1950s, the Willys-Overland Company in Toledo was simultaneously producing its famous Jeep —once again in heavy demand during the Korean War — and a new line of vehicles aimed at the burgeoning mass-consumer market.

A

B

While accelerating mechanization steadily increased productivity in mines from Glouster (A) to New Lexington (B), it also contributed to drastic declines in employment. Between 1950 and 1970, the state's employed miners dwindled by nearly one-third. Not until the nation's energy crisis of the mid-1970s would hopeful signs of resurgence appear. But adversity had become a way of life, and—as they had for generations—Ohio coal miners remained a breed apart during the postwar decades. The gloom, isolation, and extreme danger of their working-world continued to spawn a unique dignity, independence, clannishness, and militancy—traits evidenced in the stolid gaze of a seasoned veteran (C), in the haunted eyes of a young Bethesda miner in 1980 (D), or in the comradery of a crew awaiting their shift in the pits (E). Miners again exhibited their stubborn combativeness during the 1978 United Mine Workers strike. Rank and filers defiantly scorned an initial settlement (F)—one which members in Ohio rejected by a four-to-one margin—and ignored President Carter's back-to-work order under the Taft-Hartley Act, before finally ratifying a contract after 111 days.

C

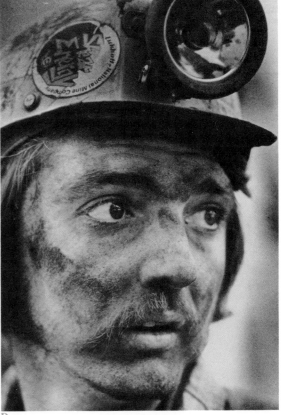

D

F

E

behind a series of locally-based efforts to buy the steel plants and to shape legislation which would force employers to consider the social implications of plant closings. Whether such efforts would succeed was unclear by 1980.

There were some positive signs in the economic picture. Ohio's position as a transportation crossroads still placed it in an attractive position in the center of major population concentrations. The energy crisis revived Ohio's lagging coal industry, making Toledo the leading coal-handling port in the nation by 1980, and in light of shortages in the western states the state's water resources became an increasingly important consideration. Although Ohioans paid a price in underfunded education and social programs as a result of having one of the lowest tax rates in the nation, those low rates would attract cost-conscious businesses. When foreign firms began investing more heavily in the American economy and even established branch plants in the United States by the late seventies, it was not coincidental that some targeted Ohio. In 1979, for instance, Honda opened a motorcycle plant in Marysville and later announced that an auto plant would follow in 1983.

Following the Second World War, an accelerating surge of technological advancement generated increasingly complex alterations in the world of work. As in previous eras, transformations did not occur evenly in all workplaces, nor were all workers affected equally. But, whether real or potential, an advanced stage of technological change was clearly in the making in all sectors of the economy — redefining old problems, creating new concerns, and remolding workers' lives.

Three primary elements comprised this ongoing technological revolution. First, automation intensified dramatically. Building upon the mechanization of industry in the nineteenth century and the mass-production techniques of the early-twentieth century, postwar automation consisted of the use of electronic or other automatic equipment to control the continuous and integrated operation of any production system. From data processing in office work to automatic assembly processes at General Motors' Lordstown plant, automation spread through various Ohio industries. In 1963, United Automobile Workers Union president Walter Reuther testified to automation's awesome impacts. Reuther pointed out that in 1927 a Ford engine block had taken three weeks to machine. By the early 1950s, the company's automated Cleveland plant turned out an engine in 14.6 minutes. But, by 1960, the plant was almost totally rebuilt, because the engine line was already obsolete. Closely linked to automation was the application of increasingly sophisticated computerization, which, by 1980 had already passed through three generations of

Skilled construction workers have moved from job to job for generations. Potter Wickware, a pipe welder from California who had worked on the Alaskan pipeline, also spent time at the Zimmer nuclear power plant in the Ohio River Valley. In a 1979 *New York Times* article, he explained his mobility and something of the modern welder's craft:

The work was said to be clean and of high quality, the working conditions good, and the pay would come to $107 a day . . . . Every welder who wants to work on the job must pass the proficiency test. This consists of welding two pieces of pipe together to make a sample of your work. The finished weld must be clean strong and uniform. Upon completion it is given a thorough X-ray examination. If you pass you get to stay on the job; if you fail, down the road you go . . . . Nuclear welding is the action of hands and brains working on fine materials. It's mostly a physical, a visual-kinetic skill, but there's also an esthetic component. With a delicate motion of the hand and wrist you urge the arc along the joint, adding molten filler metal, drop by drop. The welding power comes from a generator to the torch, whence it is applied by hand to the metal. The torch is a streamlined, precise apparatus, fed by an array of lightweight hoses and cables, with a needle-sharp tungsten electrode that focuses the electic arc to a fine point. Like a tiny lightning bolt that you hold in your hand, the arc melts a region of the joint. All your attention is directed at this puddle of steel, about the size of a child's fingernail, inches away from your face. For the welder, intent upon the moment, with the hiss of the argon gas purge blowing through the torch head, with the slight, high-pitched buzz of the arc and its ionizing, ozonous odor, its penetrating brilliance muted by the filter glass of his face shield, but casting big shadows on the walls of the booth, the process is hypnotic, fascinating.

This is your entire experience; to coax, to implore this glowing blob of metal to stay clean and to flow smoothly into the contour of the joint. At last, as the rippled surface of the weld cools, its native silver color is tinged with a play of temper colors; straw-yellow, rose, blue and violet.

I finished my test by the end of the day and sent it out to be X-rayed that night. The next morning . . . I hung around . . . waiting for my results. Finally they came: a note that said '9-2334 acceptable.' That was me.

When James J. Childs published *PRINCIPLES OF NUMERICAL CONTROL* in 1965 he anticipated that the development, which dated only to the early 1950s, would dominate the machine tool market by 1970. That prediction missed the mark, but the spread of this technique was rapid, as the following excerpt from the second edition of Child's book indicates. Were he to look back today on what he wrote then, it is likely that he would be even more surprised, for in the interim robotics has emerged to supplement numerical control.

There are probably few manufacturing technologies that are as encompassing and have advanced as rapidly as has numerical control. In less than a decade the number of operating machines has grown from a few hundred to over fourteen thousand; and while this still represents a relatively small share of the total number of outstanding machines, the significant fact is that numerical control installations have been increasing on an average of approximately 35 per cent per year. What is most significant, however, is not that numerical control sales are rapidly increasing but that the capability to direct versatile machines, automatically, from numerical data is advancing into other manufacturing and engineering areas, thus greatly improving the efficiency and extending the capabilities of these areas.

The computer's role, which was initially to assist in the calculations required for preparing tapes, is being extended to cover the design of parts as well as the planning and control for the manufacture of these parts. Further, several different types of numerical control machines may now be instructed simultaneously by a single computer — both on-site and at remote locations. Feedback arrangements, amounting to special-purpose computers, have also been developed, that are capable of measuring variable characteristics at the workpiece and then automatically overriding the original programmed commands in order to obtain optimum performance.

There is little doubt that numerical control is about to enter the era of the fully-automatic factory. However, thus far, only the threshold has been approached, and it is expected that a number of years will be required before the technical and personnel problems can be resolved.

development. The appearance of tiny silicon wafers called microchips during the 1970s permitted storage of even larger amounts of information and dramatic reductions both in the size of computers and their cost. Finally, the gradual application of lasers to industrial production within the last twenty years has emerged as the third component of the technological revolution.

For workers in countless occupations, these developments had profound implications. The combination of automated and computer-controlled processes caused a significant reduction in the number of manufacturing workers needed for particular jobs. Though national increases in population and consumer spending after World War II stimulated absolute increases in manufacturing employment, overall the proportion of all workers in manufacturing jobs began to decline by the 1950s—with little indication that the trend would ever reverse. In numerous occupations, workers' roles have changed enormously. At Sun Oil's automated-flow refinery in Toledo, for example, the passage of crude oil through the various refining steps is handled entirely from a centralized location, where technicians and computers control valves, temperatures, and mixtures. A manual-operation crew has been relegated to backup status. Similarly, in more and more supermarkets automatic scanners read and register pre-coded prices of groceries, at the same time keeping track of inventory. The clerk's responsibilities primarily consist of handling non-coded items such as fresh vegetables and pushing the total button. In other industries, workers' former skills are being assumed by robots — the latest step in the merger of automatic machinery and computer technology.

Confronted by dismal employment prospects, workers displayed a strong sense of community as they demonstrated in Columbus in 1979 to support a bill which aimed to soften the blow of plant closings (left). A 1980 effort to promote Youngstown displayed a similar spirit (right).

Robotics, as it is termed, provides a consistency of performance in tasks such as welding and material handling which fascinates cost-conscious employers faced with inflation, high interest rates, and stiff foreign competition.

Although it may be true that, in the long run, the technological revolution continuously creates new jobs, one constant in the post-World War II era has been the resurgence of traditional working-class fears that machines would eliminate the need for people in various jobs. Rather than affecting factory workers alone, this job-insecurity struck vastly different groups of wage-earners. As the baby-boom generation passed through the public schools and local districts found themselves hard-pressed to sustain enlarged staffs, interest spread, for example, in the use of teaching machines. Essentially computers programmed to handle certain kinds of learning tasks, the machines were initially greeted with fear by many teachers. University professors fretted about replacement by videotaped lectures. UAW officials touring Datsun's automated plant in Japan were awe-struck by the fact that it was ninety-seven percent automated — with few humans about, labor costs had been slashed precipitously. The implications for well-paid auto workers in rapidly aging and uncompetitive American plants became obvious.

Since the late nineteenth century, workers in industry, offices, and retail establishments had

Semi-automatic pumps had transformed work at Cincinnati's Hudepohl Brewing Company by the post-war era (A), but in a range of other fields more than mechanization and refined mass-production techniques were applied. Indeed, entirely new categories of workers had emerged. As automatic procedures spread, console operators appeared in various firms, such as New Philadelphia's Warner and Swasey plant in 1980 (B). The escalating use of computers — many of which were assembled at NCR's Dayton facility in the mid-1960s (C) — altered other work-worlds as well. By the 1970s, while public employees mastered the complexities of Columbus' computerized water system (D), secretaries armed with word processors formed the vanguard of an "information revolution" (E).

dealt with the application of systematic and scientific management principles epitomized by Frederick W. Taylor. In the post-World War II era, the essential elements of Taylorism were implemented in broader and broader circles, magnifying the time-worn issue of job-control. In essence, the issue of the manner in which work shall be performed involves clashes between managements' right to control production versus the workers' degree of autonomy, dignity, and sense of personhood. Over the decades, skilled artisans, who had been most affected by management efforts to gain control of their knowledge, had waged a series of bitter struggles over the job-control issue. Conflict of that sort has not been repeated on the same scale, but in factories and offices there has been

By the 1960s computerized billing systems revolutionized the work of many clerical employees. An Ohio Bell vice president explained this to a conference on automation in 1964:

Another area of . . . mechanization or automation in Ohio Bell, is in the billing job. The job already is highly mechanized. We have progressed from the quill pen to the typewriter, the addressograph, the billing machine, and tabulating cards. We issue somewhat over 1 million bills a month, and we bill well over 8 million long distance calls. And when you issue millions of anything you have a production process. It has been said that the billing job in the telephone industry is the one most like a factory job. At Ohio Bell we use about 30 tons of punched cards and spend $18,000 per month for cards and paper for the billing process. Rather than the clerk with the high stool, the green eyeshade and the quill pen, the typical telephone accounting employee today is best visualized as a personable young woman deftly manipulating stacks of tabulating cards.

As the next step, a large-scale computer is now being placed in service in Cleveland to compute, print bills and post customer accounts. This equipment is much faster than a tabulating card system and for most purposes uses magnetic tapes rather than cards. Here again the routine repetitive operations are being mechanized. Cleveland bills are now being issued by the computer, and customer account treatments have been started. When the customer returns the bill stub with his payment, an optical scanner is used to read the bill stub and post the account. In the billing and accounting conversions, no employee displacement problems are anticipated other than retraining and reassignment, since other computer projects requiring additional record preparation work will be fitted into our schedule.

a continuation—though in different and sometimes more subtle forms — of the contest between management and employees. Alienation, depersonalization, and frustration in the workplace—popularly termed "blue-collar blues"—became issues of widespread public concern.

By the 1960s, many workers and observers alike had concluded that Taylorism had outlived its usefulness, that the quality of a person's working life should be of paramount concern, and that workplaces should be humanized and safe. Reflecting pressures which flowed upward from the rank and file, through unions, to state legislatures and Congress, demands surfaced to protect occupational health and safety. During the 1930s and 1940s, such problems had taken a backseat to more pressing issues such as security, wages, and war. During the 1960s, consciousness of air and water pollution, the increased use of toxic substances in production as well as a twenty-nine percent increase in industrial accident rates, reversed this tendency. Within a decade passage of three crucial pieces of federal legislation had major impacts on workers in Ohio and elsewhere: the Coal Mine Health and Safety Act of 1969 and the Black Lung Benefits Act of 1972, both pressed for by the Black Lung Association and Miners for Democracy, as well as the Occupational Safety and Health Act of 1970, championed by the Steelworkers, the Oil, Chemical and Atomic Workers, the UAW, the AFL-CIO, and Ralph Nader.

Although some sociologists and political scientists proclaimed the end of the working class in the 1950s, wage earners knew otherwise. They might describe themselves as middle-class in response to pollsters' questions, but they also knew that they were set apart from most salaried employees in several distinct ways. As a result of unionization, wages in manufacturing, construction, transportation, and various other fields increased substantially in the postwar era. Important fringe benefits such as sup-

Meat cutting in Cincinnati had always been a highly subdivided occupation. Power-driven saws eased the heavier physical work involved (right). Compared to earlier days, however, the most notable differences by the postwar era were the general cleanliness of the operations and the watchful presence of federal inspectors (far right).

A

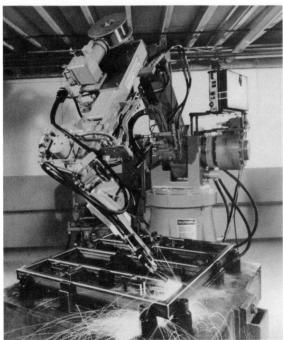

B

C

The introduction of robots in Ohio industry began in the 1970s, usually to perform specific functions such as welding (A & B). The concept was hardly new, Henry Ford having envisioned "automatic welding machines" in 1931. Still, in the quest to heighten efficiency and thus reduce costs, robotics represented a quantum leap in mechanization. The use of robots conjured up images of workplaces devoid of humans, yet that notion was exaggerated. For, while it was clear that their widespread use would dramatically reduce reliance on human production workers, the often fragile and erratic "mechanical men" still depended on "mere mortals" for construction and direction (C). In any case, by 1980, only a very limited number of robots actually had been installed on the state's shop floors.

plemental unemployment benefits developed as well. But the reality of unemployment and sporadic work remained a persistent danger. Too often overtime and a wife's paycheck became absolutely crucial just to make ends meet, rather than to enjoy greater luxury. Brief examination of several specific situations highlight the profound changes in working environments and the perplexing problems which resulted.

Describing the assembly line as the classic symbol of powerlessness, Ohio author Sherwood Anderson wrote in 1931: "It is the belt. The belt is boss. It moves always forward." Assembly lines changed during the following half century in ways incomprehensible to scientific management practitioners of earlier decades. But the delimited nature of worker-control on the line remained a poignant fact. Although the assembly line continued to symbolize wage-earner powerlessness, persistently high levels of absenteeism, slowdowns, and numerous wildcat strikes suggested that modern workers would persist in carving out autonomy and clinging to dignity.

The case of production employees at General Motors' Lordstown plant was perhaps the most publicized. Built in the mid-1960s, the facility represented "the state of the art" in automation at the time. In 1966 it turned out about sixty cars per hour. Five years later, with further modifications to the line to meet the challenge of small imports then gaining a larger share of the domestic market and with a new management team in place, the pace stepped up to over one hundred cars per hour. Crackdowns on absenteeism, a renewed concern with productivity, and management's willingness to confront the militant United Auto Workers Union Local 1112 all generated a showdown which international union chieftains could scarcely control. At first workers staged slowdowns. As grievances stacked up for several years without resolution, this tactic spread. In 1972 the Lordstown workers struck, gaining tremendous publicity, and making alienation a national issue. Equally important, the strike dramatized spreading anti-authoritarianism among rank and filers toward both union leaders and corporate

managers — a rebelliousness which reflected general tendencies in the larger society. Many of the Lordstown workers were young, long-haired, and veterans of the Vietnam conflict. Though the strike achieved only marginal gains, this generation of workers had discovered the lessons of their predecessors. As former auto-worker Al Nash succinctly noted, militancy in its broadest sense serves as "a form of control indicating to management that there are limits they dare not trespass lest the workers react in a slowdown or wildcat strike. The militancy of the worker and the common resentment that he shares with his colleagues against the company reduced markedly his degree of estrangement, isolation, meaninglessness, and powerlessness on the job."

Problems of an entirely different nature arose for textile workers at the Columbus Coated Fabrics plant, a subsidiary of the Borden Chem-

By the 1960s, a renewed surge of concern about occupational health and safety problems—especially those involving increasing amounts of toxic industrial wastes (A)—led to a variety of protective measures. In 1978, a foundry worker at Buckeye Steel Castings in Columbus had been issued a complete set of safety devices — hard hat, protective glasses, ear plugs, and particle mask (B). Painters at Dayton's Frigidaire plant in 1964 wore specially designed hoods to prevent respiratory ailments (C).

A B

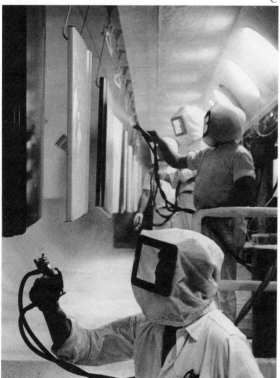

C

ical Company. Relations between the local unions and the company had been acutely strained for many years. But in 1973, new disputes relating to extremely hazardous working conditions emerged. The company, which employed about 950 workers to print and dye fabrics, introduced a new chemical in their production process. Apparently as a result, incidents of "paralysis" began to develop among workers in one department. Diagnosed as peripheral neuropathy or neuritis of unknown toxic origin, these cases caused a shutdown of the department and a gradual layoff of over 300 employees. After extensive investigation by federal and state occupational health officials and lengthy negotiations, workers returned to their jobs with new work rules, protective clothing, and safety procedures.

Nevertheless, rank-and-file fears for their lives and suspicions of management policies spawned an even stronger adversarial relationship between labor and company officials. Consequently, when contract negotiations broke down in February, 1974, Textile Workers Locals 487 and 487-A struck. Ostensibly, the dispute centered upon management's rejection of union demands for a cost-of-living clause and formation of a Joint Labor-Management Committee to develop a health and safety program. However, as explained by an NLRB examiner, the controversy was actually rooted in fundamental differences between modern management and a new generation of workers. The situation was akin to those which had emerged repeatedly after the late nineteenth century:

Columbus Coated Fabrics started out as a small midwestern family-owned operation and developed into a large enterprise. In much of the company's history the ownership was also the management. There was close contact with the employees and the Company's attitude was both benevolent and paternal. Labor disputes have been at a minimum and were resolved within a framework of conciliation, adjustment and mutual understanding.

Presently the Company was sold and became part of a corporate conglomerate. The new management had a different business orientation and a different philosophy regarding labor relations. No real communication developed between the union and the management. Controversies

During the late 1970s, serious challenges by foreign competitors, escalating labor costs, and the deterioration of outmoded plants spurred renewed interest in robotics by American automobile manufacturers — once the world's envied leaders in advanced technology. While robot welders appeared on AMC's Jeep line at Toledo (left), General Motors utilized robot-teams equipped with special sensing probes to inspect tolerances on car bodies (above). Whether such accelerated efforts would enable the severely depressed industry to regain its former glory remained an open question in 1980.

Conditions on the notorious Vega assembly line at Lordstown generated thousands of unresolved worker-grievances during the early 1970s, as management insisted on churning out more than one car per minute — regardless of the human cost involved.

erupted and became emotional, resulting in a deep sense of frustration on each side. Consequently, the prospects increase that the present strike will be long and bitter before a settlement results.

The examiner's prediction proved accurate. A bomb exploded inside the plant in March, when the company threatened to move out machinery and close the Columbus facility. In addition to filing an unsuccessful "runaway shop" grievance with the NLRB, the union launched a boycott of all Borden products—an effort which ultimately failed due to complaints from employees in other Borden plants who feared resultant layoffs. The strike dragged on into the summer, when, as the union leadership had warned all along, the company announced plans to close the plant and move production to its facility in North Andover, Massachusetts. Perhaps prodded by that threat, both local unions ratified a compromise settlement by July 1. Nonetheless, frictions persisted into the next decade, over such issues as racial discrimination, the company's deactivation of the Joint Safety Committee, unresolved safety-related grievances, and—as alleged by one local activist — a general "degradation of production employees."

The activities of Cincinnati local 1495 of The Textile Workers Union of America, one of the

pioneers in occupational health, further illustrate the various difficulties encountered by unions in this area. The national union began its concern with safety when accident rates in textiles only leveled off during the 1950s, while those in other industries had declined. By 1963, local 1495 had formed a safety committee to investigate complaints of various hazards at the Stearns and Foster Company. Results of the study quickly spurred the union into active involvement in the occupational disease area. Initially mild concern with ammonium hydroxide fumes, for instance, escalated into distress upon the discovery that a noxious "smog" shrouded an entire department. Over a one-year period the committee lodged several grievances, only to be told by the company that such fumes were not a safety problem *per se*. The frustration of union representatives was evident in a statement issued during the fall of 1964, which noted that fans now blew the formerly localized smog from one building to another and made all workers ill: "We have been talking about this all last summer and here we are again. Can't something be done?" A year later, nothing had been done. In September, 1968, the local discussed the continuing problem of smoke and fumes in the plant, even after a visit by a state inspector. Similar complaints arose over glaze running on the floor and clogging drains in another department. The committee first complained about the safety and health hazard in late 1963, but by January, 1965, a frustrated committeeman wrote that the problem had still not been rectified: "Most of the time it's so slippery you can hardly stand. Not only that, but you must walk or wade through all this slop." Nor had corrective measures been taken nine months later, despite repeated demands by the union.

Meanwhile, the discovery that the Stearns and Foster plant contained high levels of cotton dust — which caused byssinosis or "brown lung" — provided yet another health issue around which rank-and-file Textile Workers rallied. The dread of brown lung and—as with the other safety grievances — the union's inability to protect their members triggered serious intraunion factionalism, slowdowns, and a 1968 wildcat. But still the problems went unresolved. An OSHA report of early 1972 advised that dust levels arising from mattress production in the plant were seventeen times higher than recommended levels. In September 1972 the local received the results of another government test on dust levels in the plant, which indicated that some local union members would have to be examined for brown lung disease. Four years later, the company's vice president for industrial relations complained of proposed new OSHA standards for cotton dust. The firm had previously argued successfully that the particular kind of dust generated by work with its mattresses did not fall under existing legislation. The new regulations, however, gave the company "considerable cause for alarm." According to the vice-president, the firm had already spent $675,000 in OSHA-related expenses and another $115,000 to comply with Environmental Protection Agency regulations. Further costs for controlling cotton dust would "obviously have an impact on the future operations of the company, including such things as work practices" he hinted darkly. Obviously, health and safety would be a long-running issue, without easy resolution.

As in the past, machinists continued to work in a broad range of industries and at a variety of skill levels. Throughout the post World War II era, management refined its efforts to gain control of the handicraft skills machinists often developed over a working lifetime. Some sense of the tension between machinists and managers is evident in the following excerpt from a grievance filed at a Toledo machine shop in 1951. Referring to a proposed time study plan on which a new incentive program would be based, the union noted:

1. The men feel that they are journeymen, not piece or production workers.

2. The pressure of the extremely close timing are not inductive of accurate or quality workmanship.

3. The mental stress and strain, also, dissension caused by stop watch timing, is an unhealthy and unproductive condition for both employees and employer. We feel that an equitable bonus can be installed without the use of a stop watch.

By the 1960s and 1970s a new stage in this lengthy battle over skills emerged—the numerical control of machine tools. Regarded by some authorities as the "most significant new development in manufacturing technology since Henry Ford introduced the concept of the moving assembly line," numerical control meshed engineering job-design techniques with computer technology to fundamentally alter the machinists' craft in numerous factories.

In the steel industry, too, working conditions have changed dramatically in the years since World War II. With the exception of the era from 1890 to the First World War, perhaps no other period has seen such a dramatic alteration in the working environment of steelworkers. Between 1940 and 1959, the capacity of Ohio steel mills increased by sixty-eight percent,

Occupational health was not a new issue, but in the decades after World War II it assumed a new and significant role among workers' concerns. The Ohio Environmental Council outlined the breadth of the problem:

Most toxic substances have their origin in the workplaces of America. The factories, farms and mines are generally responsible for the entrace of a substantial portion of toxics into the environment. Indeed, occupational exposure is generally believed to be one of the most serious of any environmental exposures to toxic substances.

Workers are exposed to substances contacting their skin and contaminating their clothing. These same clothes, if worn home, can become a source of contamination to the entire family.

The air in many American workplaces contains varying concentrations of many dusts, gases, vapors, fumes, and mists to which many workers are exposed.

From workplaces, discharge of toxics into the air, water, and disposal sites translates an occupational health problem into an environmental, community health problem.

Workers are on the front lines of exposure and for this reason, action taken to reduce human exposure to toxic substances must begin in the workplaces of America. Through the concerted efforts of labor unions, business interests and government regulatory agencies such as OSHA and NIOSH (National Institute for Occupational Safety and Health), an effective fight can be launched to clean up the environment and reduce environmentally related diseases in our society.

In March, 1980, local IAM and UAW members jointly struck Columbus Auto Parts.

Even as robots, numerical control, and computers spread through the world of work, highly skilled machinists remained crucial at certain stages of production in many plants. Attuned to the nuances of fine-tolerance metal working, this man shaped part of a machine tool at Warner and Swasey in New Philadelphia.

243

A

B

Not all workers in the Age of Affluence moved to the suburbs. "Irish Town" and other housing in the Cleveland Flats during the late 1940s looked much as it had a generation earlier (A & B). Twenty years later, in 1967, Cleveland's slum-housing reflected the lost grandeur of bygone wealth (C). A certain sameness was apparent, too, in the housing of workers adjacent to steel mills in Cleveland (D) and Youngstown (E).

C

D

E

A

from over seventeen thousand net tons to nearly twenty-nine thousand net tons. During the same period, however, the number of plants operating in Ohio declined from twenty-one to twenty, and the state's share of total capacity in the country dropped slightly from 21.2 to 19.6 percent. Meanwhile, the number of production workers nationwide climbed only ten percent while that of administrative, professional, and clerical workers in the industry leaped by eighty percent. In Ohio production workers dropped by twenty-three percent and non-production workers rose twenty-two percent. Between 1940 and 1958, output per wage earner rose by roughly fifty percent. Prior to 1947, the steelworkers had secured a clause in their contracts which protected local work practices. But throughout the years after 1947, the major steel firms pressed to regain control. Arguing the need for productivity increases, management turned to technological modifications, pointed to the dangers of foreign competition, and urged intervention by the federal government.

In 1959, half-a-million steelworkers—61,000 of whom worked in Ohio—staged one of the industry's longest and most difficult strikes, affecting eighty-five percent of national steel production. Proposed work-rules changes were the major issue. This walkout differed significantly from strikes of the 1930s. Old adversarial relations had softened and, in Niles and Warren at least, one company even furnished materials for strikers' picketline shanties. By August, however, the hardship of the long strike was evident, and by November whole families were showing up at the special union kitchen set up to feed pickets. In other parts of Ohio District 26, similar hardship prevailed. The strike finally drew to a close after 110 days, with President McDonald negotiating a contract which included substantial wage and fringe benefit increases. While the majority of the national membership voted to accept the settlement, District 26 had the distinction of rejecting the companies' final offer by the highest percentage of any district in the country. According to one local union president, nearly ninety-seven percent of those voting turned it down.

As the strike neared an end, *New York Times* labor reporter A.H. Raskin detailed the tugs and pulls operating on steelworkers. "In the steel towns the pinch of financial distress is beginning to be acute, despite the millions of dollars in the union treasury and the additional millions made available to it by sister unions." Raskin also noted the crucial point that kept unionists out: "The one issue on which they remain firm is their resistance to giving their employers an uncurbed right to cut work crews or make other shifts in work practices in the interest of greater efficiency. The willingness of the companies to submit the question to arbitration has brought little evident lessening of workers' apprehension over any 'backward step' on this highly emotional issue."

Under David McDonald's leadership, the union subsequently negotiated a series of contracts regarded as innovative by some observers. Concessions on productivity issues, however, did not allay rank and filers. In 1965, they turned to I. W. Abel in hopes of exerting more influence on the direction of bargaining. But Abel continued in the path of McDonald, pledging further productivity in 1971 and in 1973, agreeing to bar industry-wide strikes, and endorsing binding arbitration of grievances.

In the immediate postwar period, the future of the steel industry had not seemed grim. One cause of the industry's basic optimism was U.S. Steel's continuous seamless pipe mill in the Lorain (Ohio) Works of the National Tube Division. Number 4 Seamless Mill represented a dramatic step forward in steel technology and, for the twenty-seven men involved, a dramatic change in their work. Social scientist Charles Walker observed the three crews closely and reported on how their working lives were molded by the machines so closely integrated into the new mill. Although not a fully automatic factory, the seamless mill represented a step in that direction. Walker noted:

The semi-automatic character of the work environment is . . . apparent. It is quite unlike the old mills where physical labor and manual control of tool and product prevailed. The top men, man-

B

C

D

E

drel mill operator and the sizer-reducer, are partly technicians, partly coordinators of operations. The furnace discharger has a characteristically mixed job, half of it consisting in watching truly automatic equipment, the charger, the other half in manually operating the levers and buttons of the discharger. The complex system of conveyors and moving tables which take the product through its complete work-flow cycle is wholly automatic, characterized by electric eyes, timing devices, limit switches, rotary controls, and so forth. Jobs like the bar inserter's and the strippers are wholly automatic performed by machinery without the operators lifting a hand. But they must 'watch' and, if anything goes wrong, intervene with manual correction. In the long road toward the wholly automatic factory there will be many jobs like these. . . .

Under the new system, three nine-man teams produced four times as much as twenty twenty-five man teams did in old seamless mills. Increased productivity was only one aspect of the job that changed. To the men involved, the altered job content was most noticeable. Most found the job less demanding physically, but more of a burden mentally. After a period of adjustment, most said they preferred the new mechanisms. Still, there were problems. Because the new layout took considerably more space, the men were more distant from one another, a fact which altered social relations within the plant. "In Number 1 we used to have a lot of fun — those on the furnace, anyhow," one man complained. "Over here in Number 4 there is too much tension. It was more like a home atmosphere in the old mills. You work

alone in Number 4. It is against the rules for anybody to talk to me while I'm operating. On Number 1 there was a group of us on the furnace. We got to know each other good." In terms of working conditions, other aspects of the jobs were more satisfactory. Safety provisions were improved, lighting better, and fewer crew members were exposed to intense heat and dirt. "It's like living in a small, dark bedroom for years and then going into a nice big light bedroom," one worker explained. "You would never want to go back to the old hole." Changes in the work process, however, did produce considerably more smoke in the plant and that emerged as a principal grievance within a short time. Over time the men became accustomed to the nature of the machinery and learned how to control it more precisely. As production stepped up, indeed, some workers learned that the automatic speed controls were an hindrance. "The engineers designed that mill to run automatic," one man explained. "When we go above that speed, the equipment prevents us from going any faster, because there are automatic kickoffs. So we have to throw it on manual if we want to reach really high speed. . . ." Other jobs, however, had not been fully automated and for these workers as production increased so did the work load.

By the 1960s and 1970s, the steel industry was plagued by technological obsolescence, foreign competition, and plant closings. Despite persistent rank-and-file discontent, company pressures for productivity steadily reduced the size of the steel workforce. Technological in-

Since their 1973 contracts had contained no cost-of-living clauses, the wage rates of URW members slipped downward relative to other industrial workers. In an attempt to achieve equity, especially with auto workers, the URW in 1976 launched a massive strike involving nearly 70,000 workers against Firestone, Goodyear, Goodrich, and Uniroyal. Coming within a month after a nationwide Teamsters' strike had achieved wage and benefit increases worth approximately thirty percent over three years, the URW action caused grave concern among inflation-watchers. Sporadic violence testified to the intensity of feelings. After 141 days — the industry's longest walkout — the URW won increases of about thirty-six percent over three years plus an unlimited cost-of-living clause.

novation had originally been the cause, but by the Vietnam Era plant closings explained the greatest proportion of job losses in the industry.

Much the same pattern unfolded in the rubber industry. Technological developments lowered production employment by twenty-nine percent between 1947 and 1961. As long as automobiles sold well, however, the domestic companies had little difficulty. But in the wake of the 1973 oil embargo, the spreading use of long-wearing radial tires, and a decline in U.S. auto sales, crisis soon washed over the industry. The United Rubber Workers, which saw its membership plummet eighteen percent between World War II and the early 'sixties, held firm for

established practices and in a mammoth 1976 strike which lasted 141 days actually won additional concessions. As it turned out, the strike accelerated the exodus of rubber companies from Akron. Within the space of a few years, Firestone, Goodyear, and Goodrich had all ceased manufacturing operations, idling nearly 30,000 workers.

Negotiations at General Tire in 1978 and 1979 pointed to the path that more and more negotiations would follow. In return for promises that the company would build a new facility in Akron, the union agreed to alter time-honored seniority provisions in the contract and allow the company to change work rules and job clas-

In 1973, the URW sought substantial pay increases from the major rubber companies, all of which had enjoyed record profits the previous year. Goodyear settled without a strike, granting a sixteen percent raise over three years and a ''thirty-and-out'' retirement clause. However, at Firestone and B.F. Goodrich (right) workers had to walk out before they secured wage increases and improved fringe benefits.

sifications as well. Workers would accept a wage reduction and a new wage curve designed to increase productivity. Despite such concessions, General Tire would find it impossible to resist the lure of the Sunbelt and the pressures of inflation, high interest rates, and the auto recession; it, too, began to phase out its operations. By October, 1980, General Tire's sixty-five-year-old truck tire plant was the only tire-making facility still operating in the city.

Despite changes in the law, political climate, and the economy, organizing the unorganized remained a difficult job. Charles H. Brush, then a business agent for the Bakery and Confectonary Workers Union, Local 57, Columbus, described one campaign in 1949-50:

. . . we worked long hours in organizing, and a lot of it was done in the evenings; we used the grass roots methods of organizing. Working in the bakery so long myself . . . I did know some people in all the bakeries. And we would go to their homes, after their work was over, whatever time it would be, bakery work was all kinds of crazy hours. Some would be late in the evening, some would be in the mornings before they even went to work. We'd go to their homes and talk to them, tell them the advantage of unionisn, and we would get an authorization card signed by them and, of course, while we were there we would pick up names of their co-workers . . . as many as we could, where they lived, and we would also go to their homes. One bakery in particular, the Felber Biscuit Company . . . in Columbus, they had approximately 300 employees, and it was a long drawn out job . . . but we were able to find some who were enthusiastic enough . . . that they would help us, would take some of the cards and get them signed for us. At that time the National Labor Relations Board has two elections; after you got 30% of the employees signed up you could apply for a recognition election but . . . we figured that we should have at least 65% signed up in order to win . . . . After the recognition election . . . then they had an election for a union shop . . . Now, at the Felber Biscuit Company we won the recognition and they had to recognize us as a bargaining agent for the employees, but we lost the union shop election. The results were that only those that wanted to belong to the union joined, and those that didn't care, they didn't have to join, pay dues, and we had to wait a full year before we could hold an election . . . . Well, when that happens, then you've just got to live with the people for a whole year because you possibly have maybe half of them that are dues paying members, and the other half are not. So . . . a year later we applied again, and we won it . . . overwhelmingly, because we had done a job for the people during that period of time, had constant contact. So, it was a grass roots method that we did use in the organizing efforts . . . Organizing is the lifeblood of any union . . . .

Although the major rubber firms would retain Akron as their corporate headquarters, the city's glory days as the world's ''tire capitol'' were gone.

Between 1945 and 1980, then, work worlds altered in fundamental ways. Evident especially in manufacturing, the application of technological refinements continued the long process of increasing the productivity of a declining portion of the workforce. By the 1960s, automation accelerated remarkably, followed in the 'seventies by robotics. Gradually, too, the application of computer and other technologies spread into other areas of the economy, reshaping the skills required of employees and reinforcing the tendency for more and more workers to toil in the production of services — everything from providing information to servicing coin-operated dispensing machines. The shift would have profound implications for the state's labor unions.

World War II completed the organization of the mass-production industries begun during the 1930s. Within two years the labor movement had reached what turned out to be the apex of its strength. In 1945, organized labor counted fully thirty-six percent of nonagricultural workers as members. Over the next three decades, that proportion gradually declined. By 1978, despite dramatic increases in the numbers of unionists and the expansion of trade unionism into government and white-collar sectors of the economy, only twenty-four percent of the nonagricultural workforce was unionized. When all workers are included, the decline was even more dramatic— from twenty-seven percent in 1958, to twenty-five percent in 1968, and twenty-one percent in 1978. Within Ohio the proportion of the nonagricultural workforce which was unionized remained higher than the national average, but here too the decline was painfully evident. Between 1970 and 1978, Ohio union membership fell by over nine percent. In 1970, 36.4 percent of nonagricultural workers had been organized. Eight years later only 29.5 percent were in unions (see Table 5-K). All Midwestern industrial states witnessed a weakening of union strength during this period, yet none matched Ohio's decline. In fact, it was the sharpest drop in the nation for a major industrial state. Reasons for organized labor's subsidence are numerous, some stemming from factors within the union movement itself, and others relating to the context within which the movement has operated since the Second World War.

Political factionalism within unions has always existed, but seldom has it proved so devastating as it did in the years after 1945, when anti-Communist hysteria ripped apart a number of unions. During the war itself, the issue of Communism had been muted because of the fact that Russia and the United States were allies against Germany and because the American Communist Party supported President Franklin D. Roosevelt's policies. After the war, relations between the U.S. and the Soviet Union soured, and by the late 1940s the presence of Communists or apparent Communists in the labor movement—especially the CIO—was viewed as a political liability. Evidence of the tension within the Ohio CIO units surfaced by 1946 and showed up initially in the Industrial Union Councils of several cities. The IUCs were directly affiliated with the national CIO office and as friction between left and right-wing factions intensified, the national office moved to contain the battle. In Portsmouth, for example, the purportedly left-wing Shoe Workers Union dominated the IUC, much to the displeasure of members of the Steelworkers Union. After several steel locals threatened to withdraw from the Council altogether, the CIO sent regional director Robert J. Davidson to investigate the situation. His report made no mention of specific activities by alleged Communists, but did point to the effects of controversy within the Council. A coordinated Political Action Committee program, he noted, had not been developed and because of the factionalism, organizational efforts among non-unionized workers in the Portsmouth vicinity had been totally neglected. Davidson's recommendations reflected CIO policy during the early stages of the unfolding conflict:

. . . IT IS VITALLY IMPORTANT in the interest of the entire CIO in Portsmouth and surrounding territory that their [sic] be no further contention or conflict. . . . It is absolutely not permissible to have any group of CIO Locals operating in a capacity dual to that of the Council. The authority of the Portsmouth Council should be recognized by all CIO Locals in the city and they should undertake to cooperate fully with its officials in order to advance the interests of the CIO in this area.

One of the contributing causes of bickering and friction within the Council has been a tendency on the part of certain delegates to bring controversial issues to the floor on which the CIO has not declared its position, and which are remote from the interest of the workers in the Portsmouth area. Our Councils are a forum for a free discussion of all issues with which they may choose to concern themselves consistent with CIO policy, and no rules could or should be laid down which attempt to prescribe what subjects could be discussed by Councils and what ones could not.

the Ohio AFL-CIO is...

a voluntary federation of Local Unions and Central Labor Councils representing the working men and women of Ohio. Like our parent body — National AFL-CIO — the Ohio AFL-CIO primarily serves as a legislative voice for the Local Unions and individual members we are privileged to represent.

While workers have long had rights to join Unions, those "rights" were virtually meaningless until governments granted Unions collective bargaining rights. Today, our Unions are still controlled by governments, and our effectiveness can be limited by government edicts. The wages, job security, and everyday lives of Union members are even affected by actions of governments. Therefore, the Ohio AFL-CIO must stand a constant vigil to protect and improve governments that confront us.

Since its formation in 1958, the Ohio AFL-CIO has been extremely active in pursuit of this goal. Anti-Union "right-to-work" (for less) zealots were turned back in Ohio in 1958, and the 1960s were spent protecting workers' rights during a series of hostile sessions of the General Assembly. The decade of the 1970s has been devoted to improving and advancing government assistance to workers thru fairer taxation; higher unemployment insurance for laid-off workers; better Workers' Compensation benefits for injured workers and their families; protection of family budgets in the marketplace; and a fair energy policy to protect jobs while providing essential utility services at the most reasonable costs.

Every Local Union knows that to be effective today requires the support of the greatest number of eligible workers at its place of jurisdiction. The "Union of Unions" in Ohio — the Ohio AFL-CIO — must likewise have the support of the greatest number of Local Unions in Ohio to do the best job possible representing all working people.

With strong support from all Local Unions, the following Ohio AFL-CIO services can become better:

LEGISLATIVE SERVICES
All Officers and Staff personnel of the Ohio AFL-CIO lobby in the General Assembly in behalf of legislation affecting workers. Face-to-face meetings are held with State Senators and Representatives to inform them of Labor's position on issues, and formal testimony is presented at various Committee hearings. Legislative policy is formulated at biennial Ohio AFL-CIO Conventions when rank-and-file delegates act upon Resolutions. This policy is then implemented by the Ohio AFL-CIO through its lobbying at the Legislature.

COPE
The key to effectiveness in the Ohio General Assembly is Labor's work supporting political candidates who sympathize with problems of working families — and opposing politicians who would pass legislation to harm workers. The Ohio AFL-CIO's Committee On Political Education (COPE) is recognized as one of the most effective units in the entire nation. Our voter registration and get-out-the-vote campaigns have become models for all other state AFL-CIO's to follow. Our computerized data processing system has assisted local Central Labor Councils to more effectively communicate with Union members, and to translate endorsements of political candidates into meaningful victories.

PUBLIC RELATIONS
The Ohio AFL-CIO publishes a monthly magazine (focus) and a weekly newsletter (News and Views). focus has won national labor journalism awards nearly every year since it was conceived in 1968. It is delivered to the homes of more than 800,000 Trade Unionists in Ohio. News and Views comments on legislative activities and other Union matters of interest to Local Union officers. Both publications are circulated to all Ohio daily and weekly newspapers, radio and TV stations and all labor publications in the state. News Releases explaining the Ohio AFL-CIO's position on various topics are released as warranted. And pamphlets, reports and special brochures are prepared for conferences and seminars.

COMPENSATION
The Ohio AFL-CIO assists Local Unions in representing their members in handling and processing of claims for unemployment insurance and workers' compensation. It also conducts annual weekly Institutes for training Local Union members in the handling of such claims. The Ohio AFL-CIO publishes an annual textbook explaining latest changes in the Workers' Compensation law and a Work Comp "Facts" handbook. Besides the statewide training Institute, many local seminars are conducted where Local Union members receive training on compensation laws. The Ohio AFL-CIO's activities in compensation, bolstered by its constant lobbying in the General Assembly, have helped make Ohio's compensation law and benefit levels the best in the nation.

COMMUNITY SERVICES
In many cases, the problems Union members experience off the job are just as difficult as the ones encountered on the Job. Therefore, the Ohio AFL-CIO supports a Community Services program where Local Union representatives are trained to work with the many voluntary health, welfare, recreation or family agencies that help people in need. A biennial Community Services Institute is conducted to train more Union representatives in this field, and considerable effort is made to place full-time Labor representatives on staffs of various community agencies to assure that the voice of working people is heard.

CIVIL RIGHTS
The Ohio AFL-CIO has long been a champion of civil rights for all people. Over the years, the Ohio AFL-CIO has played a major roll in efforts to eliminate racial prejudice and discrimination. We have accomplished this task with cooperation of the NAACP, National AFL-CIO Civil Rights Dept., Ohio Civil Rights Commission, and the A. Philip Randolph Institute. A statewide conference is held biennially to execute policy in this field. In recent years, sexual discrimination has become a major issue, and the Ohio AFL-CIO again is working to assure that women workers have the same rights as men workers. We have established several local committees to deal with "women's issues," and conduct a special Women's Conference biennially to discuss these issues and adopt policy that will be in the best interest of our women members.

ohio afl-cio

On the other hand it is of vital importance to the entire CIO that a working harmony be restored in the Portsmouth Council, and it is my earnest advice to all delegates to the Council that they concentrate their time and attention on matters directly related to the interest of CIO members in Portsmouth and vicinity and that they refrain from stirring up issues which are secondary or of slight importance to the Trade Union movement, and which may have the effect of creating hard feelings.

In Cleveland the left-right factional squabble became so bitter that the CIO sent George De-Nucci, the CIO regional director for central Ohio, to mediate their disputes. When that proved impossible, DeNucci took over the IUC

As detailed in this flyer, the Ohio AFL-CIO had implemented wide-ranging political and educational programs to promote the diverse interests of its members by the late 1970s.

as administrator for the national office in the fall of 1946. The split in Cleveland dated, as it had in Portsmouth, from 1944, when the Cleveland IUC endorsed Arnold Johnston — the head of the Ohio Communist Party—as an independent candidate for the local school board. When Amalgamated Clothing Worker and Steelworker locals threatened to resign from the Council, the endorsement was reversed. In 1946 a similar issue arose and nearly half of the membership threatened to withdraw. It was at that point that DeNucci arrived. As national columnist Marquis Childs commented:

> But, politically speaking, the damage has already been done. The public quarrel has supplied the Republicans with effective documentation for the cry of communism. In the past that cry has sounded pretty hollow. Now, however, faithfully reported from day to day, is the story of an intrigue, dominated by Communists and fellow travelers, to dictate the policy of one of the chief labor organizations in the state. The Republicans are using this handy campaign ammunition to the utmost.

By 1948, the controversy had become more heated, not only in Portsmouth and Cleveland, but in numerous union strongholds across the state as well. A key point of contention was the presidential candidacy of Henry Wallace, a former vice-president during Roosevelt's third administration. Wallace had been nominated by the newly-formed Progressive Party and campaigned on a platform which called for the continuation of New Deal reforms, enforcement of free-speech rights for political dissidents, and an end to heightening tensions with the Soviet Union. Within the highly-charged atmosphere of Cold War America, however, these liberal proposals were not politically popular — especially since Wallace received the ill-fated endorsement of the Communist Party. The third-party candidate consequently fell victim to

guilt-by-association, with both himself and his supporters branded as communist sympathizers. At a political rally in Cleveland, for example, Wallace was greeted with eggs, tomatoes, and obscenities from a hostile mob. For CIO leaders — most of whom supported the re-election of President Truman, because of his and the Democratic Party's opposition to the Taft-Hartley Act—the election became a litmus test of loyalty. From national headquarters to local union halls, cleavages widened between Wallace-supporters opposed to the accelerating Cold War, and unionists convinced that such activists were actually tools of an international Communist conspiracy. Though Wallace was soundly defeated, conservative CIO officials marked his backers within the organization as disloyal to the union cause, as possible traitors to their country, and, therefore, as targets for disciplinary action.

Using the Wallace campaign and alleged communist-domination as justification, the 1949 CIO convention expelled four "left-wing" unions and leveled charges against ten others, most of which were also purged within the next two years. The United Public Workers; United Office and Professional Workers; the Food, Tobacco, Agricultural and Allied Workers; and the International Union of Mine, Mill and Smelter Workers were the first to go. Then followed the West Coast Longshoremen, Marine Cooks, Communications Association, Fishermen, Fur and Leather Workers, United Electrical Workers, Transport Workers Union, and Farm Equipment Workers. By thus succumbing to the anti-communist hysteria which was sweeping the nation—and, in some cases, manipulating the issue to rid the organization of inveterate policital opponents—CIO leaders incurred the loss of nearly a million purged members.

A bitter strike in 1949 at the Selby Shoe Company, Portsmouth's major employer, brought together several features of the postwar situa-

In the winter of 1955-1956, the IUE confronted Westinghouse in a strike which lasted six months. Pickets from Locals 724 and 760 at the firm's Lima facility blocked entrances to prevent cars from entering the plant.

tion. The United Shoe Workers, who represented the employees, had previously been accused of left-leaning tendencies and of dominating the local industrial union council. The company president pleaded, over the radio, that economic realities precluded the wage and cost-of-living increases demanded by the union. More important, given the rising concern about Communist infiltration, were company accusations about left-wing relationships among the local union leaders. Leaders, they charged, had refused to sign the non-Communist affidavits required under the Taft-Hartley Act of 1947. As the strike lengthened into the summer, the company stepped up its attacks, effectively using radio broadcasts every other day. The union also took to the air, and to complicate matters further, the AFL Boot and Shoe Workers Union entered the fray with charges of Communism directed against the CIO affiliate. The AFL union, moreover, contested representation rights and this halted negotiations in mid-July. Despite further AFL accusations of Communism, the United Shoe Workers won a decisive victory in the representation election—the third such confrontation between the two groups since 1937.

Considerable conflict over the Communist issue also occurred during the 1948 Univis Lens strike in Dayton. Led by United Electrical Workers Local 768, workers struck in late April when their first contract, negotiated in June 1947 after a heated confrontation with the firm and its company-sponsored union, expired. Between May 5 and August 2, pickets numbering from ten to as many as two thousand gathered before plant entrances despite an injunction. Serious violence erupted on several occasions, especially after the company initiated a back-to-work movement in late June. In the midst of this, a group of employees filed for a decertification election. The UE narrowly lost the July 23 election to "no union." The company refused to negotiate with the local, too, because its officials had refused to sign the Taft-Hartley non-Communist affidavit. Its strategy shaped by a number of UE International union representatives, the local countered that employees had been intimidated and that the results represented collusion between Univis Lens and the National Labor Relations Board. As these accusations were being investigated, picketing continued. Now Univis Lens strikers were joined by sympathizers from other plants. When the plant reopened on July 27, violence erupted and the Montgomery County Industrial Union Council threatened a general strike, despite pleas by city officials. Governor Thomas J. Herbert and Mayor Louis Lohrey both tried to mediate the conflict, but the membership refused to ratify the resulting agreement on August 1. Fearing renewed violence, Herbert sent in three thousand troops, tanks, and an armored troop carrier. This effectively weakened picketers' efforts to continue blocking the resumption of work. At this juncture, Michigan Congressman Clare E. Hoffman began hearings on the strike in Dayton and Washington, pulling

Repeated confrontations with strikebreakers led to the arrest of a number of UE pickets.

Police protect workers entering the Univis Lens plant in Dayton during the turbulent 1948 UE strike.

key UE local leaders and international representatives away from the scene. Although his findings were not reported to the House Committee on Education and Labor until December, the approach evident in the final report was manifest during the hearings. Hoffman believed that "the methods and the procedure followed in some labor disputes, strikes, and picketing, since the introduction of the sit-down technique in Michigan in 1937, run parallel to those employed by the Communists in inciting rioting, creating civil strife in connection with their propaganda, and efforts to further the interests of their party in other countries." Since UE officials refused to sign the non-Communist affidavit and since they figured importantly in the Univis Lens strike, it followed that the strike posed a Communist threat. (The same logic had been evident in a May 1948 UE strike at the Hoover Company in Canton.) The presence of troops in Dayton, meanwhile, sapped the strength of the strikers. The back-to-work movement gained daily and on August 10 em-

UE representatives huddle during talks with Governor Herbert on July 31, 1948.

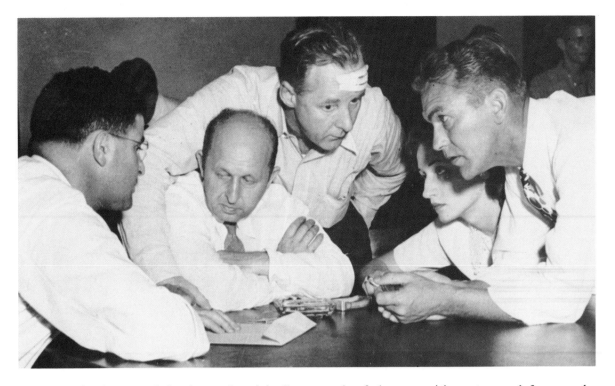

ployees gained some of the demands originally advanced. The ninety-day old Univis Lens strike was over and UE Local 768 had lost its representation rights.

The Univis Lens strike reflected long-standing factionalism in the UE between the left and right wings. In addition, external opponents of Communism had for some time made the UE a focal point of their investigations. The House Un-American Activities Committee, for example, began to probe UE in mid-1947 while the national CIO leadership was also moving toward a harsher stand on left-wing unions. Despite his opposition in principle to the non-Communist oath, for instance, CIO President Phillip Murray advocated signing it by the fall of 1947. When UE officers Julius Emspack and Albert Fitzgerald formally supported Henry Wallace and resigned from the CIO's Political Action Committee because of its opposition to third party activities in 1948, this cemented official CIO disapproval of the UE. Although

much of the opposition stemmed from rank-and-file actions in different communities, James Carey, then CIO secretary, served as a rallying point for UE insurgents. Carey and other opponents of the left-wing became bolder after Truman won reelection in 1948, proclaiming flatly that "labor did it." Left-wing unions which had backed Wallace became further discredited at the 1948 CIO convention when Murray, by now firmly allied with the Democratic Party, openly attacked opposition to Truman and the Marshall Plan. He did not single out the large UE, but the direction was obvious. By 1949 events moved rapidly, climaxing in November when UE and three other unions were expelled and the CIO chartered a new organization, the International Union of Electrical Workers. The UE convention that September in Cleveland merely provided evidence of the intensity of the left-right split within the union and suggested the coming CIO actions. Following the UE convention, opponents in the left-wing began to

After National Guard troops arrived in August, the strike was lost. The Guard dispersed pickets with tear gas (below) and assured free access to the plant for employees who sought to return to work (right).

Teamster strikes often involved violence. Coal haulers in Somerset turned to state police for protection during the 1950 dispute (left). In 1970 a wildcat strike erupted among owner-haulers dissatisfied with the terms of the National Master Freight Agreement. Ohio strikers (below) held out longer than most, ultimately prompting Governor James A. Rhodes to call out the National Guard. When the strike ended, the same guardsmen were sent to Kent State University to handle student demonstrations against the invasion of Cambodia.

work for secession while the UE administration began to withhold per capita payments to the CIO.

Whether in membership or prestige, the total cost of the Communist controversy to the labor movement is difficult to measure precisely. While nearly one million members were expelled from the CIO, for example, the majority probably remained in the movement by joining "acceptable" unions. However, by focusing the attention of the combatants on this issue, internal struggles detracted from the time available for organizing drives. Furthermore, because the conflict unfolded during the early stages of the Cold War, the association of unionism with Communism provided many employers with potent ammunition to thwart union growth.

Political factionalism involving the issue of Communist influence was largely restricted to the state's CIO unions during the late-1940s. But contests for office and disagreements over policy issues within unions persisted throughout the era, thus further contributing to organized labor's gradual decline. Constant involvement in factional disputes and rivalries inevitably distracted attention from organizing the unorganized and, in some instances, from adequately servicing members. The severity of such disputes varied from union to union, yet existed in nearly all. The most notable battles took place within the UE, as already noted, but most unions in the state experienced internal conflicts of one sort or another.

Within the Teamsters, a union whose growth was not hurt by factional squabbles, one of the most interesting conflicts involved locals in Cincinnati. James Luken, a former milk driver who became president of his own local and then of the powerful Cincinnati Joint Council, resisted the centralizing tendencies of both International president Jimmy Hoffa and William Presser, head of the Ohio Teamsters Joint Council. In 1961, to the surprise of many, Luken withdrew his locals from the International and went independent. Luken had opposed former Team-

ster's president, Dave Beck and was equally vocal in opposition to Hoffa. His support of John Kennedy in 1960, at a time when his brother Robert was investigating the Teamsters, did nothing to ease tensions between Luken and Hoffa. In several unions the factionalism involved heated battles for the national union presidency. Such was the case in the Steelworkers and the Mine Workers. During the postwar era, the most important of these struggles for Ohio workers involved the mid-1960s contest between David McDonald of the Steelworkers and I. W. Abel of Ohio for the union presidency.

Inter-union factionalism, which also played a role in limiting the growth of the labor movement after World War II, affected both AFL and CIO unions, especially in the first decade of the period. Both labor bodies, for example, fielded unions in the same industries and direct competition for workers increased the cost of organizing. Jurisdictional squabbles figured as well. Although notions of exclusive jurisdiction still persisted within the labor movement, in practice the concept was breaking down as

While unions emerged from the war more acceptable to many employers, deep-seated opposition persisted and sometimes posed a distinct threat to the jobs of workers interested in starting a local union. One activist reported just such a situation to the secretary of the Newark Federation of Labor in December, 1947:

Two weeks ago I was going to get in touch with you concerning Union and Fibreglass [sic]. Right now it sounds a little funny speaking of the two in the same breath.

Still . . . I'd like you to try once again to have a voting at Fibreglass pro or con union. Of late I've been conversing with various men in and around the plant and most of them want the A.F. of L. Of course there are some who will vote non-union . . . . If by any chance you want a group of names claiming to be for the union I will try to give you as many as possible.

It is impossible for me to come to your office as I have been 'notified' my job would become [in]valid were I caught trying to incite unionism in the plant.

I'm willing to chance it if you advise possibilities.

Pickets jumped rope outside the B.F. Goodrich plant in Akron in 1952, a year of considerable unrest among workers. A company attempt to decertify the URW among office workers triggered a plant-wide shutdown in protest.

more and more unions broadened their structures and became conglomerates with a mixed membership, neither wholly craft nor industrial in nature. In the late 'forties, for example, the Carpenters found themselves competing with Iron Workers, Machinists, and several other craft unions. The ouster from the CIO of unions accused of being Communist-dominated heightened such competition, the case of the two unions in the electrical field being but one example. The UAW also aggressively invaded UE preserves, went after Mine, Mill and Smelter Worker locals in several cities such as Cleveland, and tackled the Farm Equipment Workers. The Steelworkers confronted the MMSW as well, foreshadowing the eventual merger of the two unions. The refusal of a number of left-wing unions to sign the Taft-Hartley anti-Communist affidavit provided a convenient wedge for these ventures because the NLRB would not honor representation rights in such cases. The tendency was opportunistic as much as political, however, and pointed toward the emergence by the 1970s of more and more conglomerate unions. The increasing cost of organizing workers, the anti-labor environment, and the shrinking size of the labor movement forced increasing numbers of mergers as time passed.

A lengthy strike by the CIO's Mine, Mill and Smelter Workers in 1948-49 suggested the complex nature of factionalism within the labor movement. When Local 536 struck the American Zinc Oxide plant in Columbus in mid-August, 1948, the left wing within the CIO was already under attack. The refusal of Mine and Mill leaders to sign the anti-Communist affidavit provided an opening for the rival AFL Chemical Workers Union. Though the Mine and Mill union had won an earlier representation election, the Chemical Workers seized on the company's refusal to bargain with its rival. As tension mounted on the picket line, the AFL union gradually built strength, and won a wage agreement with the company. In mid-December

Even as the Teamsters' Union surpassed a record 2.5 million members, making it the largest union in the country, dissent spread within its ranks. The Professional Drivers' Council and the Teamsters for a Democratic Union, formed in 1977, charged national leaders with corruption and anti-democratic practices, campaigned for election of business agents and stewards, improved grievance handling, rank-and-file control of pension funds, and elimination of multiple salaries. By the time the two groups, now merged, held their 1980 convention in Cleveland, little progress had been made toward those goals.

the firm recognized the Chemical Workers as the bargaining agent and discharged all striking members of the Mine and Mill union. Repeated clashes increased after the turn of the year when the plant reopened. Gradually, the CIO's support of the Mine and Mill union dwindled, and by April, 1949, the strike had been lost.

The merger in 1955 of the American Federation of Labor and the Congress of Industrial Organizations, regarded by many labor leaders as a kind of panacea which would solve the difficulties of a beleaguered labor movement, did not end factional disputes, jurisdictional battles, or political disagreements. Despite the compelling pressures to combine, in fact, two decades of rivalry, intense personality clashes, and mutual suspicion slowed the process of merger at the state level and thus compounded the problems organized labor had in coping with issues of common concern. That weakness would leave labor vulnerable. In the Buckeye state formal unification of the AFL and CIO did not occur until 1958. Disagreements over officers of the new state organizations, as well as the issue of jurisdiction, proved difficult stumbling blocks. Building and construction trade unions resisted, too, because of past raiding battles. As one observer put it: "Little empires and dynasties are beginning to tremble and sooner or later must surely come down." As of 1958 the AFL had a paid-up membership in the state of 223,339, the largest unions being the Teamsters with 29,458, the Carpenters with 16,586, Hod Carriers with 15,295, Hotel and Restaurant Workers with 14,787, and the Machinists with 13,087. The CIO, by contrast, had a paid up membership of 498,933. The largest unions were the Auto Workers with 160,343, Steelworkers with 156,192, Rubber Workers with 53,028, Electrical, Radio & Machine Workers with 51,352, and Communications Workers with 13,811. Finally, on

May 7, 1958, the new orgnization met. The last session of the AFL state organizations was marred by two fisticuff battles between opponents and proponents of merger. Local level mergers took a bit longer to put together, but eventually they too had been completed.

A delimiting factor of a different sort was racism. For a time at least, discriminatory practices probably limited the size of some unions, especially in the building trades, by denying qualified blacks equal access to available jobs in the skilled crafts. Some sense of the dimension of the problem can be seen in a report prepared by the National Urban League in mid-1946:

There is no uniformity in union practices in the building trades. . . . In one town . . . Negro and white carpenters will be found in the same local union, while in another not many miles distant, Negroes are organized in completely separate unions. Bricklayers, plasterers, cement finishers, and other workers in the trowel trades are generally accepted without serious question, although in many cities the union policy is to grant Negroes work permits rather than full union membership . . . (In Akron) There are few Negro workers in the building trades, particularly the skilled crafts. From such records as are available, it is estimated that there are 10 carpenters, 8 plasterers, 6 electricians, and 2 bricklayers. The majority of Negro craftsmen are union workmen, but they function actively only when they are able to obtain employment on union jobs. Few apprentice opportunities exist for young men. Good pre-employment training at the Hower Trade School is available, but all classes are filled with veterans, and there is a long list of applicants. . . . Definite information regarding the number of Negro building mechanics (in Cincinnati) is unavailable, although it is estimated that there are between 400 and 500 in the city. The vast majority of these workmen do not have union membership and have not been able to overcome union resistance to Negro mechanics. In the public housing construction program few Negro mechanics were able to obtain

A

B

C

While modern technology and relatively high wages had certainly eased the burden, construction work continued to be a strenuous, insecure, and often seasonal way of earning a living. During the winter of 1977, "hard hats" in Akron were fortunate to find employment, but labored under harsh weather conditions (A). In the summer heat of 1977, laborers paved Akron's streets, but may have wondered whether climbing inflation and dwindling city budgets would indeed compel them to take out that "2nd mortgage" (B). Nor did mechanization totally eliminate physical exertion, as demonstrated by a construction worker laying pipe at Rittman in 1980 (C).

Known for its aggressively interracial organizing and advanced stands on civil rights, the Mine, Mill and Smelter Workers tackled the American Zinc Oxide Company in a bitter and unsuccessful strike which stretched from August, 1948, into April, 1949.

employment. . . . Construction laborers are organized in a separate local. Cement finishers are usually accepted in the union. There are few apprenticeship opportunities . . . and pre-employment training is confined to the public schools. . . . (In Cleveland) There are approximately 32 carpenters, 57 bricklayers, 80 painters, 9 plumbers, 6 electricians, 40 plasterers . . . Negro mechanics are accepted in most unions except the Electrical Workers and Plumbers' locals. Through an off-the-record agreement with these unions, Negro plumbers and electricians are permitted to work freely for Negro clientel. . . . Plumbers have formed an association which is not affiliated with the union. . . . Opportunities for employment as apprentices and helpers are limited as is pre-employment training. Through efforts of the Cleveland Urban League, a few Negro veterans were accepted for apprenticeship in the carpenters' union. The union plans to train 3,000 carpenters in the post-war program.

Various industrial unions faced similar problems, generally because of shop-level discrimination which paralleled the evident bias within many building-trades unions. A 1947 report by the NAACP's Labor Secretary suggested as much, and hinted at how various anti-labor laws passed after World War II would be used in ways unforeseen by their sponsors:

The first suggestion of what is in store for colored people under the Taft-Hartley Act came from the National Tube Company of Lorain, Ohio. When union representatives obtained the upgrading of some colored employees, the white individuals in the shop to which they were sent objected. These persons have announced that they will utilize the Taft-Hartley Law to secure a separate bargaining unit, and, thereby, be free to carry on discriminatory policies. I visited Lorain on this matter during the past month and pledged the union involved (United Steel Workers, CIO) that we will give full cooperation in helping to prevent the dissenters from making a successful attack on the union.

Traditional blue-collar occupations were not the only areas in which blacks had difficulty finding jobs. A November, 1948, Dayton Urban League report indicated something of the problem. It described the plight of two eighteen-year-old black women who had graduated in June from Roosevelt High School with typing and stenographic skills. "The Urban League has been grooming them since September . . .

for induction into business, industry or Government. They are now ready for jobs. Each recently passed the government test in her speciality. Each prefers to work for business or industry but has been unable to find employment."

Practices varied around the state and among the unions in each locale. Some cities early-on followed the lead suggested by President Harry S. Truman's civil-rights panel in its historic report, "To Secure These Rights." In 1951, for example, the Cincinnati City Council established a commission "to prevent discrimination in employment in business and industry engaged in defense contracts." When it investigated the situation within the city itself, its report etched a grim picture of the narrow employment opportunities open to blacks of whatever skill level. "It is true that substantial improvement in interracial relations generally has been achieved here in recent years," a 1953 report noted. "At many points of community life, new understanding and cooperation have developed from both sides." Yet that made little difference. "The striking fact is that this marked change of 'climate' has not been accompanied by equal change in employment practices. We can only conclude that many white workers have become more willing to accept nondiscriminatory hiring than many employment policy makers realize." On-going investigations in other cities during the same period suggested similar difficulties.

Throughout the post-war era one particular goal for civil rights groups was to crack the apprenticeship barrier in various craft unions. The Urban League and the NAACP were active in this effort, as were the UAW, the Steelworkers and several of the left-wing unions ousted by the CIO. These groups tried to deal with the issue by pressuring individual firms, and by taking a political route at the local and state level.

By the late 1950s four presidential executive orders barred discrimination on various jobs. But these applied only to employment contracted for or by the federal government. Eighteen states had fair employment practice laws, but two provided no enforcement procedures. The Ohio Civil Rights Commission covered all but domestic servants and employees of religious, educational and charitable organizations. Yet even as the AFL and CIO merged, blacks

A

D

B

C

E   F

Black unemployment remained double that of whites into the mid-'fifties, when this Cincinnatian sought work (A). Even when available, opportunities were too often limited to the most unattractive, menial, low-paying positions. Hot, heavy, and exhausting labor in foundries—as in Wilmington (B) and Dayton in 1962 (C)—epitomized these conditions. Long-brewing outrage with such discriminatory practice eventually exploded into massive, often violent, demands by blacks for greater access to social, economic, and political advancement. Organized blacks challenged the entrenched resistance of employers and unions alike with increasingly strident tactics, such as this 1965 demonstration in Cincinnati (D). Though an excruciatingly slow process, hard-won gains were achieved in many trades and industries. By 1978, for example, skilled blacks became more common in the Akron building trades (E). By 1980, a welding teacher for Sheet Metal Workers Local 98, Columbus, was in a position to assist in the equally bitter struggles of women for economic justice (F).

noted that the Brotherhood of Locomotive Firemen and the Brotherhood of Railroad Trainmen were admitted to membership, despite the fact that their constitutions specifically barred black members.

A 1962 Urban League report summarized the Cincinnati situation, one fairly representative of opportunities for blacks within craft unions by that time:

> Contacts with six of the craft unions relative to apprenticeship training opportunities for non-whites revealed that only one has a Negro apprentice. There was no uniformity with reference to application procedures, educational requirements and method of selection. . . . There is a very strong tendency toward the selection of relatives of craftsmen which appears to be a rather consistent pattern. . . . Summarized, it might be pointed out that it is virtually impossible for a non-white applicant to enter a bona-fide apprenticeship training program. It is possible . . . for him to have the training experience under a Negro craftsman. The question of apprenticeship training selection by [white] committees, together with the possibility of the non-white applicant being re-

jected by the contractor, poses a dual problem. A third difficulty has to do with membership procedures, with many of the craft unions . . . limit [ing] the avenues for entrance. . . .

Over the course of the next eighteen years, the situation changed rather dramatically. By 1977, sixty-seven percent of all non-union blacks and other minorities—in sharp contrast to their customary apathy or hostility toward organized labor — indicated in a Department of Labor study that they would vote to unionize, if given the opportunity. The Civil Rights movement— which gained momentum in the 'sixties with the financial and political assistance of several major unions — finally had an impact on employment legislation, as activists increasingly recognized the necessity of targeting the economic sphere for primary attention. The 1964 Civil Rights Act barred job discrimination against blacks and women, as well as segregation in public accommodations, and was a critical turning point. The numbers of black apprentices in various trades increased thereafter and, in a related development, blacks pressed for participation at the leadership level in industrial unions. Some of the gains were illusory, however, for many of the increased job opportunities for black males were in the auto industry during the 'sixties. These semi-skilled positions rapidly evaporated during the 'seventies, reinforcing the tendency apparent throughout the post-World War II era for the black employment rate to run at double that of whites. As for black women, their gains seemed even more impressive, the numbers of professionals more than doubling for instance. Yet, most women entered the ranks of "female" occupations which paid less than male jobs and which were not well organized.

During the 'seventies, the paradox of apparent gains and persistent problems remained. While real advances for blacks were evident— particlarly at the upper end of the occupational scale—they were accompanied by even higher unemployment rates. Recessions in 1970-71 and, especially, 1974-75 struck all workers, but played particular havoc with blacks. Even after the economy began to climb upward, black unemployment rates remained disturbingly high. In 1977 it stood at 14.5 percent. Among black teenagers the unemployment rate was a staggering forty percent.

Bureaucratization, a related institutional rigidity, and a growing distance between leaders and the rank and file in some unions also contributed, at least indirectly, to the problems organized labor confronted after World War II. Throughout this period a tension existed between shop-floor needs and the concerns of established leaders to assure the continued legitimacy of their unions. Expressed in a variety of ways — from unauthorized walkouts to challenged elections and reform slates—rank-and-file discontent flowed from various sources. In some instances, especially within the Steelworkers and the United Mine Workers, younger members bridled at structures which appeared authoritarian. In the case of the Mine Workers,

Periodic recessions marred the steady expansion of the economy in the thirty years after World War II. When declining production idled thousands in mid-1954, a U.S. surplus food distribution center in Canton did a booming business (above). A web of social benefits ensured that temporary unemployment would not bring with it the hardships of the '30s. For many blacks, however, unemployment was a chronic problem. By the mid-'60s, welfare rights groups, such as the one shown here in Columbus in 1968, were aggressively pressing for job assistance programs (right).

corruption at the national level was an additional factor.

Yet, even where corruption and anti-authoritarianism were not involved, established labor leaders repeatedly found themselves in difficulty with the rank and file. A series of ironies helped to explain that situation. The growing complexity of collective bargaining in the post-World War II era heightened the need for experienced and skilled leadership, and so did the insistent pressure of managers who demanded that, in exchange for a slice of control, unions serve as a kind of buffer between employees and employer. These circumstances reinforced existing tendencies in the labor movement for officers to serve long terms and for power to become increasingly centralized. Both of these courses, however, had the effect of widening the distance between the perceptions of the rank and file and those of the top leadership. For instance, union chiefs often viewed technological and economic issues in terms of broad national and international trends by the late-1970s, while members were far more concerned about direct impacts on their job-security and paychecks. Thus, when union leaders argued that wage-freezes and automation were crucial in order to keep plants open and to compete successfully with foreign producers, they often faced rebellion and charges of "selling out" from angry rank and filers who were already anxious about the daily threat of inflation and unemployment. The fact that both perspectives held merit made the dilemma even more perplexing. Critics blasted organized labor for its consequent vacillation and the apparently short-sighted demands of its members. But, it must also be noted that business and political leaders suffered from the very same malady, and had to bear equal blame for failing to find effective solutions to the nation's economic quandry.

Other factors were also involved in the growing bureaucratization problem, of course, especially after 1960. Both the civil rights and feminist movements had a ripple effect in the trade union movement, as did the anti-war crusade by the late-1960s, encouraging activist currents and a questioning of entrenched practices. The changing composition of the workforce, particularly the influx of younger workers less concerned than their parents with the dominant issue of security, also played a role. But the heart of the gap rested in the establishment of elaborate grievance procedures during and after World War II and the growing tendency for arbitration to be inserted as an additional step. These procedures reflected the leadership's quest for order and discipline. The problem, frequently, was that the formal channels clogged, grievances stacked up, and rank-and-

For many workers, unions were both a vehicle of upward mobility and an organization which gave meaning to their lives. Reflecting on his long career in the labor movement, James S. Culver explained in the mid-1970s that:

The union meant an opportunity to do things for people that I would not have been able to do otherwise. It also made it possible for me to do some things for my own family, that I would not have been able to do otherwise and, to me, these are two of the principal responsibilities that an individual has, and two of the things that he ought to want to do, and if he's prevented in any way, or not given an opportunity in any way to do these things, he has a very unsatisfactory life. Therefore, I see the union as a means of enabling me, and other people who belong to the unions, of having a more satisfactory life, living better; both in terms of having more of the good things of life, and more in terms of being able to help other people in society. I know of no other way . . . a working person can do these things because he doesn't have influence . . . . He only has money, he only has power, he only has influence when he can join hands with some other worker. So, to me, unions are not something just desirable for working people, it's something that's absolutely essential.

Though drastically reduced by restrictive legislation after the early 1920s, the flow of people from abroad never ceased entirely. Here, a group of citizens-to-be participated in a 1980 naturalization ceremony in Youngstown.

Though identified by some politicians as "the silent majority," Ohio workers could be quite articulate. A local union COPE-committee chairman in Youngstown vented his pent-up frustrations in a letter to the Ohio AFL-CIO in March, 1968:

In regards to your letter of March 1, in which you asked for suggestions. Here are a few, even though I know you didn't mean it. Most of you people, forgot what the union movement was originally started for. Instead of checking with the rank and file, you our so called leaders are starting to think for us, and trying to tell us what is good for us.

The reason that six out of ten people in Ohio arent registered, is that they gave up. I could find at least a dozen familys within a two block area in the neighborhood in which I live. These people told me there is no sense in voting because all politicians are crooks, and look out for their own, and special interests.

I am and have been quite active in the political arena, having at various times held both public and union Elective office, therefore I am not just speaking thru my hat, but giving you the majority opinion of quite a few of my fellow workers.

We are getting fed up with so called liberals. If you want us to vote for Gilligan than stop telling us what a great spender he is and will be. The money these fellows spend is ours.

The average taxpayer is getting tired of Viet-Nam, foreign aid, civil rights give away programs, (600 people working on federal payroll in Mahoning County alledgedly fighting poverty) riots, Judges and the Supreme court making it harder for policemen to do a job etc etc etc. Do you know that the average taxpayer, is nicked to the tune of a minimum of 25% of his wages for various taxes.

If Gilligan wants to win he should come out for (1) Balanced Budget thru cuts in all Branches of Government. Especially give away programs. (2) Tightening up of all loopholes whereby most of the rich people, and most of the oil industry escape paying their fair share of taxes, pluss, so called non profit organizations.

Tell Gilligan to soft Pedal the civil rights malarky that is sweeping the country. We to so called white racists are getting tired of being blamed for some thing that has been aided and condoned by the politicians of this country for years.

I refer to the so called ghetto or slum. Even as I write this letter, I am hearing on the news where a negro church is trying to get a zone change in our town of youngstown. This is to permit the building of a low rent housing project, in a predominantly negro, quite nice neighborhood. Know something? these negro home owners & workers are opposing this zone change.

Even these people dont want to live with the low class, shiftless, the majority of whom are unwed mothers, and fathers who do not wish to work and are satisfied to live like pigs and be supported by us suckers.

In my opinion these people should be forced to live like human beings, deprived of the right to vote and perhaps shipped of to some reservation.

file frustrations deepened. This and the differing perceptions which members and leaders had about central issues confronting workers created a kind of crisis by the early 'sixties. As A.H. Raskin observed in 1964: "What is developing is a conflict between the individual worker's desire for a strengthened sense that he is the center of his union and the inevitable trend toward impersonality, bureaucracy, and a global view in big unions set up to balance the size of big corporations."

A Department of Labor poll conducted over a decade later, in 1977, suggested that this conflict had not been resolved. Union members stressed concern with improving grievance handling, the information provided members by their unions, and the degree of influence members could exert, as the first, second, and fourth most important areas. Concern with fringe benefits placed third, and wages, job-security, and safety and health issues followed in that order.

Whatever the divisions and other problems within the houses of labor, the major reasons for the gradually dwindling extent and power of unions related to factors outside the labor movement itself, or at least ones over which it did not have total control. From the start of the postwar period, organized business groups hoped to recoup what they regarded as the excessive incursions made by unions during the 1930s and World War II into the right to manage. Wartime militancy and the extraordinary wave of strikes which swept the nation in 1946 strengthened this sentiment and spawned a major revision of the nation's basic labor law. The Taft-Hartley Act, co-sponsored by Ohio Senator Robert A. Taft, amended the National Labor Relations Act of 1935, its shapers said, to balance the restrictions placed on management with limits on labor. Besides requiring union officials to sign an affidavit that they were not Communists, the legislation provided emergency-disputes provisions, allowed employers freer expression before employees, outlawed the closed shop, and authorized states to pass legislation which superseded federal labor law. The act also severely narrowed the kinds of actions unions could take in support of the collective bargaining functions. Banning sympathy strikes, mass picketing, secondary boycotts, and political contributions, it struck at activities long used to express class solidarity. The legislation also sought to crack down on wildcat strikes by making unions responsible if members walked out depite no-strike contract clauses. As subsequently interpreted by the courts, this particular provision has been especially critical and has reinforced the tendency for state and national-level union officials to resist rank-and-file militancy.

While organized labor promptly branded the bill as a "slave-labor bill," it did not have as much impact on established unionism in Ohio as it did on efforts to organize new workers in areas without strong union traditions. For Ohio workers, the principal impact of the Taft-Hartley Act came in the 1958 attempt to achieve a so-called "right-to-work" amendment to the state constitution. Basically, the proposal stipulated that no person could be denied, or excluded from, employment due to membership or non-membership in a labor organization — thus placing legal limitations on union-security agreements. Several factors prompted the amendment, which proponents previously had seen die in legislative committee six times. Organized labor had failed badly in 1950 in its

Fresh memories of Hitler's threat to democratic institutions and the deepening Cold War of the late-1940s provided the backdrop for an ideological confrontation between trade unionists and some business leaders. While Cleveland union members linked the 1947 Taft-Hartley Act to fascism (left), a conservative Canton firm attacked the union-shop principle by exploiting the CIO's internal controversies over Communism (below).

bid to thwart Senator Taft's reelection, despite UMW president John L. Lewis' warning that "Taft was born encased in velvet pants and has lived to rivet an iron collar around the necks of millions of Americans." The ouster of several corrupt unions from the AFL in 1956 and the publicity generated by Senator John McClellan's probing investigations into corruption also made labor seem vulnerable. Similarly encouraging to anti-union forces were labor's failure in 1956 to secure legislation allowing supplementary unemployment benefits, Indiana's passage of a right-to-work law in 1957 (the first in a northern state), and the inability of the state's two labor organizations to merge smoothly.

The Ohio Chamber of Commerce and other advocates of the legislation badly misread the situation. Indeed, the amendment campaign served to unite organized labor in Ohio, at least temporarily. Shortly after Chamber officials created Ohioans for Right-to-Work in November, 1957, state AFL, CIO, Railroad Brotherhood, and Mine Worker representatives forged United Organized Labor of Ohio. Walt Davis, editor of the *Cleveland Citizen,* assumed the job of UOLO director. This centalized direction provided crucial planning and coordination efforts, while a Toledo public relations firm and a Pittsburgh ad agency helped shape a campaign which kept the anti-labor group on the run. In addition, cities such as Toledo and Cleveland launched their own committees and individual national and international unions in the state prepared materials as well.

By contrast, the Chamber of Commerce's campaign bogged down early. Because few volunteers could be recruited, people had to be paid to gather signatures on petitions. Once the amendment had been placed on the ballot, moreover, contributions dried up, thus limiting funds for publicity prior to the election. A number of corporations did not want to jeopardize their relationships with unions. Finally, on the eve of the election, a good many Republicans also became fearful of political repercussions which might stem from opposing the suddenly united and surprisingly effective organized labor movement.

The UOLO mounted a far more effective campaign, raising over $800,000 in all and pouring volunteers by the thousands into the field. Slick media techniques alone scarcely did the

STICKY FINGERS

In a 1958 bid to secure a so-called "right-to-work" amendment to the Ohio Constitution, proponents appealed to voters with attempts to link the union shop with corruption, coercion, and other anti-democratic practices (above). Stressing the improved security, standard of living, and working conditions (above, right) which they claimed were the more accurate benchmarks of unionization, opponents successfully blocked the measure by a two-to-one margin.

job, but they did not hurt. Using a device which dialed ten phone numbers at the same time and then played a tape, public figures such as Eleanor Roosevelt, Eddie Cantor, and Harry S. Truman spoke to thousands of Ohioans. Radio programs, television spots, dozens of newspaper ads all appeared. Volunteers from unions across the state, however, made the crucial difference. They mounted the voter registration drive which brought Ohioans to the polls in record numbers. The final results startled proponents of the amendment, for in only sixteen counties did the amendment win. Overall, the

amendment went down to defeat by a two-to-one margin, and in major industrial centers such as Lucas and Cuyahoga counties by slightly higher margins. Equally important from labor's point of view, Republican candidates met overwhelming defeat for a variety of offices. Michael DiSalle unseated incumbent Governor William O'Neill who had backed the right-to-work amendment, and Stephen Young ousted Senator John Bricker.

Although Ohio labor blocked the Chamber's bid for legally enforced open shops, unions in the Buckeye state and elsewhere were affected by other pieces of postwar labor legislation. The issue of corruption within unions, for example, received considerable public attention during the 1950s, including extensive Congres-

Participation in the political process had always been one means by which workers sought to control, or at least shape, their destinies. In order to counteract rising hostility toward organized labor during the postwar era, unions again launched vigorous political action drives. Undaunted by their failure to unseat Senator Taft in 1950, the CIO continued to mobilize its 429,000 Ohio members by conducting voter registration drives for the 1952 presidential and congressional elections.

sional investigations. The problem was most acute in industries with intense competition among small firms or considerable movement of cargo. Tendencies for companies to pay for quick handling or strike-immunity dated back several decades in trucking and longshoring. Corrupt practices permeated some building-trades unions also, although anti-labor journalists vastly exaggerated the extent of graft here and in other industries. Given the existing hostility toward unions, however, it was scarcely surprising that labor, already on the defensive, would attempt to clean its own house. The issue received considerable attention from the newly formed AFL-CIO early in its history. The AFL had previously ousted the east coast longshoremen's union and in 1956 the AFL-CIO urged the Teamsters to drop any afiliations with that union. When the McClellen Committee probed into the affairs of the Teamsters, the Bakers Union, and the United Textile Workers the next year, it found sufficient abuses to warrant further concern by the AFL-CIO. By the end of 1957 the Teamsters, the Bakers, and the Laundry Workers had been expelled from the AFL-CIO, although this did not halt the adverse publicity which tarnished the entire labor movement and reinforced existing anti-union attitudes. Nor was organized labor's proposal of the Welfare and Pension Plans Disclosure Act of 1958, one offshoot of Congressional investigations of labor racketeering, successful in turning aside the legislative onslaught. In 1959 the Labor Management Report and Disclosure Act, sometimes called the Landrum-Griffin Act, passed. Several provisions of this act had also been proposed by labor—removing the bar on strikers from voting in representation elections and permitting prehiring agreements between building trade unions and employers — but others more clearly mirrored the general anti-union drift of public opinion evident by the late 1950s.

The act broadened the secondary-boycott provisions of the Taft-Hartley Act, for instance, and narrowed definitions of permissable organizational and recognition picketing. To prevent financial abuses, it also required bonding of labor officials and required the filing of detailed financial reports with the Secretary of Labor. Finally, in the belief that some labor leaders violated the rights of some union members, the

Being a union official became more and more complicated over time, as Jackie Presser of the Teamsters suggested in a 1980 interview:

How does a guy become a business agent or an officer of the local union? He runs because he's a truck driver, a dockman, a warehouseman, an auto worker, a steel worker. He has no exposure to really big business. This is big business. So some guy is popular in an auto plant, a steel mill or a machine shop what have you and he runs for office and wins the presidency of the local union and there are 2, 3, 5, 10 thousand members. The day he sits in the chair for the first time he better understand Taft Hartley and Landrum-Griffin. He better understand ERISA (Employee Retirement Income Security Act). He better understand bonding and security. And he surely should know the prudence of the investment and financial responsibility. Unfortunately [for] the limited educated truck driver, warehouseman and dockman, machinist, steel worker whatever industry you want to name that's an awesome responsibility to assume and if they are going to be good leaders they better have that whole education system behind them. Now many of them get up and say, "well you hire auditors and you hire accountants and you hire attorneys." But it doesn't work that way because when you hire the professionals they try to run your operation and then you are really going to get killed. Industry has learned to hire the best that's available to compete with the organized labor representatives going to the bargaining table. So when you catch a union with weak representation which 80% of the unions in America have, in the fields that I just mentioned, the high power fields, they are no match for the law firms . . . . They can't cope with those types of high bred attorneys . . . .

During the 1980 presidential campaign, members of Teamsters Joint Council 41 in Cleveland displayed their union's endorsement of the Republican ticket.

A minority in the organizations they had helped to erect, many labor movement veterans by the 1970s worried that young workers lacked an appreciation of the struggles union-building involved. Lola Kuntzman, for some twenty years president of the Hoover IBEW local in Canton, reflected on this problem in 1978:

. . . all of these young people coming in . . . uneducated on what the union is. They look at it as some kind of a first aid station. You don't have to ever go near it unless you're hurt and then you just run screaming and someone should wave a wand and take care of it. And this is the sad part . . . . They don't understand what a union is, what their powers are, what their restrictions are and that it's a two way street . . . . and they have no conception of what has taken place through the years. Just like your vacations, your paid holidays and all of these things. They take them for granted.

Interviewed in 1976, textile organizer Toni Podojil of Cleveland voiced similar thoughts:

I've always felt that we failed in bringing labor education to the children. And I mean . . . . that we have not been teaching them the labor movement from the third-fourth-fifth grades when they were studying their American history. We have failed all the way down the line by not having teachers going in and picking up classes and telling these young people, 'Look, this is what labor is; all this good social legislation that you've got is because of the labor movement. The forty-hour week, your vacation pay, time-and-a-half after forty hours, and none of this child labor.' We have never taught this to the children . . . . How are children going to appreciate what we went through?

Hospital workers remain among the state's lowest-paid service workers. In 1980 members of AFSCME Local 1745 struck the Cuyahoga County Hospital in an attempt to raise their wages.

Act included a bill of rights for unionists and detailed regulations to govern union elections. These laws scarcely retarded union growth by themselves. In so far as they spun out of and reinforce existing anti-union stereotypes, however, they made it all the harder for unions to operate effectively.

Despite numerous allegations, proven corruption within Ohio unions has not been extensive. Dissident members of a Columbus local of the Hod Carriers Union used the Labor Management Reporting and Disclosure Act in 1959-1961 to curb apparent financial abuses and nepotism by their officials. In 1967, in a case unique among industrial unions, a Steelworker District Commission reviewed charges of corruption in a Mansfield local. Investigations revealed the use of certain improper procedures, but no outright graft. It is possible that the charges arose originally out of a factional dispute. That appears to have been the case at a McDonald, Ohio local in 1976, when a grievance committeeman claimed excess lost time and subsequently repaid the local treasury. Of Ohio unions, the Teamsters have most often been charged with links to racketeers. Neither the jailing of international presidents Dave Beck and James Hoffa, nor the earlier ouster of the union from the AFL-CIO, deterred either the growth of the Teamsters or prevented it from developing such fringe benefits as pre-paid legal services and a national grievance system for health and safety. Charges of corruption persisted and were partially involved in the 1961 secession of Cincinnati Teamster locals from the International. Yet, even the man who led that disaffiliation noted that William Presser, then head of the Ohio Teamsters Joint Council, never used pressure tactics commonly attributed to the union. Rumors lingered, however, and affected Jackie Presser, William's son, when he became an international vice-president in 1976. While launching a public relations campaign to improve the union's image, Presser built a strong organization and developed alliances with such related trades as restaurant workers, bartenders, and bakers. Between 1967 and 1977, the Ohio Teamsters grew by forty-three percent and cultivated a high political profile.

Attitudes about unions played an increasingly important role in shaping an atmosphere in which expansion of the labor movement was difficult. Restrictive legislation, evidence of corruption, and repeated expressions about the power of "big labor" all had an effect by the 1950s. That impact lingered on after that, but with the passage of time it is likely that a more powerful notion was one which regarded unions as simply irrelevant. Paradoxically, this view developed in part because of the very successes of the labor movement in the years after the Great Depression. In a sense, organized labor has created a powerful competitor in the form of big government. It is difficult to say how much of a role this has played in the decades since World War II, but the fact that a generation of workers has grown up with numerous social benefits provided by free-spending government means that they often take those benefits for granted, rather than realizing that they came into being with the help of a labor movement that became increasingly politicized. Union battles for improved working conditions, wages, and fringe benefits are paralleled in many ways by the Occupational Safety and Health Administration, the minimum-wage laws, and, among other things, the Employee Retirement Income Security Act of 1974.

Legislation at the state level followed a similar pattern, especially since the 1960s when the

A

The resurgence of feminism in the 1960s and the subsequent demise of protective legislation — now regarded as unduly restrictive of employment opportunities — combined to open a variety of nontraditional careers to women. In 1973 women in Cleveland heard Senator Marijeanne Valiquette speak in support of the Equal Rights Amendment (A). During that decade black women found work at Youngstown Sheet and Tube (B). Other women helped to drill for gas near Goodyear's Plant 2 in Akron in 1976 (C), and worked as apprentice carpenters in Columbus in 1979. (D)

B

C

D

Ohio AFL-CIO became a powerful lobbying force. By 1980, the Ohio legislature had dealt with numerous issues of concern to workers, generally in response to the specific efforts of the state's labor movement. Most notable were the broadening of benefits first established during the 'thirties, and the introduction of new legislation to keep pace with changing social and economic conditions. Legal minimum-wage levels rose steadily and were extended to more and more classes of workers and provisions for workmen's compensation and unemployment benefits were constantly revised, the general direction being to raise the level and length of support. Legislation designed to assist displaced homemakers, normally mature women with low-level skills who were thrown into the job-market because of the death of a spouse or the dissolution of a long-term marriage, illustrated the changing nature of legislative concerns. The easing of employment restrictions on nightwork and maximum hours of work for sixteen and seventeen-year olds, in 1978, exemplified the move away from protective legislation. The 'sixties and 'seventies were noteworthy, too, for the volume of legislation barring sexual harrassment and discrimination by race, sex, and age, or because of handicap or pregnancy. In 1980, Ohio — following the lead of Connecticut the year before, and along with Michigan and Wisconsin — prohibited the awarding of state contacts to persons or firms found in violation of the National Labor Relations Act.

The perception of unions as irrelevant stemmed not only from the encompassing web of laws, but also from that all-pervasive and shaping media, television and the movies. From the 'fifties on, television exercised a profound, if subtle and indirect, influence on attitudes. Blatantly anti-union programs were rare. Probably more influential, ultimately, were prime-time shows which portrayed workers in stereotypical ways from an upper-middle class perspective and which, most important, simply left unions out altogether. The message, whether intended or not, buttressed the notion that trade unions were unnecessary institutions. As TV actor Alan Alda observed on one occasion, "The unspoken assumptions are what mold the audiences." In an era when the popularity of labor leaders plunged and suspicions about them rose, that insight seemed all the more perceptive.

Until the late 1970s, motion pictures bolstered the idea that organized labor was of peripheral importance, if only because few films even touched on the labor movement. And when unions suddenly sprang into prominence on the silver screen in 1978-79, themes in two features reflected existing images of corruption and of union leaders distant from their members, people serving their own needs not those of their members. Contrary pictures of labor did emerge during the seventies in an extraordinary outburst of documentaries, yet the audience exposed to such more realistic portrayals was, by comparison, tiny.

Another thing over which the labor movement had no control was the changing structure of the workforce (see Table 5-F). The increasing numbers of workers in the secondary labor force represented people notoriously difficult to organize because of high turnover, low level of skills, and, often, the extent of competition among workers. Such workers, moreover, traditionally fell outside the areas of labor union interest and there was thus little incentive to organize them. The most significant change in the workforce, however, was the steady and rapid decline in size of the traditional bastions of union power in the state. In 1950 manufacturing workers still represented nearly thirty-seven percent of the non-agricultural workforce; by 1980 that proportion had dropped to twenty-

Despite intensive lobbying and a march on the capitol, organized labor was unable in 1963 to thwart passage of several legislative acts which slashed unemployment compensation benefits for Ohio workers.

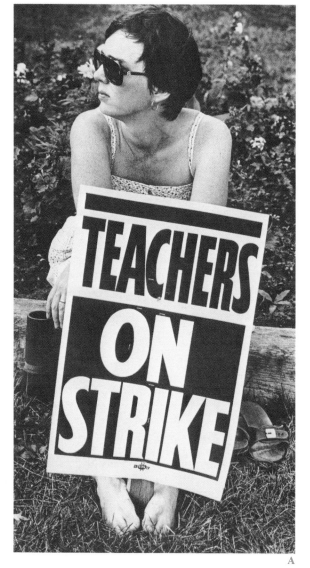

A

B

nine percent. Mining, transportation, communication and utilities, all also highly unionized industries, similarly declined in importance. Together these groups represented 45.4 percent of the nonagricultural workforce in 1950, only 24.8 percent thirty years later. Meanwhile, those sectors of the workforce which had, before 1960 at least, been little unionized expanded steadily. Wholesale and retail trade, professional and service industries, and public administration collectively represented 41.4 percent of the workforce in 1950 and 61.4 percent three decades later. Accurate data on Ohio trade union membership is difficult to obtain, but in 1964, 35.7 percent of the nonagricultural workforce was unionized; in 1980 the figure stood at only 29.5 percent (see Table 5-K). The largest growth section of the workforce was professionals, a group of workers difficult to organize at best.

In the past twenty years there has been considerable change within the traditionally non-union sectors of the workforce. The upsurge of public employee activism began in the 1960s, prompting legislators at the state and national levels to alter laws covering such workers. By 1968 thirty-eight states permitted at least some public employees to organize and bargain collectively and nine had highly detailed laws to regulate such activities. Ohio re-

mains outside the ranks of such states. Indeed, successive attempts to pass comprehensive collective bargaining bills for public employees have failed for a number of years and the prospect that such a measure can pass remains uncertain. As a result, Ohio public employees still are restrained legally from striking and bargaining collectively by the Ferguson Act of 1947.

That legal point, however, has been insufficient to restrain the militancy of public employees. An Ohio Supreme Court ruling that the act was not self-effectuating and that notices thus had to be issued to employees before termination penalties could be imposed has had the effect of limiting the use of the statute. While relatively few of the thousands of strikes which rocked Ohio between 1945 and 1957 (see Table 5-J) were called by public employees, from 1958 to 1970 the state ranked second in the nation for public sector strikes. The decade of the 'seventies was no less turbulent, the proportion of state workers who were unionized rising from 36.7 to 37.5 percent and that of local government workers from 50.9 to 53.5 percent between 1972 and 1974 alone. Walkouts by firemen, police, prison guards, teachers, refuse collectors, social workers, and hospital employees swept the state. Although often successful, such actions did not alleviate the central underlying grievance. In 1969 the starting

The combination of declining tax bases, layoffs, and inflation placed public employees in difficult positions by the '70s, evoking a startling wave of militancy which rolled across the state. Among other places, teachers struck at Lakewood in 1978 (A). AFSCME — by 1978 the largest and one of the fastest growing unions in the AFL-CIO — lobbied for passage of a collective bargaining bill for public employees (B). Among the most controversial, and bitterest, strikes were those waged by police and fire fighters. In a 1978 Lorain walkout, off-duty firemen from other communities helped with picketing (C). Frustrated by a rising taxpayer revolt and a sense that the public did not understand their needs, Bowling Green's municipal workers appealed for support in 1979 (D). It was not always forthcoming. The 1977 strike of Dayton fire fighters, for instance, generated strong anti-labor sentiment, evident in this newspaper cartoon (E).

C

E

salary for guards at Ohio's prisons was $4,900, for example, substantially lower than that of adjoining states. By mid-1975, after ten strikes, entry salaries had risen to $7,946 annually, but that figure was still lower than that paid by nearby states and, in any case, the bulk of the increases had meanwhile been wiped out by inflation. Many other public employees faced an identical quandry, as Toledo teachers demonstrated in 1978 and Cleveland teachers proved in a significant eleven-week strike in 1980.

Public employees had been a distinct minority within organized labor for decades. In 1960 they still represented barely six percent of all unionists and carried little influence within the AFL-CIO. As it became clear that unions such as the American Federation of Teachers and AFSCME were in fact the fastest growing unions in the AFL-CIO, that body in 1974 created a new Public Employees Department. Despite such gains and the evidence of flexibility in unionism, however, the increases in public sector unionism were insufficient to make up for losses in areas of traditional union strength due to technological displacement and plant closings.

Ultimately, neither laws, poor images, hostile attitudes, nor the changing composition and structure of the workforce, by themselves, explained the poor record of organized labor be-

tween 1945 and 1980. The combination of those factors, of course, was crucial, but the key element in the equation of demise was something that observers of the labor-management scene had long understood, the amazing resistance power of American capitalism. That resistance took a variety of forms in the post-war years. While some firms adopted a rigid anti-unionism stance, others learned, often with the help of consultants, to manipulate NLRB procedures so as to minimize union victories. Closely related to this latter approach was a renewed stress on improved personnel management policies. The "human relations" school of industrial relations spread in the post-war period and this interdisciplinary method, melding sociological and psychological techniques as well as aspects of the welfare capitalism Ohio firms had pioneered in the late nineteenth and early twentieth century, served to soften the harsh edges which often generated grievances among workers and thus served as the basis for unionism. The movement, what one practitioner called "preventive labor relations," gained considerable momentum in the 1970s. It involved "positive personnel management that meets the needs of people at work," the argument went, not "union busting." But if the "proper" procedures were followed then employees would "see no need for union representation . . . ." Delaying tactics, carefully designed hiring, personnel and compensation policies, and subtly structured bargaining units did, in fact, have an impact. By the seventies unions were losing more than half of all certification elections and, by 1977, an amazing seventy-six percent of all decertification elections.

The spread of economic hardship well beyond the ranks of minorities in the 'seventies represented a turning point from the pattern which had dominated for three decades after World War II. For much of that time hopes for peace, security, and prosperity were fulfilled. Real wages edged upwards. Union contracts broadened to include an amazing array of fringe benefits, and some unions—such as the auto, steel, and rubber workers — sought guaranteed annual wages. While they did not achieve that goal, a comparable gain was ultimately secured—supplemental unemployment benefits. Inflation picked away at earnings, but economic opportunities abounded in Ohio. As each year passed, more and more women entered the labor force and job opportunities for blacks also moderately expanded. Thus, total family income rose steadily. That was of central importance, since, for many workers, it made possible a move to better homes, the purchase of a new car, or television set, a college education for the kids.

Yet by the later 1950s some flaws had already appeared in the economy of abundance. Ohio's rank among manufacturing states began to slip and, as the 1960s progressed, problems intensified—foreign competition, flight to the Sunbelt, a declining production force. In the mid-1970s, as the nation sought to heal the wounds of Vietnam and Watergate, the bubble burst in the most severe recession to slice through the economy in the years after 1945. The nation recovered from the recession, but in large measure Ohio's economy remained weak. In the latter part of the 'seventies, scarcely a week passed without an announcement of another plant or store-closing. As the 'eighties began, and the election of Ronald Reagan heralded a supposedly new political and economic direction, yet another recession hit.

For the depression-generation, concerned above all with economic security, such developments were enormously disturbing. They had won seniority clauses, unemployment and disability compensation, supplemental unemployment benefits, Medicare, Medicaid, and steadily expanded Social Security coverage. While such programs tempered the sharp edges of layoffs, they did not prevent closings. And, while jobs in other sectors of the economy increased, they were less unionized and did not pay as well as manufacturing jobs. For the post-depression generation of Ohio workers, the dilemma was also acute. They had grown up with abundance and access to superior educa-

A

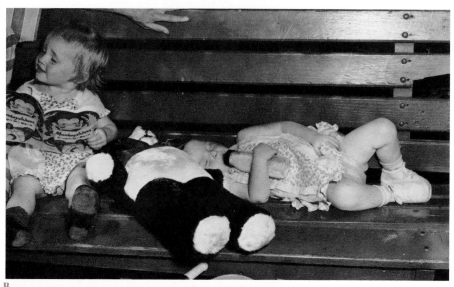

B

C

Leisure activities remained an integral part of working-class life. Company-sponsored programs — cut during the depression years to save money — were resumed by large firms as the postwar economy strengthened. Goodyear in 1960 (A) supported sports teams, while General Tire held annual picnics (B & C).

Among the numerous Ohio plants which closed in the late 1970s was Federal Glass in Columbus (right). In this case federal regulations, not foreign competition, were largely to blame. The Federal Trade Commission, purportedly to maintain competition in the industry, blocked merger plans and thus precipitated the company's decision to shut down. Fifteen hundred employees lost their jobs and joined the ranks of the unemployed (below).

In a 1980 *New York Times* article, Barberton rubber workers clearly stated the dilemma faced by many contemporary manufacturing workers. One well-paid unionist explained the benefits derived from his work:

That's what I love about this job . . . . A kid can go in there and build tires and live like a college professor, even if he never had the opportunity to go to college. You don't go in low and wait for your pay to start climbing, like you do in the professions. You start out high and you stay there. Think of the self-esteem it gives these people.

Firestone's decision to close the old Seiberling tire plant in Barberton posed a distinct threat to that way of life. Joe Albanese, president of URW Local 18, pointed out that alternative jobs were too frequently inadequate replacements:

When we were raising hell during the last election about all the good manufacturing jobs we were losing in Ohio, Governor Rhodes said, 'Well, we got 38,000 new jobs in the state last year' . . . . Well those are all jobs at McDonald's and Wendy's for the minimum wage . . . and that's just where we're headed — a nation of minimum-wage earners. Ten jobs at McDonald's isn't worth one job building tires.

tional opportunities. Now, many of them nonetheless could not find good jobs. As for young blacks and Hispanics, the predicament was crueler still. Disproportionately unskilled and poorly educated, they entered the job-market just when well-paying industrial positions were contracting and even menial jobs were becoming scarce.

Long the home of production pace-setters, Ohio had witnessed the pioneering stages of mass-production fabrication, giant steel mills, and mechanized mining. As the postwar era unfolded, that leadership role faded. An influx of foreign goods undercut Ohio-produced materials and cost-conscious managers turned southward, westward, and overseas for cheaper, non-union labor. The exodus had a snowballing effect. Partly to blame because of their militant wage demands and defense of work practices, Ohio's workers would disproportionately shoulder the burden of the effects.

Unions, the instrument of security for so many Ohio workers, faced these transformations from a weakened position. As the size of manufacturing workforces declined and the number of plant closings increased, the size and relative strength of the state's largest unions declined. The inability, in some cases the unwillingness, to organize among "new workers" in the expanding white-collar and, to a lesser extent, service sectors of the economy reinforced this tendency. Organized labor had had difficulty unifying politically through much of the postwar era and the challenges of the economy by the 1970s did not simplify that task. Labor had mounted its most effective joint effort in 1958, when it combined to defeat the right-to-work amendment. Whether or not similar unity could develop again was a moot point. As Ronald Reagan took office, there was no guarantee that organized labor would be able to withstand the anticipated assaults on the Occupational Health and Safety Administration and the numerous other social programs which it had worked for since the 'thirties. By the end of the 'seventies, in any case, one certainty had emerged — the image of an all-powerful "Big Labor" was but a mirage.

CONCLUSION

The story we have told explores the events and developments, the transformations and confrontations which make up the rich and varied history of Ohio workers. The story remains incomplete, not because workers were inarticulate, but rather because a basic limitation to the historian's craft is that the materials left by successive generations are always fragmented. Time imposes its own boundaries, and, in this instance, so has the format selected. This is an illustrated history intended for a general audience, not a monograph designed to be read only by specialists; it spans more than a century and a half, and it deals with a racially and ethnically diverse working class, spread across an entire state, which underwent a multiplicity of experiences. Moreover, rather than focusing only on workers in unions or on the job, we have sought to present a balanced discussion of Ohio working peoples in the broadest possible context. Few other studies of American workers have attempted to deal with the topic on so broad a scale. And, so far we we know, this book represents the first attempt to seriously probe the working class of a single state over such an extended period of time.

If we hastily scan the eighteen decades since Ohio achieved statehood in 1803, the enormity of what transpired becomes readily apparent. Both where and how people work and live have changed in fundamental ways. In the early years, the bulk of Ohioans toiled as farmers or farm laborers. Now, only a tiny portion of the labor force make their living in this fashion, and the overwhelming majority of the population lives in bustling metropolitan areas. The dramatic engine of change was industrialization, a process which both altered how goods are produced and re-worked the entire fabric of society. By 1920 nearly half of all nonagricultural employees in the state labored in throbbing factories which made Ohio one of the nation's industrial giants. Yet, today, empty and quiet plants dot the state, and two-out-of-every-three workers are in profession-al, service, or government jobs. Meanwhile, the hours of labor have declined substantially, life expectancy nearly doubled, opportunities for leisure and education mushroomed, and the standard of living risen incredibly, if unevenly.

Workers were scarcely powerless bits of flotsam awash in the seas of change which repeatedly

Amidst mounting public concern by the 1980s that the pressures of modern life had caused a rapid disintegration of basic family units, many working-class families maintained a unique cohesiveness and common identity which extended into the workplace. Such close bonds among work-groups traditionally played crucial roles in shop-floor behavior and labor relations. Here, two generations of the Taylor family — whose seniority ranged from forty-one to four years—posed outside the Toledo Jeep plant.

By the 1970s — in a scene inconceivable to earlier generations of steelworkers — a female employee proudly posed in the heat and grime of a Youngstown Sheet and Tube mill. Despite individual victories, however, the effort to permanently overcome sexist barriers in the workplace remained an ongoing struggle.

swept the state, transforming it from a major producer of agricultural commodities to an industrial colossus, and even now pointing it in another direction. While not all workers fully understood each of the impersonal forces swirling about them at any particular time, it is apparent that most were acutely conscious of the transformations occurring and that they actively attempted to cope with and have some impact on their world. Indeed, this interaction of the worker with the environment — whether shop-floor or community—emerges as a central feature of our study. Various documents which we have incorporated, many of them previously untapped by historians, reveal both an articulated consciousness of process and a determination to protect valued institutions, practices, and traditions. Victimized at times, workers were never merely victims; they responded, shaped, and were active participants in society. Despite their relative neglect by students of labor, Ohio workers actually were distinctly active in this regard. They provided leadership, inspiration, and guidance within the labor movement at critical points and frequently were in the forefront of developing national trends. It was no coincidence that the American Federation of Labor and international unions such as the United Mine Workers were founded in the state, that many of the turbulent conflicts which punctuate American working-class history were acted out here, or that Ohio pioneered in such fields as workman's compensation.

The diversity and the range of experiences among Ohio's working people have been illus-

The ongoing technological revolution drastically altered working environments, the composition of the labor force, and the very nature of work itself—even in many of Ohio's traditional "smokestack" industries. By the 1970s, for instance, a new generation of steelworkers—fewer in number, racially diverse, and possessing new skills—commonly monitored and regulated production at Youngstown Sheet and Tube from control rooms perched high above the hazards, heat, and filth of the mill-floor.

trated by the graphics presented here, a number of which have been reproduced for the first time. Their significance lies in what they show us about the nature of work and the lives of those who toiled between the early-nineteenth and late-twentieth century. Used as historical documents, these graphics, especially the photographs, provide an intimacy with the past that is difficult to create with the written word alone. Linked with excerpts from statements by workers themselves, they bestow texture to our narration and meaning to the bloodless statistics, crucial as they are, on which scholars too often rely to sum up life experiences.

Some elements of the story of Ohio workers remain in doubt, for in a very real sense this study has generated more questions than answers. Workers were "alive to their own interests," for instance, but it is not always clear why they chose the paths they did. The mechanisms of collective action and the intricacies of the impact of individualism remain to be explored more fully by others. Differing perceptions of success seem an especially fruitful area to probe, as notions of opportunity are one clue to the moderation normally evident among workers. Such an inquiry would also bridge the lines of sex, race, ethnicity, and religion which transect the working class, and thus contribute to a richer understanding of the absence of a generalized and sustained class-consciousness. Of related pertinence would be a systematic comparison of the standard of living across time and among different groups, and, especially important, the participation of workers and unions in the political process. Closer examination of local settings will unravel the perplexing fact that workers in different areas of the state reacted in dramatically diverse ways to essentially identical conditions. Of crucial impor-

tance will be fine-grained investigations of specific work environments, for these will provide insight into topics as varied as occupational health and safety and informal shop "rules."

Affluence during the thirty years following World War II accentuated the perennial union problem of membership apathy. James Turner, former Fair Practices Director of the United Rubber Workers, explained the issue in 1975, and in the process pointed out some of the changes in unions over the years:

You ask a person to come to a meeting now and he tells you, "Well, I'd like to come, but I promised to take the folks up to the cottage," or "I promised to take them out on the boat," or "I always watch Peyton Place at this hour," you know, "on the color television." And these are some of the things that are concrete results of the union's raising of the standard of living, the raising of the economic floor in our society and, so, they have become a victim (of their own success). He doesn't realize that had it not been for the union, he wouldn't have the cottage, he wouldn't have the boat, and he wouldn't have the color television. And I'm saying that only to the extent that the union still will be the mechanism that must be used; we just need, possibly, some new ways of communicating with people because this is not going to change. We're not going to advocate doing away with the boat; we're really going to advocate more, and more, and more, you see, of the good things in life—a part of the profit of the corporation so that they can remain stable and strong and, yet, we too can receive some of the benefits of their profits . . . . I think security is the key word . . . then they can also carefully schedule their industrial needs . . . then they can also carefully schedule their human needs, and it isn't necessary to hire great bunches of people now and then lay them off at the end of the year; more careful scheduling will eliminate this, and if you do this then you must pay the penalty through what we call supplemental unemployment benefits—while these people are off, depending upon how long they've been employed, they will get so much money each week for being unemployed.

By examining the functioning of work groups, a critical unit in shaping behavior, perhaps it will be possible to perceive why workers rejected the Industrial Workers of the World at the institutional level, yet, in effect, wove its slow-down tactics so deeply into the texture of working-class life.

The maturation of labor-management relations obviously also needs further study. A tension between employer and employee over the control of work routines and the extent of recognition to be accorded workers existed in nearly every decade. The probing of work environments will shed much additional light on what has transpired, but access to company records and interviews with management personnel will be essential if the entire account is to be told. The Ohio Labor History Project has made available a core of essential materials for an understanding of workers in Ohio, demonstrating the value of investing in the heritage of this major portion of the state's population. It would be appropriate for an Ohio Business or Industrial History Project to be launched as well. In the absence of the records that might be gathered in such a parallel undertaking, one is left to assess the actions taken by employers from alternative sources. While these are revealing, of course, they do not always explain the nuances of behavior, the rhythms of employer resistance to unions, the extent of diversity within the business community, or the degree to which management has been affected by its dealings with unions over time.

A cluster of other subjects, a host of other questions, await investigation and answers. In addition to job-related areas, we can hope that more future attention will be paid to the molding of working-class attitudes, values, and opinions—a process which has played a key role in how workers deal with their grievances and how employers, in turn, respond to their workers. Education, family, the press, and the electronic media all deserve to be examined. Similarly, racial, ethnic, and religious organizations need to be treated more fully. And, finally, recreation is a topic worthy of more attention. The bibliography will serve as a useful starting point for forays into all of these topics. While it reveals that scholars who provided the building blocks on which our own structure was erected have scarcely begun the task of writing the history of workers in Ohio, the bibliography nonetheless indicates readily available published sources. Also listed are numerous manuscript and oral history collections, as well as a range of other materials from doctoral dissertations and masters' theses to state and federal government reports.

We end this study at a time of insecurity, scarcely a new phenomenon for members of the working class. Insecurity, indeed, stands out as a recurrent theme in working-class life, whether due to the erratic course of the economy, the rhythmic fluctuations of employment in seasonal occupations such as construction, the irregularities of work in the state's mines and factories, or the persistent dilution of skills. Still, the current situation seems in some respects more grave than other times of crisis in the past. Dramatic alterations in the structure and composition of the workforce have occurred in a relatively short period of time and left growing numbers of workers in diverse industries adversely and permanently affected. There is nothing entirely new in this scenario, nor in the fact that so many workers find themselves subject to forces seemingly beyond their control. Yet this development has been accompanied by a paradoxical tendency which is difficult to assess. Even as unions have succeeded in erecting bastions of security through collective bargaining and political action, their power has eroded. What the outcome will be remains in doubt. History cannot predict the future. One thing is abundantly clear: those who condemned Cincinnati to the ash can of history, when rival metropolises arose one hundred years ago, were proven wrong. It seems likely that those who today predict Ohio's economic and urban demise, and see in currently weakened unions the end of the labor movement are similarly incorrect.

No strength without union....

APPENDIX

TABLE 2A: Population Characteristics of Ohio, 1840-1880 (in thousands)

	Total Population (TP)	Native Born	% of TP	Foreign Born	% of TP	Born in Ohio	% of TP	Native Born Outside Ohio	% of TP	Blacks	% of TP	Urban*	% of TP	Rural	% of TP
1840	1,519.5									17.3	1%	83.5	6%	1,436	94%
1850	1,980.3	1,762.1	89%	218.2	11%	1,224.4	62%	537.8	27%	25.3	1%	242.4	12%	1,737.9	88%
1860	2,339.5	2,011.3	86%	328.3	14%	1,529.6	65%	481.7	21%	36.7	2%	400.4	17%	1,939.1	83%
1870	2,665.3	2,292.8	86%	372.5	14%	1,842.3	69%	450.5	17%	63.2	2%	682.9	26%	1,982.3	74%
1880	3,198.1	2,803.1	88%	394.9	12%	2,361.4	74%	441.7	14%	79.7	3%	1,030.8	32%	2,167.3	68%

*places with more than 2500 residents

Sources: Compendium of the Seventh Census; 1860, 1870, 1880 U.S. Census; Leon E. Truesdell, Population, Second Series, Characteristics of the Population, Ohio (Washington, D.C.; U.S. Government Printing Office, 1942).

TABLE 2B. Population Changes in Ohio, 1840-1880 (in thousands)

	Total Population	% change	Native Born	% change	Foreign Born	% change	Born in Ohio	% change	Native Born Outside Ohio	% change	Blacks	% change	Urban*	% change	Rural	% change
1840-1850	+460.9	+30%									+7.9	+46%	+158.9	+190%	+301.9	+21%
1850-1860	+359.2	+18%	+249.1	+14%	+110.1	+50%	+305.2	+25%	−56.1	−10%	+11.4	+45%	+158	+65%	+201.2	+12%
1860-1870	+325.8	+14%	+281.5	+14%	+44.2	+14%	+312.8	+21%	−31.3	−7%	+26.5	+72%	+282.5	+71%	+43.3	+2%
1870-1880	+532.8	+20%	+510.4	+22%	+22.5	+6%	+519.1	+28%	−8.8	−2%	+16.4	+26%	+347.9	+51%	+185	+9%

*places with more than 2500 residents

Sources: Compendium of the Seventh Census; 1860, 1870, 1880 U.S. Census; Leon E. Truesdell, Population, Second Series, Characteristics of the Population, Ohio (Washington, D.C.: U.S. Government Printing Office, 1942).

TABLE 2C. Population Changes in Principal Ohio Counties, 1840-1880 (in thousands)

	1840-1850	% change	1850-1860	% change	1860-1870	% change	1870-1880	% change
Hamilton	+76.7	+96%	+59.6	+38%	+44	+20%	+53	+20%
Cuyahoga	+21.6	+82%	+29.3	+62%	+54	+69%	+64.9	+49%
Franklin	+17.9	+71%	+7.5	+17%	+12.7	+25%	+23.8	+38%
Montgomery	+6.3	+20%	+14	+37%	+11.8	+23%	+14.5	+23%
Lucas	+3	+32%	+13.5	+10%	+20.9	+81%	+20.7	+44%
Stark	+5.3	+15%	+3.1	+8%	+9.5	+22%	+11.5	+22%
Muskingum	+6.3	+16%	−.6	−1%	+.5	+1%	+4.9	+11%
Belmont	+3.7	+12%	+1.8	+5%	+3.3	+9%	+9.9	+25%
Columbiana	−6.8*	−17%	−.8	−2%	+5.5	+17%	+10.3	+27%
Trumbull	−7.6*	−20%	+.2	+1%	+8	+26%	+6.2	+16%
Summit	+4.9	+22%	−.1	−1%	+7.3	+27%	+9.1	+26%
Washington	+8.7	+42%	+6.7	+23%	+4.3	+12%	+2.6	+7%
Mahoning			+2.2	+9%	+5.1	+20%	+11.9	+38%
Butler	+2.6	+9%	+5.1	+16%	+4.1	+11%	+2.7	+7%
Licking	+3.8	+11%	−1.8	−5%	−1.3	−3%	+4.7	+13%
Ross	+4.6	+17%	+3	+9%	+2	+6%	+3.2	+9%

*divided in 1846 to form Mahoning County

Sources: Compendium of the Seventh Census; 1860, 1870, 1880 U.S. Census.

TABLE 2D. Population of Principal Ohio Counties, 1880 (in thousands)

	Total (TP)	Native Born	% of TP	Foreign Born	% of TP	Born in Germany	% of TP	Born in Ireland	% of TP	Born in England & Wales	% of TP	Blacks	% of TP
Hamilton	313.4	231.1	74%	82.3	26%	53.3	17%	17	5%	4.1	1%	10.5	3%
Cuyahoga	196.9	128.2	65%	68.8	35%	27.1	14%	13.2	7%	10.8	6%	2.2	1%
Franklin	86.8	75	86%	11.8	14%	6.1	7%	2.7	3%	1.6	2%	3.9	5%
Montgomery	78.6	66.3	84%	12.3	16%	7.9	10%	2.6	3%	.7	1%	1.3	2%
Lucas	67.4	50	74%	17.4	26%	8.3	12%	3.3	5%	1.3	2%	1.1	2%
Stark	64	55.4	87%	8.6	13%	4.1	6%	.6	1%	1.5	2%	.3	.5%
Muskingum	49.8	46.6	94%	3.2	6%	1.5	3%	.8	2%	.4	1%	1.3	3%
Belmont	49.6	46.5	94%	3.1	6%	1	2%	1.2	2%	.6	1%	1.6	3%
Columbiana	48.6	43.8	90%	4.8	10%	.9	2%	1.2	3%	1.9	4%	.7	1%
Trumbull	44.9	36.2	81%	8.7	19%	.9	2%	1.7	4%	4.6	10%	.3	.6%
Summit	43.9	36.7	84%	7.1	16%	2.3	5%	1.3	3%	2.1	5%	.4	1%
Washington	43.2	40.2	93%	3.1	7%	2	5%	.5	1%	.2	1%	1.2	3%
Mahoning	42.9	34.1	80%	8.8	20%	1.5	3%	2.5	6%	3.3	8%	.5	1%
Butler	42.6	36.6	86%	5.9	14%	3.7	9%	1.3	3%	.4	1%	1.1	3%
Licking	40.5	38.3	95%	2.2	5%	.5	1%	.6	2%	.8	2%	.4	1%
Ross	40.3	37.7	94%	2.6	6%	1.7	4%	.5	1%	.1	.3%	3.3	8%

Source: 1880 U.S. Census.

TABLE 2E. Growth of Ohio's Leading Manufactures,
Measured By Book Value of Products, 1850-1880

	Output ($ million)				Growth Rate		
	1850	1860	1870	1880	1850-60	1860-70	1870-80
Flour and Grist-Mill Products	14.4	24.8	25	39	+ 72%	+ 1%	+ 56%
Iron and Steel[1]	9.7	8.2	34.5	35.5	− 16%	+ 321%	+ 3%
Iron Manufactures— Miscellaneous[2]	.3	.2	2.7	1.9	− 33%	+ 1250%	− 30%
Clothing, Men's and Women's	2.8	8.9	13.2	21.3	+ 218%	+ 48%	+ 61%
Meat Packing	3.4	5.2	10.7	19.2	+ 53%	+ 106%	+ 79%
Foundry and Machine-Shop Products	NA	NA	NA	18.2			
Lumber, Sawed and Planed	3.9	6.1	10.8	16.8	+ 56%	+ 77%	+ 56%
Agricultural Implements	.6	2.8	11.9	15.5	+ 366%	+ 325%	+ 30%
Carriages and Wagons	.9	2.3	5.1	10	+ 156%	+ 122%	+ 96%
Liquors, Malt	.5	1.9	5.8	9.1	+ 280%	+ 205%	+ 57%
Furniture	NA	3.6	6.8	7.7		+ 89%	+ 13%
All Ohio Industries	62.7	121.7	269.7	348.3	+ 94%	+ 122%	+ 29%
All U.S. Industries	1019.1	1885.9	4232.3	5369.6	+ 85%	+ 124%	+ 27%

NA—not available due to changing census categories
1 pig, foundries, furnaces, forges, rolled, castings, blooms, bar, sheet, railroad
2 nails, bolts, nuts, washers, rivets, architectural, ornamental, etc.

Sources: 1850 U.S. Census of Manufactures; 1860 U.S. Census of Manufactures;
Compendium of the 10th Census; 1870 U.S. Census—Wealth and Industry;
Senate Executive Document 39, 35th Congress, 2nd Session, 1859.

TABLE 2F. Occupational Characteristics of Ohio's Workforce, 1840-1880 (in thousands)

	Persons Engaged in All Classes of Occupations*			Engaged in Agriculture*		Engaged in Nonagricultural Occupations*				
	Male	Female	Total Workforce (TW)		% of TW	Professional and Personal Services	Trade and Transportation	Manufactures and Mechanical and Mining Industries	Total	% of TW
1840	NA	NA	358	272.6	76%	5.7	12.7	67	85.4	24%
1850	530.8[a]	NA	530.8	270.4[a]	51%	NA	NA	NA	260.4[a]	49%
1860	NA	NA	645	300.4	47%	NA	NA	NA	344.6	53%
1870	757.4[b]	83.5[b]	840.9[b]	397[b]	47%	168.3[b]	78.6[b]	197[b]	443.9[b]	53%
1880	881.8[b]	112.6[b]	994.4[b]	397.5[b]	40%	250.4[b]	104.3[b]	242.3[b]	597[b]	60%

	Average Number of Wage Earners Employed in Manufacturing				
	Males Above 16 Years	Females Above 15 Years	Children	Total	% of TW
1840	NA	NA	NA	NA	
1850	47.1	4.4	NA	51.5	10%
1860	65.8	9.9	NA	75.7	12%
1870	119.7	11.6	5.9	137.2	16%
1880	152.2	18.6	12.8	183.6	19%

NA—not available due to lack of specific census data
a—15 years of age and above
b—10 years of age and above

Sources: 1840, 1850, 1860, 1870, 1880 U.S. Census; Compendium of the 7th Census; Compendium of the 10th Census.

(*Note: These figures present only a crude outline of the occupational structure. Within these broad census categories, clear distinctions are not made between employers and employees or "white collar" and "blue collar" workers.)

TABLE 2H. Population of Principal Ohio Cities, 1840-1880 (in thousands)

	Total (TP)	Born in Ohio	% of TP	Blacks	% of TP	Foreign Born	% of TP	Born in Germany	% of TP	Born in Ireland	% of TP
Cincinnati											
1840	46.3			2.3	5%						
1850	115.4	39.3	34%	3.2	3%	54.5	47%	33.4	29%	14.4	13%
1860	161	65.3	41%	3.7	2%	73.6	46%	43.9	27%	19.4	12%
1870	216.2	111.1	51%	5.9	3%	79.6	37%	49.5	23%	18.6	9%
1880	255.1	151.5	59%	8.2	3%	71.7	28%	46.2	18%	15.1	6%
Cleveland											
1840	6.1			.06	1%						
1850	17			.2	1%						
1860	43.4			.8	2%	19.4	45%	9.1	21%	5.5	13%
1870	92.8	41	44%	1.3	1%	38.8	42%	15.9	17%	10	11%
1880	160.2	79.3	50%	2	1%	59.4	37%	23.2	15%	12	8%
Columbus											
1840	6.1			.6	9%						
1850	17.9			1.3	7%						
1860	18.6			1	5%						
1870	31.3	18.3	59%	1.8	6%	7.6	24%	4	13%	1.9	6%
1880	51.7	34.9	68%	3	6%	9.1	18%	4.4	9%	2.3	5%
Dayton											
1840	6.1			.3	5%						
1850	11			.2	2%						
1860	20.1			.3	2%	5.6	28%	3.6	18%	1.3	6%
1870	30.5	18	59%	.6	2%	7.4	24%	5	16%	1.3	4%
1880	38.7	25.5	66%	1	3%	7.3	19%	4.9	13%	1.3	3%
Toledo											
1840	1.2			.03	3%						
1850	3.8			.1	3%						
1860	13.8			.2	2%						
1870	31.6	14.3	45%	.6	2%	11.1	35%	5.3	17%	3	10%
1880	50.1	26.3	52%	.9	2%	14.4	29%	9.8	14%	2.9	6%

Sources: 1840, 1850, 1860, 1870, 1880 U.S. Census; Compendium of the 7th Census; Compendium of the 10th Census.

TABLE 2G. Characteristics of the Workforce in Ohio's Principal Cities, 1860-1880* (in thousands)

	Population		Persons Engaged in All Occupations					Engaged in Manufacturing, Mechanical, and Mining Industries					
	Total	% foreign born	Males	Females	Children (under 16 yrs)	% foreign born	Total Workforce (TW)	Males	Females	Children (under 16 yrs)	% foreign born	Total	% of TW
Cincinnati													
1860	161	46%						23.2	6.3			29.5	
1870	216.2	37%	59.2	16	2.7	55%	77.9	27	5.5	1.4	57%	33.9	44%
1880	255.1	28%	74.9	20.4	5.1	38%	100.4	35.8	8.6	2.9	38%	47.3	47%
Cleveland													
1860	43.4	45%						2.8	.6			3.4	
1870	92.8	42%	25.9	3.9	.4	61%	30.2	12.7	.9	.3	64%	13.9	46%
1880	160.2	37%	45.7	9.6	1.6	53%	56.9	22.1	3.3	.9	56%	26.3	46%
Columbus													
1860	18.6							1.6	.1			1.7	
1870	31.3	24%	9	2.2	.4	37%	11.6	4.5	.6	.1	37%	5.2	45%
1880	51.7	18%	15	3.2	.5	24%	18.7	6	1	.2	27%	7.2	39%
Dayton													
1860	20.1	28%						1.6	.2			1.8	
1870	30.5	24%	8.5	1.8	.4	38%	10.7	4.5	.7	.2	38%	5.4	51%
1880	38.7	19%	11.4	2.3	.5	26%	14.2	5.9	.8	.3	27%	7	49%
Toledo													
1860	13.8							.9	.2			1.1	
1870	31.6	35%	11.2	1.6	.2	57%	13	3.9	.4	.1	50%	4.4	34%
1880	50.1	29%	14.4	2.9	.4	41%	17.7	5.1	.9	.2	42%	6.2	35%

	Engaged in Trade and Transportation						Engaged in Professional and Personal Services					
	Males	Females	Children (under 16 yrs)	% foreign born	Total	% of TW	Males	Females	Children (under 16 yrs)	% foreign born	Total	% of TW
Cincinnati												
1860												
1870	16	.5	.4	44%	16.9	22%	14.8	10	.9	60%	25.7	33%
1880	20.9	1.3	.7	36%	22.9	23%	17.2	10.5	1.4	39%	29.1	29%
Cleveland												
1860												
1870	8.1	.06	.1	49%	8.2	27%	4.8	2.9	.1	66%	7.8	26%
1880	12.3	.5	.2	42%	13	23%	10.8	5.7	.5	57%	17	30%
Columbus												
1860												
1870	2.3	.03	.03	26%	2.4	21%	2.3	1.5	.1	43%	3.9	34%
1880	4.4	.1	.1	18%	4.6	25%	4.4	2.1	.2	25%	6.7	36%
Dayton												
1860												
1870	2	.04	.1	27%	2.2	21%	1.8	1.1	.1	68%	5.8	45%
1880	2.8	.1	.1	24%	3	21%	2.6	1.3	.2	25%	4.1	29%
Toledo												
1860												
1870	2.7	.004	.02	45%	2.8	22%	4.4	1.3	.1	68%	5.8	45%
1880	4.9	.1	.1	35%	5.1	29%	4.1	1.8	.2	44%	6.1	35%

(*Note: These figures present only a crude outline of the occupational structure. Within these broad census categories, clear distinctions are not made between employers and employees or "white collar" and "blue collar" workers.)

Sources: 1860, 1870, 1880 U.S. Census: Ninth Annual Report of the State Commissioner of Statistics (Columbus: State Printer, 1865).

TABLE 2I. Population of Representative Secondary Cities in Ohio, 1840-1880 (in thousands)

		Total (TP)	Foreign Born	% of TP	Blacks	% of TP
Springfield						
	1840	2.1			.1	4%
	1850	5.1			.2	4%
	1860	7			.3	4%
	1870	12.7	2.2	17%	1.2	10%
	1880	20.7	3.1	15%	2.4	11%
Zanesville						
	1840	4.8			.2	3%
	1850	7.9			.2	3%
	1860	9.2			.4	4%
	1870	10	1.6	16%	.3	3%
	1880	18.1	2.1	12%	.9	5%
Akron						
	1840	1.7			.02	1%
	1850	3.3			.07	2%
	1860	3.5			.02	1%
	1870	10	2.6	26%	.2	2%
	1880	16.5	3.6	22%	.3	2%
Youngstown						
	1840					
	1850	2.8			.02	1%
	1860	2.8			.01	.3%
	1870	8.1	2.8	35%	.1	2%
	1880	15.4	4.8	31%	.3	2%
Steubenville						
	1840	4.3			.1	2%
	1850	6.1			.1	2%
	1860	6.2			.2	3%
	1870	8.1	1.7	20%	.3	3%
	1880	12.1	1.9	16%	.5	4%
Portsmouth						
	1840	1.9			.1	6%
	1850	4			.1	3%
	1860	6.3			.2	3%
	1870	10.6	2.1	20%	.9	8%
	1880	11.3	1.6	14%	1	9%
Mansfield						
	1840	1.3			.01	1%
	1850	3.6			.05	1%
	1860	4.6			.01	.3%
	1870	8	1.5	19%	.1	1%
	1880	9.9	1.5	15%	.1	1%
East Liverpool						
	1840	.5			.002	.4%
	1850	1.6			0	
	1860	2.1			.01	1%
	1870	3	.7	23%	.002	.06%
	1880	5.6	1.1	20%	.07	1%

Sources: *1840, 1850, 1860, 1870, 1880 U.S. Census; Compendium of the 7th Census; Compendium of the 10th Census.*

TABLE 2K. Annual Average Earnings, Expenses, and Savings of Ohio Working-Class Families, Headed Predominantly By Skilled Workers, 1877-1885

	Number of Families	Average Family Size	Total Family Earnings	Total Family Expenses	Total Family Savings	Percentage of Earnings Saved
1877	61	4.9	$568	$508	$60	10.6%
1878	140	4.6	$511	$476	$35	6.8%
1879	114	4.9	$655	$576	$79	12.1%
1880	324	4.8	$681	$552	$129	18.9%
1881	211	5.0	$788	$584	$204	25.9%
1882	500	5.0	$707	$551	$156	22.1%
1883	266	5.1	$649	$553	$96	14.8%
1885	353	4.9	$538	$489	$49	9.1%

Sources: *Annual reports of the Ohio Bureau of Labor Statistics for 1877 through 1885.*

TABLE 2J. Retail Prices of Sample Necessities in Six Ohio Cities, 1845-1880*

	Potatoes (bushel)	Flour (barrel)	Bacon (pound)	Sugar (pound)	Coffee (pound)	Butter (pound)	Beans (quart)	Eggs (dozen)	Totals	Coal (ton)	Rent—Four Room House (monthly)
Cincinnati											
1845	.42	3.68	.08	.06	.11	.14	.05	.10	4.64		
1855	1.70	8.25	.09	.07	.12	.18	.06	.12	10.59		6.00
1860	.55	5.25	.09	.08	.14	.14	.03	.10	6.38		6.00
1865	1.28	8.77	.21	.23	.35	.33	.07	.30	11.54		6.00
1875	.70	5.34	.14	.09	.24	.27	.06	.20	7.04	3.35	10.00
1880	.50	5.65	.11	.09	.16	.24	.05	.15	6.95	2.52	10.00
Cleveland											
1845	.30	4.21	.13	.08	.05	.07	.05	.08	4.97		
1855	1.16	9.58	.11	.08	.12	.15	.06	.15	11.41		
1860	.38	5.30	.11	.07	.14	.13	.03	.12	6.28		
1865	.77	9.79	.23	.21	.38	.31	.06	.26	12.01		
1875	.70	7.63	.14	.11	.25	.25	.06	.22	9.36	3.65	
1880	.52	5.96	.11	.09	.18	.22	.05	.16	7.29	4.16	
Columbus											
1845	.41	3.80	.08	.06	.08	.13	.03	.10	4.69		
1855	.89	8.73	.13	.07	.14	.21	.08	.12	10.37		
1860	.35	5.96	.13	.10	.17	.15	.04	.11	7.01		
1865	1.25	9.80	.32	.22	.41	.37	.08	.29	12.74		
1875	.77	6.36	.14	.09	.22	.24	.06	.19	8.07		
1880	.47	5.83	.11	.10	.17	.17	.05	.13	7.03	2.81	
Springfield											
1845											
1855	.25	3.25	.05	.07	.12	.07	.05	.06	3.92		5.00
1860	.30	4.00	.06	.09	.15	.10	.05	.07	4.82		5.00
1865	.85	10.00	.12	.15	.40	.25	.08	.15	12.00	3.50	5.00
1875	.50	6.00	.08	.09	.17	.13	.10	.12	7.19	3.50	12.00
1880	.70	6.00	.10	.08	.15	.13	.10	.13	7.39	4.00	12.00
Zanesville											
1845											
1855	.60	3.50	.07	.08	.15	.15	.07	.10	4.72	1.50	7.00
1860	.60	4.75	.10	.08	.15	.13	.06	.15	6.02	3.00	7.00
1865	1.00	7.50	.20	.18	.20	.33	.10	.15	9.66	3.00	9.00
1875	.75	7.00	.16	.10	.20	.20	.10	.15	8.66	2.50	8.00
1880	.60	4.00	.12	.10	.20	.20	.10	.15	5.47	2.25	8.00
Canton											
1855	.38			.06	.10	.09	.04	.08		2.00	6.00
1860	.50	5.75	.09	.08	.16	.12	.05	.10	6.85	2.00	6.25
1865	.60	7.80	.15	.16	.35	.14	.05	.10	9.35	1.68	6.00
1875	.40	7.00	.08	.09	.25	.20	.05	.16	8.23	3.00	6.00
1880	.50	6.00	.06	.08	.20	.20	.08	.10	7.22	2.25	8.00

*figures represent lowest average prices where available

Sources: Joseph D. Weeks, Report On the Statistics of Wages In Manufacturing Industries; With Supplementary Reports On the Average Retail Prices of Necessaries of Life . . . (Washington, D.C.: Government Printing Office, 1886); Seventeenth Annual Report of the Ohio Bureau of Labor Statistics . . . For 1893. (Norwalk: Laning Printing Co., 1894).

TABLE 2L. Estimated Strikes in the United States and Ohio, 1881-1885*

	OHIO					UNITED STATES				
	1881	1882	1883	1884	1885	1881	1882	1883	1884	1885
Total Strikes	40	33	48	38	63	471	454	478	443	645
Number of Establishments	190	137	199	120	293	2928	2105	2759	2367	2284
Employees Striking and Involved	11,217	16,221	12,085	13,112	35,624	129,521	154,671	149,763	147,054	242,705
% of Union-ordered Strikes	47.5	66.7	60.4	55.3	63.5	47.4	48.5	56.7	54.2	55.4
% of Strikes Totally or Partly Won by Workers	73.2	58.4	59.8	22.5	63.8	71.7	65.9	82.4	58.9	73.0
% of Nation's Strikes Occurring In Ohio	8.5	7.3	10.0	8.6	9.8					
% of Nation's Striking and Involved Workers In Ohio	8.7	10.5	8.1	8.9	14.7					

*Figures listed here do not include lockouts, and therefore are lower than those cited in Historical Statistics of the United States, I: 179.

Sources: Third Annual Report of the Commissioner of Labor, 1887, Tenth Annual Report . . . 1894, Sixteenth Annual Report . . . 1901, Twenty-First Annual Report . . . 1906.

TABLE 3A. Population Characteristics of Ohio, 1880-1920 (in thousands)

	Total Pop. (TP)	Native Born	% of TP	Foreign Born White	% of TP	Frgn/Ntv Born of Frgn/Mixed Parents	% of TP	Blacks	% of TP	Born in Ohio	% of TP	Ntv/Born Outside Ohio	% of TP
1880	3,198.1	2,803.1	88%	394.9	12%			79.7	3%	2,361.4	74%	441.7	14%
1890	3,672.3	3,213.0	88%	459.3	12.5%	1,251.0	34%	87.5	2%	2,772.0	76%	441.0	12%
1900	4,157.6	3,698.8	89%	458.7	11%	916.2	22%	97.3	2.3%	3,190.0	77%	509.0	12%
1910	4,767.1	4,169.1	88%	597.3	12.5%	1,621.6	34%	111.5	2.3%	3,547.0	74%	622.0	13%
1920	5,759.4	5,079.4	88%	678.7	11.8%	1,902.8	33%	186.2	3.2%	4,080.0	71%	983.5	17%

Sources: Censuses of 1880, 1890, 1900, 1910, 1920.

TABLE 3B. Population Changes in Ohio, 1880-1920 (in thousands)

	Total Pop.	% Change	Native Born	% Change	Foreign Born	% Change	Born In Ohio	% Change	Ntv/Born Outside Ohio	% Change	Blacks	% Change	Frgn/Ntv Born of Frgn/Mixed Parents	% Change
1880-1890	+474.3	+14.8%	+409.9	+14.6%	+64.4	+16%	+410.6	+17%	-0.7	-0.2%	+7.8	+9.8%		
1890-1900	+485.2	+13.2%	+485.8	+15.1%	-0.6	-0.1%	+418.0	+15%	+68.0	+15%	+9.8	+11.2%	-334.8	-26.7%
1900-1910	+609.6	+14.7%	+470.3	+12.7%	+138.5	+30.2%	+380.0	+12%	+113.0	+22%	+14.2	+14.5%	+705.4	+77%
1910-1920	+992.3	+20.8%	+910.3	+21.8%	+81.5	+13.6%	+533.0	+15%	+361.5	+58%	+74.7	+67.1%	+281.1	+17.3%

Sources: Censuses of 1880, 1890, 1900, 1910, 1920.

TABLE 3C. Population Changes in Principal Ohio Counties, 1880-1920 (in thousands)

County	1880 Pop.	1880-1890 pop. chgn.	1880-1890 % chgn.	1890-1900 pop. chgn.	1890-1900 % chng.	1900-1910 pop. chgn.	1900-1910 % chng.	1910-1920 pop. chng.	1910-1920 % chng.	1920 Pop.
Hamilton	313.4	+61.2	+19.5%	+34.9	+9.3%	+52.2	+12.5%	+33.0	+7.2%	493.7
Cuyahoga	196.9	+113.1	+57.4%	+129.1	+41.7%	+198.3	+45.2%	+306.1	+48.1%	943.5
Franklin	86.8	+37.3	+43.0%	+40.4	+32.6%	+57.1	+34.7%	+62.4	+28.2%	284.0
Montgomery	78.6	+22.3	+28.4%	+29.3	+29%	+33.6	+25.9%	+45.7	+27.9%	209.5
Lucas	67.4	+34.9	+51.8%	+51.3	+50.2%	+39.1	+25.5%	+83.0	+43.1%	275.7
Stark	64.0	+20.2	+31.6%	+10.6	+12.6%	+28.2	+29.8%	+54.2	+44.1%	177.2
Muskingum	49.8	+1.4	+2.8%	+2.0	+3.9%	+4.3	+8.1%	+.5	+.9%	58.0
Belmont	49.6	+7.8	+15.7%	+3.5	+6.1%	+16	+26.3%	+16.3	+21.2%	93.2
Columbiana	48.6	+10.4	+21.4%	+9.6	+16.3%	+8	+11.7%	+6.5	+8.5%	83.1
Trumbull	44.9	-2.5	-5.6%	+4.2	+9.9%	+6.2	+13.3%	+31.1	+59%	83.9
Summit	43.9	+10.2	+23.2%	+17.6	+32.5%	+36.6	+51.1%	+177.8	+164.2%	286.1
Washington	43.2	-.8	-1.9%	+5.9	+13.9%	-2.9	-6%	-2.3	-5.1%	43.1
Mahoning	42.9	+13.1	+30.5%	+14	+25%	+46.2	+66%	+70.1	+60.3%	186.3
Butler	42.6	+6.0	+14.1%	+8.3	+17.1%	+13.4	+23.6%	+16.7	+23.8%	87.0
Licking	40.5	+2.8	+6.9%	+3.8	+8.8%	+8.5	+18.1%	+.8	+1.4%	56.4
Ross	40.3	-1.0	-2.5%	+1.4	+3.5%	-.8	-2.0%	+1.5	+3.7%	41.6

TABLE 3E. Ohio's Urban & Rural Population Distribution, 1880-1920

	Urban	% of TP	Rural	% of TP
1880	1,030,769	32%	2,167,293	68%
1890	1,504,390	41%	2,167,939	59%
1900	1,998,382	48%	2,159,163	52%
1910	2,665,143	56%	2,101,978	44%
1920	3,677,136	64%	2,082,258	36%

Sources: Censuses of 1880, 1890, 1900, 1910, 1920.

TABLE 3F. Changes in the Distribution of Ohio's Population, 1880-1920 (in thousands)

	Urban*	% Change	Rural	% Change
1880-1890	+473.6	+45.9%	+0.7	+0.3%
1890-1900	+494.0	+32.8%	-8.8	-0.4%
1900-1910	+666.8	+33.4%	-57.2	-2.7%
1910-1920	+1,012	+38%	-19.7	-0.9%

Sources: Censuses of 1880, 1890, 1900, 1910, 1920.

places with more than 2500 residents

TABLE 3D. Population of Principal Ohio Counties, 1920 (in thousands)

County	Total (TP)	Native Born White	% of TP	For- eign Born	% of TP	Blacks	% of TP	Born in Germany	% of TP	Born in Ireland	% of TP	Born in England and Wales	% of TP	Born in Hungary	% of TP	Born in Italy	% of TP	Born in Poland	% of TP
Cuyahoga	943.5	641.8	68%	265.9	28%	35.4	4%	30.6	3%	10.7	1%	15.6	2%	31.7	3%	19.4	2%	37.1	4%
Hamilton	493.7	411.2	83%	48.7	10%	33.8	7%	21.1	4%	4.4	1%	2.1	.4%	3.2	1%	2.8	1%	1.3	.3%
Summit	286.1	230.8	81%	48.9	17%	6.6	2%	3.6	1%	1.1	.4%	4.0	1%	9.2	3%	3.2	1%	.7	.3%
Franklin	284.0	241.7	85%	18.2	6%	23.9	8%	4.7	2%	1.4	1%	.8	.3%	1.1	.4%	2.7	1%	.4	.1%
Lucas	275.7	228.4	83%	41.2	15%	6.1	2%	9.5	4%	1.6	1%	2.2	1%	3.1	1%	.9	.3%	10.7	4%
Montgomery	209.5	183.9	88%	15.5	7%	10.1	5%	5.2	3%	1.0	1%	.7	.3%	2.0	1%	.6	.3%	.7	.3%
Mahoning	186.3	132.0	71%	45.7	25%	8.5	5%	1.9	1%	1.8	1%	4.5	2%	4.2	2%	7.1	4%	3.6	2%
Stark	177.2	150.0	85%	24.4	14%	2.8	2%	3.1	2%	.4	.2%	1.9	1%	1.9	1%	3.2	2%	.7	.4%
Belmont	93.2	76.1	82%	15.0	16%	2.0	2%	.9	1%	.3	.4%	1.2	1%	1.6	2%	2.2	2%	3.0	3%
Lorain	90.6	69.4	77%	19.2	21%	1.9	2%	2.7	3%	.4	.4%	1.5	2%	3.9	4%	1.0	1%	2.2	2%
Butler	87.0	78.6	90%	4.9	6%	3.5	4%	1.8	2%	.2	.2%	.2	.2%	.4	1%	.4	1%	.1	.1%
Trumbull	83.9	68.8	82%	14.0	17%	1.1	1%	.5	1%	.5	1%	2.0	2%	1.1	1%	3.0	4%	.4	1%
Columbiana	83.1	74.7	90%	7.0	8%	1.4	2%	.7	1%	.3	.4%	1.9	2%	.2	.2%	1.4	2%	.1	.1%
Clark	80.7	70.0	87%	3.0	4%	7.5	9%	.9	1%	.6	1%	.6	1%	.05	.1%	.2	.2%	.04	.1%
Muskingum	58.0	54.6	94%	1.6	3%	1.8	3%	.5	1%	.1	.2%	.2	.3%	.2	.3%	.02	.03%	.1	.2%

Source: United States Census, 1920.

TABLE 3G. Population of Principal Ohio Cities, 1880-1920

	Total Pop.	% Change From Prev. Census	% Foreign Born White	% Ntv/Wht of Frn/Mxd Parents	% Ethnic	% Black
Akron						
1880	16,512					
1890	27,601	+67.2	21.7	29.3	51.0	1.6
1900	42,728	+54.8	16.7	31.0	47.0	1.2
1910	69,067	+61.6	19.2	25.1	44.3	1.0
1920	208,435	+201.8	18.2	19.1	37.3	2.6
Cincinnati						
1880	255,139					
1890	296,908	+16.4	24.0	45.0	69.0	3.9
1900	325,902	+9.8	17.8	42.9	60.7	4.4
1910	363,591	+11.6	15.6	36.4	52.0	5.4
1920	401,247	+10.4	10.7	30.3	41.0	7.5
Cleveland						
1880	160,146					
1890	261,353	+63.2	37.1	38.2	75.3	1.2
1900	381,768	+46.1	32.6	42.8	75.4	1.6
1910	560,663	+46.9	34.6	39.9	74.8	1.5
1920	796,841	+42.1	30.1	69.0	69.0	4.3
Columbus						
1880	51,647					
1890	88,150	+70.7	14.1	26.1	40.2	6.3
1900	125,560	+42.4	9.8	23.9	33.7	6.5
1910	181,511	+44.6	9.0	28.6	28.6	7.0
1920	237,031	+30.6	6.8	23.5	23.5	9.4
Dayton						
1880	38,678					
1890	61,220	+58.3	15.6	28.2	43.8	3.5
1900	85,333	+39.4	11.7	27.6	39.3	4.0
1910	116,577	+36.6	11.9	21.9	33.8	4.2
1920	152,559	+30.9	8.6	19.3	27.9	5.9
Toledo						
1880	50,137					
1890	81,434	+62.4	27.7	37.6	64.7	1.3
1900	131,822	+61.9	21.0	38.0	59.0	1.3
1910	168,497	+27.8	19.0	35.2	54.2	1.1
1920	243,164	+44.3	15.7	30.9	46.6	2.3
Youngstown						
1880	15,435					
1890	33,220	+115.2	31.7	38.8	70.5	2.0
1900	44,885	+35.1	27.2	41.0	68.2	2.0
1910	79,066	+76.2	31.4	33.7	65.1	2.4
1920	132,358	+67.4	25.6	34.2	59.8	2.9

Sources: U.S. Census, 1890, 1900, 1910, 1920.

TABLE 3H. Population of Representative Secondary Cities In Ohio

	Total Pop.	% Change From Prev. Census	% Foreign Born White	% Ntv/Wht of Frn/Mxd Parents	% Ethnic	% Black
Canton						
1880	12,258					
1890	26,189	+113.7	16.1	27.2	43.3	.4
1900	30,667	+17.1	13.1	28.1	41.2	.4
1910	50,217	+63.7	17.2	23.5	40.7	.6
1920	87,091	+73.4	16.9	19.9	36.8	1.5
Hamilton						
1880	12,122					
1890	17,565	+44.9	16.9	37.9	54.8	1.7
1900	23,914	+36.1	12.3	34.5	46.8	1.5
1910	35,279	+47.5	9.4	26.6	36.0	2.1
1920	39,675	+12.5	6.7	21.4	28.1	3.3
Lakewood						
1880	N/A					
1890	N/A					
1900	3,355		27.7	36.7	64.4	.1
1910	15,181	+352.5	25.8	32.8	58.6	.3
1920	41,732	+174.9	17.4	33.1	50.5	.2
Lima						
1880	7,567					
1890	15,981	+111.2	10.8	20.3	31.1	3.5
1900	21,723	+35.9	6.6	19.1	25.7	3.4
1910	30,508	+40.4	5.3	14.6	19.9	3.2
1920	41,326	+35.5	4.6	13.5	18.1	3.0
Lorain						
1880	1,595					
1890	4,863	+204.9	22.0	32.6	54.6	4.0
1900	16,028	+229.6	29.5	31.8	61.3	2.2
1910	28,883	+80.2	37.8	31.6	69.4	1.3
1920	37,295	+29.1	32.0	37.1	69.1	1.5
Portsmouth						
1880	11,321					
1890	12,394	+9.5	10.0	27.9	37.7	7.7
1900	17,870	+44.2	6.0	21.5	27.5	5.3
1910	23,481	+31.4	3.5	14.7	18.2	3.3
1920	33,011	+40.6	2.1	10.7	12.8	3.5
Springfield						
1880	20,730					
1890	31,895	+53.9	11.7	22.5	34.2	11.1
1900	38,253	+19.9	8.6	22.3	30.9	11.1
1910	46,921	+22.2	6.7	17.6	24.3	10.5
1920	60,840	+29.7	4.5	13.2	17.7	11.6

N/A—not available   Source: U.S. Census, 1890, 1900, 1910, 1920.

TABLE 3I. Growth of Ohio's Leading Manufactures, Measured by Book Value of Products, 1880-1920

	Output ($ Millions)					Growth Rate			
	1880	1890	1900	1910	1920	1880-90	1890-1900	1900-10	1910-20
Flour & Grist Mill Products	39	39	35.1	48.1	89.4	0%	−10%	+37%	+86%
Iron & Steel[1]	35.5	57.1	138.9	281.5	805.6	+61%	+143%	+103%	+186%
Iron/Steel-Misc. Manuf.[2]	1.9	2.4	12.4	—	23.5	+26%	+417%	—	—
Clothing, Men's & Women's	21.3	19.7	25.1	44.4	106.9	−8%	+27%	+77%	+141%
Slaughtering & Meat Packing	19.2	13.3	20.8	50.8	170.4	−31%	+56%	+144%	+235%
Foundry & Machine Shop Products	18.2	43.6	88.4	145.8	347.6	+140%	+103%	+65%	+138%
Lumber & Mill Work	16.8	28	32.8	34.6	44.5	+67%	+17%	+6%	+29%
Agricultural Implements	15.5	14.3	14	14.4	26.6	−8%	−2%	+3%	+85%
Carriages & Wagons	10	18.8	22.8	21.9	5	+88%	+21%	−4%	−77%
Liquors, Malt	9.1	15.9	18.5	25.3	25.2	+75%	+16%	+37%	−.4%
Boots & Shoes	—	11.2	18.2	31.6	71.4	—	+63%	+74%	+126%
Furniture[3]	7.7	10	9.5	16.3	35.2	+30%	−5%	+72%	—
Rubber Tires, Tubes & Rubber Goods	—	1.5	7.3	53.9	551.1	—	+387%	+638%	+923%
Automobiles, Bodies Parts	—	—	.1	38.8	379.4	—	—	+38,700%	+878%
Cars & GNL Shop Const & Repair/Steam RR Co.	—	8.1	12.9	28.6	4.7	—	+59%	+122%	−84%
Electrical Mach., Appar. & Supplies	—	68	6.5	18.8	157	—	+856%	+189%	+735%
Glass	—	56	4.5	14.4	35.2	—	−20%	+220%	+144%
All Ohio Industries	348.3	641.7	748.7	1,437.9	5,100.3	+84%	+17%	+92%	+255%
All U.S. Industries[4]	5,369.6	9,372.4	13,010.0	20,672.1	62,418.1	+75%	+39%	+59%	+202%

1—*Pig, foundries, furnaces, forges, rolled, castings, blooms, bar, sheet, railroad.*
2—*Nails, bolts, nuts, washers, rivets, architectural, ornamental, etc.*
3—*For 1910, includes refrigerators.*
4—*Includes establishments with over $500 in annual value of product.*

Sources: U.S. Censuses of 1880, 1890, 1900, 1910, 1920.

TABLE 3J. Structure of Ohio's Workforce, 1880-1920[1] (in thousands)

	Persons Engaged in All Classes of Occupations[2]			Engaged in Agriculture[3]		Engaged in Nonagricultural Occupations										
	Males	Females	Total Work-force(TW)	Number	Per-cent of TW	Mineral Mining	Profes-sional	Domestic/ Personal	Cler-ical	Public Service	Trade	Trans-portation	Manufac. & Mech. Indust.	Total	Per-cent of TW
1880	881.8	112.6	994.4	397.5	40%	5.6		250.4				104.3	236.7	597	60%
1890	1,088.6	184.2	1,272.8	401.2	31.5%	27.9	61.9	255.3				195.6	331	871.7	68.5%
1900	1,299.9	246.1	1,546	382.4	24.7%	33.3	77.1	306.4				283.9	463.8	1,164.5	75.3%
1910	1,572.3	346.7	1,919.1	419.4	21.9%	54.5	93.2	174.1	99.7	20.8	201.4	153	702.9	1,499.6	78.1%
1920	1,891.5	410	2,301.5	360.6	15.7%	59.6	117.5	161.7	190.6	32.3	246.2	173.6	959.4	1.940.9	84.3%

1—*Categories alter each census year and while it is possible to delete proprietors and supervisory personnel, doing so scarcely changes the percentage of the total workforce in each category. The figures here overestimate the proportion of wage-earners, as opposed to salaried personnel or owners, by about two percent.*
2—*10 years and above*
3—*Includes Fisheries and Forestry*

Sources: U. S. Census, 1880, 1890, 1900, 1910, 1920

TABLE 3K. Characteristics of the Workforce in Ohio's Principal Cities, 1890-1920 (in thousands)

		Population		Persons Engaged In All Occupations					Persons Engaged In Manufacturing & Mechanical					
		Total	Percent of Foreign Born	Males	Females	Children	Percent of Foreign Born	Total Work-force (TW)	Males	Females	Children	Percent of Foreign Born	Total	Percent of TW
Akron	1890	27.6	21.7%	—	—	—	—	—	—	—	—	—	—	—
	1900	42.7	16.7	13.9	3.4	—	—	17.3	6.7	1.3	—	—	8.0	46.2%
	1910	69.0	19.2	26.3	6.0	.2	—	32.3	17.6	2.4	.1	—	20.0	61.9
	1920	208.4	18.2	92.1	16.0	.5	22.7%	108.1	66.7	4.5	.1	26.3	71.2	65.9
Cincinnati	1890	296.9	24.0	94.5	30.4	—	30.6	124.9	42.1	12.8	—	28.4	54.9	43.9
	1900	325.9	17.8	103.8	37.8	6.2	21.5	141.6	46.0	15.0	3.4	23.3	60.9	43.0
	1910	363.6	15.6	124.3	48.1	4.0	17.9	172.4	59.2	16.6	1.3	15.0	75.8	43.9
	1920	401.2	10.7	134.9	50.4	1.2	12.1	185.3	66.5	14.7	.5	14.4	81.2	43.8
Cleveland	1890	261.4	37.1	83.1	19.3	—	50.0	102.4	34.2	7.0	—	43.9	41.2	40.2
	1900	381.8	32.6	122.5	31.4	5.2	43.9	153.9	55.9	10.6	2.7	48.1	66.5	43.2
	1910	560.7	34.9	194.0	54.8	6.0	45.3	248.8	109.6	18.2	1.8	36.3	127.8	51.4
	1920	796.8	30.1	273.7	73.5	2.3	39.8	347.2	165.1	18.8	.8	70.3	183.9	52.9
Columbus	1890	88.2	14.1	28.2	7.0	—	18.8	35.2	10.5	2.3	—	18.8	12.8	36.4
	1900	125.6	9.8	40.4	11.5	1.4	12.3	51.9	15.0	3.4	.7	15.2	18.4	36.5
	1910	181.5	9.0	63.7	19.5	1.2	11.2	83.2	28.8	5.1	.2	10.0	33.9	40.7
	1920	237.0	6.8	80.7	25.5	.7	8.5	106.2	37.3	5.3	.2	10.8	42.6	40.1
Dayton	1890	61.2	15.6	19.8	4.8	—	20.3	24.6	9.4	2.0	—	19.3	11.4	46.3
	1900	85.3	11.7	28.2	7.8	1.0	14.7	36.0	13.5	3.0	.5	14.5	16.5	45.8
	1910	116.6	11.9	41.2	11.4	.8	15.8	52.6	24.6	4.6	.2	10.3	29.2	55.5
	1920	120.6	8.6	53.5	15.0	.6	10.9	68.5	31.7	4.5	.1	13.8	36.2	52.8
Toledo	1890	81.4	27.7	25.8	6.1	—	36.7	31.9	9.5	1.9	—	32.5	4.4	13.8
	1900	131.8	21.0	41.0	10.6	1.6	27.9	51.6	15.3	3.0	.6	31.7	18.3	35.5
	1910	168.5	19.0	56.0	17.0	1.7	24.2	73.0	27.0	5.0	.4	20.6	32.0	43.8
	1920	243.2	15.7	86.8	23.3	.9	19.8	110.1	47.5	5.7	.3	26.1	53.2	48.3
Youngstown	1890	33.2	31.7	—	—	—	—	—	—	—	—	—	—	—
	1900	44.9	27.2	15.2	2.7	—	—	17.9	7.7	.6	—	—	8.3	46.3
	1910	79.1	31.4	30.4	5.6	0	—	36.0	19.3	1.0	0	—	20.3	56.4
	1920	132.4	25.6	46.6	8.7	.3	37.0	55.3	28.5	1.0	.1	48.5	29.5	53.3

		Engaged In Trade & Transportation						Engaged in Professional & Personal Services					
		Males	Females	Children	Percent Foreign Born	Total	Percent of TW	Males	Females	Children	Percent Foreign Born	Total	Percent of TW
Akron	1890	—	—	—	—	—	—	—	—	—	—	5.0	28.9
	1900	3.5	.7	—	—	4.2	24.3%	3.6	1.4	—	—	6.9	21.4
	1910	4.7	.6	0	—	5.3	16.4	3.8	3.1	.1	—	22.9	21.2
	1920	11.7	1.9	.2	19.9%	13.6	12.6	13.3	9.6	.2	13.1%	22.9	21.2
Cincinnati	1890	28.6	3.5	—	23.0	32.1	25.7	22.7	14.0	—	31.6	36.7	29.4
	1900	34.6	6.5	1.7	16.3	41.1	29.0	22.3	16.3	1.0	23.0	38.6	27.3
	1910	35.2	5.5	.6	14.5	40.7	23.6	28.4	25.8	1.2	12.4	54.2	31.4
	1920	36.2	6.5	.3	11.5	42.7	23.0	30.7	29.1	.4	9.2	59.8	32.3
Cleveland	1890	21.3	2.3	—	31.4	23.6	23.0	26.8	9.9	—	57.8	36.7	35.8
	1900	34.9	6.2	1.2	28.7	41.1	26.7	30.9	14.5	1.2	51.5	45.4	29.5
	1910	48.8	7.0	1.1	34.7	55.8	22.4	34.3	29.5	1.5	26.0	63.8	25.6
	1920	57.7	11.1	.6	33.0	68.8	19.8	49.6	43.6	.9	22.4	93.2	26.8
Columbus	1890	9.0	.7	—	11.3	9.7	27.6	8.3	3.9	—	18.9	12.2	34.1
	1900	13.9	2.0	.3	8.8	15.9	30.6	10.8	6.1	.3	12.4	16.9	32.6
	1910	19.6	2.1	.4	10.1	21.7	26.0	14.7	12.2	.3	6.3	26.9	32.3
	1920	24.0	3.6	.3	8.3	27.6	26.0	18.7	16.6	.2	5.9	35.3	33.2
Dayton	1890	4.9	.5	—	12.9	5.4	21.9	5.3	2.3	—	22.4	7.6	30.9
	1900	7.5	1.4	.2	10.1	8.9	24.7	6.9	3.3	.3	15.7	10.2	28.3
	1910	8.8	1.2	0	8.0	10.0	19.0	7.3	5.6	.1	5.4	12.9	24.5
	1920	10.7	2.0	.3	9.4	12.7	18.5	10.9	8.5	.2	6.2	19.4	28.3
Toledo	1890	8.5	.8	—	23.7	9.3	29.2	7.4	3.4	—	44.4	10.8	33.9
	1900	14.5	2.2	.3	19.2	16.7	32.4	10.9	4.8	.7	33.8	15.7	30.4
	1910	17.9	2.3	.4	18.3	20.2	27.7	10.5	9.6	.3	12.4	20.1	27.5
	1920	22.5	3.5	.3	15.4	26.0	23.6	16.2	14.0	.3	12.3	30.2	27.4
Youngstown	1890	—	—	—	—	—	—	—	—	—	—	—	—
	1900	3.6	.6	—	—	4.2	23.5	3.8	1.4	—	—	5.2	29.0
	1910	6.4	1.0	0	—	7.4	20.6	4.6	3.6	0	—	8.2	22.8
	1920	9.8	1.7	.1	29.6	11.5	20.8	8.0	5.9	.1	20.1	13.9	25.1

Children: Age period 10-15 years
Children not Available for 1890 (Age Groups 10-24)
Males and Females: All persons 10 years old and older
Sources: United States Census, 1890, 1900, 1910, 1920.

TABLE 3L. Strikes in The United States and Ohio, 1886-1905[1]

	Year	Total Strikes	Number of Estab-lishments	Number of Employees Striking & Involved	Percent of Strikes Ordered by Union	Percent of Strikes Totally or Partially Won by Workers	Percent of Nation's Strikes Occurring in Ohio	Percent of Nation's Striking & Involved Workers in Ohio
UNITED STATES	1886	1,432	10,053	508,044	53.3%	53.9		
	1887	1,436	6,589	379,676	66.3	55.6		
	1888	906	3,506	147,704	68.1	61.2		
	1889	1,075	3,786	249,559	67.4	67.0		
	1890	1,833	9,424	351,944	71.3	64.1		
	1891	1,717	8,116	298,939	74.8	46.6		
	1892	1,298	5,540	206,671	70.7	48.1		
	1893	1,305	4,555	265,914	69.4	64.8		
	1894	1,349	8,196	660,425	62.8	51.0		
	1895	1,215	6,973	392,403	54.3	69.3		
	1896	1,026	5,462	241,170	64.6	69.0		
	1897	1,078	8,492	408,391	55.3	89.2		
	1898	1,056	3,809	249,002	60.4	75.9		
	1899	1,797	11,317	417,072	62.1	90.5		
	1900	1,779	9,248	505,066	65.4	70.0		
	1901	2,924	10,908	543,386	75.9	67.6		
	1902	3,162	14,248	659,792	78.2	72.0		
	1903	3,494	20,248	656,055	78.8	65.5		
	1904	2,307	10,202	517,211	82.1	51.3		
	1905	2,077	8,292	221,686	74.7	52.9		
OHIO	1886	88	301	21,487	39.8%	56.8	6.1	4.2
	1887	77	244	14,264	39.0	50.8	5.4	3.8
	1888	46	93	5,583	39.1	41.9	5.1	3.8
	1889	45	90	5,275	44.4	52.2	4.2	2.1
	1890	83	311	10,544	55.4	73.3	4.5	3.0
	1891	104	349	19,781	63.5	51.6	6.1	6.6
	1892	77	291	9,596	66.2	58.8	5.9	4.6
	1893	95	386	30,447	64.2	33.4	7.3	11.5
	1894	100	554	60,802	54.0	44.8	7.4	9.2
	1895	104	631	48,235	57.7	39.1	8.6	12.3
	1896	101	312	23,926	68.3	47.4	9.8	9.9
	1897	67	210	13,019	58.2	68.6	6.2	3.2
	1898	86	258	21,370	73.3	59.3	8.1	8.6
	1899	148	357	25,338	62.8	73.9	8.2	6.1
	1900	128	386	17,725	64.0	67.9	7.2	3.5
	1901	232	1,137	63,365	62.9	63.9	7.9	11.7
	1902	190	698	21,643	66.3	72.8	6.0	3.3
	1903	283	1,329	37,093	71.0	71.3	8.1	5.7
	1904	163	760	35,735	72.4	36.6	7.1	6.9
	1905	131	571	10,444	70.9	51.5	6.0	4.7

Sources: Tenth Annual Report of the Commissioner of Labor, 1894; Sixteenth Annual Report . . . 1901; Twenty-First Annual Report, 1906.
1—The figures listed here for the U.S. are lower than those cited in Historical Statistics of the United States, I:179 because they do not include lockouts.

TABLE 3M. Local Unions In Ohio, to 1900

Union	Total #	Organized 1880-90	Organized 1890-1900
Bakers & Confectioners	7	1	6
Barbers	17		16
Bicycle Workers	10		9
Broth. Boilermkrs & Iron Shipbldrs	11		11
Bookbinders	4		4
Boot & Shoe Workers	4		4
Bakers & Confectioners	7	1	17 (sic)
Bricklayers	6	1	5
Brickmakers	3		
Broommakers	3		3
Carriage & Wagon Workers	5		5
Carpenters & Joiners	30	12	16
Granite Cutters	3	2	1
Hod Carriers	4		2
Horseshoers (Journeymen)	6	*1 1	4
Iron Molders	27	*9 7	8
Iron, Steel & Tin	41	*2 7	29
Laundry Workers	4		4
Leather Workers	3		3
Letter Carriers	12		11
Longshoremen	35	*1 1	33
Machinists	18	1	14
Metal Chippers	2		
Metal Polishers	11		11
Mine Workers	194	*1 6	156
Musicians	10	2	8
Oil & Gas Well Workers	9		9
Painters, Decorators & Paperhangers	18	3	14
Pattern Makers	4		4
Plasterers	2	*1	1
Potters	19		19
Printing Pressmen	15	2	13
Railroad Conductors	22	10	9
Railway Trackmen	4		4
Railway Trainmen	28	10	11
Sheet Metal Workers	2		2
Street Railway Employees	9		8
Steam Fitters	3		
Stereotypers	2	1	1
Stone Cutters	2	*1	1
Stone Masons	4	2	2
Stove Mounters	4		3
Stoneware Potters	3		3
Suspender Workers	2		2
Tailors	15	3	12
Teamsters	11		11
Telegraph Operators	7	1	6
Theatrical Stage Employees	8	*1	7
Tin Plate Workers	5		5
Tobacco Workers	5		4
Typographers	18	*3 4	8
Waiters	2		2
Wood Carvers	2	*1	1
Wood Workers	4		4
Wood, Wire & Metal Lathers	6		6
Miscellaneous	54	*2 2	47
TOTAL	956	*40 126	710

*Pre-1880

Organized During 1900—300
Disbanded During 1900—25

Source: Ohio Bureau of Labor Statistics, Twenty-Fourth Annual Report . . . 1900 (Columbus, 1900), 362-373.

TABLE 4A. Work Stoppages in the United States and Ohio, 1919-1945

	UNITED STATES			OHIO		
	# beginning in year	Workers involved (in thousands)	Man-days idle (in thousands)	# beginning in year	Workers involved (in thousands)	Man-days idle (in thousands)
1919	3,630	4,160	N/A	237	N/A	N/A
1920	3,411	1,463	N/A	206	N/A	N/A
1921	2,385	1,099	N/A	167	N/A	N/A
1922	1,112	1,613	N/A	73	N/A	N/A
1923	1,553	757	N/A	65	N/A	N/A
1924	1,249	655	N/A	68	N/A	N/A
1925	1,301	428	N/A	73	N/A	N/A
1926	1,035	330	N/A	68	N/A	N/A
1927	707	330	26,200	21	29	4,521
1928	604	314	12,600	27	12	1,627
1929	921	289	5,350	44	6	174
1930	637	183	3,320	33	8	116
1931	810	342	6,890	42	12	143
1932	841	324	10,500	37	19	1,815
1933	1,695	1,170	16,900	96	25	280
1934	1,856	1,470	19,600	200	81	1,381
1935	2,014	1,120	15,500	173	89	1,302
1936	2,172	789	13,900	177	125	1,743
1937	4,740	1,860	28,400	257	132	1,743
1938	2,772	688	9,150	97	44	300
1939	2,613	1,170	17,800	96	51	769
1940	2,508	577	6,700	149	30	323
1941	4,288	2,360	23,000	341	164	1,310
1942	2,968	840	4,180	238	64	317
1943	3,752	1,980	13,500	467	297	1,020
1944	4,956	2,120	8,720	549	216	705
1945	4,750	3,470	38,000	477	418	3,440

N/A—not available

Sources: Florence Peterson, Strikes In the United States, 1880-1936: Bulletin No. 651 (Washington, D.C.: Government Printing Office, 1938); Morris Hansen, Statistical Abstract of the United States, 1944-45 (Washington, D.C.: Government Printing Office, 1946); U.S. Department of Commerce. Bureau of the Census, Historical Statistics of the United States (Washington, D.C.: Government Printing Office, 1975); Division of Research and Statistics. Ohio Bureau of Employment Services, "Work Stoppages and Man-Days of Idleness In Ohio." Columbus, 1978. (Mimeographed); Monthly Labor Review, May 1937-April 1939.

TABLE 4B. Population Characteristics of Ohio, 1920-1940 (in thousands)

	1920	1930	1940
Total Population (TP)	5,759.4	6,646.7	6,907.6
Native Born[a] % of TP	4,893.2 85%	5,687.0 86%	6,047.3 88%
Foreign Born[b] % of TP	678.7 12%	649.2 10%	519.3 8%
Born in Ohio % of TP	4,077.7 71%	4,619.8 70%	5,020.9 73%
Native Born Outside Ohio % of TP	984.9 17%	1,362.3 21%	1,348.1 20%
Blacks % of TP	186.2 3%	309.3 5%	339.5 5%
Urban % of TP	3,677.1 64%	4,507.4 68%	4,613.0 67%
Rural % of TP	2,082.3 36%	2,139.3 32%	2,294.6 33%

a—native white
b—foreign-born white

Sources: U.S. Department of Commerce. Bureau of the Census. Fourteenth Census of the United States, 1920: Population, vol. B; U.S. Department of Commerce. Bureau of the Census. Fifteenth Census of the United States, 1930: Population, vol. 3; U.S. Department of Commerce. Bureau of the Census. Sixteenth Census of the United States, 1940: Characteristics of the Population, vol. 2.

TABLE 4C. Population Changes in Ohio, 1920-1940 (in thousands)

	1920-1930	1930-1940
Total Population % change	+ 887.3 + 15%	+ 260.9 + 4%
Native Born % change	+ 793.8 + 16%	+ 360.3 + 6%
Foreign Born % change	− 29.5 − 4%	− 129.9 − 19%
Born in Ohio % change	+ 542.1 + 13%	+ 401.1 + 9%
Native Born Outside Ohio % change	+ 377.4 + 38%	− 14.2 − 1%
Blacks % change	+ 123.1 + 66%	+ 30.2 + 10%
Urban % change	+ 830.3 + 23%	+ 105.6 + 2%
Rural % change	+ 57.0 + 3%	+ 155.3 + 7%

Sources: U.S. Department of Commerce. Bureau of the Census. Fourteenth Census of the United States, 1920: Population, vol. B; U.S. Department of Commerce. Bureau of the Census. Fifteenth Census of the United States, 1930: Population, vol. 3; U.S. Department of Commerce Bureau of the Census. Sixteenth Census of the United States, 1940: Characteristics of the Population, vol. 2.

Sources: U.S. Department of Commerce. Bureau of the Census. Fourteenth Census of the United States, 1920: Population, vol. B; U.S. Department of Commerce. Bureau of the Census. Fifteenth Census of the United States, 1930: Population, vol. 3; U.S. Department of Commerce. Bureau of the Census. Sixteenth Census of the United States, 1940: Characteristics of the Population, vol. 2.

TABLE 4D. Population Changes in Ohio's Principal and Secondary Cities, 1920-1940 (in thousands)

	1920-1930	% change	1930-1940	% change
Cleveland	+ 103.6	+ 13%	− 22.1	− 3%
Cincinnati	+ 49.9	+ 12%	+ 4.5	+ 1%
Columbus	+ 53.5	+ 23%	+ 15.5	+ 5%
Toledo	+ 47.6	+ 20%	− 8.4	− 3%
Akron	+ 46.6	+ 22%	− 10.3	− 4%
Dayton	+ 48.4	+ 32%	+ 9.7	+ 5%
Youngstown	+ 37.6	+ 28%	− 2.3	− 1%
Canton	+ 17.8	+ 21%	+ 3.5	+ 3%
Springfield	+ 7.9	+ 13%	+ 1.9	+ 3%
Lakewood	+ 28.8	+ 69%	− 1.3	− 2%
Cleveland Heights	+ 35.7	+ 234%	+ 4.1	+ 8%
Hamilton	+ 12.5	+ 32%	− 1.6	− 3%
Lima	+ 1.0	+ 2%	+ 2.4	+ 6%
Lorain	+ 7.2	+ 19%	− .4	− 1%
Warren	+ 14.0	+ 52%	+ 1.8	+ 4%
Portsmouth	+ 9.6	+ 29%	− 2.1	− 5%
Steubenville	+ 6.9	+ 24%	+ 2.2	+ 6%

TABLE 4E. Population of Principal Ohio Cities, 1920-1940 (in thousands)

	Total (TP)	Native-Born White	% of TP	Foreign-Born White	% of TP	Blacks	% of TP
Cleveland							
1920	796.8	522.5	66%	239.5	30%	34.5	4%
1930	900.4	597.6	66%	229.5	26%	71.9	8%
1940	878.3	614.2	70%	179.2	20%	84.5	10%
Cincinnati							
1920	401.3	328.3	82%	42.8	11%	30.1	8%
1930	451.2	368.3	82%	34.8	8%	47.8	11%
1940	455.6	374.1	82%	25.8	6%	55.6	12%
Columbus							
1920	237.0	198.7	84%	16.1	7%	22.2	9%
1930	290.6	242.3	83%	15.3	5%	32.8	11%
1940	306.1	258.3	84%	11.9	4%	35.8	12%
Toledo							
1920	243.2	199.2	82%	38.2	16%	5.7	2%
1930	290.7	243.3	84%	33.5	12%	13.3	5%
1940	282.4	242.8	86%	24.8	9%	14.6	5%
Akron							
1920	208.4	164.8	79%	37.9	18%	5.6	3%
1930	255.0	212.2	83%	31.6	12%	11.1	4%
1940	244.8	207.1	85%	25.4	10%	12.3	5%
Dayton							
1920	152.6	130.4	86%	13.1	9%	9.0	6%
1930	201.0	171.8	86%	12.0	6%	17.1	9%
1940	210.7	181.1	86%	9.3	4%	20.3	10%
Youngstown							
1920	132.4	91.8	69%	33.8	26%	6.7	5%
1930	170.0	122.8	72%	32.9	19%	14.6	9%
1940	167.7	126.4	75%	26.7	16%	14.6	9%

Sources: U.S. Department of Commerce. Bureau of the Census. Fourteenth Census of the United States, 1920: Population, vol. B; U.S. Department of Commerce. Bureau of the Census. Fifteenth Census of the United States, 1930: Population, vol. 3; U.S. Department of Commerce. Bureau of the Census. Sixteenth Census of the United States, 1940: Characteristics of the Population, vol. 2.

TABLE 4G. Occupational Characteristics of Ohio's Workforce, 1920-1940 (in thousands)

	1920	1930	1940
Persons Engaged in all Gainful Occupations			
Males	1,891.5	2,076.2	1,967.8
Females	410.0	539.6	592.8
Total Workforce (TW)	2,301.5	2,615.8	2,560.6
Persons Engaged in Manufacturing and Mechanical Industries			
Males	857.3	889.5	713.1
Females	102.1	101.8	89.4
Total	959.4	991.2	802.4
% of TW	42%	38%	31%
Persons Engaged in Trade and Transportation			
Males	363.0	490.5	388.2
Females	26.8	76.6	60.8
Total	389.8	567.1	449.0
% of TW	17%	22%	18%
Persons Engaged in Professional, Domestic and Clerical Services[a]			
Males	261.9	341.7	279.5
Females	240.2	353.1	350.4
Total	502.1	694.8	630.0
% of TW	22%	27%	25%
Persons Engaged in Coal Mining			
Total	47.8	30.6	23.3
% of TW	2%	1%	1%

a—including public service workers.

Sources: U.S. Department of Commerce. Bureau of the Census. Fourteenth Census of the United States, 1920: Population, Occupations, vol. 4; U.S. Department of Commerce. Bureau of the Census. Fifteenth Census of the United States, 1930: Population, Occupations, vol. 4; U.S. Department of Commerce. Bureau of the Census. Sixteenth Census of the United States, 1940: Population, vol. 3, The Labor Force; Occupations, Industry, Employment, and Income, part 4; U.S. Department of Commerce. Bureau of the Census. Historical Statistics of the United States. Washington, D.C.: Government Printing Office, 1975.

TABLE 4F. Population of Representative Secondary Cities in Ohio, 1920-1940 (in thousands)

		Total (TP)	Native-Born White	% of TP	Foreign-Born White	% of TP	Blacks	% of TP
Canton	1920	87.1	71.1	82%	14.7	17%	1.3	2%
	1930	104.9	88.6	85%	13.2	13%	3.0	3%
	1940	108.4	93.3	86%	11.1	10%	4.0	4%
Springfield	1920	60.8	51.0	84%	2.8	5%	7.0	12%
	1930	68.7	58.3	85%	2.1	3%	8.3	12%
	1940	70.7	60.8	86%	1.6	2%	8.3	12%
Lakewood	1920	41.7	34.4	83%	7.3	18%	.1	.2%
	1930	70.5	60.7	86%	9.7	14%	.1	.1%
	1940	69.2	61.4	89%	7.6	11%	.1	.2%
Cleveland Heights	1920	15.2	N/A		N/A		N/A	
	1930	51.0	42.7	84%	7.6	15%	.6	1%
	1940	55.0	46.5	85%	7.9	14%	.5	1%
Hamilton	1920	39.7	35.7	90%	2.7	7%	1.3	3%
	1930	52.2	48.0	92%	2.2	4%	2.0	4%
	1940	50.6	48.5	96%	1.5	3%	2.1	4%
Lima	1920	41.3	38.2	93%	1.9	5%	1.2	3%
	1930	42.3	39.4	93%	1.5	4%	1.4	3%
	1940	44.7	42.1	94%	1.1	3%	1.6	4%
Lorain	1920	37.3	24.8	67%	11.9	32%	.6	2%
	1930	44.5	30.7	70%	11.6	26%	1.0	2%
	1940	44.1	33.6	76%	9.4	21%	1.1	3%
Warren	1920	27.1	21.7	80%	4.7	17%	.7	3%
	1930	41.1	32.1	78%	6.5	16%	2.6	6%
	1940	42.8	35.1	82%	5.2	12%	2.5	6%
Portsmouth	1920	33.0	31.2	95%	.7	2%	1.2	4%
	1930	42.6	40.0	94%	.6	1%	1.9	5%
	1940	40.5	38.5	95%	.4	1%	1.6	4%
Steubenville	1920	28.5	21.8	77%	5.6	20%	1.1	4%
	1930	35.4	27.4	77%	5.2	15%	2.8	8%
	1940	37.7	30.2	80%	4.6	12%	2.8	7%

N/A—not available

Sources: U.S. Department of Commerce. Bureau of the Census. Fourteenth Census of the United States, 1920: Population, vol. B; U.S. Department of Commerce. Bureau of the Census. Fifteenth Census of the United States, 1930: Population, vol. 3; U.S. Department of Commerce. Bureau of the Census. Sixteenth Census of the United States, 1940: Characteristics of the Population, vol. 2.

TABLE 4H. Characteristics of the Workforce in Ohio's Principal Cities, 1920-1940 (in thousands)

	Population		Persons Engaged in All Occupations					Engaged in Manufacturing and Mechanical Industries					
	Total	% foreign born	Males	Females	Children (under 16 yrs)	% foreign born	Total Workforce (TW)	Males	Females	Children (under 16 yrs)	% foreign born	Total	% of TW
Cleveland													
1920	796.8	30%	273.7	73.5	2.3	40%	347.3	165.1	18.8	.8	51%	183.9	53%
1930	900.4	26%	295.9	99.1	.7	33%	394.8	153.8	21.0	.1	44%	174.8	44%
1940	878.3	20%	228.6	91.0		24%	319.6	107.2[a]	20.9			128.1	40%
Cincinnati													
1920	401.3	11%	134.9	50.4	1.2	12%	185.3	66.5	14.7	.5		81.2	44%
1930	451.2	8%	147.4	55.6	.3	9%	203.0	64.7	10.8	.04	12%	75.4	37%
1940	455.6	6%	118.6	51.4		7%	170.0	42.8[a]	9.8			52.6	31%
Columbus													
1920	237.0	7%	80.7	25.5	.7	9%	106.2	37.3	5.3	.2	13%	42.6	40%
1930	290.6	5%	93.9	35.4	.4	7%	129.3	36.7	5.7	.02	9%	42.4	33%
1940	306.1	4%	77.7	34.8		5%	112.5	24.7	5.3[a]			30.0	27%
Toledo													
1920	243.2	16%	86.9	23.3	.9	20%	110.1	47.5	5.7	.3	26%	53.2	48%
1930	290.7	12%	98.0	29.3	.2	15%	127.3	48.2	5.4	.01	19%	53.7	42%
1940	282.4	9%	71.3	27.9		10%	99.2	27.7[a]	5.6			33.3	34%
Akron													
1920	208.4	18%	92.1	16.0	.5	23%	108.1	66.8	4.5	.1		71.3	66%
1930	255.0	12%	82.5	23.9	.2	17%	106.4	49.2	6.6	.03	20%	55.8	53%
1940	244.8	10%	61.0	21.5		14%	82.6	29.1[a]	5.0			34.1	41%
Dayton													
1920	152.6	9%	53.5	15.0	.6	11%	68.6	31.7	4.5	.1	14%	36.2	53%
1930	201.0	6%	66.4	22.9	.2	8%	89.3	35.2	4.8	.01	10%	40.0	45%
1940	210.7	4%	58.5	23.1		5%	81.6	27.8[a]	5.2[a]			33.0	40%
Youngstown													
1920	132.4	26%	46.6	8.7	.3	37%	55.3	28.5	1.0	.1	48%	29.5	53%
1930	170.0	19%	52.0	12.1	.1	29%	64.1	29.8	.8	.004	39%	30.6	48%
1940	167.7	16%	43.6	12.6			56.2	22.4	1.4			23.8	42%

	Engaged in Trade and Transportation						Engaged in Professional, Clerical, and Personal Service[b]					
	Males	Females	Children (under 16 yrs)	% foreign born	Total	% of TW	Males	Females	Children (under 16 yrs)	% foreign born	Total	% of TW
Cleveland												
1920	57.7	11.1	.6	33%	68.8	20%	49.6	43.6	.9	23%	93.2	27%
1930	76.7	14.0	.4	29%	90.7	23%	61.9	63.9	.2	20%	125.8	32%
1940	29.4	9.6		12%	39.0	12%	51.4	53.7			105.1	33%
Cincinnati												
1920	36.2	6.5	.3	14%	42.7	23%	27.5	29.1	.4	9%	56.6	31%
1930	43.7	7.1	.2	8%	50.7	25%	37.1	37.7	.1	7%	74.8	37%
1940	26.8	5.3			32.2	19%	33.1	33.2			66.3	39%
Columbus												
1920	24.0	3.6	.3	8%	27.6	26%	18.7	16.6	.2	6%	35.3	33%
1930	31.0	5.1	.3	6%	36.0	28%	25.0	24.6	.1	5%	49.6	38%
1940	20.0	3.8			23.8	21%	21.2	21.2			44.5	40%
Toledo												
1920	22.6	3.5	.3	16%	26.1	24%	16.2	14.0	.3	12%	30.2	27%
1930	29.5	4.3	.1	12%	33.7	27%	19.3	19.5	.07	10%	38.9	31%
1940	18.2	3.4			21.6	22%	16.7	17.3			34.0	34%
Akron												
1920	11.7	2.0	.2	20	13.6	13%	12.3	9.5	.2	13%	21.8	20%
1930	16.9	3.2	.1	16%	20.0	19%	14.9	14.1	.1	13%	29.0	27%
1940	11.9	2.4			14.3	17%	14.1	13.3			27.4	33%
Dayton												
1920	10.7	2.0	.3	10%	12.7	19%	10.9	8.5	.2	6%	19.4	28%
1930	15.4	3.2	.2	7%	18.7	21%	14.8	14.8	.06	5%	29.6	33%
1940	10.4	2.5			12.9	16%	13.6	14.0			27.6	34%
Youngstown												
1920	9.8	1.7	.1	29%	11.5	21%	8.1	6.0	.1	20%	14.1	25%
1930	12.3	2.1	.1	21%	14.4	22%	9.4	9.2	.04	18%	18.7	29%
1940	8.4	2.1			10.5	19%	8.3	8.4			16.7	30%

Sources: U.S. Department of Commerce. Bureau of the Census. Fourteenth Census of the United States, 1920: Population, Occupations, vol. 4; U.S. Department of Commerce. Bureau of the Census. Fifteenth Census of the United States, 1930: Population, Occupations, vol. 4; U.S. Department of Commerce. Bureau of the Census. Sixteenth Census of the United States, 1940: Population, vol. 3, The Labor Force; Occupation, Industry, Employment, and Income, part 4.

a—*does not include "operative workers" (ex. brakemen, chauffeurs, locomotive engineers and firemen, etc.) which were included under "transportation category in the 1920 census.*

b—*also includes "public service workers."*

c—*1920 statistics include all persons ten years of age and above in the workforce.*

d—*1940 statistics include all persons fourteen years of age and above in the workforce.*

TABLE 4I. Growth of Ohio's Leading Manufactures, Measured by Book Value of Products, 1920-1940

	Number of Establishments[a]			Output[b] ($ million)			Growth Rate	
	1920	1930	1940	1920	1930	1940	1920-30	1930-40
Steel Works	86	88	46	626.4	817.8	609.8	+31%	−25%
Motor Vehicles, Bodies, Parts, and Accessories	281	163	101	379.4	620.4	285.7	+64%	−54%
Rubber Tires and Tubes	96	32	19	551.1	503.2	268.0	−9%	−47%
Meat Packing	141	120	158	170.3	163.2	132.5	−4%	−19%
Blast Furnace Products	42	26	23	179.2	175.1	131.8	−2%	−25%
Bread and Bakery Products	1609	1321	1072	67.2	103.2	84.3	+54%	−18%
Petroleum Refining	11	12	13	43.3	68.5	84.1	+58%	+23%
Paper and Paperboard Mills	49	53	45	55.1	80.6	67.5	+46%	−16%
Machine Tools	102	66	51	62.6	67.6	65.5	+8%	−3%
Chemicals	37	49	49	32.7	46.3	60.9	+42%	+32%
Newspaper Publishing and Printing	794	552	321	58.6	132.4	55.9	+126%	−58%
All Ohio Industries	16,125	11,855	10,070	5,100.3	6,030.0	4,580.0	+18%	−24%
All U.S. Industries	214,383	210,959	184,230	62,041.0	70,434.9	56,843.0	+14%	−19%

a—excluding hand and neighborhood industries.
b—including only those establishments with over $5,000 in annual value of product.

Sources: U.S. Department of Commerce. Bureau of the Census. Fourteenth Census of the United States. State Compendium, Ohio; U.S. Department of Commerce. Bureau of the Census. Fifteenth Census of the United States. Manufactures: 1929. vol. 3: Reports by States, Statistics for Industrial Areas, Counties, and Cities; U.S. Department of Commerce. Bureau of the Census. Sixteenth Census of the United States: 1940. Manufactures: 1939. vol. 3: Reports for States and Outlying Areas; U.S. Department of Commerce. Bureau of the Census. Abstract of the 15th Census: 1930; U.S. Department of Commerce. Bureau of the Census. Abstract of the 16th Census: 1941.

TABLE 4J. Average Number of Employees in Leading Ohio Industries, 1920-1940 (in thousands)

	1920			1930				1940			
	Salaried Personnel	Wage-Earners	Total	Salaried Personnel	Wage-Earners	Total	% change 1920-30	Salaried Personnel	Wage-Earners	Total	% change 1930-40
Steel Works and Rolling Mills	1.4	73.0	74.4	6.5	89.1	95.6	+28%	5.8	71.9	77.7	−19%
Tires and Inner Tubes	1.3	63.6	64.9[a]	7.9	55.3	63.2	−3%	5.4	29.9	35.3	−44%
Motor Vehicles, Bodies, Parts, and Accessories	1.4	45.9	47.3	6.3	57.6	64.0[b]	+35%	4.7	29.8	34.6	−46%
Bread and Bakery Products*	.3	7.4	7.7	1.2	13.6	14.8[c]	+92%	1.2	14.7	15.9	+7%
Machine Tools	.7	13.9	14.5	2.0	11.9	13.9	−4%	2.3	10.8	13.1	−6%
Men's and Boy's Suits, Coats, and Overcoats Made in Inside Factories	.4	8.7	9.1[d]	1.3	13.2	14.5[e]	+60%	.7	10.0	10.8	−26%
Refrigerators, Machinery and Equipment	.02	.1	.2[f]	1.0	3.8	4.9[g]	+3058%	1.2	9.8	11.0	+127%
Paper and Paperboard Mills	.3	6.9	7.2[h]	.9	9.2	10.3[i]	+43%	1.2	8.9	10.2	−1%
Electrical Machinery, Apparatus, and Supplies	.9	26.7	27.6	7.0	36.3	43.2	+57%	1.2	7.0	8.2[j]	−81%
Foundry and Machine Shop Products	3.5	72.2	75.8	11.2	61.5	72.7	−4%			NA[k]	
Tobacco, Cigars, and Cigarettes	.3	11.0	11.2	.2	6.2	6.4	−43%	.1	1.3	1.4	−78%
Railroad Cars, Repairs and Construction	1.2	35.3	36.4	2.6	25.5	28.1	−23%	.2	.9	1.1[l]	−96%
All Ohio Industries	30.3	730.7	761.0	112.2	741.1	853.4	+12%	87.7	598.4	686.1	−20%

*—excluding biscuit, crackers, and pretzels
a—including "rubber tires, tubes, and rubber goods, not elsewhere specified."
b—combination of categories identical to single 1940 category
c—including "bread and other bakery products."
d—including "clothing, men's, regular factories."
e—including "clothing (except work clothing) men's, youths', and boys' not elsewhere classified."

f—including "refrigerators."
g—including "refrigerators and refrigerator cabinets, exclusive of mechanical refrigeration equipment."
h—including "paper and wood pulp."
i—including "paper."
j—including "electrical appliances and electrical products not elsewhere classified."
k—not available due to changing census categories.
l—defined as "cars and car equipment—railroad, street, and rapid-transit."

Sources: U.S. Department of Commerce. Bureau of the Census. Fourteenth Census of the United States. State Compendium-Ohio; U.S. Department of Commerce. Bureau of the Census. Fifteenth Census of the United States. Manufactures: 1929. vol. 3: Reports by States, Statistics for Industrial Areas, Counties, and Cities; U.S. Department of Commerce. Bureau of the Census. Sixteenth Census of the United States: 1940. Manufactures 1939. vol. 3: Reports for States and Outlying Areas.

TABLE 5A. Population Characteristics of Ohio, 1950-1980 (in thousands)

	1950	1960	1970	1980
Total Population (TP)	7,946.6	9,707.1	10,652.0	10,797.6
Native Born (white)	6,985.1	8,502.0	9,348.2	10,500.8[a]
% of TP	87.9%	87.6%	87.8%	97.3%
Foreign Born (white)	443.2	390.9	303.3	—
% of TP	5.6%	4.0%	2.8%	—
Blacks	513.1	784.2	970.5	1,076.7
% of TP	6.5%	8.1%	9.1%	10.0%
Urban	5,578.3	7,123.9	8,025.8	8,242.9
% of TP	70.2%	73.4%	75.3%	76.3%
Rural	2,368.4	2,579.2	2,626.2	2,759.9
% of TP	29.8%	26.6%	24.7%	25.6%
Born in Ohio	5,621.8	6,734.6	6,863.1	7,782.8
% of TP	70.7%	72.3%	64.4%	72.1%
Native Born Outside Ohio	1,770.9	2,350.5	2,114.1	2,717.9
% of TP	22.3%	25.2%	19.8%	25.2%

a—native born white and non-white

Sources: U.S. Department of Commerce. Bureau of the Census. Census of the Population: 1950, vol. 2: Characteristics of the Population, part 35: Ohio; U.S. Department of Commerce. Bureau of the Census. U.S. Census of the Population: 1960—General Social and Economic Characteristics of Ohio; U.S. Department of Commerce. Bureau of the Census. 1970 Census of the Population, vol. 1: Characteristics of the Population, part 37: Ohio, section 1; U.S. Department of Commerce. Bureau of the Census, 1980 Census of the Population.

TABLE 5B. Population Changes in Ohio, 1950-1980 (in thousands)

	1950-1960	1960-1970	1970-1980
Total Population	+1,760.5	+944.9	+146.7
% change	+22.2%	+9.7%	+1.4%
Native Born (white)	+1,516.9	+846.2	+166.3
% change	+21.7%	+10.0%	+1.6%
Foreign Born (white)	−52.3	−87.6	—
% change	−11.8%	−22.4%	—
Born in Ohio	+1,112.8	+666.2	+372.5
% change	+19.8%	+9.9%	+5.0%
Native Born Outside of Ohio	+579.6	+114.4	+222.6
% change	+32.7%	+4.9%	+8.9%
Blacks	+271.1	+186.3	+106.8
% change	+52.8%	+23.8%	+11.0%
Urban	+1,545.6	+901.9	+217.1
% change	+27.7%	+12.7%	+2.7%
Rural	+210.8	+47.0	+133.7
% change	+8.9%	+1.8%	+5.1%

Sources: U.S. Department of Commerce. Bureau of the Census. Census of the Population: 1950, vol. 2: Characteristics of the Population, part 35: Ohio; U.S. Department of Commerce. Bureau of the Census. U.S. Census of the Population: 1960—General Social and Economic Characteristics of Ohio; U.S. Department of Commerce. Bureau of the Census. 1970 Census of the Population, vol. 1: Characteristics of the Population, part 37: Ohio, section 1; U.S. Department of Commerce. Bureau of the Census, 1980 Census of the Population.

TABLE 5C. Population of Principal Ohio Cities, 1950-1980 (in thousands)

	Total Population (TP)	% Change from Previous Decade	Foreign Born White % TP	Native White of Foreign and Mixed Parentage % TP	Ethnic % TP	Black % TP
Akron						
1950	274.6	+12.2%	7.7%	16.0%	23.7%	8.7%
1960	290.4	+5.7%	5.9%	12.8%	18.8%	12.2%
1970	275.4	−5.1%	4.3%	10.5%	14.8%	17.5%
1980	237.2	−13.9%	N/A	N/A	N/A	22.2%
Cincinnati						
1950	504.0	+10.6%	4.0%	12.4%	16.5%	15.5%
1960	502.6	−0.3%	3.2%	8.6%	13.8%	21.6%
1970	452.5	−10.0%	2.5%	6.3%	8.8%	27.6%
1980	385.5	−14.8%	N/A	N/A	N/A	33.8%
Cleveland						
1950	914.8	+4.2%	14.5%	30.2%	44.7%	16.2%
1960	876.1	−4.2%	10.9%	19.7%	30.6%	28.6%
1970	750.9	−14.3%	7.3%	14.0%	21.4%	38.3%
1980	573.8	−23.6%	N/A	N/A	N/A	43.8%
Columbus						
1950	375.9	+22.8%	2.9%	11.0%	13.9%	12.4%
1960	471.3	+25.4%	2.2%	6.2%	8.4%	16.3%
1970	539.7	+14.5%	1.8%	5.2%	7.0%	18.5%
1980	564.9	+4.7%	N/A	N/A	N/A	22.1%
Dayton						
1950	243.9	+15.7%	3.3%	13.5%	16.7%	14.0%
1960	262.3	+7.6%	2.3%	6.0%	8.3%	21.9%
1970	243.6	−7.1%	1.5%	4.6%	6.1%	30.5%
1980	203.6	−16.4%	N/A	N/A	N/A	36.9%
Toledo						
1950	303.6	+7.5%	6.6%	18.8%	25.4%	8.2%
1960	318.0	+4.7%	4.8%	15.6%	20.4%	12.6%
1970	383.8	+20.7%	3.0%	12.2%	15.3%	13.8%
1980	354.6	−7.6%	N/A	N/A	N/A	17.4%
Youngstown						
1950	168.3	+0.4%	12.7%	29.4%	42.0%	12.7%
1960	166.7	−1.0%	10.0%	22.7%	32.7%	19.0%
1970	139.8	−16.1%	6.2%	19.0%	25.3%	25.2%
1980	115.4	−17.4%	N/A	N/A	N/A	33.3%

N/A—not available

Sources: U.S. Department of Commerce. Bureau of the Census. Census of the Population: 1950, vol. II: Characteristics of the Population, part 35: Ohio; U.S. Department of Commerce. Bureau of the Census. U.S. Census of the Population: 1960—Detailed Social and Economic Characteristics of Ohio; U.S. Department of Commerce. Bureau of the Census. 1970 Census of Population, vol. 1: Characteristics of the Population, part 37: Ohio, section 1. U.S. Department of Commerce. Bureau of the Census. 1980 Census of Population.

TABLE 5D. Population of Representative Secondary Cities in Ohio, 1950-1980
(in thousands)

	Total Population (TP)	% Change from Previous Decade	Foreign Born White % TP	Native White of Foreign and Mixed Parentage % TP	Ethnic % TP	Black % TP
Canton						
1950	116.9	+7.9%	8.0%	N/A	N/A	6.0%
1960	113.6	−2.8%	6.4%	14.2%	20.6%	9.7%
1970	110.1	−3.1%	4.0%	11.5%	15.5%	12.5%
1980	94.7	−13.9%	N/A	N/A	N/A	16.0%
Hamilton						
1950	58.0	+14.5%	2.2%	N/A	N/A	4.9%
1960	72.4	+24.9%	1.7%	5.6%	7.3%	6.0%
1970	67.9	−6.2%	1.1%	4.2%	5.3%	6.9%
1980	63.2	−6.9%	N/A	N/A	N/A	7.7%
Lakewood						
1950	68.1	−1.6%	9.9%	N/A	N/A	0.1%
1960	66.2	−2.8%	10.0%	22.9%	32.9%	0.1%
1970	70.2	+6.1%	9.3%	19.0%	28.3%	0.1%
1980	62.0	−11.7%	N/A	N/A	N/A	0.2%
Lima						
1950	50.3	+12.4%	1.8%	N/A	N/A	6.5%
1960	51.0	+1.6%	1.6%	5.2%	6.8%	10.5%
1970	53.7	+5.3%	1.5%	4.4%	5.9%	14.9%
1980	47.4	−11.8%	N/A	N/A	N/A	20.4%
Lorain						
1950	51.2	+16.0%	15.2%	N/A	N/A	4.9%
1960	68.9	+34.6%	9.0%	22.0%	31.9%	6.4%
1970	78.2	+13.4%	6.2%	17.2%	23.4%	9.4%
1980	75.4	−3.5%	N/A	N/A	N/A	11.9%
Portsmouth						
1950	36.8	−9.1%	1.2%	N/A	N/A	3.9%
1960	33.6	−8.6%	0.9%	3.7%	4.6%	4.8%
1970	27.6	−17.8%	0.6%	2.6%	3.2%	4.7%
1980	25.9	−6.1%	N/A	N/A	N/A	5.1%
Springfield						
1950	78.5	+11.1%	1.8%	N/A	N/A	12.4%
1960	82.7	+5.4%	1.4%	4.7%	6.1%	14.3%
1970	81.9	−1.0%	1.1%	3.5%	4.6%	15.5%
1980	72.6	−11.5%	N/A	N/A	N/A	17.2%

N/A—not available

Sources: U.S. Department of Commerce. Bureau of the Census. Census of the Population: 1950, vol. II: Characteristics of the Population, part 35: Ohio; U.S. Department of Commerce. Bureau of the Census. U.S. Census of the Population: 1960—Detailed Social and Economic Characteristics of Ohio; U.S. Department of Commerce. Bureau of the Census. 1970 Census of Population, vol. 1: Characteristics of the Population, part 37: Ohio, section 1. U.S. Department of Commerce. Bureau of the Census. 1980 Census of Population.

TABLE 5E. Population Changes in Ohio's Principal and Secondary Cities, 1950-1970 (in thousands)

	1950-1960	% change	1960-1970	% change
Cleveland	−38.7	−4.2%	−125.2	−14.3%
Cincinnati	−1.4	−.3%	−50.1	−10.0%
Columbus	+95.4	+25.4%	+68.4	+14.5%
Toledo	+14.4	+4.7%	+65.8	+20.7%
Akron	+15.8	+5.8%	−15.0	−5.1%
Dayton	+18.4	+7.5%	−18.7	−7.1%
Youngstown	−1.6	−1.0%	−26.9	−16.1%
Canton	−3.3	−2.8%	−3.5	−3.1%
Springfield	+4.2	+5.4%	−.8	−1.0%
Lakewood	−1.9	−2.8%	+4.0	+6.1%
Cleveland Heights	+7.7	+4.6%	−1.0	−1.7%
Hamilton	+14.4	+24.8%	−4.5	−6.2%
Lorain	+17.7	+34.6%	+9.3	+13.4%
Lima	+.8	+1.6%	+2.7	+5.3%
Warren	+9.7	+19.4%	+3.9	+6.4%
Portsmouth	−3.2	−8.7%	−6.0	−17.8%
Steubenville	−3.4	−4.5%	−1.7	−5.3%

Sources: U.S. Department of Commerce. Bureau of Census. U.S. Census of Population: 1960. General Social and Economic Characteristics, Ohio; U.S. Department of Commerce. Bureau of Census. U.S. Census of Population: 1970.

TABLE 5F. Occupational Characteristics of Ohio's Workforce, 1950-1980 (in thousands)

	1950	1960	1970	1980[c]
Civilian Labor Force (Aged 14 or More)				
Males	2,337.9	2,554.6	2,720.9	
Females	863.2	1,152.7	1,557.9	
Total labor force (TLF)	3,201.1	3,707.4	4,278.8	
Employed Labor Force				
Males	2.232.9	2,415.8	2,623.1	
Females	826.7	1,089.1	1,480.6	
Total Employed Labor Force (TELF)	3,059.6	3,504.9	4,103.8	4,367.4
% of TLF	95.6%[b]	94.5%[b]	95.9%[b]	
Persons Engaged In Manufacturing Industries				
Males	896.3	1,046.9	1,085.5	
Females	224.0	249.0	301.9	
Total	1,120.4	1,295.9	1,387.5	1,264.5
% of TELF	36.6%	37.0%	33.8%	29.0
Persons Engaged In Mining				
Males	30.0	18.4	18.6	
Females	.6	.8	1.7	
Total	30.6	19.3	20.3	30.7
% of TELF	1.0%	0.6%	0.5%	0.7%
Persons Engaged In Transportation, Communication, and Other Utilities				
Males	208.1	194.7	191.4	
Females	31.7	34.8	48.2	
Total	239.9	229.5	239.6	223.1
% of TELF	7.8%	6.5%	5.8%	5.1%
Persons Engaged In Wholesale and Retail Trade				
Males	351.6	356.2	413.7	
Females	206.6	253.1	334.6	
Total	558.2	609.2	748.3	957.0
% of TELF	18.2%	17.4%	18.4%	21.9%

			Aggregate of Services and Government	
			1970	1980
Persons Engaged In Professional and Related Services				
Males	97.2	149.4	218.5	
Females	139.4	244.7	405.8	
Total	236.6	394.1	624.3	
% of TELF	7.7%	11.2%	15.2%	
Persons Engaged In Other Service Industries[a]				
Males	183.3	180.3	200.6	
Females	153.7	196.4	223.6	
Total	337.0	376.7	424.3	1,214.9 / 1,724.6
% of TELF	11.0%	10.7%	10.3%	29.6% / 39.5%
Persons Engaged In Public Administration				
Males	90.1	102.6	116.9	
Females	32.1	37.9	49.3	
Total	122.2	140.6	166.3	
% of TELF	4.0%	4.0%	4.1%	

a—Includes persons engaged in insurance, financial, and real estate; business and repair services; personal services; and, entertainment and related services.
b—Selected sectors are not included in these percentages.
c—Ohio Bureau of Employment Services, Division of Research and Statistics, March, 1981. Figures may not be consistent with other data sources.

Sources: U.S. Department of Commerce. Bureau of Census. Census of Population: 1950. vol. 2; Characteristics of the Population, part 35; Ohio; U.S. Department of Commerce. Bureau of Census. 1970 Census of Population, vol. 1: Characteristics of the Population, part 37: Ohio, Section 1.

TABLE 5K. Union Membership in the United States and Ohio, 1945-1978 (in thousands)

	UNITED STATES		
	Employees in nonagricultural establishments	Union membership	As % of employees in nonagricultural establishments
1945	40,394	14,322	35.5%
1947	43,881	14,787	33.7%
1949	43,778	14,300	32.6%
1950	45,222	14,300	31.5%
1952	48,825	15,900	32.5%
1954	49,022	17,022	34.7%
1956	52,408	17,490	33.4%
1958	51,363	17,029	33.2%
1960[a]	54,234	17,049	31.4%
1962	55,596	16,586	29.8%
1964	58,331	16,841	28.9%
1966	63,955	17,940	28.1%
1968	67,915	18,916	27.9%
1970	70,644	19,757	27.9%
1972	73,675	19,789	26.9%
1974	78,265	20,566	26.3%
1976	80,048	19,874	25.0%
1978	84,446	20,459	23.6%

	OHIO			
	Union membership	National rank by total membership	As % of employees in nonagricultural establishments	National rank by % of employees
1960[a]	1,000[b]			
1962				
1964	1,148	5	35.7%	10
1966				
1968	1,345	5	35.0%	9
1970	1,413	5	36.4%	4
1972	1,369	5	34.8%	8
1974	1,389	5	33.2%	8
1976	1,289	5	31.5%	9
1978	1,294	5	29.5%	9

a—Alaska and Hawaii henceforth included.
b—Includes AFL-CIO unions only

Sources: Historical Statistics . . . To 1970; U.S. Department of Labor. Bureau of Labor Statistics, Directory of International Labor Unions, 1961, 1965, 1971, 1977, 1979.

TABLE 5G.—PAGES 292 & 293

TABLE 5G. Characteristics of the Labor Force in Ohio's Principal Metropolitan Areas (SMSA's) 1950-1970 (in thousands)

| | Population | | Labor Force | | | | Employed Labor Force | | | | |
	Total	% Black	Males	Females	% Black	Total Labor Force (TLF)	Males	Females	% Black	Total Employed Labor Force (TELF)	% of TLF
Cleveland											
1950	1,128.9	9.0	449.9	191.7	N/A	641.6	432.5	183.3	9.6	615.7	96.0
1960	1,277.7	13.2	493.4	242.4	N/A	735.8	467.5	228.9	12.6	696.4	94.6
1970[a]	1,435.4	14.8	536.2	322.5	14.9	858.7	518.9	309.7	14.4	828.6	96.5
Cincinnati											
1950	691.1	N/A	259.0	113.0	N/A	372.0	248.3	108.8	9.6	357.2	96.0
1960	754.5	11.3	279.0	138.0	N/A	417.8	266.3	132.0	10.9	398.2	95.3
1970	939.7	10.3	340.0	204.0	10.3	544.0	329.4	193.9	10.0	523.3	96.2
Columbus											
1950	376.7	N/A	138.7	65.9	N/A	204.6	135.2	64.9	10.0	200.0	97.7
1960	478.6	11.1	174.3	94.7	N/A	269.0	165.9	90.8	10.8	256.7	95.4
1970	632.5	10.6	227.1	152.3	10.7	379.4	219.7	146.7	10.5	366.4	96.6
Toledo											
1950	302.3	N/A	120.5	48.6	N/A	169.2	113.4	45.1	5.9	158.5	93.5
1960	320.9	8.5	121.2	58.4	N/A	179.6	113.5	54.5	7.8	168.0	93.5
1970	474.3	7.4	175.9	101.3	7.7	277.2	169.5	96.2	7.3	265.7	95.8
Akron											
1950	305.0	N/A	121.7	45.5	N/A	167.2	115.2	43.1	5.5	158.3	94.7
1960	354.7	7.3	138.7	60.7	N/A	199.5	131.8	57.2	6.7	189.0	94.7
1970	468.3	7.3	175.3	96.7	7.0	272.0	168.8	91.3	6.7	260.1	95.6
Dayton											
1950	339.7	N/A	132.3	54.4	N/A	186.7	128.8	52.6	9.0	181.4	97.1
1960	475.5	10.0	181.2	88.4	N/A	269.6	173.4	84.3	9.4	257.7	95.6
1970	581.5	10.4	216.5	129.0	10.8	345.5	209.6	122.7	10.5	332.2	96.2
Youngstown-Warren											
1950	396.5	N/A	162.7	50.3	N/A	212.9	154.8	47.4	5.9	202.3	95.0
1960	354.0	8.4	137.1	53.2	N/A	190.3	128.5	49.5	7.6	177.9	93.5
1970	371.5	8.6	138.9	72.3	8.4	211.2	132.0	67.5	7.8	199.5	94.4
Canton											
1950	211.1	N/A	84.1	28.8	N/A	112.9	82.3	27.4	3.8	109.7	97.2
1960	237.9	4.9	91.0	37.7	N/A	128.6	85.5	35.4	4.5	121.0	94.0
1970	256.8	5.2	95.7	52.0	5.5	147.7	92.1	49.2	5.0	141.3	95.7

| | Persons Engaged In Manufacturing | | | | | Persons Engaged In Mining | | | | | Persons Engaged In Transportation, Communication, Utilities | | | | |
	Males	Females	% Black	Total	% of TELF	Males	Females	% Black	Total	% of TELF	Males	Females	% Black	Total	% of TELF
Cleveland															
1950	195.8	53.8	7.5	249.6	40.5	.5	.1	12.9	.6	.1	43.7	8.7	8.8	52.4	8.5
1960	217.0	57.6	9.4	274.7	39.4	.6	.2	5.6	.8	.1	39.1	8.7	10.7	47.8	6.8
1970	224.2	68.7	N/A	293.0	35.4	1.4	.4	N/A	1.8	.2	42.0	13.2	N/A	55.2	6.7
Cincinnati															
1950	89.6	28.4	5.2	118.0	33.0	.2	.03	7.8	.2	.1	29.1	4.3	9.0	33.4	9.4
1960	101.2	30.2	5.9	131.4	33.0	.3	.04	7.1	.3	.1	26.1	4.4	9.1	30.5	7.6
1970	130.2	40.9	N/A	171.2	32.7	.4	.1	N/A	.5	.1	29.5	7.3	N/A	36.9	7.0
Columbus															
1950	38.0	12.0	7.2	50.1	25.0	.5	.04	3.5	.5	.3	17.0	2.4	9.2	19.4	9.7
1960	52.5	14.7	6.8	67.2	26.2	.6	.06	5.9	.7	.3	15.0	3.1	7.7	18.1	7.0
1970	62.4	23.5	N/A	85.9	23.4	.8	.09	N/A	.9	.3	18.7	5.3	N/A	24.0	6.5
Toledo															
1950	48.4	12.8	3.8	61.2	38.6	.1	.02	5.5	.1	.1	14.7	1.6	4.2	16.3	10.3
1960	48.1	11.2	4.4	59.1	35.2	.1	.02	2.3	.2	.1	12.4	1.7	3.9	14.1	8.4
1970	72.1	17.5	N/A	89.6	33.7	.4	.04	N/A	.4	.2	16.5	3.4	N/A	19.9	7.5
Akron															
1950	63.1	14.1	4.9	77.3	48.8	.2	.01	7.3	.2	.1	8.5	1.7	4.3	10.2	6.4
1960	71.3	13.3	5.7	84.6	44.7	.3	.02	0.0	.3	.1	10.2	2.4	3.6	12.6	6.7
1970	83.2	18.9	N/A	102.2	39.3	.4	.02	N/A	.4	.2	12.8	3.4	N/A	16.2	6.2
Dayton															
1950	59.8	15.3	6.0	75.1	41.4	.1	.01	6.4	.1	.1	6.8	1.6	9.0	8.5	4.7
1960	77.1	20.3	5.2	97.4	37.8	.3	.02	3.4	.4	.1	8.9	2.5	7.0	11.4	4.4
1970	97.9	26.3	N/A	124.2	38.4	.5	.03	N/A	.5	.2	10.9	4.0	N/A	14.9	4.5
Youngstown-Warren															
1950	86.8	12.1	6.7	98.9	48.9	.7	.03	1.2	.7	.4	11.9	1.6	3.2	13.6	6.7
1960	70.1	10.7	7.7	80.8	45.4	.3	.03	4.0	.3	.2	8.9	1.4	3.3	10.3	5.8
1970	70.3	15.3	N/A	85.5	43.0	.2	.05	N/A	.2	.1	8.6	1.9	N/A	10.5	5.3
Canton															
1950	43.5	7.5	4.0	51.0	46.5	.5	.02	.1	.5	.4	6.9	.9	4.1	7.8	7.1
1960	45.6	7.9	3.9	53.5	44.2	.4	.03	1.3	.4	.3	6.3	.9	3.7	7.1	5.9
1970	48.0	11.3	N/A	59.3	42.0	.4	.05	N/A	.4	.3	6.6	1.6	N/A	8.2	5.8

	Persons Engaged in Public Administration					Persons Engaged in Other[b] Service Industries				
	Males	Females	% Black	Total	% of TELF	Males	Females	% Black	Total	% of TELF
Cleveland										
1950	18.2	6.0	11.3	24.1	3.9	42.3	34.9	12.5	77.2	20.1
1960	21.2	7.3	20.1	28.5	4.1	40.5	41.9	21.1	82.4	11.8
1970	26.0	9.6	N/A	35.6	4.3	50.2	52.1	N/A	102.2	12.3
Cincinnati										
1950	10.2	2.7	10.4	12.9	3.6	28.0	25.8	21.3	53.8	15.1
1960	12.1	3.5	16.4	15.6	3.9	25.6	27.3	19.0	52.9	13.3
1970	15.2	7.7	N/A	23.0	4.4	32.6	35.3	N/A	67.9	13.0
Columbus										
1950	9.4	5.3	12.9	14.6	7.3	15.8	13.8	19.4	29.6	14.8
1960	10.9	6.2	17.3	17.1	6.7	17.2	19.0	18.7	36.2	14.1
1970	14.7	8.3	N/A	23.0	6.3	24.5	27.9	N/A	52.4	14.3
Toledo										
1950	4.9	1.4	16.8	6.3	4.0	9.5	8.0	14.5	17.5	11.0
1960	5.2	1.6	20.1	6.9	4.1	9.5	10.4	17.8	20.0	11.8
1970	6.1	2.2	N/A	8.3	3.1	13.0	15.6	N/A	28.6	10.8
Akron										
1950	3.2	1.0	4.2	4.1	2.6	9.5	7.6	14.7	17.1	10.8
1960	3.6	1.3	6.4	4.9	2.6	9.9	10.3	15.4	20.2	10.7
1970	5.0	2.2	N/A	7.1	2.7	12.4	13.9	N/A	26.3	10.1
Dayton										
1950	13.3	5.3	10.8	18.6	10.3	10.2	8.7	21.0	18.9	10.4
1960	17.2	7.0	16.5	24.1	9.4	13.2	14.0	18.3	27.2	10.5
1970	17.8	7.9	N/A	25.7	7.7	16.3	19.1	N/A	35.4	10.6
Youngstown-Warren										
1950	3.9	1.2	6.4	5.0	2.5	9.5	8.2	12.4	17.7	8.7
1960	3.7	1.2	7.7	5.0	2.8	7.8	8.7	15.0	16.6	9.4
1970	4.2	1.4	N/A	5.7	2.8	8.2	9.9	N/A	18.1	9.1
Canton										
1950	1.9	.5	2.9	2.4	2.2	5.9	4.8	9.1	10.7	9.7
1960	2.1	.7	4.5	2.8	2.4	5.4	6.4	9.8	11.8	9.7
1970	2.6	.9	N/A	3.5	2.5	6.5	7.5	N/A	14.0	9.9

	Persons Engaged in Wholesale/Retail Trade					Persons Engaged in Professional and Related Services				
	Males	Females	% Black	Total	% of TELF	Males	Females	% Black	Total	% of TELF
Cleveland										
1950	73.5	45.1	7.2	118.6	19.3	20.2	30.4	9.7	50.6	8.2
1960	70.6	52.6	9.0	123.2	17.7	30.1	47.4	15.1	77.5	11.1
1970	88.0	74.9	N/A	166.9	20.1	46.9	86.9	N/A	133.8	16.1
Cincinnati										
1950	51.4	27.4	7.0	78.8	22.1	12.4	17.6	8.9	29.9	8.4
1960	46.4	28.9	8.0	72.9	18.3	17.2	26.5	14.4	43.7	11.0
1970	60.8	45.8	N/A	106.6	20.4	30.9	54.6	N/A	85.5	16.3
Columbus										
1950	27.3	16.2	6.6	43.4	21.7	10.2	12.0	6.9	22.2	11.2
1960	29.7	19.2	8.2	48.9	19.0	17.2	22.6	10.9	39.7	15.5
1970	45.0	33.0	N/A	78.0	21.3	30.9	46.3	N/A	77.2	21.1
Toledo										
1950	20.4	12.0	4.1	32.4	20.4	4.6	7.6	4.2	12.2	7.7
1960	19.1	13.8	5.2	32.8	19.5	6.8	12.5	8.9	19.4	11.5
1970	29.3	24.5	N/A	53.8	20.3	15.6	31.5	N/A	47.1	17.7
Akron										
1950	17.8	10.7	3.1	28.5	18.0	4.4	7.0	3.5	11.5	7.2
1960	18.0	14.1	5.4	32.1	17.0	6.9	13.2	6.2	20.1	10.6
1970	27.2	23.4	N/A	50.6	19.4	14.7	28.1	N/A	42.8	16.5
Dayton										
1950	18.9	12.2	7.1	31.1	17.1	5.2	7.9	11.5	13.1	7.2
1960	23.5	17.9	6.7	41.4	16.1	10.2	17.2	11.8	27.4	10.6
1970	31.6	29.2	N/A	60.8	18.3	17.3	34.3	N/A	51.6	15.5
Youngstown-Warren										
1950	20.2	13.8	3.4	34.0	16.8	5.2	8.8	3.2	14.0	6.9
1960	16.8	13.3	5.2	30.2	16.9	6.2	11.6	6.0	17.7	10.0
1970	20.2	18.7	N/A	38.9	19.5	9.2	19.4	N/A	28.6	14.3
Canton										
1950	12.3	7.8	2.1	20.1	18.3	3.1	4.9	2.1	8.0	7.3
1960	12.1	9.2	3.4	21.3	17.6	4.4	8.4	4.4	12.8	10.6
1970	14.8	12.6	N/A	27.3	19.4	6.0	14.7	N/A	20.6	14.6

Notes: a—1970 population and other statistics include only persons 16 years of age or older; 1950 and 1960 statistics include persons 14 years or older.
b—Includes persons engaged in insurance, financial, and real estate; business and repair services; personal services; and, entertainment and related services. Ohio's Metropolitan Areas are those Standard Metropolitan Areas with 250,000 or more inhabitants as of 1950.

N/A—Not Available

Sources: U.S. Department of Commerce. Bureau of the Census. Census of Population: 1950, vol. 2; Characteristics of the Population, part 35: Ohio; U.S. Department of Commerce. Bureau of the Census. U.S. Census of the Population: 1960—Detailed Social and Economic Characteristics of Ohio; U.S. Department of Commerce. Bureau of the Census. 1970 Census of the Population, vol. 1: Characteristics of the Population, part 37: Ohio, Sections 1 and 2.

TABLE 5H. Average Number of Employees in Leading Ohio Industries, 1947 to 1977
(in thousands)

	All Employees				Production Workers			
	1947	1958	1967	1977	1947	1958	1967	1977
Machinery, Except Electric	227.7	157.5	215.3	197.3	186.3	113.6	158.7	139.2
Fabricated Metal Products	122.1	113.3	149.9	164.5	102.8	85.5	116.8	127.4
Transportation Equipment	93.8	151.6	170.8	158.9	78.0	106.3	128.1	122.3
Primary Metals	177.2	153.3	169.6	142.6	156.7	127.2	140.4	116.4
Electrical Equipment	91.5	108.1	129.9	110.0	77.6	81.0	98.8	80.6
Rubber, Misc. Plastics	83.5	76.6	93.4	98.3	68.2	57.7	70.1	73.2
Food & Kindred Products	67.0	85.9	78.5	66.4	48.1	50.7	46.4	42.7
Printing & Publishing	49.9	57.9	67.1	60.0	32.9	37.6	43.2	37.0
Stone, Clay, Glass	59.7	64.4	61.1	59.0	53.4	52.9	49.4	47.6
Chemical & Allied Products	37.3	45.4	47.7	45.5	26.7	27.9	29.4	27.4
Paper & Allied Products	31.7	35.8	38.8	36.7	27.3	28.4	30.4	27.4
Instrument, Related Products	8.3	9.6	13.0	23.1	6.2	6.4	8.4	15.5
Total—All Industries	1194.6	1162.3	1397.0	1331.2	988.4	856.5	998.1	924.4

Sources: U.S. Department of Commerce. Bureau of the Census. 1977 Census of Manufacturers, Vol. 3, Table 5. 1967, Census of Manufacturers, Vol. 3, Table 5. 1958 Census of Manufacturers, Vol. 3, Table 4. 1947 Census of Manufacturers, Vol. 3, Table 4.

TABLE 5J. Work Stoppages in the United States and Ohio, 1945-1976

	UNITED STATES			OHIO		
	# beginning in year	Workers involved (in thousands)	Man-days idle (in thousands)	# beginning in year	Workers involved (in thousands)	Man-days idle (in thousands)
1945	4,750	3,470	38,000	477	418	3,440
1946	4,985	4,600	116,000	396	450	10,600
1947	3,693	2,170	34,600	274	129	2,140
1948	3,419	1,960	34,100	256	122	1,480
1949	3,606	3,030	50,500	266	245	4,430
1950	4,843	2,410	38,800	469	220	2,550
1951	4,737	2,220	22,900	402	197	1,690
1952	5,117	3,540	59,100	444	410	7,260
1953	5,091	2,400	28,300	518	218	2,390
1954	3,468	1,530	22,600	266	134	1,830
1955	4,320	2,650	28,200	434	329	2,570
1956	3,825	1,900	33,100	357	291	4,720
1957	3,673	1,390	16,500	355	151	1,580
1958	3,694	2,060	23,900	359	234	3,160
1959[a]	3,708	1,880	69,000	391	238	9,630
1960	3,333	1,320	19,100	303	101	931
1961	3,367	1,450	16,300	283	127	1,420
1962	3,614	1,230	18,600	298	75	1,110
1963	3,362	941	16,100	265	63	861
1964	3,655	1,640	22,900	340	191	2,690
1965	3,963	1,550	23,300	369	97	1,460
1966	4,405	1,960	25,400	431	184	2,190
1967	4,595	2,870	42,100	536	345	6,020
1968	5,045	2,649	49,018	573	253	4,593
1969	5,700	2,481	42,869	672	272	3,206
1970	5,716	3,305	66,414	632	333	7,458
1971	5,138	3,280	47,589	523	250	3,866
1972	5,010	1,714	27,066	520	161	2,346
1973	5,353	2,251	27,948	502	217	2,648
1974	6,074	2,778	47,991	560	205	3,335
1975	5,031	1,746	31,237	432	130	2,233
1976	5,648	2,420	37,859	549	271	4,839

a—Alaska and Hawaii henceforth included.

Sources: U.S. Department of Labor, Handbook of Labor Statistics (Washington, D.C.: Government Printing Office, 1980); Ohio Bureau of Employment Services, "Work Stoppages and Man-Days of Idleness in Ohio, 1945-1976," n.p., n.d.

TABLE 5I. Growth of Ohio's Leading Manufacturers, Measured by Number of Establishments and Value Added by Manufacture, 1947-1977

	Number of Establishments						
	1947	1954	1958	1963	1967	1972	1977
Food and Kindred Products	1879	2109	2023	1728	1455	1259	1094
Paper and Allied Products	228	273	297	306	321	368	408
Printing and Publishing	1555	1732	1815	1880	1824	1917	2081
Chemicals and Allied Products	641	683	706	743	695	701	705
Rubber and Miscellaneous Plastic Products[a]	134	190	397	479	549	772	863
Stone, Clay, and Glass Products	872	887	1084	1077	1039	1035	1081
Primary Metal Industry Iron and Steel	605	650	677	667	669	653	659
Fabricated Metal Products	1432	1828	1924	2016	2034	2178	2376
Machinery, Except Electrical	1864	2471	2588	2768	3065	3347	3683
Electric and Electronic Equipment[b]	302	365	477	495	512	574	647
Transportation Equipment	247	370	363	400	398	445	468
All Ohio Industries	12303	14550	14931	15483	15428	16396	17354
All U.S. Industries	240807	N/A	303303	311931	311140	320710	359928

Notes: a—Known as "rubber products" until 1958.
b—Known as "electrical machinery" until 1963, then as electrical equipment and supplies" until 1972.

TABLE 5I. (cont.)

	Value Added By Manufacture (in millions of dollars)						
	1947	1954	1958	1963	1967	1972	1977
Food and Kindred Products	413.2	689.4	871.6	1051.9	1306.7	1737.7	2802.3
Paper and Allied Products	199.1	297.1	343.3	449.3	552.7	670.2	1040.4
Printing and Publishing	322.3	465.6	523.9	662.2	874.6	1223.0	1687.2
Chemicals and Allied Products	347.2	566.4	714.9	956.1	1358.6	1975.4	3209.0
Rubber and Miscellaneous Plastic Products	381.2	474.7	710.1	968.7	1330.6	2001.7	2658.8
Stone, Clay, and Glass Products	293.9	480.4	623.9	740.0	852.3	1254.4	1774.8
Primary Metal Industry (Iron and Steel)	852.8	1423.9	1643.7	2197.7	2702.5	3235.0	5505.7
Fabricated Metal Products	634.7	942.9	1035.3	1345.8	2212.2	3166.1	5398.6
Machinery, Except Electrical	1251.0	1709.6	1410.5	2036.7	3253.8	3933.2	5989.2
Electric and Electronic Equipment	471.6	355.4	1143.2	1547.6	1979.1	2277.9	3654.0
Transportation Equipment	483.4	1386.7	1566.9	2459.8	2593.8	3829.6	6376.5
All Ohio Industries	6359.0	10165.1	11472.5	15506.1	20435.4	27218.5	43054.7
All U.S. Industries	74290.5	117032.3	141540.6	192082.9	261983.8	353994.0	585165.6

Sources: U.S. Department of Commerce. Bureau of the Census. 1947 Census of Manufactures, vol. III: Statistics by States; U.S. Department of Commerce. Bureau of the Census. U.S. Census of Manufactures: 1954, vol. III: Area Statistics; U.S. Department of Commerce. Bureau of the Census. U.S. Census of Manufactures: 1958, vol. III: Area Statistics; U.S. Department of Commerce. Bureau of the Census. 1963 Census of Manufactures, vol. III: Area Statistics, part 2: Nebraska-Wyoming; U.S. Department of Commerce. Bureau of the Census. 1972 Census of Manufactures, vol. III: Area Statistics, part 2: Nebraska-Wyoming; U.S. Department of Commerce. Bureau of the Census. 1977 Census of Manufactures, vol. III: Geographic Area Statistics, part 2; General Summary, Nebraska-Wyoming.

TABLE 5K.—SEE PAGE 291

BIBLIOGRAPHY

PART 1

Books and Articles

Arms, Richard G. "From Disassembly to Assembly—Cincinnati: The Birthplace of Mass-Production." *Bulletin of the Historical and Philosophical Society of Ohio* 17 (1959): 195-203.

Baily, Marilyn. "From Cincinnati, Ohio to Wilberforce, Canada: A Note on Antebellum Colonization." *Journal of Negro History* 58 (January 1973): 427-40.

Bogart, Ernest Ludlow. *Financial History of Ohio*. Urbana-Champaign: University of Illinois Press, 1912.

Brooks, Thomas R. *Toil and Trouble*. New York: Dell, 1971.

Brownlee, W. Elliot. *Dynamics of Ascent: A History of the American Economy*. 2nd edition. New York: Alfred A. Knopf, 1979.

Buchstein, Frederick D. "Josiah Warren: The Peaceful Revolutionist." *Cincinnati Historical Society Bulletin* 32 (Spring-Summer 1974): 61-71.

Buley, R. Carlyle. *The Old Northwest*. 2 vols. Indianapolis: Indiana Historical Society, 1950.

Cist, Charles. *Cincinnati in 1841*. Cincinnati: By the Author, 1841.

——————. *Cincinnati in 1851*. Cincinnati: Wm. H. Moore, 1851.

——————. *Cincinnati in 1859*. Cincinnati: By the Author, 1859.

Clark, Victor S. *History of Manufactures in the United States*. Vol. 1, Washington: Carnegie Institution, 1929; reprint ed., New York: Peter Smith, 1949.

The Columbus & Hocking Coal & Iron Co. and the Mineral Resources and Industries of the Hocking Valley. New York: Globe Stationery and Printing Co., [1883].

Commons, John R.; Saposs, David J.; Sumner, Helen L.; Mittelman, E.B.; Hoagland, H.E.; Andrews, John B.; Perlman, Selig. *History of Labour in the United States*. Vols. 1,6,7. reprint ed., New York: Augustus M. Kelley, 1966.

Commons, John R. "Labor Organization and Labor Politics." *Quarterly Journal of Economics* 21 (February 1907): 323-29.

Corns, John B. "Industrial, Invincible Ironton." *The Ohio Magazine* 3 (August-September 1907): 153-58.

Coxe, Tench. *A Statement of the Arts and Manufactures of the United States of America For the Year 1810*. Philadelphia: A. Cornman, 1814.

Davis, Harry E. "John Malvin, A Western Reserve Pioneer." *Journal of Negro History* 23 (1938): 426-34.

Davis, Lenwood G. "Nineteenth Century Blacks in Ohio: An Historical View." In *Blacks in Ohio History*, pp. 4-10. Edited by Rubin F. Weston. Columbus: Ohio Historical Society, 1976.

Dial, George. "The Construction of the Ohio Canals." *Ohio Archaeological and Historical Publications* 13 (1904): 460-82.

Dodds, Gilbert F. *Early Ironmasters of Ohio*. By the Author, 1957.

Downard, William L. *The Cincinnati Brewing Industry*. Athens: Ohio University Press, 1973.

Drake, B. and Mansfield, E.D. *Cincinnati in 1826*. Cincinnati: Morgan, Lodge and Fisher, 1827.

Erickson, Charlotte. "British Immigrants in the Old Northwest, 1815-1860." In *The Frontier in American Development*, pp. 323-56. Edited by David M. Ellis. Ithaca: Cornell University Press, 1969.

Evans, Lyle, ed. *A Standard History of Ross County, Ohio*. Chicago: Lewis Publishing Co., 1917.

Executive Council, International Typographical Union. *A Study of the History of the International Typographical Union, 1852-1963*. Colorado Springs: International Typographical Union, 1964.

Farrell, Richard T. "Cincinnati, 1800-1830: Economic Development Through Trade and Industry." *Ohio History* 77 (Autumn 1968): 111-29.

Finn, Chester E. "The Ohio Canals: Public Enterprise on the Frontier." *The Ohio State Archaeological and Historical Quarterly* 51 (1942): 1-40.

Fite, Gilbert C. and Reese, Jim E. *An Economic History of the United States*. 3rd edition. Boston: Houghton Mifflin, 1973.

Foner, Philip S. *American Labor Songs of the Nineteenth Century*. Urbana: University of Illinois Press, 1975.

Fox, Wendall P. "The Kendal Community." *Ohio Archaeological and Historical Publications* 20 (1911): 176-219.

Garber, D.W. *Waterwheels and Millstones: A History of Ohio Gristmills and Milling*. Columbus: Ohio Historical Society, 1970.

George, John J. "The Miami Canal." *The Ohio State Archaeological and Historical Quarterly* 36 (1927): 92-115.

Glaab, Charles N. "The Idea of the City and Early Ohio Growth." In *Toward an Urban Ohio*, pp. 5-12. Edited by John Wunder. Columbus: Ohio Historical Society, 1977.

Goodwin, Frank P. "The Rise of Manufactures in the Miami Country." *American Historical Review* 12 (1907): 761-75.

Green, Constance. *American Cities In the Growth of the Nation*. New York: Harper & Row, 1965.

Greer, Thomas H. "Economic and Social Effects of the Depression of 1819 in the Old Northwest." *Indiana Magazine of History* 44 (September 1948): 227-43.

Gutman, Herbert G. *Work, Culture & Society in Industrializing America*. New York: Random House, 1976.

Hall, Bowman N. "The Economic Ideas of Josiah Warren, First American Anarchist." *History of Political Economy* 6 (1974): 95-108.

Hatcher, Harlan. *The Western Reserve*. Indianapolis: Bobbs-Merrill, 1949.

Hicks, Clara Belle. "The History of Penal Institutions in Ohio to 1850." *Ohio Archaeological and Historical Quarterly* 33 (October 1924): 359-416.

History of the Ohio Canals. Columbus: Ohio State Archaeological and Historical Society, [1905].

Hook, Charles Ruffin. *Romance of Iron and Steel*. New York: Newcomen Society of North America, 1950.

Howells, William Cooper. *Recollections of Life in Ohio*. Cincinnati: Robert Clarke Company, 1895.

Jones, Robert Leslie. "Ohio Agriculture in History." *Ohio Historical Quarterly* 65 (July 1956): 229-58.

Jordan, Philip D. *The National Road*. New York: Bobbs-Merrill, 1948.

Kranzberg, Melvin and Gies, Joseph. *By the Sweat of Thy Brow*. New York: G.P. Putnam's Sons, 1975.

Lawson, A. *The Iron Industries of Ironton, and the Hanging Rock Iron Region of Ohio*. Cincinnati: Bloch & Co., 1871.

Lebergott, Stanley. *Manpower in Economic Growth: The American Record Since 1800*. New York: McGraw-Hill, 1964.

Lee, Alfred. *History of the City of Columbus, Ohio*. Vol. 1, New York: Munsell and Co., 1892.

Leet, Don R. "The Determinants of the Fertility Transition in Antebellum, Ohio." *Journal of Economic History* 36 (June 1976): 359-78.

Litwack, Leon F. *North of Slavery*. Chicago: University of Chicago Press, 1961.

Mabry, William Alexander. "Industrial Beginnings in Ohio." *Ohio State Archaeological and Historical Quarterly* 55 (1946): 242-53.

The Mahoning Valley: Its Resources, Mines, Blast Furnaces, and Rolling Mills. Youngstown: Mahoning Valley Centennial Association, [1876].

McCollam, C. Harold. *The Brick and Tile Industry in Stark County 1809-1976*. Canton: Stark County Historical Society, 1976.

Meyer, Lysle E. "Radical Responses to Capitalism in Ohio Before 1913." *Ohio History* 79 (Summer-Autumn 1970): 193-208.

Montgomery, David. "The Shuttle and the Cross: Weavers and Artisans in the Kensington Riots of 1844." In *The Many-Faceted Jacksonian Era*, pp. 114-41. Edited by Edward Pessen. Westport: Greenwood Press, 1977.

Montgomery, David. "The Working Classes of the Pre-Industrial American City, 1780-1830." *Labor History* 9 (Winter 1968): 3-22.

Morris, James M. "Communes and Cooperatives: Cincinnati's Early Experiments in Social Reform." *Cincinnati Historical Society Bulletin* 33 (Spring 1975): 20-45.

Morrow, Frank C. *A History of Industry in Jackson County, Ohio*. Wellston, Ohio: By the Author, 1956.

Neufeld, Maurice F. "Three Aspects of the Economic Life of Cincinnati From 1815 to 1840." *Ohio Archaeological and Historical Quarterly* 44 (1935): 65-80.

Newcomer, Lee. "Construction of the Wabash and Erie Canal." *Ohio Archaeological and Historical Quarterly* 46 (1937): 199-207.

North, Douglass C. *Growth and Welfare in the American Past.* 2nd edition. Englewood Cliffs: Prentice-Hall, 1974.

Peskin, Allan, ed., *North Into Freedom: The Autobiography of John Malvin, Free Negro, 1795-1880.* Cleveland: Western Reserve University Press, 1966.

Pessen, Edward. "The Egalitarian Myth and the American Social Reality: Wealth, Mobility, and Equality in the Era of the Common Man." *American Historical Review* 76 (October 1971) 989-1034.

Pessen, Edward. "Builders of the Young Republic." In *The American Worker,* pp. 56-103. Edited by Richard B. Morris. Washington: U.S. Government Printing Office, nd.

Rayback, Joseph G. *A History of American Labor.* New York: The Free Press, 1959.

Reilley, Edward C. "Politico-Economic Considerations in the Western Reserve's Early Slavery Controversy." *Ohio State Archaeological and Historical Quarterly* 52 (1943): 141-57.

Rich, David. "The Toledo Mechanics' Association: The City's First Labor Union." *Northwest Ohio Quarterly* 46 (Winter 1973-74): 12-19.

Richards, Leonard L. *"Gentlemen of Property and Standing."* New York: Oxford University Press, 1970.

Robertson, Ross M. and Walton, Gary M. *History of the American Economy.* 4th edition. New York: Harcourt Brace Jovanovich, 1979.

Rodabaugh, James H. "The Negro in Ohio." *Journal of Negro History* 31 (1946): 9-29.

Rowe, Frank H. *History of the Iron and Steel Industry in Scioto County, Ohio.* Columbus: Ohio State Archaeological and Historical Society, 1938.

Schafer, Joseph. "Was the West A Safety Valve for Labor?" *Mississippi Valley Historical Review* 24 (December 1937): 299-314.

Scheiber, Harry N. "Ohio's Transportation Revolution — Urban Dimensions, 1803-1870." In *Toward an Urban Ohio,* pp. 12-23. Edited by John Wunder. Columbus: Ohio Historical Society, 1977.

——————. "State Policy and the Public Domain: The Ohio Canal Lands." *Journal of Economic History* 25 (March 1965): 86-113.

——————. *Ohio Canal Era.* Athens: Ohio University Press, 1969.

——————. "The Pennsylvania & Ohio Canal: Transport Innovation, Mixed Enterprise, and Urban Commercial Rivalry." *The Old Northwest* 6 (Summer 1980): 105-135.

Schob, David E. *Hired Hands and Plowboys.* Urbana: University of Illinois Press, 1975.

Segal, Harvey H. "Canals and Economic Development." In *Canals and American Economic Development,* pp. 216-48. Edited by Carter Goodrich. New York: Columbia University Press, 1961.

Soltow, Lee. "The Growth of Wealth in Ohio, 1800-1969." In *Essays in Nineteenth Century Economic History,* pp. 191-207. Edited by David C. Klingaman and Richard K. Vedder. Athens: Ohio University Press, 1975.

Stephenson, Bert S. "Iron and Steel Making in Ohio." *The Ohio Magazine* 2 (January 1907): 64-72.

Stoddard, Paul W. "The Economic Progress of Ohio, 1800-1840." *Ohio Archaeological and Historical Society Publications* 41 (April 1932): 177-94.

Taylor, George R. *The Transportation Revolution, 1815-1860.* New York: Harper & Row, 1951.

Teagarden, Ernest M. "Builders of the Ohio Canal, 1825-1832." *Inland Seas* 19 (Summer 1963): 94-103.

Tyler, Alice F. *Freedom's Ferment.* New York: Harper & Row, 1944.

Vedder, Richard K. and Gallaway, Lowell E. "Migration and the Old Northwest." In *Essays in Nineteenth Century Economic History,* pp. 159-76. Edited by David C. Klingaman and Richard K. Vedder. Athens: Ohio University Press, 1975.

Wade, Richard C. "The Negro in Cincinnati, 1800-1830." *Journal of Negro History* 39 (January 1954): 43-57.

——————. *The Urban Frontier.* Chicago: University of Chicago Press, 1959.

Waite, Frederick C. "An Indenture of 1831 in Portage County, Ohio." *Ohio Archaeological and Historical Quarterly* 55 (July-September 1946): 288-92.

Wittke, Carl, gen. ed. *The History of the State of Ohio.* 6 vols. Columbus: Ohio State Archaeological and Historical Society, 1942. Vol. 2: *The Frontier State, 1803-1825,* by William T. Utter. Vol. 3: *The Passing of the Frontier, 1825-1850,* by Francis P. Weisenburger.

——————. *The Irish in America.* Baton Rouge: Louisiana State University Press, 1956.

Woodson, Carter G. "The Negroes of Cincinnati Prior to the Civil War." *Journal of Negro History* 1 (January 1916): 1-22.

Woolen, Evans. "Labor Troubles Between 1834 and 1837." *Yale Review* 1 (May 1892): 87-100.

Yasuba, Yasukichi. *Birth Rates of the White Population in the United States, 1800-1860.* Baltimore, Johns Hopkins Press, 1962.

Unpublished Studies

Aaron, Daniel. "Cincinnati, 1818-1838: A Study of Attitudes In the Urban West." Ph.D. dissertation, Harvard University, 1942.

Becker, Carl M. "Mill, Shop, and Factory: The Industrial Life of Dayton, Ohio, 1830-1900." Ph.D. dissertation, University of Cincinnati, 1971.

Beringer, Sara M. "History of Dayton's Industries." Dayton and Montgomery County Public Library, 1955. (Mimeographed.)

Chaddock, Robert E. "Ohio Before 1850." Ph.D. dissertation, Columbia University, 1908.

Demming, David W. "A Social and Demographic Study of Cuyahoga County Blacks, 1820-1860." M.A. thesis, Kent State University, 1976.

Donakowski, Conrad. "Labor in the Old Northwest, 1800-1860." M.A. thesis, Xavier University, 1959.

Dubin, Barbara H. "A Critical Review of the Social and Educational Theories of Josiah Warren and His Individualist School of Anarchism." Ph.D. dissertation, University of Illinois, 1973.

Folk, Patrick A. "The Queen City of Mobs: Riots and Community Reactions in Cincinnati, 1788-1848." Ph.D. dissertation, University of Toledo, 1978.

Gephart, William F. "Transportation and Industrial Development in the Middle West." Ph.D. dissertation, Columbia University, 1909.

Glazer, Walter. "Cincinnati in 1840: A Community Profile." Ph.D. dissertation, University of Michigan, 1968.

Lippincott, Isaac. "A History of Manufactures in the Ohio Valley to the Year 1860." Ph.D. dissertation, University of Chicago, 1914.

Matthews, James S. "Expressions of Urbanism in the Sequent Occupance of Northeastern Ohio." Ph.D. dissertation, University of Chicago, 1949.

Morris, James M. "The Road to Trade Unionism: Organized Labor in Cincinnati to 1893. Ph.D. dissertation, University of Cincinnati, 1969.

Rankin, John. "Labor Consciousness in Jacksonian Dayton, 1822-1842." University of Dayton. (Mimeographed.)

Standafer, Raymond, "History of the Miami and Erie Canal From Middletown to Cincinnati." M.A. thesis, Miami University, 1949.

Stevens H.R. "History of the Working Class in Cincinnati to the Panic of 1819." Cincinnati Historical Society. (Mimeographed.)

——————. "The Panic of 1837 in Cincinnati." Cincinnati Historical Society, 1936. (Mimeographed.)

Trew, Marion J. "A Study of the Growth of the Population of Ohio From 1790 to 1850." M.A. thesis, Miami University, 1932.

Government Records

Fifth Census of the United States, 1830. Washington, D.C.: Duff Green, 1832.

Kilbourn, John. *Public Documents Concerning the Ohio Canals Which Are to Connect Lake Erie With the Ohio River.* Columbus: Olmsted, Bailhache and Camron, 1828.

Ohio General Assembly. "An Act to Incorporate the Mechanic's Union of Springfield." 34th General Assembly, 1836. *Ohio Laws,* vol. 34.

——————. "An Act to Incorporate the Carpenters' and Joiners' Benevolent Society of the City of Cleveland." 35th General Assembly, 1837. *Ohio Laws,* vol. 35.

Sixth Census of the United States, 1840. Washington, D.C.: Blair and Rives, 1841.

U.S. Census Office. *Fourth Census of the United States, 1820: Digest of Accounts of Manufacturing Establishments in the United States, and of Their Manufactures.* Washington, D.C.: Gales and Seaton, 1823.

Primary Sources

Cincinnati, Ohio. Cincinnati Historical Society. "Bill of Prices Agreed Upon By the Journeymen Tin-Plate Workers, of Cincinnati," January 26, 1830.

Cleveland, Ohio. Western Reserve Historical Society. Roberts Family Papers.

Columbus, Ohio. Ohio Historical Society. *Constitution and By-Laws of the Mechanics' Union of Springfield*, 1836.

——————. Erasmus Gest Papers.

——————. *Memorial of the Ohio Anti-Slavery Society to the General Assembly of the State of Ohio*, 1838.

——————. Micajah T. Williams Papers.

——————. Ohio Canal Commission Correspondence.

——————. *Rapid Forge Ledger Book, 1818-1819*.

——————. *Report on Buckeye Furnace, 1934*.

——————. Sheldon Kellogg Autobiography, 1871. Description and Travel Collection.

——————. Steele Family Papers.

——————. Wilbur Stout Records.

"Journal of Cyrus P. Bradley." *In Ohio Archaeological and Historical Society Publications* 15 (1906): 207-70.

Ohio Anti-Slavery Society. *Proceedings of the Ohio Anti-Slavery Convention Held at Putnam*. New York: American Anti-Slavery Society, 1835.

"Transplanting Free Negroes to Ohio From 1815 to 1858." In *Journal of Negro History* 1 (June 1916): 302-17.

PART 2

Books, Articles, and Pamphlets:

Abbott, Edith. "The Wages of Unskilled Labor in the United States, 1850-1900." *Journal of Political Economy* 13 (June 1905): 321-69.

Aiken, William Earl. *The Roots Grew Deep*. Cleveland: Lezius-Eiles Co., 1957.

Amsden, Jon, and Brier, Stephen. "Coal Miners on Strike: The Transformation of Strike Demands and the Formation of a National Union." *Journal of Interdisciplinary History* 7 (Spring 1977): 583-616.

Anderson, Elaine S. "Pauline Steinem, Dynamic Immigrant." In *Women In Ohio History: A Conference to Commemorate the Bicentennial of the American Revolution*. The Ohio American Revolution Bicentennial Conference Series, No. 2, pp. 13-19. Edited by Martha Whitlock. Columbus: Ohio Historical Society, 1976.

Bailie, William. *Josiah Warren: The First American Anarchist, A Sociological Study*. Boston: Small, Maynard, & Co., 1906.

Bancroft, Thomas B. "Strikes in the Ohio Coal Fields." *Ohio Mining Journal* 3 (1885): 27-40.

Banla, R. E. *The Ohio*. New York: Rhinehart & Co., 1949.

Barnard, Harry. *Rutherford B. Hayes and His America*. Indianapolis: Bobbs-Merrill, 1954.

Bartha, Stephen J. "The German Element in Toledo." *Northwest Ohio Quarterly* 18 (1946): 25-38.

Baughin, William A. "Ballots and Bullets: The Election Day Riots of 1855." *Historical and Philosophical Society of Ohio Bulletin* 21 (1963): 267-73.

Baxandall, Rosalyn; Gordon, L.; and Reverby, S.; eds. *America's Working Women*. New York: Vintage Books, 1976.

Becker, Carl M. "Entrepreneurial Invention and Innovation in the Miami Valley During the Civil War." *Cincinnati Historical Society Bulletin* 22 (1964): 5-28.

——————. "The Death of J. F. Bollmeyer: Murder Most Foul?" *Cincinnati Historical Society Bulletin* 24 (1966): 249-69.

——————. "Evolution of the Disassembly Line: The Horizontal Wheel and the Overhead Railway Loop." *Cincinnati Historical Society Bulletin* 26 (July, 1968): 277-82.

——————. "A 'Most Complete' Factory: The Barney Car Works, 1850-1926." *Cincinnati Historical Society Bulletin* 31 (Spring 1973): 48-69.

Bell, Sherry S., ed. *Ohio Women*. Columbus: State of Ohio, Bureau of Employment Services, 1979.

Bemis, Edward W. "Mine Labor in the Hocking Valley." In *Publications of the American Economic Association*, Vol. 3. July 1888.

Berthoff, Rowland Tappan. *British Immigrants in Industrial America*. Cambridge, MA: Harvard University Press, 1953.

Blocker, Jack S., Jr. "Market Integration, Urban Growth, and Economic Change in an Ohio County, 1850-1880." *Ohio History* 90 (Autumn 1981): 298-316.

Bogart, Ernest L. *Financial History of Ohio*. Urbana, Ill.: University of Illinois Press, 1912.

Bremner, Robert H. *From the Depths: The Discovery of Poverty in The United States*. New York: New York University Press, 1956.

Brinkerhoff, Roeliff. *Recollections of a Lifetime*. Cincinnati: The R. Clarke, Co., 1900.

Brody, David. *The Butcher Workmen*. Cambridge, MA: Harvard University Press, 1964.

Brown, Ashley. *The History of Montgomery County, Ohio*. Chicago: W. H. Beers & Co., 1882.

Browne, Henry J. *The Catholic Church and the Knights of Labor*. Washington, D.C.: Catholic University of America Press, 1949.

Bruce, Robert V. *1877: Year of Violence*. Indianapolis: Bobbs-Merrill Co., 1954; reprint ed., Chicago: Quadrangle Books, 1970.

Buchstein, Frederick D. "Josiah Warren: The Peaceful Revolutionist." *Cincinnati Historical Society Bulletin* 32 (Spring 1974): 61-71.

Cahn, William. *A Pictorial History of American Labor*. New York: Crown Publishers, Inc., 1972.

Cebula, James E. *The Glory and Despair of Challenge and Change: A History of the Molders Union*. Cincinnati: International Molders & Allied Workers Union, 1976.

Cheek, William F. "John Mercer Langston: Black Protest Leader and Abolitionist." *Civil War History* 16 (June 1970): 101-20.

Chyet, Stanley F. "Ohio Valley Jewry During the Civil War." *Cincinnati Historical Society Bulletin* 21 (1963): 179-89.

Cincinnati Federal Writers Project of the Works Progress Administration in Ohio. *They Built a City: 150 Years of Industrial Cincinnati*. Cincinnati: Cincinnati Post, 1938.

Cist, Charles. *Sketches & Statistics of Cincinnati in 1851*. Cincinnati: W. H. Moore & Co., 1851.

——————. *Sketches & Statistics of Cincinnati in 1859*. Cincinnati: By the Author, 1859.

Clark, Victor S. *History of Manufactures in the United States*. 2 vols. New York: Carnegie Institute of Washington, 1929.

Clarke, James F. *The Present Condition of the Free People of Color of the United States*. New York: n. p., 1859.

Collins, B. W. "Economic Issues in Ohio's Politics During the Recession of 1857-1858." *Ohio History* 89 (Winter 1980): 46-64.

Colored Men of Ohio: Proceedings of a Convention of the Colored Men of Ohio. Cincinnati: n. p., 1858.

Colston, Freddie C. "The Political Behavior of the Black Legislators in the Ohio House of Representatives." In *Blacks in Ohio History*, pp. 16-25. Edited by Rubin F. Weston. Ohio American Revolution Bicentennial Conferences Series, No. 4. Columbus: Ohio Historical Society, 1977.

The Columbus & Hocking Coal & Iron Company. New York: Globe Stationery, 1883.

Commons, John R.; Phillips, Ulrich B.; Gilmore, Eugene A.; Sumner, Helen L.; and Andrews, John B., eds. *A Documentary History of American Industrial Society*. Vols. 7, 8, and 9: *Labor Movement*. Cleveland: Arthur H. Clark Co., 1910.

Commons, John R.; Saposs, David J.; Sumner, Helen L.; Mittelman, E. B.; Hoagland, H. E.; Andres, John B.; and Perlman, Selig. *History of Labor in the United States*. 4 Vols. Reprint ed., New York: Augustus M. Kelley, 1966.

Condit, Carl W. *The Railroad and the City: A Technological and Urbanized History of Cincinnati*. Columbus: Ohio State University Press, 1977.

Connaughton, Mary Stainislaus. *The Editorial Opinion of the Catholic Telegraph of Cincinnati on Contemporary Affairs and Politics, 1871-1921*. Washington, D. C.: Catholic University of America Press, 1943.

Conway, Jill. "Women Reformers and American Culture, 1870-1930." *Journal of Social History* 5 (Spring 1972): 164-77.

Cooper, Jerry M. "The Army as Strikebreaker — The Railroad Strikes of 1877 and 1894." *Labor History* 18 (Spring 1977): 179-96.

Corns, John B. "Industrial, Invincible Ironton." *The Ohio Magazine*, August-September 1907, pp. 153-58.

Cotkin, George B. "Strikebreakers, Evictions and Violence: Industrial Conflict in the Hocking Valley, 1884-1885." *Ohio History* 87 (Spring 1978): 140-50.

Croly, Herbert. *Marcus Alonzo Hanna: His Life and His Works*. New York: Macmillan, 1912.

Dabney, Wendell P. *Cincinnati's Colored Citizens; Historical, Sociological, and Biographical*. Cincinnati: The Dabney Publishing Co., 1926.

Dannenbaum, Jed. "Immigrants and Temperance: Ethnocultural Conflict in Cincinnati, 1845-1860." *Ohio History* 87 (Spring 1978): 125-39.

Davis, Pearce. *The Development of the American Glass Industry*. Cambridge, Mass.: Harvard University Press, 1949; reprint ed., New York: Russell & Russell, 1970.

Davis, Russell H. *Black Americans in Cleveland: From George Peake to Carl B. Stokes, 1796-1969*. Washington, D. C.: Associated Publishers, 1962.

Davis, S. M. "Women and Wages." *The American Journal of Politics* 4 (January 1894): 63-65.

Dawley, Allen. "Working Class Culture and Politics in the Industrial Revolution, Sources of Loyalty and Rebellion." *Journal of Sociological History* 9 (June 1976): 466-80.

Dealtry, William. *The Laborer, A Remedy for His Wrongs*. Cincinnati: R. Allison & Co., 1825.

De Pew, Chauncey M., ed. *One Hundred Years of American Commerce*. 2 vols. New York: D. O. Haynes, 1895.

Deveraux, Francis, comp. *Ohio's Manufacturers*. Columbus: W. J. Conley, 1871.

Dickson, Paul. "The Great Railroad War of 1877." *American Heritage* (February-March 1978): 56-61.

Dorn, Jacob H. *Washington Gladden: Prophet of the Social Gospel*. Columbus: Ohio State University Press, 1967.

Downard, William L. *The Cincinnati Brewing Industry*. Athens, Ohio: Ohio University Press, 1973.

Downes, Randolph C. *Industrial Beginnings, 1875-1900*. Lucas County Historical Series, vol. 4. Toledo, Ohio: Historical Society of Northwestern Ohio, 1954.

—————. *Lake Port*. Lucas County Historical Series, vol 3. Toledo, Ohio: Historical Society of Northwestern Ohio, 1951.

Doyle, W. D., ed. *Centennial History of Summit County, Ohio and Representative Citizens*. Chicago: Biographical Publishing Co., 1908.

Drumm, Carl. *A Complete History of the Scioto Marsh*. Kenton, Ohio: Kenton Republican Co., 1940.

Du Bois, W. E. B., and Dill, Augustus Granville, eds. *The Negro Artisan*. Atlanta: Atlanta University Publications, No. 17, Atlanta University Press, 1912; reprinted in *Atlanta University Publications*, Nos. 16-20. New York: Russell & Russell, 1969.

Dubofsky, Melvin. *Industrialism and the American Worker, 1865-1920*. Arlington Heights, Ill.: A. H. M. Publishing Corp., 1975.

—————. "Industrialization in Ohio's Gilded Age." In *Toward an Urban Ohio: A Conference to Commemorate the Bicentennial of the American Revolution*, pp. 23-28. Edited by John Wunder. Columbus; Ohio Historical Society, 1977.

Duffy, Thomas J. *An Early History of the National Brotherhood of Operative Potters*. East Liverpool, Ohio: The Potter's Herald Press, 1901.

Duggan, Edward P. "Labor Supply and Technological Change in the Nineteenth Century: A Comparison of Cincinnati and Birmingham, England." *Cincinnati Historical Society Bulletin* 31 (Winter 1973).

—————. "Machines, Markets, and Labor: The Carriage and Wagon Industry in Late Nineteenth-Century Cincinnati." *Business History Review* 51 (1977): 308-25.

Edwards, Richard. *Toledo Historical and Descriptive*. Toledo, Ohio: Toledo Commercial Co., 1876.

Elben, Jack E. "Analysis of Nineteenth Century Frontier Populations." *Demography* 2 (December 1965): 399-413.

Eggert, Gerald G. "A Missed Alternative: Federal Courts as Arbiters of Railway Disputes, 1877-1895." *Labor History* 7 (Fall 1966): 287-306.

Ely, Richard T. *The Labor Movement in America*. New York: Thomas Y. Crowell & Co., 1886.

Emery, Joseph. *Thirty-five Years Among the Poor, and the Public Institutions of Cincinnati*. Cincinnati: Stevens, 1887.

Erickson, Charlotte, *American Industry and the European Immigrant 1860-1885*. Cambridge, Mass.: Harvard University Press, 1957.

Evaenson, Howard N. *The First Century and a Quarter of the American Coal Industry*. Pittsburg: Koppers, 1942.

Evans, Chris. *History of the United Mine Workers of America*. 2 vols. Indianapolis: n. p., 1918-20.

Fauster, Carl U. *Libbey Glass Since 1818: A Pictorial Guide*. Toledo, Ohio: Len Beach Press, 1979.

Feck, Luke. *Yesterday's Cincinnati*. Miami: E. A. Seeman Publishing Co., 1975.

Fine, Nathan. *Labor and Farmer Parties in the United States, 1828-1928*. New York: Rand School of Social Science, 1928.

Fine, Sidney. *Laissez Faire and the General-Welfare State*. Ann Arbor: University of Michigan Press, 1956.

Fisk, William L. "The Scotch-Irish in Central Ohio." *Ohio History* 57 (1948): 111-25.

Fite, Emerson. *Social and Industrial Conditions in the North During the Civil War*. New York: The Macmillan Press, 1910.

Flint, James. *Letters From America Containing Observations on the Climate and Agriculture of Western States, the Manners of the People, the Prospects of Emigrants*. 9 vols. Cleveland: A. A. Clarke, 1904.

Foner, Eric. *Free Soil, Free Labor, Free Men: The Ideology of the Republican Party Before the Civil War*. New York: Oxford University Press, 1970.

Foner, Philip S. *The Great Labor Uprising of 1877*. New York: Monad Press, 1977.

—————. *Women and the American Labor Movement: From Colonial Times to the Eve of World War I*. New York: The Free Press, 1979.

Ford, Henry A., and Ford, Kate B. *History of Cincinnati, Ohio with Illustrations and Biographical Sketches*. Cleveland: L. A. Williams & Co., 1881.

Frohman, Charles E. "The Milan Canal." *Ohio History* 57 (1948): 237-46.

Gagel, Diane VanSkiver. "Ohio Women Unite: The Salem Convention of 1850." In *Women in Ohio History: A Conference to Commemorate the Bicentennial of the American Revolution*. Marta Whittock. Columbus: Ohio Historical Society, 1976.

Garraty, John A., ed. *Labor and Capital in the Gilded Age*. Boston: Little, Brown & Co., 1968.

Gerber, David A. *Black Ohio and the Color Line, 1860-1915*. Urbana, Ill.: University of Illinois Press, 1976.

Gibbons, Willis A. "The Rubber Industry, 1839-1939." *Annual Report of the Board of Regents, 1939-1940*. Smithsonian Institution, 193-214.

Glaab, Charles N. "The Idea of the City and Early Ohio Growth." In *Toward an Urban Ohio: A Conference to Commemorate the Bicentennial of the American Revolution*. Edited by John Wunder. Columbus: Ohio Historical Society, 1977.

Glaab, Charles, and Brown, A. Theodore. *A History of Urban America*. New York: The Macmillan Co., 1967.

Glazier, Willard. *Peculiarities of American Cities*. Philadelphia: Hubbard Bros., 1886.

Goodrich, Carter. *Government Promotion of American Canals and Railroads, 1800-1890*. New York: Columbia University Press, 1960.

Gompers, Samuel. *Seventy Years of Life and Labor: An Autobiography*. 2 vols. London; Hurst & Blackett, Ltd., n.d.

Graham, Hugh, and Gurr, Ted, eds. *Violence in America; Historical and Comparative Perspectives*. Washington: Government Printing Office, 1969.

The Great Cincinnati Riots! Being the Only Correct History of that Most Lamentable Outbreak in Ohio's Greatest City. Philadelphia: The Old Franklin Publishing House, 1884.

Green, Constance McLaughlin. *American Cities in the Growth of the Nation*. New York: Harper & Row, 1965.

Greenway, John. *American Folksongs of Protest*. Philadelphia: University of Pennsylvania Press, 1953.

Griffen, Clyde. "Occupational Mobility in Nineteenth Century America: Problems and Possibilities." *Journal of Social History* 5 (Spring 1972): 310-30.

Grisiner, Karl H. *Akron and Summit County*. Akron: Summit County Historical Society, 1952.

Grob, Gerald N. "The Railroad Strikes of 1877." *Midwest Journal* 6 (Winter 1954-55): 16-34.

—————. *Workers and Utopia: A Study of Ideological Conflict in the American Labor Movement, 1865-1900*. Chicago: Quadrangle Paperback ed., 1969.

Grossman, Lawrence. "In His Veins Coursed No Bootlicking Blood: The Career of Peter H. Clark." *Ohio History* 86 (Spring 1977): 79-95.

Grosvenor, W. M. "The Communist and the Railway." *International Review* 4 (September, 1877).

Gutman, Herbert. "An Iron Workers' Strike in the Ohio Valley, 1873-1874." *Ohio Historical Quarterly* 68 (October 1959): 353-70.

—————. "Reconstruction in Ohio: Negroes in the Hocking Valley Coal Mines in 1873 and 1874." *Labor History* 3 (Fall 1962): 243-64.

—————. "Trouble on the Railroads, 1873-1874: Prelude to the 1877 Crisis." *Labor History* 2 (Spring 1961): 215-35.

—————. *Work, Culture and Society in Industrializing America.* New York: Vintage Books, 1977.

—————. "The Worker's Search for Power: Labor in the Gilded Age." In *The Gilded Age,* pp. 38-68. H. Wayne Morgan, ed. Syracuse: Syracuse University Press, 1963.

Hall, Henry. *Report on the Ice Industry of the United States.* Washington: Government Printing Office, 1888.

Handlin, Oscar. *A Pictorial History of Immigration.* New York: Crown Publishers, Inc., 1972.

Harding, Leonard. "The Cincinnati Riots of 1862." *Cincinnati Historical Society Bulletin* 25 (October 1967): 229-39.

Hareven, Tamara K. *Anonymous Americans.* Englewood Cliffs, N.J.: Prentice-Hall, Inc., 1971.

Hatcher, Harlan. *The Buckeye Country; A Pageant of Ohio.* New York: H. C. Kinsey & Co., 1940.

Havighurst, Walter. *Ohio: A Bicentennial History.* New York: W. W. Norton & Co., 1976.

Headley, J. T. *Pen and Pencil Sketches of the Great Riots; An Illustrated History of the Railroad and Other Great American Riots.* New York: E. B. Treat, 1877.

Heywood, E. H. "The Great Strike." *Radical Review* 1 (November 1877).

Hicks, John E. *Adventures of a Tramp Printer, 1880-1890.* Kansas City, Mo: Midamericana Press, 1950.

Higham, John. *Strangers in the Land: Patterns of American Nativism, 1860-1925.* New York: Atheneum, 1969.

Hill, Joseph A. *Women in Gainful Occupations, 1870-1920.* Washington: Government Printing Office, 1929.

Hill, Norman Newell, Jr., comp. *History of Coshocton County, Ohio: Its Past and Present.* Newark, Ohio: A. A. Graham & Co., 1881.

—————. *History of Licking County, Ohio: Its Past and Present.* Newark, Ohio: A. A. Graham & Co., 1881.

Historical and Descriptive Review of the Industrial Enterprises of Dayton, Springfield, Hamilton, Urbana, Miamisburg, Piqua, Troy, and Xenia. New York: International Publishing Co., 1886.

History of Trade Unions of Columbus. Columbus, Ohio: Franklin Printing Co., 1895.

The History of Washington County, Ohio. Cleveland: H. Z. Williams & Co., 1881.

Holliday, Joseph. "Freedmen's Aid Societies in Cincinnati, 1862-1870." *Cincinnati Historical Society Bulletin* 20 (1964): 169-85.

Holt, Edgar A. *Party Politics in Ohio, 1840-1850.* Columbus: Ohio State Archaeological and Historical Society, 1931.

Hook, Charles Ruffin. *Romance of Iron and Steel: Contribution of the Central Ohio Valley.* New York: The Newcomen Society, 1950.

Howe, Henry. *Historical Collections of Ohio.* 2 vols. Columbus: n. p., 1889-91.

Hubbart, Henry Clyde. *The Older Middle West, 1840-1880.* New York: D. Appleton-Century Co., 1936.

Hughes, Langston; Melzer, Milton; and Lincoln, C. Eric. *A Pictorial History of Black Americans.* New York: Crown Publications, 1968.

Hulbert, Archer Butler. *The Ohio River: A Course of Empire.* New York: G. P. Putnam, 1906.

Hunter, Louis C. *Steamboats on the Western Rivers an Economic and Technological History.* Cambridge, Mass.: Harvard University Press, 1949.

—————. *Studies in the Economic History of the Ohio Valley: Seasonal Aspects of Industry and Commerce Before the Age of Big Business.* Smith College Studies in History, no. 19. Northhampton, Mass.: Department of History of Smith College, 1934.

Huntington, C. C., and McClelland, C. P. *History of Ohio Canals, Their Construction, Cost, Use, and Partial Abandonment.* Columbus: Ohio Historical Society, 1905.

Hutchinson, E. P. *Immigrants and Their Children, 1850-1950.* New York: John Wiley & Sons, 1956.

Ingham, John N. "Rags to Riches Revisited: The Effect of City Size and Related Factors on the Recruitment of Business Leaders." *Journal of American History* 63 (December 1976): 615-37.

Ingham, W. A. *Women of Cleveland and Their Work.* Cleveland: Cleveland Printing and Publishing Co., 1893.

International Typographical Union Executive Council. *A Study of the History of the International Typographical Union, 1852-1963.* 2 vols. Colorado Springs, Col.: International Typographical Union, 1964 (1966).

Jacobson, Julius, ed. *The Negro and the American Labor Movement.* Garden City, NY: Doubleday and Co., 1968.

James, John. "The Miner's Strike in the Hocking Valley." *Cooper's New Monthly* 1 (July 1874).

Johnson, Leland R. *An Illustrated History of the Huntington District.* Washington: U. S. Army Corps of Engineers, Government Printing Office, 1977.

Jones, Robert Leslie, ed. "Flatboating Down the Ohio and Mississippi 1867-1873." Correspondence and Diaries of the William Dudley Devol Family of Marietta, Ohio. *Ohio State Archaeological and Historical Quarterly* 59 (1950): 287-309; and 385-410.

Jones, W. H. "Welsh Settlements in Ohio." *Ohio History* 16 (1907): 194-227.

Jordan, Philip Dillon. *The National Road.* Indianapolis: Bobbs-Merrill Co., 1948.

—————. *Ohio Comes of Age 1873-1900. History of the State of Ohio,* vol. 5. Carl Wittke, ed. Columbus: Ohio Archaeological and Historical Society, 1943.

Jordan, Wayne. "The Hoskinville Rebellion, 1863." *Ohio State Archaeological and Historical Quarterly* 47 (October 1938): 319-54.

Josephson, Matthew. *Union House, Union Bar.* New York: Random House, 1956.

Keller, Vernon D. *The Commercial Development of Cincinnati.* Chicago: University of Chicago Press, 1938.

Kennedy, James H. *A History of the City of Cleveland, Its Settlement and Progress, 1796-1896.* Cleveland: Imperial Press, 1896.

Kennedy, Susan Estabrook. *If All We Did Was To Weep at Home: A History of White Working-Class Women in America.* Bloomington, Ill., and London: Indiana University Press, 1979.

Kenny, Daniel J. *Illustrated Cincinnati.* Cincinnati: Robert Clarke & Co., 1875.

Kerr, K. Austin. "The Movement for Coal Mine Safety in Nineteenth-Century Ohio." *Ohio History* 86 (Winter 1976): 3-18.

Klein, Maury, and Kantor, Harvey A. *Prisoners of Progress: American Industrial Cities, 1850-1920.* New York: Macmillan, 1976.

Kleine, W. Laird. "Anatomy of a Riot." *Historical and Philosophical Society of Ohio Bulletin* 20 (October 1962): 234-44.

Kleppner, Paul. *The Cross of Culture—A Social Analysis of Midwestern Politics 1850-1900.* New York: The Free Press, 1970.

Klingaman, David C., and Vedder, Richard K. *Essays In Nineteenth Century Economic History: The Old Northwest.* Athens, Ohio: Ohio University Press, 1975.

—————, eds. "Individual Wealth in Ohio in 1860. In *Essays in Nineteenth Century Economic History,* pp. 177-90. Athens, Ohio: Ohio University Press, 1975.

Knapp, H. S. *History of the Maumee Valley, Commencing With its Occupation by the French in 1680.* Toledo, Ohio: Blade Publishing House, 1872.

Knepper, George W. *An Ohio Portrait.* Columbus: Ohio Historical Society, 1976.

Kolehmainen, I. *A History of the Finns in Ohio, Western Pennsylvania and West Virginia.* New York: Parta Printers, Inc., 1977.

Kremm, Thomas W. "Cleveland and the First Lincoln Election: The Ethnic Response to Nativism." *Journal of Interdisciplinary History* 8 (Summer 1977): 69-86.

Kusmer, Kenneth L. *A Ghetto Takes Shape: Black Cleveland, 1870-1930.* Urbana, Ill.: University of Illinois Press, 1976.

Lane, Roger. "Crime and the Industrial Revolution: British and American Views." *Journal of Social History* 7 (Spring 1973): 287-303.

Lang, W. *History of Seneca County.* Springfield, Ohio: Transcript Publishing Co., 1880.

Larrowe, Charles P. *Maritime Labor Relations on the Great Lakes.* East Lansing, Mich.: Michigan State University, Labor and Industrial Relations Center, 1959.

Lauck, W. Jett. *Political and Industrial Democracy, 1776-1926.* New York: Funk & Wagnalls, 1926.

Lebergott, Stanley. *Manpower and Economic Growth: The American Record Since 1800.* New York: McGraw-Hill, 1964.

Lee, Alfred. *History of the City of Columbus.* New York: Munseil Co., 1892.

Leet, Don R. "Human Fertility and Agricultural Opportunities in Ohio Counties: From Frontier to Maturity, 1810-1860." In *Essays in Nineteenth Century Economic History*, pp. 138-58. Richard K. Vedder and D. C. Klingaman, eds. Athens, Ohio: Ohio University Press, 1975.

Leonard, Henry B. "Ethnic Clevage and Industrial Conflict in Late 19th Century America: The Cleveland Rolling Mill Company Strikes of 1882 and 1885." *Labor History* 20 (Fall 1979): 524-548.

——————. "Ethnic Conflict and Episcopal Power: The Diocese of Cleveland, 1847-1870." *Catholic Historical Review* 62 (July 1976): 388-407.

Levine, Louis. *The Women's Garment Workers: A History of the International Ladies Garment Workers Union*. New York: B. W. Huebsch, 1924.

Levstik, Frank R. "The Hocking Valley Miners' Strike, 1884-1885: A Search for Order." *The Old Northwest* (March 1976): 55-65.

——————, ed. "Life Among the Lowly: An Early View of an Ohio Poor House." *Ohio History* 88 (Winter 1979): 84-88.

Lippincott, Isaac. *A History of Manufacturers in the Ohio Valley up to the Year 1860*. New York: The University of Chicago Press, 1914.

Lofton, Williston H. "Northern Labor and the Negro During the Civil War." *Journal of Negro History* 34 (July 1949): 251-73.

Long, Clarence D. *Wages and Earnings in the United States, 1860-1890*. New York: National Bureau of Economic Research, 1960.

Lynd, Staughton. *American Labor Radicalism: Testimonies and Interpretation*. New York: John Wiley & Sons, Inc., 1973.

McCabe, David A., and Barnett, George E. *Mediation, Investigation and Arbitration in Industrial Disputes*. New York: Appleton, 1916.

McDonald, David J., and Lynch, Edward A. *Coal and Unionism: A History of the American Coal Miners' Union*. Indianapolis: Cornelius Printing Co., 1939.

McEwen, R. S. *The Mysteries, Miseries, and Rascalities of the Ohio Penitentiary, From the 18th of May 1852, to the Close of the Administration of J. B. Buttles*. Columbus, Ohio: J. Geary, Son & Co. Printers, 1856.

McGrane, R. C. "Ohio and the Greenback Movement." *Mississippi Valley Historical Review* 11 (March 1925): 526-42.

McKinney, James, comp. *The Industrial Advance of Dayton, Ohio and Environs*. Dayton, Ohio: Commerce Publishing Co., 1889.

McNeill, George E., ed. *The Labor Movement: The Problem of To-Day*. Boston: A. M. Bridgman & Co., 1886.

McPherson, Rosamond. *History of the Young Men's Christian Association of Dayton, Ohio, 1858-1953*. New York: Association Press, 1953.

Mansfield, Edward D. *Personal Memories, Social, Political, and Literary, with Sketches of Many Noted People, 1803-1843*. Cincinnati: Robert Clarke & Co., 1879.

Mansfield, John Brandt. *The History of Tuscarawas County, Ohio*. Chicago: Warner, Beers & Co., 1884.

Mantoux, Paul. *The Industrial Revolution in the Eighteenth Century*. New York: Harper & Row, 1961.

Marquis, A. N., ed. *Cincinnati Past and Present: Or, Its Industrial History, as Exhibited in the Life and Labors of Its Leading Men*. Cincinnati: Joblin, Maurice, & Co., 1872.

Martin, William T. *History of Franklin County*. Columbus, Ohio: Follett, Foster, & Co., 1858.

Meltzer, Milton. *Bread and Roses—The Struggle of American Labor, 1865-1915*. New York: Alfred Knopf, 1967.

Merrick, George Byron. *Old Times on the Upper Mississippi, The Recollections of a Steamboat Pilot from 1854-1863*. Cleveland: Arthur H. Clark, 1909.

Meyer, Annie Nathan, ed. *Woman's Work in America*. New York: Henry Holt & Co., 1891.

Meyer, Lysle E. "Radical Responses to Capitalism in Ohio Before 1913." *Ohio History* 79—(Summer-Autumn 1970): 193-208.

Mihok, Janet A. "Women in the Leadership Role, Past and Present, in the Public Schools of Northeastern Ohio." In *Women in Ohio History*. Marta Whitlock, ed. pp. 26-31. Columbus: The Ohio Historical Society, 1976.

Milis, Harry A. *How Collective Bargaining Works*. New York: The Twentieth Century Fund, 1942.

Miller, Zane L. "Boss Cox's Cincinnati: A Study in Urbanization and Politics, 1880-1914." *Journal of American History* 54 (March 1968): 823-38.

——————. "Ohio's Immigrants and the Rush to an Urban Setting: Ethnicity and Community in Historical Perspective." In *Toward an Urban Ohio: A Conference to Commemorate the Bicentennial of the American Revolution*, pp. 29-34. John Wunder, ed. Columbus: Ohio Historical Society for the Ohio American Bicentennial Advisory Committee, 1977.

Minutes and Address of the Convention of the Colored Citizens of Ohio, 1849. Oberlin, Ohio: J. M. Fitch's Power Press, 1849.

Minutes of the State Convention of the Colored Citizens of Ohio, 1850. Columbus: Gate & Cleveland, 1850.

Monkkonen, Eric H. *The Dangerous Class: Crime and Poverty in Columbus, Ohio, 1860-1885*. Cambridge, MA: Harvard University Press, 1975.

Monroe, Alden N. "Effects to Causes: The Evolution of a Social Agency." *Cincinnati Historical Society Bulletin* 37 (Fall 1979): 191-216.

Montgomery, David. *Beyond Equality*. New York: Vintage Books, 1967.

——————. "Gutman's Nineteenth-Century America." *Labor History* (Summer 1978): 416-429.

——————. "Strikes in Nineteenth-Century America." *Social Science History* 4 (Winter 1980): 81-104.

——————. *Workers' Control in America: Studies in the History of Work, Technology, and Labor Struggles*. Cambridge, MA: Cambridge University Press, 1979.

——————. "Workers' Control of Machine Production in the Nineteenth Century." *Labor History* (Fall 1976): 485-509.

Morgan, John M. "The Ashley's Build a Railroad." *Northwest Ohio Quarterly* 30 (Spring 1958): 82-99.

Morris, James M. "Communes and Cooperatives: Cincinnati's Early Experiments in Social Reform." *Cincinnati Historical Society Bulletin* 33 (Spring 1975).

——————. "No Haymarket for Cincinnati." *Ohio History* 83 (Winter 1974): 17-32.

——————. "William Haller 'The Disturbing Element'." *Cincinnati Historical Society Bulletin* 28 (Winter 1970).

Morris, Robert B., ed. *The American Worker*. Washington, D. C.: Government Printing Office, 1976.

Mulder, John M. "The Heavenly City and Human Cities: Washington Gladden and Urban Reform." *Ohio History* 87 (Spring 1978): 151-74.

Munn, Robert F. "The Development of Model Towns in the Bituminous Coal Fields." *West Virginia History* 40 (Spring 1979): 243-47.

Murray, Percy E. "Crusading Editor, Harry C. Smith." In *Blacks in Ohio History*, pp. 31-38. Rubin F. Weston, ed. Columbus: Ohio Historical Society, 1976.

Musselman, Barbara L. "Working Class Unity and Ethnic Division: Cincinnati Trade Unionists and Cultural Pluralism." *Cincinnati Historical Society Bulletin* 34 (Summer 1976): 129-43.

Nelson, Daniel. *Managers and Workers: Origins of the New Factory System in the United States, 1880-1920*. Madison: University of Wisconsin Press, 1975.

Nordoff, Charles. *The Communistic Societies of the United States: From Personal Visit and Observation*. London: John Murray, 1875.

Ohio State Trades and Labor Assembly. *Proceedings of the Second Annual Session*. Cincinnati: Unionist Print, 1885.

Ohioana Library. *Ohio Yearbook 1973: Women of Ohio*. Vol. 26. Columbus: Martha Kinney Cooper Ohioana Library Association, 1973.

Olin, Oscar; Allen, Ada; Brouse, Edwin W.; and Braden, James A., eds. *A Centennial History of Akron, 1825-1925*. Akron Ohio: Summit County Historical Society, 1925.

Orth, Samuel Peter. *Immigration and Labor*. New Haven, Conn.: Yale University Press, 1926.

O'Sullivan, Judith, and Gallick, Rosemary. *Workers and Allies*. Washington, D. C.: Smithsonian Institution Press, 1975.

Out of the Crucible. Pittsburgh: United Steelworkers of America, 1976.

Owen, Robert Dale. *An Address Delivered Before the Young Men's Mercantile Association*. Cincinnati: Herald of Truth Press, 1848.

Parsons, Floyd W. "Employment of Women in Mining." *Coal Age* 13 (1918): 859.

Periam, Jonathan. *The Groundswell. A History of the Origins, Aims, and Progress of the Farmers' Movement*. Cincinnati: E Hannaford Co., 1874.

The Plunder of Labor. Cincinnati: A. Moore, 1865.

Porith, Sam. *History of Cleveland*. Cleveland: S. J. Clarke, 1910.

Powderly, Terence V. *Thirty Years of Labor in America, 1859-1889*. Columbus, Ohio: Excelsior Publishing House, 1890.

Practical and Moral Justice in the Aims of Capital and Labor. Cincinnati: n. p., 1854.

Proceedings of the Convention of the Colored Freedmen of Ohio, 1852. Cincinnati: Dumas & Lawyer, 1852.

Quillan, Frank U. *The Color Line in Ohio*. New York: Negro University Press, 1913.

Raff, G. W. *The Law Relating to Roads and Highways in the State of Ohio*. Cincinnati: S. J. Clarke, 1864.

Raphael, Marc Lee. *Jews and Judaism in a Midwestern Community: Columbus, Ohio, 1840-1975*. Columbus: Ohio Historical Society, 1979.

Rayback, Joseph. *A History of American Labor*. New York: The Free Press, 1959.

Resch, John Phillips. "Ohio Adult Penal System, 1850-1900: A Study in the Failure of Institutional Reform." *Ohio History* 81 (Autumn 1972): 236-62.

Rich, David. "The Toledo Mechanics Association: The City's First Labor Union." *Northwest Ohio Quarterly* 46 (Winter 1973-74).

Richardson, Reed C. *The Locomotive Engineer, 1863-1963*. Ann Arbor: University of Michigan Press, 1963.

Rodabaugh, James H. "The Negro in Ohio." *Journal of Negro History* 31 (1946): 9-29.

——————. "The Cincinnati Riot of 1884." *Museum Echoes* 32 (December 1959): 91-94.

Robison, W. Scott. *History of the City of Cleveland*. Cleveland: Robison & Cockett, 1887.

Rodgers, Daniel T. "Tradition, Modernity and the American Industrial Workers: Reflections and Critique." *Journal of Interdisciplinary History* 7 (Spring 1977): 655-81.

——————. *The Work Ethic in Industrial America, 1850-1920*. Chicago: University of Chicago Press, 1978.

Rose, William Ganson. *Cleveland, the Making of a City*. Cleveland: The World Publishing Co., 1950.

Roseboom, Eugene H. *The Civil War Era, 1850-1873*. *History of the State of Ohio*, vol. 4. Carl Wittke, ed. Columbus: Ohio Archaeological and Historical Society, 1944.

——————. "Southern Ohio and the Union in 1863." *Mississippi Valley Historical Review* 39 (June 1952): 29-44.

——————, and Weisenburger, Francis P. *A History of Ohio*. Columbus: The Ohio Historical Society, 1969.

Roy, Andrew. "Coal Cutting Machinery in Ohio Mines." *The Ohio Mining Journal* 1 (15 May 1883): 114-19.

——————. *A History of Coal Miners of the United States*. Columbus: J. L. Trauger Printing Co., 1906.

——————. "The Origin and Results of Miners' Unions." *Ohio Mining Journal* 2 (15 February 1884): 113-20.

——————. "Sketch of the Mines and Miners of the State." Ohio Bureau of Labor Statistics. *Third Annual Report*. Columbus: Nevins and Myers, 1880.

Ryan, Daniel J. "Lincoln and Ohio." *Ohio Archaeological and Historical Review* 32 (January 1936): 1-281.

Saliers, Earl A. *The Coal Miner; A Study of His Struggle to Secure Regulated Wages in the Hocking Valley*. Bethlehem, PA: n. p., 1912.

Scheiber, Harry J. *Ohio Canal Era: A Case Study of Government and the Economy 1820-1861*. Athens, Ohio: The Ohio University Press, 1969.

——————. "Ohio's Transportation Revolution — Urban Dimensions, 1803-1870." In *Toward an Urban Ohio: A Conference to Commemorate the Bicentennial of the American Revolution*. John Wunder, ed. Columbus: Ohio Historical Society, 1977.

Schluter, Hermann. *The Brewing Industry and the Brewery Workers' Movement in America*. Cincinnati: International Union of United Brewery Workmen of America, 1910.

Schnapper, W. B. *American Labor: A Pictorial Social History*. Washington, D. C.: Public Affairs Press, 1975.

Scott, Thomas A. "The Recent Strikes." *North American Review* 125 (September-October, 1877).

Second Annual Report of Dayton-Cincinnati (Short-Line) Rail Road. Cincinnati: N. p., 1854.

Sharts, Joseph. *Biography of Dayton: An Economic Interpretation of Local History*. Dayton: Miami Valley Socialist, 1922.

Shelling, David Carl. "Relation of Southern Ohio to the South During the Decade Preceding the Civil War." *Quarterly Publication of the Historical and Philosophical Society of Ohio* 8 (1913): 2-28.

Shephard, Lee. "Steamboat Building at Cincinnati." *Historical and Philosophical Society of Ohio Bulletin* 6 (1948): 16-18.

Shepherd, Rebecca A. "Restless Americans: The Geographic Mobility of Farm Laborers in the Old Midwest, 1850-1870." *Ohio History* 89 (Winter 1980): 25-45.

Shepperson, Wilbur S. "British Backtrailers: Working-Class Immigrants Return." In *In The Trek of the Immigrants*, pp. 179-95. O. Frieiof Ander, ed. Rock Island, Ill.: Augustana College Library, 1964.

Shotliff, Don A. "The Ohio Pottery Industry: The Experiences of its Development and the Struggle for a Stabilized Wage, 1877-1900." *Northwest Ohio Quarterly* 45 (Summer 1973).

Shover, John L. "Washington Gladden and the Labor Question." *Ohio Historical Quarterly* 68 (October 1959): 335-52.

Simon, Paul, and Simon, Regina. *Cherish Our Differences: A Source Book for Cincinnati's Ethnic Heritage*. Cincinnati: Xavier University, 1978.

Slaner, Philip A. "The Railroad Strikes of 1877." *Marxist Quarterly* 1 (April-June 1937): 214-36.

Slocum, Charles E. *History of the Maumee River Basin from the Earliest Account to Its Organization into Counties*. Indianapolis: Bowen & Slocum, 1905.

Smith, Theodore G. *The Liberty and Free Soil Parties in the Old Northwest*. New York: Longmans, Green, 1897.

Smith, Thomas H., ed. *An Ohio Reader: Reconstruction to the Present*. Grand Rapids, MI: William B. Eerdman Publishing Co., 1975.

——————. *An Ohio Reader: 1750 to the Civil War*. Grand Rapids, MI: William B. Eerdman Publishing Co., 1975.

Smith, William C. "The Cincinnati Saloon, 1880-1900." *Historical and Philosophical Society of Ohio Bulletin* 19 (October 1961): 279-92.

Smith, William Ernest. *History of Southwestern Ohio: The Miami Valleys*. 3 vols. New York: Lewis Historical Publishing Co., 1964.

Soltow, Lee. "The Growth of Wealth in Ohio, 1800-1969." In *Essays in Nineteenth Century Economic History*, pp. 191-207. David C. Klingaman and Richard K. Vedder, eds. Athens, Ohio: Ohio University Press, 1975.

——————. Soltow, Lee. *Men and Wealth in the United States, 1850-1870*. New Haven, CT: Yale University Press, 1975.

Stern, Joseph S., Jr. *They Said It Couldn't Be Done*. Cincinnati: Centennial Committee, 1966.

Stevens, Harry R. "Samuel Watts Daview and the Industrial Revolution in Cincinnati." *Ohio History* 70 (1961): 92-127.

Stockton, Frank T. "The International Molders Union of North America." In *Johns Hopkins University Studies in Historical and Political Science*. Baltimore: Johns Hopkins Press, 1921.

Stone, Katherine. "The Origins of Job Structures in the Steel Industry." *Review of Radical Political Economics* 6 (Summer 1974): 61-97.

Suffern, Arthur E. *Concilation and Arbitration in the Coal Industry of America*. Boston: Houghton Mifflin Co., 1915.

Taft, Philip, and Ross, Philip. "American Labor Violence: Its Causes, Character, and Outcome." In *Violence in America*, pp. 221-301. Vol. 1. Hugh Davis Graham and Ted Robert Gurr, eds. Washington: Government Printing Office, 1969.

Taylor, David G. "Hocking Valley Railroad Promotion in the 1870's: The Atlantic and Lake Erie Railway." *Ohio History* 81 (Autumn 1972).

Taylor, George R. *The Transportation Revolution, 1815-1860*. New York: Harper & Row, 1951.

Temin, Peter. *Iron and Steel in Nineteenth-Century America*. Cambridge, MA: Massachusetts Institute of Technology Press, 1964.

Thernstrom, Stephen, and Sennett, Richard, eds. *Yale Conference on the Nineteenth Century Industrial City*. New Haven, CT: Yale University Press, 1968.

Todd, Edwin S. "The Presidential Election of 1868." *American Historical Magazine* 2 (May 1907): 151-72.

Tracy, George. *History of the Typographical Union*. Indianapolis: Hullenbeck Press, 1913.

Tunison, J. S. *The Cincinnati Riot: Its Causes and Results*. Cincinnati: Keating & Co. Printers, 1886.

Ulman, Lloyd. *The Rise of the National Trade Union: The Development and Significance of Its Structure, Governing Institutions, and Economic Policies*. Cambridge, MA: Harvard University Press, 1955.

Underwood, Paul. *Ohio's Eastern European Heritage*. Columbus: Center for Slavic and East European Studies at the Ohio State University, 1978.

Unger, Irwin. "Business and Currency in the Ohio Gubernatorial Campaign of 1875." *Mid-America* 41 (1959): 27-39.

——————. *The Greenback Era*. Princeton, NJ: Princeton University Press, 1964.

United States Potters Association. *Proceedings of the Third Convention*. Trenton, NJ: John L. Murphy, State Gazette Publishing House, 1877.

——————. *Proceedings of the Fifth Convention*. Trenton, NJ: John L. Murphey, State Gazette Printing House, 1879.

VanHorne, William E. "Lewis D. Campbell and the Know-Nothing Party in Ohio." *Ohio History* 76 (Autumn 1967): 202-21.

VanTine, Warren R. *The Making of the Labor Bureaucrat: Union Leadership in the United States 1870-1920.* Amherst, MA: The University of Massachusetts Press, 1973.

Vatter, Harold G. *The Drive to Industrial Maturity: The U. S. Economy, 1860-1914.* Westport, CT: Greenwood Press, 1975.

Vedder, Richard K., and Gallaway, Lowell E. "Migration and the Old Northwest." In *Essays in Nineteenth Century Economic History*, pp. 159-76. David C. Klingaman and Richard K. Vedder, eds. Athens, Ohio: Ohio University Press, 1975.

Vitz, Carl. "The Cincinnati Water Front 1848." *Historical and Philosophical Society of Ohio Bulletin* 6 (1948): 28-39.

Walters, Ronald G. *American Reformers 1815-1860.* New York: Hill and Wang, 1978.

Ware, Norman. *The Industrial Worker, 1840-1860.* New York: Houghton Mifflin Co., 1924; reprint ed, Chicago: Quadrangle Books, 1964.

_____. *The Labor Movement in the United States, 1860-1895.* New York: D. Appleton & Co., 1929.

Weeks, Joseph D. *Report on Strikes and Lockouts Occurring Within the United States.* Washington, D. C.: Government Printing Office, 1886.

_____. *Report on Trades Societies in the United States.* Washington, D. C.: Government Printing Office, 1886.

Weeks, Lyman. *A History of Paper Manufacturing in the United States, 1690-1910.* New York: Lockwood Journal Press, 1916.

Weisenburger, Francis. "A Brief History of Immigrant Groups in Ohio." In *In The Trek of the Immigrants*, pp. 81-93. O Frieiof Ander, ed. Rock Island, IL: Augustana College Library, 1964.

_____. *The Passing of the Frontier, 1825-1850. History of the State of Ohio*, vol. 3. Carl Wittke, ed. Columbus: Ohio Archaeological and Historical Society, 1941.

Wertheimer, Barbara Mayer. *We Were There: The Story of Working Women in America.* New York: Pantheon Books, 1977.

Wesley, Charles Harris. *Negro-Americans in Ohio.* Wilberforce, Ohio: Central State University, 1953.

_____. *Negro Labor in the United States, 1850-1925, A Study in American Economic History.* New York: Vanguard Press, 1927.

Wiebe, Robert H. *The Search for Order, 1877-1920.* New York: Hill and Wang, 1967.

Wieck, Edward A. *The American Miners' Association.* New York: Russel Sage Foundation, 1940.

Williams, Charles R., ed. *Diary and Letters of Rutherford Birchard Hayes.* Columbus: Ohio Archaeological and Historical Society, 1922.

Williams, Daniel J. *The Welsh of Columbus, Ohio: A Study in Adaptation and Assimilation.* Oshkosh, WI: By the author, 1913.

Williams, Thomas Harry. *Hayes: Diary of a President, 1875-1881.* New York: D. McKay Co., 1964.

Wing, George A. "The Development of an Industrial Base for the Cincinnati Machine-Tool Industry, 1817-1860." *Cincinnati Historical Society Bulletin* 23 (April 1965): 85-103.

Winter, James F. *A History of Northwest Ohio.* 3 vols. New York: Lewis Publishing Co., 1917.

Wittke, Carl. "Carl Schurz and Rutherford B. Hayes." *Ohio History* 55 (1956): 337-55.

_____. *We Who Built America.* Cleveland: Western Reserve University Press, 1964.

_____. "Ohio's Germans, 1840-1875. *Ohio State Archaeological and Historical Quarterly* 66 (1957): 339-54.

_____, gen. ed. *History of the State of Ohio.* 6 vols. Columbus: Ohio Archaeological and Historical Society, 1941. Vol. 3: *The Passing of the Frontier*, 1825-1850, by Francis P. Weisenburger.

_____, gen. ed. *History of the State of Ohio.* 6 vols. Columbus: Ohio Archaeological and Historical Society, 1944. Vol. 4: *The Civil War Era 1850-1873*, by Eugene H. Roseboom.

_____, gen. ed. *History of the State of Ohio.* 6 vols. Columbus: Ohio Archaeological and Historical Society, 1943. Vol. 5: *Ohio Comes of Age 1873-1900*, by Philip D. Jordan.

Woodson, Carter G. *A Century of Negro Migrations.* Washington, D. C.: The Association for the Study of Negro Life and Culture.

Works Progress Administration. *Warren and Trumbull County.* Warren, Ohio: Western Reserve Historical Celebration Committee, 1938.

Wright, Carrol D. *The Industrial Evolution of the United States.* New York: Charles Scribner's Sons, 1902.

Wynar, Lubomyr R. *Ethnic Groups in Ohio With Special Emphasis on Cleveland: An Annotated Bibliographical Guide.* Cleveland: Cleveland State University, 1976.

Yager, Elizabeth F. "The Presidential Campaign of 1864 in Ohio." *Ohio State Archaeological and Historical Quarterly* 34 (October 1925): 548-80.

Yearly, Clifton K. "The Baltimore and Ohio Strike of 1877." *Maryland Historical Magazine* (September 1956).

Yellowitz, Irwin. *The Position of the Worker in American Society, 1865-1896.* Englewood Cliffs, N. J.: Prentice-Hall, 1969.

Ziebold, Mary L. "Immigrant Groups in Northwestern Ohio to 1860." *Northwest Ohio Quarterly* 17 (1945): 65-75.

Zornow, William F. "The Ohio Democrats and the Africanization Issue in 1863." *Negro History Bulletin* 11 (June 1948): 211-14.

Unpublished Studies

Arthur, Robert W. "The Cincinnati Riot, July, 1862." Unpublished Paper, Cincinnati Historical Society, 4 July 1969.

Bain, Trevor. "The Impact of Technological Change on the Flat Glass Industry and the Union's Reactions to Change: Colonial Period to the Present." Ph.D. dissertation, University of California, Berkeley, 1964.

Barnett, Stanley. "Location and Relocation of Industry in Dayton, 1856-1880." Seminar Paper, Wright State University, 1969.

Baughin, William. "Nativism in Cincinnati Before 1860." M. A. thesis, University of Cincinnati, 1963.

Becker, Carl M. "Mill, Shop, and Factory: The Industrial Life of Dayton, Ohio, 1830-1900." Ph.D. dissertation, University of Cincinnati, 1971.

Boyd, Florence E. "Dayton, Ohio, During the Civil War." M. A. thesis, The Ohio State University, 1939.

Brown, Maude G. "A History of Organized Labor in Toledo." M. A. thesis, University of Toledo, 1924.

Burns, Frank M. "The Use of Injunction in Labor Disputes in the United States." M. A. thesis, University of Toledo, 1930.

Chelminski, David G. "The Ethnicity of the Poles in Toledo, 1830-1886." M. A. thesis, University of Toledo, 1978.

Clapp, Tom. "The Rail Strike of 1877 in Toledo." 17 December 1968. (Mimeographed.)

Clifford, Amy H. "Feminism in Ohio, 1848-1857." M. A. thesis, Kent State University, 1972.

Deem, Warren H. "The Barney & Smith Car Company: A Study of Business Growth and Decline." Unpublished Paper, 1953.

_____. "The Employers' Association of Dayton, Ohio." Unpublished Paper, Wright State University, 1953.

Dobbert, Guido A. "The Disintegration of an Immigrant Community: The Cincinnati Germans, 1870-1920." Ph.D. dissertation, University of Chicago, 1965.

Donakowski, Conrad. "Labor in the Old Northwest, 1800-1860." M. A. thesis, Xavier University, 1959.

Folk, Patrick Allen. "The Queen City of Mobs: Riots and Community Reactions in Cincinnati, 1788-1848." Ph.D. dissertation, University of Toledo, 1978.

Garlock, Jonathan E. "A Structural Analysis of the Knights of Labor." Ph.D. dissertation, University of Rochester, 1974.

Gephart, William F. "Transportation and Industrial Development in the Middle West." Ph.D. dissertation, Columbia University, 1909.

Gildemeister, Glen Albert. "Prison Labor and Convict Competition With Free Workers in Industrializing America, 1840-1900." Ph.D. dissertation, Northern Illinois University, 1977.

Goings, Kenneth W. "Blacks in the Rural North: Paulding County, Ohio, 1860-1900." Ph.D. dissertation, Princeton University, 1977.

Gold, Ruth Wood. "The Attitude of Labor in the Ohio Valley Toward the Civil War." M. A. thesis, The Ohio State University, 1948.

Goliber, Thomas J. "Cuyahoga Blacks: A Social and Demographic Study, 1850-1880." M. A. thesis, Kent State University, 1972.

Graham, Oliver D. "History of the Ohio Canal System." M. A. thesis, The Ohio State University, 1939.

Hickok, Charles T. "The Negro in Ohio, 1802-1870." Ph.D. dissertation, Western Reserve University, 1896.

Hough, Leslie Seldon. "The Turbulent Spirit: Violence and Coaction Among Cleveland Workers, 1877-1899." Ph.D. dissertation, University of Virginia, 1977.

Howell, James. "Community-Transit Relations in Dayton, Ohio, 1869-1961." M. A. thesis, The Ohio State University, 1962.

Jebsen, Harry Jr. "Cincinnati Protestant Clergy in Social and Political Reform, 1865-1915." M. A. thesis, University of Cincinnati, 1966.

Kelly, Jean. "The Historical Development of Industrial Legislation for Ohio's Women." M. A. thesis, University of Cincinnati, 1938.

Land, Mary. "The Malcontents and the Melting Pot: The Cleveland Story." M. A. thesis, Western Reserve University, 1946.

Leet, Don R. "Population Pressure and Human Fertility Response: Ohio, 1810-1860." Ph.D. dissertation, The University of Pennsylvania, 1972.

Lozier, John W. "The Hocking Valley Coal Miners' Strike, 1884-1885." M. A. thesis, The Ohio State University, 1963.

McCormick, Michael R. "A Comparative Study of Coal Mining Communities in Northern Illinois and Southeastern Ohio in the Late Nineteenth Century." Ph.D. dissertation, The Ohio State University, 1978.

Matthews, James Swinton. "Expressions of Urbanism in the Sequent Occupance of Northeastern Ohio." Ph.D. dissertation, University of Chicago, 1949.

Meyers, Kenneth W. "Congress and the Contract Labor Question, 1864-1888." M. A. thesis, University of Toledo, 1948.

Morris, James Matthew. "The Road to Trade Unionism: Organized Labor in Cincinnati to 1893." Ph.D. dissertation, University of Cincinnati, 1969.

Nelson, Thomas C. "The Alienated American; The Free Negro in Ohio, 1840-1851." M. A. thesis, University of Toledo, 1969.

Paluszak, Mary Cecelia. "The Opinion of the Catholic Telegraph on Contemporary Politics, 1831-1871." M.A. thesis, Catholic University of America, 1940.

Rose, Patricia Terpack. Design and Expediency: "The Ohio State Federation of Labor as a Legislative Lobby, 1883-1935." Ph.D. dissertation, The Ohio State University, 1975.

Ross, Steven J. "Workers on the Edge: Work, Leisure, and Politics in Industrializing Cincinnati, 1830-1890." Ph.D. dissertation, Princeton University, 1980.

Schwartz, Irving. "Dayton, Ohio, During the Civil War." M. A. thesis, Miami University, 1949.

Segal, Harvey Hirst. "Canal Cycles, 1834-1861: Public Construction Experience in New York, Pennsylvania and Ohio." Ph.D. dissertation, Columbia University, 1956.

Shotliff, Don A. "The History of the Labor Movement in the American Pottery Industry." Ph.D. dissertation, Kent State University, 1977.

Shreevastava, Mahavira. "The Industrial Development of Springfield, Ohio: A Study in Economic Geography." Ph.D. dissertation, The Ohio State University, 1956.

Steele, Herbert E. "The American Flint Glass Workers' Union." Ph.D. dissertation, The Ohio State University, 1947.

Trester, Delmer John. "Unionism Among Ohio Miners in the Nineteenth Century." M. A. thesis, The Ohio State University, 1947.

Tribe, Ivan Mathews. "An Empire of Industry: Hocking Valley Mining Towns in the Gilded Age." Ph.D. dissertation, University of Toledo, 1976.

—————. "The Ethnic and Geographic Origins of Midwestern Workingmen: The Hocking Valley Miner in the Gilded Age." October 1975. (Typewritten.)

Unstad, Lyder L. "A Survey of the Industrial and Economic Development in Central Ohio, with Special Reference to Columbus, 1797-1872." Ph.D. dissertation, The Ohio State University, 1937.

Waksmundski John. "McKinley Politics and the Changing Attitudes Toward American Labor, 1870-1900." Ph.D. dissertation, The Ohio State University, 1972.

Newspapers

Belmont Chronicle, 18 December 1884—8 October 1885.

Cincinnati Commercial, 29 April 1874—28 May 1875.

Cincinnati Enquirer, 1 March 1874—21 January 1883.

Cleveland Daily Herald, 29 August 1850.

Cleveland Plain Dealer, 7 May—12 May 1874.

East Liverpool Potters' Gazette, 4 January—1 March 1883.

East Liverpool Tribune, 15 June 1882—17 March 1883.

Eaton Labor Journal, 28 May 1884.

Hocking Sentinel, 19 January 1874—1 April 1875.

Iron Molders Journal, 1864-1866, 1873-1877, 1883-1886.

Mahoning County Register, 4 August 1864.

National Labor Tribune, 13 March 1886.

New Lexington Democratic Herald, 4 June 1874.

New Lexington Tribune, 11 June 1874.

New Lisbon Ohio Patriot, 17 August 1882—11 January 1883

Ohio State Journal, 15 September 1884—18 July 1885.

The People's Paper, January—February 1858.

Somerset Press, 7 November 1873—10 July 1874.

Workingman's Advocate, 10 January—20 June 1874.

Government Records and Documents

Ohio. *An Act Relating to Roads and Highways.* Passed by the 57th General Assembly of Ohio, 24 February 1867.

—————. *Acts for the Preservation and Repair of the National Road.* Columbus: S. & M. H. Medary, 1840.

—————. *Annual Report of the Adjutant General to the Governor of the State of Ohio, 1883.* Columbus: G- J. Brand & Co., 1883.

—————. *Annual Report of the Adjutant General to the Governor of the State of Ohio, 1884.* Columbus: G. J. Brand & Co., 1884.

—————. *Annual Report of the Adjutant General to the Governor of the State of Ohio, 1885.* Columbus: G. J. Brand & Co., 1885.

—————. State Board of Agriculture. *Second Annual Report of the Ohio State Board of Agriculture, 1847.* In, *Documents, Including Messages and Other Communications Made to the Forty-Sixth General Assembly of the State of Ohio.* Vol. 12. Part 2. Columbus: Charles Scott's Steam Press, 1848.

—————. *Eighteenth Annual Report of the Ohio State Board of Agriculture, with an Abstract of the Proceedings of the County Agricultural Societies to the General Assembly of Ohio, for the Year 1863.* Columbus: Richard Nevins, 1864.

—————. *Twenty-First Annual Report of the Ohio State Board of Agriculture to the General Assembly of Ohio for the Year 1866.* Columbus: L. D. Myers & Bros., 1867.

Ohio. Commissioner of Railroads and Telegraphs. *Sixth Annual Report.* Columbus: State Printers, 1873.

—————. *Eleventh Annual Report.* Columbus: State Printers, 1878.

—————. *Annual Report for the Year 1883.* Columbus: State Printers, 1883.

—————. *Annual Report for the Year 1887.* Columbus: State Printers, 1888.

Ohio. Commissioner of Statistics. *Annual Report to the General Assembly of Ohio for the Year 1857.* Columbus: Richard Nevins, 1858.

—————. *Fourth Annual Report to the Governor of the State of Ohio, 1860.* Columbus: Richard Nevins, 1863.

—————. *Sixth Annual Report to the Governor of the State of Ohio, 1862.* Columbus: Richard Nevins, 1863.

—————. *Seventh Annual Report to the Governor of the State of Ohio, 1863.* Columbus: Richard Nevins, 1864.

—————. *Ninth Annual Report to the Governor of the State of Ohio, 1865.* Columbus: Richard Nevins, 1866.

Ohio. Commissioner of Immigration. "Annual Report to the Governor of the State of Ohio for the Year 1863."

—————. "Annual Report to the Governor of the State of Ohio for the Year 1865."

Ohio. Department of Highways. "An Outline of the History of Ohio's Roads and Related Transportation Development." Columbus: n. p., 1849.

Ohio. Department of Inspection of Workshops, Factories, & Public Buildings. *First Annual Report of the State Inspector of Shops and Factories for the Year 1884.* Columbus: State Printer, 1885.

—————. *Eleventh Annual Report to the Governor of the State of Ohio for the Year 1894.* Columbus: The Westbote Co., 1895.

—————. "Executive Document, Message, & Annual Reports for 1864."

—————. "Executive Document, Message, & Annual Reports for 1866."

Ohio. General Assembly. *Annual Reports for 1874 Made to the Sixty-First General Assembly of the State of Ohio.* Columbus: State Printers, 1875.

—————. *Annual Reports for 1879, Made to the Sixty-First General Assembly of the State of Ohio.* Columbus: State Printers, 1880.

_____. *Documents, Including Messages and Other Communications Made to the Forty-Fifth General Assembly of the State of Ohio.* Vol. 11. Columbus: Charles Scott Press, 1847.

_____. *Proceedings of the Hocking Valley Investigation Committee of the General Assembly of the State of Ohio.* Columbus: 1885.

Ohio. Mining Commission. *Report of Messrs. Roy and Pollock, Miners' Committee to Columbus, To Urge the Passage by the Legislature of the Miners' Bill for the Ventilation and Inspection of Coal Mines.* Cincinnati: 1872.

_____. *Report of the Mining Commission.* Appointed under Joint Resolution in 1871. Columbus: 1872.

_____. Chief Inspector of Mines. "Twenty-Eighth Annual Report of the Chief Inspector of Mines to the Governor of the State of Ohio for the Year 1902."

_____. State Mine Inspector. "Third Annual Report of the State Mine Inspector, to the Governor of the State of Ohio for the Year 1876."

Ohio. Penitentiary. "Annual Report of the Directors and Warden of the Ohio Penitentiary for 1846."

_____. "Annual Report of the Directors and Warden of the Ohio Penitentiary for 1851."

_____. *Annual Report of the Directors and Warden of the Ohio Penitentiary for 1852.* Columbus: Osgood & Blake, 1853.

_____. *Annual Report of the Directors and Warden of the Ohio Penitentiary for 1853.* Columbus: Osgood, Blake, & Knapp, Printers, 1854.

_____. "Annual Report of the Directors and Warden of the Ohio Penitentiary to the Governor of the State of Ohio, for the Year 1872."

_____. "Report of the Commission on Examination into the Contract Labor System in the Ohio Penitentiary." 1884.

Ohio. Secretary of State's Office. *Annual Report of the Secretary of State to the Governor of the State of Ohio for the Year 1879.* Columbus: Nevins & Myers, 1880.

_____. *Annual Report of the Secretary of State to the Governor of the State of Ohio, for the Year 1880.* Columbus: State Printers, 1881.

_____. *Annual Report of the Secretary of State to the Governor of the State of Ohio, for the Year 1881.* Columbus: G. J. Brand & Co., 1882.

_____. *Annual Report of the Secretary of State to the Governor of the State of Ohio, for the Year 1882.* Columbus: Myers Bros., 1882.

Ohio. Secretary of State's Office. *Annual Report of the Secretary of State to the Governor of the State of Ohio for the Year 1883.* Columbus: Myers Bros., 1884.

_____. *Annual Report of the Secretary of State to the Governor of the State of Ohio for the Year 1885.* Columbus: The Westbote Co., 1885.

_____. *Statistical Report of the Secretary of State to the General Assembly of the State of Ohio, for the Year 1868.* Columbus: Columbus Printing Co., 1869.

_____. "Statistical Report of the Secretary of State to the General Assembly of the State of Ohio for the Year 1872."

_____. *Annual Report of the Secretary of State to the Governor of the State of Ohio including the Statistical Report to the General Assembly for the Year 1877.* Columbus: Nevins & Meyers, 1878.

U. S. Bureau of Labor Statistics. "1879 Annual Report."

_____. Commissioner of Labor. *The First Annual Report of the Commissioner of Labor.* Washington: Government Printing Office, 1886.

_____. *The Third Annual Report of the Commissioner of Labor, 1887.* Washington: Government Printing Office, 1888.

_____. "Twenty-First Annual Report of the Commissioner of Labor, 1906."

U. S. Congress. Senate. *Reports of the Immigration Commission; Abstracts of Reports of the Immigration Commission.* 2 vols. Washington: Government Printing Office, 1911.

_____. *Reports of the Immigration Commission; Statistical Review of Immigration 1820-1910, Distribution of Immigrants, 1850-1900.* Washington: Government Printing Office, 1911.

_____. Department of Commerce. Bureau of Census. *Abstract of the Twelfth Census of the United States, 1900.* 3rd ed. Washington: Government Printing Office, 1902.

_____. *Historical Statistics of the United States: Colonial Times to 1970.* Bicentennial ed., 2 vols. Washington, D. C.: Government Printing Office, 1975.

_____. *Immigrants and Their Children, 1920* by Niles Carpenter. Census Monographs 7. Washington: Government Printing Office, 1927.

_____. *Negro Populations, 1790-915.* Washington: Government Printing Office, 1915.

_____. *Sixteenth Census of the United States: 1940. Population, Comparative Occupation Statistics for the United States, 1870-1940,* by Alba M. Edwards. Washington: Government Printing Office, 1943.

U.S. Department of Commerce. Bureau of the Census. *Sixteenth Census of the United States, 1940. Population 2nd Series. Characteristics of the Population of Ohio,* by Leon E. Truesdell. Washington: Government Printing Office, 1942.

_____. *Thirteenth Census of the United States.* Vol. 4: *Population 1910, Occupational Statistics.* Washington: Government Printing Office 1914.

_____. Department of the Interior. *Abstract of the Eleventh Census: 1890.* 2nd ed. Washington: Government Printing Office, 1896.

_____. Department of the Interior. Census Office. *A Compendium of the Ninth Census.* Washington: Government Printing Office, 1872.

_____. *A Compendium of the Tenth Census of the United States, 1880.* Part I. Washington: Government Printing Office, 1883.

_____. *A Compendium of the Tenth Census.* Part II. Washington: Government Printing Office, 1883.

_____. *A Compendium of the Eleventh Census: 1890.* Part III. Washington: Government Printing Office, 1897.

_____. *Manufacturers of the United States in 1860; compiled from the Original Returns of the Eighth Census.* Washington: Government Printing Office, 1865.

_____. *Abstract of Statistics of Manufactures, 1850.* Washington, D.C.: Government Printing Office, 1859.

U. S. Department of the Interior. Census Office. *Population of the United States in 1860; Compiled from the Original Returns of the Eighth Census,* by Joseph C. G. Kennedy. Washington: Government Printing Office, 1864.

_____. *Report on Manufacturing Industries in the United States at the Eleventh Census: 1890.* Part I: *Totals for States and Industries.* Washington: Government Printing Office, 1895.

_____. *Report on the Manufacturing Industries in the United States at the Eleventh Census: 1890.* Part II: *Statistics of Cities.* Washington: Government Printing Office, 1895.

_____. *Report on the Manufacturing Industries in the United States at the Eleventh Census: 1890.* Part III: *Selected Industries.* Washington: Government Printing Office, 1895.

_____. *Report on the Social Statistics of Cities,* by George E. Waring, Jr. Part I: *The New England and the Middle States;* Part II: *The Southern and the Western States.* Washington: Government Printing Office, 1887.

_____. *Report on the Statistics of Wages in Manufacturing Industries; with Supplementary Reports on the Average Retail Prices of Necessaries of Life and on Trade Societies and Strikes and Lockouts,* by Jos. D. Weeks. Washington: Government Printing Office, 1886.

U. S. Department of the Interior. Census Office. *Statistics of the Population of the United States at the Tenth Census.* Washington: Government Printing Office, 1883.

_____. *Twelfth Census of the United States Taken in the Year 1900.* Vol. 2: Census Reports. Population Part II. Washington: U. S. Census Office, 1902.

_____. "Manufacturers in the Several States and Territories for the Year ending June 1, 1850. Abstract of the Statistics of Manufactures According to the Returns of the Seventh Census."

_____. Ninth Census. Vol. 1: *The Statistics of the Population of the United States,* by Francis A. Walker. Washington: Government Printing Office, 1872.

_____. Ninth Census. Vol. 1: *The Statistics of the Wealth and Industry of the United States Embracing...the Major Tables of Occupations,* by Francis A. Walker. Washington: Government Printing Office, 1872.

_____. *The Seventh Census Report of the Superintendent of the Census for December 1, 1852.* Washington: Robert Armstrong, 1853.

_____. *Statistical View of the United States, Being A Compendium of the Seventh Census.* Vol. 5: *Demographic Monographs,* by J. D. B. DeBow. New York: Gordon & Breach Science Publishers, 1854.

U. S. Department of the Interior. *Statistics of the United States (Including Mortality, Property, etc.) in 1860; Compiled from the Original Returns and Being the Final Exhibit of the Eighth Census.* Washington: Government Printing Office.

_____. Department of Labor. *Hours of Work,* by Ewan Clague. Presented to the Select Subcommittee on Labor; the House Education and Labor Committee. 11 June 1963.

Primary Sources

Cincinnati, Ohio. Cincinnati Historical Society. Iron Machine Molders Union, No. 4 Papers.

Cleveland, Ohio. Western Reserve Historical Society. Roberts Family Papers.

Columbus, Ohio. Ohio Historical Society. Garrett Coleman Papers.

_____. Columbus Typographical Union, Local No. 5 Records.

_____. *Constitution of the Workingmen's Union of Stark County, Ohio*. Canton, Ohio: John Raber, 1861.

_____. "Memorandum of Agreement, September 27, 1876, between ironworkers and laborers and the firm of Cornell Dienst and Co. to work in the Ashtabula Rolling Mill."

_____. Charles McChesney Mount Papers.

_____. Ohio AFL-CIO Records.

_____. Joseph Slight Papers.

_____. Wilbur Stout Records.

_____. *Constitution, By Laws and Rules of Order, of Washington Council, No. 1, of the Order of United American Mechanics, of the State of Ohio*. Cincinnati: Unionist Print, 1885.

Dayton, Ohio. Wright State University Archives. Dayton Typographical Union, Local 57 Papers.

PART 3

Books and Articles

Adams, Graham, Jr. *Age of Industrial Violence 1910-15: The Activities and Findings of the United States Commission on Industrial Relations*. New York: Columbia University Press, 1966.

Ameringer, Oscar. *If You Don't Weaken; The Autobiography of Oscar Ameringer*. New York: Henry Holt & Company, 1940.

Amsden, Jon, and Brier, Stephen. "Coal Miners on Strike: The Transformation of Strike Demands and the Formation of a National Union." *Journal of Interdisciplinary History* 7 (Spring 1977): 583-616.

Axinn, June, and Levin, Herman. *Social Welfare: A History of the American Response to Need*. New York: Dodd Mead & Company, 1975.

Bahna, Donald G. "The Pope-Toledo Strike of 1907." *Northwest Ohio Quarterly* 35 (Summer 1963) Part I: 106-21; 35 (Autumn 1963) Part II: 172-87.

Ball, Wilma I. "Street Trading in Ohio." *The American Child* 1 (1919-20): 123-29.

Barclay, Morgan J. "Reform in Toledo: The Political Career of Samuel M. Jones." *Northwest Ohio Quarterly* 50 (Summer 1978): 79-89.

_____, comp. *Celebrating the City: A Pictorial Essay of Toledo 1890-1940*. Toledo, Ohio: Toledo-Lucas County Public Library, 1979.

Barton, Josef J. *Peasants and Strangers: Italians, Rumanians, and Slovaks in an American City, 1890-1950*. Cambridge, MA.: Harvard University Press, 1975.

Baxandall, Rosalyn; Gordon, L.; Reverby, S.; eds. *America's Working Women*. New York: Vintage Books, 1976.

Becker, Carl M. "A 'Most Complete' Factory: The Barney Car Works 1850-1926." *Cincinnati Historical Society Bulletin* 31 (Spring 1973): 48-69.

Bell, Florence Louise. "The Social Settlement: Columbus, Ohio." *Annals of the American Academy of Political and Social Science* 4 (May 1902).

Blackford, Mansel G. "Scientific Management and Welfare Work in Early Twentieth Century American Business: The Buckeye Steel Castings Company." *Ohio History* 90 (Summer 1981): 238-58.

Brandes, Stuart D. *American Welfare Capitalism 1880-1940*. Chicago: University of Chicago Press, 1970.

Braverman, Harry. *Labor and Monopoly Capital: The Degradation of Work in the Twentieth Century*. New York: Monthly Review Press, 1974.

Brissenden, Paul F., and Frankel, Emil. *Labor Turnover in Industry: A Statistical Analysis*. New York: The MacMillan Company, 1922.

Brito, Patricia. "Protective Legislation in Ohio: The Inter-War Years." *Ohio History* 88 (Spring 1979): 173-97.

Brody, David. *Steelworkers in America: The Nonunion Era*. Cambridge, MA.: Harvard University Press, 1960; reprint ed., New York: Harper & Row, 1969.

_____. *Workers in Industrial America: Essays on the 20th Century Struggle*. New York: Oxford University Press, 1980.

Bryner, Edna. *Dressmaking and Millinery*. Cleveland: The Survey Committee of the Cleveland Foundation, 1916.

_____. *The Garment Trades*. Cleveland: The Survey Committee of the Cleveland Foundation, 1916.

Buder, Stanley. *Pullman: An Experiment in Industrial Order and Community Planning 1880-1930*. New York: Oxford University Press, 1967.

Butler, Joseph Green. *History of Youngstown and the Mahoning Valley, Ohio*. Chicago: American Historical Society, 1921.

Cary, Lorin Lee. "The Bureau of Investigation and Radicalism in Toledo, Ohio; 1918-20." *Labor History* 21 (1980): 430-40.

Canton Sesquicentennial Corporation. *Canton Sesquicentennial: 150 Years of Progress*. Canton, Ohio: Canton Sesquicentennial Corporation, 1955.

Chandler, Alfred D. *The Visible Hand: The Managerial Revolution in American Business*. Cambridge, MA.: Harvard University Press, 1977.

Consumers' League of Cincinnati. *Biennial Report March 1911-February 1913*. Cincinnati: Consumer's League of Cincinnati, 1913.

_____. *Bulletin on Conditions of Saleswomen in Cincinnati Mercantile Establishments*. Cincinnati: Consumers' League of Cincinnati, June 1915.

_____. *First Annual Report for the Year Ending February, 1907*. Cincinnati: Consumers' League of Cincinnati, 1907.

Clawson, Dan. *Bureaucracy and the Labor Process: The Transformation of U.S. Industry 1860-1920*. New York: Monthly Review Press, 1980.

Cleveland Chamber of Commerce. *Violence in Labor Disputes — First Report*. Cleveland: Chamber of Commerce, 1915.

Cleveland Chamber of Commerce. *Violence in Labor Disputes — Third Report* (January 1, 1916 to January 31, 1917). Cleveland: Chamber of Commerce, 1917.

Conlin, Joseph R. *At the Point of Production: The Local History of the I.W.W.* Westport, CT.: Greenwood Press, 1981.

Consumers' League of Ohio. "A Study in Wage Increase Made by the Minimum Wage Committee of the Consumers' League of Ohio." 1918.

Crowther, Samuel. *John H. Patterson, Pioneer in Industrial Welfare*. Garden City, N.Y.: Doubleday, Page & Co., 1923.

Davis, Jerome. *The Russian Immigrant*. New York: The MacMillan Company, 1922.

Derber, Milton. *The American Idea of Industrial Democracy, 1865-1965*. Urbana, Ill.: University of Illinois Press, 1970.

Destler, Chester McArthur. *American Radicalism 1865-1901*. Chicago: Quadrangle Books, 1946; reprinted in 1966.

Dick, William M. *Labor and Socialism in America: The Gompers Era*. Port Washington, N.Y.: Kennikat Press, 1972.

Diggins, John P. *The American Left in the Twentieth Century*. New York: Harcourt, Brace, Jovanovich, Inc., 1973.

Dubofsky, Melvyn. *We Shall Be All: A History of the Industrial Workers of the World*. Chicago: Quadrangle Books, 1969.

Duggan, Edward P. "Labor Supply and Technological Change in the Nineteenth Century: A Comparison of Cincinnati and Birmingham, England." *Cincinnati Historical Society Bulletin* 31 (Winter 1973): 263-84.

Dulles, Foster Rhea. *A History of Recreation: America Learns to Play*. 2nd ed. New York: Appleton-Century Crofts, 1965.

Eggert, Gerald G. "Coxey's March on Washington, 1894." *American History Illustrated* 12 (October 1977): 20-31.

Ewen, Stuart. *Captains of Consciousness: Advertising and the Social Roots of the Consumer Culture*. New York: McGraw-Hill Book Co., 1976.

Fairfield, E. William. *Fire & Sand; The History of the Libbey-Owens Sheet Glass Company*. Cleveland: Lezius-Hiles Co., 1980.

Fleming, Ralph Douglas. *Railroad and Street Transportation*. Cleveland: The Survey Committee of the Cleveland Foundation, 1916.

Folk, Richard A. "Socialist Party of Ohio — War and Free Speech." *Ohio History* 78 (Spring 1969): 104-54.

Foner, Eric. "Class, Ethnicity & Radicalism in the Gilded Age: The Land League & Irish-America." *Marxist Perspectives* 1 (Summer 1978): 6-55.

Foner, Philip S. *Organized Labor and the Black Worker 1619-1973*. New York: International Publishers, 1974.

Gallaway, Lowell. "The Origin and Early Years of the Federation of Flat Glass Workers of America." *Labor History* 3 (Winter 1962): 92-102.

Garraty, John A. *The New Commonwealth 1877-1890*. New York: Harper & Row, 1968.

Gerber, David A. *Black Ohio and the Color Line, 1860-1915.* Urbana, IL.: University of Illinois Press, 1976.

Gibson, R. M., and Martin, E. S. *Photographic and Industrial History of New Straitsville, Ohio.* Newark, Ohio: Ohio Advertising Company, 1907.

Gildemeister, Glen A. "The Founding of the American Federation of Labor." *Labor History* 22 (Spring 1981): 262-68.

Gilson, Mary Barnett. *What's Past is Prologue.* New York: Harper & Brothers, 1940; reprint ed., New York: Arno Press, 1980.

Gompers, Samuel. *Seventy Years of Life and Labour: An Autobiography.* 2 vols. London: Hurst & Blackett, Ltd., n.d.

Goodwyn, Lawrence. *The Populist Movement: A Short History of the Agrarian Revolt in America.* New York: Oxford University Press, 1978.

Grafowski, John J. "From Progressive to Patrician: George Bellamy and Hiram House Social Settlement, 1896-1914." *Ohio History* 87 (1978): 37-52.

Graebner, William. "Great Expectations: The Search for Order in Bituminous Coal, 1890-1917." *Business History Review* 48 (1973): 49-72.

Green, James R. *The World of the Worker: Labor in Twentieth-Century America.* New York: Hill and Wang, 1980.

Green, Marguerite. *The National Civic Federation and the American Labor Movement, 1900-1925.* Washington, D.C.: The Catholic University of America Press, 1956.

Greenstone, J. David. *Labor in American Politics.* New York: Vintage Books, 1969.

Greenwald, Maurine Weiner. *Women, War, and Work: The Impact of World War I on Women Workers in the United States.* Westport, CT.: Greenwood Press, 1980.

Griffin, John Ignatius. *Strikers: A Study in Quantitative Economics.* New York: Columbia University Press, 1939.

Gutman, Herbert G. *Work, Culture, and Society in Industrializing America.* New York: Alfred A. Knopf, 1976.

Haley, Theresa S. *Infant Mortality: Results of a Field Study in Akron, Ohio, Based on Births in One Year.* U.S. Department of Labor, Children's Bureau. Bureau Publication 72. Washington D.C.: Government Printing Office, 1920.

Herron, Robert. "The Police Strike of 1918." *Bulletin of the Historical and Philosophical Society of Ohio* 17 (1959): 181-94.

Higgs, Robert. *The Transformation of the American Economy, 1865-1914: An Essay in Interpretation.* New York: John Wiley & Sons, Inc., 1971.

Higham, John. *Strangers in the Land: Patterns of American Nativism 1860-1925.* New York: Atheneum, 1955; reprint ed., 1963.

Hiller, E. T. *The Strike: A Study in Collective Action.* Chicago: University of Chicago Press, 1928.

Himes, J. S., Jr. "Forty Years of Negro Life in Columbus, Ohio." *Journal of Negro History* 27 (April 1942): 133-54.

A History of the Activities of the Ohio Branch, Council of National Defense: How Ohio Mobilized Her Resources for the War. Columbus, Ohio: F. J. Heer Printing Co., 1919.

Hoagland, H. E. *Wage Bargaining on Vessels of the Great Lakes.* Urbana, IL.: University of Illinois Press, 1917.

Howe, Frank Henry. "Inspection of Workshops and Factories of Ohio: Prepared . . . from the Reports of Henry Dorn, Chief Inspector for the State. . . ." Vol. 1: *Historical Collections of Ohio,* pp. 208-16. Cincinnati: C. J. Krehbiel & Co., 1908.

Inciardi, James A., and Faupel, Charles E. *History and Crime: Implications for Criminal Justice Policy.* Beverly Hills, CA.: Sage Publications, 1980.

International Brotherhood of Teamsters, Chauffeurs, Warehousemen, and Helpers of America. *Teamsters All: Pictorial Highlights in Our History.* Washington: Merule Press, Inc., 1976.

Jaher, Frederic Cople, ed. *The Age of Industrialism in America: Essays in Social Structure and Cultural Values.* New York: The Free Press, 1968.

Jensen, Richard. *The Winning of the Midwest: Social and Political Conflict 1888-1896.* Chicago: University of Chicago Press, 1971.

Jones, Samuel Milton. *Letters of Labor and Love.* Toledo, Ohio: Franklin Printing and Engraving Co., 1900-01.

Karson, Marc. *American Labor Unions and Politics 1900-18.* Boston: Beacon Press, 1958; reprint ed., 1965.

Katzman, David M. *Seven Days A Week: Women and Domestic Service in Industrializing America.* New York: Oxford University Press, 1978.

Kaufman, Stuart Bruce. *Samuel Gompers and the Origins of the American Federation of Labor 1848-1896.* Westport, CT.: Greenwood Press, 1973.

Kessler-Harris, Alice. *Women Have Always Worked: A Historical Overview.* Old Westbury, NY.: The Feminist Press, 1981.

Kirkland, Edward Chase. *Industry Comes of Age: Business, Labor and Public Policy, 1860-1897.* Chicago: Quadrangle Books, 1961; reprint ed., 1967.

Laslett, John H. M. *Labor and the Left: A Study of Socialist and Radical Influences in the American Labor Movement, 1881-1924.* New York: Basic Books, 1970.

Lauck, W. Jett, and Sydenstricker, Edgar. *Conditions of Labor in American Industries: A Summarization of the Results of Recent Investigations.* New York: Funk & Wagnalls, 1917.

Lebergott, Stanley. *The American Economy: Income, Wealth, and Want.* Princeton, NJ.: Princeton University Press, 1976.

_____. *Manpower and Economic Growth: The American Record Since 1800.* New York: McGraw-Hill, 1964.

Leech, Margaret. *In the Days of McKinley.* New York: Harper & Brothers, 1959.

Livesay, Harold C. *Samuel Gompers and Organized Labor in America.* Boston: Little, Brown, & Co., 1978.

Lutz, R. R. *The Metal Trades.* Cleveland: The Survey Committee of the Cleveland Foundation, 1916.

_____. *Wage Earning and Education.* Cleveland: The Survey Committee of the Cleveland Foundation, 1916.

McKenzie, Roderick Duncan. *The Neighborhood: A Study of Local Life in the City of Columbus, Ohio.* Chicago: University of Chicago Press, 1923.

McMurry, Donald L. *Coxey's Army: A Study of the Industrial Army Movement of 1894.* Boston: Little, Brown, and Co., 1929.

Mann, Annette. *Women Workers in Factories: A Study of Working Conditions in 275 Industrial Establishments in Cincinnati and Adjoining Towns.* Cincinnati: Consumers' League of Cincinnati, 1918.

Meyer, Lysle E. "Radical Responses to Capitalism in Ohio Before 1913." *Ohio History* 79 (Summer/Autumn 1970): 193-208.

Meyer, Stephen III. *The Five Dollar Day: Labor Management and Social Control in the Ford Motor Company 1908-1921.* Albany, NY.: SUNY Press, 1981.

Miller, Zane L. *Boss Cox's Cincinnati: Urban Politics in the Progressive Era.* New York: Oxford University Press, 1968.

Millett, Stephen M. "Charles E. Ruthenberg: The Development of an American Communist, 1909-1927." *Ohio History* 81 (Summer 1972): 193-205.

Montgomery, David. "Strikes in Nineteenth-Century America." *Social Science History* 4 (Winter 1980): 81-104.

_____. *Workers' Control in America: Studies in the History of Work, Technology, and Labor Struggles.* Cambridge, MA.: Cambridge University Press, 1979.

Morris, James M. "The Cincinnati Shoemakers' Lockout of 1888: A Case Study in the Demise of the Knights of Labor." *Labor History* 13 (Fall 1972): 505-19.

Musselman, Barbara L. "Working Class Unity and Ethnic Division: Cincinnati Trade Unionists and Cultural Pluralism." *Cincinnati Historical Society Bulletin* 34 (Summer 1976): 121-43.

Nelson, Daniel. *Frederick W. Taylor and the Rise of Scientific Management.* Madison, WI.: University of Wisconsin Press, 1980.

_____. *Managers and Workers: Origins of the New Factory System in the United States 1880-1920.* Madison, WI.: University of Wisconsin Press, 1975.

_____. "The New Factory System and the Unions: The National Cash Register Company Dispute of 1901." *Labor History* 15 (Spring 1974): 163-78.

_____. *Unemployment Insurance: The American Experience 1915-1935.* Madison, WI.: University of Wisconsin Press, 1969.

Newman, Pauline M. "From the Battlefield: Some Phases of the Cloak-Makers' Strike of Cleveland." *Life and Labor* (October 1911): 292-97.

Noble, David F. *America By Design: Science, Technology, and the Rise of Corporate Capitalism.* New York: Oxford University Press, 1977.

O'Leary, Iris Prouty. *Department Store Occupations.* Cleveland: The Survey Committee of the Cleveland Foundation, 1916.

Porter, Glenn. *The Rise of Big Business, 1860-1910.* New York: Thomas Y. Crowell Co., 1973.

Preston, William, Jr., *Aliens and Dissenters: Federal Suppression of Radicals, 1903-1933.* New York: Harper & Row, 1966.

Rae, John B. *The American Automobile: A Brief History.* Chicago: University of Chicago Press, 1965.

_____. *American Automobile Manufacturers: The First Forty Years*. New York: Chilton Company, 1959.

Reagan, Patrick D. "The Ideology of Social Harmony and Efficiency: Workmen's Compensation in Ohio, 1904-1919." *Ohio History* 90 (Autumn 1981): 317-31.

Reese, William J. "The Control of Urban School Boards During the Progressive Era." *Pacific Northwest Quarterly* 68 (October 1977): 164-74.

_____. "Trade Unions and School Reform 1890-1920: A Comparison of Four American Cities." Paper presented at the Fall 1980 Social Science History Association, Columbus, Ohio, 1980.

Reiser, George F. "Toledo's State-City Free Labor Exchange." *Toledo City Journal,* 13 May 1916, sect. 2, p. 5.

Richardson, James R. "Urban Political Change in the Progressive Era." *Ohio History* 87 (Summer 1978): 310-21.

Rodabaugh, James H. "The Reform Movement in Ohio at the Turn of the Century." *Ohio Archaeological and Historical Quarterly* 54 (January-March 1945): 46-55.

_____. "Samuel M. Jones—Evangel of Equality." *Historical Society of Northwestern Ohio Quarterly Bulletin* 15 (January 1943): 17-46.

Rodgers, Daniel T. "Tradition, Modernity, and the American Industrial Worker: Reflections and Critique." *Journal of Interdisciplinary History* 7 (Spring 1977): 655-81.

_____. *The Work Ethic in Industrial America, 1850-1920*. Chicago: University of Chicago Press, 1978.

Schleppi, John R. "It Pays': John H. Patterson and Industrial Recreation at the National Cash Register Company." *Journal of Sports History* 6 (Winter 1979): 20-28.

Scott, Emmett Jay. *Negro Migration During the War*. New York: Arno Press, 1969.

Scoville, Warren C. *Revolution in Glassmaking: Entrepreneurship and Technological Change in the American Industry 1880-1920*. Cambridge, MA.: Harvard University Press, 1948.

Sharp, H. J. "Report on the Pollution of Water-Courses by Straw-Board Factories." Report of the State Board of Health, Ohio Executive Documents, 1887. In, *An Ohio Reader-Reconstruction to the Present*, pp. 64-67. Thomas H. Smith, ed. Grand Rapids, Mich.: William B. Eerdmans Co., 1975.

Sharpless, John, and Rury, John. "The Political Economy of Women's Work, 1900-1920." *Social Science History* 4 (August 1980): 317-46.

Shaw, Frank L. *The Building Trades*. Cleveland: Survey Committee of the Cleveland Foundation, 1916.

_____. *The Printing Trades*. Cleveland: The Survey Committee of the Cleveland Foundation, 1916.

Sidlo, T. L. "Socialism and Trade-Unionism, A Study of Their Relation in Cleveland." *Western Reserve University Bulletin* 12 (November 1909): 126-53.

Sklar, Robert. *Movie-Made America: A Social History of American Movies*. New York: Random House, 1975.

Slichter, Sumner H. *The Turnover of Factory Labor*. New York: 1919.

Spargo, John. *The Bitter Cry of the Children*. New York: The MacMillan Co., 1907.

Spero, Sterling D., and Harris, Abram L. *The Black Worker*. New York: Columbia University Press, 1959; reprint ed., New York: Atheneum, 1968.

Steghagen, Emma. "A Summer of Strikes in Cincinnati." *Life and Labor* (November 1913): 333-35.

Stevens, Bertha M. *Boys and Girls in Commercial Work*. Cleveland: The Survey Committee of the Cleveland Foundation, 1916.

Stone, Katherine. "The Origin of Job Structures in the Steel Industry." *Radical America* 7 (November-December 1973): 1964.

Taft, Philip. *The A. F. L. in the Time of Gompers*. New York: Harper & Brothers, 1957.

Taylor, Philip. *The Distant Magnet: European Emigration to the U. S. A.* New York: Harper & Row, 1971.

Thompson, R. S., Colvin, Wilber, and Lockwook, M. C. *Profit or Plunder, Which? A Question of the Day, A Review of the Causes of the Present Depression in Agriculture and Unrest of Labor*. Springfield, Ohio: New Era Company, 1890.

Van Tine, Warren R. *The Making of the Labor Bureaucrat*. Amherst: University of Massachusetts Press, 1973.

Vatter, Harold G. *The Drive to Industrial Maturity: The U. S. Economy, 1860-1914*. Westport, CT.: Greenwood Press, 1975.

Walker, Kenneth R. "The Era of Industrialization: Capital and Labor in the Midwest in 1901." *Northwest Ohio Quarterly* 37 (Spring 1965): 49-60.

Warner, Hoyt Landon. *Progressivism in Ohio, 1897-1917*. Columbus, Ohio: The Ohio State University Press, 1964.

Weinberg, Daniel E. "Ethnic Identity in Industrial Cleveland: The Hungarians 1900-1920." *Ohio History* 86 (Summer 1977): 171-86.

Wiebe, Robert H. *The Search for Order, 1877-1920*. New York: Hill and Wang, 1967.

Williams, W. *What's On the Worker's Mind*. New York: N. p., 1920.

Willys, John North. *How I Tackled My Three Biggest Problems*. Toledo, Ohio: Guardian Trust & Savings Bank of Toledo, n. d.

Wittke, Carl, ed. *History of the State of Ohio*. 6 vols. Columbus, Ohio: Ohio Historical Society, 1941-44. Vol. 5: *Ohio Comes of Age 1873-1900*, by Philip D. Jordan.

_____. *History of the State of Ohio*. 6 vols. Columbus, Ohio: Ohio Historical Society, 1941-44. Vol. 6: *Ohio in the Twentieth Century, 1900-1938*, by Harlow Lindley.

Wolff, Gerald W. "The Ohio Farmer-Labor Vote in the Election of 1896: A Case Study." *Northwest Ohio Quarterly* 45 (Summer 1975): 100-119.

Woltz, James M. *Safety and Welfare Work as Carried on at the Youngstown Sheet & Tube Company, Youngstown, Ohio*. Youngstown: n. p., 1915.

"Women Streetcar Conductors Fight Layoffs." In *America's Working Women*, pp. 204-07. Edited by Rosalyn Baxandall, Linda Gordon, and Susan Reverby. New York: Random House, 1976.

Wortman, Roy. "The I. W. W. and the Akron Rubber Strike of 1913." In *At the Point of Production: The Local History of the I. W. W.*, pp. 49-60. Edited by Joseph R. Conlin. Westport: Greenwood Press, 1981.

_____. "The Resurgence of the I. W. W. in Cleveland." *Northwest Ohio Quarterly* 47 (Winter 1974-75): 20-29.

Wright, Richard J. *Freshwater Whaler: A History of the American Ship Building Company and Its Predecessors*. Kent, Ohio: Kent State University Press, 1969.

Yellen, Samuel. "A Socialist Boyhood." *American Mercury* 21 (October 1930): 199-207.

Youngstown, Ohio Central Labor Union. *Illustrated History of the Central Labor Union of Youngstown, Ohio and Vicinity and Its Affiliated Organizations*. Youngstown: Central Labor Union, 1903.

Zornow, William F. "Bellamy Nationalism in Ohio 1891 to 1896." *The Ohio State Archaeological and Historical Quarterly* 58 (April 1949): 152-70.

Unpublished Studies

Anderson, Elaine S. "The Jews of Toledo 1845-1895." Ph.D. dissertation, University of Toledo, 1974.

Bahna, Donald G. "The Pope-Toledo Strike of 1907." M. A. thesis, University of Toledo, 1963.

Bindley, Joe Hoover. "An Analysis of Voting Behavior in Ohio." Ph.D. dissertation, University of Pittsburgh, 1959.

Brown, G. Maude. "A History of Organized Labor in Toledo." M. A. thesis, University of Toledo, 1924.

Cichanowicz, Stanley R. "The Kossuth Colony and Jacob D. Moskowitz—An Experiment in the Settlement of Hungarian Immigrants in Dayton, Ohio." University of Dayton. 3 December 1963. (Mimeographed.)

Cincinnati Consumers' League. "Home Work in the Clothing Industry." August 1918. (Mimeographed.)

_____. "A Study of Living Conditions in Rooming Houses." June 1916. (Mimeographed.)

Fink, Leon Reynolds. "Workingman's Democracy: The Knights of Labor in Local Politics, 1886-1896." Ph.D. dissertation, University of Rochester, 1977.

Folk, Richard A. "A Study of the Socialist Party of Ohio, 1900-1925." M. A. thesis, University of Toledo, 1965.

Grabowski, John J. "A Social Settlement in a Neighborhood in Transition, Hiram House, Cleveland, Ohio, 1896-1926." Ph.D. dissertation, Case Western Reserve University, 1977.

Harrison, Dennis. "The Consumers' League of Ohio: Women and Reform, 1909-1937." Ph.D. dissertation, Case Western Reserve University, 1975.

Holford, David. "The Great Bituminous Coal Strike of 1897 and Miners' Relief in the Hocking Valley Field." June 1975. (Typewritten.)

_____. "Mechanization and Miners' Relief: The Case of the Hocking Valley." 1976. (Typewritten.)

_____. "Mechanization, Labor Unrest, and Miners' Relief in the Hocking Valley: The Coal Strike of 1897." October 1975. (Typewritten.)

_____. "Mine Mechanization and Labor Unrest in the Hocking Valley, 1890-1900." Paper presented at the Ohio Academy of History Conference, Columbus, Ohio, 26 April 1975.

Howson, Embrey Bernard. "Jacob Sechler Coxey: A Biography of a Monetary Reformer, 1854-1951." Ph.D. dissertation, The Ohio State University, 1973.

Javersak, David Thomas. "The Ohio Valley Trades and Labor Assembly: The Formative Years, 1882-1915." Ph.D. dissertation, West Virginia University, 1977.

May, Alma. "The Negro and Mercer County." M. A. thesis, University of Dayton, 1968.

McDonald P. T. A. "A Brief History of McDonald, Ohio." 1966. Youngstown State University Library. (Typewritten.)

Musselman, Barbara L. "The Quest for Collective Improvement: Cincinnati Workers, 1893-1920." Ph.D. dissertation, University of Cincinnati, 1975.

Nash, Michael Harold. "Conflict and Accommodation: Some Aspects of the Political Behavior of America's Coal Miners and Steel Workers, 1880-1920." Ph.D. dissertation, University of New York at Binghamton, 1975.

Peterson, Joyce Shaw. "A Social History of Automobile Workers Before Unionization, 1900-1933." Ph.D. dissertation, University of Wisconsin at Madison, 1976.

Rose, Patricia Terpack. "Design and Expediency: The Ohio State Federation of Labor as a Legislative Lobby, 1883-1935." Ph.D. dissertation, The Ohio State University, 1975.

Ross, Steven Joseph. "Workers on the Edge: Work, Leisure, and Politics in Industrializing Cincinnati, 1830-1890." Ph.D. dissertation, Princeton University, 1980.

Rosswurm, Kevin Micael. "A Strike in the Rubber City: Rubber Workers, Akron, and the I. W. W., 1913." M. A. thesis, Kent State University, 1975.

Seewer, Michael. "An Interpretive History of the National Cash Register Company Strike of 1901." Paper prepared for History 475 at Wright State University. Summer 1969.

Steele, Herbert E. "The American Flint Glass Workers' Union." Ph.D. dissertation, The Ohio State University, 1947.

Tribe, Ivan M. "An Empire of Industry: Hocking Valley Mining Towns in the Gilded Age." Ph.D. dissertation, University of Toledo, 1976.

Weasner, Clyde. "A History of the Labor Movement in Cleveland from 1890 to 1896." M. A. thesis, The Ohio State University, 1933.

Whipple, James B. "Cleveland in Conflict: A Study in Urban Adolescence, 1876-1900." Ph.D. dissertation, Case Western Reserve University, 1951.

Wiliams, LeRoy T. "Black Toledo: Afro-Americans in Toledo, Ohio, 1890-1930." Ph.D. dissertation, University of Toledo, 1977.

Wortman, Roy Theodore. "The I. W. W. in Ohio, 1905-1950." Ph.D. dissertation, The Ohio State University, 1971.

Newspapers

The Cincinnati Enquirer, 27 April 1914—15 October 1918.

The Labor Advocate, 30 October 1914—30 December 1916.

The Ohio State Journal, 21 June 1905—15 January 1916.

Portsmouth Daily Times, 17 March—30 November 1914.

The Teamsters, January 1906—November 1906.

Toledo City Journal, 13 May 1916.

Government Records and Documents

Ohio. Bureau of Labor Statistics. *Tenth Annual Report, 1886*. Columbus: The Westbote Co., 1887.

_____. *Eleventh Annual Report, 1887*. Columbus: The Westbote Co., 1888.

_____. *Twelfth Annual Report, 1888*. Columbus: The Westbote Co., 1889.

_____. *Thirteenth Annual Report, 1889*. Columbus: The Westbote Co., 1890.

_____. *Fourteenth Annual Report, 1890*. Columbus: The Westbote Co., 1891.

_____. *Fifteenth Annual Report, 1891*. Columbus: The Westbote Co., 1892.

_____. *Sixteenth Annual Report, 1892*. Norwalk, Ohio: The Laning Printing Co., 1893.

_____. *Seventeenth Annual Report, 1893*. Norwalk, Ohio: The Laning Printing Co., 1894.

_____. *Eighteenth Annual Report, 1894*. Columbus: The Westbote Co., 1895.

_____. *Twentieth* (Nineteenth) *Annual Report, 1895*. Norwalk, Ohio: The Laning Printing Co., 1897.

_____. *Twentieth Annual Report, 1896*. Norwalk, Ohio: The Laning Printing Co., 1897.

_____. *Twenty-first Annual Report, 1897*. Norwalk, Ohio: The Laning Printing Co., 1898.

_____. *Twenty-second Annual Report, 1898*. Columbus: Fred J. Heer Printing Co., 1899.

_____. *Twenty-third Annual Report, 1899*. Columbus: Fred J. Heer Printing Co., 1900.

_____. *Twenty-fourth Annual Report, 1900*. Columbus: N. p., 1900.

_____. *Twenty-fifth annual Report, 1901*. Columbus: Fred J. Heer Printing Co., 1902.

_____. *Twenty-sixth Annual Report, 1902*. Columbus: Fred J. Heer Printing Co., 1903.

_____. *Twenty-seventh Annual Report, 1903*. Columbus: Fred J. Heer Printing Co., 1904.

_____. *Twenty-eighth Annual Report, 1904*. Springfield, Ohio: Springfield Publishing Co., 1905.

_____. *Twenty-ninth Annual Report, 1905*. Springfield, Ohio: Springfield Publishing Co., 1906.

_____. *Thirtieth Annual Report, 1906*. Springfield, Ohio: Springfield Publishing Co., 1907.

_____. *Thirty-first Annual Report, 1907*. Springfield, Ohio: Springfield Publishing Co., 1908.

_____. *Thirty-second Annual Report, 1908*. Springfield, Ohio: Springfield Publishing Co., 1909.

_____. *Thirty-fourth Annual Report, 1909*. Springfield, Ohio: Springfield Publishing Co., 1910.

_____. *Thirty-fifth Annual Report, 1910*. Springfield, Ohio: Springfield Publishing Co., 1911.

_____. *Thirty-sixth Annual Report, 1911*. Springfield, Ohio: Springfield Publishing Co., 1912.

_____. *Thirty-seventh Annual Report, 1912*. Columbus: Fred J. Heer Printing Co., 1915.

Ohio. Executive Documents. *Annual Reports for 1902. Made to the Twenty-Sixth General Assembly of the State of Ohio, Part II. Twenty-Eighth Annual Report of the Chief Inspector of Mines to the Governor of the State of Ohio for the Year 1902*. Springfield, Ohio: The Springfield Publishing Co., 1903.

Ohio. Department of Inspection of Workshops, Factories, and Public Buildings. *Fifth Annual Report, 1888*. Columbus: Westbote Co., 1889.

_____. *Eleventh Annual Report, 1894*. Columbus: Westbote Co., 1895.

Ohio Industrial Commission. *Job Setting in Industrial Establishments in Ohio*. Columbus: Fred J. Heer Printing Co., 1916.

_____. *Mediation of Industrial Disputes in Ohio, January, 1914, to June, 1916*. Columbus: n. p., 1916.

_____. *Plan for Adjustment of Grievances, Complaints and Differences Arising in the Shelby Shoe Company's Plant at Portsmouth*. n. p., 14 February 1914.

_____. *Preliminary Survey of Labor Camps in Ohio*. Columbus: Fred J. Heer Printing Co., 1918.

_____. Department of Investigation and Statistics. Reports 1 through 13, 1913-14. Columbus: Fred J. Heer Printing Co., and Allied Printing Trades Council, 1914-15.

_____. Reports 14 through 18, 1914-15. Columbus: Fred J. Heer Printing Co., 1915-16.

_____. Reports 19 through 27, 1915-16. Columbus: Fred J. Heer Printing Co.; and Springfield, Ohio: Springfield Publishing Co., 1916-17.

_____. Reports 28 through 35, 1915-18. Columbus: Fred J. Heer Printing Co., and Allied Printing Trades Council; and Springfield, Ohio: Springfield Publishing Co., 1916-17.

Ohio Institute for Public Efficiency. "Report of Social Survey of Portsmouth, Ohio for the Associated Charities of Portsmouth." August-September, 1916. (Typewritten.)

Ohio. Senate. *Report of the Select Committee Appointed to Investigate Causes and Circumstances of the Akron, Ohio Strike to the 80th General Assembly of the State of Ohio.* Columbus: Fred J. Heer Publishing Co., 1913.

U.S. Bureau of the Census. *Historical Statistics of the United States, Colonial Times to 1970.* 2 vols. Washington, D.C.: Government Printing Office, 1975.

_____. *People of the United States in the 20th Century,* by Irene B. Taeuber and Conrad Taeuber. Washington, D.C.: Government Printing Office, 1971.

_____. *Women in Gainful Occupations 1870 to 1920: A Study of the Trend of Recent Changes in the Numbers, Occupational Distribution, and Family Relationship of Women Reported in the Census as Following a Gainful Occupation.* Washington, D.C.: Government Printing Office, 1929.

U.S. Bureau of Labor. *First Annual Report of the Commissioner of Labor, 1886: Industrial Depressions.* Washington, D.C.: Government Printing Office, 1886.

_____. *Fourth Annual Report of the Commissioner of Labor, 1888: Working Women in Large Cities.* Washington: Government Printing Office, 1889.

_____. *Fifth Annual Report of the Commissioner of Labor, 1889: Railroads.* Washington, D.C.: Government Printing Office, 1890.

U.S. Bureau of Labor. *Sixth Annual Report of the Commissioner of Labor, 1890: Iron, Steel, and Coal.* Washington, D.C.: Government Printing Office, 1891.

_____. *Seventh Annual Report of the Commissioner of Labor, 1891.* Washington, D.C.: Government Printing Office, 1892. Vol. 2: *Cost of Production: The Textiles and Glass,* and Vol. 3: *Cost of Living.*

_____. *Sixteenth Annual Report of the Commissioner of Labor, 1901: Strikes and Lockouts.* Washington, D.C.: Government Printing Office, 1901.

_____. *Twenty-first Annual Report of the Commissioner of Labor, 1906: Strikes and Lockouts.* Washington, D.C.: Government Printing Office, 1907.

U.S. Congress. House of Representatives. *Seventh Annual Report of the Commissioner of Labor, 1891. Costs of Production: The Textiles and Glass.* Vol. 2. Part 3: *Cost of Living.* Washington, D.C.: Government Printing Office, 1892.

U.S. Department of Commerce and Labor. Bureau of the Census. *Special Reports; Occupations at the Twelfth Census.* Washington, D.C.: Government Printing Office, 1904.

U.S. Department of the Interior. Census Office. *Report of the Statistics of Wages in Manufacturing Industries.* Washington, D.C.: Government Printing Office, 1886.

_____. *Reports on Strikes and Lockouts Occurring Within the United States During the Calendar Year 1880,* by Joseph D. Weeks. Washington, D.C.: Government Printing Office, 1886.

U.S. Department of the Interior. National Park Service. ''National Register of Historic Places Inventory — Nomination form for the Kossuth Colony, Dayton, Montgomery County, Ohio.''

U.S. Department of Labor. Bureau of Labor Statistics. *Handbook of Labor Statistics 1975; Reference Edition.* Washington, D.C.: Government Printing Office, 1975.

U.S. Department of Labor. Division of Negro Economics. *The Negro at Work During the World War and During Reconstruction.* Washington, D.C.: Government Printing Office, 1921; reprint ed., New York: Negro University Press, 1969.

_____. *Negro Migration in 1916-1917,* by R. H. Leavell, T. R. Snavely, T. J. Woofter, Jr., T. B. Williams, and Francis D. Tyson. Reprint ed. New York: Negro University Press, 1969.

U.S. Industrial Commission. *Report of the Industrial Commission on Labor Legislation.* Vol. 5 of the Commission's Report. Washington, D.C.: Government Printing Office, 1900.

_____. *Report on Prison Labor.* Washington, D.C.: Government Printing Office, 1900.

_____. *Report of the Industrial Commission on the Relations & Conditions of Capital and Labor Employed in the Mining Industry.* Vol. 12 of the Commission's Report. Washington, D.C.: Government Printing Office, 1901.

Primary Sources

Akron, Ohio. Akron University. B.F. Goodrich Papers.

_____. Firestone Archives. ''Strike, Akron, 1913.''

Athens, Ohio. Ohio University Archives. United Shoe Workers, Local 117 Records.

Bowling Green, Ohio. The Center for Archival Collections at Bowling Green State University. International Association of Machinists and Aerospace Workers, District 57 Records.

_____. Toledo Central Labor Union Records.

Cincinnati, Ohio. University of Cincinnati Libraries. International Association of Machinists, District 34 Records.

Cleveland, Ohio. Western Reserve Historical Society. Hiram House Records.

_____. Moses Baskind Papers.

_____. Ignatz Koenig Papers.

_____. Max Sandin Papers.

Columbus, Ohio. Ohio Historical Society. Buckeye Steel Castings Co. Collection.

_____. Columbus Typographical Union, Local 5 Records.

_____. Council of National Defense, Ohio, Records.

_____. Arthur Garford Papers.

_____. The Godman Guild Collection.

_____. Judson Harmon Papers.

_____. Andrew L. Harris Papers.

_____. International Brotherhood of Electrical Workers, Local 54 Records.

_____. Frank Washburn Jennings Collection.

_____. George Nash Papers.

_____. Newark Area AFL-CIO Council Records.

_____. Pearl Nye Papers.

_____. Railway Trainmen, Nickle Plate Lodge 54 Records.

_____. Socialist Labor Party, Columbus Section, Minute Book, 1915-16.

_____. Joseph Slight Papers.

_____. United Brotherhood of Carpenters and Joiners, Local 660 Records.

Dayton, Ohio. Montgomery County Historical Society. Dayton Manufacturing Records.

Detroit, Michigan. American Motors Corporation Archives. American Motors Corporation Records and Historical Materials.

Kent, Ohio. Kent State University Library. East Liverpool Trades & Labor Council Papers.

_____. National Brotherhood of Operative Potters, Headquarters Papers.

Lima, Ohio. Allen County Historical Society. Labor History Collection.

Oberlin, Ohio. Oberlin College. I. W. Metcalf ''American Sabbeth Union'' Collection.

Toledo, Ohio. Toledo-Lucas County Public Library. Toledo Labor Exchange Collection.

Washington, D.C. Library of Congress. N.A.A.C.P. Papers.

Washington, D.C. National Archives. Bureau of Investigation Papers, 1908-22. File No. OG224877, Roll No. 116B. Department of Justice, Record Group 65.

Madison, Wisconsin. State Historical Society of Wisconsin. David Saposs Papers.

Oral Histories

Young, Albert. Interview 13 June 1980. Ohio Historical Society.

PART 4

Books & Articles

Abbott, William, and Glazer, Joe. *25 Years of the U. R. W.* Akron: United Rubber, Cork, Linoleum, and Plastic Workers of America, 1960.

Adamic, Louis. *My America, 1928-1938.* New York: Harper & Brothers, 1938.

Aiken, William Earl. *The Roots Grew Deep.* Cleveland: Lezius-Hiles Co., 1957.

Allen, Hugh. *The House of Goodyear, 1936.* 3rd ed. Akron: Superior Printing & Lithographic Co., 1936.

Amalgamated Association of Iron, Steel, and Tin Workers. *Journal of Proceedings of the International Lodge, 1936.* Pittsburgh: Amalgamated Press, n. d.

Ambler, Charles Henry. *A History of Transportation in the Ohio Valley.* Glendale, CA: The Arthur H. Clark Co., 1932.

American Federation of Labor. "Rubber Workers Council." *American Federationist* (July 1934): 698-99.

American Federation of Labor. *Fifty Years of Service.* American Federation of Labor, 1931.

American Iron and Steel Institute. *Yearbook of the American Iron and Steel Institute, 1937.*

Amidon, Beulah. "Toledo: A City the Auto Ran Over." *Survey* 63 (1 March 1930): 656-60.

Anderson, Sherwood. *Perhaps Women.* Boston: Horace Liveright, 1931; reprint ed., Mamaroneck, NY: Paul P. Appel, 1970.

Arnold, Joseph L. *The New Deal in the Suburbs: A History of the Greenbelt Town Program 1935-1954.* Columbus: Ohio State University Press, 1971.

Auerbach, Jerold S., ed. *American Labor: The Twentieth Century.* Indianapolis: Bobbs-Merrill Company, 1969.

——————. *Labor and Liberty: The LaFollette Committee and the New Deal.* Indianapolis: Bobbs-Merrill Company, 1966.

Augustine, Thomas. *Negro Job Progress in Akron: 1940-1950.* Akron: Akron Community Service Center, 1955.

Bain, Trevor. "Internal Union Conflict: The Flat Glass Workers, 1936-1937." *Labor History* 9 (Winter 1968): 106-9.

Ball, Wilma I. "Street Trading in Ohio." *The American Child* 1 (1919-1920): 123-129.

"John Barber, Ed Mann, and Others." In *Rank and File*, pp. 265-84. Alice Lynd and Staughton Lynd, eds. Boston: Beacon Press, 1973.

Bartlow, E. O. *Vocational Survey, Boy's and Men's Occupations Toledo, Ohio.* Toledo: Toledo Board of Education, 1939.

Barton, Josef J. *Peasants and Strangers: Italians, Rumanians, and Slovaks in an American City, 1890-1950.* Cambridge, MA: Harvard University Press, 1975.

Baughman, James L. "Classes and Company Towns: Legends of the 1937 Little Steel Strike." *Ohio History* 87 (Spring 1978): 175-92.

Baum, Vicki. *The Weeping Wood.* London: Michael Joseph, 1945.

Baxandall, Rosalyn; Gordon, Linda; and Reverby, Susan, eds. *America's Working Women.* New York: Random House, 1976.

Beasley, Norman. *Men Working; A Story of the Goodyear Tire and Rubber Company.* New York: Harper & Brothers, 1931.

Becker, Carl M. "A 'Most Complete' Factory: The Barney Car Works, 1850-1926." *Cincinnati Historical Society Bulletin* 31 (Spring 1973): 48-69.

Bell, Daniel. "Industrial Conflict and Public Opinion." In *Industrial Conflict*, pp. 240-56. Arthur Kornhauser, Robert Dubin, and Arthur M. Ross, eds. New York: McGraw-Hill, 1954.

Bell, Sherry S., ed. *Ohio Women.* Columbus: State of Ohio Bureau of Employment Services, 1979.

Bell, Spurgeon, and Watkins, Ralph J. *Industrial and Commercial Ohio.* 2 vols. Columbus: Ohio State University, 1930.

Bernstein, Irving. *The Lean Years: A History of the American Worker, 1920-1933.* Boston: Houghton-Mifflin, 1960.

——————. *The Turbulent Years: A History of the American Worker, 1933-1941.* Boston: Houghton-Mifflin, 1970.

Berry, Theodore M. "The Negro in Cincinnati Industries." *Opportunity* 8 (December 1930): 361-63.

Berthoff, Rowland Tappan. *British Immigrants in Industrial America, 1790-1950.* Cambridge, MA: Harvard University Press, 1953.

Booth, Viva, and Arnold, Sam. *Prewar, War, and Postwar Earnings, Hours, and Employment of Wage Earners in Ohio Industries, 1935-1946.* Columbus: Ohio State University, 1949.

Bowden, Witt. "Labor in Depression and Recovery, 1929-1937." *Monthly Labor Review* 27 (November 1937): 1-37.

Braeman, John; Bremmer, Robert H.; and Brody, David, eds. *The New Deal.* Vol. 2: *State and Local Levels.* Columbus, Ohio: Ohio State University Press, 1975.

Braverman, Harry. *Labor and Monopoly Capital.* New York: Monthly Review Press, 1974.

Brecher, Jeremy. *Strike.* Greenwich: Fawcett, 1972.

Bremner, Robert H. *From the Depths; The Discovery of Poverty in the United States.* New York: New York University Press, 1956.

Brito, Particia. "Protective Legislation in Ohio: The Inter-War Years." *Ohio History* 88 (Spring 1979): 173-97.

Brody, David. "Labor and Great Depression: The Interpretative Prospects." *Labor History* 13 (Spring 1972): 231-44.

——————. *Labor In Crisis: The Steel Strike of 1919.* Philadelphia: J. B. Lippincott Co., 1965.

——————. *Workers In Industrial America.* New York: Oxford University Press, 1980.

Brooks, Robert R. R. *As Steel Goes ... Unionism in a Basic Industry.* New Haven: Yale University Press, 1940.

Brophy, John. *A Miner's Life.* Madison: University of Wisconsin Press, 1964.

Brown, Rollo W. *The Hills Are Strong.* Boston: Beacon Press, 1952.

Cannon, Harry. "Collective Bargaining by the United Rubber Workers." *Monthly Labor Review* 29 (September 1939): 604-17.

Cary, Lorin Lee. "The Bureau of Investigation and Radicalism in Toledo, Ohio, 1918-1920." *Labor History* 21 (Summer 1980): 430-40.

Cebula, James E. *The Glory and Despair of Challenge and Change: A History of the Molders Union.* Cincinnati: International Molders & Allied Workers Union, AFL-CIO-CLC, 1976.

Chafe, William H. *The American Woman, Her Changing Social, Economic, and Political Roles, 1920-1970.* New York: Oxford University Press, 1972.

Chalmers, David H. *Hooded Americanism: The History of the Ku Klux Klan.* New York: Doubleday and Co., 1965; reprint ed., New York: New Viewpoints, 1976.

Cincinnati Chamber of Commerce. *The Status of the Negro in Industry and Occupational Opportunities in Cincinnati.* Cincinnati: Cincinnati Chamber of Commerce and Department of Public Welfare, 1930.

Cincinnati Federal Writers Project of the Works Progress Administration in Ohio. *They Built A City: 150 Years of Industrial Cincinnati.* Cincinnati: The Cincinnati Post, 1938.

Clapp, Tom. "Toledo Industrial Peace Board, 1935-1943." *Northwest Ohio Quarterly* 40 (Spring 1968): 50-67.

Claque, Ewan, and Claque, Couper. "The Readjustment of Workers Displaced by Plant Shutdown." *Quarterly Journal of Economics* 12 (February 1931): 309-46.

Close, J. K. "Toledo Plan for the Elimination of Strikes; Originated by Edward F. McGrady." *Annalist* 46 (October 1935): 462.

——————. "Toledo Steps Forward in Good Government and Industrial Peace." *American City* 51 (December 1936): 81.

Coates, Charles B. "Labor Boomerang in Akron." *Factory Management and Maintenance* 6 (July 1938): 38-44.

Cochran, Bert. *Labor and Communism: The Conflict That Shaped American Unions.* Princeton: Princeton University Press, 1977.

Cochran, Thomas C., and Brewer, Thomas B., eds. *Views of American Economic Growth: The Industrial Era.* 2 vols. New York: McGraw-Hill, 1966.

Colston, Freddie C. "The Political Behavior of Black Legislators in the Ohio House of Representatives." In *Blacks in Ohio History*, pp. 16-25. Rubin F. Weston, ed. Columbus: Ohio Historical Society, 1977.

Commission of Inquiry, Interchurch World Movement. *Report on The Steel Strike of 1919.* New York: Harcourt, Brace & Howe, 1920.

Committee for Industrial Organization. *How the Rubber Workers Won.* Washington, D. C.: Committee for Industrial Organization, 1936.

Commons, John R.; Saposs, David J.; Sumner, Helen L.; Mittelman, E. B.; Hoagland, H. E.; Andres, John B.; and Perlman, Selig. *History of Labor in the United States, 1896-1932.* 4 vols. Reprint Edition; New York: Augustus M. Kelley, 1966. Vol. 3: *Working Conditions & Labor Legislation*, by Dan D. Lescohier and Elizabeth Brandeis.

Commons, John R.; Saposs, David J.; Sumner, Helen L.; Mittelman, E. B.; Hoagland, H. E.; Andres, John B.; and Perlman, Selig. *History of Labor in the United States, 1896-1932.* 4 vols. Reprint Edition; New York: Augustus M. Kelly, 1966. Vol. 4: *Labor Movements*, by Selig Perlman and Philip Taft.

Conduit, Carl W. *The Railroad and the City: A Technological and Urbanized History of Cincinnati.* Columbus, Ohio: Ohio State University Press, 1977.

Conlin, Joseph R. *Bread and Roses Too: Studies of the Wobblies.* Westport, CT: Greenwood Publishing Co., 1969.

_____. "The I. W. W. and the Question of Violence." *Wisconsin Magazine of History* 51 (Summer 1968): 316-26.

Conroy, Jack. "Hard Winter." *American Mercury* 22 (February 1931): 129-137.

Cook, Philip L. "Tom Girdler and the Labor Policies of Republic Steel Corporation." *Social Science* 42 (January 1967): 21-30.

Coombs, Whitney. *The Wages of Unskilled Labor in Manufacturing Industries in the United States, 1890-1924.* Studies in History, Economics, and Public Law No. 283. New York: Columbia University Press, 1926.

Cox, James M. *Journey Through My Years.* New York: Simon and Schuster, 1946.

Crowther, Samuel. *John H. Patterson: Pioneer in Industrial Welfare.* Garden City, NY: Doubleday, Page & Co., 1924.

Dalrymple, Sherman H. "The United Rubber Workers of America." U. S. Department of Labor, Bureau of Labor Statistics. *Labor Information Bulletin* (April 1939): 4-7.

Danish, Max D. *William Green: A Pictorial Biography.* New York: Inter-Allied Publications, 1952.

Davis, Horace. *Labor and Steel.* New York: International Publishers, 1933.

Davis, Pearce. *The Development of the American Glass Industry.* Cambridge, MA: Harvard University Press, 1949.

Davis, Russell H. *Black Americans in Cleveland: From George Peake to Carl B. Stokes, 1796-1969.* Washington, D. C.: Associated Publishers, 1972.

DeAngelo, E. A. "Toledo's Manager Government and Labor." *National Municipal Review* 26 (October 1937): 484-86.

Dickason, Gladys. "Women in Labor Unions." *Annals of the American Academy of Political and Social Science* 25 (May 1947).

Douglas, Paul H. "An Analysis of Strike Statistics, 1881-1921." *Journal of the American Statistical Association* 18 (September 1923): 866-77.

Dowell, Eldrige F. *A History of Criminal Syndicalism Legislation in the United States.* Baltimore: Johns Hopkins University Press, 1939.

Drucker, Mary J. *The Rubber Industry in Ohio.* National Youth Administration in Ohio. Occupational Study No. 1. December 1937.

Dubofsky, Melvyn. "Labor Organizations." In *Encyclopedia of American Economic History: Principal Movements and Ideas,* pp. 524-551. Edited by Glen Porter. New York: Scribner's Sons, 1980.

_____. "Not So Turbulent Years: Another Look at the American 1930s." *America Studien* 24 (January 1979): 5-20.

_____. *We Shall Be All: A History of the Industrial Workers of the World.* Chicago: Quadrangle Books, 1969.

_____, and Van Tine, Warren. *John L. Lewis.* New York: Quadrangle, 1977.

Dulaney, W. Marvin. "Blacks as Policemen in Columbus, Ohio, 1895-1945." In *Blacks in Ohio History,* pp. 10-16. Rubin F. Weston, ed. Columbus: Ohio Historical Society, 1976.

Ells, H. P. "City Peace Board Aids in 23 Labor Disputes." *Public Management* 22 (May 1940): 148.

Evaenson, Howard N. *The First Century and a Quarter of American Coal Industry.* Pittsburgh: Koppers Building, 1942.

Fairbanks, Robert B. "Cincinnati and Greenhills: The Response to a Federal Community, 1935-1939." *Cincinnati Historical Society Bulletin* 36 (Winter 1978): 223-41.

Feis, Herbert. *Labor Relations: A Study Made in the Proctor and Gamble Company.* New York: Adelphi Co., 1928.

Fine, Nathan. *Labor and Farmer Parties in the United States, 1828-1928.* New York: Rand School, 1928.

Fine, Sidney. *Sit-Down; the General Motors Strike of 1936-1937.* Ann Arbor: University of Michigan Press, 1969.

_____. "The Toledo Chevrolet Strike of 1935." *Ohio History* 67 (October 1958): 326-56.

Flontek, Pete, ed. *Twelve Years of Progress, Local 1104 Lorain, United Steelworkers of America.* Lorain, Ohio: Committee for Industrial Organization, 1949.

Foner, Philip S. *American Socialism and Black Americans: From the Age of Jackson to World War II.* Westport, CT: Greenwood Press, 1977.

Fordyce, Wellington G. "Nationality Groups in Cleveland Politics." *Ohio State Archaeological and Historical Quarterly* 46 (April 1937).

Foster, William Z. *The Great Steel Strike and Its Lessons.* New York: B. W. Huebsch, Inc., 1920.

Frey, Alexander. "What's Behind the Strike?" *Harper's Monthly* 186 (January 1938): 168-78.

Fritchey, Clayton. "Relief in Ohio." *American Mercury* 31 (May 1940): 74-81.

Frost, Dayton H. *Emergency Relief in Ohio.* Columbus: Federal Relief Administration, 1936.

Gadsby, M. A. "The Steel Strike." *Monthly Labor Review* 9. (December 1919): 79-94.

Gaffey, John D. *The Productivity of Labor in the Rubber Tire Industry.* New York: Columbia University Press, 1940.

Galenson, Walter. *The CIO Challenges to the AFL.* Cambridge, MA: Harvard University Press, 1960.

_____. "The Unionization of the American Steel Industry." *International Review of Social History* 1 (1956): 8-40.

Gallaway, Lowell E. "The Origin and Early Years of the Federation of Flat Glass Workers of America." *Labor History* 3 (Winter 1962): 92-102.

"Germany and Cincinnati." *Historical and Philosophical Society of Ohio Bulletin* 20 (1962): 2-95.

Gibbons, Charles E. *Administration of the Child Labor Law In Ohio.* New York: National Child Labor Committee, 1931.

Gibbons, Willis A. "The Rubber Industry, 1839-1939." In *The Annual Report of the Board of Regents of the Smithsonian Institution Showing the Operations, Expenditures, and Condition of the Institution for the Year Ended June 30, 1940,* pp. 193-214. Washington, D. C.: Government Printing Office, 1941.

Gietschier, Steven P. "Detained, J. B. McNamara: Two Letters From the Convicted *Los Angeles Times* Bomber." *Labor History* 23 (Winter 1982): 79-89.

Girdler, Tom M. *Boot Straps: The Autobiography of Tom M. Girdler.* New York: Charles Scribner's Sons, 1943.

Glaab, Charles, and Brown, A. Theodore. *A History of Urban America.* New York: The MacMillan Co., 1967.

Goodrich, Carter. *The Miner's Freedom.* Boston: Little, Brown, 1925.

_____, et al. *Migration and Planes of Living, 1920-1934; Study of Population Redistribution.* Bulletin No. 2. Philadelphia: n. p., 1935.

Goodyear Tire & Rubber Company. *The Work of the Labor Division.* Akron: Goodyear Tire & Rubber Company, 1920.

Gordon, Max. "The Communists and the Drive to Organize Steel, 1936." *Labor History* 23 (Spring 1982): 254-265.

Grant, H. S. "General Motors Strikes Back; Toledo Plant Dismantled." *Nation* 141 (25 December 1935): 743-44.

Gray, Chester J. *Job Opportunities for Negro Youth in Columbus.* Columbus, Ohio: National Youth Administration, 1938.

Green, Howard W. *Population Characteristics by Census Tracts of Cleveland, Ohio.* Cleveland: The Plain Dealer Publishing Co., 1930.

Green, James. "Working Class Militancy in the Depression." *Radical America* 6 (November-December 1972): 1-34.

_____. *The World of the Worker.* New York: Hill and Wang, 1980.

Green, Marguerite. *The National Civic Federation and the American Labor Movement, 1900-1925.* Washington: Catholic University Press, 1956.

Greenway, John. *American Folksongs of Protest.* Philadelphia: University of Pennsylvania Press, 1953.

Gregory, Chester W. *Women in Defense Work During World War II.* New York: Exposition Press, 1974.

Grisiner, Karl H. *Akron and Summit County.* Akron: Summit County Historical Society, 1952.

Grove, S. "Toledo Defense Production Association." *American City* 57 (June 1942): 101.

Hallgren, Maruitz A. "Bankers and Breadlines in Toledo." *Nation* 134 (6 April 1932): 395-97.

Harbison, Frederick H., and King, Car. *The Libbey-Owens-Ford Glass Company and the Federation of Glass, Ceramic and Silica Sand Workers of America.* Washington, D. C.: National Planning Association, 1949.

Hardman, J. B. S. *American Labor Dynamics.* New York: Harcourt, Brace and Company, 1928.

Heald, Edward Thornton. *The Stark County Story.* Vol. 4: *Free People at Work.* Part 2: *The Suburban Era, 1917-1958.* Canton, Ohio: Stark County Historical Society, 1959.

Hill, T. Arnold. "Labor: Dayton, Ohio." *Opportunity* 23 (January 1929).

Himes, J. S., Jr. "Forty Years of Negro Life in Columbus, Ohio." *Journal of Negro History* 27 (April 1942): 133-54.

Hohman, Elmo. "Maritime Labor in the United States." *International Labour Review* 38 (August 1938).

Holmes, Robert E. "Ohio's Industrial Growth, 1900-1957, and Some Possibilities for Study." *Ohio History* 66 (July 1957): 290-99.

Hotel and Restaurant Workers. *Fifty Years of Progress: A Brief History of Our Union.* n. p., 1942.

House, John D. "Rubber Workers Unionize—Goodyear Leads the Way." *American Federationist* (May 1934): 486-88.

Howard, Donald S. *The W. P. A. and Federal Relief Policy.* New York: Russell Sage Foundation, 1943; reprint ed., New York: Da Capo Press, 1973.

Hunker, Henry L., and Wright, Alfred J. *Factors of Industrial Location in Ohio.* Columbus: Ohio State University, 1963.

Hunt, Edward E.; Tryon, F. G.; and Willits, Joseph H. *What the Coal Commission Found.* Baltimore: The Williams & Wilkins Co., 1925.

Ickes, Harold I. *The Secret Diary of Harold L. Ickes.* Vol. 2: *The Inside Struggle, 1936-1939.* New York: Simon and Schuster, 1954.

International Typographical Union. Executive Council. *A Study of the History of the International Typographical Union, 1852-1963.* 2 vols. Colorado Springs, Colorado: International Typographical Union, 1964.

Jacoby, Robin. "Feminism and Class Consciousness in the British and American Women's Trade Union Leagues, 1890-1925." In *Liberating Women's History,* pp. 137-60. Bernice Carroll, ed. Urbana, IL: University of Illinois Press, 1976.

Jacobson, Julius, ed. *The Negro and the American Labor Movement.* Garden City, NY: Doubleday, 1968.

Jenkins, William D. "The Ku Klux Klan in Youngstown, Ohio: Moral Reform in the Twenties." *The Historian* 41 (November 1978): 76-93.

Johnson, Oakley C. *The Day is Coming: Life and Work of Charles E. Ruthenberg, 1882-1927.* New York: International Publishers, 1957.

Jones, Alfred Winslow. *Life, Liberty, and Property.* Philadelphia: J. B. Lippincott Co., 1941.

Jordan, Phillip Dillon, and Kessler, Lillian. *Songs of Yesterday: A Song Anthology of American Life.* Garden City, NY: Doubleday, Doran & Co., 1941.

Keeler, Vernon D. *The Commercial Development of Cincinnati.* Chicago: University of Chicago Press, 1938.

Keeran, Roger. *The Communist Party and the Auto Workers Unions.* Bloomington: Indiana University Press, 1980.

Kelley, Florence; Leum, Clara; Clevenger, Olive; Reeder, Faye; and McMillan, Dapel Dell. *The Development in the United States of Legislation Concerning Women's Renumerative Work in Gainful Occupations.* Columbus: Pi Lambda Theta, 1939.

Kennedy, Aileen. *The Ohio Poor Law and Its Administration.* Chicago: American Public Welfare Association, 1934.

Kennedy, Susan Estabrook. *If All We Did Was to Weep at Home: A History of White Working Class Women in America.* Bloomington: Indiana University Press, 1979.

Kornbluh, Joyce, ed. *Rebel Voices: An I. W. W. Anthology.* Ann Arbor: University of Michigan Press, 1964.

Kornblum, William. *Blue Collar Community.* Chicago: University of Chicago Press, 1974.

Korth, P. A. "Auto-Lite Strike: Methods and Materials." *Labor History* 16 (Summer 1975): 412-17.

Kruchko, John G. *The Birth of a Union Local: The History of U. A. W. Local 674, Norwood Ohio, 1933-1940.* Ithaca: Cornell University, 1972.

Kusmer, Kenneth L. *A Ghetto Takes Shape: Black Cleveland, 1870-1930.* Urbana, IL: University of Illinois Press, 1976.

"Labor Board Improves Toledo Labor Picture." *American City* 56 (July 1941): 82.

"Labor Conditions in the Onion Fields of Ohio." *Labor Review* 40 (February 1935): 324-35.

Labor Research Association. *Labor Fact Book No. 3.* Labor Research Association, 1936.

Lamb, Edward. *No Lamb for Slaughter.* New York: Harcourt, Brace & World, 1963.

Larrowe, Charles P. *Maritime Labor Relations on the Great Lakes.* East Lansing: Michigan State University, 1959.

Leiserson, William M. *Adjusting Immigrant and Industry.* New York: Harper & Brothers, 1924.

Lens, Sidney. *The Labor Wars.* New York: Doubleday, 1973.

Levin, Maurice. *Income in the Various States; Its Sources and Distribution 1919, 1920, and 1921.* New York: National Bureau of Economic Research, 1925.

Levine, Louis. *The Women's Garment Workers; A History of the International Ladies Garment Workers' Union.* New York: P. W. Huebsch, 1924.

Levinger, Lee J. "Jews in the Liberal Professions in Ohio." *Jewish Social Studies* 11 (1940).

Levitt, Theodore. *World War II Manpower Mobilization and Utilization in A Local Labor Market.* Columbus: Ohio State University Press, 1951.

Lief, Alfred. *Harvey Firestone: Free Man of Enterprise.* New York: McGraw-Hill Co., 1951.

Lindley, Harlow, ed. *Ohio in the Twentieth Century, 1900-1938.* Columbus: Ohio State Archaeological and Historical Society, 1942.

Little, E. H. "The U. S. Rubber Companies' Use of Dismissal Wage." *American Management Association,* Personnel, Series No. 6, 1930.

Lovin, Hugh T. "The Automobile Workers Unions and the Fight for Labor Parties in the 1930s." *Indiana Magazine of History* 77 (June 1981): 122-149.

Lynd, Alice and Lynd, Staughton, eds. *Rank and File.* Boston: Beacon, 1973.

Lynd, Staughton. *American Labor Radicalism: Testimonies and Interpretation.* New York: John Wiley & Sons, 1973.

——————. "The Possibility of Radicalism in the Early 1930's.: The Case of Steel." *Radical America* 6 (November-December 1972): 37-64.

McCabe, David A. *National Collective Bargaining in the Pottery Industry.* Baltimore: Johns Hopkins Press, 1932.

McDonald, David J., and Lynch, Edward A. *Coal and Unionism: A History of the American Coal Miners' Union.* Indianapolis: Cornelius Printing Co., 1939.

McKenney, Ruth. *Industrial Valley.* New York: Harcourt, Brace & Co., 1939.

McKenzie, Roderick Duncan. *The Neighborhood: A Study of Local Life in the City of Columbus, Ohio.* Chicago: University of Chicago Press, 1923.

McMurray, David A. "The Willys-Overland Strike, 1919." *Northwest Ohio Quarterly* 36 (Autumn 1964): 171-181.

McQueeney, E. C. *A History of Housing the Industrial Employee in Akron.* Akron, Ohio: By the Author, 706 McQueeney Avenue, 1939.

Magdoff, Harry; Siegel, I. H.; and Davis, M. B. *Production, Employment and Productivity in 59 Manufacturing Industries.* 3 vols. Philadelphia: National Research Project of the W. P. A., 1939.

Maher, Amy G. *Ohio Wage Earners in the Manufacture of Rubber.* Toledo, Ohio: Information Bureau on Women's Work, 1930.

Mark, Mary Louise. *Negroes in Columbus Ohio.* Contributions in Social Science, No. 2. Columbus: The Ohio State University Press, 1928.

Matles, James J. and Higgins, James. *Them and Us: Struggles of a Rank-and-File Union.* Boston: Beacon Press, 1974.

Matson, R. A. "Toledo's Plan to End Strikes." *Nation's Business* 24 (July 1936): 42.

Mauer, David J. "Relief Problems and Politics in Ohio." In *The New Deal,* pp. 77-102. Vol. 2. John Braeman, Robert H. Bremner, and David Brody, eds. Columbus: Ohio State University, 1975.

Meek, Charles S. "Study of the Progress of Newsboys in School." *Elementary School Journal* 24 (February 1924): 430-33.

Mihok, Janet A. "Women in the Leadership Role, Past and Present, in the Public Schools of Northeastern Ohio." In *Women in Ohio History,* pp. 26-31. Marta Whitlock, ed. Columbus: Ohio Historical Society, 1976.

Miller, Zane L. "Boss Cox's Cincinnati: A Study in Urbanization and Politics, 1880-1914." *Journal of American History* 54 (March 1968): 823-38.

Millett, Stephen M. "Charles E. Ruthenberg: The Development of an American Communist, 1909-1927." *Ohio History* 81 (Summer 1972): 193-209.

Millis, Harry A., ed. *How Collective Bargaining Works.* New York: Twentieth Century Fund, 1942.

Mills, C. Wright. "The Middle Classes in Middle-Sized Cities." *American Sociological Review* 11 (October 1946): 520-29.

Monroe, Alden N. "Effects and Causes: The Evolution of a Social Agency." *Cincinnati Historical Society Bulletin* 37 (Fall 1979): 191-216.

Mooney-Melvin, Patricia. "Mohawk-Brighton: A Pioneer in Neighborhood Health Care." *Cincinnati Historical Society Bulletin* 36 (Spring 1978): 37-72.

Moore, H. R. *A Report on Conditions Associated With Employment in The Scioto Marsh, Hardin County.* Columbus: Ohio State University, 1939.

Moore, L. S. "Maintaining Industrial Peace; Toledo Industrial Peace Board." *Public Management* 19 (April 1937): 103-7.

Morris, Charles E. *Progressive Democracy of James M. Cox*. Indianapolis: Bobbs-Merrill Co., 1920.

Morris, Richard B., ed. *The American Worker. U. S. Department of Labor Bicentennial History*. Washington, D. C.: Government Printing Office, 1976.

Mortimer, Wyndham. *Organize*. Boston: Beacon Press, 1971.

Murray, Robert K. "Communism and the Great Steel Strike of 1919." *Mississippi Valley Historical Review* 38 (December 1951): 445-66

Musselman, Barbara L. "Working Class Unity and Ethnic Division: Cincinnati Trade Unionists and Cultural Pluralism." *Cincinnati Historical Society Bulletin* 34 (Summer 1976): 121-43.

National Industrial Conference Board. *The Cost of Living Among Wage-Earners: Cincinnati, Ohio, May, 1920*. New York: National Industrial Conference Board, 1920.

National Youth Administration. *Vocational Opportunities for Negroes in Cleveland*. Vocational Study for Negroes, No. 1., 1938.

——————. *Occupational Studies*. Vocational Study for Negroes. Series 3, nos. 1-2, 1938.

Nelson, Daniel. "The Beginning of the Sit-Down Era: The Reminiscences of Rex Murray." *Labor History* 15 (Winter 1974): 89-97.

North, Philip A. "The Auto-Lite Strike Methods and Materials." *Labor History* 16 (Summer 1975): 412-17.

Northrup, Herbert R. *Organized Labor and the Negro*. New York: Harper & Brothers, 1944.

——————, and Batchelder, Alan B. *The Negro in the Rubber Tire Industry*. University of Pennsylvania, 1969.

Nunn, W. L. "Committee Settles Their Labor Problems: Toledo Industrial Peace Board." *National Municipal Review* 29 (March 1940): 174-77.

——————. "Municipal Labor Boards of Toledo and Newark." *Monthly Labor Review* 49 (November 1939): 1045-49.

O'Brien, Larry D. "The Ohio National Guard in the Coal Strike of 1932." *Ohio History* 84 (Summer 1975): 127-144.

O'Connor, Harvey. *History of Oil Workers International Union, CIO*. Denver: Oil Workers International Union, 1950.

Olin, Oscar; Allen, Ada; Brouse, Edwin W.; and Braden, Joseph A., eds. *A Centennial History of Akron, 1825-1925*. Akron: Summit County Historical Society, 1925.

Oliver, Frank J. "Press and Industrial Peace; Toledo Plan." *Commonweal* 23 (31 January 1936): 375-76.

——————. "Quiet on the Toledo Front." *Factory Management and Maintenance* 93 (October 1935).

"One City's Plan for Industrial Peace; Toledo's Court of Arbitration." *American City* 51 (July 1936): 93.

Oppenheimer, Valerie. *The Female Labor Force in the United States*. Westport, CT: Greenwood, 1970.

Overman, William D. "The Rubber Industry in Ohio." *Ohio History* 66 (1957): 278-89.

Parker, Florence E. "Experience Under State Old Age Pension Acts in 1934." *Monthly Labor Review* 41 (1935): 303-12.

Pesotta, Rose. *Bread Upon the Waters*. New York: Dodd, Mead & Co., 1944.

Peterson, Florence. *American Labor Unions*. New York: Harper & Brothers, 1945.

Peterson, Jon A. "From Settlement to Social Agency: Settlement Work in Columbus, 1898-1958." *Social Science Review* 39 (June 1965): 191-208.

Pidgeon, Mary Elizabeth. *Changes in Women's Employment During the War*. Special Bulletin No. 20. U. S. Women's Bureau. Washington: Government Printing Office, 1944.

——————. *A Preview as to Women Workers in Transition From War to Peace*. Washington, D. C.: Government Printing Office, 1944.

——————. "Women Workers and Recent Economic Change." *Monthly Labor Review* 65 (1947).

Preston, William. *Aliens and Dissenters: Federal Suppression of Radicals, 1903-1933*. New York: Harper Torchbooks, 1966.

Preis, Art. *Labor's Giant Step: Twenty Years of the CIO*. New York: Pathfinder Press, 1972.

Rich, Frances Ivins. *Wage-Earning Girls in Cincinnati*. Cincinnati: Helen S. Trounstine Foundation, 1927.

Richardson, James F. "The City in Twentieth-Century Ohio." In *Toward An Urban Ohio*, pp. 34-44. Edited by John Wunder. Columbus: Ohio Historical Society, 1977.

Richardson, Reed C. *The Locomotive Engineer, 1863-1963*. Ann Arbor: University of Michigan Press, 1963.

Roberts, Harold S. "Negotiation of Collective Agreements in the Rubber Industry." *Monthly Labor Review* (June 1939).

——————. *The Rubber Workers: Labor Organization and Collective Bargaining in the Rubber Industry*. New York: Harper & Brothers, 1944.

Rodabaugh, James H. "The Negro In Ohio." *Journal of Negro History* 31 (1946): 9-29.

Rose, William Ganson. *Cleveland: The Making of a City*. Cleveland: The World Publishing Co., 1950.

Rosenzweig, Roy. "Radicals and the Jobless: The Musteites and the Unemployed Leagues, 1932-1936." *Labor History* 16 (Winter 1975): 52-77.

Ruffin, E. "Municipal Labor Board Settles Strikes After Action is Voted." *Public Management* 19 (September 1937): 277-78.

——————. "Toledo Assumes Responsibility for Industrial Peace." *Public Management* 18 (June 1936): 180-81.

Ruthenberg, Charles E. *Voices in Revolt: Speeches and Writings of Charles E. Ruthenberg*. New York: International Publishers, 1928.

Ryan, Mary P. *Womanhood in America*. New York: New Viewpoints, 1975.

Scharf, Lois. "Employment of Married Women in Ohio, 1920-1940." In *Women in Ohio History*, pp. 14-26. Marta Whitlock, ed. Columbus: Ohio Historical Society, 1976.

Schroeder, Gertrude G. *The Growth of Major Steel Companies, 1900-1950*. Baltimore: Johns Hopkins Press, 1953.

Shannon, Irwin V. *Southeastern Ohio in Depression and War: The Disintegration of an Area*. Columbus: The Ohio State University, 1943.

Shiner, John F. "The 1937 Steel Labor Dispute and the Ohio National Guard." *Ohio History* 84 (Autumn 1975): 182-95.

Shoenfeld, Oscar and MacLean, Helene, eds. *City Life*. New York: Grossman Publishers, 1969.

Silverburg, Louis G. "Citizen's Committees: Their Role in Industrial Conflict." *The Public Opinion Quarterly* (March 1971): 17-38.

Slavin, Richard H. "The 'Flint Glass Workers' Union vs. The Glassware Industry: Union Management Policies in a Declining Industry." *Labor History* 5 (Winter 1964): 27-39.

Smith, Thomas H., ed. *An Ohio Reader: Reconstruction to the Present*. Grand Rapids: B. Eerdmans Publishing Co., 1975.

Smith, William E. *History of Southwestern Ohio*. 3 vols. New York: Lewis Historical Publishing Co., 1964.

Sobczak, John N. "The Politics of Relief: Public Aid in Toledo, 1933-1937." *Northwest Ohio Quarterly* 48 (Fall 1976): 134-42.

Soule, George. "Liberty League Liberty." *Liberty* (24 September 1938): 15-17.

——————. "Panic Over Labor." *New Republic* 83 (23 June 1937): 175-76.

"Southern Negro in Cleveland Industries." *Monthly Labor Review* 19 (July 1924): 41-44.

Speer, Michael. "The Little Steel Strike: Conflict for Control." *Ohio History* 78 (Autumn 1969): 273-87.

"A Square Deal for Negroes — at the American Rolling Mill Company's Plant in Middletown, Ohio." *Southern Workman* 50 (May 1921): 209-16.

Stein, Rose M. "It's War in Youngstown." *Nation* 145 (3 July 1937): 12-14.

——————. "Republic Sticks to Its Guns." *Nation* 145 (12 June 1937): 668-69.

Sterling, David L. "The 'Naive Liberal,' the 'Devious Communist' and the Johnson Case." *Ohio History* 78 (Spring 1969): 94-103.

Stern, Joseph S., Jr. *They Said It Couldn't Be Done*. Cincinnati: Centennial Committee, 1966.

Sternsher, Bernard. "Victims of the Great Depression: Self-Blame/Non-Self-Blame, Radicalism, and Pre-1929 Experiences." *Social Science History* 1 (Winter 1977): 137-177.

Stokes, Thomas L. "Washington Looks at Steel." *Nation* (19 June 1937).

Stolberg, Benjamin. "Vigilantism, 1937." *Nation* 145 (August 1937): 166-68.

——————. "Big Steel, Little Strike and the CIO." *Nation* 145 (31 July 1937): 119-23.

Stone, Katherine. "The Origins of Job Structures in the Steel Industry." *Review of Radical Political Economics* 6 (Summer 1974): 61-97.

"The Story of the I. W. W. — The Fiasco at Akron." *The One Big Union Monthly* 2 (April 1920): 44-46.

Stout, Wilber. "Charcoal Iron Industry of the Hanging Rock District." *Ohio State Archaeological and Historical Quarterly* 42 (1933): 72-104.

Straw, Richard. "An Act of Faith: Southeastern Ohio Miners in the Coal Strike of 1927." *Labor History* 21 (Spring 1980): 221-38.

Suffern, Arthur E. *The Coal Miners' Struggle for Industrial Status*. New York: The MacMillan Co., 1926.

Sweeney, Vincent D. *The United Steelworkers of America Twenty Years Later*. Indianapolis: Allied Printing, n. d.

Terkel, Studs. *Hard Times*. New York: Random House, 1970.

Thompson, Fred. *The I. W. W.: Its First Fifty Years*. Chicago: I. W. W., 1955.

Throckmorton, H. Bruce. "A Note on Labor Banks." *Labor History* 20 (Fall 1979).

Toledo Council of Social Agencies. *The Toledo Relief Survey*. Toledo: N. p., 1939.

Toledo Metropolitan Housing Authority. "A Study of Housing Conditions Conducted by the Toledo Metropolitan Housing Authority." Bulletin No. 1, 1934.

Ulman, Lloyd. *The Government of the Steel Workers' Union*. New York: John Wiley & Sons, 1962.

Van Raaphorst, Donna L. "I Won't Give Up, I Can't Give Up, I'll Never Give Up: Motto of Geraldine Roberts, Founder of the Domestic Workers of America." In *Women in Ohio History* pp. 31-38. Marta Whitlock, ed. Columbus: Ohio Historical Society, 1976.

VanTine, Warren; Sickmeier, Marie Bell; and Vorys, Gail Arch, eds. *A Centennial History of the United Brotherhood of Carpenters and Joiners of America in Ohio*. Columbus: Labor Education and Research Service, 1982.

Verba, Sidney, and Schlozman, Kay Lehman. "Unemployment, Class Consciousness, and Radical Politics: What Didn't Happen in the Thirties." *Journal of Politics* 34 (May 1977): 291-323.

Vites, A. L., and Grimley, A. C. "Rubber Industry." In *The Development of American Industries*, pp. 227-44. J. Glover. New York: Prentice-Hall, 1935.

Vorse, Mary Heaton. *Labor's New Millions*. New York: Modern Age Books, 1938.

Walker, Charles R. "Life Curve of a C. I. O. Union." *Survey Graphic* (November 1938): 554-59.

_____. *Steel: The Diary of a Furnace Worker*. Boston: Atlantic Monthly Press, 1922.

Walsh, J. Raymond. *C. I. O. Industrial Unionism in Action*. New York: W. W. Norton, 1937.

Watkins, Damon D. *Keeping The Home Fires Burning*. Columbus: The Ohio Company, 1937.

Wertheimer, Barbara Mayer. *We Were There: The Story of Working Women in America*. New York: Pantheon Books, 1977.

Wesley, Charles Harris. *Negro-Americans in Ohio*. Wilberforce, Ohio: Central State University, 1953.

_____. *Negro Labor in the United States, 1850-1925; A Study in American Economic History*. New York: Vanguard Press, 1927.

Whitney, Frances R. *What Girls Live on and How: A Study of the Expenditures of a Sample Group of Girls Employed in Cincinnati in 1929*. Cincinnati: Consumers' League of Cincinnati, 1930.

Williams, Lee. "Newcomers to the City: A Study of Black Population Growth in Toledo, Ohio, 1910-1930." *Ohio History* 89 (Winter 1980): 5-24.

Williams, Pierce. "The Essence of the Steel Strike." *Survey Graphic* 26 (October 1937): 516-19.

Williams, Whiting. *What's On the Worker's Mind*. New York: Charles Scribner's Sons, 1921.

Williamson, John. *Dangerous Scot: The Life and Work of an American Undesirable*. New York: International Publishers, 1969.

Wittee, Edwin E. *The Government in Labor Disputes*. New York: McGraw-Hill, 1932.

Wolf, Harold. "The Rubber Barons Fight to the Death." *American Mercury* (June 1931).

Wolf, Howard and Wolf, Ralph. *Rubber: A Story of Glory and Greed*. New York: Covici, Friede Publishers, 1936.

Wolters, Raymond. *Negroes and the Great Depression*. Westport, CT: Greenwood Publishing Company, 1970.

Works Progress Administration. Ohio Writer's Project. *Cincinnati, A Guide to the Queen City and Its Neighbors*. Cincinnati: Wiesen-Hart Press, 1943.

_____. Federal Writers Program, State of Ohio. *The Ohio Guide*. New York: Oxford University Press, 1940.

_____. *Warren and Trumbull County*. Warren, Ohio: Western Reserve Historical Celebration Committee, 1938.

Wortman, Roy T. "An IWW Document on the 1919 Rossford Strike." *Northwest Ohio Quarterly* 43 (Summer 1971): 37-42.

Yellen, Samuel. "A Socialist Boyhood." *American Mercury* 21 (October 1930): 199-207.

Zieger, Robert H. "The Limits of Militancy: Organizing Paper Workers, 1933-1935." *Journal of American History* 63 (December 1976): 638-57.

Unpublished Studies

Bain, Trevor. "The Impact of Technological Change on the Flat Glass Industry and the Unions' Reactions to Change: Colonial Period to the Present." Ph.D. dissertation, University of California, 1964.

Baughman, James Lewis. "The 1937 Little Steel Strike in Three Ohio Communities." M. A. thesis, Columbia University, 1975.

Bruno, Gorden E. "The Function of the American Federation of Labor and the Congress of Industrial Organizations in Developing a Welfare Program for Workers in the Period 1930-1940." M. A. thesis, University of Toledo, 1950.

Chelminski, David G. "Strikebreakers, Slavs and Violence in the 1919 Willys-Overland Labor Dispute in Toledo, Ohio." Toledo, 1977. (Mimeographed.)

Clapp, Tom. "Toledo Industrial Peace Board, 1935-1943." M. A. thesis, University of Toledo, 1965.

Daugherty, Robert L. "Citizen Soldiers in Peace: The Ohio National Guard, 1919-1940." Ph.D. dissertation, Ohio State University, 1974.

Deem, Warren H. "The Employers Association of Dayton, Ohio." 1953. (Typewritten.)

Fonow, Mary Margaret. "Women in Steel: A Case Study of the Participation of Women in a Trade Union." Ph.D. dissertation, Ohio State University, 1977.

Gaither, Alexander D. "Negro Women Employed in Domestic Service in Columbus, Ohio." M. A. thesis, Ohio State University, 1938.

Gates, D. L. "A Survey and Analysis of the Content of the Relief Families of Belmont County, Ohio." M. A. thesis, Ohio State University, 1934.

Harbison, Frederick H. "Labor Relations in the Iron and Steel Industry, 1936-1939." Ph.D. dissertation, Princeton University, 1940.

Harris, Thelma. "An Investigation of a Labor Union's Policies and Membership Attitudes Toward Race and Sex." M. A. thesis, University of Akron, 1946.

Harrison, Dennis. "The Consumers' League of Ohio: Women and Reform, 1909-1937." Ph.D. dissertation, Case Western Reserve University, 1975.

House, John D. "Birth of a Union." (Mimeographed.)

Howell, James. "Community-Transit Relations in Dayton, Ohio, 1869-1961." M. A. thesis, Ohio State University, 1962.

Howson, Emery. "The Ku Klux Klan in Ohio After World War I." M. A. thesis, Ohio State University, 1951.

Huff, Clarence. "Unionization Behind the Walls." An Analytic Study of the Ohio Prisoners' Labor Union Movement. Ph.D. dissertation, Ohio State University, 1974.

Josephson, P. O. "A Study of the Influence of the FERA and the SRC upon the Administration of Relief in Eight Selected Counties." M. A. thesis, Ohio State University, 1936.

Kellogg, Jefferson Bradley. "A Study of Negro Direct Action Activity During the Depression: The Selective Buying Campaigns in Chicago, Baltimore, Cleveland, Washington, New York, and Richmond." M. A. thesis, Kent State University, 1974.

Kelly, Jean Kirkendall. "The Historical Development of Industrial Legislation for Ohio's Women." M. A. thesis, Ohio State University, 1938.

Konigsberg, R. L. "Social Factors in the Transiency of Boys." M. A. thesis, Ohio State University, 1935.

Lages, John D. "The CIO-SWOC Attempt to Organize the Steel Industry, 1936-1942; A Restatement and Economic Analysis." Ph.D. dissertation, Iowa State University, 1967.

Land, Mary. "The Malcontents and the Melting Pot; The Cleveland Story." M. A. thesis, Western Reserve University, 1946.

Leotta, Louis, Jr. "Republic Steel Corporation in the Steel Strike of 1937." M. A. thesis, Columbia University, 1960.

Levitt, Theodore. "World War II Manpower Mobilization and Utilization in a Local Labor Market: The Wartime Manpower Experience in the Columbus, Ohio Area." Columbus: Ohio State University Research Foundation, 1951.

Lezius, Walter G. "The Glass Industry in Toledo and Its Environs." Toledo Business Research, College of Business Administration, University of Toledo, 1937.

Lutz, Oscar E. "The Social Problem of the School Boy Who Works in Toledo." M. A. thesis, University of Toledo, 1923.

McMurray, David A. "The Willys-Overland Strike of 1919-1920." M. A. thesis, University of Toledo, 1964.

Marec, Ronald E. "The Fiery Cross: A History of the Ku Klux Klan in Ohio, 1920-1930." M. A. thesis, Kent State University, 1967.

Marshall, Laurie. " 'Yours for Industrial Freedom': The Socialist Party and the Labor Movement of Dayton, Ohio, 1900-1921." Cleveland, May 1971. (Typewritten.)

Mason, Harrison. "A Study of the Occuptional Opportunities for Negroes in the City of Dayton, Ohio." M. A. thesis, Wittenberg College, 1935.

Mead, John F. "An Economic Analysis of the Toledo Labor Management-Citizens Committee After Twenty Years of Operation." Ph.D. dissertation, University of Kentucky, 1955.

Millett, Stephen M. "Charles E. Ruthenberg and American Bolshevism, 1917-1921." M. A. thesis, Ohio State University, 1970.

Moore, Gilbert Wesley. "Poverty, Class Consciousness, and Racial Conflict: The Social Basis of Trade Union Politics in the UAW-CIO, 1937-1955." Ph.D. dissertation, Princeton University, 1978.

Mosier, Tana. "Brand Whitlock Homes: The Land, the People, and the Project." M. A. thesis, University of Toledo, 1981.

Mould, Beryl F. "The People of Godman Guild Neighborhood of Columbus, Ohio, 1939." M. A. thesis, Ohio State University, 1939.

Nelson, Daniel. "Origins of the Sit-Down Era: Worker Militancy and Innovation in the Rubber Industry, 1934-38." (Mimeographed.)

Nuckolls, Charles B., Jr. "The Governorship of Martin I. Davey of Ohio." M. A. thesis, Ohio State University, 1952.

Ohio Council of Social Agencies in Cooperation with the Ohio Institute for Public Efficiency for the Hamilton Chamber of Commerce. "Report of Social Survey of Hamilton, Ohio." November, 1919.

Ohio Council of Social Agencies. "Study and Advisory Report to the Mansfield Council of Social Agencies." August, 1920.

Ohio State Transient Committee. "Summary of Conditions in Ohio In Regard to Interstate Migration of Destitute Citizens." Report presented to Tolan Congressional Committee Meeting in Chicago, August 19-21, 1940.

Peterson, Joyce Shaw. "A Social History of Automobile Workers Before Unionization, 1900-1933." Ph.D. dissertation, University of Wisconsin at Madison, 1976.

Rinehart, J. D. "A Study of the Transient Problem in Columbus and Franklin County." M. A. thesis, Ohio State University, 1938.

Robert, Marcus. "Franklin D. Roosevelt, Martin L. Davey and the Little Steel Strike in Ohio." M. A. thesis, Kent State University, 1969.

Rose, Patricia Terpack. "Design and Expediency: The Ohio State Federation of Labor as a Legislative Lobby, 1883-1935." Ph.D. dissertation, Ohio State University, 1975.

Shotliff, Don A. "The History of the Labor Movement in the American Pottery Industry: The National Brotherhood of Operative Potters." Ph.D. dissertation, Kent State University, 1977.

Shreevastava, Mahavira. "The Industrial Development of Springfield, Ohio: A Study in Economic Geography." Ph.D. dissertation, Ohio State University, 1956.

Smith, Michael. "Italians in Akron, 1900-1940." M. A. thesis, University of Akron, 1973.

Snorf, Sue. "A Sociological Study of the Hungarian Settlement in Columbus." M. A. thesis, Ohio State University, 1925.

Sobczak, John N. "The Inadequacies of Localism: The Collapse of Relief in Toledo, 1929-1939." M. A. thesis, Bowling Green State University, 1975.

Sofchalk, Donald G. "The Little Steel Strike of 1937." Ph.D. dissertation, Ohio State University, 1961.

Spencer, Donald Andrew. "Job Opportunities for Negroes in the Printing and Tailoring Trades of Cincinnati." M. A. thesis, University of Cincinnati, 1940.

Steel, Herbert E. "The American Flint Glass Workers' Union." Ph.D. dissertation, Ohio State University, 1947.

Sternsher, Bernard. "The Onion Workers' Strike in Hardin County, 1934." (Mimeographed.)

Stitt, H. L. "A Study of the Woman's Party Position on Special Labor Laws for Women." M. A. thesis, Ohio State University.

Stockham, J. R. "An Analysis of Organizational Structure Aims and Tactics of the Worker's Alliance of America in Franklin County and Cuyahoga County, Ohio, and in Hennepin County, Minnesota." M. A. thesis, Ohio State University, 1938.

Stockton, Edward Jerome. "Negro Employment in Metropolitan Columbus." M. A. thesis, Ohio State University, 1956.

Terpack, Patricia Ann. "Youngstown and the 'Little Steel Strike of 1937': A Study of Community Reaction to a Labor Dispute." M. A. thesis, Ohio State University, 1971.

Traynor, C. F. "The Battle of Columbia Heights." (Mimeographed.)

Webne, Sam. "United Automobile Workers — Toledo, Ohio: A Chapter in the History of Labor Strife and Development." M. A. thesis, University of Toledo, 1949.

Willard, Tim. "Grievances, Grievance Procedure, and the Federation of Glass, Ceramic and Silica Sand Workers of America, 1933-1958." Toledo, 1978. (Mimeographed.)

Williams, LeRoy Thomas. "Black Toledo: Afro-Americans in Toledo, Ohio, 1890-1930." Ph.D. dissertation.

Wortman, Roy Theodore. "The I. W. W. in Ohio, 1905-1950." Ph.D. dissertation, Ohio State University, 1971.

Government Records and Reports

Ohio. Bureau of Unemployment Compensation. "The Ohio State Employment Service and the Negro in Defense." 1940.

––––––––––. Minority Groups Services Department. *Twenty-Three Years of Service, 1939-1962: Minority Groups Services.* Columbus: Ohio Bureau of Unemployment Compensation, 1962.

Ohio. Department of Public Welfare. "Public Aid in Ohio, 1938-1941."

Ohio. General Assembly. Joint Legislative Committee on Prisons and Reformatories. *The Penal Problem in Ohio.* Columbus: Fred J. Heer Printing Co., 1926.

U. S. Congress. Senate. On Post and Roads. *Hearings Regarding Delivery or Nondelivery of Mail in Industrial Areas.* 75th Congress, 1st session. Washington: 1937.

U. S. Congress. Senate. *The 'Little Steel' Strike and Citizens' Committees.* Report No. 151. 77th Congress, 1st session, 1937-1938.

U. S. Congress. Senate. Committee on Education and Labor. *Oppressive Labor Practices Act.* Hearings Before a Subcommittee of the Committee on Education and Labor. 76th Congress, 1st session. "A Bill to Eliminate Certain Oppressive Labor Practices Affecting Inter-State and Foreign Commerce, and for Other Purposes. 25 and 26 May 1939, and 1, 2, 5, 6, 7, and 13 June 1939. Washington, D. C.: Government Printing Office, 1939.

––––––––––. Hearings before the Subcommittee, 75th Congress, 1st session, pursuant to Sen. Res. 266. *A Resolution to Investigate Violations of the Right to Free Speech and Assembly and Interference with the Right of Labor to Organize and Bargain Collectively.* Robert M. La Follette, Jr., Chairman of the Subcommittee.

––––––––––. *Violation of Free Speech and Rights of Labor.* S. Report No. 6, Part 2, 76th Congress, 1st session, 1939.

––––––––––. *Violation of Free Speech and Rights of Labor.* Report on the Committee on Education and Labor. Pursuant to Sen. Res. 266. "A Resolution to Investigate Violations of the Right to Free Speech and Assembly and Interference with the Right of Labor to Organize and Bargain Collectively. Report No. 6, Parts 4-6. 76th Congress, 1st session, 1939.

U. S. Congress. Senate. Committee on Interstate Commerce. *"Conditions in the Coal Fields of Pennsylvania, West Virginia, and Ohio."* Hearings before the Committee on Interstate Commerce, 70th Congress, 1st session. Washington, D. C.: Government Printing Office, 1928. (2 vols.)

U. S. Department of Commerce. Bureau of the Census. *Immigrants and Their Children, 1920,* by Niles Carpenter. Census Monographs 7. Washington, D. C.: Government Printing Office, 1927.

U. S. Department of Labor. *Earnings in the Women's and Children's Apparel Industry in the Spring of 1939.* Washington, D. C.: U. S. Government Printing Office, 1940.

––––––––––. "Labor Through the Century." *Labor Department Bulletin.* No. 605. Washington, D. C.: Government Printing Office, 1933.

––––––––––. Bureau of Labor Statistics. *Characteristics of Company Unions.* Bulletin No. 634. Washington, D. C.: n. p., 1938.

––––––––––. "Digest of Material on Technological Changes, Productivity of Labor and Labor Displacement." *Monthly Labor Review* (November 1932): 1-27.

––––––––––. *Fluctuation in Employment in Ohio, 1914-1929.* Washington, D. C.: Government Printing Office, 1932.

––––––––––. "The Goodyear Tire and Rubber Company Strike." *Monthly Labor Review* (May 1936): 1288-1293.

––––––––––. "Productivity of Labor in the Rubber Tire and Iron and Steel Industries." *Monthly Labor Review* (December 1926): 28-34.

_____. *Wages and Hours of Labor in the Automobile Tire Industry, 1923*. Bulletin No. 358. Washington, D. C.: Government Printing Office, 1924.

U. S. National Labor Relations Board. "In the Matter of Republic Steel Corporation and Steel Workers Organizing Committee." Case No. C-184. Decided 18 October 1938. *Decisions and Orders of the National Labor Relations Board*, vol. 8, 1939.

U. S. Trade Commission. In the Matter of the Goodyear Tire and Rubber Company. Docket 2116, 1936.

U. S. Women's Bureau Publications. Nos.: 63, 66 Parts I and II, 98, 125, 132, 137, 143, 144, and 145.

Primary Sources

Akron, Ohio. Firestone Corporate Archives. Firestone Company Records.

_____. University of Akron. B. F. Goodrich Corporation Papers.

Athens, Ohio. American History Research Center, Ohio University Library. United Mine Workers District 6 Collection.

Bowling Green, Ohio. Center for Archival Collections, Bowling Green State University. Edward Lamb Papers.

_____. International Association of Machinists and Aerospace Workers, District 57 Records.

_____. International Typographical Union, Local No. 63 Records.

_____. Toledo Central Labor Union Records.

Cincinnati, Ohio. University of Cincinnati. International Association of Machinists and Aerospace Workers, District 34 Records.

_____. Cincinnati Historical Society. Charles P. Taft Papers.

_____. Pamphlet File.

_____. Urban League of Greater Cincinnati Papers.

Cleveland, Ohio. Western Reserve Historical Society. Marvin Harrison Papers.

_____. Hiram House Records.

_____. Whiting Williams Papers.

Columbus, Ohio. Ohio Historical Society. Brotherhood of Railroad Trainmen, Nickle Plate Lodge 54 Records.

_____. Garrett Coleman Papers.

_____. Elmer F. Cope Papers.

_____. Governor James M. Cox Papers.

_____. George DeNucci Papers.

_____. Max S. Hayes Papers.

_____. International Association of Machinists and Aerospace Workers, District 52 Records.

_____. International Brotherhood of Electrical Workers, Local 683 Papers.

_____. International Typographical Union, Local No. 5 Records.

_____. Newark AFL-CIO Council Records.

_____. Ohio Adjutant General Papers.

_____. Ohio AFL-CIO Papers.

_____. Ohio Socialist Labor Party Records.

_____. Ohio War History Commission Papers.

_____. Charles E. Ruthenberg Papers.

_____. United Brotherhood of Carpenters and Joiners of America, Local 200 Records.

_____. Youngstown Sheet & Tube Corporation Papers.

Dayton, Ohio. Wright State University Library. Ruth Herr Papers.

_____. Dayton Typographical Union No. 57 Records.

_____. I. U. E. Local 755 Records.

_____. I. U. E. Local 801 Records.

_____. I. U. E. Local 689 Records.

_____. I. U. E. District Council 7 Records.

_____. Dayton Urban League Papers.

Detroit, Michigan. American Motors Corporation Archives. American Motors Corporation Records.

_____. Archives of Labor History and Urban Affairs, Wayne State University. Charles Beckman Papers.

_____. Henry Kraus Papers.

_____. George Roberts Papers.

_____. United Rubber Workers Collection.

_____. United Auto Workers, Local 32 Collection.

_____. Mary van Kleek Papers.

Ithaca, New York. Cornell University. Amalgamated Clothing Workers Union Papers.

_____. Brotherhood of Locomotive Firemen and Engineers Papers.

Kent, Ohio. Kent State University Library. East Liverpool Trades and Labor Council Papers.

_____. International Brotherhood of Pottery and Allied Workers, International Headquarters Papers.

Madison, Wisconsin. State Historical Society of Wisconsin. David J. Saposs Papers.

New York, New York. Tamiment Library, New York University. Daniel Bell Papers.

Toledo, Ohio. University of Toledo Library. Richard Gosser Papers.

_____. Toledo Public Library. Women's Movement Papers.

Washington, D. C. Catholic University of America. John Brophy Papers.

_____. C. I. O. Local Industrial Union Councils Collection.

_____. Phillip Murray Papers.

_____. Library of Congress. John P. Frey Papers.

_____. National Association for the Advancement of Colored People Papers.

_____. Robert A. Taft Papers.

Newspapers

Cleveland Plain Dealer, 1 January 1930-7 March 1935.

Ohio State Journal, 29 October 1932-15 August 1936.

Youngstown Vindicator, 19 September-30 December 1919.

Oral Histories

Abel, Iorwith Wilbur. Interview 1975. Ohio Historical Society.

Amdur, Max. Interview 1978. Ohio Historical Society.

Beck, Carl. Interview 1974. Ohio Historical Society.

Beckman, Charles. Interview 25 July 1961. Wayne State University.

Blakely, Daniel. Interview 1976. Ohio Historical Society.

Coleman, Dick. Interview 23 June 1960. Wayne State University.

Cook, Alexander. Interview 31 August 1960. Wayne State University.

Culver, James H. Interview 1976. Ohio Historical Society.

DeNucci, G. George. Interview 1976. Ohio Historical Society.

Ditzel, Joseph. Interview 25 September, 1960. Wayne State University.

Doherty, William C. Interview 1977. Ohio Historical Society.

Eagle, Newton H. Interview 1974. Ohio Historical Society.

Elsner, Robert N. Interview 27 August 1976. Ohio Historical Society.

Ferline, Jack. Interview 1976. Ohio Historical Society.

Foster, Bert. Interview 26 July 1961. Wayne State University.

Gallagher, James P. Interview 1967. Ohio Historical Society.

Gray, Ben. Interview 1977. Ohio Historical Society.

Hogg, Charles R. Interview 1974. Ohio Historical Society.

Hogg, Charles. Interview 7 November 1974. Youngstown State University Oral History Program.

House, John. Interview 1976. Ohio Historical Society.

Humphrey, Edward. Interview 1974. Ohio Historical Society.

Jackson, Clingan. Interview 1974. Ohio Historical Society.

Jones, Orville C. Interview 1977. Ohio Historical Society.

Lamb, Edward. Interview 1979. Ohio Historical Society.

Lynch, Florence. Interview 1978. Ohio Historical Society.

Miley, Paul. Interview 24 July 1961. Wayne State University.

Morris, Russell D. Interview 1975. Ohio Historical Society.

Norris, Laird. Interview 1975. Ohio Historical Society.

Oleno, Peter. Interview 1975. Ohio Historical Society.

O'Malley, Patrick. Interview 1976. Ohio Historical Society.

Presser, Jackie. Interview 1980. Ohio Historical Society.

Ramsay, John G. Interview 1976. Ohio Historical Society.

Repasky, Edward. Interview 1976. Ohio Historical Society.

Reynolds, Finas. Interview 1976. Ohio Historical Society.

Ross, Ray. Interview 1975. Ohio Historical Society.

Roland, James. Interview 25 September 1960. Wayne State University.

Shaffer, Emmett C. Interview 19 July 1974. Youngstown State University Oral History Program.

Silvey, Ted. Interview 1976. Ohio Historical Society.

Steinhilber, Wesley M. Interview 1976. Ohio Historical Society.

Taylor, Pauline. Interview 1978. Ohio Historical Society.

Thomas, Daniel. Interview 1974. Ohio Historical Society.

White, Thomas. Interview 1974. Ohio Historical Society.

Wines, Harry. Interview 1968. Ohio Historical Society.

Young, Albert. Interview 13 June 1980. Ohio Historical Society.

PART 5

Books and Articles

"Appalachia on Cleveland's East Side." *Appalachia*, 5, no. 7 (July-August 1972). 50-51.

Aronowitz, Stanley. *False Promises: The Shaping of American Working Class Consciousness.* New York: McGraw-Hill Book Company, 1973.

Ashford, Nicholas Askounes. *Crisis in the Workplace: Occupational Disease and Injury, A Report to the Ford Foundation.* Cambridge, MA: MIT Press, 1976.

Baldwin, Deborah. "Will Youngstown Point the Way? A Devastated Steel Town Tries to Survive." *The Progressive* 42 (Oct. 1978): 40-43.

Barton, Josef J. *Peasants and Strangers: Italians, Rumanians, and Slovaks in an American City, 1890-1950.* Cambridge, MA: Harvard University Press, 1975.

Beck-Rex, Marguerite. "Youngstown: Can This Steel City Forge A Comeback?" *Planning.* (January 1978): 12-14

Bednarzik, Robert W. and Klein, Deborah P. "Labor Force Trends: A Synthesis and Analysis." *Monthly Labor Review.* (Oct. 1977): 3-12.

Behrens, Chester C. "Automation—Its Significance and Effect at The Managerial Level." *Business and Society Conference on Automation* (February 21, 1964) Columbus: Ohio State University, College of Commerce and Administration, 1964.

Berman, Daniel M. *Death on the Job: Occupational Health and Safety in the United States.* New York: Monthly Review Press, 1978.

Blume, Norman. "Union Worker Attitudes Toward Open Housing: The Case of the UAW in the Toledo Metropolitan Area." *Phylon* 34 (March 1973): 63-72.

Bok, Derek C. and Dunlop, John T. *Labor and the American Community.* New York: Simon and Schuster, 1970.

Boothe, Viva and Arnold, Sam. *Earnings and Hours of Ohio Production Workers, 1947-1951.* Columbus: Bureau of Business Research, Ohio State University, nd.

Braverman, Harry. *Labor and Monopoly Capital: The Degradation of Work in the Twentieth Century.* New York: Monthly Review Press, 1974.

Brill, Steven. *The Teamsters.* New York: Simon and Schuster, 1978.

Brody, David. *Workers in Industrial America: Essays on the 20th Century Struggle.* New York: Oxford University Press, 1980.

Cochran, Bert. *Labor and Communism: The Conflict That Shaped American Unions.* Princeton: Princeton University Press, 1977.

Colston, Freddie C. "The Political Behavior of Black Legislators in the Ohio House of Representatives." In *Blacks in Ohio History.* Edited by Rubin F. Weston. Columbus: Ohio Historical Society, 1977.

DeMaria, Alfred T. *How Management Wins Union Organizing Campaigns.* New York: Executive Enterprises Publications Co., Inc., 1980.

Dubofsky, Melvyn. "Labor Organizations." In *Encyclopedia of American Economic Movements and Ideas.* II: 524-51. Edited by Glen Porter. New York: Charles Scribner's Sons, 1980.

Dunlop, John T. "The Future of the American Labor Movement." In *The Third Century: America as a Post-Industrial Society.* Edited by Seymour Martin Lipset. Stanford: Hoover Institution Press, 1979.

Edwards, P. K. *Strikes in the United States, 1881-1974.* New York: New York: St. Martin's Press, 1981.

Eisinger, Peter K. "Black Employment in Municipal Jobs: The Impact of Black Political Power." *The American Political Science Review* 76 (June 1982): 380-392.

Fenton, John H. "Ohio's Unpredictable Voters." *Harper's Magazine* 225 (October 1962): 61-65.

Gabin, Nancy. "Women Workers and the UAW in the Post-World War II Period: 1945-1954." *Labor History* 21 (Winter 1979-80): 5-30.

Gorisek, Sue. "The Working Wounded." *Ohio Magazine* (April 1981): 34-40, 91.

Green, James R. *The World of the Worker: Labor in Twentieth-Century America.* New York: Hill and Wang, 1980.

Harris, William H. *The Harder We Run: Black Workers Since The Civil War.* New York: Oxford University Press, 1982.

Howe, Irving, ed. *The World of the Blue-Collar Worker.* New York: Quadrangle Books, 1972.

International Brotherhood of Teamsters. *What is the Teamsters Union: A Brief Look at the Largest Trade Union in the Western Hemisphere.* Washington, D. C.: International Brotherhood of Teamsters, 1977.

Jacobson, Julius, ed. *The Negro and the American Labor Movement.* Garden City, NY: Doubleday and Company (Anchor Books), 1968.

James, Ralph C. and James, Estelle Dinerstein. *Hoffa and the Teamsters: A Study of Union Power.* Princeton, NJ: D. Van Nostrand Co., Inc., 1965.

Johnson, Ralph Arthur. "World Without Workers: Prime Time's Presentation of Labor." *Labor Studies Journal* 5 (Winter, 1980): 199-206.

Kahn, E. J. Jr. *The American People.* Baltimore: Penguin Books, 1973.

Kenneally, James J. *Women and American Trade Unions.* St. Albans, VT: Eden Press Women's Publications, Inc., 1978.

Kennedy, Susan Estabrook. *If All We Did Was to Weep at Home: A History of White Working-Class Women in America.* Bloomington: Indiana University Press, 1979.

Kessler-Harris, Alice. *Out to Work: A History of Wage-Earning Women in the United States.* New York: Oxford University Press, 1982.

—————. "Where Are the Organized Women Workers?" *Feminist Studies* 3 (1975): 92-110.

Kilgour, John G. *Preventive Labor Relations.* New York: Amacom, 1981.

Kochan, Thomas A. "How American Workers View Labor Unions." *Monthly Labor Review* (April 1979): 23-31.

Levenstein, Harvey A. *Communism, Anticommunism, and the CIO.* Westport, CT: Greenwood Press, 1981.

Labor-Management Problems of the American Merchant Marine. Washington, U.S. Government Printing Office, 1955.

Larrowe, Charles P. *Maritime Labor Relations on the Great Lakes.* East Lansing: Michigan State University (Labor and Industrial Relations Center), 1959.

Levinson, David, "The Westinghouse Strike—1955-56." *Labor Law Journal* 7 (September 1956): 543-551.

"John Barbero, Ed Mann and Others," In *Rank and File.* Edited by Alice and Staughton Lynd. (Boston, 1973), pp. 265-284.

Lynd, Staughton, ed. *American Labor Radicalism: Testimonies and Interpretation.* New York: John Wiley and Sons, Inc., 1973.

McDermott, John. *The Crisis in the Working Class and Some Arguments For a New Labor Movement.* Boston: South End Press, 1980.

Main, Jeremy. "Work Won't Be the Same Again." *Fortune* (28 June 1982): 52-65.

Meissner, Martin. *Technology and the Worker: Technical Demands and Social Processes in Industry.* San Francisco: Chandler Publishing Company, 1969.

Miller, Glenn W. and Ware, Stephan B. "Organized Labor in the Political Process: A Case Study of the Right-to-Work Campaign in Ohio." *Labor History* 4 (Winter 1963): 51-67.

Miller, Herman P. *Rich Man, Poor Man.* New York: Thomas Y. Crowell Company, 1971.

Montgomery, David. "Work." In *Encyclopedia of American Economic History: Principal Movements and Ideas* Edited by Glen Porter. New York: Charles Scribner's Sons, 1980, III: 958-83.

—————. *Workers' Control in America: Studies in the History of Work, Technology, and Labor Struggles* Cambridge: Cambridge University Press, 1979.

Morris, Richard B., ed. *The American Worker: The U.S. Department of Labor Bicentennial History.* Washington, D.C.: U. S. Government Printing Office, 1976.

Northrup, Herbert R. and Rowan, Richard L. "Multinational Union Activity in the 1976 U. S. Rubber Tire Strike." *Sloan Management Review* 18 (Spring 1977): 17-28.

Nugent, Walter. *Structures of American Social History.* Bloomington: Indiana University Press, 1981.

Ohio Environmental Council. *Ohio Toxic Substances Referral Guide.* Columbus: Ohio Environmental Council, 1982.

Papier, William. "Employment Problems in Ohio." *Agenda for Management* 1 (Winter 1979): 2-6.

Peck, Sidney M. *The Rank-and-File Leader.* New Haven, CT: College and University Press Service, 1963.

Peterson, Gene B., Sharp, Laure M., and Drury, Thomas F. *Southern Newcomers to Northern Cities—Work and Social Adjustment in Cleveland.* New York: Praeger Publishers, 1977.

Raphael, Marc Lee. *Jews and Judaism in a Midwestern Community: Columbus, Ohio, 1840-1975.* Columbus: Ohio Historical Society, 1979.

Rezier, Julius. *Automation and Industrial Labor.* New York: Random House, 1969.

Ripley, Randall B. *The Implementation of CETA in Ohio.* Washington, D.C.: U. S. Government Printing Office, 1977.

Roberts, Patti. "An Introduction to Comparable Worth." *New Labor Worth* 4 (Fall 1982): 1-18.

Rothschild, Emma. *Paradise Lost: The Decline of the Auto-Industrial Age.* New York: Vintage Books, 1973.

Scholozman, Kay Lehman and Verba, Sidney. *Injury to Insult: Unemployment, Class, and Political Response.* Cambridge: Harvard University Press, 1979.

Scott, Rachel. *Muscle and Blood.* New York: E. P. Dutton & Co., Inc., 1974.

Seligman, Daniel. "Who Needs Unions?" *Fortune* (12 July 1982): 52-56, 61, 64, 66.

Sexton, Patricia. "A Feminist Union Perspective." In *Auto Work and Its Discontents.* Edited by B. J. Widick. Baltimore: Johns Hopkins University Press, 1976, 369-389.

Slavin, Richard H. "The Flint Glass Workers' Union vs. The Glassware Industry: Union Management Policies in a Declining Industry." *Labor History* 5 (Winter 1964): 27-39.

Staudohar, Paul D. "Prison Guard Labor Relations in Ohio." *Industrial Relations* 15 (May 1976): 177-190.

Terkel, Studs. *Working.* New York: Pantheon Books, 1972.

United Electrical, Radio and Machine Workers Of America (UE-CIO). *We Fought for our Union! The Story of the Univis Strike.* (Cleveland: UE—District 7, n.d.

Wagoner, Harless D. *The U.S. Machine Tool Industry From 1900 To 1950.* Cambridge, MA: MIT Press, 1968.

Walker, Charles R. *Toward the Automatic Factory: A Case Study of Men and Machines.* New Haven, CT: Yale University Press, 1957.

Whitlock, Marta, ed. *Women In Ohio History.* Columbus: Ohio Historical Society, 1976.

Widick, B. J., ed. *Auto Work and Its Discontents.* Baltimore: The Johns Hopkins University Press, 1976.

Unpublished Studies

Buss, Terry F. and Redburn, F. Stevens. "Shutdown: Public Policy for Mass Unemployment." Youngstown State University, Center for Urban Studies, 1981.

Dickes, Allen. "The Development of the Port of Toledo, 1946-1966." M. A. thesis, University of Toledo, 1970.

Emspak, Frank. "The Break-Up of the Congress of Industrial Organizations, (CIO), 1945-1950." Ph.D. dissertation, University of Wisconsin, 1972.

Filippelli, Ronald Lee. "The United Electrical, Radio and Machine Workers of America, 1933-1949: The Struggle for Control." Ph.D. dissertation, Pennsylvania State University, 1970.

Fonow, Mary Margaret. "Women in Steel: A Case Study of the Participation of Women in a Trade Union." Ph.D. dissertation, Ohio State University, 1977.

Gross, Elizabeth E. "A Twenty-Five Year Historical Study of the Labor-Management-Citizens Committee, 1946-71." M.A. thesis, University of Toledo, 1971.

Huff, Clarence Ronald. "Unionization Behind the Walls: An Analytic Study of Ohio Prisoners' Labor Union Movement." Ph.D. dissertation, Ohio State University, 1974.

Lathrope, Donald E. "The Toledo Labor-Management-Citizens Committee, 1945-1953: A Descriptive and Analytic Study." Ph. D. dissertation, University of Pittsburgh, 1955.

Miller, James D. "The Impact of Automation on the United Rubber Workers of America." M. A. thesis, Kent State University, 1964.

Shreevastava, Mahavira Prasada. "The Industrial Development of Springfield, Ohio: A Study in Economic Geography." Ph.D. dissertation, Ohio State University, 1956.

Skalski, Anne. "A Rank and File Challenge to the Leadership of the Engineman's Brotherhoods: The Rise and Fall of the Consolidated Committee of Enginemen, 1946-1949." M. A. thesis, University of Toledo, 1971.

Steele, Herbert E. "The American Flint Glass Workers' Union." Ph.D. dissertation, Ohio State University, 1947.

Stocks, Anthony H. "Employment Shifts in the Youngstown-Warren Metropolitan Area in the Year Following Black Monday." Typescript. Youngstown State University, Center for Urban Studies, January 1979.

Government Records and Documents

Ohio. Bureau of Employment Services. *Employment, Payroll, and Earnings Under Ohio Unemployment Compensation Law By County. 1943-1971.*

—————. *Employment, Payroll, and Earnings Under the Ohio Unemployment Compensation Law By County. 1972-1980.*

—————. Division of Research and Statistics. *Ohio Labor Force Estimates By County, By Month Since 1967.* (1981).

—————. *Ohio Labor Force Estimates By County, By Month, 1970-1977.* (1978).

Ohio. Bureau of Unemployment Compensation. *Manpower and Employment Trends in Ohio.* Typescript (of report by William Papier,), 1 May 1964.

Ohio. Department of Industrial and Economic Development. *Statistical Abstract of Ohio, 1960.* (1960).

Ohio. Department of Industrial Relations. *Ohio Wage-Hour Study: Laundry Industry.* February, 1960.

Ohio. Development Department. *Labor Force in Ohio.* (1968).

—————. *Manufacturing in Ohio.* (1967).

—————. *Ohio Economic Regions.* (1965).

—————. *Ohio Manufacturing.* (1965).

—————. *Population and Housing in Ohio.* (1968).

Ohio. Governor's Committee on Migrant Labor. *Migratory Labor in Ohio Agriculture: A Report by the Governor's Committee, November 1964.*

—————. *Migratory Labor in Ohio Agriculture: A Report by the Governor's Committee, December 1965.* (1966).

—————. *Migratory Labor in Ohio Agriculture: The 1966 Report of the Governor's Committee.* (1967).

—————. *Migratory Labor in Ohio Agriculture, Report of the Governor's Committee, August 1968.*

Ohio. Un-American Activities Commission. *Report of the Un-American Activities Commission State of Ohio, 1951-1952.* (1953).

U.S. Bureau of the Census. *Census of Manufacturers: 1958.* Vol II, Part 2.

—————. *Historical Statistics of The United States, Colonial Times to 1970, Bicentennial Edition.* Washington, D.C.: Government Printing Office, 1975.

U.S. Department of Commerce. Bureau of the Census. *1977 Census of Manufacturers, Geographic Area Series — Ohio.* Washington, D.C.: U.S. Government Printing Office, 1980.

—————. *United States Census of Population, 1950: Detailed Characteristics — Ohio.* Washington, D.C.: U.S. Government Printing Office, 1952.

—————. *1980 Census of Population and Housing, Preliminary Reports —Ohio.* Washington, D.C.: U.S. Government Printing Office, 1981.

—————. *1972 Census of Manufacturers — Ohio.* Washington, D.C.: U.S. Government Printing Office, 1975.

—————. *Statistical Abstract of the United States, 1961.* Washington, D.C.: U.S. Government Printing Office, 1961.

—————. *Statistical Abstract of the United States, 1971.* Washington, D.C.: U.S. Government Printing Office, 1971.

U.S. Department of Labor. "Background Statistics Bearing on the Steel Dispute." Typescript, August 15, 1979.

—————. *Handbook of Labor Statistics 1967.* Washington, D.C.: U.S. Government Printing Office, 1967.

—————. *Handbook of Labor Statistics 1968*. Washington, D.C.: U.S. Government Printing Office, 1968.

—————. *Handbook of Labor Statistics 1970*. Washington, D.C.: U.S. Government Printing Office, 1970.

—————. *Handbook of Labor Statistics 1975*. Washington, D.C.: U.S. Government Printing Office, 1975.

—————. *Manpower Report of the President*. Washington, D.C.: U.S. Government Printing Office, 1967.

U.S. Department of Labor. Bureau of Labor Statistics. *Directory of National Unions and Employee Associations, 1979*. Washington, D.C.: U.S. Government Printing Office, 1980.

—————. *Occupational Earnings and Wage Trends in Metropolitan Areas, (July) 1969- (June) 1970, No. 2 of 3*. Washington, D.C.: n.p., June, 1970.

U.S. Department of Labor. Women's Bureau. *1975 Handbook on Women Workers*. Washington, D.C.: U.S. Government Printing Office, 1975.

U.S. House of Representatives. Committee on Education and Labor. *Investigation of Univis Lens Co. Strike, Dayton, Ohio*. Committee Report No. 20, December 29, 1948.

Primary Sources

Akron, Ohio. University of Akron. Communications Workers of America, Local No. 4303 Records.

—————. B.F. Goodrich Corporation Papers.

Athens, Ohio. American History Research Center, Ohio University Library. United Shoe Workers of America, Local No. 117 Records.

Bowling Green, Ohio. Center for Archival Collections, Bowling Green State University. International Association of Machinists and Aerospace Workers, District 57 Records.

—————. International Typographical Union, Local No. 63 Records.

—————. Edward Lamb Papers.

—————. Toledo Central Labor Union Papers.

Cincinnati, Ohio. Cincinnati Historical Society. Urban League of Greater Cincinnati Papers.

—————. University of Cincinnati. Amalgamated Clothing and Textile Workers Union, Local No. 1495 Records.

—————. Cincinnati AFL-CIO Council Records.

—————. International Association of Machinists and Aerospace Workers, District No. 34 Records.

Columbus, Ohio. Ohio Historical Society. Amalgamated Clothing and Textile Workers of America, Local No. 487 Records.

—————. Leland Beard Papers.

—————. Robert Bollard Papers.

—————. Bricklayers, Masons and Plasterers' International Union of America, Local No. 55 Records.

—————. Elmer Cope Papers.

—————. Glass Bottle Blowers Association of the United States and Canada, Local No. 33 Records.

—————. International Association of Machinists and Aerospace Workers, District No. 52 Records.

—————. International Brotherhood of Electrical Workers, Local No. 2020 Records.

—————. International Typographical Union, Local No. 5 Records

—————. Newark AFL-CIO Council Records.

—————. Ohio Adjutant General Papers.

—————. Ohio AFL-CIO Council Records.

—————. Ohio Socialist Labor Party Records.

—————. Ohio War History Commission Papers.

—————. United Brotherhood of Carpenters and Joiners of America, Local 200 Records.

—————. United Industrial Workers of the Seafarers International Union of America Records.

—————. United Steelworkers of America, District No. 27, Sub-District No. 5 Records.

Dayton, Ohio. Wright State University Library. Dayton Urban League Papers.

—————. International Union of Electrical, Radio and Machine Workers, District Council No. 7 Records.

—————. International Union of Electrical, Radio and Machine Workers, Local No. 755 Records.

—————. International Union of Electrical, Radio and Machine Workers, Local No. 801 Records.

Detroit, Michigan. Archives of Labor History and Urban Affairs, Wayne State University. Charles Baker Papers.

—————. Richard Gosser Papers.

—————. Sam Pollock Papers.

—————. U.A.W. Local 1112 Collection.

—————. United Rubber Workers Collection.

Ithaca, New York. Cornell University. Brotherhood of Railway Trainmen Collection.

Kent, Ohio. Kent State University. East Liverpool AFL-CIO Council Records.

—————. International Brotherhood of Pottery and Allied Workers, International Headquarters Records.

—————. International Union of Electrical, Radio and Machine Workers, Local No. 717 Records.

—————. Pauline Taylor Papers.

—————. United Steel Workers of America, Local 1307 Records.

—————. United Steel Workers of America, Local 1375 Records.

—————. Rebecca Williams Community House Collection.

—————. Youngstown Urban League Papers.

New York, New York. Tamiment Library, New York University. Daniel Bell Papers.

Toledo, Ohio. Toledo-Lucas County Public Library. Vertical Files.

—————. University of Toledo. T.J. McCormick Papers.

Washington, D.C. Catholic University of America. John Brophy Papers.

—————. C.I.O. Local I.U. Councils Collection.

—————. Phillip Murray Papers.

—————. Library of Congress. National Association for the Advancement of Colored People Papers.

—————. Robert A. Taft Papers.

Oral Histories

Baumgardner, Francis Lee. Interview 1976. Ohio Historical Society.

Brush, Charles H. Interview 1975. Ohio Historical Society.

Burch, Dorothy. Interview 1976. Ohio Historical Society.

Culver, James H. Interview 1976. Ohio Historical Society.

Kuntzman, Lola. Interview 1978. Ohio Historical Society.

Luken, James. Interview 1976. Ohio Historical Society.

Podijil, Tony. Interview 1976. Ohio Historical Society.

Presser, Jackie. Interview 1980. Ohio Historical Society.

Ramsay, John. Interview 1976. Ohio Historical Society.

Stephens, Butler R. Interview 1976. Ohio Historical Society.

Taylor, Pauline. Interview 1978. Ohio Historical Society.

Turner, James. Interview 1975. Ohio Historical Society.

Wornstaff, Leothar. Interview 1976. Ohio Historical Society.

CREDITS

We are extremely grateful to the dozens of organizatons, depositories, individuals, and publications which provided the thousands of images considered for this work. Unfortunately, however, limited space did not permit the utilization of many excellent graphics. For the images finally selected, locations on a particular page are signified by (T) top, (C) center, (B) bottom, (L) left, and (R) right. The contributions of the following sources are identified by abbreviation:

ABJ—*Akron Beacon Journal*
ACHS—Allen County (Ohio) Historical Society
ACTWU—Courtesy of the Amalgamated Clothing and Textile Workers Union
AFL-CIO—American Federation of Labor and Congress of Industrial Organization
AFSCME—Courtesy of AFSCME Ohio Council 8, Columbus, Ohio
ALHUA—The Archives of Labor History and Urban Affairs, Wayne State University
AMC—American Motors Corporation
AZ—Allen Zak
BGSU—Courtesy of Center for Archival Collections, Bowling Green State University
BB—Benjamin Butterworth, *The Growth of Industrial Arts* (Washington, D.C.: G.P.O., 1888).
CAC—Cincinnati AFL-CIO Labor Council
CCHS—Courtesy, Clark County Historical Society Collections, Clark County Historical Society
CD—*The Columbus (Ohio) Dispatch*
CDMC—Courtesy of the Chillicothe Division of The Mead Corporation
CE—*The Cincinnati Enquirer*
CHS—Courtesy of the Cincinnati Historical Society
CM—Courtesy of Cincinnati Milacron
CMM—Campus Martius Museum, Ohio Historical Society
CP—Culver Pictures
CPD—*Cleveland Plain Dealer*
CPL—Cleveland Picture Collection, Cleveland Public Library
CR—*Canton Repository*
DJH—*Dayton Journal Herald and Daily News*
DMC—Dayton and Montgomery County Public Library
DPD—Courtesy of Delco Products Division of General Motors Corporation
ELHS—East Liverpool Historical Society, on deposit at the Ohio Historical Society's Museum of Ceramics
FTR—The Firestone Tire & Rubber Company
GTR—The General Tire & Rubber Company
HB—Hudepohl Brewing Company
HW—*Harper's Weekly*
IH—International Harvester Archives
IUE—International Union of Electrical, Radio and Machine Workers
JP—Jay Paris
KC—Courtesy of Kahn's and Company, Cincinnati, Ohio
LC—Library of Congress
LCHS—Lake County Historical Society
LG—Courtesy of Lunn Gallery/Graphics International
LI—*Leslie's Illustrated*
MC—Courtesy of Marietta College Dawes Library, Fischer Collection, Marietta, Ohio
MM—The Massillon Museum
MOC—Marathon Oil Company
NARS—National Archives and Records Service, Audiovisual Archives Division, Still Photo Section
NC—Courtesy Mrs. Nelson McCoy
NCR—Courtesy of NCR Corporation
NYHS—New York Historical Society
OB—Photo-MODERN MEDIA CORP./O. Bosworth
ODD—Courtesy of the Ohio Department of Development
OEPA—Courtesy of the Ohio Environmental Protection Agency
OHS—Ohio Historical Society
OI—Owens-Illinois
OU—Ohio University Library/Archives & Special Collections
PLC—Public Library of Cincinnati and Hamilton County
PW—Photoworld
RL—Courtesy of the Ramsayer Library, Stark County Historical Society
TLCPL—Toledo-Lucas County Public Library
UPI—United Press International
WRHS—Courtesy of the Western Reserve Historical Society
WS—The Warner & Swasey Company, Gradall Division (a subsidiary of Bendix Corp.)
WSU—Department of Archives and Special Collections, University Library, Wright State University

INDEX